MUSIC IN MEDIEVAL EUI

*This book is dedicated in gratitude, respect, and friendship
to Bryan Gillingham*

Music in Medieval Europe

Studies in Honour of Bryan Gillingham

Edited by

TERENCE BAILEY
University of Western Ontario, Canada

ALMA SANTOSUOSSO
Wilfrid Laurier University, Canada

ASHGATE

Published by
Ashgate Publishing Limited
Gower House
Croft Road
Aldershot
Hants GU11 3HR
England

Ashgate Publishing Company
Suite 420
101 Cherry Street
Burlington, VT 05401-4405
USA

Ashgate website: http://www.ashgate.com

British Library Cataloguing in Publication Data
Music in medieval Europe : studies in honour of Bryan
    Gillingham
    1.Music – 500-1400 2.Music – 15th century
    I.Gillingham, Bryan II.Bailey, Terence III.Santosuosso,
    Alma
    780.9'02

Library of Congress Cataloging-in-Publication Data

Music in medieval Europe : studies in honour of Bryan Gillingham/
    edited by Terence Bailey and Alma Santosuosso.
        p. cm.
    Includes bibliographical references and indexes.
    ISBN 0-7546-5239-4 (alk. paper)
    1. Music – 500-1400 – History and criticism. 2. Gillingham, Bryan.
    I. Gillingham, Bryan. II. Bailey, Terence. III. Santosuosso, Alma
    ML172.M874 2006
    780.9'02 – dc22

                                                        2005037691

ISBN-13: 978-0-7546-5239-7

Printed and bound in Great Britain by TJ International Ltd, Padstow, Cornwall.

Photograph of Bryan Gillingham by Jack Coghill

*The editors acknowledge gratefully
the unfailing help and advice of Kathryn Puffett and Sara Gruen.
We also wish to thank John Shepherd, Carleton University, Heidi May and
Pete Coles*

Contents

List of examples

List of figures

List of tables

List of contributors

Terence Bailey is Professor Emeritus at the University of Western Ontario. He has written books and articles on the early medieval liturgy, principally on the Ambrosian rite of Milan. Most recently he has completed an edition and study of the transitoria.

Rebecca A. Baltzer is Professor of Musicology in the School of Music at the University of Texas at Austin. Her interests include medieval chant, liturgy, music, manuscripts, and the culture of Gothic France (Paris), focusing particularly on the Notre-Dame school. She is the editor of the fifth volume (*Les Clausules à Deux Voix*) of *Le Magnus liber organi de Notre-Dame de Paris*.

James Borders is the Associate Dean for Graduate Studies at the University of Michigan. His interests extend to rock and contemporary popular music, but have centred on the development of plainchant. He has published an edition of eleventh-century chants from the Italian abbey of Nonantola.

James John Boyce, O. Carm., teaches at Fordham University in New York. His research concentrates on music and liturgy, particularly that of the Carmelites. Ten of his articles have been assembled in his book *Praising God in Carmel: Studies in Carmelite Liturgy*.

John Caldwell, author of *The Oxford History of English Music*, is Professor of Music at Oxford University. He has published editions of keyboard music and, recently, the book *Editing Early Music*.

László Dobszay, member of the Hungarian Academy of Sciences, Institute for Musicology, is Professor at the Liszt Ferenc Music Academy. His numerous publications are mostly devoted to central European chant studies, hymnody, and Hungarian folk songs. His most recent book is *Corpus Antiphonarum: Europai örökség és hazai alakítzás* [Corpus Antiphonarum: European Heritage and Hungarian Creation].

Joseph Dyer is Professor of Music History at the University of Massachusetts in Boston. His research centres on medieval Roman liturgy and music. His many articles include studies on Old Roman chant, performance practices (including the singing of psalms), and chant theory. He is the author of the central article 'Roman Catholic Church Music' in *New Grove*.

Barbara Haggh is Professor of Musicology at the University of Maryland at Baltimore. Her work includes studies on sacred music in the Middle Ages and Renaissance and editions of offices for the saints. Her most recent book is *Two Offices for St Elizabeth of Hungary: Gaudeat Hungaria and Letare Germania*.

Jane Morlet Hardie is an Honorary Research Associate for Medieval Studies at the University of Sydney. Her research, focused on Spanish liturgical music, has appeared in numerous articles and most recently in her book *The Lamentations of Jeremiah: Ten Sixteenth-Century Spanish Prints*.

David Hiley, author of *Western Plainchant: A Handbook*, is Professor of Music History at Regensburg University. His studies are concerned with plainchant families (Norman chant, English chant traditions) and offices of the saints. He has edited a number of facsimiles of important chant manuscripts.

Andrew Hughes is Professor Emeritus at the University of Toronto. He has published editions of medieval music, bibliographies, electronic databases, and offices of the Saints. He is the author of *Late Medieval Liturgical Offices: Resources for Electronic Research*.

David Hughes, the author (with John Bryden) of *An Index of Gregorian Chant*, is Professor Emeritus at Harvard University. His numerous articles have centred on the Gregorian chant repertory, modal theory, and medieval polyphony.

Michel Huglo, author of *Les tonaires*, is Emeritus Director of Research at the CNRS in Paris. He has published widely in all aspects of medieval musicology, including music theory and chant. Some of his many, many important articles have been collected into a series of books by Ashgate.

Theodore Karp is a specialist in the songs of the trouvères, twelfth-century polyphony, and the Gregorian tract repertory. He is Professor Emeritus at Northwestern University. His most recent book is *The Polyphony of Saint Martial and Santiago de Compostella*.

Thomas B. Payne is Associate Professor of Music at the College of William and Mary in Virginia. His research interests centre on the music and poetry of medieval Paris. His recent book, *Les organa à deux voix ... Le Magnus liber organi de Notre-Dame de Paris*, is an edition of fifty of these compositions.

Dolores Pesce, whose principal interest is the theory of medieval music, is Associate Professor of Music History at Washington University in St Louis. Her *Guido of Arezzo's* Regule rithmice, Prologus in antiphonarium, *and* Epistola ad Michahelem is a critical edition with translations of three important treatises.

Alejandro Enrique Planchart is Professor Emeritus at the University of California at Santa Barbara. He has published many articles on a wide range of musical topics from Giuseppe Tartini to Guillaume du Fay to tropes, his special interest in the latter dating from his early and influential study, *The Repertory of Tropes at Winchester*.

Alma Santosuosso is Professor of Music History at Wilfrid Laurier Univer-sity in Waterloo, Ontario. She is the author of *Letter Notations in the Middle Ages*, and she has produced several studies on medieval theoretical manuscripts.

Ruth Steiner, Professor Emerita at the Catholic University of America in Washington DC, has published many important studies and articles on Gregorian chant and the Roman office. She was the founder of CANTUS, which, still ongoing, prepares and publishes in electronic form inventories of manuscripts containing the chants of the Divine Office.

William John Summers' interests go beyond medieval English music to include Spanish music of the Alta California and the Philippines. His most recent book is *English Fourteenth-Century Polyphony: Facsimile Edition of Sources Notated in Score*. He is Professor of Music History at Dartmouth College.

Philip Weller, Lecturer in Music at the University of Nottingham, is particularly interested in the cultural history of music from the Middle Ages to the twentieth century. He has written on Janequin, Binchois, Lassus, and Lejeune, among others, and on medieval and Renaissance historiography.

Bibliographical abbreviations

AMw	*Archiv für Musikwissenschaft*
AH	Analecta hymnica medii aevi, ed. C. Blume and G. M. Dreves. 55 vols plus indexes. Leipzig, 1886–1922; reprinted Frankfurt am Main, 1961, indexes 1978
AnnM	Annales musicologiques, 1953–1977
CAO	*Corpus antiphonalium officii.* Rerum ecclesiasticarum documenta, Series maior, Fontes 7–12. Rome, 1963–1979.
CSM	Corpus scriptorum de musica. The American Institute of Musicology, 1950–
EG	*Etudes grégoriennes*, 1954–
EMH	*Early Music History*, 1981–
FS Anderson	*Gordon Athol Anderson (1929–1981) in memoriam von seinen Studenten, Freunden und Kollegen.* ed. Luther Dittmer. Henryville, PA: Institute of Medieval Music, 1984
FS Hucke	*De Musica et Cantu – Studien zur Geschichte der Kirchenmusik und der Oper: Helmut Hucke zum 60 Geburtstag*, ed. Peter Cahn and AnnBKatrin Heifer. Musikwissenschaftlichen Publicationen 2. Hildesheim, 1993
FS Levy	*Study of Medieval Chant: Paths and Bridges, East and West. In Honor of Kenneth Levy*, ed. Peter Jeffery. Woodbridge, 2001
FS Steiner	*The Divine Office in the Latin Middle Ages,* ed. Rebecca A. Baltzer and Margot Fassler. Oxford, 2000
GS	M. Gerbert, *Scriptores ecclesiastici de musica sacra potissimum.* 3 vols. 1784 (facs. 1931, 1963)
IMS	Institute of Mediaeval Music
JAMS	*Journal of the American Musicological Society*
JM	*The Journal of Musicology*
MGG	*Die Musik in Geschichte und Gegenwart*, ed. Friederich Blume. 14 vols. Kassel, 1949–1968. Supplements in 2 vols, 1973, 1979. Index, 1986
MMMA	Monumenta monodica medii aevi. Institut für Musikwissenschaft der Universität Erlangen-Nürnberg, 1965–
MQ	*The Musical Quarterly*
NG	*New Grove Dictionary of Music and Musicians*, 2nd edn, ed. Stanley Sadie and John Tyrrell. 29 vols. London, 2001
PL	Patrologia cursus completus, i. Series latina, ed. J.-P. Migne. 221 vols. Paris, 1844–1864
PM	Paléographie musicale. Solesmes, 1889–
RB	*Revue bénédictine*
StM	*Studia musicologica: Academiae scientarum hungaricae*, 1961–

VMK   Veröffentlichungen der musikhistorischen Kommission. Munich: Bayerische Akademie der Wissenschaften, 1977–

Chapter 1

Two paradigms of orality: the office and the mass

László Dobszay

The hotly debated questions of the 'Urgeschichte' of the Gregorian chant (i.e. 'the question concerning its origin and development' as formulated by Apel),[1] the relationship of the Carolingian period to the Roman heritage, the priority of the Old Roman and Gregorian versions, the problems of orality, the influence of the invention of notation, the notion of essential and 'trivial' variants, the role of improvisation and verbatim music memory, the study of 'generative rules', the possibility (or impossibility) of getting an overall view of an age prior to the employment of notation: all these are, in reality, different aspects of one and the same question. Moreover, after reading the literature over and over again and comparing the opposing views, I am inclined to regard the discords as apparent only. It is as if it were the case merely that the old, more or less naïve, approaches to the whole set of questions had been attacked at *different points* in the past three or four decades, with the understandable consequence that each attacker exaggerated his results or had reservations about the results of others, without taking all of the elements of the argument into consideration.

Apart from some unavoidable one-sidedness of the different presentations, a new consensus among researchers seems to have taken shape at the end of the twentieth century. It has not yet appeared in written form, but it lies hidden in the apparently conflicting conclusions of scholars. It goes without saying that this consensus does not affect all *details*; moreover, there are some intractable problems to which answers will always remain tentative, more in the nature of probabilities than well-founded conclusions. The kind of consensus I am talking about cannot be expected to include agreement on such points.

The great questions enumerated above are, in fact, about the same thing, and it does not matter where we start the survey. The key concept may be the strength of memory in any oral music culture. Helmut Hucke and Leo Treitler, creators of the

---

[1] Willi Apel, *Gregorian Chant* (Bloomington, IN, 1958), pp. 74–83, 507, and 'The Central Problem of Gregorian Chant', *JAMS* 9 (1956), pp. 118–127; James McKinnon, *The Advent Project: The Later-Seventh-Century Creation of the Roman Mass Proper* (Berkeley, 2000), pp. 14–15.

'New Historical View',[2] saw much more clearly than anyone else before them that the issue of the origin of chant can be discussed only in the context of oral tradition. They realized that anything one has to say on this theme should be in harmony with the laws of an oral culture and the ways in which production, preservation, and memory work in that environment. They provoked opposition, not so much by holding this view, but by extending it to different periods of the long history, including the age of the manuscripts. The major concern of these two scholars was, in fact, not whether the music recorded in the manuscripts or the structure of a late production (a trope, for example) should be regarded as an outcome of improvisation (understood in any sense), but whether the manuscripts could offer any information regarding the periods prior to their emergence.

On the other hand, when David Hughes, Kenneth Levy, and others referred to the homogeneity of the Gregorian tradition and gave precedence to music script in the process of unification,[3] it was not their intention to deny the importance of oral tradition. They meant to confront their colleagues with the fact that the freedom of variation manifested in the codices is much narrower than could be supposed in an improvisatory oral culture. For them the most important feature of chant transmission was the essential homogeneity of the *written* tradition. They offered a formula for

---

[2]Helmut Hucke, 'Gregorianischer Gesang in altrömischer und fränkischer Überlieferung', *AMw* 12 (1955), pp. 74–87; 'Zu einigen Problemen der Choralforschung', *Die Musikforschung* (hereafter *Mf*) 11 (1958), pp. 385–414; 'Karolingische Renaissance und gregorianischer Gesang', *Mf* 28 (1975), pp. 4–18; 'Towards a New Historical View of Gregorian Chant', *JAMS* 33 (1980), pp. 437–467; 'Gregorianische Fragen', *Mf* 41 (1988), pp. 304–330. Leo Treitler, 'Homer and Gregory: The Transmission of Epic Poetry and Plainchant', *MQ* 60 (1974), pp. 333–372; 'Centonate Chant: Übles Flickwerk or *E pluribus unus*?', *JAMS* 28 (1975), pp. 1–23; 'Oral, Written, and Literate Process in the Transmission of Medieval Music', *Speculum* 56 (1981), pp. 471–491; 'The Early History of Music Writing in the West', *JAMS* 35 (1982), pp. 237–239; 'Orality and Literacy in the Music of the Middle Ages', *Paragon: Bulletin of the Australian and New Zealand Association for Medieval and Renaissance Studies* 2 (1984), pp. 143–175. See also Peter Jeffery, *Re-Envisioning Past Musical Cultures: Ethnomusicology in the Study of Gregorian Chant* (Chicago, 1992), pp. 11–50, and Leo Treitler, 'Sinners and Singers: a Morality Tale', *JAMS* 47 (1994), pp. 137–171, and Peter Jeffery's response: *JAMS* 49 (1996), pp. 175–179.

[3]David Hughes, 'Evidence for the Traditional View of the Transmission of Gregorian Chant', *JAMS* 40 (1987), pp. 377–404. See also Leo Treitler in 'Communications', *JAMS* 41 (1988), pp. 566–575, and 'The Implications of Variants for Chant Transmission', in *FS Hucke*, pp. 65–73; Kenneth Levy, 'Charlemagne's Archetype of Gregorian Chant', *JAMS* 40 (1987), pp. 1–30 (also in Levy, *Gregorian Chant and the Carolingians* (Princeton, 1998), pp. 72–108); Alejandro Planchart, 'Old Wine in New Bottles', in *FS Hucke*, pp. 41–64; McKinnon, *The Advent Project*, pp. 374–403; Apel, *Gregorian Chant*, pp. 76–77; Kenneth Levy, 'On Gregorian Orality', *JAMS* 44 (1990), pp. 185–227 (also in *Gregorian Chant and the Carolingians*, pp. 141–177). See also Communications by Hendryk van der Werf in *JAMS* 42 (1989), pp. 432–444, and David Hughes in *JAMS* 44 (1991), pp. 517–524.

compromise when they conceded that the unity of the codices may derive from the previous stability within the *oral* practice.

Two well-known facts speak against any tendency to exaggerate the importance of notation in the fixing of the chant repertory. The first is that manuscripts were not used in the actual singing. Anyone familiar with the behaviour of singers will know that a book in the master's hand is not an effective means of arriving at homogeneity and avoiding the process of *Umsingen*. The second fact is even more convincing. The adiastematic neumatic notation was not capable of recording the most essential features of the tunes: the neumatic signs viewed in themselves could be interpreted in many different ways. The most essential support they could offer to memory was the co-ordination of the *written* words and the *memorized* tune. These adiastematic manu-scripts were, in fact, *textbooks* whose weakness with respect to the pitches had to be corrected by the strength of memory. Consequently, any description of the history of chant and its transmission that makes a sharp dividing line at the point of the intro-duction of neumatic notation is faulty.

Most scholars agree that the chant put in writing in the course of the ninth century was a music that had earlier been fixed in the living practice.[4] In other words, the repertory was retained in memory by means of oral tradition during the decades between the Frankish reception and the first notated manuscripts. This statement has psychological-perceptual implications: history has demonstrated what memory *was* capable of; it follows that memory *is* able to retain a large repertory that contains many, sometimes elaborated melodies.[5] And if memory could preserve such a complex reper-tory in the eighth and ninth centuries, it is illogical to deny this possibility with regard to a smaller and stylistically more homogeneous repertory during the earlier centuries.

What was this memory like?[6] Was it reconstructive or did it preserve music like a sound recording? Those who argue in favour of the one method or the other do not in most cases refer to the same set of examples. The arguments for the 'reconstruction according to generative rules' have been taken not from the sphere of introits, offer-tories or communions, but from an analysis of graduals, tracts, responsories, and antiphons.[7] There is, however, an essential difference between the two groups of genres. Many pieces in the latter group are adaptations of a model, a melody type, to

---

[4]See Kenneth Levy, 'Plainchant before Neumes', in *Gregorian Chant and the Carolingians* (Princeton, 1998), pp. 195–213; David Hughes, 'From the Advent Project to the Late Middle Ages: Some Issues of Transmission', in Sean Gallagher *et al.*, eds, *Western Plainchant in the First Millenium: Studies in the Medieval Liturgy and its Music* (Aldershot, 2003), pp. 181–198; and Andreas Pfisterer, *Cantilena Romana. Untersuchung zur Überlieferung des gregorianischen Chorals* (Paderborn, 2002).

[5]This contradicts Apel, *Gregorian Chant*, p. 76.

[6]See Jeffery, *Re-Envisioning Past Musical Cultures*, pp. 87–107.

[7]See the literature listed in note 2.

different texts. The tracts and many of the graduals and alleluias are the products of thinking in terms of genres and their musical types.[8]

The genres themselves offer alternatives in each case. Though the melody of an antiphon may be more or less predetermined by the given type, its details are not. The Old Roman or Ambrosian parallels confirm clearly that the identity of a piece depends more upon its underlying type melody than upon a particular elaboration. On the other hand, Gregorian tradition, in spite of regional differences and some occasional anomalies, demonstrates a homogeneity even with respect to minor details. In other words, an item lived in general consciousness principally as a melody type, and only secondarily as a fixed series of pitches.[9] On the one hand, we see antiphons with different words but similar music, and in all three of the main chant traditions we observe, along with this unity of type, the dissimilarity of the individual chants – eloquent witness that memory is attached to types rather than to actual elaboration. On the other hand, we encounter the testimony of the Gregorian manuscripts with their fixed combinations of melodies and text, each chant an independent entity, yet all only slightly different appearances of the same 'tune'. The musical remembrance of antiphons was not one single and homogeneous moment, but a complex process combining different psychological and historical layers.

These remarks are more or less valid for responsories, tracts, and the like.[10] But introits, offertories, and communions do not in any discernible way belong to genre types (except for the late contrafacta) – and this is an important difference that calls for explanation. Some scholars are inclined to explain typological coherence as a result of

---

[8]David Hiley, *Western Plainchant: A Handbook* (Oxford, 1993), pp. 71–73, 77–80, 82–88, 91–99, 132–133; see also the earlier literature cited there.

[9]See François-Auguste Gevaert, *La mélopé antique dans le chant de l'église latine* (Ghent, 1895); Peter Wagner, *Einführung in die gregorianischen Melodien III: Gregorianische Formenlehre* (Leipzig, 1921), pp. 304–305; Walter Howard Frere, Introduction to *Antiphonale sarisburiense* (London, 1901–1924; reprinted 1966); Helmut Hucke, 'Musikalische Formen der Offiziumsantiphonen', *Kirchenmusikalisches Jahrbuch* 37 (1953), pp. 7–33; László Dobszay, 'Experiences in the Musical Classification of Antiphons', in *International Musicological Society, Study Group Cantus Planus, Papers Read at the Third Meeting, Tihany, Hungary, 19–24 September 1988* (Budapest, 1988), pp. 143–156, 'The Types of Antiphons in Ambrosian and Gregorian Chant', in Bryan Gillingham and Paul Merkely, eds, *Chant and its Peripheries: Essays in Honour of Terence Bailey* (Ottawa, 1998), pp. 50–61, and *Corpus Antiphonarum: Europai örökség és hazai alakítás* [Corpus Antiphonarum: European Heritage and Hungarian Creation], (Budapest, 2003); Michel Huglo and Joan Halmo, 'Antiphon', in *NG2*, vol. 1, pp. 735–748; Edward Nowacki, 'Antiphon', in *MGG*, vol. 1, pp. 636–660; László Dobszay and Janka Szendrei, *Antiphonen*, MMMA 5 (Kassel, 1999), 22*–27*, 43*–114*; Terence Bailey and Paul Merkley, *The Antiphons of the Ambrosian Office* (Ottawa, 1989); Edward Nowacki, 'Studies on the Office Antiphons of the Old Roman Manuscripts' (Ph.D. diss., Brandeis University, 1980), and 'The Gregorian Office Antiphons and the Comparative Method', *JM* 4 (1985), pp. 243–275.

[10]Apel, *Gregorian Chant*, pp. 312–363.

later standardization;[11] but why should such a tendency prevail in one group of genres and not in the other?

And we may go further. Taking the office antiphons again as an example, it will be apparent that the description I have just given is not valid for the entire repertory. There is a group of such antiphons that fully demonstrate 'typological creativity'. In another group features such as typical melodic lines, or the linking of melodic lines and stereotypical motives, can be explained by the vocabulary and grammar of a genre type, while the formation of the melody as a whole is individual. In a third group the individual pieces are nearly or completely independent from each other; such is the case for introits as well.[12]

The three groups have markedly different liturgical spheres and only the contrafacta cross the borders. To the sphere of St Benedict's rule belong the first set of antiphons, those that follow the principle of *type*. The chants of the second group are almost completely missing from the Old Roman repertory, apart from some items borrowed from the Gregorian. The members of the third group are for the most part compositions for the new services of the early Middle Ages.[13] This means that the first manuscripts[14] already contain a *complex* repertory – which is another powerful argument against linking the origins of the chant repertory to the origins of the notation. A repertory produced within two or three – or even four or five – decades could not possibly demonstrate such immense stylistic differences within liturgical categories. The memory that preceded written records consisted of different kinds of recollection, with strata of different depths.

The kind of relationship observed in the first group of antiphons is not to be found in introits, offertories, and communions.[15] But it must be true for them, too, that at an earlier phase of their existence the same sort of relationships were in some sense present – that is to say, that in the general consciousness abstract forms were understood to lie behind individualized pieces. Evidence of this stage is the structural identity of the same pieces elaborated differently in the Old Roman, Gregorian, and Ambrosian versions[16] (the hypothesis of simple borrowing can be ruled out in most

---

[11]Edward Nowacki, 'Contantinople – Aachen – Rome: The Transmission of *Veterem hominem*', in *FS Hucke*, pp. 95–115 (especially 109–115). Cf. Thomas Connolly, 'Introits and Archetypes: Some Archaisms of the Old Roman Chant', *JAMS* 25 (1972), pp. 165–174, and Hucke, 'Gregorianischer Gesang', pp. 74–87.

[12]The three groups are separated in Dobszay and Szendrei, *Antiphonen*.

[13]László Dobszay, 'Concerning a Chronology for Chant', in Gallagher *et al.* (eds), *Western Plainchant in the First Millenium*, pp. 217–229.

[14]*CAO*, vols 1–4.

[15]Apel, *Gregorian Chant*, pp. 310–311, 363–375; McKinnon, *The Advent Project*, p. 198.

[16]Hendrik Van der Werf, *The Emergence of Gregorian Chant: A Comparative Study of Ambrosian, Roman, and Gregorian Chant*, 2 vols (Rochester NY, 1983) and 'Communications', *JAMS* 42; Hughes, 'Communications', *JAMS* 44; McKinnon, *The Advent Project*, pp. 198–207; Robert J. Snow, 'The Old-Roman Chant', in Apel, *Gregorian Chant*, pp. 487–492; László Dobszay, 'The Debate about the Oral and Written Transmission of Chant', *Revista de*

cases). As common antecedents one should not suppose an *Urform*, but rather the abstract melodic type itself – realized differently from the outset by different executants and different communities.

Since creation from type – something that is common in the first genre group – never occurs in the second, we cannot avoid the conclusion that we are dealing with two different performing practices and/or epochs. The following insights gained from the history of liturgy support this view. Roughly speaking, the first set of genres is the outcome of the practice of musically uneducated, but liturgically well-versed communities headed by musically trained leaders: what was sung was produced more or less like folk music. The second group is the joint product of communities of musically educated professional singers. To put it simply, the early office is completely dominated by *usus*, while the mass-proper was a step towards *ars*, a step taken while the conditions of an oral culture still prevailed.

The music of the early office was produced and maintained by secular or monastic communities. In both cases the chanting of untrained singers was directed by quasi-professional leaders, the precentors (successors of the ancient *psalmistae*). The functioning of memory in such a community may have worked in two different ways. In the first, the community being instinctively familiar with the musical language and the musical *types*, the precentors suggested the actualization of this common knowledge – the combination of melody types and text – by means of introductory intonation.[17] In the second case the adaptation of music to text was fixed, and the chants were taught and memorized as individual melodies isolated from the common musical language, i.e. from the raw material offered by *types*. Such fixity may have been required by liturgy (e.g. in the case of the oldest mass ordinary), but the number of cases was limited, and the long-term transmission of such melodies was guaranteed by frequent, regular use.

The items of the mass-proper (with the exception of the chants between the lessons) have developed under special conditions. Their individuality is understandable if we suppose that they were the property of the schola, i.e. a *group* of singers acting in a professional way from its beginnings.[18] These idiosyncratic pieces required a radically different method of remembering. The style, the formulas, and the frequent linking of elements might help the memory to some extent, but only rote learning and appropriate rehearsal could ensure a satisfactory group performance.

Musicología 16 (1993), pp. 706–729, and *Ólatin liturgiák énekei* [Chant in the Old Latin Liturgies], Egyházzenei Füzetek [Church Music Guide Books], series 1, vol. 13 (Budapest, 2004), pp. 38–44.

[17]Edward Nowacki, 'The Performance of Office Antiphons in Twelfth-century Rome', *IMS, Cantus Planus* (1988), pp. 79–91.

[18]James McKinnon, ed., *Antiquity and the Middle Ages from Ancient Greece to the Fifteenth Century* (Englewood Cliffs NJ, 1990), pp. 109–117, and 'Lector Chant Versus Schola Chant: A Question of Historical Plausibility', in Janka Szendrei and David Hiley, eds, *Laborare fratres in unum*, Spolia berolinensia 7 (Berlin, 1995), pp. 201–211.

This performance practice is not at odds with the observations gained from the comparison of Old Roman, Gregorian, and Ambrosian repertories. The structures of the chants might exist as abstractions out of which the continuous work of the various scholae crystallized an exact form of the melody. The same abstract structures appear *differently* in different repertories but are preserved *uniformly* within each of the three branches of the tradition.

It is clear that the two paradigms I am proposing (spontaneous elaboration from *type* and the transmission by memory of distinct melodies) reflect two practices that differ sociologically and historically. The exceptions do not contradict this. The interlectionary chants of the mass-proper are documented in the earliest period of the liturgy and we know that they were solo pieces (occasionally with refrains sung by the community). There was no reason, under the circumstances of quasi-professional transmission from psalmist to psalmist, why the fixing of a solo piece – at least within a given community – should go beyond the measure established automatically by the regularly recurring tunes, texts, and liturgical events. Consequently it is easy to understand why the earliest layer of the relevant genres of interlectionary chant reflects the same combination of re-creation and fixity we have observed in the office genres. Indeed, to some extent the office – overseen by trained singers in monasteries or cathedrals – itself went over to the realm of *ars*, and the new repertory of office chants thus grew increasingly to resemble those of the 'memory type' in the mass-proper.

Transitions between the two categories of memory are perfectly possible. Both fit in well with the remnants of the music culture from antiquity, the oldest religious rituals, and ethnomusicological traditions; the Cantus Romanus – indeed, all Old Latin chant – derives from the same world as these. On the one hand we have an example from the Jews. Zoltán Simon, an eminent expert in Jewish liturgical chant has given a detailed illustration of the use of what he calls 'tonal microstructures' realized differently by different singers in different communities.[19] While these microstructures remained identical over a very long time, the elaboration continued without abatement. The changing features (the ornamentation) may be in accord with the feast, the region, or the singer's individual inclination; however, *within* this steadily changing musical world some prayers get a stable form (at least for a given community), depending on the requirements of the liturgical situation. On the other hand, in his new book Theodore Karp, while presenting examples of both categories of memory,[20] draws our attention to the strict system of training singers to acquire the vast melodic material of the Vedas, note by note, in their exact and fixed form.

What I have had to say in this chapter is neither for nor against the 'New Historical View'. I suppose that in the course of the long history of chant several kinds of tendencies prevailed, several methods of music production and several types of memory

---

[19] Ágoston Schmelowszky, *Rövid bevezetés a zsidó liturgiába* [A Short Introduction to the Jewish Liturgy], Egyházzenei Füzetek [Church Music Guide Books], series 1, vol. 13 (Budapest, 2002), pp. 53–62.

[20] Theodore Karp, *Aspects of Orality and Formularity in Gregorian Chant* (Evanston IL, 1998), pp. 16–27.

played a role in shaping the different parts of the repertory and of different performance practices.

Let us look at these practices backwards through history. The Gregorian melodies
were canonized by the Solesmes editions of the twentieth century, but these were
preceded by the different traditions of the post-Tridentine period. The Carolingian age
had wanted to fix and canonize the Gregorian repertory, and it was successful inasmuch as a given text has ever since been associated with what is essentially the same
melody. The *res facta* thus produced spread within the Roman rite from England to
Hungary, from Norway to Sicily. The success was owed partly to notation and perhaps even more to the living practice; but the day-to-day practice also produced
differences that cannot be neglected, whether derived from regional dialects (represented, probably, in the oldest manuscripts and affecting, eventually, the whole repertory), or from the tonal reinterpretations of many chants, not to speak of 'trivial'
variants, that worked against fixation and unity. Furthermore, a great many of these
differences may derive, not from *Zersingen* (and still less from *Zerkopierung*) of an
archetype, but from the wealth of variation allowed in an era prior to the first official
encoding of the melodies. (A parenthetical remark: we cannot take for granted that
'essential' and 'trivial' had the same meaning for a singer of the eighth and ninth
century as they have for a scholar in the twentieth. For those early singers, even large-
scale tonal differences may have been considered 'trivial';[21] something else may have
been regarded as the essence of the melody.)

These are hypotheses. It is certain, however, that in the centuries prior to the Carolingian fixing of the repertory, the essence of a melody was not so much a defined series
of pitches as an abstract melodic structure, i.e. the coordination of textual and melodic
articulation, the set of pitches used, the skeleton of motives and melodic lines, the
order of cadences, etc. It goes without saying that this stage in the development of
chant was preceded by a moment or moments of fixity. Fixity can be seen best in the
mass-proper (and, of course, in the analogous genres of the office); but even where
'typical melodies' were employed, some stability would be required for each community, at least in the distribution of words over these schemata.

Going back a step further, we may say that the first of many subsequent fixations
established the word–melody combination. The background of this 'first fixation' is
the use of free, textually undetermined models, ready to be combined with any appropriate text in order to receive their *ad hoc* shape in this combination: τόπος became
opus.

And though such seems to be the freest possible state of existence of the Latin
liturgical chant, the practice entailed restrictions, those that determined 'how it is
usually done'. To give another example: according to the well-known Jewish anecdote, a precentor applied, after a long absence, to the rabbi for permission to sing at

---

[21]Jean Claire, 'Les répertoires liturgiques latins avant l'octoéchos. I. L'office férial romano-
franc', *EG* 15 (1975), pp. 5–192. László Dobszay, 'Antiphon Variants and Chant Transmission',
StM 45 (2004), pp. 67–93.

musical services. The rabbi chose a text at random and asked him chant it. When the man was finished, the rabbi gave him the required permission: 'Well, you have not forgotten the appropriate *trop*' (i.e. the authorized tone to which it should be sung). Although the freedom that cantors were allowed in the Jewish liturgical practice seems unlimited, a knowledge of the correct *trop* was a prerequisite. Such performance practices were universal: the alternation between variation and stability is continuous, a part of the process of creation.

How then should we reformulate Apel's 'central question' on the birth of Gregorian chant? The various historical snapshots we have viewed raise an even more central question. What *is* Gregorian chant? We may select one of many moments in time and say Gregorian chant is a Frankish creation. But that would mean projecting the attitudes of the second millennium backwards to the past. Gregorian chant has been studied for decades by scholars trained in western schools of musicology. They expect answers to the questions 'Show us *the* melody of *Puer natus est*' and 'Tell us when, where, and by whom it was made; we can date the chant repertory only after all items have been documented in this way'. (By the way, it is not by chance that Gregorian studies have dealt mostly with the mass chants: their individuality was closer to Western expectations.) With regard to the first millennium, however, this approach is unrealistic.[22]

Willi Apel had doubts about the ability of memory to transmit chant. He wrote:

> It is entirely unthinkable that a collection of melodies even approximating the size and elaboration of the Gregorian repertory could have been transmitted, to say nothing of 'preserved', orally over two or three centuries.[23]

To answer him we need to consider what is the essence of chant. How old is the Greek temple? Is the temple something built in such-and-such a year on such-and-such a spot, or is the Temple the original concept, the inspired design, the idea according to which it was constructed? If Gregorian chant is a set of tunes that were transmitted in exactly the same form, note for note, then Gregorian chant did not originate in the eighth or ninth century but only at the end of the nineteenth. If it is a well-defined repertory with clearly identifiable melodies, but with many variants of equal authority, its origin is rightly sought in the Carolingian age. If it is the aggregate of assigned texts, each associated with a stable melodic structure, then its emergence, layer by layer, probably preceded the Carolingian age by centuries. According to the thinking of the ancient world the essence of music was the set of compositional means, types, typical motives,

---

[22]Benjamin Rajeczky, 'Népdal-történet és gregorián-kutatás', [Ethnomusicology and Chant Research], in Béla Gunda, ed., *Festschrift für Zoltán Kodály* (Budapest, 1943), pp. 308–312; 'Gregorián, népének, népdal' [Gregorian Chant, Folk Hymn, Folk Song], in *Magyar Zenetörténeti Tanulmányok* [Studies in Hungarian Music History] (Budapest, 1969), pp. 45–64; 'Choralforschung und Volksmusik des Mittelalters?', *Acta musicologica* 46 (1974), pp. 181–192.

[23]Apel, *Gregorian Chant*, p. 76.

outlines of melodic shape, a generally understood tonal organization – in sum, a musical language that was able to serve any text and ready to be fixed if required. In view of *this* musical essence, Gregorian chant may precede the first notations by as much as half a millennium. And this reality, when perceived through analysis, is not *less* real than the concrete elaboration of pieces found in the manuscripts. The scholarly disputes about the reliability of memory and the validity of reconstructing the past through study of the written sources is itself the mirror of the musical complexity I have been trying to deal with. The scholars who disagree have merely been focusing on different moments in this complexity.

Chapter 2

Salamanca to Sydney: a newly-discovered manuscript of the *Lamentations of Jeremiah*

Jane Morlet Hardie

In mid-2002 the Rare Book Room of Fisher Library at the University of Sydney acquired two manuscript choirbooks from Minet Frères of Brussels.[1] Both of these volumes contained plainchant written in a notation typical of Spain in the sixteenth century. One, a kyriale/antiphoner (Fisher RB add. ms 327, henceforth referred to as Fisher 327) has some fragments in Aquitanian notation pasted into the covers as part of the binding.[2] The other volume, Fisher RB add. ms 335 (henceforth Fisher 335), containing chant for the *Lamentations of Jeremiah*, does not appear to have been reported anywhere, and has not yet been studied.[3]

From the earliest days of printing in Iberia, manuscript and print have been inextricably intertwined in the transmission of the *Lamentations of Jeremiah*, and Fisher

---

An earlier version of this chapter was given as a paper to the Symposium of the International Musicological Society in Melbourne in July 2004.

[1] I would like to thank Clare Thornley for alerting me to the acquisition. I would also like to thank Neil Boness, the Rare Book Librarian at Fisher Library in the University of Sydney, for allowing me unrestricted access to Fisher RB add. ms 335.

[2] Fischer 327 has been mistakenly described as a *gradual*, and appears to be the work of at least two scribes. Kathleen Nelson is making a study of the Aquitanian fragments in this manuscript, and I am making a full study of the rest of the manuscript

[3] I would like to thank James Boyce, O. Carm., for his helpful discussion of the Salamanca Cathedral manuscripts and their possible relationships to the Sydney sources. For a number of years I have been working on Iberian manuscripts and early prints containing plainchant for the *Lamentations of Jeremiah*. In late 2003 I completed a book containing a study of some of these sources, together with editions of the *Lamentations* as they are preserved in ten sixteenth-century Spanish prints. This study was published by Bryan Gillingham. See my *The Lamentations of Jeremiah: Ten Sixteenth-Century Spanish Prints*, IMS Collected Works, vol. 22 (Ottawa, 2003). It seems particularly fitting that this article should be written in honour of Bryan Gillingham, for it was his publication of work by both Boyce and myself that aided in the identification of this manuscript.

335 is no exception. In the present study I argue that this source uses texts that establish a *terminus a quo* of 1572, and chants and notation that suggest a *terminus ad quem* of 1582. The texts of the manuscript relate it to a number of other contemporary manuscripts and prints, and the chant relates it to an earlier manuscript tradition from Toledo and a later print from Salamanca. I discuss ways in which the manuscript and print traditions for this commemorative ritual interacted on the Iberian peninsula before 1600 and explore the notion that Fisher 335 may be one of the missing manuscripts from a series of sixteenth-century choirbooks made for and now housed at the Cathedral of Salamanca. I want also to suggest that this source is related to another print now in the Houghton Library at Harvard University.

Fisher 335 is a vellum choirbook of forty-eight folios measuring 41 x 30 cm. This volume has a full, contemporary, brown morocco binding over wooden boards, with blind-stamped decorations around the sides with four brass studs, and a brass boss in the centre surrounded by blind-stamped flowers. The edges are decorated with twenty-eight brass nails and reinforced with brass corners. The entire volume is devoted to the readings (*lectios*) for matins in the *triduum sacrum* and includes chant for the *Lamentations of Jeremiah*, notated in square notation on a five-line stave. Seventy decorated initial letters (thirty-five in red, three in black, and twenty-one in red and blue) are scattered throughout the book. Minet Frères in Brussels do not appear to have kept records of their purchase of either of the two manuscripts.[4]

Using physical evidence (the notation, letter decoration, and the bindings) and the contents (the texts and the chant), I am able to offer some precise information on this manuscript and to provide it with a context in a tradition of other manuscript and printed books of the *Lamentations of Jeremiah* in Spain.

Spanish source material containing the *Lamentations* can be categorized by type (such as breviary, antiphonal, passional), by form (manuscript or print), or by liturgical use (pre- or post-Pius V, *nuevo rezado*).[5] One of the common liturgical books in Spain

---

[4] I contacted Derek Minet to ask whether he had any records regarding the background or provenance of the manuscripts. He was unable to provide any information.

[5] For an extensive discussion of the typologies, history, historiography, and other issues relating to the manuscript liturgical book see Eric Palazzo, *A History of Liturgical Books from the Beginning to the Thirteenth Century* (Collegeville MN, 1998). Categorization of books by type (breviary, antiphonal, passional, and so on) is at best inexact, for many books contain material that defies classification in this way. For example music for the *Lamentations* sometimes occurs in books that do not normally contain chant. The initial letters for the *Lamentations* may be found with musical notation in some Bible manuscripts. Paul Ludwig identified two such Spanish sources (the Bible of Burgos, tenth century, from the monastery of Saint Pierre de Cardeña, folios 236r–238r) and León, *codex catedral 6*, also from the tenth century (fol. 50^V). See Paul Ludwig, 'Lamentations notées dans quelques manuscrits bibliques', *EG* 12 (1971), pp. 127–130 (especially 128). The chant incipits in the Bible of Burgos appear to be the same as, or related to, those of the Huesca manuscript sources of the *Lamentations*. In comparison with the rate of production and survival of breviaries (where the bulk of *Lamentations* texts are found) the number of extant antiphonals (books of music for the office) is very

was the passional or *officium hebdomadae sanctae*. This normally contained some or all of the texts and music for either or both the mass and office from Palm Sunday to Easter Day. Since Holy Week was, and is, such an important period of commemoration in Spain, and its attendant rituals are so rich and complex, it made sense to isolate this material in a single, easily transportable volume.[6] Accordingly, in some cases all of the Holy Week material would be together in one volume (*officium hebdomadae sanctae*), and in others several books would have been used together to complete the liturgy.

It is not only the distinctions between liturgical books that are blurred. The relationship between print and manuscript is similarly indistinct. Manuscripts were, of course, influenced by others belonging to different traditions, but also, especially the later ones, by prints.[7]

Another way of categorizing has to do with changing liturgical priorities, different text traditions, and liturgical geography. In the Iberian peninsula traditional notions of typology have less meaning, and distinctions between manuscript and print almost none at all, except where idiosyncrasies or errors might aid in establishing relationships between sources. Manuscripts are usually earlier than printed books and reflect the variety of text usage that characterized Spanish regional and local practice before the breviary of Pius V (1568). Although the 1568 breviary introduced a standardized liturgy, the exemption from text changes obtained by Philip II for Spanish Lands resulted in alterations, and additional text variation was introduced by the Quignon

---

small. The reasons for this may be varied, but it is certainly true that breviaries, whether manuscript or later printed sources, were produced in larger numbers than were books containing music. The latter were more expensive to produce, and since singing of the chant by a choir was almost certainly taught by rote, normally only one book would have been required for each place.

[6] One can only wonder what percentage of material produced has survived and whether this is a representative sample. Speculation about reasons for the survival of early manuscripts and books must remain just that, and may relate to function and politics as much as to serendipity. Certainly the more elaborately produced and decorated sources (produced for presentation, to record a particular repertory, to celebrate an important place or patron and so on) seem to have had a better chance of survival than plainer ones used every day. For a more extensive discussion of the matter see my 'Liturgical Books for Use in Spain 1468–1568: Puzzles in Parchment and Print', *Musica antiqua* 9 (1991), pp. 279–319.

[7] The earliest appearances of the *Lamentations* seem to be in the Bible of Burgos (tenth century) and in Aquitanian sources from Huesca and elsewhere; the latest known manuscript appears to be an eighteenth-century copy of a sixteenth-century original from Santa Cruz Campezo (ms 1, fols 93r–96r). See Carmen Rodriguez Suso, *La monodia litúrgica en el País Vasco (fragmentos con notación musical de los siglos XII al XVIII)* (Bilbao, 1993). I have written elsewhere about relationships between Toledan and Córdoban manuscripts and prints. See my 'The Past in the Present: Some Liturgico-musical Relationships between Toledo, Rome and Andalucía', in László Dobszay, ed., *The Past in the Present*, 2 vols (Budapest, 2003), vol. 2, pp. 207–222.

Breviary and later text modifications by Gregory XIII (1572).[8] Texts that followed the modifications of Gregory XIII were identified as belonging to the *nuevo rezado* (The New Prayer), and became enormously influential and widespread in the later sixteenth century.[9] Idiosyncratic text patterns transcended the distinctions between manuscript and print, and provide one of the most valuable aids to placing and sometimes even to dating a tradition.

The foregoing observations about manuscript and early printed liturgical books in Spain apply in some measure to Fisher 335. It contains part of the material normally found in a passional or *officium hebdomadae sanctae*, with texts and music for the first nocturn of matins (*lectios* 1–3*)* and the texts for the second and third nocturns (*lectios* 4–9) for each of the three days (Holy Thursday, Good Friday, and Holy Saturday) of *tenebrae*. There are no responsories. These features identify Fisher 335 as a practical book for use by a choir or choirmaster, a book from which the melodies for the *Lamentations* (nocturn 1, *lectios* 1–3) would have been learned and the texts for the *lectios* of the second and third nocturns read. Since it contains only a small part of the matins services for each of the three days it would have been used along with a breviary, an antiphonal, or some other book containing the full *officium hebdomadae sanctae*. The contents – music for the readings of the first nocturn and text only for the second and third nocturns (*lectios* 4–9) – might indicate that only the first nocturn was to be sung.

The music is written on a red five-line stave. This is typical of chant manuscripts of Spanish origin, and part of a tradition of Spanish manuscript production from at least the fourteenth century.[10] The otherwise unremarkable square notation contains what appear to be mensural (rhythmic) signifiers that are found also in manuscripts from Toledo and elsewhere in Spain from the fourteenth century to about 1600.[11] The style and colours of the decoration are also seen generally in widely dispersed manuscripts of Spanish origin from the thirteenth century on. Fisher 335 thus lies centrally within a known tradition of Spanish chant manuscript production that prevailed in Spain from about 1300 to 1600. To date and place it more precisely it is necessary to look more closely at the texts, details of the chant (and its notation) and the binding.

I noted above that one of the ways of categorizing liturgical books in Spain had to do with changing liturgical priorities and their concomitant text traditions. This is particularly true for the *Lamentations of Jeremiah*, whose texts by the sixteenth cen-

---

[8]For more on these text modifications see my *Lamentations of Jeremiah*, pp. xxvi–xxxi.

[9]For more on the *nuevo rezado* see Jaime Moll, 'Plantino, los Junta y el "privilegio" del nuevo rezado', in Hans Tromp and Pedro Peira, eds, *Simposio internacional sobre Cristóbal Plantino* (Madrid, 1990), pp. 9–23.

[10]For example, the mss Toledo, catedral reservado 6, 7, and 8.

[11]I believe that the incipiently mensural notation seen in this manuscript and in a Salamanca print of 1582 makes explicit much of what was implied in the notation of earlier Toledo sources. For more on this and the theoretical background to the use of mensural notation in these sources see my 'Proto-mensural Notation in Pre-Pius V Spanish Liturgical Sources', *StM* 39/2–4 (1998), pp. 195–200.

tury in almost all cases represented some contraction of the earlier medieval tradition in which the whole of the *Lamentations* were read over the three days of the *triduum*. The way this played out in Spain was that in each geographical area different verses would have been read, according to the dictates of local use.[12] Such variety makes it possible, by a consideration of the exact cursus of texts used, to suggest a geographical provenance for many books. Since by 1568 the variety of local text traditions gave way (at least in principle) to the new requirements of the breviary of Pope Pius V and his bull, *Quod a nobis*, it becomes possible in some cases not only to place but also to date books according to the texts used.

The texts for all of the readings and the chant in Fisher 335 are those of the *nuevo rezado* of Gregory XIII. Since this precise combination of texts was not used earlier, the manuscript can be assigned a date *post* 1572. Other early sources of these texts include manuscripts and prints from Leiria (1575), Lisbon (1575), Toledo (1576), Córdoba (*ca* 1576), and Salamanca (1582).[13] Indeed, after 1572 the *nuevo rezado* texts were in common use throughout Spain and Portugal, and they are still found in some modern breviaries.[14]

While these *nuevo rezado* texts can provide a *terminus a quo* for Fisher 335, their subsequent wide use prevents us from using them to place the source. This can be done with some precision through an examination of the combinations of texts and particular chants.

I have observed elsewhere that with regard to the *Lamentations of Jeremiah* many more text versions than chant versions seem to have been used in Spain.[15] Indeed the chants belong to a small number of families, related either to Toledo or to Aragón,[16] families that reveal a great deal of overlap between manuscript and print. Melodies

---

[12]I have published elsewhere on the details of this situation. See my 'Lamentations in Spanish Sources before 1568: Notes Towards a Geography', *Revista de musicología* 16 (1993), pp. 912–942.

[13]Manuel Cardoso, *Passionarium iuxta Capellae Regiae Lusitaniae consuetudinem. Accentùs rationem integre observans* (Leiria: Antonio de Mariz, 1575); Fratre Stephano, *Liber Passionum et eorum quae a Dominica in Palmis, usque ad Vesperas Sabbathi sancti inclusive, cantari solent* (Lisboa: Simon Lopez, 1595); *Passionarium romanum con canto toledano* (Toledo: Juan de la Plaça, 1576; London. BL 3366.dd.10); Córdoba catedral, *Libros corales*, mss 64 and 70 (formerly mss O-29 and O-30), *Liber primo* and *Liber secundus de tenebrae* and *Officium hebdomadae sanctae* (Mathias Gastius: Salamanca 1582; Chicago Newberry Case VM 2148.92 C36). The Newberry Library holds two copies of this publication. Subtle differences between them indicate different printings.

[14]On the texts of the *nuevo rezado* and their introduction into Spain see Moll, 'Plantino'. Moll makes the point that these texts had not been adopted in Toledo by 1574. The *Passionarium* (Toledo: Juan de la Plaça, 1576) is the first Toledo book to use these texts. For a discussion of this see my 'The Past in the Present'.

[15]See my *Lamentations of Jeremiah*, pp. xxxi–xliii.

[16]For a discussion of the families of chant and their relationships to each other and the printers who reproduced them see *ibid.*, pp. xxxi–xliii.

from the small number of surviving versions were used in sources from more than one regionally based text group, and by more than one printer or group of printers. Manuscripts and prints were obviously copied one from another. Normally this makes it much more difficult to place the chants than the texts. Fisher 335 contains chant that has so far been found in only one other source from the period, namely the *Officium hebdomadae sanctae* printed in Salamanca by the successors of Mathias Gast in 1582.[17] Gast's 1582 *Officium* appears to have been one of the most widely used Holy Week books of the *nuevo rezado*, and many copies survive. The texts of the *Lamentations* in Fisher 335 (*nuevo rezado*) are the same as those in the Gast.[18]

I have already documented and discussed sources (both manuscript and print) in which *nuevo rezado* texts are used with the simpler, traditional Toledo chant;[19] only in the Salamanca print of 1582 and Fisher 335 do we find these texts used together with this expanded and elaborated chant version of the Toledo tradition that became associated with Salamanca. The chant in Fisher 335, whose pitches are identical to those of the printed source, allows us to place the manuscript confidently as part of the Salamanca tradition. This is particularly significant in light of James Boyce's comment that 'the vast majority of chants and choirbooks used in Salamanca are no longer extant and it is somewhat difficult even to estimate the full extent of chants or even the full number of choirbooks in use in any one period'.[20]

---

[17]*Officium hebdomadae sanctae* (Salamanca: Mathias Gastius, 1582). The printery of Gast and his heirs, like those of Brocar, Eguía, Coci, and Najera, involved a web of family relationships and played an influential part in the sixteenth-century history of printing in Spain. Gast himself started printing in the printery of Juan de Junta in Salamanca (where he married Juntas's daughter Lucrecia). At the death of Juan de Junta he began a business associateship with his mother-in-law and printed under the name of *Herederos de Juan de Junta*. In 1558 he commenced printing under his own name. After his death in 1577 his business was carried on by his widow, their children, and other members of the extended family who worked as *Herederos de Matías Gast*. Gast was also active as a bookseller in Antwerp, Medina del Campo, and Burgos. For more on his businesses and relationships see the articles on Gast, Junta and their related print shops in Juan Delgado Casado, *Diccionario de impresores españoles (siglos XV–XVI)* (Madrid, 1996). These business details are typical. All of the surviving prints of *Lamentations* chant from the sixteenth century can be linked to one or other of a very small group of printers. Printers were related through dynasty, professional partnership, or inter-marriage, and their materials moved with them from place to place. Books of *Lamentations* whose text patterns and therefore *use* separated them from one another can be related through the re-employment of music type that circulated within a family or professional grouping. Thus, while large numbers of text-only materials survive, representing a wide variety of printers, the music sources comprise a surprisingly small and tightly-knit group.

[18]See my *Lamentations of Jeremiah*, pp. lii–liii.

[19]For a full discussion of sources using *nuevo rezado* texts with traditional Toledo chant and their relationships to earlier traditions see my 'The Past in the Present'.

[20]James Boyce, 'Newly-discovered Manuscripts for an Old Tradition: The Salamanca Choirbooks', *International Musicological Society Study Group Cantus Planus. Papers read at Estergom and Visegrád* (Budapest, 1998), pp. 9–28, especially 13–14.

The Salamanca connection may be even stronger. In 1993 Boyce published a catalogue of the manuscript choirbooks now housed in the *Archivo* of Salamanca Cathedral.[21] Four of the fifty-two manuscripts he catalogued (mss 5, 6, 7, and 8) were 'newly discovered' sources, and two of them, mss 5 and 6, are relevant to the story of Fisher 335. According to Boyce, mss 5 and 6 belong to a subgroup of ten pre-Tridentine sources that form part of this collection. In a subsequent series of studies, which included the publication of facsimiles of mss 5 and 6, he discusses the liturgical history of Salamanca and observes that the series of pre-seventeenth-century manuscripts now in the cathedral archives appears to be incomplete.[22] Boyce also discovered that Salamanca, mss 5 and 6 (both pre-Tridentine) were designed to be used together, as they contain complementary material. Noting that the two books between them repeat much of the same material, he writes that the reason for this

> lies in the format of codex 6, designed for the use of the cantor or *schola*, a small group of singers ... The fact that codex 6 existed for the use of the cantor or *schola* alone means that another set of manuscripts (and perhaps two, one for each side of the choir) had to be in use for the remaining cathedral canons, indicating that no expense was spared in providing the necessary materials for rendering the Divine Office. The limited contents of each codex give some idea of the large number of choirbooks which had to be in use in the cathedral during this period.[23]

The most interesting of these sources for this present study is Salamanca, ms 5, for it contains text and some chant material for the *triduum*, including texts for the *Lamentations* and responsories with chant. Extracts of the chants for the *Lamentations* together with cues from ms 5 for the responsories are in ms 6.[24] In ms 5 the cursus of texts for the *Lamentations* is that for the pre-Tridentine practice from the Toledo tradition.[25] In the margins opposite the texts of the *Lamentations* may be seen the incipits for an alternate cursus that brings this manuscript in line with the revised post-Triden-

---

[21] James Boyce, *Catálogo, archivo de música gregoriana, cantorales: 52 manuscritos, siglos XIV–XIX* (Salamanca, 1993). In a recent private communication Boyce said 'after my initial publication of the fifty-two choirbooks they discovered another four; last year they discovered a further nineteen, bringing the total of the collection to seventy-five'. These 'new' sources remain to be assessed.

[22] See James Boyce, *Salamanca, Archivo de la catedral, 5,6,7,8: Printouts from an Index in Machine-Readable Form* (Ottawa, 2001), and *Catálogo*.

[23] For more on these two manuscripts and their probable dating to before the fifteenth century see Boyce, *Salamanca Cantus Printouts*, pp. xxiii–xxv. See also 'Newly-discovered Manuscripts', *passim*.

[24] The music in Salamanca ms 6 is the 'simple Toledo' (fols 63v–64v). The notation here employs the same use of *dobles* (to signify longer note values) as other pre-Tridentine Toledo sources (Toledo, catedral mss reservado 6, 7, 8, and the printed *Passionarium toletanum* 1516).

[25] In ms 5 the first verse for *lectio* 2 on Holy Saturday has been mistakenly copied from *lectio* 1 and has been crossed out (fol. 157$^\text{V}$). For tables of the full texts of the *Lamentations* in many more Spanish sources see my *Lamentations of Jeremiah*, pp. xlix–li.

tine liturgy of the *nuevo rezado*. Fisher 335 contains all the melodies for the texts indicated in the margins of the updated ms 5. This coincidence does not in itself prove anything. However the orthography (including the use of the same *custos* in both manuscripts), the decoration, and the bindings lead me to propose that Fisher 335 is a manuscript from Salamanca Cathedral, and was the source of the music (or a copy of this source) intended to be used with the corrected ms 5 in the revised liturgy for the *triduum* at Salamanca Cathedral.

A comparison of the notation in the Salamanca mss 5 and 6, along with that in Fisher 335 and the Salamanca print of 1582, is instructive. The notation of Salamanca mss 5 and 6 is clearly earlier than that of both Fisher 335 and Salamanca 1582. Fisher 335 employs the *punto con dos plicas* and *dobles* so characteristic of proto-mensural sources from the earlier Toledo sources up to the Salamanca print. These two signs do not appear in Salamanca mss 5 and 6, whose notation does not seem to carry any mensural significance. Similarly, the notation of Fisher 335 is similar to, but simpler than, that of Salamanca 1582. This latter contrasts with the Toledo manuscript and early printed notational tradition of incipiently mensural signs that appear, for example, in the mss Toledo, catedral reservado 6, 7, and 8, and in the 1516 printed *Passionarium Toletanum*. In contrast to the notational practices of the earlier Toledo tradition and what is found in the later Salamanca print (1582), Fisher 335 does not have any dotted notes indicating longer values, or lozenges between breves indicating shorter or in any case altered values, but indicates longer note values with *longae*, *dobles* and *puntos con dos plicas*. Like the earlier Toledo sources and Salamanca 1582, Fisher 335 uses vertical lines to indicate word separation.[26]

If indeed Fisher ms 335 was the one used with Salamanca ms 5 (or even if it was a later copy) it could have been the exemplar for the printer of Salamanca 1582. But a careful examination of both the manuscript and printed sources does not lead to such a tidy conclusion. Given a tradition in Spain in which manuscripts both provided the exemplars for printed books and were copied from them, we must tread cautiously. While Fisher 335 employs the same type of notation as the print, the subtle differences between this manuscript and ms 6 suggest that the notation of the former is slightly earlier than that of the publication. At this point I am only prepared to say that these two sources are roughly contemporaneous, and that either one might have been the model for the other.

For additional help in establishing a *terminus ad quem* for Fisher 335 it is necessary to look elsewhere, firstly to the bindings and then to questions of ownership. The binding is typical of Spain in the sixteenth century, and similar to that of other chant books of the middle to late sixteenth century, when Spanish binders developed their

---

[26]For a comparison of the opening folios of the *Lamentations* in Fisher 335 with the beginning of the Salamanca print of 1582 see *ibid.*, Plate 1, p. vii. See especially the initial A in *Aleph*, the use of dotted notes in Salamanca 1582, and a *doble* in Fisher 335 expressed as a *punto con dos plicas* in Salamanca 1582.

own characteristic variations on the work of their Italian and French models.[27] Some of these variations are particularly relevant to both Fisher 335 and other choirbooks that may be related to it.[28] Gone are the elaborate geometrical patterns typical of the Mudejar bindings, and in their place come covers whose fields are defined by series of rectangles, often with a lozenge or cross design in the centre made from repeated patterns of a small stamp. Within each of the rectangular bands thus defined appear elaborate blind-stamped designs consisting of flowers or other vegetation, animals, rosettes, and often a series of heads (*cabecitas*). Typically some of these components are enclosed in a circle composed of blind-stamped dots (*ruedas*), and comprise repeating patterns of, for example, three different heads (defined by styles of headgear – cap, helmet, and so on) interspersed with three different flower patterns. The whole series then repeats as many times as is necessary to fill the required space. Some bindings add to this a coat of arms or other heraldic mark, while others alternate motifs of a number of animals with floral designs. In his introduction to the *Exposición de Encuadernaciones Españolas Siglos XII al XIX*, Francisco Hueso Rolland identifies bindings made by or for university libraries as being typical of this mid sixteenth-century tradition and regards Salamanca as one of the most important centres. According to Hueso Rolland, material of all types was gathered to be bound here at Salamanca, and, although this material may have originated in various places and not all from the same time, the 'school' of binding from Salamanca gave the books the appearance of a common origin.[29]

---

[27]For a general discussion of the characteristics of sixteenth-century Spanish bookbindings see Mathilde López Serrano, *La encuadernación española* (Madrid, 1972), pp. 56–65, and Plates 14–20. Further material on bindings and binders in sixteenth-century Spain may be found in the following: Guillermo Antolín, 'Notas acerca de la encuadernación artistica del libro en España', *Boletin de la Real Academia de la Historia* 89 (1926), pp. 294–308, and 'La encuadernación del libro en España', *Revista de archivos, bibliotecas y museos* 26 (1922), pp. 651–659; Clara Louisa Penney, *An Album of Selected Bookbindings* (New York, 1967); Vicente Castañeda, *Ensayo de un diccionario biografico de encuadernadores españoles* (Madrid, 1958), and 'Exposición de encuadernaciones de la Colección Lázaro Galdiano', *Boletin de la Academia de la Historica* 106 (1935), pp. 377–388; Manuel Rico y Sinobas, *El arte del libro en España* (Madrid, 1941); Carlos Romero de Lecca, ed., *Ochos siglos de encuadernacion española* (Brussels, 1985); Francisco Hueso Rolland, *Exposición de encuadernaciones españolas siglos XII al XIX. Catálogo general ilustrado* (Madrid, 1934).

[28]Medieval bindings that had been characterized by the use of flowers in the Gothic style or elaborate geometric patterning in the Mudejar style gradually gave way to bindings in a completely different style, emanating at first from Italy (in particular Florence and Venice), and then filtered through the famous work of anonymous binders who worked for the French Jean Grolier (1479–1565). See López Serrano, *Encuadernación española*, pp. 57ff. She identifies Salamanca, Alcalá de Henares, Toledo, Valladolid, Granada, Barcelona, and Valencia as the principal centres of production, each with some of its own distinguishing characteristics.

[29] Of these bindings, and those from Alcalá de Henares Hueso Rolland says:

Casi todas están con las conocidas ruedas de cabecitas; es decir, una rueda, que con guirnaldas de follage o simples roleos, llevan encerradas series de medallones, con cabecitas, unas coronadas, otra

In the absence of other specific information providing a *terminus ad quem* for Fisher 335, the bindings offer further clues regarding its placing and dating and may relate this source to a number of other roughly contemporary chant books. Among such books (both manuscript and print) to which this manuscript may be related through its binding are an earlier well-known *Passionarium toletanum* printed for Toledo in 1516,[30] the *Passionarium* printed in Burgo de Osma by Fernández Diego de Corduba in 1562,[31] and the other Fisher manuscript from Spain (Fisher 327). The Burgo de Osma source, of which only ten copies are known to have survived, is particularly interesting, for the bindings on the copy of this print now in the Houghton Library at Harvard University offer a particularly splendid example of the Salamanca (or possibly Alcalá de Henares) type.[32] The binding of Fisher 327 belongs to the same family and additionally contains metal bosses of a Dominican design on the front and back covers. Between them these four sources show all of the characteristics described by Hueso Rolland except for the presence of coats of arms and animal motifs normally

---

con un casco; a veces, se cambian estos tipos y se llega también a poner anímalitos en estos circulos; con frequencia se usan también las guirnaldas o roleos solos, o grijos enlazados. Con las ruedas que marcan estos dibujos, se trazen los clásicos encuadernamientos, tipicos españoles que repetidos varias veces, dejan una entrecalle libre, a propósito para poner algún motivo decorativo; finalmente, el espacio central, lleva en sus esquinas cuatro florones marcados con un hierro, que repetido cuatro veces, en forma de cruz, traza el florón central; con excepción se estampa algún superlibris heráldico; muestra de éstos son los del Rey Felipe II, en seco o en oro, pues ambos se empleaban indistintamente.

A este tipo especialmente pertenece alguna de hechas en Alcalá de Henares, 'cuya decoración está formada por tres grecas de rueda, en la cual aparecen tres pequeñas cabezas, alterando con tres escudos', pertenecientes respectivamente a los Cardinales, Cisneros, Tavera, y al Arzobispo Fonseca, lo que nos hace suponer que dichas cabezas reproducen las imágines de los personajes a que corresponden los escudos. [R. Miguélez de Mendiluce, 'Exposición de encuadernaciones artisticas de la biblioteca de la Universidad', *Boletin de bibliotecas y bibliografía*, Madrid, vol. 1, p. 48.]

See Hueso Rolland, *Exposición de encuadernaciones*, pp. 62–64.

[30]*Passionarium toletanum* (Alcalá de Henares: Arnao Guillem de Brocar, 1516; London, BL C.35 K10). Although this book was printed earlier than the other sources to which it may be related through the bindings, Spanish books at that time were often enclosed in simple parchment covers awaiting a more formal and elaborate binding. An example of a printed book that remains in such a simple parchment cover is one of the Newberry Library Chicago copies of the Salamanca 1582 print of the *Officium hebdomadae sanctae* discussed above.

[31]'Passionarium oxomense noviter excussum: cui accessit cerei paschalis, fontisque benedictionis officium cum alijs.' Burgo de Osma: Didacus Fernández de Corduba, 1562; Harvard University (Houghton Library Typ 560.62.262F).

[32]This book from Burgo de Osma may be related to the Fisher manuscript by more than just its binding. The print may be one of a series of books produced as a result of reforms in the liturgy. This series grew from a modification of the Toledo tradition, and its decoration belongs to the same tradition as Salamanca ms 5, the Fisher manuscript and the later (1582) Salamanca print. Compare for example the elaborately decorated initial letters D, C, H, A, and J in all four sources. I am currently preparing a study of the print of 1562 within its liturgico-musical context.

associated with Toledo.[33] I consider that the bindings of Fisher 335 and 327 (with its Dominican brass bosses) link both of these manuscripts most positively with the Salamanca school in the latter years of the sixteenth century, and very probably to each other.[34]

Following the manuscript from Salamanca Cathedral to Fisher Library in Sydney leads to the question of ownership. Here the detective story is only just beginning. A number of handwritten inscriptions (some dates, and possibly some signatures) can just be discerned with the aid of ultraviolet light and a strong magnifying glass on the endpapers and folio 1 of Fisher 335. Possibly the most interesting of these, in the light of the Dominican connection suggested by the binding of Fisher 327, is the hand-written name 'Antoni da Costa *predicador*', that is, *Dominican*. At the same time the word the word *conbencual* (conventual) is also just discernible beneath the name and in the same writing. This seems to signal a connection to Franciscan Conventuals, notwithstanding the fact that they had all but disappeared in Spain following the bull, *Ite vos*, of Leo X in 1517, but of course it could simply signal ownership by a convent.[35] Other barely visible names and inscriptions include 'Antonio Sanchez', 'Fongas Fernandez Galano [?]oroio', 'Lucas [?] Iriaia abogado [lawyer]' and 'Dr Juan Pedro Segovia'. Minet Frères suggested that the manuscript was possibly from Segovia. In my opinion none of the evidence regarding the manuscript's origin and production can support such a view. The only reference to Segovia seems to be the handwritten name 'Dr Juan Pedro Segovia' on the endpaper; this, like the other handwritten inscriptions is more likely to refer to ownership than origin.[36] In a later hand on the front pastedown (verso) is Maria de los Angeles. On the last folio (48[V]) we find Muntanir [?] Parinya, Abril 1 (primero), and in different writing on the recto pastedown the date 1834. Again the name 'Antonio' appears on folio 48[V], and I believe that more faded or scraped handwriting would become visible here with the use of more advanced technology. At this point I am unable to shed further light on any of these inscriptions, and a full history of ownership of the manuscript awaits further information.

---

[33]Bindings from Toledo are often characterized by their use of the gold stamping of the *escudo* of that city, and those from Medina del Campo by contents bound for the New World. For more on this see Hueso Rolland, *Exposición de encuadernaciones españolas*, pp. 63–64.

[34]In discussing Salamanca, catedral mss 5–8, James Boyce refers to payment records of 1614 for the binding of twelve liturgical manuscripts (mss 11–22). These records suggested to him that manuscripts 5–8 were no longer in use in 1614 when the new books were bound. See Boyce, *Salamanca Cantus Printouts*, p. xxiii. A connection with Medina del Campo could also be argued for the Fisher manuscripts. See Plate XI of Penney, *Album of Selected Bookbindings*, which shows a binding from '?Medina del Campo ca 1600' that is very like that of Fisher 327, with the same Dominican brass bosses.

[35]The intials 'AHP ?traict' and 'HMRP' (also in the same ink and writing) seem to be part of this same inscription. These letters have no obvious significance with reference to religious houses. AHP could simply refer to a library (*Archivo Histórico Provincial?*).

[36]It could be a name (Juan Pedro) plus a place (Segovia), or it could just be the name Juan Pedro Segovia.

To sum up, Fisher RB add. ms 335 is a manuscript of the subtype of passional, common in the sixteenth century in Spain. Its contents form part of the *triduum sacrum* and include texts from the *nuevo rezado* and music from the late sixteenth century, the expanded and elaborated Toledo chant used in Salamanca. It would have been used along with other sources to complete the liturgy. The manuscript dates from after 1572, and may perhaps be dated to *ca* 1582, if it provided the model for, or was copied from, the *Officium hebdomadae sanctae* printed by the successors of Mathias Gast in Salamanca in 1582. This manuscript and the *kyriale/antiphoner* Fisher ms 327 very likely form part of the series of sixteenth-century choirbooks made for and now preserved in Salamanca Cathedral. Marginal annotations in Salamanca, catedral ms 5, suggest that the Fisher 335 was used with earlier pre-Tridentine books to update the pre-Tridentine source in accordance with the directives of the *nuevo rezado*. Perhaps Dominicans in Salamanca copied it for a private owner or for general cathedral use. The bindings are most probably from the Salamanca University school of bookbinding and from before 1600. On the other hand (although to my mind less likely) it could have been copied from the Salamanca print somewhere other than Salamanca. It may at one time have been owned and used in Segovia. The latest date noted in the manuscript is 1825, after which it dropped from view for almost two centuries until it turned up in the shop of a Brussels dealer in rare books and manuscripts. Its purchase by the Fisher Library was a piece of the most startling serendipity. It is now in Sydney, where I hope to unravel its history further.

Chapter 3

Gregorian responsories based on texts from the *Book of Judith*

Ruth Steiner

The *Book of Judith* describes a decisive event – a turning point – in a war in the Middle East.[1] The king of Assyria has created a powerful coalition of nations and, ambitious for even greater power, has gone to war against another king, who is himself the leader of a coalition. The second army is vanquished and its leader killed, but pockets of resistance remain. The king is angry and orders the leader of his troops, Holofernes, to seek out the resisters and force them to surrender. After making appropriate preparations, the force sets out; and one after another, the groups of resisters either surrender or are destroyed. It has been said that all wars are holy: certainly that is the case in this instance, for as each group surrenders it is compelled to abandon its gods and worship as a god the king of the aggressors.

When the Israelites learn of this, they turn immediately to their God; they fast and pray and make burnt offerings.[2] They also prepare for war: they seal off the mountain passes, establish defenses on the hilltops, and lay traps in the surrounding plains. One member of the opposing force has urged restraint; he is expelled and left for the Israelites to find. After being captured by them he outlines the strategy planned by the enemy.

The advancing army is now immense, and one by one the Israelites' defenses fail. There is a siege, their water supply is cut off, and they begin to wonder whether God has abandoned them. They cannot bear the thought of seeing their women and children die of thirst, and they plead with Uzziah, one of their leaders, to yield to Holofernes. Uzziah asks them to wait five days; if God does not help them within that time, he will surrender.

At this point a new figure unexpectedly enters the scene, a wealthy widow named Judith, who is pious, beautiful, and respected for her wisdom. She invites Uzziah and two other elders of the town to come to her house and there she addresses them

---

[1] For a summary, see Carey A. Moore, *Judith: A New Translation with Introduction and Commentary*, The Anchor Bible 40 (Garden City NY, 1985), pp. 31–37.

[2] *Ibid.*, p. 153: 'although the Israelites made some military preparations against Holofernes, ... their primary response was a religious one'.

earnestly. Don't issue ultimatums to God, don't tell Him He must act within five days, she says, but instead ask Him for help. She reminds them that they have always been faithful, they have never honoured any other god. They should remember that God has put the people of Israel to the test before; she reminds them of Abraham and Isaac. And then she tells the elders that she has a plan, and she believes it will work.

During the Middle Ages, the Old Testament was read (chanted to a lesson tone) during the service of matins in the Divine Office.[3] This reading, known as the 'lectio continua', began with Genesis on Septuagesima in the pre-Lent period. *Judith* was not read until late summer; the books preceding it were Job and Tobit, and after it came Esther.[4] The books were divided into lessons, and the reading of a single book would extend over several days or weeks, depending on its length. Often (especially in breviaries) the lessons were condensed. Each was followed by a responsory. Sometimes its text would recapitulate or seem to comment upon the lesson that preceded it, but more typically the responsories formed a separate, independent series that was coherent in itself, although related to the lessons through quotations from or references to the story.[5] On occasions when the reading of a book such as *Judith* continued on a second day, or a third, the texts of the lessons would change, but the original set of responsories would continue to be used.[6]

To return to the story of Judith and her plan: in what she says to the elders at this point are words that were incorporated into a responsory, *Nos alium deum nescimus*. The full text of the chant can be found in Appendix I in the reading of number 7237 in *CAO*.[7] It is the second in the series of responsories 'De Judith' in the twelfth-century antiphoner of the cathedral of Florence preserved today in the library of the

---

[3]For an outline of matins see L. Collamore, 'Charting the Divine Office', in *FS Steiner*, pp. 3–11. See also László Dobszay, 'Offizium', in *MGG*, vol. 2, p. 7, cols 593–609; and Ruth Steiner and Keith Falconer, 'Matins', in *NG2*, vol. 16, pp. 128–129.

[4]There was some variation in this over time; see Mario Righetti, *L'anno liturgico: il breviario*, Storia liturgica 2, 3rd edn (Milan, 1969), pp. 751–759, and Brad Maiani, 'Readings and Responsories: The Eighth-century Night Office Lectionary and the *Responsoria prolixa*', *JM* 16 (1998), pp. 254–282.

[5]Helmut Hucke, 'Das Responsorium', in Wulf Arlt and Max Haas, eds, *Gattungen der Musik in Einzeldarstellungen* (Berne, 1975), p. 171: 'Diese Zyklen stehen meist in Beziehung zu Lektionszyklen, aber nicht in dem Sinne, dass bestimmte Responsorien zu bestimmten Lesungen gehören, sondern dass die Lesungen und Responsorien einander entsprechende, jeweils in sich geschlossene Zyklen bilden.'

[6]Maiani speaks of 'the need for additional responsories when the books they accompany were reassigned or given extended reading time in the Lectionary of Ordo XIIIa'; see 'Readings and Responsories', p. 281. In his comments on Hartker's antiphoner in *CAO* René-Jean Hesbert links the number of responsories to the number of lessons, explaining additional chants (if any) as 'provenant de traditions diverses, et employés *ad libitum*, ou pendant la semaine et durant les octaves' (*CAO* 2, p. viii).

[7]Texts of antiphons are given in vol. 3 of this work, texts of responsories in vol. 4.

Arcivescovado of that city.[8] As the responsories that follow it in that source are mentioned in the text below, each will be accompanied by a number indicating its position in the series.

The source of the opening of *Nos alium* is not the Vulgate; that is, it does not come from the translation made by St Jerome in Bethlehem in 398.[9] Instead it comes from an earlier Latin translation – the so-called Old Latin – that was made from the Greek version of the *Book of Judith* that is found in the Septuagint.[10] Because the Old Latin text of *Judith* was adopted for use in the Gallican church, being employed in worship there before the imposition of Gregorian chant and associated liturgical practices, it seems plausible that at least the text of this responsory has Gallican roots.[11] The verse of the chant, on the other hand, is taken from the Vulgate. This is an interesting point, and I shall return to it later.

---

[8]A cursory description of the manuscript along with a detailed list of the chants in it was prepared at The Catholic University of America for the CANTUS database by Keith Glaeske, Charles Downey, and Lila Collamore. It is available online at http://publish.uwo.ca/~cantus. See also Marica Tacconi, 'Antifonario, con tonario di Oddone d'Arezzo', in Lorenzo Fabbri and Marica Tacconi, eds, *I Libri del Duomo di Firenze. Codici liturgici e Biblioteca di Santa Maria del Fiore (secoli XI–XVI)* (Florence, 1997), pp. 213–214; and Marica Tacconi, 'Liturgy and Chant at the Cathedral of Florence: A Survey of the Pre-Tridentine Sources (Tenth–Sixteenth Centuries)' (Ph.D. diss., Yale University, 1999), pp. 208–223.

Although CANTUS is primarily an online, frequently updated database designed for swift consultation and easy downloading, books featuring eight CANTUS indexes have been published by the Institute of Mediaeval Music since 1992. The books have been widely distributed, reviews of them have appeared in leading journals, and they have enabled scholars unfamiliar with the Internet to learn about CANTUS and the access it provides to sources of the Divine Office. Professor Gillingham's decision to support CANTUS by becoming its publisher has contributed significantly to its success.

[9]By his own account, the work was done in a single night. Because the only available Semitic text was in Aramaic, a language Jerome had not learned, he first had a translation made orally from that language into Hebrew; and as he listened to that he dictated his Latin version to his secretary. He says that he focused his efforts on 'rendering the sense of it rather than a literal translation', expressing in Latin 'only those readings which I could find in Chaldean [i.e. Aramaic] without doing violence to the sense'. And he confesses to having 'cut out the most faulty variant readings of the many manuscripts' (Moore, *Judith*, pp. 95–96, quoting translations made for him by Ruth Pavlantos). The quotations from Jerome come from his 'Preface to *Judith*' published in Robert Weber, ed., *Biblia sacra iuxta vulgatam versionem*, 2nd edn (Stuttgart, 1975), vol. 1, p. 691: 'Huic unam lucubratiunculam dedi, magis sensum e sensu quam ex verbo verbum transferens. Multorum codicum varietatem vitiosissimam amputavi; soli ea quae intellegentia integra in verbis chaldeis invenire potui, latinis expressi.'

[10]On the many differences between the two see Moore, *Judith*, pp. 94–100.

[11]Pierre-Maurice Bogaert, ed., *Judith*, Vetus Latina: die Reste der altlateinischen Bibel 7/2 (Freiburg, 2001), pp. 50–51. I thank Monica Blanchard for calling this book to my attention at a time when it had just arrived in the Catholic University library and was not yet catalogued.

A typical medieval antiphoner provides eight responsories for the period of the year during which the *Book of Judith* is read in the Divine Office; however, some give nine, and some fewer. The eight responsories are quite stable. (This is evident in both Hesbert's *Corpus antiphonalium officii* and the CANTUS database.)[12] The texts of seven of the eight can be shown to have been drawn from the Bible, and all seven come from passages where there is direct quotation of the speech of characters.[13] The singing of the responsories is thus in effect and to a limited extent a dramatization of the story rather than a retelling of it. I shall mention them as I go through the rest of the story.

Judith's strategy requires a face-to-face confrontation with Holofernes, and that requires careful preparation. She knows she must seek divine aid; she prostrates herself and puts ashes on her head before beginning to pray. Her long prayer in chapter 9 is the source of two responsory texts. The first, *Domine deus qui conteris bella* (R. 3;14 *CAO* 6942), takes as its point of departure verses 10 and 11 of the Vulgate version. The second, *Dominator domine caelorum* (R. 4; *CAO* 6488), is almost entirely a literal quotation from the Old Latin.[15] A remarkable feature of these two chants is that they are sung to virtually the same melody, a theme frequently used for responsories in mode 2.[16]

---

[12]For a comparative presentation of the responsories *de Judith* in *CAO* see item number 134 in vol. 1, pp. 388–389, and vol. 2, pp. 736–737.

[13]Online versions of the Vulgate have rendered the old printed biblical concordances obsolete. One such offering that was particularly useful for this project is that provided by the Scholarly Text and Information Service (SETIS) at the University of Sydney. The address is http://setis.library.usyd.edu.au. It has the advantage of including the books of the Apocrypha, of which Judith is one, and of containing the Gallican Psalter, rather than the Psalter 'iuxta Hebraeos', which was rarely, if ever, drawn on for the texts of chants. (No searchable online version of the text known as the Roman Psalter is yet available, though it would be of significant practical use for chant scholars. I thank Professor Terence Bailey for kindly helping me to surmount this obstacle.) For the various translations of the book of Psalms into Latin see James W. McKinnon, 'Jerome', in *NG2*, vol. 13, pp. 10–11. For attempts by various scholars to explain why Judith is regarded as deuterocanonical see Moore, *Judith*, pp. 86–91.

[14] Such references are to the responsory texts given as an appendix to this article.

[15]In the absence of a complete modern edition of the Old Latin text of Judith it is difficult to determine exactly what the Urtext may have been, and thus any conclusions concerning the extent to which texts were modified when they were adapted for use in chants must be regarded as tentative. The numbering of verses in Moore's English translation of the Septuagint text does not correspond to that in Pierre Sabatier's edition of the Old Latin, *Bibliorum sacrorum Latinae versiones antiquae; seu Vetus Italica*, 2nd edn (Paris–Reims, 1751), vol. 1, part 2, pp. 746ff. Sabatier's numbers are employed here.

[16]Wagner used one of them to demonstrate the melody, Frere the other. See Peter Wagner, *Einführung in die gregorianischen Melodien, III: Gregorianische Formenlehre* (Leipzig, 1921), p. 336; Walter Howard Frere, *Antiphonale sarisburiense* (London, 1901–1924), vol. 1, pp. 6–7, and vol. 3, p. 320; and especially Hans-Jørgen Holman, 'The Responsoria Prolixa of the Codex Worcester F. 160', (Ph.D. diss., Indiana University, 1961), vol. I, pp. 87, 90–91.

Having concluded her prayer, Judith prepares for her mission. She removes her drab clothing (she is a widow, and she has been in mourning), bathes, perfumes herself, arranges her hair, and puts on a beautiful dress. Accompanied by her very capable maidservant, she goes to the enemy camp and gains entry. She remains there for three days, having been given permission to go out each night to purify herself and to pray. Holofernes has found her fascinating, and on the fourth day he arranges for her to dine with him alone. He is utterly overwhelmed by her beauty and her presence, so much so that he drinks too much, more than he has ever drunk before on one occasion, and he falls asleep. Judith seizes her opportunity, cuts off his head, and gives it to her servant, who puts it into a bag. Then the two women hide the headless corpse and leave the camp as they have on each of the preceding three nights.[17]

When they reach the city of the Israelites, Judith calls out to the watchmen, using words that are echoed in one of the responsories: *Vos qui in turribus estis, aperite portas* (R. 5). Some of the people have feared that she might have defected to the enemy; she has foreseen this, and to reassure them she pulls the head of Holofernes from the sack and holds it up, saying *Laudate dominum deum nostrum* (R. 6).

Uzziah is among those in the crowd, and he greets her warmly with the words *Benedixit te dominus in virtute sua* (R. 7). Without Holofernes to lead them, the Assyrians are quickly defeated. The book ends with Judith singing a hymn of praise – the Canticle of Judith, which has a history of its own – that is evoked and concisely paraphrased in a chant text, but not quoted, except for a very few words. The chant begins *Adonai domine deus magne et mirabilis* (R. 8). The text is perhaps traceable to the Old Latin.

A number of manuscripts present the chants in the same order as the Florence antiphoner, preceding them with one that begins *Tribulationes civitatum* (R.1), a text that evokes the scene described in the first part of the book, thus seeming to belong here at the beginning of the series. A new critical edition of the Old Latin text of the book of Judith is in progress; the first fascicle was published in 2001. The editor is familiar with the text of this responsory, and he finds in it two features that seem to come from a source other than the Vulgate, perhaps the Old Latin. One is the word *Tribulationes*, and the other is a reference to the impossibility of flight.[18]

---

[17]The opportunity to depict a seductively dressed, beautiful, and purposeful woman gazing at (or at least standing close to) the bloody head of a tyrant has attracted many painters, some of them quite renowned, to the story of Judith. Perhaps the best known depiction (dated 1901) is that of Gustav Klimt, who clothed her in an intricately decorated gown that is open in front. Another approach to the subject matter was taken by Artemesia Gentilleschi in 1612–1613; she showed the horrifying act as it was taking place, with Holofernes bleeding copiously. I am indebted to Donald F. Henderson for proposing the story of Judith as a topic for interdisciplinary discussion.

[18]Bogaert, *Judith*, p. 51. Maiani finds the melody of *Tribulationes* atypical, and uses that as the basis for his assertion that this chant was a later addition to a pre-existing series of seven chants. For his valuable comments on Holman's analysis of *Tribulationes*, see Holman, pp. 276–277.

In the responsories for Judith are four features that are difficult to explain. The use of the Old Latin is one, the combining of Old Latin texts in the responsories with verses from the Vulgate is the second, and the various arrangements in which the responsories appear in the sources is the third. The fourth will be discussed later; the different arrangements can be taken up now.

In one arrangement the responsories are placed in the order in which their source texts occur in the Bible. Using the the numbers given above for them (1 through 8) facilitates a comparison of that order with other arrangements. This biblical order is found in sources from the cathedral of Florence (as already demonstrated); Worcester Cathedral; St Denys; Notre-Dame, Paris; the monastery of San Eutizio, Norcia; and Benevento.[19] There are variations on this; some are shown below:

1 2 3 4 5 8 7 6   (Cambrai 38 – the last three chants are in reverse order)
1 2 3 5 6 7 8   (Paris, BNF, lat. 1090 – note that 4 is omitted)
1 2 4 3 5 6 8   (Toledo 44.2 – note that 7 is omitted, and 4 and 3 are
                    reversed)
1 2 3 6   (Florence, Bibl. Laurentiana, conv. sopp. 560 – an
                    abridged series, found in a source that is conservative in
                    other respects)[20]

A different arrangement of the same responsories appears in some sources, and it too appears occasionally in variant forms. The main series is found in the Antiphoner of Charles the Bald and in sources from Weingarten, Cluny, and northern France (in the French antiphoner referred to by Hesbert as G): 8 1 7 2 4 3 5 6.[21]

Occasionally a ninth responsory, *Recordare* (represented by 9* in the lists that follow), is added to this series, as in the following examples.

8 1 7 9* 2 4 3 5 6 (Hartker)
8 1 7 2 9* 4 3 5 6 (Bamberg and Krainburg, Carniola (now Kranj), Slovenia)

---

[19]The sources in question are as follows (when information concerning one of them comes from *CAO*, that is indicated; otherwise all information comes from the online version of CANTUS): Worcester, Cathedral, F. 160 (*ca* 1230, from the Cathedral of Worcester); Paris, BNF lat. 17296 (twelfth century, from Saint-Denys, *CAO*); Paris, BNF lat. 15181–2 (*ca* 1300, Cathedral of Notre-Dame, Paris); Rome, Bibl. Vallicelliana, C. 5 (late eleventh or twelfth century, originally from Rome); Benevento, Bibl. cap. 19 and 20 (twelfth century, from Benevento).

[20]These sources are Cambrai, BM 38 (*ca* 1230–1250, from Cambrai Cathedral); Paris, BNF lat. 1090 (late twelfth century, from Marseille); Toledo, Archivo y Biblioteca Capítulares, 44.2 (end of eleventh century, from Aquitaine); and Florence, Bibl. Medicea-Laurenziana, conv. sopp. 560 (late twelfth century, from Vallombrosa).

[21]Paris, BNF lat. 17436 (between 860 and 880, from Compiègne, known as the antiphoner of Charles the Bald, *CAO*); Stuttgart, Württembergische Landesbibliothek, HB.I.55 (twelfth or thirteenth century, from Weingarten); Paris, BNF lat. 12601 (late eleventh century, from near Amiens but representing the use of Cluny); and Durham, Cathedral Library, B. III. 11 (eleventh century, from northern France, *CAO*).

8 1 7 2   9* 3 4   5 6   (Pavia)
8 1 7 2   3   4 9* 5 6   (Rheinau and Zwiefalten)[22]

One remarkable variant, in Piacenza 65, is the series 8 1 7 3 5 6, which omits the responsories that have the most evident borrowings from the Old Latin.[23]

What is most striking here is not the relative disorder at the end of the series nor the occasional introduction of 'Recordare', but the strong disagreement concerning the beginning of the series. What could be the reason for it? One principle in textual scholarship is that a reading that is difficult to understand should not be dismissed, but studied; it may reveal more than one whose meaning is self-evident. It is easy to understand why manuscript editors might have chosen to place the chants in the order of the episodes of the Bible to which they refer. It is not easy to understand why the order beginning 'Adonai domine deus' was adopted; hence that is the one that invites additional consideration. But first both the music and the texts of these chants need to be examined.

The music for most of the chants makes use of standard formulas in traditional ways. There are formulas of two types: those for the respond, and those for the verse. The formulas for the verses follow the system of the ecclesiastical modes – the verse of a chant is sung to the formula for responsory verses of chants in the mode to which the respond belongs. Those for the responds are more varied, though they lend themselves to codification through a system devised by W. H. Frere and improved upon by Hans-Jørgen Holman.[24] In the medieval practice, the respond is sung first, and followed by the verse, which itself is followed by a refrain consisting of the last part of the respond. This repetendum is usually indicated by a single word that shows where the refrain begins. Florid passages are used to define phrases and clarify the structure of the text. The musical settings thus promote intelligibility; they assist in the projection of the text and make it easier to understand. What they do not do is underline the meaning of individual words and phrases.

As Frere pointed out, *Domine deus* and *Dominator domine* have essentially the same melody, and that for *Nos alium deus* is very similar.[25] The texts of the first two come from the same passage, the prayer Judith utters before she prepares to go to Holofernes's camp; *Domine deus* is based on the Vulgate version of *Judith*, while *Dominator domine* comes from the Old Latin. There's no significant difference between the music that we have for the Old Latin text and the music that we have for the

---

[22]St Gallen, SB 390–91 (*ca* 1000, from St Gallen), *CAO*; Bamberg, Staatsbibliothek, lit. 25 (*olim* ED.IV.11, late thirteenth century, from Bamberg Cathedral); Ljubljana, Nadskofijski arhiv (Archiepiscopal Archives), 17 and 18 (last decade of fifteenth century); Monza, Basilica di S. Giovanni Battista – Biblioteca Capitolare e Tesoro, 15/79 (twelfth century, from St Mayeul, Pavia); Zürich, Zentralbibliothek, Rh. 28 (thirteenth century, from Rheinau, *CAO*).

[23]Piacenza, Basilica di S. Antonino – Biblioteca e Archivio Capitolari, 65 (twelfth century, from the Cathedral of Piacenza).

[24]See Holman, 'The Responsoria Prolixa', vol. 1, pp. 63–75.

[25]Frere, *Antiphonale sarisburiense*, vol. 1, pp. 6–7.

text from the Vulgate, and thus it appears that if there was once a Gallican melody for *Dominator domine*, it has been lost. Of the five other responsories, *Tribulationes civitatum* reveals the greatest flexibility in the way pre-existing melodic formulas have been drawn on in the setting of the text.[26]

Most of the texts of these chants are not original, nor are they lengthy quotations of Biblical passages; instead, they are centonized. The examples below will help to clarify what is meant by this. In *Benedixit te dominus* the respond is made up of two separate selections from chapter 13 of the Vulgate translation of *Judith*; one comes from verse 22, the other from the end of verse 25; and the verse consists of two other selections made from the same source – the first part of verse 24, and the first part of verse 25:

22b benedixit te dominus in virtute sua quia per te ad nihilum redegit inimicos nostros ...	[**Resp.**] Benedixit te dominus in virtute sua qui pro te ad nihilum redegit inimicos nostros ut non deficiat laus tua de ore hominum.
24 benedictus dominus qui creavit caelum et terram qui te direxit in vulnere capitis principis inimicorum nostrorum	[**V.**] Benedictus dominus qui creavit celum et terram
25a quia hodie nomen tuum ita magnificavit ut non recedat laus tua de ore hominum ...	quia hodie nomen tuum ita magnificabit.

The entire text of *Nos alium deus* comes from chapter 8, verse 19, of the Old Latin, with a few words omitted. The verse comes from the Vulgate, the end of verse 14 and the beginning of verse 16.

[Old Latin] 19b nos autem alium deum nescimus praeter eum, in quo speramus, quia non despiciet nos, nec auferet salvationem, & misericordiam suam a nobis, & a genere nostro.	[**Resp.**] Nos alium deum nescimus praeter dominum in quo speramus qui non despiciat nos nec amovit salutem suam a genere nostro
[Vulg.] 14b et indulgentiam eius lacrimis postulemus ...	[**V.**] Indulgentiam eius profusis lacrimis postulemus
16a et ideo humiliemus illi animas nostras ...	& humiliemus illi animas nostras. [**R.**] Qui non ...

---

[26]Maiani, 'Readings and Responsories', pp. 276–281, sees in this, along with other features of its style, a reason for assigning it to a group of later chants.

The first of the examples above presents a chant in which both the respond and the verse have texts taken from the Vulgate reading of *Judith*. The chants *Domine deus qui conteris* and *Vos qui in turribus* are of the same type, and one would expect all of the other responsories to be like them. This is not the case. The second example above, in which the respond is taken from the Old Latin text of *Judith* and the verse from the Vulgate *Judith*, has a counterpart in *Dominator domine*. This is perhaps the most interesting pair of chants in the series, for reasons to be discussed below. Yet another possibility is demonstrated in the respond *Laudate dominum deum*, which has a text from the Vulgate *Judith* and a verse taken from the Roman Psalter.[27] *Tribulationes montium* also has a verse from a psalm; the (presumably Gallican) source of that responsory text, like that of *Adonai domine deus*, has yet to be identified. The verse of the latter responsory is taken from the Vulgate *Judith*. The following summarizes this information.

Responsory perhaps adapted from the Old-Latin *Judith*, verse from the Vulgate *Judith*	**R.** 8 Adonai domine deus
Responsory perhaps adapted from the Old-Latin *Judith*, verse from the Roman Psalter	**R.** 1 Tribulationes montium
Responsories from the Old-Latin *Judith*, verses from the Vulgate *Judith*	**R.** 2 Nos alium deum **R.** 4 Dominator domine
Responsories from the Vulgate *Judith*, verses from the same source	**R.** 3 Domine deus qui conteris **R.** 5 Vos qui in turribus **R.** 7 Benedixit te dominus
Responsory from the Vulgate *Judith*, verse from the Roman Psalter	**R.** 6 Laudate dominum

It is thus evident that for this series of responsories, the texts at least were compiled from diverse sources. It should be remembered that the verses of the *Judith* responsories are much less stable than are the responds; for example, in *CAO* four different verses are given for *Nos alium deus*.[28] (The verses that have been analysed here are those present in the Florence Antiphoner.) This suggests that the two traditions are separate, with the texts of the responds being more firmly established than those of the verses. This leads to another question: could some of these respond texts

---

[27]Concerning this translation of the book of Psalms, which antedates that of the Gallican Psalter and is usually the one drawn on in the texts of chants, see McKinnon, 'Jerome'.

[28] *CAO* 4, 308 (chant number 7237).

have originated in chants of a different genre, such as the antiphon, where there were no verses?

The order in which the *Judith* responsories appear in the second group of sources (responsory from the Old Latin *Judith*, verse from the Vulgate *Judith*), that is, the order that begins 8 1 7 2 4, brings to the forefront chant texts that have certain features in common. Two of the five – 2 and 4 – come directly from the Old Latin text of *Judith*, and two others – 8 and 1 – appear to have some connection with it. Three of the four just mentioned have endings that are not typical of Gregorian responsories. Number 8, *Adonai domine deus*, ends 'exaudi preces servorum tuorum'. Number 1, *Tribulationes*, ends 'domine miserere'; and Number 4, *Dominator domine*, ends 'exaudi orationem servorum tuorum'. Thus the fourth of the series of questions antici-pated above presents itself. These three chants, or rather the respond sections (not the verses) of these three chants, seem to belong to a genre in which it is customary to end with a petition. What could it be?

In the Gallican church, the book of Judith was read during Rogations,[29] services in which worshippers pray to God for help. There's a series of Rogation antiphons in the Aquitanian gradual Paris, BNF lat. 903, and antiphons in this series are often presented in music reference works as examples of Gallican chant. What they have in common with the prayer Judith utters in chapter 9, and with these respond texts, is that they ask God for help.

Thus it may be that the four chants 8, 1, 2, and 4 are Gallican rogation antiphons that were absorbed into Gregorian matins, along with the reading of the book of Judith, by being given verses, and by having Gregorian melodies adapted to them.[30] Two verses, those for *Adonai* and *Tribulationes*, were taken from the Roman Psalter; the other two came from the Vulgate version of *Judith*. In places where there was hesitation about juxtaposing chant series known to have been drawn from the two different traditions, the Gallican chants were hidden from view by being filed away in correct Biblical order; in other places where this was not a concern, the series was allowed to begin with the Gallican texts and the powerful word, *Adonai*, which is still used by devout Jews as a substitute for God's real name.

This is clearly not the last word on this subject. The explanation given above does not take into account the fact that responsory 7, *Benedixit te dominus*, which is entirely on Vulgate texts, stands near the beginning of the series, among the chants identified as partly Gallican. Next to nothing has been said here about *Recordare*, for which the evidence in the sources is so complex as to suggest that it merits a study of its own.

---

[29] Bogaert, *Judith*, p. 51.

[30] *Ibid.*, p. 50, states it thus: 'Tout se passe comme si, dans ANT-M et RES-R [the Moz-arabic antiphoner and the Responsorium Romanum], un vieux fonds était submergé par des apports tirés de la Vulgate.' In the CANTUS database are references to two antiphons that have texts identical to those of the respond parts of two of the responsories under discussion: *Adonai domine deus* and *Nos autem*. Only one source for the antiphon *Nos autem* has been found so far, the Aquitanian antiphoner Toledo 44.2. *Adonai domine deus* is well known.

However, the diversity in the points of origin of the Judith respond and verse texts, and the fact that they appear in two very different arrangements in the sources, are in striking contrast with the relatively conservative use of traditional 'Gregorian' music for them. The texts and their verses were selected from several different traditions – the Old Latin *Judith*, the Vulgate *Judith*, the Roman Psalter, and perhaps also a Gallican collection of votive antiphons. They were shaped into a conventional series of office responsories by having well-known Gregorian melodies and melodic formulas adapted to them. Judith transformed her appearance from that of a modest widow to that of a *femme fatale* as part of a plan to commit the murder that would save her people. The goal of those who clothed these texts with music appears to have been nothing more than that of making the responsories that tell her story seem on the surface relatively uniform and conventional – except perhaps for *Tribulationes montium*. If that was indeed their purpose, they were successful.

Appendix
Responsory texts

R. 1 (7779) Tribulationes civitatum audivimus quae passae sunt, et defecimus; timor et ebitudo mentis cecidit super nos et super liberos nostros: ipsi montes nolunt recipere fugam nostram; domine, miserere.

V. Peccavimus cum patribus nostris; injuste egimus, iniqitatem fecimus.

Refrain. domine

R. 2 (7237) Nos alium deum nescimus, praeter dominum in quo speramus, qui non despiciat nos, nec amovet salutem suam a genere nostro.

V. Indulgentiam illius fusis lacrimis postulemus, et humiliemus illi animas nostras.

Refrain. qui non

R. 3 (6492) Domine deus, qui conteris bella ab initio, eleva brachium tuam super gentes quae cogitant servis tuis mala, et dextera tua glorificetur in nobis.

V. Allide virtutem eorum in virtute tua, cadat virtus eorum in iracundia tua.

Refrain. et dex

R. 4 (6488) Dominator domine coelorum et terrae, creator aquarum, rex universae creaturae tuae, exaudi orationem servorum tuorum.

V. Tu, domine, cui humilium semper et mansuetorum placuit deprecatio.

Refrain. exau

R. 5 (7913) Vos qui in turribus estis, aperite portas: dominus omnipotens fecit virtutem, et victoriam dedit de inimicis nostris.

V. Laudate dominum deum nostrum, qui non deseruit presumentes de se.

Refrain. et victoriam

R. 6 (7078) Laudate dominum deum nostrum, qui non deseruit sperantes in se, et in me adimplevit misericordiam suam quam promisit domui Israhel.

V. Confitemini domino quoniam bonus, quoniam in seculum misericordia eius.

Refrain. quam

R. 7 (6253) Benedixit te dominus in virtute sua, qui per te ad nihilum redegit inimicos nostros, ut non deficiat laus tua de ore hominum.

V. Benedictus dominus qui creavit coelum et terram quia hodie nomen suum magnificavit

Refrain. ut non

R. 8 (6043) Adonai, Domine deus magne et mirabilis, qui dedisti salutem in manu feminae, exaudi preces servorum tuorum.

V. Benedictus es, domine, qui non relinquis praesumentes de te, et de sua virtute gloriantes humilias.

Refrain. ex

Chapter 4

Modes and modality: a unifying concept for Western chant?

John Caldwell

Research during the last forty or so years on the eight-mode system in both East and West has very properly focused on the documentary evidence. Outstanding contributions have included Michel Huglo's volume *Les tonaires*, Terence Bailey's *The Intonation Formulas of Western Chant*, and, much more recently, Peter Jeffery's magisterial survey 'The Earliest Oktōēchoi'.[1] One effect of this, as regards the Western chant repertories, has been a strong emphasis on the role of the Franks in adopting such a system, and on the lack of any documentation to suggest that other repertories were affected by it. In particular it has been denied that it bore any relevance to large parts (if to any) of the Old Roman repertory, and it is not uncommon to read assertions that modal organization was unknown outside the Frankish sphere.

As a consequence of this emphasis, there has been a parallel and ongoing search for simpler forms of modality, or tonal organization however it may be named, not only in the non-Gregorian repertories but also in the earlier stages of the Gregorian repertory itself (to the extent that 'earlier stages' are discernible).[2] Much stress is laid on inconsistencies in the Gregorian application of the system and on the evidence they seem to provide that it was mechanically imposed on a repertory not actually designed for it. There is some truth in this, but it is not the whole truth, and the current emphasis often seems to have the effect of deflecting attention from the analytical realities of those chant repertories that have been recorded in pitch-specific notation.

The approach taken in this chapter is somewhat different. It takes as its point of departure the common elements in the fully notated chant repertories: those, that is, in which the actual pitches either are unambiguously recorded or can be recovered by

---

[1] Michel Huglo, *Les tonaires: inventaire, analyse, comparaison* (Paris, 1971); Terence Bailey, *The Intonation Formulas of Western Chant* (Toronto, 1974); Peter Jeffery, 'The Earliest Oktō-ēchoi: the Role of Jerusalem and Palestine in the Beginnings of Modal Ordering', in *FS Levy*.

[2] I use the terms Gregorian and Old Roman conventionally; by 'the earlier stages of the Gregorian repertory' I mean what might be inferred about these on analytical and other grounds, as distinct from any of the specific details afforded by the Old Roman repertory, which may indeed have had a separate origin as well as being self-evidently 'late' in its surviving form.

inference. No account is taken of repertories (in particular the Old Hispanic) for which this is not the case. At the same time the evidence from Francia predates the unambiguous notation of pitch in Gregorian chant, encouraging us to believe that the tonal system of other ambiguously notated repertories may after all have conformed to the same principles.

The simplistic assertion (not found, needless to say, in the writings of reputable scholars) that Gregorian chant 'has' modes while others do not clearly contradicts the view that the modes were imposed on a Gregorian repertory not designed for them. If the latter is the case, then the Gregorian repertory is no more 'modal' than the others, except to the extent that it may have been wilfully manipulated to conform to the system. That Gregorian chant underwent some modifications to suit the needs of pitch-specific notations is not in doubt, but that is just as likely to be true of other repertories similarly notated.

The notation of pitch, as of rhythm, arises from theory, in the West as in the East. The concept of mode is not dependent on such theory, but the theory of pitch relations, at least in the Middle Ages, always takes cognizance of modes. Setting aside for the moment the earliest Frankish evidence for the eight-mode system, including that of Aurelianus of Réôme, we should start our investigation with the earliest writings to envisage a comprehensive system of pitches, the *De harmonica institutione* of Hucbald and the anonymous *Musica* and *Scolica enchiriadis*.[3]

Hucbald stands apart from the Enchiridian authors and does not invoke numerical ratios to define the nature of a tone and a semitone, from which, as he points out, all other intervals derive. No doubt his readers would have been able to supplement his definitions, based on familiar chants and on the tuning of organs, by reference to the Boethian or early medieval monochord. But he did describe ways in which the musical scale could be analysed and notated, using the terminology of the diatonic perfect system of the ancient Greeks and another more 'ecclesiastical' system of tetrachords, relating both to the properties of known chants. The two systems were connected, in that both occupied the tonal region based on the range later identified as $A - a'$ (including 'round' b), and were based on a series of alternately conjunct and disjunct tetrachords. The ancient system (typically descending) was based on the series $a'-e'$, $e'-b$, $a-e$, $e-B$, A, together with an additional tetrachord, $d'-a$, conjunct with the next lower one, $a-e$. All these tetrachords were of the form TTS (tone, tone, semitone) descending. The 'ecclesiastical' system was a kind of mirror image of this, ascending

---

[3]No implications as to relative chronology are intended by the order in which these writings are discussed. For Hucbald I have used *GS*, vol. 1, pp. 103–121a (at 'protenditur'), using the corrections supplied in *Hucbald, Guido, and John on Music*, transl. Warren Babb (New Haven, 1978), pp. 45–46, and for the Enchiridian treatises, Hans Schmid, ed., *Musica et Scolica enchiriadis una cum tractatulis adiunctis recensio nova post Gerbertinam altera ad fidem omnium codicum manuscriptorum*, VMK 3 (Munich, 1981), with the translation by Raymond Erickson, *Musica enchiriadis and Scolica enchiriadis* (New Haven, 1995).

in the form *A–d, d–g, a–d′, d′–g′, a′*, with a conjunct tetrachord *g–c′*, all in the form TST.[4]

Curiously enough, Hucbald reverts to the ancient system in discussing the modes in relation to the note series, with the result that he cannot speak (as the Enchiridian authors do) of a *tetrachordum finalium*. His understanding is nevertheless that the notes we call *d, e, f,* and *g* 'perfect' the 'four modes or tropes, which we now call tones, that is to say the protus, deuterus, tritus, and tetrardus'. Each of these four notes (*chordae*), he goes on to say, is fitted to 'rule over' the tropes in pairs, a principal or authentic and a lateral or plagal. 'Consequently any melody whatsoever is perforce classified under some one of these four pairs of modes, however variously it ranges about, whether far afield or close [to the final]. These four notes are called "finals", since everything that is sung ends among them.'[5]

Hucbald was evidently anxious to relate ecclesiastical music as far as possible to the ancient system inherited from Boethius; he seems to have been unaware of the theoretical potential of the alternative, ascending, system of tetrachords of the form TST, although he implies them in the passage immediately following the one just cited.[6] Indeed, from his treatise alone it might be inferred that the form of this tetrachord was merely a consequence of turning the ancient system on its head. But the Enchiridian treatises, which also use tetrachords of the form TST, seem to indicate otherwise.

For the Enchiridian authors, the TST tetrachord is an unexplained 'given'. The arrangement is purely disjunct, so that outside the central octave *d–g, a–d′*, we encounter *b flat* beneath and *f′ sharp*, and even *c″ sharp*, above. It is difficult to support the argument that this arrangement was designed to accommodate these flat and sharp

---

[4]Either form of scale could be understood both ascending and descending; I have emphasized the descending form of the ancient scale and the ascending form of the medieval scale in order to demonstrate their complementarity. In the Middle Ages ascending scale forms became paramount.

[5]'Quatuor a primis tribus [i.e. following the first three notes of the ascending scale], id est, lichanos hypaton, hypate meson, parypate meson, lichanos meson, quatuor modis vel tropis, quos nunc tonos dicunt, hoc est, protus, deuterus, tritus, tetrardus, perficiendis aptantur: ita ut singulae earum quatuor chordarum geminos sibi tropos regant subiectos, principalem, qui et autentus, et lateralem, qui plagius appellatur [...] ita ut ad aliquem ipsarum quatuor quamvis ultra citraque variabiliter circumacta, necessario omnis, quaecumque fuerit, redigatur cantilena. Unde et eaedem finales appellatae, quod finem in ipsis cuncta, que canuntur accipiant'. *GS*, vol. 1, p. 119a, corrected from *Hucbald, Guido, and John on Music*, 46, with the latter part of the text as translated there on pp. 38–39.

[6]'Ad quarum [i.e. the notes *d e f g*] exemplar caetera nihilominus tetrachorda, quorum unum inferius, tria superius eminent, spatia, vel qualitatem deducunt sonorum'. His further reference to final notes a fifth higher than those previously mentioned as obligatory (i.e. *a, b natural, c′, d′*) is ambiguous, but may refer to genuine alternatives, as is attested for Eastern chant, rather than to transpositions of the mode itself. (An example, though later, of a mode 1 chant ending on *a* is the Kyrie 'Cunctipotens genitor deus'.)

pitches in chant (the Enchiridian authors were entirely innocent of this nomenclature, of course) and a good deal easier to believe that it arose as an extrapolation of a disjunct system originally covering no more than the central octave.[7] Hucbald had solved this problem by making the lower and higher tetrachords conjunct, while his additional conjunct tetrachord *g–c'* validated the note that was to become *b flat*, which was not present in the Enchiridian system and later regarded as a corruption by the Cistercians.

The Enchiridian treatises have been studied principally in relation to the 'dasian' system of notation which they use, and for their descriptions of early polyphonic practice. The former is indeed a close concomitant of the tetrachordal scale, the structure and nomenclature of which is our principal concern, but its details need not be repeated here. It needs to be emphasized again that translations into modern (or in the present case Guidonian) pitch nomenclature are purely for the sake of convenience and formed no part of the Enchiridian musical cosmos.

The first point to mention – and it is important – is that in the *Musica enchiriadis* the terms *protos* or *archoos*, *deuteros*, *tritos*, and *tetrardus* [*sic*] are in the first instance applied to the notes (*ptongi*) of any tetrachord. The tetrachords in their disjunct arrangement are then set out and their constituent notes given the names *graves*, *finales*, *superiores*, and *excellentes*. A little later the same numerical adjectives, as applied to the notes of the *tetrachordum finalium*, are said to 'rule' and 'conclude' the *melum*[8] of the four *toni* and their respective *subiugales*. A little later still we are told that the 'vis primi soni → primi toni virtutem creet, qui protus autentus dicitur', and similarly for the remaining three: this is the first time that the Greek ordinal numerals are used in this treatise to indicate 'modes' rather than notes. This 'force' is exerted in each case by the tendency of a melody, schematically represented by its enechematic formula,[9] to descend towards the prescribed *finalis*.

It is probably not a coincidence that the terms *protos*, *deuteros*, *tritos*, and *tetartos* seem to refer in medieval Greek theory indifferently to notes and to 'modes'; indeed it is in the last resort uncertain what the primary musical significance of *ēchos* actually was. We are hampered by the fact that although the *ēchos* nomenclature itself is very early, the theory that supports it is not found before the fourteenth century. This theory is further marked by a failure to define the intervallic relationship between the notes of a tetrachord: our best evidence for the intended relationship is actually that provided

---

[7]The view that the dasian scale was devised with the needs of chants containing low *B flat* and high *f' sharp* was firmly articulated by Nancy C. Phillips in her dissertation, '*Musica* and *Scolica enchiriadis*: The Literary, Theoretical, and Musical Sources' (New York University, 1984), especially pp. 470–497. The difficulty is that it does not explain why these pitches should have been privileged over the equally necessary low *B* and the even more necessary high *f*.

[8]Chapter 3; Hans Schmid, ed., *Musica et Scolica enchiriadis*, p. 7. The author uses the terms *melos* and *melum* indifferently, in this case in the space of a single line.

[9]*Ibid.*, p. 15. The enechematic formulae here lack their distinctive syllables and are identical but for their placement on the eight-note grid, descending in each case to the *finalis* from the note a fifth above according to the pattern 5 4 3 4 3 2 1.

by the Enchiridian treatises, for we may assume that these represent a modification of contemporary Greek practice.

Although medieval Greek theory is ambiguous, it does offer an explanation for the terms 'authentic' and 'plagal', the latter indeed being applied to the notes belonging to the lower of the two disjunct tetrachords. The object of the Greek system was not to define a *finalis* but to arrive at the starting note of a melody. The enechematic formulae fall into two classes. Those said to belong to the *kyrioi* (the term in our sources for what Western writers call the authentic modes) start on the fifth above the (Western) *finalis*, to which they may fall before reverting, in any event, to the starting note. If a particular melody in any one mode starts on a different note, it begins with the appropriate intervallic sign. The *enēchēmata* belonging to the plagal *ēchoi* both begin and end on the (Western) *finalis*.[10]

The Western versions of these formulae differ primarily in causing each of the authentic formulae to end on the *finalis* and not on the fifth above. They signify a profoundly different approach to the analysis of melodic behaviour, an analysis that presupposes an orientation towards a goal rather than the expression of inherent and omnipresent characteristics. (To digress for a moment, it would seem that this has become the defining feature of Western music – a constant provisionality that achieves its resolution only at the conclusion of a piece.) But that this understanding was not universal amongst early Western musicians is borne out by the observations of some of them that certain melodies appeared to begin in one mode and end in another.

It is the thesis of this essay that the eight-mode system is inherent in the structure of the octave in the form of two disjunct tetrachords of the form TST. Its eight constituent notes are defined according to the relationship between the two tetrachords (yielding the opposition authentic/plagal) and according to the relationship between the notes within a tetrachord. The characteristics of a mode are defined in relation to these notes, the role of which may also, but need not, be that of its *finalis*.

Several questions of consequence arise. First, were the *ēchoi* simply the notes from which the modes arose, or were there, at the outset, well defined melody-types for which the eight-mode system provided a means of recognition and a mechanism for starting them off? Second, did Western musicians recognize similar melody-types in

---

[10] Of course these few remarks do not do justice to the variety and complexity of the Greek theoretical materials. A complete coverage would have to take into account two different traditions, that known as the *Hagiopolites*, with its ten modes, and the so-called *Papadike*, with its references to four *mesoi* in addition to the four authentic and four plagal modes. From the fourteenth century, in any case, identifiable 'masters' added their distinctive contributions. Ancient theory is transmitted solely in medieval manuscripts, some of which also contain medieval theory, which may imply a certain symbiosis. Finally there are those medieval theorists who simply reformulated ancient theory in their writings. The poor state of the earliest manuscripts, making it necessary for scholars in the field to consult sources of the sixteenth, seventeenth, eighteenth, and even nineteenth centuries, is compounded by the situation with regard to editions: although this is now being remedied, some reliance still has to be placed on older collections of doubtful accuracy and unsatisfactory arrangement.

their own repertory, or did they merely adapt a theoretical system that made sense only by virtue of the adoption of the same (or a similar) note series as that used by the ancients? Third, how were deviations from, and extensions to, the basic octave structure handled in terms of modal theory? Finally, to what extent is it legitimate to apply the concepts developed by the Franks to the structures of other Western chant repertories?

(1) The intuitive answer to the first question is that the modal system arose (at any rate in Eastern chant) as a recognition of well defined melody-types. It is difficult to believe that as early as the seventh, or at least the eighth, century there was available to hymnographers a formalized scale structure that would have enabled them to define a mode in its terms.[11] At that period it seems altogether more likely that there were recognized melody-types, distinguishable by a nomenclature that already embraced the concept of the 'plagal' but unsupported by the technical sophistication of later theory. We can only guess how far these types resembled those later defined by the eight-mode system.

And yet the very existence of the term 'plagal', or at least its abbreviation, at this early date is troubling. It is not borrowed from ancient theory, and is best explained by the position of the plagal *ēchoi*, considered as notes, in the double tetrachord. But we do not know exactly what *ēchos* meant in the seventh or eighth century. Again it is not a term of ancient theory. If it can be translated as 'sound', in what sense is that term being used? Although the possibility appears remote, one cannot rule out a system by which the correct way to start a song was in some way guaranteed by reference to a note within a definite scale; nor can one rule out a primitive form of solmization to aid the pitching of the notes within the scale and a series of formulae to help in getting the song started.

In all probablility the two factors – a repertory of melody-types and a mechanism for ensuring their correct performance – went hand in hand. One would expect the former to precede the latter, but the nomenclature itself, which is the only evidence for recognized melody-types in any case, suggests that by the time it first appears the two aspects had come to be complementary. A lack of evidence for the underlying musical structure of the Christian chant of that period will probably prevent the question from ever being decided.

(2) Did Western musicians recognize in their own repertory melody-types conforming to those defined by the eight modes of Greek chant? It would seem not. The eight-mode system was at first associated principally if not exclusively with the *kanôn*, a stanzaic form not represented in Western liturgy. However, the *troparia* or verses of the *kanôn* were originally responses (all sung to the same melody) to a portion of a canticle, and so are in some sense analogous to the Western antiphon, as also is the

---

[11]The earliest documented evidence for the modal nomenclature appears to be that attached to a *kanôn* in a papyrus of the seventh or eighth century from the Fayyum; Manchester, John Rylands Library, pap. 466; see Colin H. Roberts, *Catalogue of the Greek and Latin Papyri in the John Rylands Library, Manchester*, vol. 3 (Manchester, 1938), pp. 28–35 and plate 1. The designation (not very easy to make out, it must be confessed) is for mode 1 plagal.

stichēron, which bore a similar function in psalmody.[12] All these are forms of liturgical intercalation, and it could therefore be that modal classification was somehow linked to the manner in which the psalms or canticles were sung. Unfortunately the question to what extent and how psalms and canticles were sung in the Greek Church is itself a matter of controversy.[13] Even so, the Frankish formulation of a system whereby the tonality of a psalm or canticle was inextricably bound up with that of its refrain ensured its permanent usefulness.

(3) If my thesis is correct, Western modality was bound up with the adoption of an octave scale made up of two disjunct tetrachords of the form TST. At an early stage (though not necessarily at the outset), theorists adopted the concept of the *finalis* as an overriding criterion for the association of modal pairs. The notion of *ambitus* or range in relation to a *finalis* was less systematized. The *enēchēmata* and the more extended versions of these formulae do not convey the impression of a formal differentiation of range as regards the authentic modes and their plagal counterparts. Many of the modal allocations in tonaries and antiphonals are not easy to understand in terms of range, especially where the range of a melody is limited: they suggest, rather, that the identification of mode rested on conventions deriving from the less tangible aspects of melodic behaviour.

While limited range might create problems with regard to modal classification, the same could be true of an *ambitus* beyond the octave. Moreover, if the *ambitus* of a chant melody lay more than one note outside the central octave at either end, there was a theoretical problem in terms of tetrachordal structure. It would seem that medieval Greek theory did not take full cognizance of this: one could in principle modulate indefinitely, in either direction, from one tetrachord to another by way of disjunction (the tonal pattern being repeated at the interval of a fifth). The dasian scale of the Enchiridian treatises merely sets out these possibilities in the form of a continuous scale. But it raises the question of the intervals actually performed in a melody of wide range – a question never fully resolved in medieval Greek theory.

In western theory the theoretical problem was resolved by reverting either to the ancient Greek scale or to the alternative tetrachordal scheme proposed by Hucbald and taken up by a group of German theorists of whom Hermannus Contractus was the most prominent. These tetrachordal structures were in due course superseded everywhere by Guido of Arezzo's hexachords; but they are important historically, for they created the flexibility introduced by the note we now call *b flat*, also accounted for in the full Guidonian system by means of the 'soft' hexachord.

The dasian scale, of course, does not include *b flat*, and it is of interest that the note is rare even in some repertories notated by means of the 'Guidonian' staff. But the existence of *b flat*, although it remained controversial, permitted the notation of melodies with an element of semitonal alternation at one or other degree of the modal

---

[12]See Simon Harris, 'The "Kanon" and the Heirmologion', *Music and Letters* 85 (2004), pp. 175–197.

[13]*Ibid.*, p. 189.

scale. These alternations can occur at the second, third, fourth, fifth, sixth, or seventh degree of the scale if the *finalis* is respectively on the note *a*, *g*, *f*, *e*, *d*, or *c*. The location of a second-mode melody on *a*, or of a fourth-mode melody on *a* or *b natural*, furthermore, permits the non-existent *b flat* to be notated as *f*.[14]

Melodies notated on *a*, *b natural*, or *c'* were regarded as transpositions or relocations of melodies in modes 2 and 4 (on *a*), 4 (on *b*) and 5 and 6 (on *c'*, the former requiring an upward extension of the system). *c* (or even *c'*) was also occasionally used as the *finalis* of melodies in mode 7, providing the possibility of *b natural* (or *b' natural*) in the scale. In principle the *finales f* and *g* are reciprocal, offering different possibilities within the 'major' scale; but while there are indeed examples, both monophonic and polyphonic, of transposition from one to the other, the nomenclature of the modes seems to have remained rooted to the *finalis* actually employed, whatever the structure of the melody.

Medieval musicians therefore solved the 'problem' of the *b flat* by ignoring it for the purposes of modal classification. The note did not of itself create a transposition, but was regarded as a mobile element that could be made available at any point of the scale except the *finalis* itself.[15] However, it is tempting to conjecture that the four *parapteres* mentioned by Aurelianus as having been added by Charlemagne to the number of the modes may have had something to do with the *b flat* and more specifically to have reflected the *synemmenon* tetrachord that permitted the *b flat* in Hucbald's scale. Of course we should have to accept that this tetrachord had a real existence long before he can have written his treatise; but it is in any case the thesis of this essay that the double TST tetrachordal structure lay at the root of the modal system.

The existence of the *synemmenon* tetrachord (*g a b flat c'*) at an early date would both offer a ready explanation for the creation of the *parapteres* and an explanation for their later rejection, since it proved possible (for Western theorists, at least) to accommodate the *b flat* without extending the eight-mode system at all. The only possible exception lay in the *tonus peregrinus* or *tonus novissimus*, as the writer of the *Commemoratio brevis* calls it. These terms do not refer to the very distinctive psalm melody associated with this 'tone', but to the modality of the rather small number of antiphons to which it is assigned. They do indeed employ the *finalis g* with constant *b flat*, and were later regarded as a variant of the eighth mode.[16] If the *parapteres* were

---

[14] An example of a fourth-mode melody on *b* is the communion antiphon *Ab occultis meis*: Montpellier, Faculté de médecine ms, H 159, fol. 57, followed by two others of the same type.

[15] As far as I know the first theorist to use a flat signature (and indeed a two-flat signature) as an indication of transposition was Johannes Tinctoris in his *Liber de natura et proprietate tonorum*. It was specifically rejected by Marchetus of Padua, who stated that (for example) if the introit *Statuit ei* were notated on G with a flat signature it would be proper to mode 1 by virtue of its structure, but improperly assigned to it on the grounds of its location. See *GS* 3, p. 108.

[16] Two examples are cited, 'In templo domini' and 'Nos qui vivimus', with corresponding psalm verses; but since the notation is dasian, the note *b* remains 'natural'. Terence Bailey, ed.,

intended to accommodate the *synemmenon* tetrachord, it may have been with the object of securing a conjunct tetrachord above that of the finals for melodies ending on *d*, *e*, *f*, or *g*.

Although the *parapteres* were not necessarily equivalent to the *mesoi* of medieval Greek theory, it may be worth noting that the latter are described by John Laskaris as the notes (or modes, *ēchoi*) corresponding to *f*, *g*, *d*, and *e* respectively: they are placed midway between between the plagal and the authentic pitches of the *protos*, *deuteros*, *tritos*, and *tetrartos* respectively, but with the two latter relocated to a position in a lower pair of tetrachords.[17] It is possible that these 'modes' entailed a tetrachord attached conjunctly to the plagal tetrachord *d–g*, this being the reason for transferring the third and fourth *mesoi* to the lower pitch. The neumed *enēchēmata* assigned to the *parapteres* in Bamberg, Staatsbibliothek, ms lit. 5, fol. 5[r], as printed by Bailey,[18] unfortunately do not shed any light on this matter.

(4) The problem of the *parapteres* is something of a side issue in the present context. More germane is the extent to which the modal classification adopted by Frankish theorists is relevant to other repertories.

As a preliminary to the discussion it should be noted that the assertion that the modal system was not recognized outside the Frankish sphere is an *argumentum e silentio*. If this system was introduced by Greek musicians it is on the face of it surprising that it had not penetrated Italy or Gaul before it reached Francia. Greek-language chants from southern Italian sources of Latin chant presumably arrived with a modal identity, although this is not stated in the manuscripts.[19] It should also be remembered that almost all we know about early Roman liturgy and chant derives from Frankish copies of the relevant documents. There is nothing about the earliest tonaries from Francia that would preclude their material having reached their compilers from

---

Commemoratio brevis de tonis et psalmis modulandis (Ottawa, 1979), pp. 54–57; Schmid, *Musica et Scolica enchiriadis*, p. 165.

[17] Christos J. Bentas, 'The Treatise on Music by John Laskaris', *Studies in Eastern Chant* 2 (1971), pp. 21–27. There are further details in Laskaris's short treatise, but they are very hard to interpret.

[18] *The Intonation Formulas of Western Chant*, 96. These formulae are likely to be an artificial reconstruction. A further difficulty in identifying the *tonus peregrinus* with one of the Carolingian *parapteres* is its description in the *Commemoratio brevis* as a 'tonus novissimus'.

[19] The principal examples, in both transliterated Greek and Latin, are three antiphons for the Adoration of the Cross on Good Friday: 'Proskynumen ton stauron su / Adoremus crucem tuam', 'Ton stauron su proskynumen kyrie / Crucem tuam adoramus domine', and 'Enumen se / Laudamus te'. In addition there is a processional chant, 'Panta ta etni / Omnes gentes' and 'Otin to stauron / O quando in cruce'. See Thomas F. Kelly, *The Beneventan Chant* (Cambridge, 1989), pp. 89–90 and elsewhere. Other significant importations include the Greek Alleluias in the (Old) Roman rite of vespers in Easter week. Egon Wellesz, *Eastern Elements in Western Chant* (Copenhagen, 1947), identified 'Otin to stauron' as a second-mode chant in the Byzantine tradition, corresponding more or less in tonality to the versions preserved in Latin manuscripts.

Rome.[20] The case for a purely Frankish reception of Eastern modal theory rests largely on semi-mythical statements by Aurelianus of Réôme.

However, it is not the purpose of this chapter to posit a non-Frankish origin for Western modal theory. The object rather is to emphasize the extent to which the tonal system common to all pitched sources of Western chant renders some form of modal identity inescapable. Modal identity preceded the unambiguous notation of pitch in Francia by some considerable length of time, but it is clarified by the emergence of pitched notations.

Outside Francia a similar process took place, except that for some repertories, for the most part at least, the transition to fully pitched notation never took place. This generalization applies to Mozarabic chant and to the Old Beneventan. The latter reper-tory, insofar as it survives, is notated diastematically but without clefs.[21] The Milanese and Old Roman sources, however, employ a form of staff with clefs on the Guidonian model.

The achievement of Guido and his close contemporary the author of the *Dialogus de Musica* needs no commentary here.[22] Paradoxically, while enabling the melodic character of any chant to be unambiguously appraised, they at the same time obscured the patterns that had previously kept it on the rails, so to speak. Their fundamental innovation was to recognize octave duplication in the notation, a principle that has remained with us ever since.[23] With the addition of the note gamma (Γ) below *A*, modal identity could be defined, as it was in the *Dialogus*, by collocations of notes in ascending order. These are not, in this case, octave species, but inclusive repertories that in most cases extend beyond the octave and include both *b flat* and *b natural*.

The equation of the modes with ancient octave scales, on the other hand, was an innovation of a somewhat earlier generation of Frankish theorists. The theoretical preference for 'modus' over 'tonus' is already explicit in the *Scolica enchiriadis*. A correlation between ancient and medieval scales was also attempted by medieval Greek theorists, though there was more than one set of identifications and the practical

---

[20]These are the 'Tonary of St Riquier' (ms Paris, BNF lat. 13159, fol. 167^{r-v}, incomplete) and the document 'De octo tonis' that lies behind the eighth chapter of Aurelian's *Musica Disciplina*. These are fully discussed in Huglo, *Les tonaires*, pp. 25–29, 47–56. For Aurelian himself, see the edition by Lawrence Gushee, CSM 21 (Rome, 1975).

[21]In a recent (unpublished) paper Matthew Peattie has identified a body of cleffed chants containing Beneventan melodic formulae; these could help to resolve the problem of transcribing from uncleffed Beneventan sources; 'Traces of Old Beneventan Chant in a South Italian Office for the Dedication of a Church' (Toronto, 19 March 2004).

[22]J. Smits van Waesberghe, ed., Guido d'Arezzo, *Micrologus*, CSM 4 (Rome, 1955); Dolores Pesce, ed., *Guido d'Arezzo's* Regule rithmice, Prologus in Antiphonarium, *and* Epistola ad Michahelem: *A Critical Text and Translation* (Ottawa, 1989); *Dialogus de Musica* in *GS*, vol. 1, pp. 252–283, especially 259–263.

[23]There are partial exceptions to this generalization in the Enchiridian treatises and in Hucbald. But in neither case did these lead to a permanent system of notation.

outcome was limited.[24] In the West, however, the idea of mode as an octave species, combining a species of fourth and a species of fifth, became the overriding one, leading to a more rigid correlation between *ambitus* and mode – counterbalanced, it is true, by a streak of inventiveness that threatened to subvert the tyranny of the *ambitus* and to render the distinction between authentic and plagal difficult to sustain.

This newer understanding of mode, influential though it became, has little relevance for the Italian repertories that have been considered to invite analysis outside the eight-mode scheme altogether. Their survival in pitched notations, however, confirms their underlying structure in terms of an expanded tetrachordal scale. The upward and downward extensions that are found, for example, in Old Roman chant may or may not indicate an acceptance of a conjunct relationship of tetrachords above and below the central octave. It is more likely that the principle of octave duplication was being tacitly observed in practice without recourse to specific theoretical models. The structure of the central octave itself, however, implies a link, at a fundamental level, with the eight-mode system.

In one sense, the question might seem to be of minor importance. Chants can be sung from the notation as it stands, without theoretical baggage. Yet questions arise. How are psalms to be sung with the antiphons of the mass and office? It has been suggested that some of the 'euouae' formulae that accompany these antiphons, with or without a verbal incipit, have been influenced by Frankish practice.[25] This may be so to a certain extent, and it may possibly have resulted in modifications to the original melodic form of the antiphons themselves; at the same time the use of non-Frankish formulae is not in itself an argument against an eight-mode system.

Then again, scholars generally concur in an eight-mode classification of the office responds, based on an analysis of the melodies of their verses (if by no other criteria);[26] and a study of the Old Roman invitatories exhibits the same relation to the modal system as the Frankish (that is, that there are no chants corresponding to modes 1 and 8, and varying numbers of melodic types and associated psalmodic formulae corresponding to the remainder). Finally, the large element of correlation between the Old Roman and the core Gregorian repertories as they have come down to us is

---

[24]The *Hagiopolites* treatise lists the names of the eight modes (the four *kyrioi* followed by the four *plagioi*) as respectively Hypodorios, Hypophrygios, Hypolydios, Dorios; Phrygios, Lydios, Mixolydios, Hypomixolydios; see J. Raasted, ed., *The Hagiopolites: A Byzantine Treatise on Musical Theory* (Copenhagen, 1983), p. 13. This looks like a misapplication of the Western medieval series of octave species from *A–a* to *a–a'* (as in *Alia musica*; see *GS* 1, 127), with Hypomixolydian substituted for Hypermixolydian, as later in the West, to allow for its identification with the fourth plagal mode (octave *d–d'*). The *Papadike* is said to incorporate the Western order: Dorios, Phrygios, Lydios, Mixolydios, followed by their 'hypo' equivalents; but the list is again disordered in Vatican, BAV Barb. lat. 300; see L. Tardo, *L'antica melurgia bizantina* (Grottaferrata, 1938), p. 152.

[25]Joseph Dyer, 'Old Roman Chant', in *NG2*, vol. 18, pp. 381–385; Paul Cutter and Brad Maiani, 'Responsory', 3, in *ibid.*, vol. 21, pp. 222B224.

[26]This too has been ascribed to Frankish influence; Dyer, 'Old Roman Chant'.

suggestive of a common element in the underlying structure of chants of all types that can be expressed only in terms of a common modality.

It is for this reason that I am sceptical of attempts to analyse, for example, the repertory of Old Roman antiphons in ways that run counter to accepted modal terminology, however revealing these analyses may be in other ways.[27] Two points arising from analyses on modal lines, such as those of Claire and Bernard, seem to me important. First, the absence of any mode within a genre does not invalidate the terminology, which is rooted in aspects of chant language that transcend genre; secondly, the invention of additional categories (such as 'archaic Mi') is unnecessary, since the modal system can accommodate such chants as readily as any others. And any treatment of antiphons (whether of the mass or the office) should take into account the evidence of the *differentiae*; the eight-mode system does not depend on a correlation between antiphon and psalm melody as strict as that eventually achieved by the Franks.[28]

The underlying unity of the Gregorian and Old Roman melodic stock, reinforced as it is by common approaches to composition in formulaic types of chant, is a further reason to allow the eight-mode system its place in the classification of the latter. In the case of Milanese chant a common element is much less in evidence, although it does exist and may be more widespread than is usually suspected. As long ago as 1891 the monks of Solesmes presented the gradual/psalmellus *A summo caelo* synoptically in its Gregorian, Old Roman, and Milanese versions. There are other examples of this 'protus plagalis on *a*' melodic type in the Milanese repertory.[29] There are parallels too between the Roman introit and the Milanese ingressa,[30] while Bailey has found in the

---

[27]Edward Nowacki, 'Studies on the Office Antiphons of the Old Roman Manuscripts' (Ph.D. diss., Brandeis University, 1980). An analysis on 'modal' lines, carried out by John Claire and summarized by Philippe Bernard, has been reproduced in the introduction to the facsimile edition *Biblioteca apostolica vaticana S.Pietro B 79*, ed. Bonifacio Giacomo Baroffio and Soo Jung Kim (Rome, 1995), vol. 1, p. 33. It reveals an absence of antiphons in modes 3 and 8 but distinguishes two forms of mode 6, identifying in addition an 'archaic Mi' (reciting on E), as well as assigning all the chants on A to mode 4. However, the totals fall short of the number of antiphons actually in S. Pietro B 79 (1055 as against Nowacki's 1111; most of those not accounted for are melodies with E *finalis*).

[28]In his interesting article 'The Modes before the Modes: Antiphon and Differentia in Western Chant', in *The Study of Medieval Chant*, pp. 131–145, Keith Falconer suggests that the *differentia* played an important part in classifying chant melodies prior to the establishment of the eight-mode system, in which they played a crucial role. As can be seen, my view is that a coherent system of *differentiae* was a valuable outcome of modal organization rather than its raison d'être.

[29]PM, series I, vol. 2, (Solesmes, 1891), pp. 6–8. They have been identified and studied by Helmut Hucke, 'Die Gregorianische Gradualweise des 2. Tons und ihre ambrosianischen Parallelen', *AMw* 13 (1956), pp. 285–314.

[30]PM I, vol. 2, pp. 8–10, quoting the introit/ingressa *Resurrexi*.

Milanese Cantus parallels with both Old Roman and Old Beneventan chant.[31] There is a strong correlation between some of the Milanese responsories and those of the Roman rite, including the one with which all Roman antiphonals begin, *Aspiciens a longe*. This responsory (though not its verses, which are examples of the seventh responsorial tone in all three traditions) is an 'original' rather than a 'typical' respond (in Frere's terminology), so that its melodic comparability is all the more notable.

Nor should one confine oneself to equivalent genres in seeking evidence of common melodic material. The Gregorian/Old Roman offertorium *Ad te domine levavi* is closely matched by the similarly texted Milanese ingressa and confractorium for the first Sunday in Advent. The confractorium relates to the Roman verse *Dirige me* and recapitulates the latter part ('Etenim universi') of the ingressa, just as in the Roman offertorium, but here only after the major part of the liturgy has intervened. The fact that the strong stylistic characterization of each genre of Gregorian chant is less in evidence in the non-Roman repertories (and to a certain extent even in Old Roman chant) makes the possibility of cross-references between genres (which do of course occur even in Gregorian chant) all the more likely.

One could ascribe such resemblances to 'Gregorian influence', but it is then difficult to account for the musical differences between the various versions. Scribes were quite capable of copying Gregorian melodies if required to do so, as is the case throughout the Old Roman Gradual of St Cecilia. Such Gregorianization must often have taken place on textual grounds rather than on purely musical ones, but the evidence suggests that, where this was so, the melodies themselves were copied exactly, or at least as exactly as one would expect. It is much easier to account for the differences between melodies that are fundamentally comparable by attributing them to a common stock that has been developed locally in different ways. Indeed the existence of three versions of a chant allows the possibility of arriving at – admittedly speculative – earlier forms of such melodies.

Similar considerations apply to the Milanese antiphon repertory, which has been studied and classified in relation to melodic type by Bailey and Merkley.[32] Earlier studies were strongly influenced by the accommodation arrived at in relatively modern times in order to obtain an 'authentically' Milanese method of psalmody; but although the scheme outlined in the modern *Liber vesperalis* has been shown to be inauthentic, it is difficult to arrive at a clear understanding of the medieval system, and the extent to which it may have been influenced at some point by Gregorian practice. The point to be made again here is that the apparent flexibility of the system, and its relation to a small number (thirty) of stem melodies, are not necessarily incompatible with the notion of an eight-mode system.

---

[31] Terence Bailey, *The Ambrosian Cantus* (Ottawa, 1987). There is in any case a strong correlation between the Old Roman and Gregorian tract, which is analogous to the Milanese cantus; Emma Hornby, *Gregorian and Old Roman Eighth-Mode Tracts* (Aldershot, 2002).

[32] Terence Bailey and Paul Merkley, *The Antiphons of the Ambrosian Office* (Ottawa, 1989), and *The Melodic Tradition of the Ambrosian Office-Antiphons* (Ottawa, 1990).

Much has been made, in studies of melodic type, of the possibility that Frankish chant was adapted to fit the system of eight modes. The suggestion offered here is that, if there was adaptation, it is likely to have been made in order to accommodate the tonal system as such rather than the modes individually, and in that context to be no less applicable to the non-Frankish repertories insofar as we can read them. The primary contribution of the Frankish theorists was perhaps not the adoption of an eight-mode system but the harnessing of ancient theory to a body of chant that was already modally classified. One of the most far-reaching aspects of this development was the recognition of the *synemmenon* tetrachord as an integral feature of the note series, enabling some parts of the inherited repertory at least to be preserved notationally as sung, leaving other traditions to apply such refinement in performance without notation. It is striking that the Guidonian notation of the Old Roman and Milanese chant eschews the *b flat*, although it would seem likely to have occurred in performance. These repertories do, on the other hand, employ transpositions which have the effect of creating a conjunct tetrachord *d–g*, yielding the note *f* as the equivalent of *b flat* in untransposed modes, without of course permitting a transferred alternation of *b* and *b flat* such as the Frankish system allowed.

The melodic characteristics and note series associated with the modes are (in this view) not an arbitrary grafting of a medieval Greek system on to a repertory unsuited to it but the consequence of inheriting a tonal system that (probably not coincidentally) was found by the Franks in the Carolingian era to be more or less compatible with what they encountered in Boethius. This led in turn to modifications of modal theory itself. While the evidence for modal classification is certainly confined to Frankish sources, its relevance is (I suggest) to any body of music that can claim a link with the medieval Greek system of disjunct tetrachords. The evidence that this link applies to Western chant generally is indeed incomplete and circumstantial: it is necessary to make assumptions concerning the prior history of repertories appearing in readable form (or in any form) only in the eleventh century, if then; and as regards the bulk of, for example, the Mozarabic repertories, it is entirely speculative. But it is at least a hypothesis worth considering, the consequence being, I suggest, an understanding of Western chant generally that at the very least does not exclude its analysis in terms of the eight-mode system.

Chapter 5

Réôme, Cluny, Dijon

Barbara Haggh and Michel Huglo

The *Musica disciplina*,[1] the Dijon tonary (Montpellier, Bibliothèque de l'Université, Faculté de médecine, ms H. 159),[2] and the musical repertory of Cluny have each

---

Barbara Haggh wrote the chapter, contributed the research on Aurelian's *Musica disciplina* and the sources from Réôme and Cluny, and compiled the table. An earlier version of her contribution to this book was read at Columbia University in March 2001, as 'The Introduction of the Cluniac Practice far from and near to Cluny'. Michel Huglo contributed the analysis of the Vatican manuscript and of the tonary added to the Montpellier manuscript, as well as information and bibliography about the Montpellier manuscript, sources from St Bénigne in Dijon, and processionals.

[1]Edited by Lawrence Gushee, *Aureliani Reomensis* Musica disciplina, CSM 21 (Rome, 1975). To the literature on the treatise cited in *NG2* and the revised edition of *MGG*, add Barbara Haggh, 'Traktat *Musica disciplina* Aureliana Reomensis: proweniencja I datowanie' [Musica disciplina Aureliani Reomensis and the Problem of the Date and Origin of the Treatise]', translated from English into Polish by Katarzyna Naliwajek, *Muzyka* [Journal of the Institute of Musicology, Polish Academy of Sciences] 45 (2000), pp. 25–78 (with English summary), and 'Aurelian's Library', *International Musicological Society Study Group Cantus Planus: Papers Read at the Ninth Meeting, Esztergom & Visegrád, 1998* (Budapest, 2001), pp. 271–300. Note that on p. 294 the cited manuscript in Valenciennes should be ms 404, not 386; on p. 295 Bede, *De arte metrica*, is not cited in Aurelian at viii.36; Macrobius should be omitted from the table on pp. 298–299; and, on p. 299, Sergius's *Explanatio* is cited in Aurelian at xix, not xvix. Barbara Haggh is preparing a monograph on Aurelian's treatise.

[2]Manuel Pedro Ferreira, 'Music at Cluny: The Tradition of Gregorian Chant for the Proper of the Mass. Melodic Variants and Microtonal Nuances' (Ph.D. diss., Princeton University, 1997), pp. 167–174; *H. 159, Montpellier: Tonary of St Bénigne of Dijon*, transcribed and annotated by Finn Egeland Hansen (Copenhagen, 1974); Finn Egeland Hansen, 'Editorial Problems Connected with the Transcription of H 159, Montpellier: Tonary of St Bénigne of Dijon', *EG* 16 (1977), pp. 161–172; *The Grammar of Gregorian Tonality: An Investigation Based on the Repertory in codex H 159, Montpellier*, 2 vols (Copenhagen, 1979). Michel Huglo, 'Grundlage und Ansätze der mittelalterlichen Musiktheorie', in Thomas Ertelt and Frieder Zaminer, eds, *Geschichte der Musiktheorie*, 11 vols (Darmstadt, 2000), vol. 4, pp. 98–100 (especially Table 5); 'Le tonaire de Saint-Bénigne de Dijon (Montpellier H. 159)', *AnnM* 4 (1956), pp. 7–18,

prompted study.[3] Features common to the Dijon tonary and Cluny repertory have been identified,[4] however, the treatise *Musica disciplina* has never been considered in relation to the chant of Dijon or Cluny.

Here we claim that it should be. A list of abbots from the abbey of St Jean de Réôme in Moutiers-St-Jean, a hagiographical *libellus*, and other evidence indicate that strong ties once existed between Réôme, Dijon, and Cluny. To test the implications of this evidence, we compare Aurelian's tonary to the repertories of the Montpellier manuscript, the Ordinal of Fécamp, and two antiphoners from Cluniac houses. In a recent study, Bryan Gillingham claimed that 'Cluny was a central force for musical creativity in medieval Europe'. In this study we suggest new lines of inquiry for investigating the antecedents.

In his prologue Aurelian, from the abbey of St Jean de Réôme, dedicates the treatise to Bernardus, archcantor and soon to be archbishop.[5] In a recent study evidence was presented that Bernard was a nobleman trained at the court of Louis the Pious, later abbot of Réôme and bishop of Autun, waiting to be installed as archbishop of Lyon.[6] The abbey of Réôme was not part of the diocese of Langres in Aurelian's day, as is still assumed even in well-intentioned reference works,[7] but was royal property, which explains why the nobleman Bernard was appointed as its abbot.[8] Aurelian's treatise gains significance because this new evidence establishes a direct line of influence from the Carolingian court to Réôme, whence Aurelian came.

---

especially p. 9 and note 2, and the facsimile opposite p. 17; *Le graduel romain: les sources* (Solesmes, 1957), p. 75; *Les tonaires* (Paris, 1971), pp. 328–333. Nancy Phillips, 'Notationen und Notationslehren von Boethius bis zum 12. Jahrhundert', in Ertelt and Zaminer, *Geschichte der Musiktheorie*, vol. 4, especially pp. 352, 468–469 and 565–572. *Vatican City, ms. Vat. lat. 10673*, PM 14 (1931), p. 9; *Antiphonarium tonale missarum, XIe siècle: Codex H. 159 de la Bibliothèque de l'Ecole de médecine de Montpellier*, PM 8 (1901).

[3]See Michel Huglo and Manuel Pedro Ferreira, 'Cluniac Monks', in *NG2*, vol. 6, pp. 63–65.

[4]Ferreira, 'Music at Cluny'.

[5]Gushee, *Aureliani Reomensis*, p. 53.

[6]Haggh, 'Traktat', pp. 51–53.

[7]Jane Bellingham, 'Aurelian of Réôme', in *NG2*, and Marie-Hélène Jullien and Françoise Perelman, eds, *Clavis scriptorum latinorum medii aevi: auctores Galliae, 735–987*, vol. 2 (Turnhout, 1999), p. 202.

[8]See Neithard Bulst, *Untersuchungen zu den Klosterreformen Wilhelms von Dijon (962–1031)*, Pariser historische Studien 11 (Bonn, 1973), p. 61: 'Im Jahre 885 wurde von Kaiser Karl III das Kloster Moutier-St-Jean, das wohl seit dem 8. Jahrhundert Königskloster gewesen war, an die Bischöfe von Langres zurückgegeben.' Bulst examines at length on pp. 61–65 the list of abbots, which he consulted in Roverius. Gushee had placed Réôme under the Crown in his dissertation, but did not observe its significance for the career of Bernardus or for the content of Aurelian's treatise; see Lawrence Gushee, 'The *Musica disciplina* of Aurelian of Réôme: A Critical Text and Commentary' (Ph.D. diss., Yale University, 1963), p. 5 n. 2, also p. 21 n. 1.

That Carolingian nobility should have laid claim to the Abbey of St Jean de Réôme should not surprise, because it was, with Flavigny, one of the oldest in Burgundy, founded *ca* 440,[9] and its patron saint, St Jean (d. *ca* 544, feast 28 January), was the godfather of Clovis, the first Christian king of France.[10] The abbey was led by an illustrious series of abbots whose names appear in only one surviving source, a list written in the second half of the thirteenth century into a earlier hagiographical *libellus* from Réôme.[11] The section of the list that concerns us is transcribed here:

Ms Semur-en-Auxois [15–20 kilometres from the abbey of St Jean de Réôme], BM 1, fol. 76[r] [tenth century, with later additions]

> 76[r]: Bernardus augustod[unensis] ep[iscopu]s
> Lotharius fili[us] caroli [861–865]
> Hu[m]marus lugdune[n]s[is] ep[iscopu]s
> Carlomanus fili[us] caroli
> Vulpo
> Vulphardus
> Ingebrannis

---

[9]On the abbey see the historical notes in Paris, AN, carton M 723, dossier 24, pièce 205 (25 fols), and ms Paris, BNF lat. 12676, fols 282–286. See Pierre Gasnault, 'Le projet de diction-naire de tout l'Ordre de Saint-Benoît de Dom Charles Petey de l'Hostallerie', *Revue Mabillon*, nouvelle série 13 [74] (2002), p. 64. The abbey joined the Congregation of St Maur in 1636.

[10]See Society of Bollandists, eds, *Bibliotheca hagiographica latina (BHL)* (Brussels, 1898–1899, reprinted 1992), nos 4424–4431.

[11]Ms Semur-en-Auxois, BM 1, is described by Auguste Molinier, *Catalogue général des manuscrits des bibliothèques publiques de France*, vol. 6 (Paris, 1887), pp. 296–298, and Alfred Vittenet, *L'abbaye de Moutier-St-Jean* (Mâcon, 1938), pp. xv–xvii. An undated eighteenth-century catalogue of the manuscripts of Réôme, probably written by Dom Plancher, now Paris, BNF, Collection de Bourgogne, ms 9, fol. 123[v], lists this manuscript as item one: 'Un ancien manuscrit sur velin de sept à huit cens ans contenant la vie de st Jean de Réôme, les leçons qu'on lit en ses festes, et deux chartes, une du grand Clovis et l'autre de son fils Chlo-taire, en faveur dud[it] monastère'. The manuscript is surely from the abbey of St Jean de Réôme or destined for it, given the extent of the liturgical material for St Jean and its elaborate illuminations. François Avril, in a private communication of 29 July 1997, places the script *ca* 1000 and finds the illumination appropriate for a Burgundian origin at the end of the tenth century. The manuscript begins with a neumed *historia* for St Jean de Réôme and a full-page initial and includes a complete set of readings for his *natalis* and the eight days of its octave as well as his *vita* and miracles. The end of the manuscript is comprised of copies of the most important early charters for the history of the abbey and of lists of bishops of Langres and abbots of Réôme. The transcription of the latter list published in Petrus Roverius, *Reomaus, seu historia monasterii Sci Johannis Reomaensis [...]* (Paris, 1637) is not entirely accurate (see Haggh, 'Traktat', pp. 51–53 and Illustration 1). On hagiographical *libelli* see Guy Philippart, *Les légendiers et autres manuscrits hagiographiques* (Turnhout, 1977).

Aurelian[us]

Guillermus abbas s[an]c[t]i benigni divione[n]s[is]:

    Iste guillelmus fuit primus abbas monasterij fiscanensis rothomagensis
dyocesis. Et obijt. Anno domini. M. Xxxiijo. Cepit autem regere
monasterium sancti benigni divionensis. Circa annum domini
millesimum.

Sanctus maiolus abbas Cluniacensis

Heldricus sancti maioli discipulus: Iste heldricus presidebat. Anno domini.

    Millesimo iijo. Et fuit presidens tribus monasteriis uno et eodem tempore
scilicet monasteriis sancti germani autissiodorensis reomensis. Atque
flavigniacensis.

This list includes many prominent abbots. Among those after Bernardus are two sons of Charles the Bald, Lothar (861–865) and Carloman (ruled France 879–884); the latter was abbot of St Amand and of Lobbes as well as of Réôme.[12] Of interest here are the names of St Maiolus (d. 994) and Guillaume de Volpiano (d. 1031).[13] Maiolus was abbot of Réôme (*ca* 983–992) and fourth abbot of Cluny (954–994). He brought Guillaume to Cluny from northern Italy. Guillaume, abbot of Réôme (*ca* 992–1002) and of St Bénigne of Dijon (990–1031), had spent two years at Cluny before establishing St Bénigne after its model. His reforms extended to more than eighty monasteries, especially in Normandy and indirectly in England, as in Winchcombe and Gloucester. Maiolus's second Italian disciple, Heldricus, was abbot of Réôme, Flavigny, and of St Germain of Auxerre, but not of Cluny.

Another manuscript, Biblioteca apostolica vaticana [BAV], Reg. lat. 493, an eleventh-century compilation of hagiographic *libelli*, corroborates the association between Réôme and Cluny. Of special interest in this manuscript are the lives of the abbots of Cluny and other items surely from Cluny, such as the sermon by St Odo for the feast of St Peter on 29 June (fol. 41^V), a life of St Maiolus which is not in BHL (fol. 80^r), another life and *transitus* of St Maiolus by Syrus, this one in BHL 5177 (fol. 88^r), a description of Odilo's election as fifth abbot of Cluny in 994 (fol. 99^V), and the hymn by St Odilo composed for St Maiolus, his predecessor (fol. 100^V; AH 50, 299). As in the Semur manuscript, the life of St Jean de Réôme that follows on fols 105^r ff is

---

[12]Ms Valenciennes, BM 148, was in the library of St Amand by the second half of the twelfth century. Gustav Becker publishes a twelfth-century library of the Cluniac abbey of Anchin, with an *Aurelius de tonis* (Becker, *Catalogi bibliothecarum antiqui* (Bonn, 1885; reprinted Hildesheim, 2003), p. 248, catalogue 38, item 121), but according to Philippe Grierson this catalogue is from Lobbes. See Grierson, 'La bibliothèque de St Vaast d'Arras au XIIe siècle', *RB* 52 (1939), pp. 117–140, and other alternatives considered by Nancy Phillips, '*Musica* and *Scolica enchiriadis*: The Literary, Theoretical, and Musical Sources' (Ph.D. diss., New York University, 1984), p. 526.

[13]Neithard Bulst gives 1031. See his important monograph, *Untersuchungen*.

divided into twelve lessons, with a homily for the third nocturn (fol. 112^r), the recitation of his miracles (fol. 117^r), and hymns for matins and vespers (fol. 121^{r-v}: hymnum ad nocturnos *Contio fratrum pietate* (AH 52, 210), ad vesperum *Sacra dies infunditur* (AH 43, 198)). The responsories and antiphons of the office (fol. 121^v) are entered in Cluniac neumes (not French neumes as in the Semur manuscript)[14] and lack *differentiae* and even, towards the end of the office, entire chants. Following is a second life of St Jean (fols 124^v ff), which was to be read in the refectory and not in the choir. After the material for St Jean, there follow a life of St Odilo by Petrus Damianus (fol 136^r), who visited Cluny in 1063, and two biographies of St Hugo, sixth abbot of Cluny from 1049–1109 (fols 142^r ff). Nevertheless, a few non-Cluniac works find their way into this compilation, such as a neumed office for St Agylus of Rebais, the patron saint of a monastery not attached to Cluny but which followed the rule of St Columban. The cult of St Jean de Réôme also reached Dijon: a mass for the saint is in the thirteenth-century ordinal of St Bénigne.[15] Indeed, martyrologies and calendars from Réôme, Dijon, and Cluny would surely further confirm the close associations between these abbeys.[16]

Other evidence complements that of the liturgy. Art historians have observed Cluniac influence on the abbey of Réôme during the years when construction was underway on Cluny III (1088–1030). The abbey of St Jean de Réôme was rebuilt in Cluniac style under abbot Bernard II (1109–1133). One of the 'Moutiers masters' had worked at Cluny before moving to Moutiers-St-Jean (location of the abbey of Réôme) around 1125.[17]

A copy of Aurelian's treatise was in the library of Cluny in the twelfth century, and the treatise was disseminated to other Cluniac houses. The earliest comprehensive catalogue of the Cluny library to survive was written between 1158 and 1161, under the abbacy of Hugues III. No. 464 is a compilation including the *Musica disciplina*.[18]

---

[14]Jacques Hourlier, 'Remarques sur la notation clunisienne', *Revue grégorienne* 30 (1951), pp. 231–240.

[15]Abbé Chomton, *Histoire de l'église Saint-Bénigne de Dijon* (Dijon, 1900), pp. 419ff (edition of the ordinal, p. 421).

[16]A martyrology and calendar of St-Jean-de-Réôme written at the abbey in the first half of the eighth century is in ms Paris, BNF lat. 14086. See Pierre Salmon, 'Le martyrologe-calendrier conservé dans le ms. L. 14086 de Paris et ses origines,' *RB* 56 (1945–1946), pp. 42–57.

[17]See Charles T. Little, 'From Cluny to Moutiers-St-Jean: The Origin of a Limestone Fragment of an Angel at the Cloisters', *Gesta* 27 (1988), pp. 23–29; Neil Stratford, 'La sculpture médiévale de Moutiers-St-Jean (Saint-Jean-de-Réôme)', *Congrès archéologique de France, 144e session: Auxois-Chatillonais* (Paris, 1989), pp. 157–201; cf. Christian Sapin, ed., *Abbaye Saint-Germain d'Auxerre: intellectuels et artistes dans l'Europe carolingienne, 1Xe–XIe siècles* (Auxerre, 1990), pp. 281–283.

[18]No. 464: 'Volumen in quo continetur Boetius de consolatione philosophie, et laus sive musice discipline Aureliani, monachi Sancti Johannis Reomensis.' Published in Léopold

The fact that this item names Aurelian and describes him as being from Réôme indicates that Cluny had a copy of the treatise with the prologue that now survives only in its earliest source, ms Valenciennes, BM 148. The prologue was surely included in the copy Aurelian sent to Bernardus, abbot of St Jean de Réôme. One should also note the presence of a copy of the Life of St Jean de Réôme in the Cluny library.[19] A later version of Aurelian's treatise cites the text of *Descendit de caelis,* the Christmas responsory reformed at Cluny, and we have already placed the treatise at St Amand, which became Cluniac in 958.[20]

A further link between Réôme, Dijon, and Cluny is a common interest in Boethius's *De institutione musica.* Aurelian acknowledges Boethius by name and cites him often; he also cites glosses transmitted in the *Glossa maior.*[21] An important source for the *Glossa maior,* ms Paris, BNF n.a. lat. 1618, was written at St Bénigne in the eleventh century and includes early paleofrank or early French neumes on fols 69r, 70^v, and 91^{r-v}.[22] The widespread presence in this region of manuscripts of Boethius with and without the *Glossa maior* may explain both Guillaume de Volpiano's letter notation and microtonal signs in the Montpellier manuscript, which are borrowed from the Table of Alypius transmitted by Boethius.[23] Manuel Pedro Ferreira concluded that the use of microtonal signs in the Cluny gradual ms Paris, BNF lat. 1087 might reflect new applications of familiar neumes following the reading of ancient Greek theory. Both Boethius's *De institutione musica* and his *De arithmetica* were in the Cluny

---

Delisle, *Le cabinet des manuscrits de la Bibliothèque impériale,* vol. 2 (Hildesheim, 1978; reprinted of Paris 1874 edn), p. 477.

[19]No. 297 (Delisle, *Le cabinet,* p. 469): 'Volumen in quo continetur vita Johannis Remensis [*recte:* Reomensis] abbatis, passiones sancti Jacobi et fere omnium apostolorum, passiones sanctorum Laurentii et Vincentii, cum duobus sermonibus sancti Augustini de [eodem] sancto, vite Launomari abbatis, Ambrosii, Audoeni, Germani, episcoporum, passio sanctorum Georgii monachi ac Natalie, et in finem una homelia de evangelio Simile est regnum celorum in festo sancte Scholastice.'

[20]On St Amand see Dietrich W. Poeck, *Cluniacensis Ecclesia: der cluniacensische Klosterverband (10.–12. Jahrhundert)* (Munich, 1998), pp. 448–449. The revised Aurelian manuscript, Oxford, Bodleian Library, ms Canonici misc. 212, is discussed and edited by Gushee in *Aureliani Reomensis,* pp. 30–34, 45–46, 136–153 and *passim,* the revised *Descendit* on p. 138 (reconsidered in Haggh, 'Traktat', pp. 63–68).

[21]Haggh, 'Aurelian's Library', pp. 275–278.

[22]Described in *RISM B III 1,* p. 126, and *RISM B III (Recueils imprimés XVI–XVII siècles),* pp. 235–236.

[23]Michael Bernhard and Calvin M. Bower, eds, *Glossa maior in institutionem musicam Boethii,* 3 vols (Munich, 1993–1996). See also Nancy Phillips, 'Notationen', in Ertelt and Zaminer, *Geschichte der Musiktheorie,* pp. 560–572, especially the signs on p. 566 and her commentary on p. 568.

library in the twelfth century.[24] The quilisma, which had microtonal consequences at Cluny, is described by Aurelian.[25]

This evidence suggests that the chants Aurelian describes in his treatise, whose first known witness is the Valenciennes manuscript of *ca* 875–885, might have found their way into the liturgy of Cluny (founded in 909) and beyond.[26] Did they?

The following table lists the chants cited by Aurelian, in the order in which they occur in his treatise, and indicates concordances with the St Riquier tonary (Paris, BNF lat. 13159), the Dijon tonaries,[27] the ordinal of Fécamp,[28] and two antiphoners from Cluniac houses now in Paris, BNF lat. 12044 (early twelfth century, complete antiphoner from the Cluniac monastery of St Maur des Fossés) and lat. 12601 (1064–1095, a summer breviary from the Cluniac monastery of St Taurin l'Échelle in Picardy).[29] The Norman abbey of Fécamp is of interest, because Guillaume de Volpiano, abbot of St Bénigne, was its first abbot and reformed it beginning in 1001.

From this table we can conclude, first, that the tonaries of St Riquier and Aurelian have in common only four chants and the inclusion of items for the mass. More significant are the concordances with Montpellier and especially Fécamp. There are also points of contact between Aurelian's tonary and the small added tonary of St

---

[24]Ms Paris, BNF n.a. lat. 2662, is a tenth-century copy of Boethius's music treatise and no. 24 in the Cluny library catalogue; see Delisle, *Le cabinet*, pp. 477–478. See also Ferreira, *Music at Cluny*, pp. 174–185 (on Greek theory, including but not exclusive to, Boethius) and 241–282 (discussion of microtonal neumes with reference to the notations of Laon, St Gall, and Chartres). The microtonal signs are found only in chants for the mass.

[25]'Tremulam adclivemque emittunt vocem' and 'tremula emittitur vox' (Gushee, *Aureliani Reomensis*, p. 95). Cf. Ferreira, *Music at Cluny*, pp. 147–148, 255–258 (especially 258): '[in most cases] when a clivis follows a quilisma and is followed by a structural *fa* note, the lower note of the clivis is sharpened', and Phillips, 'Notationen', pp. 384–385.

[26] The destination of the Valenciennes manuscript is not known, but was surely not the abbey of St Amand, since an office for the Annunciation added just after the treatise is unrelated to the office used at St Amand (discussion forthcoming in the monograph by Barbara Haggh). The destination of Aurelian's treatise was the abbey of St Jean de Réôme, and Aurelian presumably knew its chant repertory, since he calls himself 'de Réôme'.

[27]See Michel Huglo, 'Grundlage', in Ertelt and Zaminer, *Geschichte der Musiktheorie*, p. 98, Table 5.

[28]David Chadd, ed., *The Ordinal of the Abbey of the Holy Trinity, Fécamp (Fécamp, Musée de la Bénédiction, ms 186)*, 2 vols, Publications of the Henry Bradshaw Society, vols 111 and 112 (London, 1999 and 2002). One should also compare the thirteenth-century antiphoner-hymnary of ms Fécamp, Rouen, BM, A 190 (245) and its complete tonary (see Huglo, *Les tonaires*, p. 232).

[29]Both indexed for CANTUS, where they are described in detail, with bibliography. See http://publish.uwo.ca/~cantus/.

Bénigne.[30] (The gradual *Venite filii* and the offertory *Benedictus es domine* with microtonal signs in the Dijon tonary are not in Aurelian.) Moreover, Montpellier includes every item for the mass cited by Aurelian.

Comparison of Aurelian's chants with those in the ordinal of Fécamp also reveals few differences: Fécamp lacks only the responsory *Recordare mei domine*, the invitatory antiphon *Deus magnus dominus*, and four Magnificat antiphons *per annum*.

More differences exist between Aurelian/Fécamp and the antiphoner of St Maur des Fossés. (The summer breviary of St Taurin l'Échelle in Picardy excludes chants for the winter, which explains the smaller number of its concordances to the other sources.) St Maur des Fossés lacks twelve antiphons, eight responsories, and six responsory verses present in the other two sources. Yet a common point between St Bénigne of Dijon and Cluny (and also St Germain des Près, St Martin de Tours, and Sts Vanne and Hydulphe) was their fidelity to the older type of processional with antiphons, while some cathedrals and monasteries adopted the new type of processional with responsories.[31] This was because Cluny continued to sing the entire night office with all of its responsories, while others moved the singing of responsories to processions.

An abbey associated with St Bénigne as well as with Réôme was St Germain of Auxerre: Maiolus, abbot of Cluny, reformed St Germain in 987–989 (it became Cluniac in 972), and Heldricus, his pupil, was abbot there and at St Bénigne. A Life of St Maiolus (BHL 5179) centonizes the metrical Life of St Germain of Auxerre, of which a copy was in the Cluny library.[32] An anonymous sermon about St Maiolus centonizes excerpts from John Scot's *Periphyseon*, an anonymous sermon in honour of St Jean de Réôme, works by St Augustine, and Heiric of Auxerre's miracles of St Germain.[33]

The connection to St Germain d'Auxerre explains the presence of an office for St Urban in the Dijon tonary.[34] In 862 monks from St Germain went to Rome as an embassy and brought back the relics of Pope Urban and the martyr Tiberius. On their return they passed by St Maurice d'Agaune and brought along the relics of St Maurice

---

[30]This office tonary is on p. 8 of the facsimile in PM 8 (index on p. 11). The antiphons that appear in both and are also assigned to the same tone are *Innuebant patri eius*, fourth tone, fifth differentia (p. 8, col. C); *Vobis datum*, sixth tone (col. C); *Veni domine visitare nos*, seventh tone, seventh differentia (col. D); *Loquebantur* seventh tone, fifth differentia (col. D); *Stella ista*, seventh tone, fourth differentia (col. D); *Vivit dominus*, seventh tone, fourth differentia (col. D); *Dixerunt discipuli*, seventh tone, sixth differentia (col. D); *Lux de luce*, eighth tone, second differentia (col. D).

[31]See Michel Huglo, *Les manuscrits du processionnal, RISM B XIV 2*, Index II.1 (Munich, 2004).

[32]Delisle, *Le cabinet*, p. 475, no. 426.

[33]See Sapin, *Abbaye Saint-Germain d'Auxerre*, pp. 277–283. Heldricus is depicted in Paris, BNF lat. 12302 on fol. 1[r].

[34]On p. 9 in the facsimile edition.

and the head of Innocent, one of his martyred companions. In 865 the crypts of St Germain of Auxerre were consecrated.[35]

In sum, the close correspondence between the repertories of chant described by Aurelian of Réôme and those transmitted in manuscripts from Dijon, Fécamp, and St Maur-des-Fossés is explained by significant historical associations between the abbeys of Réôme, Dijon, and Cluny, notably those resulting from abbots being affiliated with more than one house.[36] Nevertheless, it will now be necessary to examine the melodies and tonal assignments of these repertories in order to identify the cases where the musical and liturgical traditions are separate. Further investigations of this kind and also into the histories and local practices of these very old Burgundian abbeys,[37] particularly on their martyrologies, calendars, liturgies (even isolated neumed chants), and customaries, may better show how the chant and liturgy of the powerful abbey of Cluny was formed and confirm the central role of the Burgundian region in the development of Gregorian chant in the ninth and tenth centuries.[38]

---

[35]Sapin, *Abbaye Saint-Germain d'Auxerre*, p. 290. Huglo and Hansen were not aware of this translation. See Hansen, *H. 159, Montpellier: Tonary of St Bénigne of Dijon*, p. 35*. On p. 37* Hansen observes that the Dijon tonary also has *Venit ad Petrum* with the famous *Caput* melisma, which is not in Bukofzer's list of sources. See Manfred Bukofzer, 'Caput: A Liturgico-Musical Study', in *Studies in Medieval and Renaissance Music* (New York, 1950), pp. 217–310.

[36]Ferreira, *Music at Cluny*, concluded on p. 284 that 'Cluny has strong links with Brittany and some relation to Laon', but notes (p. 285) that 'Cluny was open to outside influence, especially from the Aquitaine, probably through personal connections and exchanges with affiliated houses there [we add: particularly Moissac]'.

[37]Joseph Perry Ponte III, 'Aureliani Reomensis, *Musica disciplina*: A Revised Text, Translation, and Commentary' (Ph.D. diss., Brandeis University, 1961), in a thorough examination of the chant of Aurelian's tonary, concludes that the chants most resemble those of the Hartker Codex. Contacts between Burgundy, southern Germany, and St Gall were already important in the early ninth century. See Joachim Wollasch, 'Das Patrimonium Beati Germani in Auxerre', in Gerd Tellenbach, ed., *Studien und Vorarbeiten zur Geschichte des Grossfränkischen und Frühdeutschen Adels*, Forschungen zur Oberrheinischen Landesgeschichte 4 (Freiburg-im-Breisgau, 1957), pp. 185–224.

[38]We need to reconfigure our early history of chant, taking central Gaul into account as much as the Carolingian court and the centres from which we have manuscripts. Note the conclusions presented by Kenneth Levy in 'Gregorian Chant and the Romans', *JAMS* 56 (2003), pp. 5–41 (p. 41: '[...] still under Pippin or later under Charlemagne, the Franks rejected the ROM music and, in their effort to establish GREG, turned to familiar Gallican chants, which tended to have fixed, memorable melodies.').

Table 5.1: Aurelian, Dijon, Fécamp, St Maur-des-Fossés

A = antiphon, Alv = alleluia verse, Co = communion, F = Ordinal of Fécamp, Gr = gradual, Grv = gradual verse, Hy = hymn, Int = introit, Intv = introit verse, Inv = invitatory, M = Dijon tonary, Of = offertory, Ofv = offertory verse, R = responsory, Rv = responsory verse, StR = tonary of St Riquier

Chants are in the order of their appearance in *Musica disciplina*, and second appearances are signalled. Chapter titles follow Gushee's edition, but spellings of the chant are normalized.

II.12 Inclina domine, Int	M, F		
II.14 Confessio, Int	M, F		
II.15 Circumdederunt me, Int	StR, M, F		
II.16 Puer natus, Int	M, F		
IV.2 Exclamaverunt ad te, Int	StR, F		
IV.4 Rex eterne domine, Hy	F	12044	
X De authentu proto			
Gaudete in domino, Int	M, F		
Justus es domine, Int	M, F		
Suscepimus deus, Int	M, F		
Super flumina Babilonis, Of	M, F		
Posuisti domine, Gr	M, F		
Sacerdotes eius, Gr	M, F		
Dominus dabit, Co	M, F		
Amen dico vobis, Co	M, F		
Tria sunt munera, R	F	12044	
Reges T[h]arsis, Rv	F	12044	
Recordare mei domine, R[39]			
Exsurge domine non, Rv			
Domine, ne in ira tua, R	F	12044	
Timor et tremor, Rv	F	12044	
Peccantem me cotidie, R	F		
Deus in nomine tuo, Rv	F		
Tradent enim vos, A	F	12044	12601
Fulgebunt iusti, A	F	12044	12601
Misso Herodes, A	F	12044	12601
Mihi vivere Christus, A	F	12044	12601

---

[39]*CAO* 7511: only in E.

XI De plagis proti

Dominus inluminatio mea, Int	M, F		
Dominus fortitudo, Int	M, F		
Ad te domine levavi, Of	M, F		
Exiit sermo inter fratres, Co	M, F		
Vos qui in turribus, R	F	12044	12601
Laudate dominum deum nostrum, Rv	F	12044	12601
Sanctificavit Moyses, Of	M, F		
Oravit Moyses, Ofv	M		
Hic est fratrum amator, R	F	12044	12601
Ecce quam bonum, Rv	F	12044	12601
Veni domine et noli, R	F	12044	
O sapientia, A	F		
Juste et pie vivamus, A	F	12044	

XII De autentu deutero

Confessio [et pulchritudo], Int	M, F		
Dum clamarem, Int	M, F		
Deus tu convertens, Of	M, F		
De fructu operum, Co	M, F		
Venite exultemus domino, Inv[40]	F		
Regem venturum dominum, Inv	F		
Regem apostolorum, Inv	F	12044	12601
Regem martyrum dominum, Inv	F	12044	12601
Regem magnum, A	F		
Audite verbum, R	F		
A solis ortu, Rv	F		
Peccavi super numerum, R	F	12044	12601
Quoniam, Rv	F	12044	
Declara super nos, R	F	12044	
Declaratio sermonum, Rv	F	12044	
Hec est generatio, A	F		
Pulchra es et decora, A	F	12044	12601
Malos male perdet, A	F	12044	

XIII De plagis deuteri

Resurrexi, Int	M, F

---

[40]Note that Aurelian cites many invitatory antiphons. See Ruth Steiner, 'Reconstructing the Repertory of Invitatory Tones and Their Uses at Cluny in the Late Eleventh Century', in *Musicologie médiévale: Notations-Séquences*, studies put together by Michel Huglo (Paris, 1987), pp. 175–182. This study was reprinted as article 4 in Ruth Steiner, *Studies in Gregorian Chant*, Variorum Collected Studies Series (Aldershot, 1999).

Eduxit [eos] dominus, Int	M, F		
Justus ut palma, Of	M, F		
Memento verbi, Co	M, F		
Christus natus est nobis, Inv	F	12044	
Christus apparuit nobis, Inv	F	12044	
Adoremus deum, Inv	F	12044	12601
Ipsi vero non congnoverunt, Inv	F	12044	
Adoremus dominum, Inv	F	12044	12601
Hodie si vocem domini, Inv	F	12044	
Rex noster adveniet, R	F		
Ecce agnus dei, Rv	F	12044	
Angelus domini vocavit, R	F	12044	
Et benedicentur, Rv	F	12044	
Ecce agnus dei, R	F	12044	
Hoc est testimonium, Rv	F	12044	
Ecce agnus dei, Rv	F	12044	
Exultabunt sancti, Gr	M, F		
Cantate domino, Grv	M, F		
A summo caelo egressio, Grv	M, F		
Tollite portas principes, Gr	M, F		
Quis ascendet, Grv	M, F		
Haec dies, Gr	M, F		
Confitemini domino, Grv	M		
Isti sunt triumphatores, R	F	12044	12601
Isti sunt qui venerunt, Rv	F	12044	12601
Vidi coniunctos viros, R	F	12044	12601
Vidi angelum dei, Rv	F	12044	12601
Maria et flumina, A	F	12044	
Mane surgens Iacob, A	F	12044	12601
Nox praecessit, A	F		
Justi autem, A	F		
Innuebant patri eius, A	M, F	12044	12601
Habitabit in tabernaculo, A	F	12044	12601
Sanctis qui in terra, A	F	12044	12601
Omnes gentes quascunque, A	F		
Omnis terra adoret te, A	F		

XIIII De autentu trito

A solis ortu, Rv	F		
Circumdederunt me, Int	StR, M, F		
Ecce deus adiuvet me, Int	StR, M, F		
Inmittit angelum dominus, Of	M, F		
Quis dabit ex Sion, Co	M, F		
In manu tua domine, Inv	F	12044	12601

Obsecro domine, R	F		
A solis ortu, Rv	F		
Vestri capilli capitis, A	F	12044	

XV De plagis triti

Omnes gentes plaudite, Int	M, F		
Stetit angelus, Of	M, F		
Exultavit ut gigas, Co	M, F		
Aspiciebam in visu, R	F		
Ecce dominator dominus, Rv	F	12044	
Potestas eius potestas, Rv	F	12044	
Reges T[h]arsis et insule, R[41]	F	12044	
Reges Arabum et Saba dona, Rv	F	12044	
A facie inimici, Rv	F	12044	
Gaude Maria, R	F	12044	12601
Gabrielem, Rv	F	12044	12601
O quam gloriosum, A	F	12044	12601
Puer Jesus, A	F	12044	
Vobis datum, A	F	12044	
Quare detraxistis, A	F		12601

XVI De autentu tetrardi

Puer natus, Int	M, F	
Audivit dominus, Int	M, F	
In virtute tua, Of	M, F	
Dicite pusillanimes, Co	M, F	
Non sit vobis vanum, Inv	F	12044
Deus magnus dominus, Inv		
Aspiciens a longe, R[42]	F	
Quique terrigena, Rv	F	
Dixit Judas fratribus, R	F	12044

---

[41]This responsory (*CAO* 7522) is unusually short and lacks its repetendum. It is found especially in Eastern manuscripts.

[42]This responsory (*CAO* 6129) was not sung in Lyon or Cluny. It was banned by Agobard because of its non-Biblical text, but Aurelian cites it, as does the ordinal of Fécamp (see Chadd, *Ordinal*, vol. 1, p. 48; omitted from index). There were writings by Agobard in the library of Cluny (Delisle, *Le cabinet*, p. 468, no. 273). See Michel Huglo, 'Les remaniements de l'antiphonaire grégorien au IXe siècle: Helisachar, Agobard, Amalaire', in *Atti del XVIII Convegno di Studi sul tema 'Culto cristiano e politica imperiale carolingia'*, *Todi, 9–12 ottobre 1977* (Todi, 1979), p. 106 (reprinted in *Sources du plainchant et de la musique médiévale*, Variorum Collected Studies Series (Aldershot, 2004), vol. 1, no. 11), and 'Les livres liturgiques de la Chaise-Dieu', *RB* 87 (1977), pp. 322–323 (reprinted *Sources du plainchant*, vol. 3, no. 4).

Cumque abisset Ruben, Rv	F		
Iste est frater vester, R	F	12044	
Adtollens autem Joseph, Rv	F	12044	
Veni hodie ad fontem, R	F	12044	
Igitur puella, Rv	F	12044	
Dixit autem David, R	F[43]	12044	12601
Cumque extendisset, Rv	F	12044	12601
Surge Aquilo, A	F	12044	12601
Si vere fratres, A	F	12044	
Constitues eos, A	F	12044	
Habitabit in tabernaculo, A	F	12044	12601
Sanctis qui in terra, A	F	12044	12601
Veni domine visitare nos, A	M, F		
Ante t[h]orum, A	F	12044	12601
Gaude Maria, A	F	12044	12601
Loquebantur, A	M, F	12044	
Fidelia omnia, A	F	12044	
Regnum tuum domine, A	F	12044	12601
Sicut locutus es, A	F		
Stella ista, A	M, F	12044	
Vivit dominus, A	M, F	12044	12601
Nos qui vivimus, A[44]	F	12044	12601
Martyres domini, A	F	12044	12601
Angeli domini, A	F	12044	12601
Gaude Maria, A	F	12044	12601
Dixerunt discipuli, A	F	12044	12601

XVII De plagis tetrardi

Ad te levavi, Int	M, F		
Si ambulavero, Of	M, F		
Vox in rama, Co	M, F		
Iste homo, R	F		
Ecce homo sine querela, Rv	F		
Montes Gelboe, R	F	12044	12601
Omnes montes, Rv	F	12044	
Ab omni via mala, R	F	12044	
A iudiciis tuis, Rv	F	12044	
Servus tuus, R	F	12044	

---

[43]In the edition (Chadd, *Ordinal*, vol. 1, p. 315), but omitted from the index.

[44]Aurelian and Regino of Prüm assign this antiphon and the next two to the seventh tone, whereas other tonaries consider it to be in the eighth (see Huglo, *Les tonaires*, p. 395).

Ut discam mandata tua, Rv	F	12044	
Videntes Joseph, R	F	12044	
Cumque vidissent Joseph, Rv	F	12044	
Dixit Ruben fratribus, R	F	12044	
Merito haec patimur, Rv	F	12044	
Merito haec patimur, R	F	12044	
Dixit Ruben fratribus, Rv	F	12044	
Repleti sunt omnes, A	F	12044	
Dum medium silentium, A	F	12044	
Gloria in excelsis, A	F	12044	
Exsultavit spiritus, A[45]			
Lux de luce, A	M, F	12044	
O ineffabilem virum, A	F	12044	12601
Missus sum ad oves quae, A	F	12044	
Lumen ad revelationem, A	F	12044	
Martyrum chorus, A	F		

XVIIII De plagis proti

Immola deo sacrificium, Rv	F	12044	
Erue a framea deus, R	F	12044	
De ore leonis libera me, R	F	12044	
De autento deuteri			
Ecce dominator, Rv	F	12044	
De plagis deuteri			
Ps. Beati immaculati, Intv	M		
In ecclesiis benedicite, R	F	12044	
Alleluia! Audivimus eum, R[46]		12044	
Ecce quam bonum, Rv	F	12044	12601
De autentu trito			
Ps. Diligam te domine, Intv	M		
A solis ortu, Rv	F		
Et misericordia ejus, A[47]			

---

[45]Magnificat antiphon *per annum*. These disappeared after the creation of antiphons with texts taken from the Gospels of the Sundays after Pentecost, which are found only in Gregorian antiphoners and not in the Old Roman antiphoners. On this subject see Amalarius, *De ordine antiphonarii* (Jean-Michel Hanssens, ed., *Amalarii episcopi opera liturgica omnia*, Studi e Testi 138–140 (Vatican, 1948, 1950)), vol. 3, ch. 68, and Michel Huglo, 'Le chant *vieux-romain*', *Sacris erudiri* 6/1 (1954), p. 121 (reprinted in *Sources du plainchant*, vol. 2, no. 1).

[46]*CAO* 6069. This alleluiatic responsory is for the Farewell to the Alleluia of the Septuagesima office, a possibly Gallican custom that was suppressed by Pope Alexander II (1061–1073). The responsory nevertheless remained in ms Paris BNF lat. 12584, a manuscript very close to the antiphoner of St Maur des Fossés used here.

De plagis triti

Ps. Noli emulari, Intv	M		
Et dixit: nequaquam, Rv	F	12044	
Fecit potentiam A[48]			

De autentu tetrardo

In omnem terram, Rv	F	12044	12601
Dixit paterfamilias, A	F	12044	
Virgo dei genitrix, A	F		
Dum staret Abraham, R	F	12044	

De plagis tetrardi

Neque inrideant me, Intv[49]	F		
Magi veniunt ab oriente, R	F	12044	
Iste est qui ante deum, R	F		
Et erexit cornu, A[50]			

XX.34

Cives apostolorum, R	F	12044	12601
Emitte domine, Rv			
In omnem terram, Rv	F	12044	12601

---

[47] Magnificat antiphon *per annum.*

[48] Magnificat antiphon *per annum.*

[49] Aurelian calls this a *versus introituum*, but it is the third phrase of the introit *Ad te levavi* (see the entry in the Table above). Compare Aurelian: 'V. Neque inrideant me inimici mei; etenim universi qui te expectant *non erubescant*' (Gushee, *Aureliani Reomensis Musica disciplina*, p. 128) with Eugene Cardine, *Graduel neumé* (Solesmes, 1966), p. 1, '[...] *non erubescam*: neque irrideant me inimici mei: etenim universi qui te exspectant, *non confundentur*' (emphasis ours).

[50] Magnificat antiphon *per annum.*

Chapter 6

The first dictionary of music: the *Vocabularium musicum* of ms Monte Cassino 318

Alma Santosuosso

Monte Cassino, Archivio della Badia, ms 318, with its encyclopaedic collection of medieval theoretical writings, is well known to musicologists. The contents include, among other things, the complete works of Guido of Arezzo and many other treatises and excerpts from earlier theorists, tonaries, two neume tables, and musical compositions. It also contains the first dictionary of music, its word list concerned primarily with musical instruments and their players.

Copied by a single scribe, the codex comprises 300 pages measuring 260 x 165 mm. On the last page there is a thirteenth-century *ex libris* of S. Maria de Albaneto. Most scholars have considered the codex to be a mid-eleventh-century product from this house, which is located less than a kilometre from the monastery of Monte Cassino. However, both the dating and origin of MC 318 were recently questioned by Francis Newton in his monumental study of the scriptorium and library at Monte Cassino.[1] He determined that 'nothing in the script or decoration [of MC 318] has any connection with the Albaneto products that survive'. He considered two possibilities: either MC 318 originated at Monte Cassino but was penned by a scribe whose training was at another centre, or it originated at that other centre but was given to Monte Cassino as a gift during the Desiderian (1058–1087) or Oderisian period (1087–1105). As for the date, Newton suggests 'after 1070 at least' if it was written at Monte Cassino and 'if of another centre, perhaps, but not necessarily, a little later'. Newton believes that sometime during its history, the codex was lent to Albaneto and later returned to Monte Cassino. Like other Cassine manuscripts, MC 318 has page rather than folio numeration.

The contents of the manuscript have been indexed by many scholars, including Mauro Inguanez, Paolo Ferretti, Adrien de la Fage, Joseph Smits van Waesberghe,

---

[1]Francis Newton, *The Scriptorium and Library at Monte Cassino 1058–1105* (Cambridge, 1999). For Newton's dating of Monte Cassino 318 and his remarks about provenance see p. 373.

Pieter Fischer, Paul Merkley, and Dolores Pesce.[2] As well, an index is available on the internet site of the *Lexicon musicorum latinum medii aevi*. In 2001 Angelo Rusconi wrote a short article giving an overview of the structure and contents of MC 318.[3] Although an author or a title has been assigned to most of the music theory texts in MC 318, some remain to be identified.

Musicologists have studied MC 318 extensively. I will mention here only the more important of the numerous books and articles.[4] The tonaries were examined by Michel Huglo, Paul Merkley, Clyde Brockett, and Katarina Livljanic;[5] Paolo Ferretti and Michael Bernhardt dealt with the notation;[6] and Christian Meyer and Joseph Smits van Waesberghe published the monochord divisions.[7] The famous *O Roma nobilis*, popular even today as a pilgrimage hymn, was examined by Bryan Gillingham and Bernard Peebles; other musical compositions of MC 318 have been edited by Karl-Werner Gümpel and Michael Bernhard.[8] As for the major theoretical treatises, MC 318 was used in the critical editions of *Musica enchiriadis* and other important works,

---

[2]Mauro Inguanez, *Codicum casinensium manuscriptorum catalogus cura et studio monachorum S. Benedicti archicoenobii Montis Casini* (Rome, 1915–1951); Paolo M. Ferretti, 'I manoscritti musicali gregoriani dell'archivio di Montecassino', *Casinensia* 1 (1929), pp. 187–203; Adrien de la Fage, *Essai de diphthérographie musicale* (Amsterdam, 1964; reprint of 1864 Paris edn); Joseph Smits van Waesberghe, ed., Guido Aretinus, *Micrologus*, CSM 4 (1955); Pieter Fischer, ed., *Italy*, vol. 2 of *The Theory of Music from the Carolingian Era up to 1400*, ed. Joseph Smits van Waesberghe with the collaboration of Pieter Fischer and Christian Maas (Munich, 1968); Paul Merkley, *Italian Tonaries* (Ottawa, 1988); Dolores Pesce, *Guido of Arezzo's* Regule rithmice, Prologus in antiphonarium, *and* Epistola ad Michahelem (Ottawa, 1999).

[3]Angelo Rusconi, 'Il cod. 318 di Montecassino: note sulla struttura e sul contenuto', in Michael Bernhard, ed., *Quellen und Studien zur Musiktheorie des Mittelalters* 3 (Munich, 2001), pp. 121–144.

[4]I am currently working on a detailed index and bibliographical study of MC 318, which will appear with a facsimile of the codex.

[5]Michel Huglo, *Les tonaires* (Paris, 1971); Merkley, *Italian Tonaries*; Clyde W. Brockett, *Anonymi de modorum formulis et tonarius*, CSM 37 (Rome, 1997); Katarina Livljanic, 'Modalité orale et modalité écrite: attribution modale des antiennes dans l'antiphonaire et le tonaire de Monte Cassino', *EG* 30 (2002), pp. 5–51.

[6]Ferretti, 'I manoscritti', pp. 193–195. Michael Bernhard, 'Die Überlieferung der Neumennamen im lateinischen Mittelalter', in *Quellen und Studien zur Musiktheorie des Mittelalters* 2 (Munich, 1997), pp. 81–82. See also my *Letter Notations in the Middle Ages* (Ottawa, 1989).

[7]Christian Meyer, *Mensura monochordi. La division du monocorde IXe–XVe siècles* (Paris, 1996); Joseph Smits van Waesberghe, *De musico-pedagogico et theoretico Guidone Aretino* (Florence, 1953).

[8]Bryan Gillingham, *Secular Medieval Latin Song: An Anthology* (Ottawa, 1993), and *A Critical Study of Secular Medieval Latin Song* (Ottawa, 1995); Bernard N. Peebles, 'O Roma nobilis', *American Benedictine Review* 1 (1950), pp. 67–92; Karl-Werner Gümpel, 'Spicilegium rivipullense', *AMw* 35 (1978), pp. 58–59; Michael Bernhard, *Clavis Gerberti. Eine Revision von Martin Gerberts Scriptores ecclesiastici de musica sacra potissimum*, Part 1, VMK 7 (Munich, 1989).

including those by Aurelian, Regino, Berno, and Guido of Arezzo.[9] Two of the shorter texts, *His ita perspectis* and *Omnes autenti*, have been published by Mark Leach and Karl-Werner Gümpel, respectively, and a small group of writings brought out by Adrien de la Fage.[10] Most of the works just mentioned consider the general relationships between texts of MC 318 and those found in other manuscripts; more recently, Dolores Pesce, Christian Meyer, Katarina Livljanic and I have studied the relationships between MC 318 and other Italian codices.[11]

Among the unique collection of materials found in MC 318 is the dictionary of music on the last three pages. Although the manuscript is generally in excellent condition, there are two damaged pages which are especially difficult to read. Unfortunately, these (pages 298 and 300) comprise the beginning and end of the *Vocabularium musicum*. The dictionary is in two parts. The first (pp. 298–300), which will be referred to as List A, is arranged roughly in alphabetical order with the definitions taken from several different sources. The second section, List B, occupies the lower three-quarters of page 300 and includes words and definitions only from Isidore of Seville (*ca* 560–636), primarily from his *Etymologiarum sive Originum libri XX*, Book 3, *De musica*.[12]

The Monte Cassino dictionary was first published by Adrien de la Fage (1864) and more recently by Angelo Rusconi (2001).[13] La Fage rearranged the list by putting all of the items in alphabetical order, which resulted in a useful modern edition; but by not following the original word order he deliberately obscured the rationale used by the scribe in constructing the dictionary. In his study of MC 318 Rusconi published the dictionary following the original word order of the codex, where the two lists are dis-

---

[9]Hans Schmid, ed., *Musica et Scholica enchiriadis una cum aliquibus tractatulis adiunctis*, VMK 3 (Munich, 1981); Lawrence Gushee, ed., *Aurelianus Reomensis,* Musica disciplina, CSM 21 (Rome, 1975); Sister Mary Protase LeRoux, 'The *De harmonica institutione* and *Tonarius* of Regino of Prüm' (Ph.D. diss., The Catholic University of America, 1965); Michael Bernhard, *Studien zur Epistola de armonica institutione des Regino von Prüm* (Munich, 1979); Joseph Smits van Waesberghe, *Bernonis Augiensis abbatis de arte musica disputationes traditae*, Part A: *Bernonis Augiensis de mensurando monochordo*, and *Quae ratio est inter tria opera de arte musica Bernonis Augiensis*, Divitiae Musicae Artis A/6A and B (Buren, 1978, 1979), and also Waesberghe, ed., *Aretinus,* Micrologus; Pesce, *Guido of Arezzo's* Regule rithmice.

[10]Mark A. Leach, '*His ita perspectis.* A Practical Supplement to Guido of Arezzo's Pedagogical Method', *JM* 8 (1990), pp. 82–101; Karl-Werner Gümpel, 'Spicilegium rivipullense', pp. 58–59; La Fage, *Essai de diphthérographie*, pp. 393–408.

[11]See my *Firenze, Biblioteca nazionale centrale, Conventi Soppressi, F.III.565* (Ottawa, 1994); Pesce, *Guido of Arezzo's* Regule rithmice; Meyer, *Mensura monochordi*; Livljanic, 'Modalité orale', pp. 5–51.

[12]All subsequent references to Isidore's *Etymologiarum* will be to Book 3, *De musica*; unless otherwise identified. Chapters are indicated by Roman numerals, while Arabic numbers indicate the sentence number in W. M. Lindsay's edition (Oxford, 1962).

[13]La Fage, *Essai de diphthérographie*, pp. 404–407. Rusconi, 'Il cod. 318', pp. 138B141.

tinct.[14] The word list and definitions do not reflect the vocabulary of eleventh-century music theorists; instead, as I shall demonstrate, they are dependent on the usage of several earlier writers. Both La Fage and Rusconi recognized certain passages from Isidore of Seville's *Etymologiarum*, which is the primary source for the *Vocabularium musicum*, but neither scholar dealt with the overall organization of the list nor realized the diversity of medieval writings from which the definitions were taken. Table 6.1 reproduces the *Vocabularium musicum*.

In order to understand the dictionary, I have tried to find the original source for each word and its definition. Four entries are from Biblical commentaries: St Ambrose defined 'armonia' in his *Expositio evangelii secundum Lucam*, and the description of 'chorus', 'organus', and 'timpanus' are drawn from the *Expositio psalmorum 150*, verse 4 of Cassiodorus (*ca* 490–583). I have found correspondences between other items in the dictionary and excerpts from the same author's *Institutiones divinarum et saecularium litterarum*, from Isidore's *Etymologiarum*, and from the *De universo* of Rabanus Maurus (*ca* 780–856). One of the two definitions of 'organum' is from *De orthographia liber* of the Venerable Bede (b. 672 or 673; d. 735). There are also two quotations taken from Odo of Arezzo, part of the definition of 'musica', and the description of a monochord.

Of the fifty-three words on List A (pp. 298–300), Cassiodorus's explanation of the genres of musical instruments (percussion, strings, and winds) is the longest entry. In his *Institutiones* he described the percussion instruments as being made of metal, the instruments of tension as using strings, and wind instruments as those that 'produce a vocal sound when filled by a stream of air'.[15] The musical instruments listed include the cithara, cymbalum, fistula, lyra, nablum, organum, pandyrea, psalterium, sambuca, sistrum, tintinnabulum, tuba, and tympanum. Many of these are mentioned in the Book of Psalms, and these same instruments (and others) are cited in Isidore's *Etymologiarum*. Another group of words relates to singing: armonia, concentus, chorus, melodia; certain types of sounds are also described: clangor, melos, melops. We find, as well, the *de rigueur* definition of 'musica'.

As its starting point, the *Vocabularium musicum* uses Isidore's discussion of the threefold division of music and all the musical instruments he mentions. Both parts of the dictionary contain vocabulary drawn primarily from chapters 18–22 of his *Etymologiarum*, Book 3, *De musica*. In chapter 19 Isidore writes: 'The first [division of music] is the harmonic, which consists of singing; the second, the organic, which is produced by blowing; and the third, the rhythmic, in which the music is produced by the impulse of the fingers.'[16] In chapter 20 he discusses the harmonic division, and in

---

[14] Rusconi, 'Il cod. 318', pp. 138–141.

[15] R. A. B. Mynors, ed., Cassiodorus, *Institutiones musicae* (Oxford, 1937), p. 144, section 6. Subsequent references to the *Institutiones musicae* are to this edition.

[16] Isidore, *Etymologiarum*, xix, 1–2; Leo Treitler, ed., *Strunk's Source Readings in Music History*, rev. edn. Isidore's text was translated by William Strunk Jr. and Oliver Strunk, revised by James McKinnon (New York, 1998), pp. 150–151.

connection with his definition of euphony – 'sweetness of the voice' – he derives 'melody' from the word *mel* (honey).

The words found on List A that were taken from Isidore's chapter 20 include 'armonia', 'melodia', and the related 'melos' and 'melopse'. Both 'euphonia' and 'vox' are defined subsequently, in the little word list derived exclusively from his writings. The organic division refers to instruments 'which come to life and produce a musical pitch when filled by a stream of air'.[17] In chapter 21 Isidore gives 'organ' as the generic name of all musical vessels. He continues with descriptions of the tuba (trumpet), tibias, calamus (reed), fistula (pipe), sambuca (type of harp), and pandoria (panpipes).

As we have seen, all of these instruments, as well as 'organum', appear in List A. Four of the terms, 'tuba', 'tibiae', 'calamus', and 'organum', are found also on List B, but only two, 'organum' and 'tibiae', have identical definitions on both lists. The third division of music (rhythmic) has 'to do with strings and striking, to which are assigned the different species of cithara, also the tympanum, the cymbal, the sistrum, vessels of bronze and silver, others whose hard metal yields an agreeable clanging when struck and other instruments of this nature'.[18] Isidore also mentions the psaltery, tintinnabulum (bell), and the symphonia (drum). He puts strings and percussion instruments together in the same category, and all of the above-mentioned appear in the dictionary. Of this group, only 'cymbala' and 'sistrum' recur on List B.

Items in List A are defined in different ways. Some are described by a single word (for example, 'calami' by 'casia', 'fidicen' by 'cithara', and 'nablum' by 'psalterium'), while others ('calamus', 'concentor', 'chorus', and 'fistula') have short explanations. Certain musical instruments ('lyra', 'monocordum', 'psalterium', 'simphonia', 'timpanus') have longer definitions, as does 'musica'. In some cases the scribe repeated words: 'concentus' has two definitions, while 'armonia', 'organum', and 'tibiae'[19] have three each. In a few cases etymologies are attempted, or bilingual equivalents: 'calamus graece, latino canna', 'lyra: genus citharae, dicta *apo tou lyrin*', 'musica: a musis per derivationem *apo tou moys* appellata est *moys* graece et latine *aqua*'. In one case, curiously, two words are used in immediate succession to define each other: 'calami: casia' and 'casia: calami'. Certain instruments and their respective players are grouped together on the list; for example, 'calamaula', 'calamaularius', 'calami', 'casia', and 'calamus'; 'sambucus', 'sambucista', and sambuca'; and 'tuba', 'tubicinor', and 'tubicines'. Three words – 'fidicen', 'fidicula', and 'fidis' – share a single definition, simply, 'cithara'.

The first entry in the dictionary – 'armonia' – is subsequently listed twice more and is defined by quotations from two different sources. The first definition – 'Armonia est modulatio vocis', etc. (see below) – is partly taken from Isidore's *Etymologiarum*, xx, 2. The second, 'Armonia est conveniens' etc. is a direct quotation from St Ambrose's

---

[17]Treitler, *Strunk's Source Readings*, p. 152.

[18]Isidore, *Etymologiarum*, xxii, 1; Treitler, *Strunk's Source Readings*, p. 153.

[19]The second and third definitions of 'tibiae' are illegible.

Expositio evangelii secundum Lucam, his commentary on chapter 8, verse 18.[20] The passage from St Ambrose appears earlier in MC 318, on pages 68–69, with some of the same interlinear glosses.

Three authors are called upon for the definition of 'organum'. The first and longest definition is from Cassiodorus's *Expositio psalmorum 150*, verse 4; the second from Isidore's *Etymologiarum*, xxi, 2; and the third from Bede's *De orthographia liber*.

Cassiodorus is the source of several definitions on List A. Those for 'chorus', 'organus', and 'timpanus' are direct quotations from his *Expositio psalmorum 150*, which recommends that God be praised with musical instruments. He defines the three words in his explanation of verse 4: *Laudate eum in tympano et choro, laudate eum in chordis et organo.*[21] Another two passages are from his *Institutiones*: the description of the three genera of musical instruments and 'cithara'. The quotation describing the genera duplicates that found earlier in ms 318, on pages 45–46. Both appearances have the same gloss, 'id est ascensu vel descensu, in gravitate vel acumine'; this does not appear in the published edition of Cassiodorus's text.[22]

Two other words are given interlinear glosses that have appeared earlier in MC 318.[23] In his discussion of the diapason's consonance Cassiodorus describes the ancient cithara as having eight strings 'quia apud veteres cytharae ex octo cordis constabant'.[24] This quotation is found on page 48 and is moreover employed in the dictionary as the definition of 'cythara'. Sometimes the definitions of the wind instruments and their respective players ('buccinor, cantor'; 'calamaula, canna de qua canitur'; 'tubicinor, tuba cano vel sono') use vocabulary relating to singers. Cassiodorus had described wind instruments as producing a vocal sound (*sonum vocis*) and this perhaps suggested the use of 'canere' in some instances.

All of the citations from Cassiodorus's *Institutiones* that appear in the dictionary are found earlier in MC 318 as well.[25] By contrast, although the word list is reliant overall on Isidore's *Etymologiarum*, only citations from his chapter 20, concerning the types of voices, are found earlier in MC 318 (on pp. 68–69).

Although Isidore's *Etymologiarum* is clearly the inspiration for the dictionary, it may be that his text was known only through the commentary written by Rabanus Maurus in his *De universo* (also known as *De rerum naturis*). Rabanus, one of the leading scholars of the ninth century, served as abbot of Fulda (822–842) and later as archbishop of Mainz (847–856). *De universo*, an extensive encyclopedia of twenty-

---

[20]*Ambrosii opera omnia*, PL 15.

[21]Cassiodorus, *Expositio psalterium*, Psalm 150, v. 4. *Opera omnia Cassiodori*, PL 70.

[22]Cassiodorus, *Institutiones*, p. 144, section 6.

[23]Eight interlinear glosses appear earlier in MC 318 in the quotation concerning the three instrumental generas. Only two of them, 'sensum' (.i., 'sonum') and 'species' (.i. 'figurae'), are found in the dictionary. (Words in brackets prefaced by .i. (*id est*) are interlinear glosses which appear above the previous word.)

[24]Cassiodorus, *Institutiones*, p. 145, section 7.

[25]In MC 318 pages 43–46 and 47–49 have excerpts from Book II, chapter 5, sections 1, 2, 3, 5, 6, and 7. Pages 55–56 also have quotations from Cassiodorus.

two books based on lengthy excerpts from Isidore's *Etymologiarum* – to which he added commentaries – was compiled during the years 842 to 847. Between 1022 and 1023 an illustrated copy of Rabanus's text was produced at Monte Cassino. Leo Marsicanus, the librarian and leader of the abbey's scriptorium, listed this book as *Rabanum ethimologiarum* in his eleventh-century catalogue.[26] The codex, ms Monte Cassino 132,[27] is still in the library.

Two of the quotations of the dictionary rely on *De universo*. One finds the origin of 'nablum: psalterium' in Book 18, chapter 4, *De musica et partibus eius* ('psalterium sed Hebraice nablum'),[28] and the definition of 'concentor' in Book 4, chapter 5, *De clericis* ('qui consonat: qui autem non consonat non concinit, nec concentor erit').[29]

List A is certainly indebted to Isidore in its choice of words and in the way certain words are described. But of the twenty-two taken from the *Etymologiarum*, only fourteen have definitions paraphrased or excerpted from his text. Direct quotations are employed only for 'tibiae'. The definitions of a few others – 'armonia', 'musica', 'lyra', 'simphonia' – start with Isidore's explanation but continue with textual interpolations. The compiler either inserted his own words or chose passages from other sources. For example, 'musica' begins with Isidore's explanation of how the term is derived from the Muses, but the phrase 'est moys graece et latine aqua significat' intrudes. This phrase appears earlier in MC 318, on page 90, in a section captioned, 'De genere musis'.[30] The text resumes with Isidore's explanation that the Muses were so named 'from inquiring into the power of songs and the measurement of pitch'. Then, 'veraciter canendi scientiam et facilis (.i. possibilis) a perfection canendi via' is inserted. The latter is taken from the Magister's response to the question 'Quid est musica?' in Odo of Arezzo's *Dialogus de musica*.[31] In that work, music is defined as 'the science of singing truly and the easy road to perfection in singing'. It is interesting that when the compiler chose definitions from other sources (Ambrose, Cassiodorus, Bede, and Odo of Arezzo) he always used direct quotations.

Isidore's descriptions of musical instruments vary. Sometimes he describes what the instrument looks like, or from what material it is made, or he qualifies its sound: 'clangor' appears twice, used to describe the sound of a trumpet. For other instruments he mentions where they were invented and at times gives an etymology of their names.

---

[26] Newton, *Scriptorium*, p. 20.

[27] Diane O. Le Berrurier, *The Pictorial Sources of Mythological and Scientific Illustrations in Hrabanus Maurus's* De rerum naturis (New York, 1978). Newton, *Scriptorium*, pp. 20, 301.

[28] PL 111.

[29] PL 111. This also appears in Isidore, *Etymologiarum*, Book 7, xii, *De clericis*. PL 82, no. 28.

[30] The etymologogy of the phrase 'Musica dicitur a moys, quod est aqua' was studied by Noel Swerdlow, who showed three derivations: the association of Muses and music; Muses and water; Moses and water. See Swerdlow, 'Musica dicitur a moys, quod est aqua', *JAMS* 20 (1967), pp. 3–9.

[31] Odo of Arezzo, 'Veraciter canendi scientia, et facilis ad canendi perfectionem via', *GS*, vol. 1, p. 247, MC 318, p. 218.

The specific occasions for playing certain instruments also interested him. The variety of his explanations is reflected by the compiler of the dictionary, even when the description is not taken from Isidore. For example, a bell ('tintinnabulum') is distinguished as having a sound like the 'bleating of sheep', while the 'rattling of iron' describes a cymbal ('cymbalum'). Isidore described the 'sambuca' as a type of drum, but in the dictionary it is first identified as a rustic cythara, then as a drum. 'Pandyrea' and 'sistrum' are referred to as genres of instruments.

The contents of list B (the separate smaller dictionary of thirteen items beginning on page 300) are reliant on a single source, Isidore's *Etymologiarum*.[32] The words in List B are presented in roughly the same order as they appear in Isidore's text; the compiler abridged the selections by omitting certain clauses or the last few words of sentences. The words chosen for the dictionary are in keeping with the overall plan of List A on the previous two pages in that all of the entries are related to musical instruments and singing. The entries begin, as already noted, with Isidore's definition of 'musica', its origin, and its three parts – harmonics, rhythmics, and metrics. His threefold division of music is followed by a description of how sound is caused; then 'voice' and 'euphony' are defined. Several of the same words – 'calamus, cymbala, organum, sistrum, tibiae, tuba' – appear in the earlier word list; however, the definitions are the same for only two, 'tibiae' and 'organum'. 'Musica' and 'armonia' also recur but with Isidore's explanation only. There are four words that are not part of a musical vocabulary: 'tragedi', 'tragediae', 'arithmetica', and 'arithmeticus'. Isidore's definition of 'arithmetica' appears in his *Etymologiarum*, in Book 3, chapter 1, of his *De mathematica*, 'tragedi', in Book 8, chapter 5 (*De poetis*).

Rusconi demonstrated that several of the shorter entries in the *Vocabularium musicum* came from earlier medieval glossaries. In his investigation of ms Monte Cassino 439, a tenth-century miscellaneous codex from Monte Cassino, he found nine words in MC 318 that corresponded with those in the *Glossarium Abstrusa* and another one in the *Glossarium Abolita*.[33] Rusconi presented the musical terminology found in these two glossaries in tables, and this information is presented below in List A of Table 1.[34]

The interlinear glosses found on virtually every page of MC 318 are insights into another layer of medieval thought. The scribe entered them in a small but clear hand for hundreds of words throughout the manuscript. Paul Merkley comments that 'the writing between the lines seems roughly contemporary with the main text'[35] and Rusconi agrees. Both scholars have observed that most of the interlinear glosses tend to be synonyms, not corrections or comments.[36] Rusconi argued that the scribe was familiar with the vocabulary of music theorists, and he included another table in his article

---

[32] The items were selected from chapters 15, 18, 19, 20, 21, and 22 of Isidore's *Etymologiarum*, Book 3, *De musica*.

[33] Rusconi, 'Il cod. 318', p. 127.

[34] *Ibid.*, pp. 142–144.

[35] Merkley, *Italian Tonaries*, p. 121.

[36] Rusconi, 'Il cod. 318', p. 126.

listing the glossed terms that he found in the second part of MC 318. Two of these terms, 'melodia' and 'concentum', appear in the dictionary with the same definitions.[37]

A short summary might be helpful. The scribe compiled two dictionaries of musical terms relating to musical instruments and singing. The choice of words in both reflects the influence of Isidore's *Etymologiarum* but the first dictionary has definitions quoted from other writers, including St Ambrose, Cassiodorus, Rabanus Maurus, Bede, and the late-tenth-century author Odo of Arezzo.[38] Of these, St Ambrose (from his *Expositio evangelii secundum Lucam*), Cassiodorus (from his *Institutiones*), and Odo of Arezzo (from his *Dialogus de Musica*) are cited earlier in the codex. Among the longer definitions on List A are three – 'chorus', 'organum', and 'timpanus' – from Cassiodorus's *Expositio psalmorum 150*. It seems significant, therefore, that the scribe did not include more detailed descriptions of the other biblical instruments (cymbalum, tuba, psalterium, and cithara) also discussed by Cassiodorus. The second word list, more narrowly confined to selections from Isidore, complements the first, amplifying the contents of MC 318 by providing a *compendium* of information from his *Etymologiarum*. The *Vocabularium musicum* of MC 318, the first dictionary of music, reveals both the breadth and the limitations of the medieval scholars who interested themselves in the *musica mundana*.

Table 6.1: Vocabularium musicum of ms Monte Cassino 318

Whenever possible I indicate the original source from which the word and definition were taken and include references in footnotes. For those definitions that appear earlier in the codex, I give the page number in MC 318. An asterisk after a word indicates that it appears in Isidore's *Etymologiarum*. I also indicate those words found in the two glossaries, *Abstrusa* and *Abolita*, published by Rusconi. Words glossed earlier in the codex and presented in Rusconi's table are shown with a 'Rus' placed after the definition. Finally, I confirm La Fage's and Rusconi's statement that the dictionary has many grammatical mistakes as do the interlinear glosses.[39]

Abbreviations:

Etym	Isidore, *Etymologiarum*. When the definitions are not direct quotations but are paraphrases of Isidore, I present Isidore's text as found in Lindsay's edition in a footnote.
*	Word appears in Isidore's *Etymologiarum*
Inst	Cassiodorus, *Institutiones*

---

[37]*Ibid.*, pp. 136–137.

[38]Isidore quotes a passages from Virgil's *Aeneid* that also appears in the dictionary.

[39]La Fage, *Essai de diphthérographie*, p. 408; Rusconi, 'Il cod. 318', pp. 126–127.

Exp	Cassiodorus, *Expositio psalmorum 150*
RM	Rabanus Maurus, *De universo*
GA	*Glossarium Abstrusa*
GAbo	*Glossarium Abolita*
Rus	Word and gloss found in Rusconi's table

LIST A

Armonia*: est modulatio vocis; vel competens (.i. conveniens) conjunctio. Vel ex multis
    vocabulis apta modulatio aut concordia plurimorum sonorum. [cf. *Etym* xx, 2[40]]

Armonia: est conveniens et apta (.i. congrua) rerum omnium dicitur commissa connexio
    (.i. coniunxio). Armonia: est cum fistulae organi per ordinem copulatae (.i.
    coadunate), legitimae tenent gratiam cantilenae, chordarumque aptus (.i. congru-
    um) servat ordo (.i. tenor) concordiam. [two definitions of 'armonia' by St
    Ambrose, *Expositio evangelii secundum Lucam*;[41] found also in MC 318, pp.
    68–69]

Bucinor: cantor

Calamaula: canna de qua canitur [*GA*, 'canna de quo canitur']

Calamaularius: ipse qui de canna canit [*GA*, 'ipse qui de canna canit']

Calami: casia

Casia: calami

Calamus graece, latine canna

Calamus*: arundo in sudibus; sudes, fustes utraque parte acuti

Clangoris*: vociferationis [*GAbo*, 'vociferans: clamans'; 'Clangor', *Etym* xvii, 20;
    xxi, 26]

Concentus: multorum canentium compositae [Rus, 'Concentum: multorum cantantium']

Concentus: simul in unum cantus [*GA*, 'concentus: simul cantus']

Concentor*: qui consonat; qui non consonat nec concinet (.i. consonet), nec concentor
    (.i. consonator) erit. [RM, *Etym*[42]]

Chorus: est plumimarum vocum ad suavitalis motum temperata collectio [*Exp*, 1052D]

Cymbalum*: est aeri sonitus vel crepitus ferri.

Cythara*: apud veteres cytharae octo chordis constabant [*Inst*, 7, 145, 11–12; found also
    in MC 318, p. 48]

Fistula*: tibia vel folium calamus aromatum

Fistulor: sibilor [*GA*, 'fistulor: sibilo']

Fidis: cithara, deorsum habet cavatum et sex chordas habet

Fidiculae: chordae [*GA*, 'fidiculae: chordae cithare']

---

[40]*Etym* xx, 2: 'Harmonica est modulatio vocis et concordantia plurimorum sonorum'.

[41]St Ambrose, *Expositio evangelii secundum Lucam*, book 8, v. 18, no. 3. *Ambrosii opera omnia*, PL 15; see also my *Firenze, Biblioteca nazionale centrale, Conventi Soppressi, F.III.565* (Ottawa, 1994). See fol. 99[v].

[42]Rabanus Maurus, *De universo*, book 4, chapter 5, PL 111. *Etym*, Book 7, vii (*De clericis*), 28: 'Concentor autem dicitur quia consonat: qui autem non consonat, nec concinit, nec cantor nec concentor erit'.

Fidicula: citharoedus [*GA*, 'fidicula, fidicen: citharoedus']

Fidis: chordae citharae

Fidicula* et fidicen*: cythara [*GA*, 'Fidicula, Fidicen: Citharoedus'; *Etym* xxii, 4]

Jubilate: cantate

Lyra*: genus citharae, dicta *apo tou lyrin*, id est varietate carminum; unde poetae *lyrici* dicuntur, quod diversos sonus efficiat; sonum cantionum (.i. canticum) tuarum non auditum[43] [cf. *Etym* xxii, 8]

Musica*: A musis per derivationem *apo tou moys* appellata est; moys graece et latine aqua significat, eoquod per eam quaerebatur virtus carminum et vocis modulationis; quia veraciter canendi scientia et facilis (.i. possibilis) ad perfectionem canendi via, omnis generis musicorum[44] [compiled from *Etym* xv, 1, and Odo of Arezzo]

Musicorum instrumentorum genera sunt tria: percussionalia, tensibilia, inflatilia Percussionalia sunt acitabula aenea et argentea, vel alia quae metall<ic>o rigore percussa reddunt cum suavitate tinnitum. Tensibilia sunt chordarum fila, sub arte religata, quae ammoto plectro percussa, id est in ascensu vel descensu, in gravitate vel acumine, delectabiliter sensum (.i. sonum) reddunt; in quibus sunt species (.i. figurae) citha<ra>rum diversarum. Inflatilia sunt quae, spiritu reflante completa, in sonum vocis animantur; ut sunt tubae, calami, organa, pandyria, et caetera hujusmodi [*Inst*, 144, sections 5 and 6]

Melodia*: dulcis cantus vel suavitas vocis[45] [*Etym* xx, 4; Rus, 'Melodia: dulcia sona']

Melos: dulcis sonus

Melopse: dulcissime

Monochordum: lignum longum, quadratum in modum capsae; et intus concavum in modum (.i. figuram) citharae; super quem posita chorda sonat; cujus sonitu varitates vocum facile (.i. possibile) comprehendis [Odo of Arezzo, *Dialogus de musica*; *GS* 1, 247; found also in MC 318, p. 218]

Nablum: Psalterium[46] [RM, 18, 4]

Organum: est quasi turris quaedam, diversis fistulis fabricata, quibus, flatu follium, vox copiosissima (.i. abundantissima) destinatur (.i. disponatur). Et ut eam modulatio (.i. dulcatio) decora (.i. munda?) componat, quibusdam ligneis ab interiore parte construitur, quas disciplinabiliter magistrorum digiti reprimentes, grandisonum efficiunt (.i. con<ficiunt>?), et ut suavissimam cantilenam [*Exp*, 1052]

---

[43]*Etym* xxii, 8: 'Lyra dicta *apo tou lyrin*, id est varietat vocum, quod diverso sonos efficiat'.

[44]*Etym* xv, 1: 'Musica per derivationem a Musis. Musae autem appellatae *apo tou moys*, id est a quaerendo, quod per eas, sicut antiqui voluerent, vis carminum et vocis modulatio quaereretur'. Rabanus Maurus: 'Est moys graece et latine aqua'. Odo of Arezzo: 'Veraciter canendi scientia et facilis ad canendi perfectionem via'. *GS*, vol. 1, p. 247; MC 318, p. 218.

[45]*Etym* xx, 4: 'Euphonia est suavitas vocis. Haec et melos a suavitate et melle dicta'.

[46]Rabanus Maurus, *De universo*, book 18, chapter 4: 'Psalterium, quod Hebraice nablum. Grace autem Psalterium'. PL 111.

Organum*: vocabulum est omnium vasorum musicorum. Hi tamen quibus folles
    adhibentur, alio nomine nuncupantur[47] [*Etym* xxi, 2]

Organarius: qui agatur organum[48] [Bede, *De orthographia liber*]

Organum: unius musici proprie nomen est; sed generaliter omnia musicorum vasa: id est
    tubae, calami, fistulae, cithara, psalterium, lyra, et cetera[49] [Bede, *De
    orthographia liber*[50]]

Psalterium*: genus musicorum, in modum litterae factum, et ipse est artis quae
    vulgo canticum dicitur, quod ebrei decacorda usi sunt propter numerum decalogi
    legis[51] [cf. *Etym* xxii, 7]

Psaltem: citharistam psallentem qui pulsaret ut per hoc excitatus esset spiritus eius

Psaltes: psalmicen

Psalmista: psalta

Psaltera: cantrix

Plaudite: gaudate

Pandyrea*: omnium generis musicorum in se factum

Simphonia*: genus musicae artis; est enim lignum concavum ex parte utraque extensa[52]
    [cf. *Etym* xxii, 14]

Sistrum*: genus musicae artis

Scypha: canna

Sambucus: saltator [*GA*, 'sambucus: saltator']

Sambucista: qui in cithara rustica canit [*GA*, 'sambucistria: qui (quae) in cithara rustica
    canit']

Sambuca*: genus citharae rusticae et symphoniae in musicis [cf. *Etym* xxi, 7[53]]

Tuba*: bucinum

Tubicinor: tuba cano vel sono

Tubicines: qui tuba canunt

Tibia*: excogitata in Frigia feruntur [*Etym*, xxi, 4]

Tibiae: ad?

Tibiae: quasi tubae sunt ?gitatione et species ?

Tibites: tibicines

---

[47]*Etym*, xxi, 2: 'folles adhibentur, alio *Graeci* nomine *appellant*'. This definition is
duplicated on page 300.

[48]Bede, 'Organarius autem est qui utitur organo'. PL 90, col. 140C.

[49]*Etym*, xxi, 2: 'Organum vocabulum est generale vasorum omnium musicorum'; xxi, 1:
'Secunda est divisio organica ... ut sunt tubae, calami, fistulae, organa, pandoria, et his similia
instrumenta'.

[50]Bede, 'Organum: unius musici proprie nomen est; sed generaliter omnia musicorum vasa
organa possunt dici ... citharum, psalterium, lyram, etc'. PL 90, col. 140C.

[51]*Etym*, xxii, 7: 'Psalterium, quod vulgo canticum dicitur ... in modum D literae. Psalterium
autem Hebraei decachordon usi sunt propter numerum Decalogi legis'.

[52]*Etym*, xxii, [?]: 'Symphonia vulgo appellatur lignum cavum ex utraque parte pelle
extensa ...'.

[53]*Etym* xxi, 7: 'Sambuca in musicus species est symphoniarum'.

Tibicines: aves concinentes et qui tibia canunt [*GA*, 'tybicen: qui in tibia canit']

Timpanus: est quasi duobus modiis solis capitibus confectus super eos tensi corii resultatio sonora, quod musici disciplinabili mensura percutientes, geminata resonatione modulantur [*Exp*, 1052D]

Timpanum* dicitur quod medius sit; timpanum enim extentum de pelle vel corio efficitur.[54] [cf. *Etym* xxii, 10]

Timpanistrales: juvenculae sunt quae cum timpanis cantant.

Tintinnabulum*: a sono, sicut balatus ovium.

LIST B Quotations from Isidore, *Etymologiarum*, Book 3 *De Musica*:

Musica appellata est *apo tou mason*, id est a quaerendo; quod per eam vis carminum et vocis modulatio quaeritur. [*Etym*, xv, selected from 1]

Musicae <p>arte<s> sunt tres harmonica, rhythmica, metrica. Harmonica est quae discernit in sonis acutum et grave; rhythmica (.i. numeraria) est quae requirit in cursione verborum utrum bene sonus, an male cohaereat (.i. constringat); metrica est quae mensuram diversorum metrorum probabili ratio<ne> (.i. sede quod ad omnem mensuram pertinet) cognoscit ut, verbi gratis, heroici, iambici, etc. [*Etym*, xviii, 1–2]

Materies cantilenarum triformem esse cernitur; prima est harmonia quae ex vocum cunctibus[55] [*sic*] constat, secunda organica quae ex flatu constat; tertia rhythmica quae ex pulsu digitorum sonum recipit. Nam a voce editur sonus, sicut per fauces; aut a flatu, sicut per tubam; aut a pulsu, sicut per cytharum. [*Etym*, xix, selected from 1 and 2]

Prima divisio musicae armonica dicitur, id est modulatio vocis. Armonica enim est concordantia plurimorum sonorum. Vox est aer spiritu verberans, unde et verba sunt nuncupata. [*Etym*, xx, selected from 1 and 2]

Euphonia est suavitas vocis. Haec et melos dicitur a suavitate et melle.[56] [*Etym*, xx, 4]

Tuba: a Tyrrhenis inventa; unde dicitur 'Tyrrhenusque tubae mugire per aethera clangor'. [*Etym*, xxi, selected from 3 with Isidore's quotation from Virgil's *Aeneid*, 8, 526]

Tibia: excogitatas in Frigia feruntur. [*Etym*, xxi, 4]

Calamus nomen est proprium arboris; a calando, id est vocando,[57] voces vocatur. [*Etym*, xxi, 5]

Organum: vocabulum est generale omnium vasorum musicorum, qui tamen quibus folles adhibentur, alio nomine nuncupantur.[58] [cf. *Etym*, xxi, 2]

Chordas: autem dictas a corde; quia, sicut pulsus est cordis in pectore, ita pulsus chordae in cithara, Has Mercurius excogitavit. [*Etym*, xxii, 6]

---

[54]*Etym* xxii, 14: 'Tympanum est pellis vel curium ligno ex una parte extentum. Est enim pars media symphoniae in similitudinem cribi. Tympanum autem dictum quod medium est ...'.

[55]This word should be 'cantibus'.

[56]*Etym*, xx, 4: 'Haec et melos a suavitate et melle dicta'.

[57]*Etym*, xxi, 5: 'id est *fundendo* voces vocatus'.

[58]*Etym*, xxi, 6: 'folles adhibentur, alio *Graeci* nomine *appellant*'.

Cymbala: Graece ballematia dicuntur; ergo cymbala dicta quia simul percutiuntur.[59]
   [*Etym*, xxii, 11]
Tragedia : gentilium fabulae, vel carmina poetarum.
Tragedi: quia in canendo praemium hircus, qui graece *tragos* dicitur. [*Etym*, Book 8 (*De poetis*, 5)]
Sistrum: ab inventore erat vocatum, quia Isis, regina Aegyptiorum invenisse eum dicitur.[60] [*Etym*, xxii, 12]
Arithemetica: disciplina numerorum, qui graeci numerum *rhytmum* vocant. [*Etym*, Book 3 (*De mathematica*, 3, 1)]
Arithmeticus: id est numerarius.

---

[59] *Etym*, xxii, 11: 'Dicta autem cymbala, quia cum ballematia simul percutiuntur; cum enim Graeci dicunt σύν, βαλά ballematia'.
   [60] *Etym*, xxii, 12: 'Sistrum ab inventore erat vocatum. Isis *enim* regina Aegyptiorum *id genus* invenisse *probatur*'.

Chapter 7

The twilight of troping

Theodore Karp

The essay presented in this chapter is one of three by this author that share the purpose of bringing to attention an important German printed gradual, issued in Würzburg in 1583 and entitled:

GRADUALE
HERBIPOLENSE
IUSSU ATQUE AUTHO-
RITATE REVERENDISSIMI IN CHRI-
sto Patris, Principis & Domini, D. IULII
Episcopi Herbipolensis & Franciae Orientalis Ducis emen-
datum meliorique ordine quàm hactenus dige-
stum, auctum & locupletatum, sumtuq[uam]
eiusdem excusum
ANNO, M.D. LXXXIII

The volume is worthy of attention for a variety of reasons. It contains a remarkably full series of sequences, many of which are of Notkerian origin.[1] In addition, it features a sizeable although much more limited group of *proper* tropes.[2] Nearly twenty years had passed since most, if not all, of these two kinds of pieces had been banned by the Council of Trent, and long after *proper* tropes had disappeared from the average late medieval and Renaissance source. We have slowly been accumulating information, particularly with regard to the use of sequences in both Germany and France, warning us not to overemphasize the effects of the liturgical legislation of the Council, and these tropes provide additional evidence in this regard. The Tridentine legislation undoubtedly had great force in Italy but was evidently less stringently observed or ignored in other countries. Although we would likely prefer to deal with pitch-readable sources created before 1300, the *Herbipolense* remains valuable inasmuch as it is

---

[1] See my 'Some Notkerian Sequences in Germanic Print Culture of the Fifteenth and Sixteenth Centuries', in Sean Gallagher, James Haar, John Nádas, and Timothy Striplin, eds, *Western Plainchant in the First Millenium* (Aldershot, 2003), pp. 399–428.

[2] I have mentioned these in 'A Serendipitous Encounter with St Kilian', *Early Music* 28 (2000), pp. 226–237.

frequently either the only diastematic source or one of a very small handful to permit reliable readings of a sizeable proportion of its paraliturgical content.

Table 7.1 presents a condensed account of the tropes contained within the *Herbipolense*. (When multiple elements are present in a set of tropes, these are delineated by slashes.)

Table 7.1: Tropes of the *Herbipolense*

Occasion	Chant	Function	Trope(s)
Nativity III	Puer natus	Introit	Hodie cantandus
St Stephen	Etenim	Introit	Eia collevi te[3] in protomartyris / Insurrexerunt / Invidi[4] lapidibus / Suscipe meum
John Evangelist	In medio	Introit	Quoniam dominus / Ut sacramentum / Qui eum / Quo inspirante / Inde nos moniti
Innocents	Ex ore	Introit	Hodie pro domino
Innocents	Anima nostra	Offertory	Gaudeamus laetantes
Innocents	Vox in Rama	Comm.	Veneranda praesentis
Epiphany	Ecce advenit	Introit	Ecclesiae sponsus / Jesus quem / Vidimus stellam / Cui soli debetur
Epiphany	Reges Tharsi	Offertory	O Redemptor omnium cui reges
Easter	Te deum		Quem quaeritis
John the Baptist	De ventre matris	Introit	Angelo praenunciante
John the Baptist	Justus ut palma	Offertory	Nativitatem venerandi
John the Baptist	Tu puer	Comm.	Hodie dilectissimi patres
St Kilian	Multae	Introit	Haec est alma dies / Qui pro Christo pius / Virtutes scilicet / Eya Charissimi gloriam
St Lawrence	Confessio	Introit	Hodie caelesti igne succensus
Assumption	Vultum tuum	Introit	Hodie sanctissima virgo

---

[3]*Sic.* The preferred reading, as given in vol. 1 of *Corpus troporum*, Studia Latina Stockholmiensia, edited under the direction of Ritva Jonsson (Stockholm, 1975), is *Eia conlevitae*. The splitting of the second word in the *Herbipolense* is documented by the small vertical stroke that marks the end of each word in this source. The same reading appears in an earlier Gradual issued in Würzburg in 1496 by Georg Reyser.

[4]*Sic.* The preferred reading is *Individiose*. The *Herbipolense* is the only known source to omit the last two syllables. The musical organization hints at an unintentional omission of text, and indeed the full text is present in the Reyser Gradual of 1496.

St Michael	Benedicite	Introit	Hodie regi archangelorum / Ipsum collaudantes / Vim habentes / Ad impletes / Cernere queis
St Burchard	Statuit	Introit	O Hiereus katha tin taxin / Ut vigeat summus / Inter primates / Grex tuus
Dedication	Terribilis	Introit	Sanctus evigilans Jacob / Vere dominus est / Quae Christi

For the Temporale, there are five introit tropes, two offertory tropes, and one communion trope. In addition, we have a late version of *Quem quaeritis*, which was employed in this source to preface the *Te deum*. There are seven sets of introit tropes for the Sanctorale, together with one each to embellish the offertory and communion. One notices immediately that all of the small group of tropes for the Temporale fall within the early part of the church year, from Christmas through Epiphany. There is nothing for the time between Epiphany and Easter or for the period following Easter to the end of the church year. For the Sanctorale the situation is opposite. The earliest of this group of tropes is for St John the Baptist, whose feast day falls on 24 June, long after Easter. The remainder are still later in the calendar. One cannot help but wonder what other tropes might have been known earlier in the Würzburg area, and what prompted decisions to retain those that were selected while omitting others.

The construction of a full historical context for the trope content of the *Graduale Herbipolense* is impeded by lacunae in our bibliographical studies. The editors and contributors responsible for the enormously useful *Corpus troporum* have laboured long and valiantly to provide a bibliographic base for the study of tropes, but this series is not yet complete. Additional valuable information concerning Germanic tropes may be had in Andreas Haug's *Troparia tardiva, Repertorium später Tropenquellen aus dem deutschsprachigen Raum.*[5] Haug concerns himself with tropes found in over one hundred manuscripts, but does not treat those found in prints. Moreover, we lack counterparts to Haug's work for the areas of Western Europe. Nevertheless, using available materials, we can reach a provisional assessment of the contribution made by the *Herbipolense* to our knowledge of the broader history of tropes and troping.

We may begin by noting the existence of a Würzburg tradition of troping whose surviving musical content is documented in three sources. The earliest of these is the ms M p th f 165 of the Würzburg University Library, a fourteenth-century gradual with tropes and sequences in Gothic notation. This source was brought to the attention of scholars by Volker Schier in his article 'Propriumstropen in der Würzburger Dom-

---

[5]MMMA, Subsidia 1 (1995).

liturgie'.[6] The second of the three sources is a *Graduale Wirczeburgense* published by
Georg Reyer in 1496. Useful information concerning the volume is provided in an
approbation that, together with an engraving showing a bishop with sword and crozier
surrounded by two kneeling angels and with a coat of arms at the left, is found on the
verso of a leaf. One is prompted to think that the recto side would normally have
served for a title page. However, no formal title page survives, and the appellation that
I use is found in a handwritten scrawl. The last of our sources is obviously the *Graduale Herbipolense* itself. The publisher of this volume unfortunately chose not to
identify himself. It is thought-provoking to find that the source with the greatest
number of tropes is the latest, while that with the fewest is the earliest. Were these
sources from the tenth to the thirteenth centuries, one might hypothesize that the additional materials found in the latest source were created after the earlier sources had
been completed. But this can scarcely be the case in the present instance. Several of
the tropes given in the prints but lacking in the Würzburg manuscript have concordances in one or another source of the High Middle Ages. I have no solution to offer for
this puzzle.

A preliminary survey of those concordances presently available in the volumes of
Corpus troporum indicates, as might be expected, that the repertory of the *Herbipolense* is largely Germanic. Among the concordances provided for the first nine tropes
or trope-sets by the research team of *Corpus troporum* one notes promptly that only
one trope-set and one large prefatory trope are clearly non-Germanic. The first of these
embellishes *Etenim sederunt*, the introit for St Stephen. Among sources from east of
the Rhine, only mss London, BL Add. 19768, and Paris, BNF lat. 9448, contain this
group in this order. The former originated in Mainz, the latter in Prüm. The Bamberg
Staatliche Bibliothek ms lit. 5 contains the elements in a slightly different order. The
more numerous westerly sources may contain the same elements or most of them, but
with some change. *Insurrexerunt, Invidi[ose] lapidibus*, and *Suscipe meum* customarily occur as a group, headed up by either *Hodie Stephanus martyr caelos* or *Hodie
inclitus martyr Stephanus*, while *Eia conlevitae* often occurs elsewhere among the
concordant sources, either immediately following or – more frequently – at a later
point. The relationship between the Herbipolense and Add. 19768 with regard to the
transmission of this trope-set is further made clear since only they employ the word
beatissimi rather than *protomartyris* for the opening element. Moreover, only these
two manuscripts, together with Paris 9448, employ the word *iniuste* rather than *iniqui*
in the second element. In the transmission of the trope *O redemptor omnium cui reges*
only Add. 19768 and the Herbipolense use *eia* rather than *sancta* as the final word,
and only these two sources and Bamberg 5 employ the verb-form *offerent*. On the
other hand, Add. 19768 is the only source to close *Eia conlevitae* with the word

---

[6]*Kirchenmusikalisches Jahrbuch* 76 (1991), pp. 3–43. The manuscript contains music for
the initial trope and the following seven trope-sets given in the *Herbipolense*, and these are
given in transcription by Schier. The author also collates information from textual sources,
including the *Rubricae missae*, the *Breviarium missae*, the *Directorium Herbipolense*, the
Breviarium chori sancti Kiliani, and the *Breviarium chori sancti Johannis in Hauge*.

cecinerunt, while the *Herbipolense* uses the idiosyncratic *concinite*, which is closer to the preferred reading *concinamus*. And the reading of *collevi te* is unique to the Herbipolense. While Add. 19768 does contain twelve of the eighteen trope elements present in the *Herbipolense*, it lacks the five elements of the introit trope for *In medio ecclesiae*, as well as the single element of the offertory trope for *Anima nostra*. The prefatory trope is the well-known *Quem quaeritis*, for Easter Sunday. Although there are some ten early German sources for this piece, they are outnumbered by the thirteen Aquitanian sources and nineteen Italian sources. One must also take into consideration some six Beneventan sources, together with four of insular origin, three from France, and two from Spain. We may note further that none of the Germanic sources listed in either the *Corpus troporum* or Haug's *Troparia tardiva* is diastematic. To appreciate fully the nature of the melody as it is known east of the Rhine one must turn to either the Reyser Gradual of 1496 or the *Graduale Herbipolense*.

In establishing the links that connect the *Herbipolense* with its past, we may note that Bamberg Staatliche Bibliothek ms lit. 5 contains eighteen of the nineteen elements for the Temporale, while Berlin Staatsbibliothek ms theol. lat. 4°11 contains fifteen of the elements present in the *Herbipolense*, lacking only the four trope elements for *Etenim sederunt* just mentioned. Ms St Gall, SB 381, contains one fewer of these elements. Yet the *Herbipolense* is not a direct descendant of any of the known surviving tropers. This conclusion is substantiated by an examination of the concordances for the trope elements of the set for St Kilian, the patron saint of Würzburg. According to information kindly provided by Gunilla Iversen and Brian Möller Jensen of *Corpus troporum*, the opening element, *Haec est alma*, is known only through mss Munich, BS clm 14083 and 14845, while the former source was until recently the only source known to contain the entire set. Another link between ms Munich, BS clm 14083 and the *Herbipolense* arises from the fact that the earlier source was one of only ten sources to follow *Quem quaeritis* with the *Te deum*, whereas the number of sources presenting other pairings are more than six times greater. Nevertheless, ms Munich, BS clm 14083, is known to contain concordances for only nine of the trope elements for the Temporale present in the *Herbipolense*, while the harvest in ms Munich, BS clm 14845, is much smaller still.

In a small congratulatory essay in honour of a person who has done so much for medieval musicology, it is not possible to discuss each of the eighteen tropes or tropesets. Thus I will focus on those tropes for which the fewest sources are currently known. Not surprisingly, these are all within the Sanctorale. Among the sources whose contents are explored by Haug in the *Troparia tardiva*, not one contains the trope-set for St Kilian, St Michael, or St Burchard. The first of these, for the patron saint of Würzburg, was made available in the previously cited article, 'A serendipitous encounter with St Kilian'. Burchard (*ca* 965–1025) was also venerated in Würzburg; his *Decretum*, written *ca* 1008–1012, was a highly influential work on canon law.

The introit chosen for the mass for St Burchard is *Statuit ei dominus*, which appears in four of the sources of the *Antiphonale missarum sextuplex* as the introit for St Marcellus, Pope. Among these, the *Corbiensis* (ms Paris, BNF lat. 12050) classifies the melody then known as *Authenticus protus*; presumably this was a forebear of the first-mode melody surviving in later medieval sources and in modern books. Indeed, this is its main assignment in the *Herbipolense*; its later appearance is given only in cues. The melody opens with a typical first-mode gesture, leaping up from the final to the fifth degree and continuing on to the seventh degree before subsiding to a brief recitation on the fifth. This outline forms the basis of the opening of *O Hiereus*, the initial element of the trope-set. The same outline is utilized again at the midpoint, and an equally broad gesture that may be regarded as a derivative occurs towards the end. This element attracts attention not only for its vigorous motion, ranging three times up and down the octave, and for its florid setting of the text, but also for the use of Greek text. Although the musical readings of the *Herbipolense* and the Reyser print seem generally to be quite close to one another, in this instance the two sources give differing transliterations from the Greek and different text underlay. The Reyser print delays the appearance of the final syllable of the first main word (Hiereus) for several notes; it falls out instead on the tone given in the *Herbipolense* for the initial syllable of the word following (kathatintaxin).

The syllables for this word are then redistributed so that they follow one another more closely, and the final syllable is prolonged slightly. The result draws attention away from the musical parallelism between the first two broad musical gestures, and I thus feel that the reading in the *Herbipolense* is likely to be the one originally intended.

Surveying the remaining elements of the trope-set, we continue to find a close relationship between the tonal organization of trope and that of the corresponding phrase from the introit. Care is taken to ensure that each trope element ends with the tone that will ensue from the segment of the introit that follows. We may also note a further gestural relationship between the opening of the trope element, *Inter primates*, and the corresponding introit phrase, *Ut sit illi*. The unusual degree of melodic activity found in the opening element dissipates somewhat in the elements following, but remains considerable nonetheless (see Example 7.1).[7]

Melodies of quite different character are employed for the trope-set associated with the mass for the dedication of the Church of St Michael. The introit for this occasion, *Benedicite dominum omnes Angeli ejus* (see Example 7.2), is also among four mss of the *Antiphonale missarum sextuplex*.[8] The church alluded to was constructed in Rome on the Via Salaria, and the dedication is mentioned in four masses in the Leonine Sacramentary of the early seventh century. The Corbie manuscript classifies the chant in *Authenticus deuterus*, and this is indeed the classification encountered in both medieval and modern sources.

---

[7]We may note that this trope-set was employed in Western Europe at least in the Chartrain tradition in its original function associated with St Marcellus. See the citation in Yves Delaporte, *L'ordinaire chartrain du XIIIe siècle*, Société Archéologique d'Eure-et-Loire, Mémoires 19 [1952–1953], p. 192.

[8]It likely appeared in two others, but was lost owing to damage to the manuscripts.

The melody for *Benedicite dominum* opens on the third degree of the mode and ascends to the sixth. There is an extended recitation on this degree at the opening, which is emphasized to a lesser degree in the later development. Most of the chant circulates in the fourth between *g* and *c'*. There is twice an upward extension to the seventh degree, but only at the very end does the chant descend to the final, which is touched in the last three neumes.

The various trope elements reflect the nature of the host melody. These are fairly modest melodies, frequently using only one tone per syllable, and they too develop primarily within the same fourth, *g–c'*. Indeed, the modal final appears only at the

Example 7.1: *O Hiereus / Statuit ei*

beginning of the fourth element, which itself ends on the fifth degree of the mode. The identity between the last tone of each trope element and the initial tone of the ensuing segment from the host chant that was consistently present in the trope-set for

Example 7.2: *Hodie regi archangelorum / Benedicite domino*

St Burchard is lacking here. This trope-set is of passing interest because of the presence of an element that precedes the psalm verse; such interpolations apparently occur only infrequently.

The prefatory trope *Hodie caelesti* for the mass for St Lawrence furnishes our third example. In this instance the introit *Confessio et pulchritudo* serves as the host chant. Among the sources constituting the *Antiphonale missarum sextuplex*, this chant is assigned to Feria V of the first week of Quadragesima and, secondarily, to the mass for St Lawrence and the mass for St Cesarius. Unlike our previous examples, a second diastematic source is known for this trope, namely ms Munich, UB 2°156.[9] The two readings present an unusual contrast with one another, as shown in Example 7.3.

The trope opens with a gesture very similar to that employed in the host chant. The closeness is not as striking in the reading of the *Herbipolense* as it might otherwise be, because this print omits the second tone of the introit melody, as given in the *Moosburger Graduale*, in ms Graz, UB 807,[10] as well as in modern books. (This tone is lacking also in the reading of ms Leipzig, UB St Thomas 391.[11]) This gesture is especially frequent among third-mode chants, as a perusal of the Bryden and Hughes *Index of Gregorian Chant*[12] will promptly indicate. The Index shows, however, that there are a number of first-mode chants that employ a comparable gesture; it is modally ambiguous. There is, of course, no modal ambiguity to *Confessio et pulchritudo*, if viewed as a whole. The *Herbipolense* reading preserves a modal unity between trope and host chant, as is normal, while the *Moosburger* reading would have it that no such unity existed. This is an unusual set of circumstances, and I regard the latter reading as mistaken.

The scribe of the *Moosburger Graduale* placed the tropes in a separate section near the end of the volume, just before the kyriale. The reading of *Hodie caelesti*, found on fol. 252[V], stands out from its fellows on the same side of the leaf by being the only trope to employ notated flats. But if we turn back overleaf, we find that the trope-set *Gaudent trium maximarum pulchra*, consisting of two equivalent halves, opens in first mode and uses multiple flats, as is appropriate for a chant associated with the introit *Suscepimus deus*. Below this, we find another trope-set, *Hodie resurrexit dominus*, that also opens with a descending second followed by an upward leap of a fourth. The second half, which prefaces the final singing of the *Resurrexi* – a fourth-mode chant – continues with a brief upward ascent roughly comparable to that of *Hodie caelesti*. This trope-set also opens on *d*, as does the host chant. Proceeding to tropes on the following folio, we find that *Hodie laetemur fratres devoti* also opens with the gesture that we have been discussing, as is appropriate for a trope associated with the first-

[9]David Hiley, ed., facsimile edition, *Moosburger Graduale, München, Universitätsbibliothek, 2° Cod. ms. 156*, Veröffentlichungen der Gesellschaft für bayerische Musikgeschichte (Tutzing, 1996).

[10]Facsimile edition in *PM* 17.

[11]Facsimile edition by Peter Wagner, in *Publikationen älterer Musik* 5 and 7.

[12]John Bryden and David Hughes, eds, 2 vols (Cambridge MA, 1969), 89ff.

mode introit, *Statuit ei dominus*. This picture of seeming consistency of practice is, fortunately or unfortunately, shattered by another trope found on fol. 253^r, namely *Hodie fratres angelici*, which is associated with the third-mode introit, *Benedicite dominum*. This trope is situated beginning on *e* and concluding on *g*, providing a modal unity between trope and host chant, as is normal. (The same arch occurs in the *Herbipolense* reading of *Hodie caelesti*.)

Taking the various elements examined above into consideration, I offer the hypothesis that the scribe of the *Moosburger Graduale* allowed himself to be influenced by the readings of two trope-sets that he had just finished writing on the recto of the same leaf. These began the opening gesture on *d*, as befitting their individual circumstances, and he simply followed suit, not pausing to reflect on the different environment for the trope that he was now working on. When he reached the end of the trope, he provided a cue for the introit, *Confessio et pulchritudo*, a cue that is somewhat longer than that provided in the following example. He begins the introit a second lower than is customary, realizes that he is dealing with a third-mode chant, and reaches the second neume by means of an idiosyncratic upward leap of a fifth. He continues on his way without further cares, and all is well with the world. The downward shift of the melody is facilitated by the fact that the second degree above the modal final, which is crucial in this case for modal identification, does not appear in either of the two available

Example 7.3: *Hodie caelesti / Confessio et pulchritudo*
        a *Herbipolense*
        b *Moosburger*

Example 7.3 continued

readings. Whether or not my proposed explanation is valid, the example demonstrates
clearly the need for further work on the role of gesture within the trope repertory and
for additional information regarding the tonal interaction between trope and host chant.

Example 7.4: *Angelo praenunciante / De ventre matris*
     a *Herbipolense*
     b *Moosburger*

The last three examples to be examined are tropes associated with the introit, offertory, and communion for the mass for St John the Baptist. Andreas Haug lists three late diastematic sources for the introit trope *Angelo praenunciante*, but I have had access to only one, namely the *Moosburger Graduale* (see Example 7.4). The introit for this mass is the well-known *De ventre matris*, a first-mode chant. As in the preceding examples, this introit is found among the manuscripts of the *Antiphonale missarum sextuplex*. It is classified in *Authenticus protus* in the *Corbiensis*, ms Paris, BNF lat. 12050. The readings of the *Herbipolense* and the *Moosburger Graduale* for *Angelo praenunciante* are reasonably close; the occasional variants involve details of melodic movement and do not affect the overall tonal structure. Allowing for minor changes, the opening of the trope mirrors the somewhat similar opening of the chant.

The offertory trope *Nativitatem venerandi praecursoris Christi* (see Example 7.5) presents more challenging problems. The host chant is *Justus ut palma*, another of the chants documented in the *Antiphonale missarum sextuplex*. In these textual sources, the chant is associated with both the mass for St John Apostle and that for St John the Baptist. I suspect that the first of these assignments is the earlier of the two. The only other known diastematic source for this trope is the Reyser Gradual of 1496. (It is necessary to distinguish between this work and a trope with a similar textual beginning, *Nativitatem venerandam sancte genitritis*, a melody in the first maneria associated with the introit *Gaudeamus omnes*.)

Example 7.5: *Nativitatem venerandi / Justus ut palma*

The melody of concern to us here returns us to the problems of tonal organization in connection with the two readings for *Hodie caelestis*. The trope *Nativitatem venerandi* opens on low *A*. As in *Hodie caelestis*, it descends a second and leaps up a fourth, continuing the ascent until it reaches the sixth above the lowest note. An ensuing descent leads to a duplication of the opening gesture, but this duplication begins in the middle of the second word, suggesting that we may be dealing with happenstance rather than a planned structural event. This time the ascent continues until we reach an octave above the opening tone. There is a relaxation that leads downward and a circling motion that ends on *f*, the opening tone of the offertory in the reading of the *Herbipolense*.

We may note an obvious concern for a smooth connection between the trope and the host chant. And the chant is obviously subject to modal classification. While the *Corbiensis* (ms Paris, BNF lat. 12050) frequently provides modal classifications for introits and communions, chants that employ psalm verses, it does not do so for the other items of the mass-proper. It would appear that the earliest classification now known appears in the ms Montpellier, Faculté de médecine H 159, generally thought to have been compiled in the early eleventh century. In this source, the offertory appears among the chants of the deuterus maneria; the manuscript does not distinguish here between the authentic and plagal forms. This classification is followed in modern books, which treat the melody as being in mode 4. And the *Herbipolense*, together with other medieval sources consulted ends the chant on *e*. Should the earliest performers of the trope have thought along modal lines – a fragile hypothesis – they would have been aware of connecting with a deuterus maneria. But how might the trope have been understood? We have seen that the opening melodic gesture is equivocal in nature, occurring in both first- and third-mode contexts. If we imagine the trope located a fourth higher than written, it would begin on *d*, and proceed *d–c, f, g–a, a, g, g, f–e, d, c, f, g–a, a–g–f, g, g–a, a*, etc. This provides a satisfactory realization providing that we are willing to posit the ongoing use of *b flats*. But it does not suit the modal classification of the chant. On the other hand, we could imagine the trope located a fifth higher than written. In that event, it would open *e–d, g, a–b, b, a, a, g–f sharp*[!], *e, d*. And we would need to utilize *f sharp* on a fairly frequent basis. Such a solution would be compatible with the modality of the chant, but show disregard for normal medieval treatments of the gamut. Furthermore, we are still left with the puzzle of determining the reason for the abnormally low opening. Chants that open on *A* generally proceed directly upward to *d* without any diverting motion. The Montpellier reading for *Justus ut palma*, together with other similar medieval readings, at least open on *e* and touch on this tone occasionally before the final cadence. The *Herbipolense* reading, on the other hand, seems to go to lengths to avoid the employment of *e* in any significant structural point until we reach the final cadence. With this in mind, we may well question the significance of a deuterus modal classification for the piece. It seems to tell us nothing about its tonal organization beyond the fact that its last three neumes center on *e*. The *Herbipolense* reading does not go down below *d*, and it goes as high as the *d'* one octave above. This is not a modal octave. The same is true of other medieval readings such as the one in the

Montpellier manuscript and in readings utilized in modern books. However inconclusive these musings may be, they do point to the importance of being able to link a trope melody with a version of the host chant, at least from the same region, if not indeed from the same source. We can stick a modal label on this combination of trope and chant, but this label carries very little meaning.

While the tonal tension between trope and host chant that we have been considering appears to be infrequent, the example is not unique. We may recall the lengthy prefatory trope *Hodie cantandus*, that is the first of the tropes in all three Würzburg sources. While associated with the seventh-mode introit *Puer natus est*, this trope opens on *d* and descends a second before ascending to the fourth degree.[13] Following a leap downward that takes us to the initial level and is followed by an emphasis on *d*, the range of the trope gradually expands to the upper seventh. Nevertheless, the tone *d* continues to be emphasized as a tonal centre throughout the opening phrases. It is entirely apt to describe the melody as being in first mode, utilizing *b flat*. The two later segments each begin on the fifth degree. The first of these explores the upper pentachord, ascending even to *e'*, before wending downward and ending with a firm cadence on *d*. The second turns downward immediately, reaching *d* and the second below before ascending, reaching the upper *c'* and using *b flat* no fewer than six times. It then provides a turn below *g* and concludes on this tone, which, as is well known, constitutes the opening tone of *Puer natus*. A tension has been generated between the tonal organization of the trope and that of the host chant. The frequent use of *b flat* in the trope contrasts not only with its absence from *Puer natus*, but with its rarity among seventh-mode chants in general.

Our final example is of simpler nature. The prefatory trope *Hodie dilectissimi patres et fratres* (see Example 7.6) associated with the communion *Tu puer propheta* is not known to survive in any diastematic source outside of Würzburg. (It is, to be sure, present in the Reyser Gradual of 1496.) The host chant is documented in all manuscripts of the *Antiphonale missarum sextuplex* with the exception of the Monza cantatorium. It is consistently associated with the mass for St John Baptist and with no other. The modal classification given in the *Corbiensis* is *Authenticus protus*. The trope has a fairly simple melody, clearly situated in first mode. It opens and closes on *d* and emphasizes this tone on a periodic basis. The range fills the full modal octave with an extension to the *subtonum*.

The achievements of this chapter are necessarily modest. Nevertheless, I hope that the reader will come away with a better appreciation of the extraordinary longevity of tropes in areas of conservative Germanic practice. Together with the transcriptions published earlier by Volker Schier, the six examples presented here are capable of permitting a better informed view of tropes cultivated east of the Rhine. Previous work in the area of tropes has emphasized the important southern French

---

[13]Transcriptions of this trope are available both in Volker Schier, 'Propriumstropen in der Würzburger Domliturgie', pp. 11f., and in Nicole Sevestre's contribution to vol. 1 of *Corpus troporum* ('Tropes du propre de la messe: Cycle de Noel'), pp. 294–297.

contributions, and to a lesser extent those from Italy. Moreover, we have a slightly enlarged view of tropes for offertories and communions. We have been able to examine both the strong positive influence exercised by host chants on their associated tropes, as well as two instances of great independence in the respective tonal constructions of tropes and their host chants. We have been spurred to consider more carefully the importance of formulaic gestures as unifying factors within the repertory. It is my hope that the very limitations of this chapter may act to spur future study of this fascinating area.

Example 7.6: *Hodie dilectissimi / Tu Puer propheta*

Chapter 8

To trope or not to trope? Or, how was that English Gloria performed?

William John Summers

The creation of polyphonic music for the mass ordinary texts in fourteenth-century England was unquestionably the major compositional pursuit, if the surviving fragmentary sources are to be taken as an accurate reflection of practice.[1] Some other striking observations can be made about English polyphony from this century. Virtually every composition is anonymous and carries a sacred Latin text or texts. Roughly two-thirds of the entire repertory is based upon plainsong melodies and/or *cantus prius*

---

[1] An inventory of the music manuscript sources and their contents from this century can be found in my 'English Fourteenth-century Polyphonic Music: An Inventory of the Extant Manuscript Sources' (hereafter 'Inventory'), *JM* 8 (1990), pp. 173–227. This inventory was a companion to 'Fourteenth-century English Music, a Review of Three Recent Publications' (hereafter 'Review'), pp. 118–141, which dealt with the strengths and shortcomings of modern performing editions of English fourteenth-century music and the impaired historiography implied in their creation. Other recently published studies of English polyphonic music from this century are: Peter M. Lefferts, *The Motet in England in the Fourteenth Century* (hereafter *Motet*) (Ann Arbor, 1986), especially pp. 223–234, and my 'The Effect of Monasticism on 14th-century English Music' (hereafter 'Effect'), in Marc Honneger and Paul Prevost, eds, *Actes du XIIIe Congrès de la Société Internationale de Musicologie, Strasbourg ... 1982*, vol. 1 (Strasbourg, 1986), pp. 119–142, and 'The Establishment and Transmission of Polyphonic Repertoires in England, 1320–1399' (hereafter 'Transmission'), in Angelo Pompilio *et al.*, eds, *Atti de XIV congresso della Società internazionale di musicologia*, vol. 3 (Bologna, 1990), pp. 659–672. See also Andrew Wathey, ed., *International Inventory of Musical Sources*, vol. B4 (1–2) Supplement (Munich, 1993), which makes known a number of recently rediscovered fourteenth-century fragments. Facsimile volumes devoted to this music are my *English Fourteenth-Century Polyphony: Facsimile Edition of Sources Notated in Score* (hereafter *English Fourteenth-century Polyphony*) (Tutzing, 1983). See also Frank Harrison and Roger Wibberley, eds, *Manuscripts of Fourteenth-century English Polyphony: A Selection of Facsimiles* (hereafter HW) (London, 1981). Transcriptions of a great deal of the music can be found in Frank Harrison, Ernest Sanders, and Peter Lefferts, eds, *Polyphonic Music of the Fourteenth Century* (hereafter *PMFC*), vols 15–17 (Monaco, 1980, 1983, 1986).

facti.[2] The highly diverse liturgical rankings of the ubiquitous cantus firmi embedded within the liturgical polyphony may suggest that this music was used relatively frequently within the mass and in the office on a variety of major feasts. The approximately ninety surviving manuscript fragments from the fourteenth century, the largest number from any European region, suggest that music was recorded in many types of ecclesiastical institutions, though it has become increasingly clear from recent studies that the greatest identifiable use of polyphony may have been made in the greater monasteries throughout the century.[3] The study of the manuscript types that transmit this music (and their place within the culture of writing in medieval England) is in its infancy.[4] One shocking fact about this large body of fragments is the recognition that no two sources appear to have been produced by the same hand. All are unique witnesses in that respect. Having said this, it is important to note that approximately forty per cent of the fragments have at least one piece that is concordant with another manuscript source.

English composers from this century appear to have focused their efforts almost exclusively upon three genres: the motets in the English- and French-influenced styles; the three-voice, freely-composed settings with double-stanza devotional texts, known as English cantilena; and the three-voice compositions with texts for the mass ordinary and the office, the largest single group.[5] This concentration seems somewhat surprising given the fact that the mass-proper chants embedded within most of the liturgical polyphony had been sung traditionally by the choir, not by soloists.

Along with this emphasis upon these unchanging texts, English liturgical polyphony became noticeably more homogeneous stylistically, perhaps reflecting a discernible but as yet underexplored trend towards rigorously defined and carefully controlled liturgical ritual, which is clearly outlined in the increasingly detailed discussions of these rites in the surviving service manuals from the major monasteries and both monastic and secular cathedrals.[6] With this narrowing focus upon the mass ordinary (and to a lesser extent the office) came the sustained cultivation and retention

---

[2]It is even difficult, if not impossible, to develop any picture concerning the process by which concordant settings were transmitted. In certain instances it can be shown that one setting is more recent than another, a fact most easily determined by notational innovations (e.g. the famous motet in honour of Thomas of Canterbury). See Lefferts, *The Motet*, p. 145. Here too the actual lines of transmission are obscure.

[3]See my 'Effect', especially pp. 105–112, and Lefferts, *The Motet*, pp. 9–13.

[4]See my 'Transmission', especially pp. 660–661.

[5]For the most recent scholarly opinions on these genres available in a reference work see my 'Cantilena', 'Manuscripts of Polyphonic Music', and 'Worcester Fragments', in *Medieval England, an Encyclopedia* (here after *Medieval England*) (New York, 1998), pp. 160–161, 448–489, and 818–819. See also Peter M. Lefferts, *The Motet* and 'Old Hall Manuscript', in *Medieval England*, pp. 527–529, and 560 respectively.

[6]See my 'Art Music in Fourteenth-century England: The Historiographic Conundrum of Vernacular Autism', in Nancy van Deusen, ed., *Tradition and Ecstasy: The Agony of the Fourteenth Century* (Ottawa, 1999), pp. 251–272.

of a highly uniform musical sound ideal, seen in the nearly universal use of a sophisticated three-voice compositional style employing both discant and free techniques.[7]

Given the general musical uniformity of the corpus of liturgical music, there is one subset within the music for the mass, the Gloria, *Spiritus et alme*, that seems not entirely to follow the standardizing trend towards setting entire liturgical texts with polyphony. A small number of tropes with the text *Spiritus et alme* carry three-voice polyphonic music for the trope text only.[8] The one, fragmentary, manuscript source central to the transmission of these works is Brussels, Bibliothèque royale, ms II 266 (see Figures 8.1 and 8.2). Although no information has been reported concerning its ·medieval origins, its contents have concordance with a number of other manuscript fragments (see Table 8.1). This unusually wide and uncharacteristic distribution of the works in question suggests that this music made its way into a communication network of some considerable reach.[9] If the rate of concordances is any indication of popularity, certain of these brief works are among the most popular settings with mass texts.

Also worth noting are the unusual versions of the *Spiritus et alme* text present in Br 266, as well as the high quality of the music composed for these versions. One setting makes use of the plainchant melody normally associated with this text. The other two resemble the free compositional practices associated with English cantilena.[10] Two other Glorias with the *Spiritus et alme* trope have also come down to us, carrying the plainsong in the middle voice, one – which exhibits sophisticated mensural practices – from Durham Cathedral.[11] (See Table 8.2.)

---

[7]See my 'The Repertory of Three-Voice Music Notated in Score from Fourteenth-Century England: English Discant and Free Settings' (Ph.D. diss., University of California, Santa Barbara, 1978), vol. 1, pp. 330ff.

[8]Denis Stevens, 'Polyphonic Tropes in Fourteenth-Century England', in Jan La Rue *et al.*, eds, *Aspects of Medieval and Renaissance Music* (New York, 1966), pp. 768–784, and Bernhold Schmid, *Der Gloria-Tropus Spiritus et alme bis zur Mitte des 15 Jahrhunderts* (hereafter *Spiritus et alme*) (Tutzing, 1988), especially pp. 109–111, 144–161. See also my 'Inventory', p. 178, and the concordances provided there.

[9]This point was argued in my 'Effect', pp. 110–113.

[10]There are settings with the common text, *Spiritus et alme*; troped versions of this text, *Spiritus concordie spiraculum*, etc.; and settings with the cantus firmus (DRc Co/Ca and WOcro 5117/1). For localities of the surviving sources see Table 8.1. I do not agree with Schmid's contention that the settings without the cantus firmus actually paraphrase the plainsong. Such a free use of the original would be inconsistent with the principles of discant so regularly employed throughout the repertory. See Schmid, *Spiritus et alme*, pp. 155–159.

[11]See my 'A New Source of Medieval English Polyphonic Music', *ML* 58 (1977), pp. 404–413.

Figure 8.1: Brussels, Bibliothèque royale ms II 266, fol. 1^r

Figure 8.2: Brussels, Bibliothèque royale ms II 266, fol. 1ᵛ

Table 8.1: Inventory of the contents of Br 266 indicating concordant sources

---

B-Br 266, Brussels, Bibliothèque royale, II 266, (*olim* Coussemaker), provenance unknown. *RISM* BIV^2, pp. 45–47

  1 (F) fol. 1 [*Spiritus almifice*] *Maria sine crimine*
      concordant with GLr 149, 2; Ob 14, 7
      EFP, pl. 1; *PMFC* XVI, no. 31
      expansion of the Gloria trope *Spiritus et alme*, for feasts of the Virgin

  2 (F) fol. 1–1^v *Spiritus et alme*
      EFP, pls 1–2; *PMFC* XVI, no. 27
      trope text only

  3 (F) fol. 1^v *Spiritus procedens a patre*
      concordant with GLr 149, 1; OB 14, 6; Onc 362, 13
      EFP, pl. 2; *PMFC* XVI, no. 32
      expansion of the trope *Spiritus et alme*

  4 (F) fol. 2 *Salve virgo singularis*
      concordant with Lbl 38651, 1
      EFP, pl. 3; *PMFC* XVII, no. 40
      sequence in honour of the Virgin

  5 (F) fol. 2–2^v *Mutato modo geniture*
      Preclusa viaque nature
      concordant with Cgc 334, 5; Cgc 512, 8; Lbl 38651, 10
      EFP, pls 3–4; *PMFC* XVII, no. 36
      in honour of the Virgin

  6 (F) fol. 2^v *Beata es Maria*
      EFP, pl. 4; *PMFC* XVII, no. 39
      in honour of the Virgin

GB-Cgc 334, Cambridge, Gonville and Caius College, 334/727, provenance unknown. *RISM* BIV^1, pp. 465–467

  1 (D) fol. i [*Sanctus*] ... *gloria tua* (incomplete)
      EFP, pl. 5; *HW*, pl. 109
      for lesser double feasts

  2 (D) fol. i–i^v Sanctus
      EFP, pls 5–6; *HW*, pls 109–110; *PMFC* XVI, no. 47
      for lesser double feasts

  3 (D) fol. ii [*Te deum...mi*]*sericordia tua* (incomplete)
      EFP, pl. 7; *HW*, pl. 111; *PMFC* XVI, no. 93
      for use at Matins on major feasts and elsewhere

4 (F) fol. 199 *Mater Christi nobilis*
Ut sic possint vivere (final versicle)
concordant with Ob 548, 1
EFP, pl. 8; *HW*, pl. 112; *PMFC* XVII, no. 24
in honour of the Virgin

5 (F) fol. 199–199ᵛ *Mutato modo geniture*
Preclusa viaque nature
concordant with Br 266, 5; Cgc 512, 8; Lbl 38651, 11
EFP, pls 8–9; *HW*, pls 112–113; *PMFC* XVII, no. 36
in honour of the Virgin

6 (F) fols 199ᵛ–200ᵛ *Includimur nube caliginosa*
Cupiditas vincendo virtuosa
concordant with Lbl *62132A,* 3
EFP, pls 9–11; *HW*, pls 113–115; *PMFC* XVII, no. 34
in honour of the Virgin

7 (F) fol. 201–201ᵛ *Stella maris illustrans*
De fundete fluento
EFP, pls 12–13; *HW*, pls 116–117; *PMFC* XVII, no. 33
in honour of the Virgin

8 (F) fols 201ᵛ–202 *O ceteris preambilis*
Quam plurium prelaudibilis
EFP, pls 13–14; *HW*, pls 117–118; *PMFC* XVII, no. 32
in honour of the Virgin

9 (F) fol. 202–202ᵛ *Virg[o valde] virtuosa*
[V]irg[a Iesse] generosa
EFP, pls 14–15; *HW*, pls 118–119; *PMFC* XVII, no. 29.
in honour of the Virgin

GB-Cgc 512, Cambridge, Gonville and Caius College, 512/543, Norwich,
Benedictine? *RISM*, BIV¹, pp. 468–471

1 (MP) fols 246ᵛ–247 *Mulier magni meriti*
Multum viget virtus
T[*enor*]
HW, pls 120–121; *PMFC* XV, no. 25
in honour of St Katherine (feast on 25 November)

2 (MP) fol. 247ᵛ *Princeps apostolice*
concordant with DRc 20, 4
HW, p. 142
for the common of Apostles

3 (MP) fols 248^V–249 *Virgo Maria patrem*
   O stella marina
   Virgo Maria flos divina
   Flos genuit regina
   concordant with Cpc 228, 2, one voice only
   HW, pls 124–125; *PMFC* XVI, no. 97
   in honour of the Virgin

4 (MP) fols 252^V–253 *Tu civium primas*
   O cuius vita
   Tu celestium
   Congaudens
   HW, pls 124–125; *PMFC* XVI, no. 98
   in honour of St Peter (feast on 29 June)

5 (MP) fols 253^V–254 *Suspira mirentis*
   Meroris stimulo
   T[enor]
   HW, pls 126–127; *PMFC* XV, no. 26
   in honour of the Holy Spirit at Pentecost

6 (MP) fols 254^V–255 *Thomas gemma Cantuarie*
   Thomas cesus in Doveria
   P[rimus Tenor]
   S[ecundus Tenor]
   concordant with Ob 862 9 [*WF*, no. 67]; Pru 119, A4
   HW, pls 128–129; *PMFC* XIV, no. 61
   in honour of Sts Thomas of Canterbury and Thomas of Dover (feast on 29
   November)

7 (MP) fol. 255^V *Doleo super te*
   Absolon fili mi
   T[enor]
   HW, pl. 130; *PMFC* XV, no. 27
   on David's lament

8 (F) fol. 256 *Mutato modo geniture*
   Preclusa viaque nature
   concordant with Br 266, 5; Cgc 334, 5; Lbl 38651, 10
   EFP, pl. 16; *HW*, pl. 131; *PMFC* XVII, no. 36
   in honour of the Virgin

9 (MP) fols 256^V–257 *Orto sole serene*
   Origo viri iam
   O Virga Iesse
   T[enor]

concordant with DRc 20, 7
HW, pls 132–133; *PMFC* XV, no. 33
in honour of the Virgin at Christmas

10 (F) fols 257ᵛ–258 *Salamonis inclita mater*
Dei sapiencia
concordant with NYpm 978, 5
EFP, pls 17–18; *HW*, pls 134–135; *PMFC* XVII, no. 37
in honour of the Virgin

11 (F) fols 258ᵛ–259 *Ave celi regina virginum* [two-voice version]
concordant with Cpc 228, 7
HW, pls 136–137; *PMFC* XVII, no. 38
in honour of the Virgin

12 (MP) fol. 259ᵛ *Patrie pacis*
Patria gaudencium
T[enor]
HW, pl. 138; *PMFC* XV, no. 28
in honour of the Virgin

13 (F) fol. 260–260ᵛ *Ave caro Christi*
passaque fuisti
EFP, pl. 19; *HW*, pl. 139; *PMFC* XVII, no. 21
in honour of Christ

13a(D) fol. 260–260ᵛ *Ad rose titulum*
[cf. appears in Yc xvi. N. 3,]
EFP, pls 19–20; *HW*, pls 139–140; *PMFC* XVII, 19
in honour of the Virgin

14 (F) fol. 262 *Gemma nitens*
HW, pl. 141; *PMFC* XVII, no. 20
in honour of the Virgin

GB-GLr 149, Gloucester, County Record Office, D. 149, provenance unknown.
RISM BIV², pp. 222–223

1 (F) fol. 1 [*Spiritus procedens*] ... *manens celi gloriam*
concordant with Br 266, 3; Ob 14, 6; Ob 362, 13
EFP, pl. 42; *HW*, pl. 165; *PMFC* XVI, no. 32
expansion of the trope *Spiritus et alme* in honour of the Virgin

2 (F) fol. 1–1ᵛ *Spiritus almifice consecrans*
concordant with Br 266, 1; Ob 14, 7
EFP, pls 42–43; *HW*, pls 165–166; *PMFC* XVI, no. 31
expansion of the trope *Spiritus et alme* in honour of the Virgin

GB-Lbl 38651, London, British Library, Additional 38651, Benedictine, St
Albans? *RISM* BIV2, pp. 238–239, 375–378

1   (F) fol. 1 *Salve virgo singularis*
    concordant with B-Br 266, 4
    EFP, pl. 72; *PMFC* XVII, no. 40
    in honour of the Virgin

2   (F) fol. 1^V ... *numinis et rivos*
    EFP, pl. 73

3   (F) fol. 2 *Astrorum altitudinem totamque*
    Iusta sedem propaginem immensam
    EFP, pl. 74

4   (D?) fol. 2 *Deo gratias*
    EFP, pl. 74; *PMFC* XVI, no. 71

5   (D) fol. 2^V Kyrie
    EFP, pl. 74; *PMFC* XVI, no. 25

6   (F) fols 3^V–4 *Et in terra*
    EFP, pls 76–77; *PMFC* XVI, no. 38

7   (D) fol. 4^V *Alleluia, Virga Iesse*
    EFP, pl. 78; *PMFC* XVI, no. 78
    for feasts of the Virgin in paschal time

8   (D) fol. 4^V textless (kyrie)
    EFP, pl. 78; *PMFC* XVI, no. 10

9   (F) fol. s54 *Mutato modo geniture*
    Preclusa virtus
    concordant with B-Br 266, 5; Cgc 334, 5; Cgc 512, 8
    HW, pl. 79; *PMFC* XVII, no. 36
    in honour of the Virgin

10 (F) fol. s54^V ... *pneu ... plua co ...*
    ... ...

    EFP, pl. 79a

Explanation of the abbreviations:

RISM = *Répertoire international des sources musicales*
F = free composition

EFP = *English Fourteenth-Century Polyphony: Facsimile Edition of Sources Notated in Score*, ed. William John Summers, Münchner Editionen zur Musikgeschichte 4 (Tutzing, 1983)

PMFC = *Polyphonic Music of the Fourteenth Century: English Music for Mass and Office* (I), ed. Frank L. Harrison, Ernest H. Sanders, and Peter M. Lefferts, vol. 17 (Monaco, 1983)

D = English discant setting
MP = motet notated in parts
s = page section

Table 8.2: English appearances of the *Gloria, Spiritus et alme*

---

1   Brussels, Bibliothèque royale, ms II 266 (provenance unknown) [GLr 149; Onc 362; Ob14; Cgc 334; Cgc 512; Lbl 38651]

    1   (F) [*Spiritus almifice*] *Marie sine crimine* [GLr 149, 2; Ob 14, 7]
        EFP, pl. 1; edition in *PMFC* XVI, pp. 54–57

    2   (F) *Spiritus et alme*
        EFP, pls 1–2; edition in *PMFC* XVI, pp. 42–46

    3   (F) *Spiritus procedens a patre* [GLr 149, 1; Ob 14, 6; Onc 362, 13]
        EFP, pl. 2; edition in *PMFC* XVI, pp. 58–62

2   Durham, Cathedral, Communars Cartulary, flyleaf, (Benedictine, Durham Cathedral?)

    1   (D) *Gloria, Spiritus et alme*
        EFP, pls 40–41; edition in *PMFC* XVI, pp. 37–41

3   Gloucester, County Record Office, ms D. 149 [Br 266; Ob 14; Onc 362] (provenance unknown)

    1   (F) [*Spiritus procedens*] ... *manens celi gloriam* [Br 266; GLr 149, 1; Ob 14, 6; Onc 362, 13]
        EFP, pl. 42, *MFP*, pl. 165; edition in *PMFC* XVI, pp. 58–62

    2   (F) *Spiritus almifice consecrans* [Br 266, 1; Ob 14, 7]
        EFP, pl. 177; edition in *PMFC* XVI, pp. 54–57

4   Oxford, Bodleian Library, Bodley ms 384, (Royal, St George's Windsor?)

    1   (F) *Gloria, Spiritus et alme*
        EFP, pl. 148; edition in *PMFC* XVI, pp. 47–50

3 (F) *Gloria, Spiritus et alme*
    EFP, pl. 149; edition in *PMFC* XVI, pp. 51–52

4 (F) *Gloria, Spiritus et alme*
    EFP, pl. 149; edition in *PMFC* XVI, p. 53

5 Oxford, Bodleian Library, Arch. Seldon B. 14 (provenance unknown) [Br 266; GLr 149; Onc 362; Lbl 1210; NOr 299; Ob 55; Ob 25]

    6 (F) *[Spiritus procedens] ... manens celi gloria* [Br 266, 3; Onc 362, 13; Glr 149, 1]
        EFP, pl. 178; edition in *PMFC* XVI, pp. 58–62

    7 (F) *Spiritus almifice* [Br 266, 1; Glr 149, 2]
        EFP, pls 177–176; edition in *PMFC* XVI, pp. 54–57

6 Oxford, Bodleian Library, New College ms 362 (provenance unknown) [Br 266; GLr 149; Ob 14]

    13 (F) *Spiritus procedens* [Br 266, 3; GL149, 1; Ob 14, 6]
         EFP, pl. 197, HW, pl. 93; edition in *PMFC* XVI, pp. 58–62

7 Worcester, County Record Office ms 705: 349 BA 5117/1 (xiv) (provenance unknown)

    1 (F?) *Spiritus concordie spiraculum*
        EFP, pl. 206; edition in *PMFC* XVI, pp. 63–64

Bibliographic abbreviations:

MFP = *Manuscripts of Fourteenth Century English Polyphony*, ed. Frank Harrison and Roger Wibberley, Early English Church Music 26 (London, 1981)

PMFC = *Polyphonic Music of the Fourteenth Century*, vol. 16

Those that carry the trope text only would have required some significant intervention by a precentor or ruler of the choir to render them suitable for a liturgical performance. In these cases the necessary text and music may have been supplied most simply either by the choir or soloists singing the missing text in plainsong (the solution proposed in the editions proffered in the series *Polyphonic Music of the Fourteenth Century*).[12] No other liturgical text is transmitted in such an incomplete state in fourteenth-century English musical sources, though there is one responsory and an alleluia that preserve only the soloists' portions of a text (or parts thereof) in polyphony.[13]

---

[12] *PMFC* XVI, pp. 42–46 (Br 266, 2), 54–57 (Br 266, 1), and 58–62 (Br 266, 3).
[13] See my 'Inventory', pp. 195–196, 205; 'Review', plate 78.

These settings too would have required additional music for a liturgically complete performance during the office and mass, though much less music would be needed for them to be complete. It is very difficult to imagine that these short musical segments from the Gloria would have been sung alone, say as separate devotional works within a votive service. There is clearly no precedent in the remaining corpus for compositions that are this brief, even among the settings with devotional texts.

The lineage and origins of these snippet-like works has perplexed scholars since the mid-1940s. Most, including myself, simply noted their existence without further questions. One recently discovered circumstance may shed some light upon the paternity of these puzzling settings. Peter Lefferts noticed that two versions of one textually complete Gloria exist, one with the *Spiritus et alme* trope and the other without the trope.[14] Both works had been known for quite some time and had been published in transcription and facsimile without notice of their relationship.[15] Examples 8.1 and 8.2 provide the concluding music from the two versions from two different sources, London, BL, ms Cotton XXIV (Lbl XXIV), and Oxford, Bodleian Library, ms Bodley 384. The polyphony for the ritual text is largely the same, with only minor variants. The troped version carries additional music and text.[16]

At present it is not possible on notational and/or paleographical grounds to determine which version was composed first. It seems fairly certain that one did not serve as the direct model for the other. On the grounds of musical conciseness (a trait shared by the other Glorias in Lbl XXIV), I would propose that the untroped version came first, but there is nothing to prove that the troped version did not already exist when the scribe of the British Library fragment recorded it without the trope and its music. Bodley ms 384 may in fact have been notated by a later hand than Lbl XXIV. That, however, would not necessarily settle anything concerning the priority of either version.

No other instance of this kind of transformation has been previously identified in the English liturgical repertory, though other very interesting experiments took place in this corpus.[17] This unusual occurrence of two different versions of the same work may provide evidence of a practice, both notational and performing, that was more widely employed than this one incident would suggest. Could it be that the settings of *Spiritus et alme* that survive with polyphony for the trope text only in Br 266 were originally part of complete polyphonic settings? Were the troped segments 'harvested' from longer compositions and transmitted together as a small 'collection' so that they could be 'reinserted' into existing polyphonic, modally compatible, non-troped Glorias on those occasions when the trope was required? If this was the case, that would mean

---

[14]This was first reported on in print in my 'Inventory', p. 191.

[15]See my 'Review', pp. 118ff.

[16]These excerpted examples from an anonymous Gloria, *Spiritus et alme*, and from another version of this Gloria without trope, are derived from *PMFC* XVI, pp. 52 and 74, respectively. See also my 'Review', plates 58–65, pp. 148–149.

[17]Ernest Sanders reconstructs a three-voice Agnus dei setting from two voice parts found in Pierpont Morgan Library ms 978, in *PMFC* XVI, pp. 155–158.

that the scribe of BR 266 may well have had access to a number of liturgically complete, troped settings from which to undertake the harvest. This would also suggest that these snippets were perceived by this particular scribe to be of special usefulness. The implication is clear that there was every intent to make use of these for performance. There must also have been some confidence on the part of the scribe that informed singers would make the necessary musical allowances to produce smooth couplings if 'reinsertions' in fact took place.

It has been assumed in the past that the *Spiritus et alme* snippets were to be completed in liturgical performance by adding plainsong. Could it not also be the case that the notated polyphony for the trope text may have served as a set of composed pillars which were to be connected by the ritual text sung in improvised polyphony *supra librum,* a practice documented in contemporary English theoretical sources, and known as singing by the 'sight system'?[18] If this was the case, it would suggest that free and discant musical procedures were employed in the performance of the same piece in the case of the snippets not composed upon a plainsong. Whichever of the three performance solutions was adopted, the existence of the two versions of the one complete Gloria (in both a troped and an untroped version) provokes some fascinating questions about the performance of all of the other settings of *Spiritus et alme*, not to mention their composition, transmission and use.

If the composed pillars in Br 266 did serve as fixed points in what may have been an improvised performance, do they not also shed light, albeit indirectly, upon the quality of the polyphony skilled singers would have been expected to improvise in order to complete a Gloria for which only particularly well-wrought troped portions were notated? One also wonders, by extension, if all of the remaining complete settings of this troped Gloria could have been performed without their tropes as musically complete works? Was this an English 'medieval' view of Gloria, *Spiritus et alme*? The survival of this small number of seemingly unrelated works within a larger category of the liturgical repertory once again reminds us of the crushing impact of the loss of all substantive English polyphonic music books from the fourteenth century. It also provides a tantalizing glimpse into a musical culture that was greatly preoccupied with liturgical and devotional music in honour of the Virgin. Clearly, the various versions of the *Spiritus et alme* trope transmitted in the Brussels fragment suggest that this portion of the original parent source drew from a particularly rich vein of Marian trope texts. The usefulness and desirability of these tropes appear to be confirmed by the fact that at least one setting was circulated widely. Just how they were to be sung and rendered as part of a liturgically complete setting leads to some rather remarkable speculation concerning their use within the mass. Theoretically they could have been inserted into already existing, modally compatible, notated settings, or they could have been completed by the singing of chant, or by soloists singing polyphony *supra librum*. These extremely varied possibilities suggest an experimental, perhaps even an avant-garde, performing tradition that freely mixed the notated and the oral traditions,

---

[18]See Brian Trowell, 'Sight, Sighting', in *NG2*, vol. 23, pp. 371–372.

a phenomenon that has gone unnoticed until now, and for which there is no comparable continental corollary.

To be sure, tropes of many kinds were well known to those who celebrated the *Opus dei* in fourteenth-century England. They played a special role in the chant sung in secular and regular venues, both as markers of the solemnity of certain feasts and as commentary upon the importance of a particular saint or occasion. The troped polyphonic compositions discussed here, when taken together, suggest a number of things about the use and performance of polyphony at mass, not the least important being the apparent liberty scribes took with at least one of the existing settings and the amount of musical experimentation that may have taken place in their production and performance. The uniqueness and distribution of these settings could suggest also that each is, in fact, a one-of-a-kind experiment that did not produce any significant lineage. The focus on trope texts for the Virgin also gives us reason to believe that the more specialized settings, especially for the Gloria, were composed for use in her votive mass, as well as for the capitular mass on Mary's regular feast days. Their limited numbers, unusual format, and in one case seemingly wide dissemination, suggest that this was a class of composition that received special attention from talented composers and singers.

The Brussels fragment contains a repertory exclusively in honour of the Virgin. In this respect it is atypical. There are, to be sure, other manuscript sources that contain Glorias only, or motets only. Given the importance of the Mary Mass at this time, however, this remnant may be a lone witness of a type of music manuscript which has left little trace, echoing the rarity of the survival of the only liturgically complete Gloria to survive with and without the *Spiritus et alme* trope. Br 266 is the only fragment that contains special music excerpts that would have been completed in performance by recourse to the singing of long stretches of additional music, either in chant or in improvised polyphony, or through their insertion into existing polyphonic Glorias. This unusual performance practice, within the broad context of a musical culture which appears to have prized consistency and stylistic uniformity above all else, remains perplexing.

It is curious that we have now gained a clearer understanding of the reason for the existence of certain unusual settings in Br 266 by a chance survival of two works that appear in contexts that are entirely typical. Although we may never answer all of the riddles that this particular source poses, its survival provokes us to ponder the musical practices it suggests, ever mindful that the questions might always remain more useful than the answers.

Example 8.1: From London, BL, MS Cotton XXIV (Lbl XXIV)

Example 8.2: From Oxford, Bodleian Library, MS Bodley 384

Chapter 9

Why Marian motets
on non-Marian tenors?
An answer

Rebecca A. Baltzer

In the early thirteenth century, some fifteen Latin items from the earliest layers of Notre-Dame motets exhibit a peculiar characteristic: their upper parts are in praise of the Virgin, but their tenors are based on chants that are not Marian at all. They are *proper* to major occasions in the spring half of the year, going from the feast of St John the Evangelist on 27 December to the feast of SS. Peter and Paul on 29 June (see Table 9.1).

Table 9.1: Marian motets on non-Marian tenors (fifteen motets on seven major feasts;[1] feasts of the Temporale are in capitals)

---

1 John, apostle and evangelist (Duplum, 27 December)

   Motet 69: *Serena virginum* / *Manere* – à4 in F, fol. 235[r], among à3 conductus
   T from M 5 gradual *Exiit sermo* **V.** *Sed sic eum*

2 Holy Innocents (Duplum, 28 December)

   Motet 97: *Exaltavit sydere* / *Liberati* – à2 in W2, fol. 181[r]
   T from M 7 gradual *Anima nostra* **V.** *Laqueus contritus*

---

[1] A sixteenth early motet with Marian upper parts over a non-Marian tenor first appears in the manuscript Châlons-sur-Marne, Archives départementales, 3.J.250, fol. 6[r]–6[v]: the three-voice conductus motet *O quam sancta, quam benigna* / *Et gaudebit* (Motet 317), based on a Perotinian-style clausula for the Pentecost alleluia *Non vos relinquam* (M 24). I have discussed the significance of this example in 'The Polyphonic Progeny of an *Et gaudebit*: Assessing Family Relations in the Thirteenth-century Motet', in Dolores Pesce, ed., *Hearing the Motet: A Conference on the Motet in the Middle Ages and Renaissance* (Oxford, 1996), pp. 17–27.

3   EPIPHANY (Duplum with vigil, 6 January)

Motet 101: *Et illumina eximia mater / Et illuminare* – à2 in W2, fol. 180ᵛ
Motet 103: *Remedium nostre miserie / Et illuminare* – à2 in W2, fol. 185ʳ
T from M 9 gradual *Omnes* **V.** *Surge et illuminare*

4   EASTER Annuum festum (27 March)[2]

Motet 133: *Virgo gignit genitorem / Domino quoniam* – à2 in W2, fol. 189ᵛ
T from M 13 gradual *Hec dies* **V.** *Confitemini*
Motet 221–222: *Salve, salus hominum / O radians stella / Nostrum* – à3 double
motet in W2, fol. 186ʳ
Motet 229: *Radix venie / Immolatus est* – à3 in F, fol. 385ʳ
Motet 230: *Ave Maria, fons leticie / Immolatus est* – à2 in W2, fol. 156ʳ
Motet 232: *Stupeat natura / Immolatus est* – à2 in W2, vol. 177ᵛ
T from M 14 all. *Pascha nostrum*

5   ASCENSION (Duplum, 5 May)

Motet 309: *Salve, mater, fons ortorum / Captivitatem* – à2 in F, fol. 401ᵛ, and
W2, fol. 176ᵛ (music lacking)
T from M 23 all. *Ascendens Cristus*
Motet 321: *Virgo virginum regina / Et gaudebit* – à2 in W2, fol. 187ᵛ
T from M 24 all. *Non vos relinquam*

6   Nativity of John the Baptist (Duplum with vigil, 24 June)

Motet 372: *Prima cedit femina / Mulierum* – à2 in W2, fol. 184ʳ
Motet 386: *Virgo mater salutis / Johanne* – à2 in W2, fol. 189ʳ
Motet 391: *Ave, plena gratie / Johanne* – à2 in W2, fol. 178ʳ
T from M 29 all. *Inter natos mulierum*

7   Peter and Paul, apostles (Duplum with vigil, 29 June)

Motet 398: *Regis veri regia / Pro patribus* – à2 in W2, fol. 176ʳ
T from M 30 gradual *Constitues* **V.** *Pro patribus*

For a long time I thought these motets were simply an aberration. Why would someone at Notre-Dame consider it appropriate to 'interrupt' the Easter Alleluia *Pascha nostrum* with a motet on *nostrum* in praise of the Virgin? Next, I thought that such motets were probably not sung as part of the parent organum, but detached from their original surroundings they might have been performed as part of Marian commemorations at the end of processions. But now I wish to advance another idea: that

---

[2]The movable feasts of the Temporale assume the date of Easter to be 27 March (the earliest possible date, and that on which it usually appears in Paris calendars), and the other feasts are positioned with reference to that date.

Rebecca A. Baltzer

they were indeed intended to be performed as part of their parent organum, even when their texts had not much to do with the occasion being observed. The reason for this tells us something important about the message that the clergy of this cathedral wished to convey to the populace of Paris.

Of the fifteen motets under consideration here, only three are found in the Florence manuscript; the rest are in W2.[3] On chronological grounds we are probably justified in assuming that the motets found first in F are slightly earlier than those found first in W2, so let us begin with a look at what is surely the earliest example: Motet 229, *Radix venie*, on the tenor *Latus* from the Easter Alleluia *Pascha nostrum*.[4] This motet is a three-voice conductus motet, with the same text in both upper parts, found in the first fascicle of motets in the Florence manuscript:

Tenor chant: M 14 alleluia *Pascha nostrum*

Pascha nostrum   Christ our Paschal Lamb
immo**latus** est Christus.   is sacrificed for us.

Motet 229: *Radix venie* / (*Immo*)*latus* (*est*)
à3 conductus motet in F, fol. 385ʳ [à3 source clausula]

Radix venie,   Root of pardon,
Vena gratie,   life-blood of grace,
Vie dux et portus,   leader and harbor of the way,
Porta patrie,   gateway to Heaven, [to the Father,]
Veri solis ortus,   origin of the true star,
Thronus glorie,   the throne of glory,
Summi regis cella,   chamber of the highest king,
Iesse virgula,   **the stem of Jesse,**
Ex qua flos est ortus   **from whom the Flower has arisen,**
Salvans secula,   **saving all generations,**
Clara maris stella,   bright star of the sea,
Lucis specula,   watch-tower of light,
Mortis exterminium,   the end of death,
Salus mentium,   health of the mind,
Claustra pandens celica   David's key unlocking

---

[3]The Florence manuscript (hereafter F) was published in facsimile by Luther A. Dittmer as *Firenze, Biblioteca Mediceo-Laurenziana, Pluteo 29,1* (Brooklyn, 1966–1967); there is also a color microfiche version with introduction by Edward H. Roesner, *Antiphonarium, seu, Magnus liber organi de gradali et antiphonario*, Codices illuminati medii aevi 45 (Munich, 1996). W2 is Wolfenbüttel, Herzog August Bibliothek, ms 1099 (Heinemann 1206), published in facsimile by Dittmer as *Wolfenbüttel 1099 (1206)* (Brooklyn, 1960).

[4]A transcription is available in Hans Tischler, *The Earliest Motets (to circa 1270): A Complete Comparative Edition*, 3 vols (New Haven, 1982), vol. 1, no. 20. Motet numbers are those assigned by Friedrich Ludwig and catalogued by Friedrich Gennrich in his *Bibliographie der ältesten französischen und lateinischen Motetten*, Summa musicae medii aevi 2 (Darmstadt, 1958).

Clavis davitica,	the celestial barriers,
Caput hostis terens	war-like Judith
Iudith bellica,	bruising the head of the enemy,
Lignum vite ferens	**flowering tree bearing**
Arbor florida,	**the Tree of Life;**
Pigras move mentes,	move our indolent minds
Fove corda languida!	and sustain our faint hearts![5]

Let us recall that the Virgin is depicted in medieval art as a witness to the Crucifixion, but in the Gospel accounts she has no direct part in the events of the Resurrection. In the text of *Radix venie*, however, amid the traditional Marian epithets, a connection is made between the flowering of the rod of Jesse, which resulted in the Incarnation, and the flowering of the Cross, which resulted in the Resurrection. In the first passage highlighted in the translation, Christ is the flower arising from the stem of Jesse; this is a direct recall of one of the most important office responsories in the Paris liturgy, *Styrps Yesse*, whose text is by Fulbert of Chartres: 'The stem of Jesse produced a twig and the twig a flower, and above the flower rested the nourishing Spirit.' 'The Virgin Mother of God is the twig; the flower, her son; and above this flower rested the nourishing Spirit.'[6] In *Radix venie*, the flowering tree is the *lignum crucis*, the wood of the Cross, and Christ is the Tree of Life. Thus the two great events celebrated in Christianity, Incarnation and Resurrection, are wonderfully linked in a text that emphasizes the Virgin's great role in the Incarnation and, by extension, her joint role in salvation.

There is a two-voice Latin contrafact of this motet in W2, *Ave Maria, fons leticie*, that also links the Incarnation through Mary with salvation through the Resurrection. It calls directly for praise of the Virgin on Easter, since she unlocked the gates of Heaven, and provides access to the King of Glory, who was sacrificed to end all sacrifice:

Motet 230: *Ave Maria, fons leticie / (Immo)latus (est)*
à2 in W2, fol. 156ʳ [à3 source clausula]

Ave Maria,	Hail, Mary,
Fons letitcie,	fount of joy,
Virgo pura, pia,	virgin pure and holy,
Vas munditie,	vessel of chastity,
Te voce varia	may the joyous people
Laudet sobrie	praise thee in various
Gens leta sobria.	yet restrained voices.
Gaudens varie	Rejoicing for many blessings,

---

[5]Translation by Gordon A. Anderson, *The Latin Compositions in Fascicules VII and VIII of the Notre-Dame Manuscript Wolfenbüttel Helmstadt 1099 (1206)*, 2 vols (Brooklyn, 1972; 1976), vol. 1, p. 157.

[6]**R.** Styrps Yesse virgam produxit virgaque florem, et super hunc florem requievit spiritus almus. **V.** Virgo dei genitrix virga est, flos filius eius.

Promat ecclesia	let the Church express
Laudes hodie;	its praise today;
Sonet in Maria	let the voice of the Church
Vox ecclesie.	resound in Mary.
Hec solvit scrinia	She has fulfilled the prophecies
Ysaie,	of Isaiah,
Reserans ostia	unlocking the once-closed
Clausa patrie,	gates of heaven,
Via dans eximia	granting access by a wonderful way
Regem glorie,	to the King of Glory,
Qui sola gratia	who by grace alone,
Plenus gratie	and full of grace,
Factus est hostia,	was made sacrifice,
Finis hostie.	the end of all sacrifice.[7]

Another feast of the Temporale, Ascension Day, is represented by the second Marian motet in F, motet 309: *Salve, mater, fons ortorum*, a two-voice motet on the tenor *Captivitatem*. Once again, in medieval art the Virgin is assumed to have been present with the disciples when Christ ascended into Heaven; see for example in the Florence manuscript on folio 381 the upper half of the initial that depicts this traditional scene. But the text of *Salve, mater* makes no effort to link up with the idea of the Ascension; it is purely a piece of praise and petition to the Virgin:

Tenor chant: M 23 alleluia *Ascendens Cristus*

Ascendens Christus in altum,	Christ ascending on high,
captivam duxit captivi**tatem**,	led captivity captive,
dedit dona hominibus.	and gave gifts unto men.

Motet 309: *Salve, mater, fons ortorum* / *(Captivi)tatem*
à2 in F, fol. 401^V, and W2, fol. 176^V (music lacking in W2)

Salve, mater, fons hortorum,	Hail, Mother, fount of the living,
Vellus Gedeonis,	fleece of Gideon,
Porta celi, spes reorum,	gateway of heaven, hope of sinners,
thronus Salomonis,	throne of Solomon,
Virga florens florem florum,	stem flowering the Flower of flowers,
Quam vis aquilonis	whom the force of the northwind
Numquam ledit, unguentorum	never harms, storehouse of unguents,
Cella plena bonis,	full of good things,
Nescia predonis	Virgin ignorant of the plunderer [of
Virgo, scala peccatorum,	virginity], ladder for sinners,
Per quam Babylonis	through whom ceases the yoke of
Iugum cessit et laborum	Babylon and the law of
Lexque pharaonis,	Pharaoh's labours,

---

[7]Translation by Anderson, *The Latin Compositions*, vol. 1, p. 156, with my emendations. Transcription in Tischler, *The Earliest Motets*, vol. 1, no. 20.

Septem reple donis	fill us again with thy sevenfold gifts
Pronos tuis sonis!	by thy sweet intercession for us.
Lilium convallium,	Lily of the valley,
Florens rosa,	flowering rose,
Fragrans sicut lilium,	fragrant as the lily,
Speciosa,	fair virgin producing
Virgo promens filium,	a son of noble birth;
Generosa	for God hast thou
Deo prodis genitum.	borne an offspring.
Lux mundo iocosa,	Joyous light to the world,
Tu post puerperium	thou, specially chosen
Speciosa,	and full of grace, after
Nescisti discidium	childbirth knew not
Gratiosa.	the separation [of sin].
Pro te Christo sit laus explosa,	Through thee to Christ let praise resound,
Tibi cum mentis dulci prosa.	to thee with sweet thoughts of the mind.[8]

The third of these Marian motets found in the Florence manuscript, *Serena virginum*, is built on a tenor from the gradual for the feast of St John the Evangelist on 27 December. The Virgin has two important connections to John the Evangelist: not only are the Virgin and St John shown at the foot of the Cross during the Crucifixion,[9] but the two are also depicted as petitioners for mankind before Christ in Judgement.[10] The motet *Serena virginum* is unusual in that it is a four-voice conductus motet in the Florence manuscript that is placed among three-voice conductus, which it resembles exactly until its tenor unexpectedly appears at the end.[11] Its lengthy Marian text sounds all the Marian themes that occur in such abundance in sequences, conductus, and

---

[8]Translation by Anderson, *The Latin Compositions*, vol. 1, pp. 261–262, with my emendations. Transcription in Tischler, *The Earliest Motets*, vol. 1, no. 41.

[9]Following the Gospel account in John 19:25–27. This scene is frequently the subject of a full-page miniature in thirteenth-century Paris missals; for examples see Robert Branner, *Manuscript Painting in Paris during the Reign of Saint Louis: A Study of Styles* (Berkeley, 1977).

[10]As on the tympanum of the central portal of the west front of Notre-Dame itself; see Figure 9.4.

[11]*Serena virginum* is also found à3 in ms London, BL Egerton 2615 (LoA), fols 74[v] (without text) and 92[r]; and as an à3 conductus (without tenor) in W1, old fol. 13[r]. For a facsimile of fol. 92[r] in LoA, see Mark Everist, *French Thirteenth-Century Polyphony in the British Library: A Facsimile Edition of the Manuscripts Additional 30091 and Egerton 2615 (folios 79–94[v])* (London, 1988). For W1, see J. H. Baxter, *An Old Saint Andrews Music Book* (London, 1931; reprinted New York, 1973), and Martin Staehelin, ed., *Die mittelalterliche Musik-Handschrift W1: Vollständige Reproduktion des 'Notre-Dame'-Manuskripts der Herzog August Bibliothek Wolfenbüttel Cod. Guelf. 628 Helmst*, Wolfenbütteler Mittelalter Studien 9 (Wiesbaden, 1995). Transcriptions are in Tischler, *The Earliest Motets*, vol. 1, no. 9; Gordon A. Anderson, *Notre-Dame and Related Conductus: Opera Omnia*, 9 vols (Henryville, PA, 1979–1988), vol. 1, pp. 1–3; and Anderson, *The Latin Compositions*, vol. 2, pp. 106–116.

motets in the Paris liturgy, but again it shows no effort to relate to the text of the gradual *Exiit sermo* or to the feast of St John in general:

Tenor chant: M 5 gradual *Exiit sermo* V. *Sed sic eum*

R. Exiit sermo inter fratres, quod discipulus ille non moritur: et non dixit Jesus: non moritur.	**R.** A saying went abroad among the brethren, that that disciple should not die; and Jesus did not say: He should not die.
V. Sed: Sic eum volo **manere** donec veniam: tu me sequere.	**V.** But: So I will have him to remain till I come: Follow thou me.[12]

Motet 69: *Serena virginum / Manere*
à4 conductus motet in F, fol. 235^r, among à3 conductus

Serena virginum,	Bright star of virgins,
Lux plena luminum,	light full of light,
Templum trinitatis,	temple of the Trinity,
Puritatis	chamber
Specialis thalamus,	of rare purity,
Archa nove legis,	ark of a new covenant,
Thronus novi regis,	throne of a new king,
Vellus, quod rigavit,	fleece which bedewed
Qui nostrum portavit	him who bore
Saccum nostram	our grief,
Carnem vestiens.	clothed in our flesh;
Nesciens	Not knowing the touch of man,
Virum deum paris,	thou didst bear God,
O Maria, mater pia,	O Mary, Holy Mother,
Stella maris, singularis,	peerless star of the sea,
Stella, cuius radius	star whose beam
Nubem pressit,	drove away the cloud
Quam impressit	that Eve's guilt
Eve culpa prius,	impressed, at a time
Istud nulla caritas	when no love or purity
Meruit aut castitas,	was found worthy,
Sed simplex humilitas	but that of the simple humility
Ancille.	of a handmaiden.
O mamille	O breasts,
Quarum vene fluunt plene	whose milk and honey o'erflow,
Mundo lac et mella.	plenteously filling the whole world!
Gens misella, tollite	Wretched people, take away the jar
Vas fellitum, vas mellitum	steeped in gall and drink from the jar
Bibite;	flowing with sweet honey.
Ecce, lac infantium,	Lo, the milk of infants!
Ecce, manna mundo pium,	Lo, holy manna of the world!
Ecce, pie flos Marie	Lo, the Flower of the Holy Virgin

---

[12]Translation by Anderson, *The Latin Compositions*, vol. 1, p. 211.

Virginis.	Mary! [= Christ]
Seminis	Renowned stem
Abrahe stirps inclita,	of Abraham's seed,
Balsamus mellita,	honey-sweet balsam,
Calamus condita,	crushed calamus,
Nardus myrra trita.	nard-oil and bruised myrrh:
O pia,	the snares of the hunter,
Laquei predonis,	the scorching of Babylon
Torrens Babilonis,	and Sampson's Delilah draw us
Dallida Samsonis,	to unstable and wayward actions;
Hostem, mundum,	put down the enemy, the world,
Vas immundum,	the unclean vessel
Bellica, pacifica,	and strife;
Spes reorum,	hope of sinners,
Lux celorum,	light of the heavens,
Virgo regia.	queenly virgin,
O Maria,	O Mary,
Cecis via,	road to the blind,
Nostra tympanistria,	our tambourinist,
In hoc salo	in this tempest,
Nos a malo	save us from evil,
Salva, stella previa,	O star that guides us,
Ut concordis	so that we with harmonious
Vocis, manus, cordis	voices and joyful acclamations
Plausu leti trino	shall sing a threefold
Benedicamus (domino).	Benedicamus domino.[13]

This tendency to ignore the liturgical context of the tenor chant is increasingly evident in the other Marian motets among these fifteen, especially those found first in W2. I include only two more as examples, one for the feast of John the Baptist, *Prima cedit femina*, and one for the feast of Saints Peter and Paul, *Regis veri regia*. Both are characteristic in their Marian themes, the first depicting Mary as the new Eve and the second praising Mary as the Queen of Heaven, but neither has anything to do with the themes of the feast being celebrated.

For the Nativity of John the Baptist (Duplum with vigil, 24 June):

Tenor chant: M 29 alleluia *Inter natos mulierum*

Inter natos **mulierum** non surrexit maior Johanne Baptista.	Among those born of women there has risen none greater than John the Baptist.

Motet 372: *Prima cedit femina / Mulierum*
à2 in W2, fol. 184[r]

Prima cedit femina	The first woman yields

---

[13]Translation by Anderson, *The Latin Compositions*, vol. 1, pp. 213–214.

Serpentis consilio;	to the counsel of the serpent;
Plange, femina!	weep, woman!
Sed tu, domina,	But thou, Mistress,
Medicine nuntio,	a remedy being announced,
Credis, dei filium	believe, and conceive
Concipis in gremio.	the Son of God in thy bosom.
Tibi psallat contio	To thee the whole congregation
Laudantium.	sings praise.[14]

For Peter and Paul, apostles (Duplum with vigil, June 29):

Tenor chant: M 30 gradual *Constitues* V. *Pro patribus*

R. Constitues eos principes super omnem terram: memores erunt nominis tui, domine.	**R.** Thou shalt make them princes over all the earth: they shall remember thy name, O Lord.
V. Pro patribus tuis nati sunt tibi filii: propterea populi confitebuntur tibi.	**V.** Instead of thy fathers, sons are born to thee: therefore shall people praise thee.

Motet 398: *Regis veri regia / Pro patribus*
à2 in W2, fol. 176ʳ

Regis veri regia	In the royal palace of the true King,
Recolit in gloria	the whole host
Virginis eximie,	of the heavenly train
Dei matris gaudie,	is uplifted in the glory
Preconia	of the peerless Virgin,
Celestis militie,	joyful Mother of God,
Ubi canunt omnia	where all the thousands
Milia:	sing:
Felix es, O Maria,	Happy art thou, O Mary,
Ex te sol iustitie	from thee the Sun of Justice
Ortus est, qui gaudia	has arisen, who gave
Sue dedit ecclesie.	joy to his Church.[15]

What I believe all fifteen of these motets have to tell us is that the clergy of Notre-Dame simply did not wish to let certain major feasts go by without some overt assertion of the Virgin's role in salvation, regardless of what else was being celebrated. The feasts included in Table 9.2, 'The Virgin in the Liturgy of Notre-Dame', comprise almost sixty per cent of the feasts of annual and duplex rank in the early thirteenth-century calendar of the cathedral. And as the remarks at the end of the table indicate,

---

[14]Translation by Anderson, *The Latin Compositions,* vol. 1, p. 309, with my emendations. Transcription in Tischler, *The Earliest Motets*, vol. 1, no. 27.

[15]Translation by Anderson, *The Latin Compositions*, vol. 1, p. 257; transcription in Tischler, *The Earliest Motets*, vol. 1, no. 133.

the Virgin's presence was frequently and regularly asserted in the liturgy of processions, on ferias and feasts of three lessons, and on every Saturday as well.[16] In sum, the Virgin loomed much larger in the liturgy of Notre-Dame than the four major Marian feasts alone would indicate, and her nearly pervasive presence was not an accident.

Table 9.2: The Virgin in the liturgy of Notre-Dame

Date	Principal Marian feasts	Other occasions with a Marian component	Feasts with Marian motets
December		Advent season	
4 December		Reception of the Relics	
25 December		Christmas	
27 December			John the Evangelist
28 December			Holy Innocents
1 January		Circumcision	
6 January			Epiphany
2 February	Purification		
25 March	Annunciation		
27 March			Easter
5 May			Ascension
15 May			Pentecost[17]
24 June			Nativity of John the Baptist
29 June			Peter and Paul
15 August	Assumption		
22 August	8ve Assumption		
8 September	Nativity BVM		
15 September	8ve Nativ. BVM		
1 November		All Saints' Day	

In addition, literally dozens of processions every year (almost every procession that occurred) concluded with a memorial to the Virgin consisting of an antiphon, a versicle and response, and a collect as the procession returned to the choir. By at least 1200 the Little Office of the Virgin (including all eight canonical hours) was performed on all ferias and feasts of three lessons. By at least 1200 there was a Saturday Office of the Virgin which included a mass in honour of the Virgin as well.

---

[16]See my 'The Little Office of the Virgin and Mary's Role at Paris', in *FS Steiner* (New York, 2000), pp. 463–484.

[17]See note 2.

At the time of Notre-Dame's construction the paramount and overriding message that the clerical hierarchy wanted to communicate was the idea that Mary was the Mother of God and the sinner's best avenue to salvation. More than anything else, they wanted the visitor to know that the Virgin was the Mother of God, and, through her, in *this* cathedral church built in her honour, salvation could be found. In their view Christendom offered no better patron than the Virgin Mother of God, because Mary's role in the Incarnation was the central fact about her, the starting point for any consideration of her by the faithful, and the ultimate reason for her veneration.[18]

Had we world enough and time, we could look at all the other Marian texts used in this cathedral, be they inherited chants carefully placed to emphasize certain themes, or the more contemporary repertories of sequences, conductus, and motets in honour of the Virgin, to see how her role was envisioned. But for now we can do no better than to consider the west front of Notre-Dame, an artistic enterprise directly contemporary with the earliest Notre-Dame motets, for a summary of the clergy's motivation.[19] For the western façade (see Figure 9.1), with its three great portals and its gallery of kings, was designed, much like a giant billboard, to give a graphic depiction of all that the visitor needed to know about salvation – a preview, as it were, of what was offered inside.

But the west façade of Notre-Dame offers the viewer something unique for its time: *this is the first Gothic cathedral to devote the whole west front to the Virgin Mary's role in salvation.* The story begins with the row of kings that spans the façade of the west front just above the portals. These are the twenty-eight kings of Judah, and they comprise a horizontal Jesse Tree, the first to appear on a cathedral façade. The Jesse Tree represents the twenty-eight generations of royal ancestors of Christ and the Virgin as enumerated at the beginning of Matthew's Gospel. As a liturgical text, this 'Liber generationis' was read on two important occasions during the church year at Notre-Dame: at the end of Christmas matins, and again as the Gospel in the mass on the Nativity of the Virgin, 8 September. It is meant to remind the faithful that Mary is the Mother of God.

---

[18]See my 'Aspects of Trope in the Earliest Motets for the Assumption of the Virgin', *Current Musicology* 45–47 (1991), pp. 5–42; this volume was also edited by Peter M. Lefferts and Brian Seirup and published separately as *Studies in Medieval Music: Festschrift for Ernest H. Sanders* (New York, 1990).

[19]I have discussed and annotated this subject much more fully in a forthcoming article, 'Notre-Dame and the Challenge of the Sainte-Chapelle in Thirteenth-Century Paris'. For excellent photographs of Notre-Dame by Max Hirmer see Willibald Sauerländer, *Gothic Sculpture in France, 1140–1270*, translated from the German by Janet Sondheimer (New York, 1972), plates 40–41 and 144–156. Plate 144 shows a broad view of the west front. See also the lavishly illustrated *Notre-Dame de Paris* by Alain Erlande-Brandenburg (Paris, 1991).

Figure 9.1: Lower west front of Notre-Dame, Paris

The right doorway, the so-called Sainte-Anne portal (see Figure 9.2),[20] picks up where the gallery of kings, the horizontal Jesse Tree, leaves off, for here the Virgin and Child represent the 'twig' and the 'flower' that grew from the stem of Jesse, 'and above this flower rested the nourishing Spirit' – the visible cloud above the holy figures. This portal gives centre stage to the idea of the Marian aspect of Incarnation – not just Incarnation of the Son of God, but also Incarnation through the Mother of God.

This figure of the Virgin relates not only to Fulbert of Chartres' Responsory *Styrps Yesse* quoted above but also to the Old Testament Lesson for the mass on the vigil of the feast of the Assumption. It is taken from Solomon's Book of Wisdom, or Ecclesiasticus, chapter 24:14–17. While in its biblical context it represents the discourse of Wisdom, there is no doubt that as a lesson in the liturgy it was taken to apply to the Virgin herself:

> From the beginning and before the world I was created, and unto the world to come I shall not cease to be, and in the holy dwelling-place I have ministered before him. And thus I was established in Syon, and in the holy city likewise I rested, and in Jerusalem was my power. And I took root in an honourable people, and in the portion of my God his inheritance, and my abode is in the full assembly of saints.[21]

---

[20]See also Sauerländer, plate 40. The debt of this portal to one on the west front of Chartres Cathedral has been discussed by Kathryn Horste, ' "A Child is Born": The Iconography of the Portail Ste.-Anne at Paris', *Art Bulletin* 69 (1987), pp. 187–210.

[21]The translation is from the Douai/Reims version of the Vulgate.

Figure 9.2: The Sainte-Anne or southwest portal

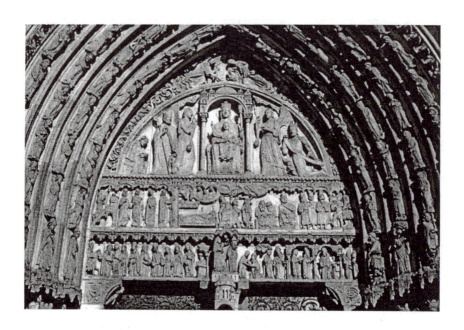

(Reiterated frequently, this lesson was also used in the weekly Saturday mass for the Virgin, and a continuation of the passage was used in the mass on the Assumption and on the Nativity of the Virgin.)

Thus on the Sainte-Anne portal, Mary is represented as the Mother of God; on the left door, known as the Coronation portal, she appears in her other great role as the Queen of Heaven (see Figure 9.3).[22] In early Christian apocryphal literature, upon her death the Virgin was bodily resurrected and assumed into heaven, where she was enthroned at the right hand of her son and was crowned Queen of Heaven. This storied event was commemorated in the feast of the Assumption of the Virgin, set on 15 August. It is no accident that at Notre-Dame of Paris the Assumption of the Virgin is the most important saint's feast in the liturgical calendar and the only one that is ceremonially on a par with the three great feasts of the Lord: Christmas, Easter, and Pentecost.[23] The Coronation portal, then, has as its theme the Assumption and Coronation of the Virgin. But it, too, has veiled reference to Mary the Mother of God. In the centre of the lower lintel appears the Ark of the Covenant, placed in a Gothic tabernacle on an altar. Three Old Testament patriarchs flank it on the viewer's left and three Old Testament kings on the right. This band of the lintel represents the Old Law and its witnesses, for what the Ark of the Covenant contains are the tablets of the Law

---

[22]See also Sauerländer, plates 152–153.
[23]See my 'Aspects of Trope', especially pp. 5, 7, and 8.

given to Moses. While in one sense the Ark of the Covenant was considered a pre-figuration of the Assumption of the Virgin, it was also considered a prefiguration of the Nativity of Christ. The Ark of the Covenant containing the tablets of the Law is the Old Testament prefiguration of the womb of the Virgin containing Christ incarnate.[24] This is even suggested by the dual architectural canopies superimposed over the trumeau sculpture of the Virgin and Child and the ark directly above her.

Figure 9.3: The Coronation or northwest portal

On either side of the central portal of Christ in Judgement (Figure 9.4) are the statues of Ecclesia and Synagogue – Ecclesia on Christ's right hand, the Synagogue on his left (Figure 9.1).[25] The Synagogue of course represents the Old Law, the Old Testament, while Ecclesia represents the New Law, the New Covenant. But on another level the Synagogue represents Eve, and Mary is the Church. The equation between Mary and the Church is made in many different ways. Both Mary and the Church are spoken of as the Bride of Christ, and Christ is the new Adam. Both as the Mother of God and as the Church, Mary is the *templum deitatis*, the temple of divinity. And the Virgin, as the vessel of Incarnation, is the restorer of salvation lost by Eve.

In her two principal roles, as Mother of God and Queen of Heaven, the Virgin is placed on both sides of the central portal, Christ in Judgement. But Mary has a role in the Last Judgement also. Just as the Virgin and St John are frequently depicted at the

---

[24]This idea is echoed in line six of *Serena virginum* (see above), where the Virgin is referred to as 'archa nove legis' (ark of the New Law).

[25]Also in Sauerländer, plate 144.

Figure 9.4: The Judgement or central portal

foot of the Cross in crucifixion scenes, so too are they depicted here as intercessors on bended knee before Christ in Judgement, who shows the wounds of crucifixion as two angels hold the instruments of his Passion.[26] Here the Virgin, again on Christ's right, is shown doing what she was most frequently petitioned to do: persuading her son to save the penitent sinner.

But the Virgin is also depicted (and not by accident) symbolically above the Last Judgement, untouched by it, with the great western rose as a giant halo behind her and the infant Christ as she is flanked by angels (Figure 9.1).[27] Here at the figural apex of the cathedral façade, Mary is the apex of a great triangle rising from the Coronation portal and the Ste Anne portal – a trinity – on the western front, surrounding and encompassing her son, who sits in Judgement in the centre. On this façade Christ is completely enveloped by his mother. Not only does this recall the miracle of Incarnation, it offers hope to those sinners who see that the Virgin can intervene on their behalf. She is their avenue to heaven. But she is also the Church, and it is through the Church, inside the *templum deitatis*, that she becomes accessible. The building, like Mary herself, was meant to be the house of God and the gate of heaven, the Hôtel-Dieu where sinful mortals can be restored to health. When you are enfolded in the church you are in the womb of the Virgin, the place where God became man, and this awesome event of Incarnation is recollected in the mass every day at the high altar – at the Virgin's altar.

---

[26] Also *ibid.*, plates 145 and 147.

[27] *Ibid.*, plate 144.

On the cathedral's west front Mary is shown in all her roles: as the Mother of God, as the Queen of Heaven, as the Church, as the restorer of salvation (the new Eve), as intercessor to Christ in Judgement, and as the supreme mediatrix between heaven and earth. This represents a *summa* of her position both within and without the world, both in time and beyond time, in the Eternal Present that is God's time. She was there before God entered time at the Incarnation, and she will still be there after time stops at the Last Judgement. ('From the beginning and before the world I was created, and unto the world to come I shall not cease to be ...'.) For the human viewer, much as it was thought to be for God himself, this sweep of time framed by eternity is all visible in a single glance at the west front of Notre-Dame. We see here a kind of peculiarly Marian All-Time, an idea particular to this cathedral, since it expressed the Notre-Dame clergy's view of the role of their church in their city, their world.

The concept of All-Time is a twelfth-century Victorine idea put forth in the writings of Hugh and Richard of St-Victor at the Augustinian abbey on Paris's Left Bank.[28] It is clear that in the latter part of the twelfth century, at the time the design for the west front of Notre-Dame was being formulated, Bishop Maurice of Sully and the cathedral hierarchy were heavily influenced by Victorine thinking on this matter. Margot Fassler has pointed out that the twelfth-century Victorines hoped to reform the cathedral chapter into an Augustinian community like their own.[29] Though they did not succeed in this attempt, aspects of their religious thought had nonetheless a powerful effect on the bishop and clergy of Notre-Dame, who did not hesitate to embrace what served their own mission. But because their emphasis was upon the Virgin, they gave the concept of All-Time a specifically Marian focus. We may summarize this belief as follows: Through the Virgin as Mother of God, salvation came into the world; through the Virgin as Queen of Heaven, sinners could be lifted out of this world. With the Virgin's help, they could surmount their earthly existence and gain access to eternity. This place, this *templum deitatis*, was the intersection between time and eternity for mankind. And at that still point, at that moment of transfer and exchange, the agent of transfer – the mediatrix both ways, from heaven to earth and from earth to heaven, *mediatrix a priori et a posteriori* – was the Virgin Mother of God.

The Notre-Dame clergy believed that their overriding mission was to elucidate the Virgin's role in salvation to those around them, in every way possible – to make this idea perspicuous. In their zeal to fulfil this mission, the clergy did not hesitate to assert the role of the Virgin on feasts from the end of December to the end of June – that

---

[28]See C. Stephen Jaeger, *The Envy of Angels: Cathedral Schools and Social Ideals in Medieval Europe, 950–1200* (Philadelphia, 1994), chapter 9, 'Humanism and Ethics at the School of St. Victor', pp. 244–268; and, more extensively, Margot Fassler, *Gothic Song: Victorine Sequences and Augustinian Reform in Twelfth-Century Paris* (Cambridge, 1993), especially chapter 9, 'The Augustinians of Paris and the Politics of Reform'.

[29]For more on the idea of All-Time and the Victorine influence on the cathedral see Fassler, *Gothic Song*, pp. 187 ff. See also Fassler, 'Representations of Time in *Ordo representacionis Adae*', in Daniel Poirion and Nancy F. Regalado, eds, *Contexts: Style and Values in Medieval Art and Literature* (a special issue of *Yale French Studies*), New Haven, 1991, pp. 97–113.

period of the church year in which she normally figured least in terms of her own feasts. In asserting the Virgin's role in this way, the clergy perhaps unwittingly opened the floodgates for the rising tide of Marian motets on non-Marian tenors that surged through the latter part of the thirteenth century. But that same rising tide is one indication that the cathedral of Paris succeeded in conveying the message about itself and its patron saint – that both should be considered the *domus dei et porta celi*: the house of God and the gate of Heaven.

Chapter 10

Consecrating the house: the Carmelites and the office of the dedication of a church

James John Boyce, O. Carm.

In his *Liber beneficiorum Diocoesis Cracoviensis* the Polish chronicler, Jan Długosz noted the arrival of the Carmelites in Krakow where 'they erected a monastery outside the city [walls] of Krakow in the western part next to the common labourers, [an area] which until now is called "on the Sand"'.[1] The designation 'outside the walls' (*extra muros*) was normally used to identify this convent in papal documents and other written records concerning the Carmelite presence in Krakow, the earliest of which is the decree of Boniface IX, dated 5 January 1401[2] giving apostolic confirmation to the convent (including the church, bell-tower, and cemetery) that they had recently established for the celebration of the liturgy and the spread of the Christian cult in Krakow.

The original group of Carmelites came from Prague as part of the progressive expansion of the Upper German province to which they belonged. They brought with

Research on this topic was made possible by a Louis Herman Rogge and Susan Hamilton Rogge Research Grant for 1996–1997 and by a Faculty Fellowship from Fordham University for the academic year 2003–2004, which I acknowledge with deep gratitude. I also wish to acknowledge the kindness of the late Fr. Leszek Pawlak, O. Carm., Prior Provincial of the Polish province, and of the Carmelite community of Krakow for their gracious hospitality during my visits there.

[1]Jan Długosz, *Liber beneficiorum Dioecesis Cracoviensis* (Wyd. Przeździeckiego) (1864), p. 475: 'monasterium extra urbem Cracoviensem in parte occidentali iuxta cerdones, quod hactenus vocatur ad Arenam constituunt'; quoted in O. dr. Bronisław Alfons Tomaszewski, Ord. Carm., 'Dzieje Klasztoru OO. Karmelitów na Piasku w Krakowie', Wydanie II (Kraków, 1970), unpublished doctoral dissertation, p. 5.

[2]*Bullarium Carmelitanum plures complectens summorum Pontificum Constitutiones ad Ordinem Fratrum Beatissimae, semperque Virginis Dei Genitricis MARIAE de Monte Carmelo spectantes*, Nunc primo in lucem editum, duasque in partes distinctum A Fratre Eliseo Monsignano ejusdem Ordinis Procuratore Generali pars prima, duplici indice exornata (Rome, 1715), vol. 1, p. 156.

them three choirbooks, newly made in the Prague convent, to be used for the celebration of the office in their new locale. They probably also brought graduals for the celebration of mass, but these have not survived. Of the choirbooks, two remain in the convent as the first two in a collection of manuscripts now numbering twenty-five,[3] while the third is now in the Biblioteka Zakładu Narodowego im. Ossolińskich, ms. (Rkp) 12025/IV,[4] in Wrocław (Breslau).

While no documents recounting the dedication of the new Carmelite church have survived, the liturgical chants found in the Wrocław manuscript show us how the office for the occasion was celebrated. An additional manuscript now known as ms. 3 (rkp. perg. 15), dated to 1468, contains chants for the Office of the Dedication as celebrated in Krakow. The general prescriptions for celebrating this office were stipulated in an ordinal compiled by a German Carmelite, Sibert de Beka, and first promulgated for use in the Order by the General Chapter of London of 1312.[5] Sibert's ordinal contained the incipits for every prayer, chant, and psalm for every day of the church year, generally ensuring a uniform tradition throughout the Order, but declined to impose a universal musical practice as the codex of Humbert of Romans had done for the Dominicans.[6] While the Carmelite liturgical tradition normally featured a high degree of uniformity from one area to another, the Feast of the Dedication is one of the rare occasions wherein practices among the Carmelites of Krakow digressed from standard Carmelite observance. The purpose of this chapter is to examine these differences and offer some commentary on the possible reasons for them. I will: 1) discuss the feast in terms of its background in the Jewish and Christian traditions, 2) comment upon general Carmelite practice, 3) show the distinctiveness of the Krakow Carmelite usage, and 4) offer some suggestions as to why the Krakow Carmelites chose such an independent approach.

---

[3]I discussed this collection of manuscripts in 'The Carmelite Choir Books of Krakow: Carmelite Liturgy before and after the Council of Trent', *StM* 45 (2004), pp. 17–34. In that article I listed the manuscripts in chronological order from ms 1 in 1397 to ms 25 in the nineteenth century, indicating the appropriate references to a different numbering used in a handlist made by Jan Gołos; I indicated his numbering as Rkp, the abbreviation for 'Rękopis', the Polish word for manuscript. For such references in this article I indicate my numbering by 'MS' and the Gołos numbering by 'rkp'; 'perg' is his indication for the parchment manuscripts.

[4]The manuscript is described in *Inwentarz Rękopisów Biblioteki Zakładu Narodowego im. Ossolińskich we Wrocławiu*, Tom III, Rękopisy 11981–13000, opracowały i przygotowały do druku Amelia Dician i Janina Loret-Heintsch pod redakcją Adama Fastnachta (Wrocław, Warszawa, Kraków, 1966), pp. 24–25.

[5]R. P. Benedict Zimmerman, O.C.D., *Ordinaire de l'ordre de Notre-Dame du Mont-Carmel par Sibert de Beka (vers 1312), publié d'après le manuscrit original et collationné sur divers manuscrits et imprimés* (Paris, 1910), p. 368.

[6]Humbert's codex is discussed in William R. Bonniwell, O. P., *A History of the Dominican Liturgy, 1215–1945* (New York, 1945), especially pp. 85–97.

1 Background to the feast and to the Carmelite liturgy

The feast for the dedication of a church finds its origins in the rededication of the temple in Jerusalem, after the Babylonian exile, by Judas Machabeus in 164 BC after its defilement by Antiochus Epiphanes, at which time the date for its annual celebration was fixed on the twenty-fifth day of Kislew and during its octave. This feast of the dedication of the temple could be celebrated on the anniversary in all synagogues throughout the land as well as in the temple itself.[7] The dedications of particular Christian basilicas are important, since they provide important links between individual churches and the Church as a whole. Thus the dedication of St John Lateran, the pope's own church, celebrated on 9 November each year, serves as a reminder of the primacy of Peter and the unity of the Church as a whole. The dedication of the basilica of St Mary Major in Rome is closely related to the feast of Our Lady of the Snows, one of the many Marian feasts celebrated within the Carmelite tradition and one celebrated with particular solemnity by the Carmelites of Krakow. For the Carmelites church dedications also recalled the church of the Holy Sepulchre and their own origins on Mount Carmel in the Latin Kingdom. Holy Sepulchre was the seat of the Latin Patriarch of Jerusalem, who included in his jurisdiction the church built on the site of Solomon's temple.

As residents of the Latin Kingdom the Carmelites participated in and contributed to its spiritual life, first by celebrating mass together and reciting the psalms privately in the manner of hermits, according to the original rule which they received from Albert of Jerusalem (1206–1214),[8] then with the full choral office according to the revised rule of 1247, which established them as mendicants. The imposition of the choral office required them to develop a *proper* office for the feast of the dedication of a church. By this time they had begun to establish themselves throughout western Christendom, growing to ten provinces by the time of the General Chapter of London of 1281.[9]

---

[7]For a discussion of the feast of the dedication of a church, with particular emphasis on the church of St John Lateran, see *Butler's Lives of the Saints*, Complete Edition, edited, revised and supplemented by Herbert Thurston, S. J., and Donald Attwater (New York, 1963), vol. 4, pp. 299B301; also see Adolf Adam, *Foundations of Liturgy: An Introduction to its History and Practice* (Collegeville, MN, 1992), pp. 340–341, and Adolf Adam, *The Liturgical Year, its History & its Meaning after the Reform of the Liturgy* (New York, 1981), pp. 183–185.

[8]Albert of Jerusalem has been discussed by Verne L. Bullough, 'Albert of Jerusalem, St.', in the *New Catholic Encyclopedia* vol. 1, p. 258; the most useful studies of the Carmelite rule are Hugh Clarke, O. Carm., and Bede Edwards, O.D.C., eds, *The Rule of Saint Albert* (Aylesford and Kensington, 1973) and Carlo Cicconetti, O. Carm., *La regola del Carmelo* (Rome, 1973).

[9]P. Ludovicus Saggi, O. Carm., 'Constitutiones Capituli Londinensis Anni 1281', *Analecta ordinis Carmelitarum* 15 (1950), pp. 203–245.

2 General Carmelite practice

The commemoration of the dedication of a church was celebrated each year by the local community, with prescribed services for both mass and office throughout the day. Sibert de Beka gave the list of chants for the Dedication in a separate section of his ordinal, presumably because the date for the celebration could vary according to local custom. His instructions included both the dedication itself and its annual commemoration:

> Officium Dedicationis ecclesiae in primo anno inchoandum est in missa. In hora vero quae sequitur missam et deinceps in omnibus horis usque ad completorium sequentis diei fiat officium totum duplex, sic quod primae vesperae dedicationis sint in ipsa die qua fit dedicatio, et in nocte sequente matutinum cum ix lectionibus et in crastino vesperae secundae. Octava vero, si celebranda fuerit in hoc primo anno, celebrabitur revoluta hebdomada eo die quod dedicato facta fuit... . Fratres de conventu in quo festum hujusmodi celebratus tam intus quam extra faciant officium de dedicatione, fratres etiam dum hospites sunt praesentes in conventu aliquo faciant officium sicut in conventu tam de festis dedicationis quam de aliis, quamvis per ordinem generaliter non fiant. Postquam vero recesserint de conventu, redeant ad officium consuetum.[10]

The Office of the Dedication of a church is begun, in the first year, with mass. In the office following mass, and thereafter in all the offices up until compline of the following day, should be 'totum duplex'.[11] [Beginning with mass means] that [in the first year] the first vespers of the dedication will be on the same day as the dedication [itself]. Matins with nine lessons [will be] in the following night, and second vespers on the following day. As for the octave, if it were to be celebrated in this first year, it will be in the following week on the same day as the dedication... . The friars[12] of the convent in which a [dedication] feast is being celebrated – both those residing and [those from] outside – should [all] take part. When friars are present in any convent as guests, they should celebrate the office just as [it is celebrated] in that convent, and as for feasts of the dedication so for others, even if [such is] generally not done throughout the order. Of course, after they have left the convent, they should return to their customary practice.

The normal practice in Sibert's ordinal is that mass occurs between prime and terce, thus somewhere in the morning, which is not surprising, given the requirements for fasting. In the case of the dedication feast one can presume a similar schedule, although it might depend on the convenience of the presiding bishop, since the fasting regulations would be determinative here too. The order of the liturgical day then followed the mass, which initiated the celebration, beginning with first vespers on that

---

[10]Zimmerman, *Ordinaire*, p. 60.

[11]The term 'totum duplex' or 'principal double' means that all the texts and chants for the office hours and mass are *proper*; see Andrew Hughes, *Medieval Manuscripts for Mass and Office: A Guide to their Organization and Terminology* (Toronto, 1982), p. 275, par. 1001.

[12] The term 'friars' describes the members (both priests and brothers) of mendicant orders, as opposed to monks or canons.

evening and concluding with second vespers on the next evening. The feast was celebrated on each of the six following days and repeated yet again on the octave.

3 A distinctive Carmelite practice in Krakow

Studies of the Carmelite office have examined extant manuscripts from Mainz (1430s), Florence (1390s), Pisa (first half of the fourteenth century),[13] and Krakow (1397 + 15th century)[14] and have shown that what was prescribed in Sibert's ordinal was generally carried out in practice in the individual houses of the order with remarkable fidelity. The later codex from Krakow, ms 3 (rkp. perg. 15), goes beyond Sibert's directions in prescribing the matins chants to be used during the octave: chants from the first nocturn for days 2 and 5, from the second nocturn for days 3 and 6, and from the third nocturn for day 4 and Saturday;[15] thus the office was performed in its entirety on the day itself and in part on the octave day and the intervening days. In the Wrocław manuscript the entire series of chants is in the original hand, while the first vespers chants are also included at the beginning of the manuscript in a revising hand from the eighteenth century.[16]

Table 10.1 lists the chants for this feast (first column) in the ordinal of Sibert de Beka,[17] their liturgical position in the office (second column), then (in the remaining columns) the mode of each chant as it appears in the Carmelite choirbooks that contain music for the feast. These are **MaiC**, Mainz, Dom- und Diözesanmuseum, codex C, fols 178^V–195^V a choirbook datable to the early 1430s for use in Mainz; **Kra3**, Krakow, Carmelite Monastery, codex 3 (rkp. perg. 15), fols 76^V–80^V, dated to 1468;

---

[13]The contents of these manuscripts have been discussed by Paschalis Kallenberg, O. Carm., *Fontes liturgiae Carmelitanae, investigatio in decreta, codices et proprium sanctorum* (Rome, 1962), especially pp. 244–247 (Pisa antiphonals), pp. 247–256 (Florence antiphonals) and 256–259 (Mainz antiphonals). My articles on these three sets of manuscripts were originally published as 'Two Antiphonals of Pisa: Their Place in the Carmelite Liturgy', *Manuscripta* 31 (1987), pp. 147–165; 'The Carmelite Choirbooks of Florence and the Liturgical Tradition of the Carmelite Order', *Carmelus* 35 (1988), pp. 67–93; and 'Die Mainzer Karmeliterchorbücher und die liturgische Tradition des Karmeliterordens', *Archiv für mittelrheinische Kirchengeschichte* 39 (1987), pp. 267–303, and reprinted as 'The Carmelite Choirbooks of Mainz and the Liturgical Tradition of the Carmelite Order', in my *Praising God in Carmel* (Washington DC, 1999).

[14]The Krakow Carmelite manuscripts have been discussed in my article 'The Carmelite Choir Books of Krakow', pp. 17–34.

[15]This rubric occurs on folio 80^V of ms 3 (rkp. perg. 15).

[16]Krakow, mss 1 (rkp. perg. 12) and 2 (rkp. perg. 14) and the Wrocław manuscript were revised in 1743 under the direction of Fr. Bonaventure Kiełkowicz, O. Carm., to conform to the directives of the Council of Trent, but nonetheless generally respect the integrity of the original chant. See my article 'The Carmelite Choir Books of Krakow' for this discussion.

[17]Zimmerman, *Ordinaire*, pp. 60–62.

Wro, Wrocław, Biblioteka Zakładu Narodowego im. Ossolińskich, Rkp 12025/IV,[18] a manuscript dated to 1397 and one of the three written in Prague and brought to Krakow for the foundation of the new convent in that year; and **Pisa**, Convento de Santa Maria del Carmine, codex D, fols 89–100, stemming from the first half of the fourteenth century. A perusal of Table 10.1 shows that while for this feast both the Pisa and Mainz manuscripts conform with great fidelity to the prescriptions of Sibert's ordinal, and even share musical characteristics, many of these prescribed chants either do not occur in the Krakow manuscripts or are assigned a different position. The two Krakow codices are, however, generally consistent with each other.

Most of the differences occurred in matins. Table 10.2 shows the chant incipits in the two Krakow codices and contrasts them with the incipits from Sibert's ordinal. These differences between the Krakow tradition and the general Carmelite tradition can be divided into three categories: a) instances where an entirely different chant is used in Krakow, b) cases where the same responsory is used but with a different verse, and c) instances where the same responsory is used but in a different liturgical place.

a) All the manuscripts use the well-known *Terribilis est locus iste* as the first vespers responsory, a chant that is normally repeated as the ninth matins responsory as well. While both the Pisa antiphonary and the ordinal of Sibert use *Terribilis* at matins, the Mainz and Krakow manuscripts prefer a different and rather unusual chant, *Benedic domine domum istam et omnes habitantes* and its verse *Conserva domine in ea*; moreover this verse is not set to the standard tone for the fifth mode but instead employs a newly-composed melody, consistent with the tradition of rhymed-office responsories. *Benedic domine domum* is a significant departure from Sibert's ordinal. Among the matins chants in Krakow that are not found in Mainz and Sibert are the antiphons *Aedificavit* (MA1.3), *Templum domini sanctum est* (MA3.2), and *Benedicta gloria domini* (MA3.3), and the responsory *Sanctificavit dominus tabernaculum suum* (MR2.3). Conversely, a number of chants prescribed in Sibert's ordinal are not found at all in the Krakow sources, for example, the antiphon *Cum evigilasset* (MA1.3).

b) Numerous responsories in the Krakow Carmelite sources feature the same responsory prescribed by Sibert de Beka, but with a different verse: thus for the responsory *In dedicatione templi* (MR1.1) Sibert's prescribed verse, *Obtulerunt sacrificum*, is assigned in Pisa, but Mainz and Krakow prefer *Fundata est domus domini*; Sibert prescribed that the responsory *Benedic domine domum istam aedificata* be used as MR2.1 along with the verse *Domine si conversus fuerit*, sung also in Pisa, while the Krakow manuscripts use it as MR1.3 with the verse *Qui regis Israel*; the closely related responsory *Benedic domine domum istam et omnes habitantes* (MR3.3),

---

[18]The manuscript is described in *Inwentarz Rękopisów Biblioteki Zakładu Narodowego*, pp. 24–25.

unique to the Mainz and Krakow Carmelite codices, has also a unique verse *Conserva domine*. All of these responsories except *Benedic ... habitantes* are derived from the standard repertory for the feast of the dedication, and have counterparts in *CAO*;[19] the difference is that Sibert's ordinal and the Krakow manuscripts use the tradition differently, choosing an alternative verse in each case from the options available in the standard repertory for each responsory.

c) A number of chants in the Krakow practice have different assignments in the Sibert tradition; thus the antiphon *Vidi Jacob scalam summitas* is found in Sibert as MA1.2 but used in Krakow as MA2.2; the antiphon *Erit mihi dominus in deum* is assigned as MA2.3 in Sibert, but as MA1.2 in Krakow; the responsory *Mane surgens* is prescribed in Sibert as MR1.3 and used in Krakow as MR2.1.

A search of the CANTUS index[20] suggests that in a couple of instances these alternate responsory verses are unique to the Krakow Carmelite sources; neither *Benedic ... habitantes* nor its verse *Conserva* occurs in any of the sources currently indexed in CANTUS, nor in the standard list of such chants from rhymed offices.[21] The special melody of the verse (rather than the standard tone for the fifth mode), also marks the responsory as unique. Similarly, *Haec est domus domini*, the verse to *Domus mea domus orationis*, and *Qui regis Israel*, the verse to *Benedic domine ... quae aedificata* are not to be found in the *CAO* sources.

The Krakow tradition includes two alternate forms of the responsory *Benedic domine*, which are of special interest for this study. The first is MR1.3, where the text follows the *CAO*:[22] *Benedic Domine, domum istam quam aedificavi nomini tuo; venientium in locum istum exaudi preces in excelso solio gloriae tuae*. The verse, *Qui regis Israel*, however, does not occur as one of the options in *CAO* for this responsory. A quite distinct responsory with the same incipit occurs in MR3.3 in Wrocław and also in Mainz, Dom- und Diözesanmuseum, codex C:[23]

Benedic domine domum istam et omnes habitantes in illa sitque in ea sanitas humilitas sanctitas castitas virtus victoria fides spes et caritas benignitas temperantia patientia spiritualis disciplina et obedientia. Per infinita secula. v. Conserva domine in ea timentes te pusillos cum majoribus. v. Gloria patri et filio et spiritui sancto.

Bless O Lord this house and all those who dwell in it and let there be in it health, humility, holiness, chastity, virtue, victory, faith, hope and charity, goodness, temperance, patience, spiritual discipline and obedience. Through unending ages. v. Keep safe

---

[19]*CAO*, vol. 4, *Responsoria, versus, hymni et varia*.

[20]This electronic index is available at http://publish.uwo.ca/-cantus/o

[21]See AH.

[22]*CAO*, vol. 4, p. 60, no. 6235.

[23]The responsory begins on p. 196 in the Wrocław manuscript and on fol. 191[V] in Mainz, Codex C.

O lord in it those who fear you, the young ones along with the older. v. Glory be to the
Father and to the Son and to the Holy Spirit.

Since this prayer refers not only to those who will come to the church but also to the
religious life of the community, it is at least reasonable to presume that it may have
been written within and for the Carmelites. Reinforcement for this hypothesis may be
seen in the references to virtues such as humility, holiness, and chastity, which enable
both individual religious and the general community to flourish, and to spiritual
discipline and obedience, which are essential for the good order of a religious house.
Since it forms an important part of the Mainz and Krakow version of the dedication
feast, I include below the version of this responsory from the manuscript Wrocław,
Biblioteka Zakładu Narodowego im. Ossolińskich 12025/IV, pp. 196–197. While in
the manuscript the *b flat* is indicated only a few times, and in a later hand, the piece is
so clearly in fifth mode that I have flattened the *b* throughout. The responsory seems
carefully crafted: the text phrases and musical phrases correspond; the tonality is never
ambiguous, although, as is often the case in responsories, a melismatic section (in this
instance at 'per infinita secula') exploits both the authentic and plagal ranges of the
tritus.

4 Explaining the differences

A comparison of the chants for the feast of the Dedication reveals a polarity between
Sibert's ordinal and the Pisa and Mainz manuscripts on the one hand, and the Krakow
codices on the other. While the Mainz tradition generally follows the standard Carmelite usage, its chants in a few instances are closer to Krakow practice than to the overall
tradition of the Order. Given the general stability of the official tradition and the overall fidelity of these manuscripts to it, these differences are noteworthy and suggest that
either the rite had evolved over time or was observed differently in central Europe.

The differences may relate to the late foundation of the Krakow convent, and are
probably regional. The convent of Pisa was founded in 1249,[24] and the Carmel of
Mainz dates to the year 1285;[25] since both houses predate the ordinal of Sibert de

---

[24] Joachim Smet, O. Carm., *The Carmelites, A History of the Brothers of Our Lady of Mount Carmel*, vol. 1: *ca 1200 until the Council of Trent* (revised edition. Darien IL, 1988), p. 26.

[25] The first datable event in the history of the Mainz Carmelite convent is 24 February 1285, when a certain Gisla, the widow of Ernst von Eberbach, bequeathed a half silver mark to the Carmelites for the construction of their convent; in 1290 Archbishop Gerhard II of Mainz officially accepted the Carmelites into his diocese, confirming by letter the convents of Frankfurt, Kreuznach, and Mainz. See *50 Jahre Karmeliter wieder in Mainz 1294–1974* (Mainz, 1974), pp. 17–18, as well as Pater Clemens Martini, *Der deutsche Carmel, ein Gesamt-überblick über die Provinzen von Niederdeutschland, Oberdeutschland und Sachsen des Stammordens u. l. Frau vom Berge Karmel in Deutschland, über die Tätigkeit u. das Wirken dieses Ordens auf deutschem Boden*, vol. 1 (Bamberg, 1922), p. 157.

Beka, their liturgies presumably reflect Carmelite practice at the time it was compiled. Our source for the Pisan Carmelite tradition (Pisa, Carmine, ms. D) dates to the years

Example 10.1:   Wrocław, Biblioteka Zakładu Narodowego im. Ossolińskich
12025/IV, pp. 196–197

The responsory "Benedic domine domum istam"

Table 10.1: Chants for the dedication of a church in the ordinal of Sibert de Beka and Carmelite manuscripts

Incipit Sibert	Chant	MaiC	Kra3	Wro	Pisa	
Sanctificavit dominus	VA1	1	1	1+	1	VA= (first) vespers antiphon
Domus haec sancta Jerusalem	VA2	3	3		2	
Gloriosum et terribile nomen	VA3	4	4		3	
Benedictus es in templo	VA4	1	5		1	
In dedicatione hujus templi	VA5	1	6		1	
Terribilis est locus iste non	VR	2	2	2	*	VR=(first) vespers responsory
Cumque evigilasset Jacob a	VV01	2	2	2		VV=(first) vespers responsory verse
Gloria patri et filio et	VV02	2	2	2		
Urbs beata Jerusalem*	VH	*	*	*	*	VH=(first) vespers hymn
Domum tuam domine decet	VW	*	*	*	*	VW=(first) vespers versicle
O quam metuendus est locus	VAM	6	6	6	6	VAM=(first) vespers Magnificat antiphon
[Templum hoc sanctum]	M I	5	-	-	-	M=matins
[Filiae Sion currite adsunt]	M I	2	-	-	-	I=invitatory antiphon
Exsultemus domino regi summo	M I	2	4	4	2	
Angulare	MH	-	*	-	*	
Tollite portas principes	MA1.1	3	3	3	3	
Vidit Jacob scalam summitas	MA1.2	7	-	-	7	
Cum evigilasset Jacob a somno	MA1.3	7	-	-	7	
Domum tuam domine decet	M W1.	*	*	*	*	

In dedicatione templi	MR1.1	1	*	1	1
Obtulerunt sacrificium super	MV01	1	-	-	1
Fundata est domus domini	MR1.2	2	1	2	2
Venientes autem venient cum	MV01	2	-	-	2
Mane surgens Jacob erigebat	MR1.3	4	-	-	4
Vidit Jacob scalam summitas	MV01	4	-	-	4
Gloria patri	MV02	-	1	1	4
Non est hic aliud nisi domus	MA2.1	7	7	7	7
Erexit Jacob lapidem in	MA2.2	7	-	-	7
Erit mihi dominus in deum et	MA2.3	4	-	-	7
Haec est domus domini	MW2.	*	*	*	*
Benedic domine domum istam	MR2.1	8	-	-	8
Domine si conversus fuerit	MV01	8	-	-	8
O quam metuendus est locus	MR2.2	1	1	1	1
Mane surgens Jacob votum	MV01	1	-	-	1
Orantibus in loco isto	MR2.3	8	-	-	8
Domine exaudi orationem meam	MV01	8	-	-	8
Gloria patri et filio et	MV02	-	-	-	8
Qui habitat in adjutorio	MA3.1	8	-	8	8
Domum istam protege domine et	MA3.2	3	-	-	3
Fundata est domus domini	MA3.3	8	-	-	8
Beati qui habitant in domo	MW3.	*	*	*	*
Lapides pretiosi omnes muri	MR3.1	7	7	7	7
Haec est domus domini	MV01	7	-	-	7
Domus mea domus orationis	MR3.2	1	1	1	1
Domum tuam domine decet	MV01	1	-	-	1
Terribilis	MR3.3	-	*	-	2

Incipit Sibert	Chant	MaiC	Kra3	Wro	Pisa	
Cumque	MV02	-	*	-	2	
[Benedic domine domum istam]	MR3.3	5	-	5	-	
[Conserva domine in ea]	MV01	5S	-	5S	-	
Gloria patri et filio et	MV02	5S	-	5S	-	
Domine dilexi	M W	*	*	*	*	
Domum tuam domine decet	LA1	7	7	7	7	L=lauds
Haec est domus domini	LA2	1	1	1	1	
Domus mea domus orationis	LA3	1	1	1	1	
Bene fundata est domus domini	LA4	8	8	8	8	
Lapides pretiosi omnes muri	LA5	1	1	1	1	
Urbs beata Jerusalem	LH	*	*	*	*	
Domus mea domus orationis	LW	*	*	*	*	
Mane surgens Jacob erigebat	LAB	4	4	4	4	LAB=benedictus antiphon
Domum tuam domine	TR	r	r	r	r	T=terce
In longitudine dierum	TV01	r	r	r	r	
Gloria patri et filio et	TV02	r	-	-	r	
Haec est domus domini	TW	*	*	*	*	
Haec est domus domini	SR	r	r	r	r	S=sext
Bene fundata est supra firmam	SV01	r	r	r	r	
Gloria patri et filio et	SV02	r	-	-	r	
Beati qui habitant in domo	SW	*	*	*	*	
Beati qui habitant in domo	NR	r	r	r	r	N=none
In saecula saeculorum	NV01	r	r	r	r	
Gloria patri et filio et	NV02	r	-	-	r	
Domus mea domus orationis	NW	*	*	*	*	

V2=second vespers

Chant	Code					
Domum tuam*	V2A1	*		*[26]	*[27]	*
Haec est domus domini	V2A2			*		*
Domus mea domus orationis	V2A3			*		
Bene fundata est domus domini	V2A4			*		
Lapides pretiosi omnes muri	V2A5			*		
Terribilis est locus iste non	V2R			*		*
Cumque evigilasset Jacob a	V2V01					
Gloria patri et filio et	V2V02					
Urbs beata Jerusalem	V2H			*		*
Domum tuam*	V2W	*		*		*
Zachaee festinans descende	V2AM	8		8		8

+   a rubric indicates that this chant begins the list of [standard] first vespers chants

*   rubric

[]   not in Sibert's ordinal

---

[26] The rubric prescribes that the lauds chants be repeated here.

[27] The rubric prescribes that the five [lauds] antiphons be used here, along with the responsory and hymn from first vespers.

Table 10.2: A comparison of matins chants for the dedication feast in the Krakow tradition and the general Carmelite liturgy

Chant	Krakow	Kra3	Wro	Sibert
M I	Exsultemus domino regi summo	4	4	Exsultemus domino regi summo
MH	Angulare	*	-	Angulare
MA1.1	Tollite portas principes			Tollite portas principes
MA1.2	Erit mihi dominus in deum	4T	4T	Vidit Jacob scalam summitas
MA1.3	Aedificavit Moyses altare	6	6	Cum evigilasset Jacob a somno
M W1.	Domum tuam domine decet	*	*	Domum tuam domine decet
MR1.1	In dedicatione templi	1	1	In dedicatione templi
MV01	Fundata est domus domini	1	1	Obtulerunt sacrificium super
MR1.2	Fundata est domus domini	2	2	Fundata est domus domini
MV01	Benedic domine domum istam	2	2	Venientes autem venient cum domum istam
MR1.3	Benedic domine domum istam	8	8	Mane surgens Jacob erigebat
MV01	Qui regis Israel intende qui	8	8	Vidit Jacob scalam summitas
MV02				
MA2.1	Non est hic aliud nisi domus	7	7	Non est hic aliud nisi domus
MA2.2	Vidit Jacob scalam summitas	7	7	Erexit Jacob lapidem in
MA2.3	Erexit Jacob lapidem in	7	7	Erit mihi dominus in deum et
MW2.	Haec est domus domini	*	*	Haec est domus domini
MR2.1	Mane surgens Jacob erigebat	4	4	Benedic domine domum istam
MV01	Cumque evigilasset Jacob a	4	4	Domine si conversus fuerit
MR2.2	O quam metuendus est locus	1	1	O quam metuendus est locus
MV01	Vere dominus est in loco isto	1	1	Mane surgens Jacob votum

MR2.3	Sanctificavit dominus	3	3	Orantibus in loco isto
MV01	Haec est domus domini	3	3	Domine exaudi orationem meam
MA3.1	Qui habitat in adjutorio	8	8	Qui habitat in adjutorio
MA3.2	Templum domini sanctum est	2	2	Domum istam protege domine et
MA3.3	Benedicta gloria domini de	7	7	Fundata est domus domini
MW3.	Beati qui habitant in domo	*	*	Beati qui habitant in domo
MR3.1	Lapides pretiosi omnes muri	7	7	Lapides pretiosi omnes muri
MV01	Structura muri ejus de lapide	7	7	Haec est domus domini
MR3.2	Domus mea domus orationis	1	1	Domus mea domus orationis
MV01	Haec est domus domini	1	1	Domum tuam domine decet
MR3.3	Benedic domine domum istam	-	5	Terribilis est locus iste
MV01	Conserva domine in ea	-	5S	Cumque evigilasset Jacob
MV02	Gloria patri et filio et	-	5S	Gloria patri et filio et
M W	Domine dilexi	*	*	Domine dilexi

* = rubric

1312–1342[28]; it is one of the earliest Carmelite antiphonaries. Since, of those manuscripts under consideration, this is the closest in time to the ordinal of Sibert, it is the most likely to follow its directives in detail. Even though the Mainz manuscript dates to the early 1430s,[29] the convent itself was well established by that time and therefore presumably loyal to the older tradition.

An inscription in the Wroclaw manuscript states that it was made in Prague in 1397 to be brought along with two other antiphonaries to Krakow for the foundation of the new house. We may thus expect it to reflect the tradition received from the German Carmelites who founded the Prague convent and also the tradition that the Prague Carmelites established for the new convent in Krakow. Not surprisingly, Krakow ms 3 (rkp. perg. 15) agrees with Wrocław (except for the responsory *Benedic domine ... habitantes*): it was made in Krakow in 1468, perhaps copied directly from the Wroclaw manuscript, which by this time reflected a localized Polish Carmelite observance. The Wrocław inscription is highly informative for our purposes: in addition to giving the date of the feast of St. Wenceslaus (28 September) in 1397 for the completion of the manuscript, the dedication lists several people who were important for its production, including brother Hartmann of Tachau, who was then in his eighteenth year as prior of Prague ('fratris Hartmanni de Tachovia protunc prioris pragensis Anno officii sui XVIII°') and brother Procopius, the cantor who directed the choir for forty-six years and was a son of Prague[30] ('item frater procopius cantor hic rexit chorum xlvi annis et maxime pragensis ...').

The Prague convent itself was founded in 1347 as part of the expansion of the German Carmelite province, the sixteenth house in the order of foundation.[31] If by 1397 Fr. Procopius had been directing the choir for forty-six years, he would have begun these duties around 1351, making him one of the early vocations for the new convent: a native of Prague, and proud enough of his origin to want it mentioned in the dedication.

---

[28]Paschalis Kallenberg, O. Carm., in *Fontes liturgiae Carmelitanae*, p. 214, dated this manuscript to the first half of the fourteenth century and suggested that it predated 1342; I confirmed this dating, based on the absence of the feast of the Three Marys, accepted into the liturgy at the General Chapter of Lyons in 1342, in my article, 'Two Antiphonals of Pisa', pp. 147–165.

[29]A single leaf extracted from Mainz, Dom- und Diözesanmuseum, Codex A, now ms Munich BS, clm. 29 164/13 contains a dedicatory notice for the manuscript with the date 1430; an identical dedicatory page in Mainz, Codex B, gives the date 1432; see Fritz Arens, 'Ein Blatt aus den mainzer Karmeliterchorbüchern', *Jahrbuch für das Bistum Mainz* 8 (1958–60), pp. 341–346, and my article 'Die mainzer Karmeliterchorbücher', pp. 267–303, for this discussion.

[30]The inscription page is an unnumbered folio; the verso side begins the antiphonary proper, numbered as page 1 in the revisions of the later hand of the eighteenth century. The first part of this inscription has been transcribed in *Inwentarz Rękopisów Biblioteki Zakładu Narodowego*, p. 24.

[31]P. Adalbert Deckert, O. Carm., *Die Oberdeutsche Provinz der Karmeliten nach den Akten ihrer Kapitel von 1421 bis 1529* (Rome, 1961), p. 29.

Bohemian saints and individuals figured more prominently in these manuscripts than in the general Carmelite tradition (consider that they contain rhymed offices for St Wenceslaus and St Ludmila,[32] and the rhymed office for Our Lady of the Snows, some of whose chants were written by John of Jenstein, archbishop of Prague). The presence of such local material is perhaps owing to the influence of figures such as Fr. Procopius, influence that probably explains the unusual latitude exercised in the celebration of the Feast of the Dedication as well.

This feast was of great importance to the German Carmelites, for whom the fourteenth century was a period of rapid expansion: after the foundation of the convent of Prague in 1347 houses were established in Lienz (1349), Tachau (1351), Neudstadt a. d. Saale (1352), Vienna (1360), Schweinfurt (1367), Straubing (1368), Budapest (1372), Gdańsk (1380), Striegau (in lower Silesia, near Wrocław, 1382), Abensberg (1392), Voitsberg (1395), and Krakow (1397),[33] thus eleven convents between the foundation of the Prague and Krakow houses, within a span of only about fifty years. The expansion was substantial enough that shortly after the foundation of the convent of Prague the German province was split into two, with the new houses now falling under the jurisdiction of the Upper German province, with headquarters at Bamberg.[34]

Conclusions

The Feast of the Dedication of a Church generally celebrated the ongoing apostolic activity of the church; for the Carmelites it celebrated their striking progress as a mendicant order. In the case of the new foundation in Krakow (as presumably for all the others) the new establishment required the production of at least some new service-books. The celebration of the Carmelite dedications is in one respect special, for it customarily included friars from other communitites, perhaps, on occasion, from other provinces, travelling to take part. We have seen that there are important differences between Krakow usage and the general Carmelite tradition in the assignment of chants that, although widely used in the chant tradition, were generally not part of the Order's practice. Although other similar departures may well be discovered, those of Krakow seem to be unique, and all the more remarkable, given the generally uniform liturgical observance within the order throughout the medieval period. One of the local productions seems to have been the prayer cited above, 'Bless, O Lord, this house and all those who dwell in it'. The Carmelite convent of Krakow, still thriving after more than six hundred years of unbroken religious life, is a sign that this prayer has been answered.

---

[32] This office is the same as the one edited by Dominique Patier, 'L'office rythmique de Sainte Ludmila', *EG* 21 (1986), pp. 49–96.

[33] Deckert, *Die Oberdeutsche Provinz*, pp. 29–38.

[34] *Ibid.*, p. 29.

Chapter 11

A historical context for Guido d'Arezzo's use of *distinctio*

Dolores Pesce

Chapter 8 of the *Micrologus* contains a perplexing statement: 'Omnes itaque modi distinctionesque modorum his tribus aptantur vocibus [*C D E*].'[1] In an earlier publication I offered an explanation for Guido's emphasis on *C D* and *E*.[2] This chapter brings together my conclusions on the significance of *C D* and *E* for Guido and my speculation on what he meant by *distinctio* in light of its music theoretical usage before and after.[3]

In Table 11.1, column 1, 'language analogy' refers to a tradition that hinges in some way on making analogies between grammatical and musical language or shows a particular concern for how text is articulated within the musical phrase. In 1989 Calvin Bower provided an overview of the language analogies made by ten medieval writers, including Guido.[4] In 1998 Karen Desmond refined Bower's table in the context of her

---

[1]Joseph Smits van Waesberghe, ed., *Micrologus*, CSM 4 (Rome, 1955), p. 127. Letter designations are used in accordance with the system formulated in the *Dialogus de musica* (*ca* 1000): Γ *A B C D E F G* (known as *graves*), with lower-case letters for the next octave, *a* through *g* (known as *acutae*), and double letters for *aa* through *dd* (known as *superacutae*). In the *graves*, the note *B* occurs only in the natural form, so capital *B* has this sole meaning. In the *acutae* and *superacutae* both the natural and flat forms of *b* were used, designated by a square b and round b respectively. In this study, the words 'b natural' and 'b flat' will be used in place of these two forms.

[2]Dolores Pesce, ed., *Guido d'Arezzo's Regule rithmice, Prologus in antiphonarium, and Epistola ad Michahelem: A Critical Text and Translation with an Introduction, Annotations, Indices, and New Manuscript Inventories* (Ottawa, 1999), pp. 26–27.

[3]To date, no entry for *distinctio* has appeared in Michael Bernhard, ed., *Lexicon musicum Latinum medii aevi. Wörterbuch der lateinischen Musikterminologie des Mittelalters bis zum Ausgang des 15. Jahrhunderts* (Munich, 1992–).

[4]Calvin Bower, 'The Grammatical Model of Musical Understanding in the Middle Ages', in Patrick J. Gallacher and Helen Damico, eds, *Hermeneutics and Medieval Culture* (Albany NY, 1989), pp. 133–145.

discussion of Guido's *Micrologus*, chapter 15.[5] In the Table I have added several writers to these earlier overviews, and further subdivided the ways in which the grammatical terms are used.[6]

Hucbald, in his *De harmonica institutione*, stresses that, just as letters allow us to recognize sounds and *distinctiones* in words, notes do likewise in music:

> Nunc ad notas musicas, quae unicuique chordarum appositae non minimum studiosis melodiae conferunt fructum, ordo vertatur. Hae autem ad hanc utilitatem sunt repertae, ut sicut per litteras voces et distinctiones verborum recognoscuntur in scripto, ut nullum legentem dubio fallant iudicio; sic per has omne melum annotatum, etiam sine docente, postquam semel cognitae fuerint, valeat decantari.[7]

> Let our course turn next to the written musical signs, which, placed by each of the string names, bring no slight profit to students of music. As the sounds and differences of words are recognized by letters in writing in such a way that the reader is not led into doubt, musical signs were devised so that every melody notated by their means, once these signs have been learned, can be sung even without a teacher.

In this case, *distinctio* does not carry a technical grammatical meaning, but a non-technical meaning of 'difference'. In medieval grammar, *distinctio* refers to a major division of a sentence, that is, a grammatical unit. Furthermore, by the time of the music writings under consideration, grammar had absorbed terminological usages from rhetoric, that included the word *distinctio*. In the tradition of the Roman rhetorician Fabius Quintilian, Isidore of Seville defined the period, which he equated with *distinctio*, as follows: 'a period ought not to be longer than can be delivered in a single breath'.[8] Thus, *distinctio* could mean a major division of a sentence or a mark of division, that is, a clause or the punctuation marking a clause. Both meanings appear in Aurelian's *Musica disciplina*. First he discusses singing the verse 'Ecce agnus dei ecce':

> ... Unde quidam hunc male distingunt, auferentes a rudibus intellectum, ita canentes:

> V. 'Ecce agnus dei ecce,' facientes in '-ce' distinctionem. Cum potius conservandum sit sensus quam modulatio, quidam vero in sexta syllaba distingunt, scilicet in '-i' ut 'Ecce agnus dei.' Estque musica licentia ut in ea littera quae maiorem obtinet numerum, scilicet '-a-', longiorem, se necessitas cogit, effici modulationem, et pro

---

[5]Karen Desmond, '*Sicut in grammatica*: Analogical Discourse in Chapter 15 of Guido's *Micrologus*', *JM* 16 (1998), p. 471.

[6]I have excluded the *Musica enchiriadis*, which appeared in the charts of Bower and Desmond, because it does not include *distinctio* within its terminology.

[7]*GS* vol. 1, p. 117; as translated by Warren Babb in Claude V. Palisca, ed., *Hucbald, Guido, and John on Music. Three Medieval Treatises* (New Haven, 1978), pp. 35–36.

[8]See Desmond, '*Sicut in grammatica*', pp. 472–473, 478.

Table 11.1: Contexts for *distinctio*

	Language analogy	General rules for endings or beginnings of phrases	Enumerated phrase endings per mode	Dividing tone of octave *cursus*	Starting tone of octave *cursus*
Hucbald	notes compared to sounds and *distinctiones* of words				
Aurelian	concern for text sense in positioning of *distinctio* (as cadence and melisma)				
Scolica enchiriadis	*cola, commata* – 'display certain suitable *distinctiones*'				
Commemoratio brevis	tonary context: *medietas* or *distinctio* for medial cadence; also uses *membrum*				
Modorum sive tonorum ordo			Yes		
De organo (Schmid, 207)	*cola, commata* = major and minor *distinctiones*				

Treatise				Modal final	Terminology / phrasing
Dialogus de musica				importance of modal final for phrase beginnings and endings	
De musica (GS I: 275–77)					*vox, syllaba, pars, distinctio*; issue of similar, balanced phrasing
Guido, *Micrologus*				importance of modal final for phrase beginnings and endings; range for phrase beginnings and endings, depending on whether authentic or plagal	*litterae, syllabae, partes, pedes, versus*; *phthongi, syllabae, neumae, distinctiones*; issues of balance and proportion; refers to tenor on *syllaba, pars, distinctio*
De modorum formulis				range for phrase beginnings and endings, depending on whether authentic or plagal	
Berno, *De mensuro monochordo*			Yes		'A chant has *cola* and *commata*, that is membra and incisiones, which we call *distinctiones* of song, on these (enumerated tones).'
Wilhelm	Yes				
Aribo				importance of modal final for phrase beginnings and endings; range for phrase beginnings, endings, and differences of tones, depending on whether authentic or plagal*	*vox, neuma, distinctio*; separately refers to tenor on *syllaba, pars, distinctio*; similarity and balance of voices, *neumae, distinctiones*
Vivell commentary		Yes		modal properties recognized at end of *distinctiones* or of whole song	

	Language analogy	General rules for endings or beginnings of phrases	Enumerated phrase endings per mode	Dividing tone of octave *cursus*	Starting tone of octave *cursus*
Quaestiones in musica	*syllaba, pars, distinctio,* including mention of tenor on each	importance of modal final for phrase beginnings and endings; range for phrase beginnings, endings, and differences or tones, depending on whether authentic or plagal*			
John Cotton (ch. 10)	grammarians *used* tonus for verbal accent (grave, circumflex, acute) or for *distinctio:* Donatus recognized three *distinctiones* or *pausationes: colon, comma, periodus*				

* In the expression 'principia dico distinctionum, et fines ac tonorum differentiae' (CSM 2:15 and *Quaestiones*, pp. 36–17), Aribo and the anonymous writer who copied this passage may intend 'differentiae' to refer to saeculorum amen endings.

duabus vel tribus constare syllabis (at tamen non tam fortiter initium exprimitur modulationis).[9]

Some, taking their cue from the untutored, punctuate this verse badly when they sing 'Ecce agnus dei ecce', making a pause after '-ce', even though the sense should be preserved more than the melody. Some pause after the sixth syllable, on '-i', in 'Ecce agnus dei'. It is allowed in music that, on a vowel of longer quantity, as for example '-a-', a longer melody may be made, if it is called for, and extended over two or three syllables, but a melody is not so greatly prolonged at its beginning.

and then the verse 'Cantate Domino':

Fit enim hoc in una parte, fit et in duabus. Fit in una parte orationis in secunda syllaba post primam distinctionem, veluti in hoc versu gradalis responsorii: V. 'A summo caelo egressio eius,' primam post distinctionem quae desinit in '-lo,'incoante altera quae est 'egressio,' post primam syllabam quae est 'e-' secunde distinctionis [in secunda syllaba videlicet] quae est ['-gres-'] ...[10]

This [a tremulous inflection] may be performed on one word, or it may be performed on two. It is performed on a single word on the second syllable after the first phrase, as in this verse of a gradual response, V 'A summo caelo egressio eius', namely, after the first phrase, which ends on '-lo-', at the beginning of the second phrase, which is 'egressio [eius]', after the first syllable, which is 'e-', of the second phrase [namely on the second syllable], which is ['-gres-'] ...

In the latter instance, Aurelian uses *distinctio* for a grammatical unit. But in the former, *distinctio* refers to where the breaks or separations (that is, punctuation marks) occur within the text sense, implying secondarily where it is appropriate to place 'a longer melody' or melisma. Another treatise that allows for both grammatical and rhetorical meanings is the anonymous *Dialogus de musica*:

Distinctiones quoque, id est loca, in quibus repausamus in cantu, et in quibus cantum dividimus, ...[11]

The *distinctiones*, too, that is, the places at which we pause in a chant and at which we divide it ...

Several treatises attempt to distinguish musical phrases of different sizes through analogy to large and small language divisions. To quote Bower, 'Generally speaking, *distinctiones* are said to be broken down into *cola*, which, in turn, are broken down

---

[9]Lawrence Gushee, ed., *Aureliani Reomensis musica disciplina*, CSM 21 (Rome, 1975), pp. 97–98. My translation does not follow the edition's punctuation of 'cum potius conservandum'.

[10]*Ibid.*, pp. 98–99. I have adopted the phrase 'tremulous inflection' from Joseph Ponte's translation in Aurelian of Réome, *The Discipline of Music*, Colorado College Music Press Translations 3 (Colorado Springs, 1968), p. 34.

[11]*GS*, vol. 1, p. 257.

into *commata*, although the terms *comma* and *colon* are sometimes reversed in the hierarchy of parts'.[12] The *Scolica enchiriadis* attempts no systematic analogy between language and music, but simply appropriates the terms *cola* and *commata* for larger and smaller musical phrases, respectively.[13] The treatise found in Gerbert's *Scriptores*, vol. 1, pp. 265–302, under the title *De musica*, following the anonymous *Dialogus de musica*, refers to a larger range of constituent parts, namely *vox, syllaba, pars, distinctio*. A *vox* (pitch) would correspond to a letter in the writing of text. Although this anonymous author does not carry through the full range of language–music analogies, he introduces a concern with the way the constituents of any one subdivision relate to one another:

> ... si eius syllabas et partes ac distinctiones similes feceris, eius difficultatem tolli et dulcedinem augeri videbis ... [14]

> ... if you would make its syllables and parts and *distinctiones* similar, you will see that its difficulty is removed and its sweetness increased ...

Thus the author emphasizes the desirability of similar, balanced, phrasing, which is also the subject of Guido's *Micrologus*, chapter 15. Guido introduces the topic with an analogy between two hierarchies:

> Igitur quemadmodum in metris sunt litterae et syllabae, partes et pedes ac versus, ita in harmonia sunt phtongi, id est soni, quorum unus, duo vel tres aptatntur in syllabas; ipsaeque solae vel duplicatae neumam, id est partem constituunt cantilenae; et pars una vel plures distinctionem faciunt, id est congruum respirationis locum.[15]

---

[12]Bower, 'The Grammatical Model', p. 134.

[13]Hans Schmid, ed., *Musica et Scolica enchiriadis: una cum aliquibus tractatulis adiunctis: recensio nova post Gerbertinam altera ad fidem omnium codicum manuscriptorum*, VMK 3 (Munich, 1981), p. 83:

> Cola autem dicimus maiores particulas, duo seu tria vel plura commata continentes, quae et oportunas quasdam sui distinctiones prebent. Porro commata sibi in levationibus ac positionibus coherentia colon peragunt. Tamen est interdum, ubi indifferenter colon sive comma dici potest.'

This author follows *commata* with the qualifier 'which also display certain suitable *distinctiones* among themselves'. Here *distinctiones* appears to be used as a synonym for the non-technical word 'differences'.

[14]*GS*, vol. 1, p. 277; on p. 275 the author introduces his schema of *vox, syllaba, pars*, then continues:

> Distinctio vero in musica est, quantum de quolibet cantu continuamus, quae ubi vox requieverit, pronuntiatur. Item sicut una pars locutionis aut duae vel plures sensum perficiunt, et sententiam integram comprehendunt, ut cum dico *quid facis?* respondes *lego, sive lectionem firmo, sive aliquam sententiam quaero*: ita una, duae vel plures ex his musicae partibus versiculum, antiphonam vel responsorium perficiunt, nec tamen suorum numerorum significationem amittunt. Et sicut multae et diversae sententiae ad volumen usque concrescunt: ita multae et diversae cantilenae antiphonarum cumulatae perficiunt.

[15]Waesberghe, *Micrologus*, pp. 162–163.

Just as in verse there are letters and syllables, parts and feet and lines, so in music there are phtongi, that is, sounds, of which one, two, or three are grouped in syllables; one or two of the latter make a neume, which is a part of a song; and one or more parts make a phrase, that is, a suitable place to breathe.

This is to say that *litterae, syllabae, partes, pedes,* and *versus* in language correspond to *phtongi, syllabae, neumae,* and *distinctiones* in music. In Guido's hierarchy *distinctio* means a musical phrase. Like the author of the anonymous *De musica,* he stresses equal phrase lengths, but he also considers desirable proportional relationships between phrases. He talks about the increasingly longer *tenores* or 'holds' on the last notes of a *syllaba, pars,* and *distinctio,* respectively. In short, he gives a great deal of attention to details of performing a chant well.[16]

Earlier, in chapters 8, 11, and 13, Guido contributes a new context for discussing *distinctiones.* Chapter 8 introduces the equivocal reference to modes and *distinctiones* of modes. Chapter 11 presents the idea that the beginning of a chant, the end of all its phrases or *distinctiones,* and even their beginnings should 'cling' to the final pitch by relating to it through one of the six *consonantiae:*

Per supradictas nempe sex consonantias voci quae neumam terminat reliquae voces concordare debent. Voci vero quae cantum terminat principatum eius cunctarumque distinctionum fines vel etiam principia opus est adhaerere.[17]

The other pitches should have a harmonious relationship with the pitch that ends a neume by means of the six consonances already mentioned. The beginning of a chant and the end of all its phrases and even their beginnings should cling to the pitch that ends the chant.

Chapter 13 complements chapter 11 by specifying the range into which the beginnings and endings of *distinctiones* fall in authentic and plagal melodies:

... ut in plagis quidem minime licet vel principia vel fines distinctionum ad quintas intendere, cum ad quartas perraro soleat evenire. In autentis vero, praeter deuterum, eadem principia et fines distinctionum minime licet ad sextas intendere; plagae autem proti vel triti ad tertias intendunt, et plagae siquidem deuteri vel tetrardi ad quartas intendunt.[18]

Thus in plagal modes one may least of all rise either in beginnings or endings of phrases to the fifth degree [above the final], although one may very rarely rise to the fourth [degree]. In authentic modes, however, except the deuterus, one may least of all rise in these beginnings and endings of phrases to the sixth degree. However, those of

---

[16]*Ibid.* In the sentence 'Sunt vero quasi prosaici cantus qui haec minus observant, in quibus non est curae, si aliae maiores, aliae minores partes et distinctiones per loca sine discretione inveniantur more prosarum' (p. 171), 'distinctiones' may refer to phrase endings rather than to the phrase itself.

[17]*Ibid.,* p. 140.

[18]*Ibid.,* pp. 154–155.

plagal protus and tritus rise as high as the third, and those of the plagal deuterus and tetrardus rise as high as the fourth.

Guido states that beginnings or endings of *distinctiones* rise to the fifth or sixth above the final in authentic modes and to the third or fourth above the final in plagal modes. As Table 11.1 shows, the general rules of chapters 11 and 13 for beginnings and endings of *distinctiones* also appear in the anonymous *Dialogus de musica*, *De modorum formulis* (attributed to Guido by Coussemaker), and then later in Aribo and the anonymous *Quaestiones in musica*, whose author borrowed from Aribo, among others.[19]

Before taking up Guido's reference in chapter 8, I want to examine one other anonymous writing, *Modorum sive tonorum ordo*, found in Gerbert *Scriptores*, vol. 1, pp. 124b–125b, and re-edited by Hans Schmid. The author of *Modorum* enumerates relevant tetrachords and *distinctiones* for each of the eight modes. The following excerpt treats the second:

> Secundus tropus habet tetrachorda duo, meson et hypaton, distinctiones proprias parhypate hypaton [*C*], lichanos hypaton [*D*], aliquando mese [*a*] et lichanos meson [*G*], in propriam interdum et parypate meson [*F*]. Ipse namquam per sinemmena currit.[20]

Thus, the second mode has two tetrachords, meson and hypaton, proper *distinctiones* on *C D*, sometimes on *a* and *G*, sometimes on *F*. In the Ancient Greek Greater Perfect System, whose language the author has appropriated, the combined meson and hypaton tetrachords cover the range *B–a*, roughly the *A–a* octave expounded for this mode by later writers; as to the *distinctiones*, the writer presumably refers to phrase endings, for after enumerating relevant *distinctiones* for all eight modes he says:

> ... quia eodem modo distinguitur cantilena quo et sententia, quippe tenor spiritus humani per cola et commata discurrendo requiescit, verum cantilenae corpus arsi et thesi, id est, elevatione sonorum et positione, completur, donec periodo, id est clausula sive circuitu, suis membris distincta terminetur.[21]

---

[19]See *Dialogus de musica*, GS, vol. 1, pp. 257–258; *De modorum formulis*, in Edmond de Coussemaker, *Scriptorum de musica medii ævi novam seriem a Gerbertina alteram*, 4 vols (Paris, 1864–1876; reprinted Hildesheim, 1963), vol. 2, p. 81, also edited by Clyde W. Brockett in CSM 37 (Neuhausen, 1997), p. 58; Joseph Smits van Waesberghe, ed., *De musica Aribonis*, CSM 2 (Rome, 1951), pp. 13–15, 21, 53–54, 56; Rudolf Steglich, ed., *Die Quaestiones in Musica; ein Choraltraktat des zentralen Mittelalters und ihr mutmasslicher Verfasser, Rudolf von St. Trond (1070–1138)* (Leipzig, 1911), pp. 35–37. Aribo also refers to phrase similarity and balance, and *tenores* on phrase endings, in response to Guido's chapter 15; see *De musica Aribonis*, 48–51, 56, and 68–70; the *Quaestiones* author refers to the same issues, p. 62.

[20]See Schmid's edition of *Modorum sive tonorum ordo* in his volume *Musica et Scolica enchiriadis*, p. 182.

[21]*Ibid.*, p. 183.

... because a song is taken apart like a sentence, the tenor of the human breath certainly finds rest as it moves through *cola* and *commata*. Indeed the body of a song is put together from arsis and thesis, that is from the rising and falling of the sounds, until it is brought to a close through a period, that is, through a clausula or circumlocution set off through its members.

That is, this writer is concerned with constituent parts of a chant and how they end.

Berno, in his *De mensurando monochordo,* also enumerates specific tones for phrase endings, and he implies that in a given mode, beginnings of chants as well as *distinctiones* or phrase endings use these tones. This excerpt is taken from his discussion of mode two:

Secundus modus ascendit ad H., raro autem ad M.. vel I.; remittitur ad A.; possidens primam inter A. et H. diapason speciem, supra vero rarenter vocem. Et hi sunt primus magister eiusque discipulus. Magistri autem cantus incipitur sex nervis, scilicet C.D.E. F.G.H.; habet vero cola et commata, id est membra et incisiones, quas distinctiones cantus apppellamus, in eisdem.[22]

The second mode ascends to *H* [*a*], rarely however to *M* [*b natural*] or *I* [*b flat*]; it returns to *A*; possessing the first species of octave between *A* and *H* [*a*], it grows less above this pitch. And these are the master and its first follower. The chant of the master is begun however on six strings, namely *C D E F G H* [*a*]; it has cola and commas, that is clauses, which we call the *distinctiones* of chant, on these [enumerated tones].

We now turn to Guido's statement in chapter 8:

Omnes itaque modi distinctionesque modorum his tribus aptantur vocibus. Distinctiones autem dico eas, quae a plerisque differentiae vocantur. Differentia autem idcirco dicitur, eoquod discernat seu separet plagas ab autentis, caeterum abusive dicitur. Ergo omnes aliae voces cum his aliquam habent corcordiam, seu in depositione seu in elevatione, nullae vero in utroque se exhibent similes cum aliis, nisi in diapason. Sed horum similitudinem omnium in hac figura quam subiecimus, quisquis requisierit, reperire poterit.

And thus all modes and *distinctiones* of modes are connected with these three pitches [*C D E*]. But I use the word *distinctiones* in the sense that *differentiae* is used by others. But insofar as *differentia* is used in this way – that is, it defines or separates plagal chants from authentic – it is used improperly. Therefore all other pitches have some concordance with these three, whether in ascent or descent; but no pitches show themselves similar to other pitches in both directions, except at the octave. Anyone who seeks can find the similarity of all of these pitches in this diagram which follows.

In this context *distinctio* may simply mean a phrase, as it does in the later chapters 11, 13, and 15. Accordingly, one can translate *omnes itaque modi distinctionesque*

---

[22] Waesberghe, ed., *Bernonis Augiensis Abbatis de Arte musica disputationes tradita, Pars A. Bernonis Augiensis De mensurando monochordo*, Divitiae musicae artis A/6a (Buren, 1978), p. 111.

modorum his tribus aptantur vocibus as 'all modes and phrases of modes are connected with these three pitches', meaning that all phrase endings within a mode, whether final or not, are in consonant agreement with *C*, *D*, and *E*. This interpretation would support Guido's primary emphasis (in this chapter) on related tones, to which I shall return. But Guido's juxtaposition of the words *distinctiones* and *differentiae* may have an additional implication.

Used in a technical sense, *differentiae* refers to the formulas with which a psalm tone ends, identified by the words 'seculorum amen'; it is commonly held that they were provided in order to ensure the smooth transition between the last note of the psalm tones and the first note of the following antiphons. Beginning in the ninth century, antiphons were grouped according to *differentiae* in liturgical books called tonaries. According to the *New Grove* entry, 'Antiphons that belong to the same melodic family are usually assigned the same psalm termination. However, it is not clear whether the choice was made because of some structural characteristic of the antiphon's melody, or merely because antiphon and cadence were associated traditionally.'[23] In his article 'Tonaries and Melodic Families of Antiphons' Paul Merkley writes, 'Mode was a late imposition on chant, but the *differentiae*, or something like them, must have been intrinsic to the practice [of chant classification] from the earliest period on'.[24] Yet in some early tonaries (of which Paris, BNF lat. 4995 is a good example) only the *Noeane* texts[25] and a series of chant text incipits are present, without provision for 'seculorum amen' formulas. Merkley goes on:

> These chant incipits are identifiable with known antiphons, and the number of them for each mode suggests that each stands for a group of antiphons with a common melodic incipit, in other words, that each antiphon may be a *differentia*.

Furthermore, the early use of the word *differentia* was not linked exclusively to a 'seculorum amen' formula, but also could refer to 'a list of antiphons in a tonary' in which each antiphon represents a melodic family.[26] At the time of Guido's writings, both usages of the word *differentia* were current.[27] Returning to Guido's statement in chapter 8:

---

[23]Terence Bailey, in *NG2* online, Psalm, II, 7 (iv).

[24]Paul Merkley, 'Tonaries and Melodic Families of Antiphons', *Journal of the Plainsong and Mediaeval Music Society* 11 (1988), p. 17.

[25]Michel Huglo, in *NG* online, 'Tonary', 2, gives this explanation for *noeane*:

> Byzantine intonation formulae (*enechemata*), with nonsense 'words' set to them as identifications of the individual modes, are found in all tonaries until the mid-eleventh century, and in some as late as the 12th. These formulae end with long melismas on the 'words' noenoeane, for the authentic modes, and noeagis, for the plagal modes, and were introduced into Carolingian Francia.

[26]Merkley, 'Tonaries and Melodic Families', pp. 19, 23.

[27]One can draw this conclusion from the data provided by Merkley in 'Tonaries and Melodic Families', pp. 17–23.

But I use the word *distinctiones* in the sense that *differentiae* is used by others. But insofar as [the word] *differentia* is used in this way – that is, it [*differentia*] defines or separates plagal chants from authentic – it is used improperly.

In all of his writings, Guido never refers specifically to 'seculorum amen' formulas, so we can not be sure whether he intends *differentia* to mean such a formula or an antiphon melodic family in Merkley's sense.[28] But we do know that in the *Micrologus*, chapter 13, he refers to the melodic formulas beginning 'Primum quaerite regnum dei'[29] by which one recognizes the modes, then segues into his discussion of ranges for beginnings and endings of *distinctiones* in authentic versus plagal melodies. If Guido intended *differentiae* to have the technical meaning of endings of psalm tones, then he is saying that he considers it improper to use these endings as the criterion for separating authentic from plagal melodies. Instead, to distinguish authentic and plagal it is proper to use *distinctiones* – that is, to look at how all of a chant's phrases unfold in terms of melodic gesture and range. If this reading of Guido is correct, then he has also given us, parenthetically, a way of distinguishing authentic and plagal chants that is different from that used by cantors, who related an antiphon to its *differentia*.

I want now to consider the anonymous commentary on Guido's *Micrologus*, *Commentarius anonymus in Micrologum Guidonis Aretini*, edited first by Cölestin Vivell and re-edited by Smits van Waesberghe.[30] In the course of this treatise, the author systematically discusses what Guido meant in the *Micrologus*, including chapter 8. As though anticipating the question posed in the present article, he inserts several paragraphs preceding Guido's puzzling statement on *distinctiones*. He begins by relating *distinctiones* to mode:

Et distinctiones vocat modos per affinitatem, cum omnes modi distinctiones possint vocari.[31]

---

[28]In the *Micrologus* transmission, Waesberghe indicates that one thirteenth-century manuscript, Vienna, ONB, 2503, contains the gloss 'differentiae vocantur, hoc est saeculorum amen'. Waesberghe, *Micrologus*, p. 127.

[29]*Ibid.*, pp. 150–157. 'Primum quaerite' are model antiphons, introduced with the *noeane* intonation formulae and ultimately displacing them. These antiphons, of unknown origin (they were not drawn from liturgical books), are based on New Testament texts as a literary elaboration of the numbers of the modes. See Huglo, 'Tonary', 2.

[30]P. Cölestin Vivell, ed., *Commentarius anonymus in Micrologum Guidonis Aretini* (Vienna, 1917); Joseph Smits van Waesberghe, ed., *Expositiones in Micrologum Guidonis Aretini; Liber argumentorum, Liber specierum, Metrologus, Commentarius in Micrologum Guidonis Aretini*, Musicologica Medii Aevi 1 (Amsterdam, 1957). Desmond discusses the dating of this treatise in her article '*Sicut in grammatica*', pp. 474–475. Whereas Waesberghe dated it to between 1070 and 1100, Desmond states that it was probably contemporaneous with Aribo's *De musica*, citing a private communication with Gabriela Ilnitchi dating it earlier rather than later within Waesberghe's time frame.

[31]Waesberghe, *Expositiones*, p. 124.

And one calls *distinctiones* modes through affinity, because all modes can be called *distinctiones*.

Still puzzled, we then read,

> Legitimae enim finales omnes in authentis cantibus sunt et modi et distinctiones suorum cantuum; modi quia in ipsis finitur cantus, distinctiones vero sunt quia distinguunt plagas ab authentis, ut a .D. in .d. est per diapason legitimus cursus authenti proti, cum plagalis eius sit ab .A. in .a.; et similiter in aliis authentis erunt finales per naturam et distinctiones et modi. In plagis vero finales per affinitatem erunt distinctiones, sed non modi, ut in proto plagali ab .A. in .a. erit cursus eius distinctus, sed non in .A. erit finis cantus nisi omissa omnino plagalis natura fiat authentus, qui solus finalem suum debet habere et distinctionem cantus sui et modum.[32]

> All legitimate finals in authentic chants are both modes and *distinctiones* of their chants – modes because on these a chant is ended, *distinctiones* because they distinguish plagals from authentics, so that from *D* to *d* is, through the octave, the legitimate cursus of authentic protus, while its plagal is from *A* to *a*; and similarly in other authentics there will be natural finals and *distinctiones* and modes. However, in plagals finals through affinity are *distinctiones*, but not modes, so that in plagal protus from *A* to *a* will be its distinct cursus, but the end of a chant will not be on A unless, entirely by negligence, the nature of plagal should become authentic, which alone ought to have its final, the *distinctio* of its chant and mode.

According to this anonymous author, the *D* final of authentic protus also identifies the mode and the starting tone or *distinctio* of the octave cursus *D* to *d*. For a plagal mode, however, its *distinctio* does not match up with its mode or final: thus, plagal protus has an *A* to *a* cursus, but the starting tone or *distinctio* of that cursus, *A*, is not the natural final or mode; rather *D* plays that role.[33]

Holding this opinion, the author then glosses Guido's statement as follows:

> *Omnes modi* naturales, ut .F.G., *et distinctiones modorum*, ut .a.b [natural], *aptantur* per aliquam concordiam *his tribus vocibus* .C.D.E. gravibus et acutis. Et bene liber has quattuor .F.G.a.b [natural]. dicit omnes modos et distinctiones, quia post .C.D.E., quibus has dicit concordare, non sunt aliae voces praeter illas quattuor.[34]

> All natural modes such as *F G*, and *distinctiones* of modes such as *a b* [*natural*], are adapted through some concordance to these three pitches *C D E*, graves and acutae. And the book is quite right to call these four, *F G a b* [*natural*], all the modes and *distinctiones*, because after *C D E*, with which it says these are in concord, there are no other pitches except those four.

---

[32]*Ibid.*, pp. 124–125.

[33]For a discussion of my understanding of 'finales per affinitatem' see my *The Affinities and Medieval Transposition* (Bloomington, IN, 1987), p. 33.

[34]Waesberghe, *Expositiones*, p. 126.

The anonymous author reminds us that *F* and *G* are natural finals, and then refers to *a* and *b* *[natural]* as *distinctiones* – in his terms, starting points of octave cursus, but not natural finals. At this point, we might consider the anonymous author's explanation of Guido's meaning reasonable, except for the fact that Guido does not speak in terms of octave cursus; in chapter 13 he mentions the usual range of authentics as an octave or a ninth, or even a tenth; plagals go down and up a fifth. He does not refer solely to the octave, but recognizes approximately an octave span for each mode.

To return to the anonymous commentary, its author next extrapolates on Guido's statement juxtaposing *distinctiones* and *differentiae*. The commentator acknowledges that *distinctiones* do, in fact, distinguish authentic and plagal chants:

> *Differentia autem dicitur* quaelibet vox dicta distinctio, ut .a.b [natural]., *eo quod discernat*, quia cum eisdem speciebus diatessaron et diapente constat quilibet plagalis quibus et authentus, tamen per distinctionem hoc modo discernitur alter ab altero, quod omnis plagalis eandem speciem diatessaron habet sub finali quam authentus habet post diapente super finalem.[35]

> But *differentia* is used for any named *distinctio* pitch such as *a b* *[natural]* for the reason that it distinguishes, because while any authentic and its plagal accord with the same species of diatessaron and diapente; yet this is the way one is distinguished from the other, namely that each plagal has the same species of diatessaron under the final as the authentic has, after the diapente, above the final.

So, a modal *distinctio* indicates an octave cursus, whose constituent diatessaron and diapente are arranged in a way that 'distinguishes' it as authentic or plagal. If the diatessaron is on top, the mode is authentic; if the diatessaron is on the bottom, the mode is plagal. Furthermore, the exchange of diatessaron and diapente creates a different octave species. Thus, within the *D* to *d* cursus for authentic protus, the diapente *D–a* is topped by the diatessaron *a–d*; when the positions are exchanged, so that *A–D* is on the bottom, the new octave species is *A–a*, the cursus for plagal protus.[36]

With this our dilemma grows greater. Guido understood completely the integral relationship of diatessaron and diapente to the octave: in chapter 5 of *Micrologus* he states that the diapason is the interval created when a diapente and diatessaron are combined, and this understanding resurfaces in chapter 18, when he presents the

---

[35]*Ibid.*, p. 126.

[36]Wilhelm of Hirsau used the terminology differently, in that he applied *distinctio* to the dividing point of the octave cursus, that is, where the constituent diapente and diatessaron intersect: 'Autenticus protus qui est a D. in d. mediam distinctionem habet in a. Subiugalis eius qui est ab A. in a. mediam distinctionem ponit in D. Qui si iungantur, ut indifferenter sit protus, ascendit ab A. in d. duas continens distinctiones medias, id est D. et a'. Denis Harbinson, ed., *Willehelmi Hirsavgensis Musica*, CSM 23 (1975), p. 33. Wilhelm allows that the authentic and plagal forms may be combined, in which case there are two *distinctiones* for that particular mode; in this case protus from *A* to *d* has *distinctiones* on *D* and *a*.

principles of organum.[37] But nowhere in any of his treatises does he use the species terminology that appears in the anonymous commentary. Thus we are left with a speculation that Guido could have conceived of *distinctio* as the starting tone of the distinguishing octave for each mode, whether or not he recognized the octave's constituent diatessaron and diapente.

The anonymous commentator ends his discussion as follows:

> Dixi causam quare distinctiones vocentur differentiae; *caeterum*, id est sed tamen est dictum *abusive*, quia non est in usu apud musicos ut distinctiones differentiae vocentur[38]

> I have given the reason why *distinctiones* are called *differentiae*; there is 'another' teaching, but notwithstanding, it is 'improper' that *distinctiones* are not usually called *differentia* by musicians.

Thus the anonymous commentator dismisses the use of the word *differentiae* for the concept of *distinctiones* (as he defines it). Unfortunately, he provides no verification for our understanding that *differentiae* are psalm-tone endings. Certainly the paragraph at issue is not one of Guido's clearest expositions, but the commentary on it is noteworthy for its thoroughness.[39] If the commentator is right that Guido used *distinctio* to mean the starting tone of an octave cursus, we have tapped into another aspect of Guido's theory.

I turn now to Guido's accompanying figure with focus on *C D E*, shown in Figure 11.1. Richard Crocker took the view that Guido was arguing for only three finals rather than the traditional four on *D E F G*, and that Guido considered only the immediate ascent from the final, that is, up two tones from *C*, up a tone and semitone from *D*, and up a semitone and tone from *E*. All other pitches mimic one of these.[40] For several reasons, I disagree with Crocker's conclusion. In the first place, chants are not restricted to two degrees above the final, and movement below the final has to be considered as well: thus *F* (which has a semitone below) and *G* (with a tone below) cannot be conflated with *C*. Secondly, in chapter 11 of the same treatise Guido states that there are four modal finals, *D*, *E*, *F*, and *G*. Thirdly, in his last treatise, the *Epistola*, Guido still stresses the importance of four modal categories, and is reluctant even there to discard a traditional means of identifying a chant's mode by matching up its ending with well-known melodic formulas (such as 'Primum querite') that link to

---

[37]See Waesberghe, *Micrologus*, pp. 107–113, 196–208.

[38]Waesberghe, *Expositiones*, pp. 126–127.

[39]This thoroughness compares with that of another anonymous writer whose work *Liber specierum* is edited by Waesberghe in the same volume, *Expositiones*, pp. 31–58. The author writes simply: 'Chapter 36. De distinctionibus: "Quod sunt distinctiones? Distinctiones autem dico eas quae a plerisque differentiae vocantur." Chapter 37. De differentia.: "Quid est differentia? Differentia autem idcirco dicitur eo quod discernat seu separet plagas ab autentis; ceterum abusive dicitur"' (p. 50).

[40]Richard Crocker, 'Hermann's Major Sixth', *JAMS* 25 ([s. l.], 1972), pp. 24–25.

the four finals on *D E F* and *G*.[41] Finally, the immediate context for the *C D E* diagram, that is, what precedes in chapters 7 and 8 and what follows in chapter 9, has to do primarily with how pitches are related and secondarily with the applicability of that relationship to mode.[42]

Figure 11.1: Diagram at the end of *Micrologus*, chapter 8

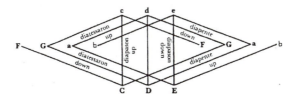

Specifically, in chapter 7 Guido links *D E F* with the respective pitches a fourth below (that is, *A B C*) and a fifth above (that is, *a b natural c*); each pair of tones such as *D* and *A* (*a*) shares a particular configuration of tones and semitones within the range of a sixth – Guido says that each pair shares an *affinitas*. In chapter 8, Guido adds that there are other related pitches: *E* with *a* and *G* with *C* and *D* – what he calls *aliae affinitates* or 'other affinities.' Guido introduces chapter 8 with this statement:

Si quae aliae sunt affinitates, eas quoque similiter diatessaron et diapente fecerunt.[43]

Whatever other affinities there are, they are produced likewise by the diatessaron and the diapente.

Thus, at the outset of the chapter and in the diagram that ends it, Guido stresses the relationship of tones separated by fourths and fifths. Why does he put *C D E* as the central focus?

Simply put, *C*, *D*, and *E* are the three contiguous pitches in the gamut that neatly summarize all these affinities. The neatness lies in the fact that the primary shared movement with the pitch a fifth above is an ascent, and with the pitch a fourth above, a descent. As Figure 11.2 shows, *C* shares ascent of a sixth with *G* and descent of a fourth with *F*; *D* shares ascent of a fifth with *a* and descent of a fifth with *G*; *E* shares ascent of a fourth with *b natural* and descent of a sixth with *a*. Since *F* shares movement only with *C*, and *B* only with *E*, neither the contiguous tones *A*, *B*, and *C* nor *D*, *E*, and *F* would encompass all the relationships that *C*, *D*, and *E* do.

---

[41]See my *Guido d'Arezzo's* Regule rithmice, pp. 498–509.

[42]See my discussion, *ibid.*, pp. 20–27.

[43]Waesberghe, *Micrologus*, p. 122.

Figure 11.2: Shared movements between pitches

	with pitch a fifth above			with pitch a fourth above
C	G	(share ascent of a sixth)	F	(share descent of a fourth)
D	a	(share ascent of a fifth)	G	(share descent of a fifth)
E	[*b natural*]	(share ascent of a fourth)	a	(share descent of a sixth)

In conclusion, we can with some degree of certainty understand why Guido placed *C*, *D*, and *E* in a central position within his Chapter 8 diagram. He had recognized their pivotal position in summarizing the *affinitates* among the seven pitches, an understanding that he reinforced with the words, 'all other pitches have some concordance with these three ...'. His earlier allusion to 'all modes and *distinctiones* of modes' continues to puzzle. He most likely meant, in the loosest sense, all phrase endings within a chant, whether final or not; or he may have understood a *distinctio* as the starting tone of an octave cursus that identifies mode, as explained by the anonymous commentator. The latter would suggest a focus on the octave that has not been attributed to Guido. I remain open to this possibility. But perhaps as significantly, my study has shown that a writer after Guido worked to reconcile Guido's theory of related tones to his own octave-oriented concept of mode. He did so successfully and his theory deserves further study.

Chapter 12

The musical text of the introit *Resurrexi*

David Hughes

The introit *Resurrexi*, idiomelic like most others, has a musical text that varies from one source to another in much the same way as other chants do – the variants are rarely (in this case never) of any musical consequence, and are scattered about in what seems to be a largely random fashion. In *Resurrexi*, however, the music shows what appears at first to be a rather striking peculiarity. Of its four phrases (three really, plus the double alleluia at the end), the first and last are relatively stable in their transmission, with only a few variants, while the second and third have noticeably more variants, to the extent where almost every place that has left written music preserves a very slightly different form of the melody at some point or other in those phrases. The aim of this study is to examine first what sorts of melodic differences may be found in the variants and how their presence may be explained, and, second, why different parts of the same chant were received differently. I should make it clear at the outset that these questions are indeed going to be examined, and not necessarily answered.

The basis for the remarks following has been the collation of a fairly large number of manuscripts (about one hundred and ten). I do not think that a larger collation would significantly change my conclusions. The emphasis has been on French manuscripts of the eleventh century or later, but the earliest French sources as well as early ones from other areas (notably those from St Gall and Bamberg) have been available and were consulted as seemed appropriate. A list of the French manuscripts and their sigla as used here will be found in the Appendix.

It will be useful to begin with an analysis of the melody. (The reader will find the whole of *Resurrexi* in Example 12.1, with the musical text of the famous Dijon mass-tonary, Montpellier, H. 159. The division of the example into numbered segments, mostly of one syllable each, will make subsequent discussion easier.) The chant is in the deuterus plagal mode, with a final on *e*. Like many chants in this mode – and indeed more than most – the melody is 'about' the conflict between the final *e* and the *f* a second above, which is the principal tone from any reasonable point of view. Now this already opens a rather dangerous door: the replacement of *e* by *f* is one of the commonest of melodic variants (it will be discussed later). Indeed it might be argued that deuterus chants have a greater tendency towards variance than the chants of other maneriae, in part for that reason.

Example 12.1: Introit, *Resurrexi*, Dijon mass-tonary, Montpellier, H. 159

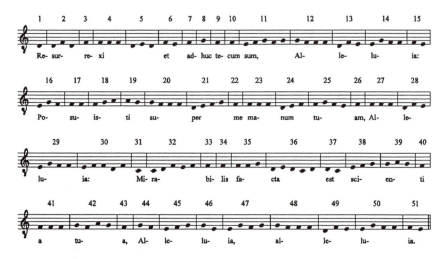

The first phrase establishes the critical third *df* in the first ten segments, then abruptly asserts *eg* in the eleventh, to descend stepwise from the *g* to the *e* at the alleluia (12–15), using a cadence typical of *e*-mode chants. All this at least is straight-forward enough: it serves to introduce the principal actors, the *f* and the *e*, decorated, as is so often the case, by thirds. The second phrase slightly expands the range, introducing the new third *fa*, and then retreating to *df*. The pivotal *f* is now surrounded by thirds on either side, again a common procedure. The concluding alleluia of the second phrase (28–30) begins as a repetition of the first alleluia, but with the ending on *e* replaced by an alternating *df* figure. This functions as a kind of deceptive cadence, both creating variety and averting a premature sense of finality that might have arisen had the normal cadence been used again. The third phrase expands the range still further, this time down to *c*, and its first half (31–37) seems to have the palindromic outline *cdfdc*. Thus the *d*, essentially an ornamental tone below *f*, is now itself ornamented, not by a lower third, for obvious reasons, but by a second. The second part (38–43) has the shape *egfgf*. As in the first phrase, the ascent to *g* permits the deployment of the standard cadence, and the final double alleluia (44–51) recalls the alleluia at the end of the first phrase. This all seems clear enough: I cannot see any problems with the analysis, nor indeed any other reasonable way in which the piece might be read. But also I cannot see much reason for the middle phrases to vary while the outer ones are relatively stable. Of course the inner phrases expand the range somewhat, and the more notes one uses the more chance there is for variation. But surely this is restricted to the details, and any sudden larger-scale variation must be owing to these details, for the overall shape does not appear to allow for it.

What sorts of variants might we expect to find in a chant? Naturally this is a question that has been discussed before,[1] but a brief restatement may be convenient. First let us consider the troublesome matter of the change from *e* to *f* (or *b* to *c*). It is generally considered that this is primarily a chronological and geographic phenomenon: early manuscripts, especially, though not exclusively, Aquitanian and Beneventan ones, have the lower notes (*es* and *bs*, deuterus tones, as I have called them[2]), while later, and especially Eastern, ones have the higher.[3] This is in a general way true enough, but there are innumerable instances that contradict the general rule. It is precisely such instances that prevent us from merely ignoring variants of this type with the comment, 'But this is a late manuscript so, of course, it has *f*'. At most one can say, 'But this is manuscript X, and X almost always has *f*', emphasizing the 'almost'. Obviously, however, a chant anchored on the thirds *df* and *eg* is overwhelmingly likely to show such variants, whatever their cause (one might compare the *g*-mode introit *Puer natus*, where such semitonal variants are scarcely to be found). It should also be noted that it is frequently (not always) impossible to detect variants of this sort in *adiastematic* manuscripts.

Unlike the problematic *e/f* variant, the others make for relatively plain sailing. The commonest is without doubt the change between a third progressions, scalewise and open. This is commonest in minor thirds, particularly those of the DF or AC species, and perhaps commoner in ascending than in descending motion.[4] (The term 'filling of a third' is often used, and is perfectly reasonable if one empties it of any notion of priority.) Following this, in no particular order, we find: the insertion or omission of an anticipation (e.g. D FG versus D DFG), the insertion or omission of an auxiliary (CDF F versus CDFE F), changes of pitch other than E to F, and finally addition or subtraction of one or more notes other than anticipations or auxiliaries (e.g. DEFG versus DG).[5] This catalogue is sufficient for a consideration of *Resurrexi*. Although much less

---

[1]See my 'Evidence for the Traditional View of the Transmission of Gregorian Chant', *JAMS* 40 (1987), pp. 383–386, and, more recently, Manuel Pedro Ferreira, 'Music at Cluny: The Tradition of Gregorian Chant for the Proper of the Mass. Melodic Variants and Microtonal Nuances', (Ph.D. diss., Princeton University, 1997), pp. 142–150. There are of course many other contributions to this subject, notably the numerous studies by Leo Treitler.

[2]Notably in my 'Guido's *Tritus*: An Aspect of Chant Style', in *FS Levy*, pp. 207–221.

[3]See Luigi Agustoni, 'Die Frage der Tonstufen SI und MI', *Beiträge zur Gregorianik* 4 (1987), pp. 47–101, and (especially) Dom Joseph Gajard, 'Les récitations modales des 3ᵉ et 4ᵉ modes dans les manuscrits bénéventains et aquitains', *EG* 1 (1954), pp. 9–45.

[4]Since the thirds favoured for this variant are those containing Es and Bs, it is entirely possible that there is a connection between the two types of variants. Until and unless this can be established, however, it will be better to treat them separately.

[5]I do not include here, as I did earlier, a separate category consisting of the reassignment of a note or group of notes to a different syllable. The manuscripts are often unclear about what notes go with which syllable, and it seems safer to treat each case on its own merits. As always, in the absence of a clear difference, no variant is assumed. When it is clear that one manuscript has, say, *fg fff* and another *f gfff* the readings will be treated as two separate variants.

often, many chants (including this one) show more aggressive changes, which can only be regarded as recompositions on a small scale.[6]

One needs to know one further characteristic of the non-semitonal variants: the overwhelming majority occur in only one or a very few sources. There are of course many exceptions, and we shall see a number of them shortly. But by and large the variants are abnormalities: of the 150 or so readings found in *Resurrexi*, about seventy per cent occur in three or fewer sources, and over fifty per cent in only one. Moreover, when three manuscripts share a reading, the chances are very good that they are *not* three related manuscripts – three from Chartres, for example, or from Paris – but rather three manuscripts without discernible interconnections. In *Resurrexi* we find Par3, Lig2, and Cha2 sharing a reading, or Par6, Sno1, and a manuscript from Verona. Again, there are exceptions, often important ones, but they are just that: exceptions to the normal rule. The implications of this are obvious. If Par3, Lig2, and Cha2 alone hit on a specific reading (in the event, the replacement of the *dfd* in segment 2 by *dfe*), and if (as is the case) we can show that this is a random grouping of inherently unrelated manuscripts, then the three sources must have adopted the reading independently, whether as a matter of preference or as a mere error. Sometimes the sources sharing a reading permit a possible but not necessary grouping. Thus for segment 6 one reading has five witnesses: Cam5, Kin, Ric2, Tie, and Vaa1. All of these but Tie are manuscripts from Picard monasteries. This leads one to assume that it is a local Picard reading, but the absence from the list of other sources with the same sort of provenance leaves the matter in some doubt all the same.

In what follows the readings found in very few sources will be given relatively little attention, except where they appear to be attempts at recomposing a part of the melody. Otherwise, whether they are correct notations of slightly aberrant singing traditions, or mere errors (or descendants of earlier errors) they do not seem to lead anywhere. Their only importance – if indeed it is an importance – is that they augment the number of readings in whatever segment they occur, and this may possibly have something so say about the perceived difficulty of the musical text at those points.[7]

---

[6] A spectacular example of recomposition may be found in the cadences of the *Alleluia Dies sanctificatus*. See my 'The Alleluias *Dies sanctificatus* and *Vidimus stellam* as Examples of Late Chant Transmission', *Journal of the Plainsong and Medieval Music Society* 7 (1998), pp. 1–28.

[7] If such readings are in fact errors it is curious that they are never corrected: I have yet to see a marginal or other indication that the musical text is wrong in one or two particular notes. Corrections do appear in the rare instances where a larger section of the chant is inadvertently omitted. When minor variants occur, did the singers perform the unusual reading anyway? Or did the cantor teach the proper version to his choir despite the reading of the manuscript? Indeed the whole notion of 'error' needs more attention than it has received. A scribe is un-likely to have looked at a pes and written a virga. Perhaps he *heard* the virga without looking at the exemplar at all. Or perhaps the 'error' goes back to a local variation antedating the surviving manuscripts from that place. (And of course behind that lurks the evil question: how did the variation arise?)

When the number of sources is somewhat larger the same random appearance of the sources often persists. Thus for one of the readings in segment 2 we find twenty-two manuscripts, namely Agv1, Agv2, Cam5, Cat4, Cha5, Cyr, Far, Kin, Mor3, Mor4, Niv1, Nof, Noy1, Pro3, Pro4, Que, Ric2, Sno1, Sno3, Sno4, Sno6, and Tur3. Clearly the reading was at home in Sens, but otherwise about the best that can be said for such a list is that it contains no Norman or Parisian sources. Most of it appears wholly miscellaneous. As a result, those who examine variants in the hope of finding relationships among sources will often come away – at least as far as the later manuscripts may be concerned – with nearly empty hands. Still, even miscellany is not necessarily neutral, and a study of the musical variants in *Resurrexi* is not wholly without meaning.

It may be convenient to begin with the first – relatively stable – incise, and examine what we find there. The opening *d* seems to have no competitors.[8] Since the *d* is not a tone of theoretical importance in the deuterus, this is vaguely encouraging: at least in pitch-specific manuscripts, no one seems to have been playing modal games with the music by making the chant begin on its final. Segment 2 represents the opposite end of the spectrum, and for a fairly obvious reason. Dij1 has *dfd* here – not merely one third but two, virtually inviting scribes[9] to add internal passing tones.[10] Their response was predictable. We find *fd* (twenty sources), *defed* (twenty-two), and *dfed* (thirty). Oddly, *defd* seems not to occur, but several other readings do: *fd*, to avoid repeating the opening *d* (fifteen sources); *dfe*, raising the second *d* to *e* (three); *efed* (again avoiding the first *d*), and the curious *ffe*, the latter two with only one witness apiece. In short, there are three readings that command significant support (amounting altogether to more than half of the manuscripts), and three others that are isolated. But this was surely a very tempting place.

Segment 3 is also inviting. Dij1 has a single *f*, and one might expect that some sources would have *e* instead. Indeed there are some that do, but only five where the note can be unequivocally identified: Alb, Tou, and Yrx from Aquitaine, and Clu2 and Rem2 from the north. Again, it is possible that the adiastematic sources conceal other traditions in which *e* was sung, but they cannot now be discovered. Segment 4, generally a tristropha on *f*, seems virtually invariable (I have not, however, counted repercussions): only Tie replaces the strophic neume with a little turn around *f – efgf –* and since Tie has the original unfilled thirds of segment 2, this reading is not without a certain merit. Segment 5 is another opportunity for an *e/f* variant, but only six manuscripts, none of them Aquitanian, elect to raise the *e*. No doubt the majority understand that there is already enough emphasis on *f*.

This brings us to the end of the first half-phrase, in which the only point of significant variation was the tempting thirds of segment 3. The second half, segments

---

[8] 'Seems to have' is necessary here, since the unheightened sources may perfectly well conceal a pitch variation not preserved in later versions.

[9] For the sake of simplicity, I shall use 'scribe' here to designate the person responsible for the version actually sung, whether it was in fact the copyist, or the cantor, or someone else.

[10] Here it would seem that the unfilled version is in fact the earlier, since it is compatible with the notation of the earliest sources, including the Eastern ones.

6–11, is also fairly stable. The only variant reading with significant support is in segment 7, where over sixty manuscripts add an anticipatory g to the f on the first syllable of *adhuc*. Like the passing tones in segment 2, this is a perfectly acceptable ornament. Also, in segment 9, fourteen manuscripts have g instead of f, delaying the f by a syllable. This too seems relatively harmless. In segment 11, no variant readings at all are found, at least in these manuscripts. This says something for the musicality of the scribes: while perhaps the exact shape of the figure here is not critical, the arrival on the pitches *efg* certainly is, since it is the first unequivocal assertion of the E mode. The unanimity is impressive.

It is so also in the alleluia that follows. There are one or two variant readings with few witnesses in segments 12 and 13, but only in 14 is there a more serious disagreement. Here several of the adiastematic sources have a torculus resupinus, signifying a rise, a fall, and another rise before the final *fe* of segment 15. Now the majority reading *egff* is clearly incompatible with this pattern, since it replaces the rise of a second with a unison. Fortunately a few of the diastematic manuscripts give what is almost certainly the solution: they have *egef*.[11] A few sources give still another version, *fgff*, raising the first *e*, and producing what to my ear is a less satisfying cadence.

Beginning with the next phrase, there are more readings altogether, and, notably, more competing readings with significant manuscript support. Of the five occurring in segment 16, one – *fgf* for *egf* – is supported in seventy sources. (Of course, adiastematic sources may also have it, but there is no way of telling.) In the very next segment, another sixty-odd manuscripts agree on a reading, in this case *ef* rather than *ff*. It may come as no surprise that the majority (though by no means all) of those with the first variant also have the second: the f in segment 16 apparently made the bistropha *ff* seem redundant (although there are many chants that have such figures). This introduces a complexity of method. In cases like the present one, the presence of a specific reading in segment n increases the probability of another specific reading in segment n +1 (or, much less often, some later point). When that increase approaches one hundred per cent we should then speak of a single variant, not two. The issue is of relevance

---

[11]Fortunately also the same variation appears in many other chants, all of which confirm that *egef* is the closest approximation that may be represented on a staff. This common *e*-mode cadence may often have been sung with the third note slightly 'sharpened' in early times. Whether it was merely the general tendency to replace *e* with *f* that caused the change, or whether other forces were at work is at present unknown. But the pitch of the *e* within this neume may have been uncertain – a bit sharper, perhaps, than the usual *e*, leading naturally enough to the unison version. There is a certain literature on the use of pitches smaller than a semitone in chant. See for example Joseph Gmelch, *Die Vierteltonstufen im Messtonale von Montpellier*, Veröffentlichungen der gregorianischen Akademie zu Freiburg 6 (Eichstatt, 1911); Dom Jacques Froger, 'Les prétendus quarts de ton dans le chant grégorien et les symboles du ms H. 159 de Montpellier', *EG* 17 (1978), pp. 145–179; Ferreira, 'Music at Cluny', pp. 236–276; and my own 'An Enigmatic Neume', in Bell Yung and Joseph S. C. Lam, eds, *Themes and Variations: Writings on Music in Honor of Rulan Chao Pian* (Cambridge MA, 1994), pp. 24–29.

here, since it is precisely in this phrase and the succeeding one that variant readings seem abnormally numerous. While there remains the same number of readings, it now appears that at least a large part of the support for the *ef* reading in segment 17 was inevitable: the *fgf* of the preceding segment requires it. The number of significant variants thus decreases by one.

Much the same point is made by segments 17 and 18 taken together. Those sources having the *ef* reading in 17 overwhelmingly do *not* have the *efga* (rather than *fga*) in the next. The scribes correctly see that two consecutive syllables beginning *ef* are not desirable at this point in the chant. Instead they write *effga*, or much more often, *efga*. Virtually every manuscript then continues in segment 19 with *gag* rather than the *ag* of Dij1. More than forty manuscripts agree on the same readings over all four segments (16–19), so that one could very nearly speak of the block of segments as a single point of variance rather than four.

With segment 21 we come to one of the most fertile points of the phrase: there are in all ten different readings, most of them with only weak manuscript support. The reading of Dij1, with slightly fewer than half the sources, is an obvious temptation: *defg*, preceded by a tristropha on *f* in segment 20. The most obvious variation on this is the omission of the *e* in the third, and in fact fifty-five manuscripts have *dfg* (not one has *deg*: one's sense that this is unnatural is shared by the scribes). Far behind in frequency come the readings with only two notes, led by *fg*, used in Paris and in four miscellaneous sources. Most of the eleven manuscripts having this reading have already added a *d* to the tristropha on *f* in the preceding segment: hence their sequence of notes is the same as that of the *dfg* manuscripts, but slightly displaced in time. Some unheightened manuscripts also have two rising notes, but since there are witnesses as well for *eg*[12] and *df* one cannot be sure what they intend. And finally there is an assortment of readings with only one or two witnesses: these include *fgf, dfe, def, dfgf,* and so on. All of them are perfectly possible musically, but their isolated occurrences make it likely that they are no more than aberrations even so.

In the next segment (22) the single *f* looks ripe for replacement by *e*, but only two of the French sources, the Aquitanian Alb and Yrx, do this.[13] Since most of the manuscripts have ended the previous segment on *g*, they clearly wish to avoid the *ge* connection here just before another tristropha on *f*. The latter (segment 23) is quite uniform, except that twenty-five manuscripts attach a *d* to the end of it, and then leave out the *d* at the beginning of the next segment. But in this segment (24) Dij1 has *def*, and almost fifty sources *df* only. These latter, added to the twenty-five sources just mentioned, reduce the *def* reading to minority status. There are also two other readings for this segment, *ef* and *dfe*, each with only one witness.

---

[12]This improbable reading occurs in only two closely related manuscripts, Rop and Bec, and is probably part of a local singing tradition.

[13]It is possible that Per1 can be read as having an *e* here, but the heightening of the manuscript is not dependable enough to be anywhere near sure. Given the absence of any other northern sources with the reading, it seems better to assume that Per1 has the usual *f*.

Segments 25 and 26 establish a deceptive cadence on *f* that will then lead to an alleluia with an even more deceptive cadence. The first of these segments is another case of multiple readings with weak manuscript support. There are five altogether, replacing the *fgfe* of Dij1 with *egfe, fgf, gf, fg*, and even *g* alone. Of these, *gf* has fifteen witnesses, including all the Paris manuscripts; *fg* is the Sens reading, and the rest are either unica or miscellaneous. There is some regionality there, but the twelve manuscripts with an *e* reading in segment 26 are another odd assortment, with Alb and Yrx from Aquitaine and a miscellany of northern sources. Too many, I should think, for a mere error. Perhaps modal thinking is involved here: the phrase *ought* to end on *e*, the more so since the alleluia following does not.

The real deceptive cadence is made in the following segments. Segments 27 and 28 repeat in inverse order the *dfe* and [*g*]*fff* found in 13 and 14 to prepare for the standard *egff fe*. As before, the *egff* is *egef* in some early sources, whereas *fgff*, which had four witnesses in the first cadence, now has thirty-four. While the list is again miscellaneous, with sources ranging from Lyon to the Channel coast, such a large number shows that the reading is not pure accident. It would be my guess that here the scribes are looking ahead to the *dffdf* of segment 30 and harmonizing, so to speak, segment 29 with those pitches: this is not going to be an E cadence, they think, so why make one here? In any event, segment 30 brings the 'deception' – the *dffdf*.[14] There are eight other readings, but none with more than two witnesses. Even filling in the opening third attracts only three sources, all early ones. Two unrelated manuscripts, Otu2 and Par12, share a reading that results from either error or stubbornness: they have *fe* (Otu2 is *adiastematic*, but these are probably the pitches intended). This of course replaces the deceptive cadence with the standard cadence used to end the other phrases. Did two scribes merely look at the wrong places in their exemplar? Or did they independently decide that *fe* was the correct cadence for any phrase of this chant on *e*? Meanwhile Foi alone has recomposed the cadence entirely: segment 29 reads *fffe* (or *fffd*: the last note is an uncertain liquescent), and 30 *ded*. Perfectly musical, to be sure, but one wonders where the idea came from – certainly this is not an 'error'. Again, a figure with a total of three minor thirds is a likely target for variation, but in this case few of the variants involve filling either of them.

The final phrase introduces the note *c* for the first time, and it is surely no accident that the single note *c* of segment 31 and the *c* that opens a four- to six-note group in 32 are both unanimously copied.[15] The rising figure in segment 32 is also nearly unanimous, although there are three variants with one witness each. Segments 33 and 34, repeated *f*s in northern manuscripts, are *es* in Aquitaine, not surprisingly. The un-

---

[14]These are the pitches given by Dij1. In its neumatic notation, it has a trigon plus a virga. Two St Gall sources have a trigon here also. The translation of the trigon, an obscure and difficult neume, into a unison plus a third below is the orthodox Solesmes interpretation. But see my 'An Enigmatic Neume', *passim*, for other possibilities.

[15]Another blow to the theory that error is the primary cause of variants. If variant readings are no more than random errors in copying, why do they cease at important points like this one and segment 11 earlier?

heightened sources may also have intended *e*, but there is no way of knowing. Segment 35 neatly demonstrates the danger of simple solutions. The reading of Dij1 is *ffg*, and one might expect the Aquitanian sources to have *efg*. In fact they do not, but keep to the *ffg*, while over sixty northern sources do in fact have *efg*. Thus, while in fact Aquitanian manuscripts often have *es* and *bs* where northern ones raise these by a semitone, there are cases where the reverse is true. Both sets of readings seem to be musically satisfactory, and for the same reason. The northern and Aquitanian manuscripts follow the two recitational notes (*f*) in segments 33 and 34 differently. The reader may wish to try the effect of *f f ffg* or *e e efg*. Both seem to me less than convincing, even though the first is the reading of Dij1 and many other manuscripts.

Segments 36 and 37 now make the medial cadence marking the end of the first half of this phrase. In all cases but one this is on *c* (the exception is an *e* in Evr3: this looks like an error, but probably is not: see below), and the preparation is a turning figure around *d*. The latter is of five notes in most manuscripts, but 35 expand it in various ways to six or seven. Most of the Parisian sources have the seven-note version, as do the two each from Cambrai and Noyon. It was therefore probably a part of earlier singing traditions of those places, not merely a random alteration.

The melody needs now only to mount from the *c* up to *g* to prepare the final descent to *e* on the twofold alleluia that will conclude the text. There are only six syllables in which to do this, so the motion must take place quickly. The universal solution is to climb up to the *g* at once, in segment 38, then ornament it with *f* and *a*. Thus the normal form of segment 38 is *efg*, leading to more *g* in the next segment. About twenty-five manuscripts have four notes instead of three, either *cefg* or *defg* (there are some *adiastematic* sources where one cannot be sure which is meant). Neither of these variants creates a problem: one merely repeats the preceding cadence tone, and the other fills the third between *c* and *e*. The shorter form, *ef*, seems less convincing, and is found only in Cat4, a manuscript abounding in unique readings, many of them even odder than this one. Two others deserve mention. It was noted that Evr3 stood alone in making the previous cadence on *e* instead of *c*. Here it stands with only two other manuscripts (Lig3 and Noy2) in replacing the turning figure around *d* with the single note *g*. It rather looks as if Evr3 has recomposed the phrase (not perhaps wholly for the better) by raising the cadence tone and thereby permitting an immediate and economical leap up to *g*. At the same place all of the later Chartres sources plus only Lig2 and Foi contribute their own recomposition, also a terse one. They have a leap, *cg*, in segment 38, which changes the feel of the phrase considerably, but is certainly not impossible. Then, having got to the *g* in segment 39, they leap back down to *d* in segment 40 (Per1 and Pro1 have *e*) before rejoining the rest on *f* thereafter.

The question that arises here is: how did such a notable alteration get into the Chartres tradition? It is difficult to see it as an error, surely, or even as a correction (perhaps theoretically derived? but what theory might be involved here?). Alterations of this sort are not especially common, but they are not really rare either. It is clear that there were occasional special happenings in the otherwise ordinary process of transmission.

The tristropha on *f* of segment 41 also has a competitor. Thirteen manuscripts, almost all from the northeast, have *ef* here instead. Many but not all of these,[16] plus over fifty others, had made a similar substitution in segment 17. The very similar succession of notes in segment 26 is not, however, varied in this way. No doubt this is because the tristropha here is the beginning of a new phrase ('alleluia'), whereas the other two cases are internal. Nine manuscripts (six of them Parisian) were willing to change the opening of a new phrase in segment 27 to *gfff*, but not one would begin with the *ef*. It will no doubt be difficult for us to appreciate fully the differences: perhaps the scribes saw the *egff* coming in segment 29 and did not wish to anticipate. The choices are in any event delicate ones. The variant *gfff* cannot (or at least does not) occur here in segment 41, because it will be used (as it was in segment 12) to begin the final alleluia (segment 48). Thus if the Paris scribes felt that there were already enough *f*s in the phrase, the *ef* was perhaps the only option open to them.

The internal cadence in segments 41 and 42 is remarkable for its almost total stability. One might have expected to find ways of settling on *g* that were different from the *gfag g* of Dij1, but there is nothing.[17] The most obvious candidate would be *gag*, but that figure was used only three syllables earlier. Once again, the reader might wish to attempt different versions: my own efforts brought me absolutely nothing – the received version seems unattackable.

The final double alleluia need only descend from the *g* through *f* to the conclusion on *e*. That its last cadence should rhyme with the first E cadence is not imperative, but it makes good musical sense, and is found universally. The first syllable of the first alleluia generally ends on *f* as a passing tone. A miscellaneous gaggle of fourteen manuscripts has merely a *g* instead of the usual *gf*. It may be that inconsistency in the notation of liquescents is involved, and that at least some of the thirteen scribes intended the *f* as a liquescent between *g* and *e*. Segment 45 then reverses the motion with *efg*, without any competition, while segment 46 perches on *g* to begin the downward motion with *e* or *f* and prepare the half cadence ending the first alleluia. Here we find a situation similar to that in segment 44: a large number of sources – indeed the majority (over eighty) – have a liquescent *g*, rather than the explicit *ge* of Dij1. Thus there may be no variant at all, although I am inclined to suspect that many of the liquescent readings were intended to represent *gf* instead of *ge*.[18] Probably not the majority, however: the reading of Dij1 in segment 47 – *egfg* – is a minority version. Almost thirty sources fill in the third, with *efgfg*, and forty-nine change the opening note to give *fgfg*. Of these the first is possible (as is the reading of Dij2) regardless of the choice made in the preceding segment. But the *fgfg* seems to me almost to require

---

[16]Coc1, Kin, Nof, Van1, and Van2 have the reading in segment 41 but not segment 17.

[17]To be sure, Cat4 rewrites the cadence as *gfgaga ag*, but this is scarcely an improvement. The same manuscript gives us yet another *ag* in segment 44.

[18]The length of the liquescent 'tail' seems sometimes to be an indication, but it is uncertain how much faith one should have in it.

an *e* to end the preceding syllable.[19] There are also three other versions, each with a single witness. They range from the bizarre (*faga* in Rem4, quite possibly a real error) to the innocuous (*fgf* in Rom; certainly not an improvement). Thus all of the manuscripts but one agree that the half cadence should end on *g*, preparing for the final cadence to come.

This, as has been noted, is a repetition of the alleluia at the end of the first phrase. There are, however, slight changes in the pattern of variants. It may be remembered that the penultimate neume of the earlier cadence (segment 14), while normally *egff*, admitted two variants. One was *fgff*, given by four sources: Agv1, Clu2, Rem2, and Rom. Of these, only two, Clu2 and Rom, joined now by Bec,[20] Fra2, and Pro4, have the same version in segment 50. Conversely, the sixteen manuscripts having *egef* in segment 14 are precisely the same as those that have the same figure in segment 50. Meanwhile, in the segments preceding the cadence (13 and 49), the number of sources in agreement remains almost the same, but they are not always the same sources, as is shown in the following:

Table 12.1: Agreement of sources in segments 49 and 13

segment 49	segment 13
Cam2	
	Cam3
Cat4	
Clu3	Clu3
Far	
Lig2	Lig2
Lyo3	Lyo3
Orl	Orl
Par3	
	Par6
Pro3	Pro3
Pro4	Pro4
Pro5	Pro5
Sno1	Sno1
Sno3	Sno3
Sno6	Sno6
Tur4	

---

[19] A third reading, found only in Clu3 and Jum1, has *effg*. This, like the lemma, is comfortable with either version of segment 47.

[20] The cadence is rather casually written in Bec: *egff* may have been intended.

It is not that unusual for scribes to change their minds about how to treat a figure occurring more than once in a chant. While on the whole they remember what they have done before and reproduce it in later repetitions, there are many instances of this sort of inconsistency.[21] In this case, two of the manuscripts, Cam2 and Cat4, are notable for erratic behaviour. The others, however, are respectable and usually reliable. In no case, either here or in the cadence of phrase 1, does the *df* variant precede the *fgff* figure: in other words, the scribes were sensitive to the potential redundancy involved.

The list above is also a good example of the sort of distribution often found with readings not widely used. The clear association of the reading at Sens (Sno1, Sno3, Sno6, and Pro3) is obvious, and it seems likely that it was from Sens that the reading spread to Provins (Pro4 and Pro5). But it is hardly probable that the remaining manuscripts in the list were influenced by the Senonese practice. The difference is so small – only the insertion or omission of an anticipatory note – that Cambrai, Langres, Lyon, and the rest merely tripped over the reading, as it were. Only when (and if) we find more examples of associations such as this one will it become reasonable to speak of groups including both Cambrai in Picardy and Lyon in the south.

Needless to say, the final *fe* is invariable (unless perhaps the adiastematic manuscripts conceal some highly unlikely variant). While change of final does occur once in a while, it would be particularly surprising here, where the melodic structure is so carefully arranged to provide for an ending on *e*.

The second object of this study – to try to discover why the inner phrases of *Resurrexi* contained many more variants than the first phrase – has to some extent already been answered. Obviously, variants occur most often in melodic contexts that favour them. Thus the presence of numerous thirds, for example, in some part of a chant will probably serve to generate variants – but almost all chants have 'numerous thirds'. In *Resurrexi* the second phrase in particular has a very large number of variants with significant manuscript support and even more readings with only few witnesses. It would be hard to say that there are more obvious temptations to vary in the second phrase than in the first. Yet a comparison (omitting the alleluias) shows how strong the contrast is. The variants totalled in the second column of Table 12.2 are shared by ten or more manuscripts; in the third column are any others shared by fewer.

Thus in the first phrase there are six variants with significant support and fifteen others; in the second those numbers are doubled, to twelve and thirty-one. To be sure, we have seen that in some cases variants occur in chains, so that readings in one segment almost automatically produce specific readings in the segment(s) following: this reduces the contrast somewhat, but still leaves a considerable difference between the two areas of the chant. The scribes seem to have perceived certain figures as relatively inviolable, others as subject to arbitrary change, sometimes for reasons we can see and appreciate, sometimes in ways we cannot yet recover. In the case of stable figures variants may still arise, but they will typically have few witnesses, while in the less

---

[21]For a brief discussion of this point, see my 'The Alleluias', pp. 109–111.

Table 12.2: Frequency of variants

	Variants in ten or more mss	Variants in fewer than ten mss
Segment 1	none	none
Segment 2	three variants, with 19, 22, and 30	four
Segment 3	none	three
Segment 4	none	one
Segment 5	none	three
Segment 6	one variant with 10	one
Segment 7	one variant with 49	one
Segment 8	none	one
Segment 9	one variant with 14	none
Segment 10	none	one
Segment 11	none	none
Segment 16	one variant with 72 manuscripts	four
Segment 17	one variant with 62	one
Segment 18	two variants, one with 18, one with 57	one
Segment 19	one variant with 84[22]	one
Segment 20	one variant with 17	four
Segment 21	two variants, one with 55, one with 11	nine
Segment 22	none	none
Segment 23	one variant with 25	one
Segment 24	two variants, one with 49, one with 28	four
Segment 25	one variant with 15	six

fixed ones some variant readings will win considerable support, and the number of readings found in only a small number of manuscripts will increase. Sometimes it is easy enough to see that a certain figure will be subject to much variation: segment 2 is an excellent example, with its thirds waiting to be filled in. Elsewhere the matter is more obscure. Segment 21 with its *d[e]fg* suggests variation, but hardly so much as to generate eleven different readings.

The evidence of other chants is similar, but generally lacks the contrast between phrases with many variants and those with few. In *Puer natus* from the third Christmas mass there are hardly any instances of multiple readings until 'im*p*erium', where Dij1 has *bd'e'f'*. Here both the filling of the third and the semitonal variant are possible. Both in fact occur, with considerable support; and, as is common for whatever reason,

---

[22]Obviously in cases like this it is Dij1 and its few followers that have the 'variant', but it seems best to avoid changing the terminology.

there are also a half dozen other readings with three or fewer witnesses. In the offertory of the same mass, *Tui sunt celi*, the last syllable of 'preparatio' has no fewer than fourteen readings, three of them with significant support, the rest with seven or fewer witnesses. Here the reason is less obvious. Dij1 has *gagfe* (continuing with *fed* for the same syllable). Two other well-supported readings are *gagf*, merely leaving out the lower auxiliary, and *gabagf*, adding an auxiliary at the top (the *b* is probably to be sung as *b flat*) and omitting the lower one, with a dozen other weakly supported versions. The temptation to vary is a good deal less clear here, but one basic phenomenon is the same: when a passage generates more than two supported readings, weakly attested readings multiply.

Less frequently, two competing readings cohabit with a large number of weak competitors. Thus in the communion *Viderunt omnes*, still from the principal Christmas mass, we find at 'ter*rae*' *gfage* in Dij1, and nearly eighty manuscripts change the *e* to *f*. But there are also nine other readings, none with more than one to three witnesses. These represent all sorts of tinkering with the basic musical idea: *gfagfg*, *geagf*, *gfagfgf*, and a set in which the opening two pitches are a second higher: *agbag*, *agbaga*, *agage*, and so on. What about: 'The occurrence of more than three readings with significant support is infrequent', but such agreement does occur from time to time, as in 'salu*t*are' of the same chant, where five readings have more than ten witnesses, with nine others weakly supported.

Thus it would appear that the difference in number of variants between the first and second phrases of *Resurrexi* is the result of nothing more than the fortuitous crowding of inherently variable elements in the second phrase. One is forced to conclude that the scribes found certain passages apt for change, whether because typically variable elements – thirds, or *es* and *bs* – were present, or perhaps because the received version was in some way problematic. In some cases we can see what the problem or the incitement may have been. The alterations found to be particularly appropriate have numerous witnesses; others found favour with only a few scribes.[23] Still, despite all of the changes, the music remains entirely recognizable in all its versions. What is more, the scribes were almost invariably musical: almost never does one find a reading that is really unsatisfactory. Given the number of copies we have, and, even more, the vast amount of time over which these copies are spread, there is abundant reason to be grateful for their work.

---

[23]In both cases the manuscripts witnessing a given reading are generally a miscellaneous group, indicating that the changes occurred independently in different places (or that there was a great deal more contact between different singing traditions than we now suppose). Sometimes a minority reading becomes dominant or universal at one or more places (Paris, for example, or Paris and Chartres), but even in such cases it will almost always occur also in unrelated sources. Readings that are clearly deliberate revisions seem (when we have enough manuscripts) most likely to become universal at their presumed place of origin and least likely to occur in unrelated sources.

During the writing of this chapter I was unaware of the study by Alejandro Planchart on the Easter chants. While there is no real overlapping, Planchart presents an analysis of *Resurrexi* that differs somewhat from mine.[24]

Appendix
List of sources consulted

Siglum	Library	Type	Provenance[25]	Date
Agv1	Angers, BM 96	gradual	Angers	12
Agv2	Angers, BM 97	gradual	Angers (St-Aubin)	12 in.
Alb	BNF lat. 776	gradual	St-Michel de Gaillac?	12
Aux1	BNF lat. 17312	missal	diocese of Auxerre	13 1/2
Bar	BNF n.a. l. 1890	missal	Barbechat (Loire Atlantique)	12 4/4
Bec	BNF lat. 1105	missal	Le Bec-Hellouin	13 2/2
Cal1	Chaumont, BM 44	gradual	Cistercian (Auberive?)	13
Cam2	BNF lat. 17311	missal	Cambrai	14
Cam3	Cambrai, BM 234	missal	Cambrai	12
Cam4	Cambrai, BM 60	gradual	Cambrai	11–12
Cam5	Cambrai, BM 61	gradual	Lille	12
Cat1	BNF lat. 845	missal	Châlons-en-Champagne	14 2/2
Cat4	BNF lat. 866	missal	Châlons, use of Troyes	15 2/2
Cha1	Chartres, BM 47	gradual	Redon (use of Chartres)	10
Cha2	BNF lat. 17310	missal	Chartres	14 in.
Cha5	Chartres, BM 520	missal	Chartres	13
Clu1	BNF lat. 1087	gradual	Cluny	11 1/2
Clu2	Brussels, BR II 3824	gradual	Sauxillanges	12
Clu3	Cambridge, Fitzwilliam Museum 369	missal	Lewes Priory	13 2/2
Coc1	BNF lat. 17307	missal	St-Corneille deCompiègne	12
Coc2	BNF lat. 16823	missal	St-Corneille de Compiègne	13 2/2
Coc3	BNF lat. 17318	missal	St-Corneille de Compiègne	12 in.
Coc4	BNF lat. 16828	gradual	St-Corneille de Compiègne	14

---

[24] Alejandro Enrique Planchart, 'The Opening Chant of Easter in the Latin West', in Bianca Maria Antolini and Teresa M. Gialdroni, eds, *Studi in onore de Agostino Ziino in occasione del suo 65° compleanno* (Lucca, 2003), pp. 63–98.

[25] The provenance and date given here are for the most part those found in standard publications, notably *Les sources* (*Le graduel romain*. II: *Les sources* (Solesmes 1957–1962)) and Victor Leroquais, *Les sacramentaires et les missels manuscrits des bibliothèques publiques de France* (Paris, 1924). Where more recent material is readily available, I have used it – for example David Hiley, 'The Norman Chant Traditions – Normandy, Britain, Sicily', *Proceedings of the Royal Musical Association* 107 (1980–1981), pp. 1–33, but I make no claim to have noticed, let alone solved, all of the problems involved.

Coc5	BNF lat. 17329	gradual	St-Corneille de Compiègne	13
Cor1	BNF lat. 18010	gradual	Corbie	11–12
Cyr	BNF lat. 10511	gradual	St-Laurent de Longré?	12 ex.
Den1	B. Mazarine 384	gradual	St-Denis	11
Den2	BNF lat. 1107	missal	St-Denis	13 2/2
Den3	BNF lat. 10505	missal	St-Denis	14
Den4	BNF lat. 9436	gradual	St-Denis	11 med.
Der1	Reims, BM 217	missal	Reims, St-Denis	14
Der2	Reims, BM 266	gradual	Reims, St-Denis	15
Dij1	Montpellier, Faculté de médecine H. 159	tonary	Dijon	11
Dij2	Brussels, BR II 3823	gradual	Souvigny	13
Évr1	Rouen, BM 385 (A166)	missal	Montaure, dioc. of Évreux	13 1/2
Évr2	BNF lat. 15616	missal	Paris, use of Évreux	13 1/2
Évr3	BNF n.a.l. 1773	missal	Évreux	13 in.
Far	B. Mazarine 405	missal	St-Faron de Meaux	13 1/2
Fle1	Angers, BM 91	gradual	Angers	10
Foi	BNF lat. 9437	missal	Foicy	12 ex.
Fra2	BNF lat. 10503	gradual	Franciscan	13
Ind	Clermont-Ferrand, BM 73	missal	St-Flour?	14
Kin	Douai, BM 90	missal	Anchin	12
Jum1	Rouen, BM 267 (A401)	missal	Jumièges	12
Lan	Laon, BM 239	gradual	Region of Laon	*ca* 930
Lat	BNF lat. 12053	missal	Lagny	11
Lig2	Sémur, BM 6	missal	Langres	13 1/2
Lig3	Avallon, BM 1	missal	Langres	1419
Lig4	Troyes, BM 155 (fols 180ff)	missal	Langres	12
Lil	Lille, BM 26	cantatorium	St-Pierre, Lille	14
Lyo3	Lyons, BM 513	gradual	St-André, Lyon	14
Mal1	BNF lat. 1132	gradual	St-Martial, Limoges	11–12
Mic	Orléans, BM 121	missal	St-Mesmin, Micy	13 1/2
Mor1	BNF lat. 13254	gradual	Chelles	12
Mor3	BNF lat. 13253	gradual	St-Maur-des-Fossés	13
Mor4	BNF lat. 12584	gradual	St-Maur-des-Fossés	11
Nar	BNF lat. 780	gradual	Narbonne	11
Niv1	BNF n.a.l. 1235	gradual	Nevers	12
Nof	BNF lat. 17320	missal	North of France (use of Compiègne)	14
Noy1	BL Egerton 857	gradual	Noyon	12

Orl	Orléans, BM 119	missal	Orléans	14 in.
Otu1	Autun, BM, S. 12	gradual	North of France	12
Otu2	Autun, BM 167	missal	Autun (Benedictines)	11
Otu3	Autun, BM 10	missal	Autun	12
Par3	B. Ste-Geneviève 93	missal	Paris	12 ex.
Par4	BNF lat. 1112	missal	Paris	*ca* 1225
Par5	BNF lat. 9441	missal	Paris	13 med.
Par6	BNF lat. 15615	missal	Paris (Sorbonne)	13
Par7	BNF lat. 830	missal	Paris (St-Germain)	13 2/2
Par8	BNF lat. 861	missal	Paris	14 1/2
Par13	B. Mazarine 411	missal	Paris (Notre Dame)	14 (*ca* 1380)
Par26	BL add. 38723	missal	Paris	13
Par27[26]	Baltimore, Walters Art Gallery, W 302	missal	Paris	14–15
Per1	Troyes, BM 894	missal	Chartres (St-Père)	12 1/2
Pic	Limoges, BM 2	gradual	Poitiers? Fontevrault?	14 in.
Pro1	Provins, BM 12	missal	Chartres (St-Père)	12
Pro3	Provins, BM 13	gradual	Sens	13
Pro4	Provins, BM 228	missal	Provins	13 2/2
Pro5	Provins, BM 227	missal	Provins	13
Que	Brussels, BR 19389	missal	Quesnart	13
Rem1	Reims, BM 221	missal	Reims	12
Rem2	Reims, BM 224	missal	Reims (Chapter)	14 2/2
Rem4	Troyes, BM 1951	missal	Reims	12 2/2
Rem6	Laon, BM 236	missal	Reims	11
Ren	BNF lat. 9439	missal	Rennes	12 1/2
Ric2	Douai, BM 114	gradual	Marchiennes	14
Rog1	BNF lat. 904	gradual	Rouen	13
Rog2	Rouen, BM 277 (Y50)	missal	Rouen	13 1/2
Rog4	Rouen, BM 249 (A280)	gradual	Paris, for the use of Eu	12
Rog5	Rouen, BM 250 (A233)	gradual	Jumièges	14
Rom	Toulouse, BM 94	missal	?	14
Rop	Leningrad, o V I6	gradual	Meulan	12–13
Sam1	Valenciennes, BM 1221	missal	St-Amand	12 ex.
Siv	B. Ste Geneviève 99	gradual	Senlis	13
Sno1	BNF lat. 10502	missal	Sens	13 1/2

---

[26] I have previously referred to this manuscript as Wal1.

Sno3	Provins, BM 11	missal	Sens	13 1/4
Sno4	Troyes, BM 1047	missal	Sens? (use of Troyes)	12
Sno6	BL add. 30058	missal	Sens	13
Soi1	Baltimore, Walters Art Gallery, W 128	missal	Soissons	13?
Teo	Reims, BM 264	gradual	St-Thierry	12
Tie	Chaumont, BM 45	gradual	Montier-den-Der	12
Tou	BL Harl. 4951	gradual	Toulouse	11
Tur3	BNF lat. 9434	missal	Tours	11
Tur4	Orléans, BM 117	missal	Tours St-Venant	13 med.
Vaa1	Cambrai, BM 75	gradual	St-Vaast	11
Vaa3	Arras, BM 444 (888)	missal	St-Vaast	13
Van1	Verdun, BM 758	missal	Verdun (St-Vanne)	12 med.
Van2	Verdun, BM 759	missal	Verdun (St-Vanne)	13 1/2
Vic1	BNF lat. 14452	gradual	Paris (St-Victor)	13 1/4
Vir	Verdun, BM 98	missal	Verdun	14 in.
Yrx	BNF lat. 903	gradual	St-Yrieix	11
Zog1	Troyes, BM 522	missal	Champagne?	11

Chapter 13

Chants for four masses in the *Editio princeps* of the *Pontificale romanum* (1485)

James Borders

For some time I have been preparing a synoptic edition of plainchant in manuscripts of the *Pontificale romanum*, liturgical books with chants,[1] rubrics, prayers, and readings for rituals over which only a bishop could legitimately preside. These services include clerical ordinations and the consecration of bishops, abbots, abbesses, and nuns, the dedication of a church and a cemetery; and the consecration of an altar and other cult objects. The edition will cover three related recensions identified by Michel Andrieu as Roman pontificals of the Twelfth Century, pontificals of the Roman Curia of the Thirteenth Century, and the pontifical of William Durandus, compiled *ca* 1293–1295.[2] They contain approximately seventy-five, fifty, and one hundred notated items respectively, most taken over from the antiphoner or the gradual. The edition will complement Andrieu's critical study of texts and sources, examining the mechanics of music transmission and assessing the changing *melos* of plainchant in the later Middle Ages in a limited, though still large, number of sources with established relationships.

As research on this project extended into the later fifteenth century its scope expanded to include early prints of the Durandus pontifical (henceforth PWD), which the Roman Catholic Church eventually imposed on all dioceses. The *editio princeps*, published in Rome in 1485 and edited by papal master of ceremonies Agostino Patrizi Piccolomini and his assistant and eventual successor, Johannes Burckhard, was an ambitious project of music printing for its time, especially compared with the missals

---

[1]Giacomo Baroffio focuses attention on the role of music in printed liturgical books of this kind in 'I libri con musica: sono libri di musica?', in *Il canto piano nell=era della stampa: Atti del Convegno internazionale di studi sul canto liturgico nei secoli XV–XVIII, Trento – Castello del Buonconsiglio, Venezia – Fondazione Ugo e Olga Levi, 9–11 ottobre 1998*, ed Giulio Cattin, Danilo Curti, and Marco Gozzi (Trent, 1999), pp. 9–12.

[2] *Le pontifical romain au moyen-âge*, 4 vols, Studi e Testi 86–88, 99 (Vatican, 1938–1941). For a general history of the *Pontificale romanum* see Cyrille Vogel, *Medieval Liturgy: An Introduction to the Sources*, trans. and rev. William Storey and Niels Rasmussen (Washington, DC, 1986), pp. 225–256.

that dominate the incunabula period.[3] Its publisher and the founder of its music type, Stephan Plannck, set not just those chants typically found in PWD manuscripts but a number that were not, including the propers for three masses: for the consecration of a bishop, an abbot, and an altar (without church dedication). Together with a fourth set of mass chants for the reconciliation of a church or cemetery, four of which were notated typically in earlier recensions of the pontifical for church dedication, we have a limited collection of twenty-two melodies with which to assess, as I shall argue, the work of an anonymous music editor in the early modern period, and material appropriate for an essay honouring a modern publisher of both music and text. The genres, incipits, and normal liturgical assignments of these items are listed in Table 13.1.

Table 13.1   Mass chants in the *Editio princeps* of the *Pontificale Romanum* (1485) with concordances in the *Missale Romanum* (1570)

Function, genre, incipit	Liturgical assignment, *Missale Romanum* (1570)
Consecration of a Bishop	
Int. *Benedicat te*	n.a.
Gr. *Imola deo sacrificium*	n.a.
All. *Diffusa est*	Lucia; Mary Magd.; Anna
Tr. *Desiderium*	Ignatio; Matt.; Com. pont. mart.; Com. mart. non pont
Off. *Benedic anima mea*	Fer. vi Qtr. Temp. Quadr.
Com. *Messis quidem*	n.a.
Consecration of an Abbott	
Int. *Tibi dixit*	Fer. III post Dom. II Quadrag.
Gr. *Miserere mei deus miserere*	Ash Wednesday
All. *Lauda anima mea*	Dom. III post Pascha
Off. *Sperent in te*	Fer. III post Dom. Passionis; Dom. IV post Pent.
Com. *Redime me deus*	Fer. III post Dom. Passionis

---

[3]Kathi Meyer-Baer, *Liturgical Music Incunabula* (London, 1962), pp. ix–xi. The Plannck pontificals of 1485 and 1497 are described on page 38 and shown in plates 5 and 6. See also Donald William Krummel and Stanley Sadie, *Music Printing and Publishing* (New York, 1990), s.v. 'Plannck, Stephan'. For a summary of the contents of the 1485 edition see Marc Dykmans, *Le pontifical romain révisé au XVe siècle*, Studi e Testi 311 (Vatican, 1985), pp. 108–123.

Consecration of an Altar (without Church Dedication)

Gr.	*Tollite hostias*	Fer. V post Com. Passionis
All.	*Redemptionem*	Dom. III post Pascha
Off.	*Sanctificavit Moyses*	Dom. XIX post Pent.
Com.	*Tollite hostias*	Dom. XIX post Pent.

Reconciliation of a Church or Cemetery

Gr.	*Locus iste*	Dedication of a Church (Anniversary)
All.	*Adorabo*	Dedication of a Church (Anniversary)
All.	*Bene fundata est*	Dedication of a Church (Anniversary)
Off.	*Domine deus in simplicitate*	Dedication of a Church (Anniversary)
Com.	*Domus Mea*	Dedication of a Church (Anniversary)

Before examining these chants and assessing the music editorial activity I believe they represent, two major problems with their readability, indeed reliability, must be discussed. First, many passages cannot be transcribed with complete confidence. Text underlay is generally problematic, and it is sometimes difficult to determine the exact pitch levels of some passages, given problems in the alignment of the red staves and black notation, which were printed in separate impressions and in that order. Other lines of music seem to be a second or third too high or too low. Scribal customs of ligation, moreover, had only a limited impact on Plannck's selection of music type. He used only five basic shapes – *virga, punctum*, a lozenge-shaped note, *podatus*, and *clivis* – which he combined to create three-element and compound neumes. Thus, for instance, an ascending three-note *scandicus* might be printed as three single notes (in various combinations) or as a *podatus* plus single note (or vice versa), provided the *podatus* covered no more than a third: Plannck's two *podatus* fonts spanned a second and a third.[4] One might excuse such a rudimentary approach to notating chant, given the early date of Plannck's activity, very near the origins of music printing in Italy, but this does not mitigate the problems with the melodies. Finally, the position of C clef[5] is also sometimes odd, with some chants evidently pitched at some interval higher than was typical of prior manuscript versions. Of course, this observation assumes that such versions exist, which brings us to the second major problem: over a third of all the 1485 chant melodies, and more than half the mass chants, cannot be traced to sources earlier than Plannck's edition.[6] I will label these melodies 'untraditional'.

[4]By the 1497 edition Plannck had cut a *podatus* font spanning a fourth. For example, see in this edition fol. 138[V]: '*adorate*' and '*Revelabit*'; fol. 156[r]: '*inestimabile*' and '*est*'.

[5]Plannck used only the C clef for the mass chants, but the F clef elsewhere.

[6]See my 'The 1485 *Pontificale romanum* and its Chants', in *Il canto piano nell=era della stampa*, pp. 13–28. An early fifteenth-century northern Italian pontifical (Oxford, Bodleian Library, Canonici ms 375), which contains fewer chants than most other PWD manuscripts, does preserve some melodies resembling untraditional printed ones (Borders, 'The 1485

Although some differences in music and text are typical of chants in manuscripts of the *Pontificale romanum* from one recension to the next, the degree of difference encountered in Plannck's edition is unusual. For some texts there are untraditional melodies as well as revised and abbreviated ones (although many of the simpler antiphons in the *editio princeps* are just as they are usually found elsewhere). Given the technical problems just mentioned, transcribing the untraditional melodies would be an unacceptably provisional enterprise, were it not for surviving manuscript copies of the 1485 edition, two of which were consulted for this study (US-CAh Typ. 217 and I-Rvat Ott. lat. 501, the latter having been commissioned by Bishop Jean Vitez for King Mathias Corvin of Hungary).[7] Although the scribes of these deluxe books occasionally substituted traditional PWD settings for untraditional ones, they more frequently recopied the print versions intelligibly, clarifying text underlay and ligation. Sometimes they also moved clefs and changed intervals, pitch levels, and finals.

Our controls are not limited to manuscript copies: the *Pontificale romanum* was itself printed nine more times before the mid-sixteenth century, once by Plannck himself (1497), once in Brescia (1503), five times in Venice (by Giunta, in 1510, 1515, 1520, 1543, and 1544), and twice more in Lyons (1511 and 1542).[8] In all editions up to 1543 the chants of the *editio princeps* are reprinted with minor changes in ligation, text underlay, and, here and there, melody. In 1543, an anonymous Giunta music editor revised many untraditional melodies along lines that the scribes of the manuscript copies had followed two generations earlier. (It would not be surprising to learn that such a manuscript were at hand, along with the 1520 edition from which he worked.)[9] His most important contribution was bringing the chants into conformity with widely understood rules of modality. Where an earlier untraditional melody did not conform to his taste or understanding, he substituted a traditional setting that had circulated in PWD manuscripts. The 1543 edition became the basis for later printed pontificals until the 1595–1596 Roman edition, which reflected changes associated

---

Pontificale romanum and its Chants', pp. 17, 25–26). Such resemblances, though not always close, nonetheless suggest an effort on the part of this and perhaps other music scribes to 'reform' plainchant in the PWD in Italy in the decades before the *editio princeps*.

[7] For information on US-CAh Typ. 217 (Cambridge, MA, Harvard University (Houghton) Library, Typ. 217), I-Rvat Ott. Lat. 501 (Vatican, BAV, Ottob. lat. 501), and other manuscript copies of the *editio princeps* see Dykmans, *Le pontifical romain révisé*, pp. 124–126. Dykmans dates the two sources consulted here to the 1490s. Small differences between Plannck's editions of 1485 and 1497 further prove that the manuscripts were copied from the first edition. For example, in the communion *Messis quidem*, the conjunction *sed*, lacking in 1497, is found in 1485 and both manuscripts.

[8] These are listed in Borders, 'The 1485 *Pontificale romanum*', p. 21, Table 2. The Lyons editions were based on the Giunta books that immediately preceded them chronologically. No exemplars of the 1515 and 1544 Giunta editions survive.

[9] Again, small melodic and text differences distinguishing the prints suggest the editor's working procedure. It was probably a general practice that type was set from the immediately preceding edition.

with the Council of Trent.[10] A comparison of readings in the *editio princeps* with later sources thus permits us to make sense of the earliest printed melodies, to see beyond the available materials to the recompositions and revisions in the lost printers' copies. If, as I argue, the untraditional, revised, and abbreviated settings are authentic, we have proof of chant reform in Rome more than a century before the (in)famous Medicean gradual (1614–1615) and even, for that matter, a still earlier reform edition published by Angelo Gardane in Venice (1591).[11] Let us now turn to the mass chants themselves.

Presentation

For our purposes, the most obvious difference between the *editio princeps*, manuscript copies, and later editions on one hand, and fourteenth- and early fifteenth-century PWD manuscripts on the other, is the provision of four complete sets of mass-propers. Earlier sources provided a mass for the dedication of a church,[12] which – except for its introit (*Terribilis est locus iste*) – agrees with the 1485 mass for the reconciliation of a church or cemetery. In addition to these, three *proper* chants for the consecration of a bishop were notated typically in the medieval PWD: the introit *Benedixit te* (*sic*), gradual *Imola deo sacrificium*, and communion *Messis quidem multa*.[13] These items had no place in medieval Temporal or Sanctoral cycles (see Table 13.1) and were thus unfamiliar to bishops, singers, and scribes, and this presumably necessitated their neumation. By no means should we conclude that they were later compositions. Their use in what is obviously the same consecration ritual is indicated by incipits in the ninth-century Senlis *antiphonale missarum* and in early pontificals.[14]

---

[10]There are no mass chants in the 1595–1596 edition (Rome); reprinted as *Pontificale romanum: Editio princeps (1595–1596)*, ed. Manilo Sodi and Achille Maria Triacca, Monumenta Concilii Tridentini (Vatican, 1997). Luca Marenzio and Giovanni Andrea Dragoni edited the chants in this *Pontificale romanum*.

[11]Annarita Indino, 'Il Graduale stampato de Angelo Gardano (1591)', in *Il canto piano nell=era della stampa*, pp. 207–221. See also Marco Gozzi, 'Il graduale di Angelo Gardano (1591)', in Laura Dal Prà, ed., *Un museo nel Castello del Buonconsiglio: Acquisizioni, contributi, restauri* (Trent, 1995), pp. 399–414.

[12]Michel Andrieu, *Le pontifical romain au moyen âge* (1. *Le pontifical romain du XIIe siècle*, 2. *Le pontifical romain de la curie au XIIIe siècle*, 3. *Le pontifical de Guillaume Durand*), Studi e Testi 86–88 (Vatican, 1938–1940), vol. 88, pp. 477–478 (lib. 2, cap. II, 100–108) and 516 (lib. 2, cap. VI, 19–26).

[13]*Ibid.*, pp. 380–389 (lib. 1, cap. XIV, 22, 24, 57). The text and music differences between the introit *Benedixit te*, found in PWD manuscripts, and *Benedicat te*, found in prints, are discussed below.

[14]In Senlis, however, the communion *Euntes predicate evangelium* is indicated for this proper; *Messis quidem* is assigned here for the consecration of more than one bishop. René-Jean Hesbert, *Antiphonale missarum sextuplex* (Brussels, 1935), pp. 171, 171 quat. and 172. The formulary for the service in the late tenth-century Romano-Germanic pontifical, the forerunner

Text differences

For the most part, comparison reveals only minor differences in text between *proper* mass chants in the 1485 *editio princeps* and other sources (not just pontificals but earlier and later graduals and missals). Variants are generally limited to case endings or the omission and/or substitution of a few words. The largest number of such text differences, as indicated below in facing columns, is found in the introit for the consecration of an altar, *Dicit dominus sermones mei.*

1485, editio princeps: text variants, other sources (in parentheses)[15]

Dicit dominus sermones mei	none
quos dedi in os tuum	os *meo* (*AMS*); os *tuum* (Chartres; Sarum)
non deficient de ore tuo	none
adest enim nomen tuum	*adest ... tuum* om. (*MR*; MED)
et munera tua accepta erunt	none
super altari meo.	*altare meum* (Chartres, Sarum; *MR*; MED)
	altari meo (*AMS*)

In general, at least some sources earlier than 1485 agree with each other (as with '*os tuum*' and '*altari meo*'); later printed books with mass-propers, particularly the *Missale romanum* (1570) and Medicean gradual (1614–1615), stand apart from the print tradition of the *Pontificale romanum*.[16] However, the texts of two mass chants in

---

to all the Roman pontificals, included *Benedixit te* and *Messis quidem*, but not *Imola deo*; the gradual *Memor sit omnis sacrificii* was assigned instead. Cyrille Vogel and Reinhard Elze, eds., *Le pontifical romano-germanique du dixième siècle*, 3 vols, Studi e Testi 226, 227, and 269 (Vatican, 1963, 1972), vol. 1, pp. 208 (lib. LXIII, cap. 6), 213 (lib. LXIII, cap. 22), and 226 (lib. LXIII, cap. 60).

[15]Abbreviations are as follows: *AMS*: *Antiphonale missarum sextuplex*; Chartres: David Hiley, ed., *Missale carnotense (Chartres codex 520)*, MMMA 4 (1992); Sarum: Walter Howard Frere, ed., *Graduale sarisburiense: A Reproduction in Facsimile of a MS. of the 13th Century* (London, 1894; reprinted Farnborough, 1966); *MR*: Manlio Sodi and Achille Maria Triacca, eds, *Missale romanum: Editio princeps (1570)*, Monumenta liturgica concilii tridentini (Vatican, 1998); MED: *Editio medicea* (1614–15), 2 vols, available in facsimile as *Graduale de tempore iuxta ritum sacrosanctæ romanæ ecclesiæ: Editio princeps (1614): Edizione anastatica e appendice ...* and *Graduale de sanctis iuxta ritum sacrosanctæ romanæ ecclesiæ: Editio princeps (1614): Edizione anastatica e appendice*, ed. Giacomo Baroffio, Eun Ju Kim, and Manlio Sodi, Monumenta studia instrumenta liturgica 10–11 (Vatican, 2001); *GT*: *Graduale triplex* (Solesmes, 1979).

[16]Two similar examples: the final two words of the 1485 offertory *Domine deus in simplicitate* (*Domine deus in simplicitate cordis mei letus obtuli universa et populum tuum qui repertus est vidicum ingenti gaudio deus israel custodi hanc voluntatem Domine deus*) are lacking in *MED*, but present in *MR*. Some medieval sources, including *Sextuplex*, conclude with '*Domine deus*', others do not. The gradual respond *Locus iste* in 1485 includes the conjunction

1485 disagree extensively with all other known counterparts. The first text, also assigned to the consecration of an altar, is the alleluia verse *Redemptionem*. Here Psalm 110.9 is continued, and the verse text is twice as long as the version cited below from the graduals and missals of the *GT* (but also found in *Sextuplex*, Chartres, Sarum, *MR*, and MED):

1485: *Redemptionem misit dominus populo suo mandavit in eternum testamentum suum.*

GT: *Redemptionem misit dominus populo suo.*

Whether the long verse was transmitted in some late medieval chantbooks is uncertain, but it does not appear in Karlheinz Schlager's edition of late alleluias.[17] Finding it in the manuscripts of a given place or time might provide a useful clue to the provenance of chants in the *editio princeps* or the origins of their editor.

The second chant, the introit *Benedixit te / Benedicat te*, unassigned in the yearly liturgical cycle (see Table 13.1) but here specified for the consecration of a bishop, is extensively reworked in 1485. Its text is compared below with that found in authoritative manuscript sources of the PWD:

PWD *Benedixit te hodie deus et unxit te oleo letitie pr[a]e consortibus tuis memor esto nominis domini dei tui.*

1485 *Benedicat te hodie dominus deus et respiciat super te servum suum et det tibi fortitudinem ad resistendum inimicis ecclesie sancte sue.*

The text of *Benedixit te* (PWD) stems from Psalm 44.8, but in the 1485 edition biblical metaphor gives way to direct entreaties for God's help against the Church's enemies in non-scriptural, prayer-like language. The text was part of a sweeping revision of the service for the consecration of a bishop by Piccolomini and Burckhard,[18] without doubt a product of their editorial intervention, if not authorship.

Melodic settings

Given the transformation of this introit text for the first edition, it seems only reasonble that the music editor would provide *Benedicat te* with a new, that is, untraditional, setting. Having for whatever reason rejected the first-mode melody of *Benedixit te* in PWD manuscripts (compare Examples 13.1 and 13.2), he may have drawn inspiration from the third-mode introit *Benedicite dominum* (*GT*, p. 607). Both incorporate the *g–a–c'* intonation figure of the psalm-tone ('*dominus deus*'; '*et det tibi*') and inflected

---

'*et*' lacking in other sources available to me (*Locus iste a deo factus est inestimabile sacramentum et irreprehensibilis est*).

[17]*Alleluia-Melodien II ab 1100*, MMMA 8 (1987).

[18]Dykmans, *Le pontifical romain révisé*, pp. 113–114.

recitation. *Benedixit te*, however, centres mainly on *g* ('*super te*'; '*ad resistendum inimicis ecclesia sancte*') rather than the reciting pitch, *c'*, and demonstrates, arguably, a more classical Gregorian approach that preserves the traditional architecture of the reciting-tone. It is enlightening to see in Example 13.2 how the ligation in manuscript readings (represented here by I-Rvat Ott. lat. 501 and indicated by slurs) clarifies the reading of the print, in which the text underlay is unclear.

Example 13.1: Introit, *Benedixit te hodie* (Paris, BNF, ms lat. 733, fol. 23ʳ)

The choice of mode III for an untraditional setting was not unusual, particularly among the mass chants. According to Table 13.2, which compares putative modes and ranges in the 1485 edition (in the column immediately right of the incipits) with those assigned in the *GT* (far left column) and the two manuscript copies, seven of thirteen

Table 13.2 Comparison of mode (1485 and GT), final, and ambitus in editions and manuscript copies of the *Pontificale Romanum*

Genre	Incipit	mode 1485	final 1485	ambitus 1485	final CAh	ambitus CAh	final Ott.	ambitus Ott.	final 1543	ambitus 1543	mode GT	Comments
Int.	*Benedicat te*	III	e	e–c'	e	e–c'	e	e–c'	e	e–c'	no	UNTRADITIONAL; PWD (I)
Gr.	*Imola Deo sacrificium*	V	c	A–a	f	d–d'	f	d–d'	f	d–d'	no	version of TRADITIONAL
All.	*Diffusa est*	VIII	g	f–e'	g	f–e'	g	f–e'	g	f–e'	VIII	version of TRADITIONAL
Tr.	*Desiderium*	VIII	g	d–d'	g	d–d'	g	d–d'	g	d–d'	VIII	version of TRADITIONAL
Off.	*Benedic anima mea*	III	a	g–g'	f	f–e'	e	d–d'	f	f–e'	V	UNTRADITIONAL
Com.	*Messis quidem*	II	a	d–d'	a	d–d'	a	d–d'	g	d–d'	no	UNTRADITIONAL; PWD (II)
Int.	*Tibi dixit*	I	A	g–e'	d	c–a	d	c–a	d	c–a	III	UNTRADITIONAL
Gr.	*Miserere mei Deus miserere*	I	a	a–g'	a	a–g'	d	d–c'	d	d–c'	I	version of TRADITIONAL
All.	*Lauda anima mea*	VIII	a	g–g'	a	g–g'	g	f–f'	g	f–e'	VIII	version of TRADITIONAL
Off.	*Sperent in te*	III	f	f–e'	f	f–e'	e	e–d'	e	e–d'	III	version of TRADITIONAL
Com.	*Redime me Deus*	I	a	g–g'	a	g–g'	d	c–c'	g	TRAD	VII	UNTRADITIONAL
Int.	*Dicit dominus sermones*	III	c'	g–f'	g	TRAD	c'	g–f	g	d–c'	I	UNTRADITIONAL
Gr.	*Tollite hostias*	V	c'	c'–a'	f	f–d'	c'	c'–a'	f	TRAD	V	version of TRADITIONAL
All.	*Redemptionem*	VIII	a	g–f	d	c–b	a	g–f	g	f–e'	II	UNTRADITIONAL
Off.	*Sanctificavit Moyses*	III	e	e–g'	e	e–g'	e	e–g'	e	e–g'	V	UNTRADITIONAL
Com.	*Tollite hostias*	III	e	d–d'	e	c–e'	e	d–d'	e	A–a	IV	UNTRADITIONAL

										TRAD	TRAD	
Int.	*Dum sanctificatus*	III	a	g-f'	e	c-b	a	g-f'	e	TRAD	III	UNTRADITIONAL
Gr.	*Locus iste*	V	a	g-f'	d	c-b	a	g-f'	f	TRAD	V	version of TRADITIONAL
All.	*Adorabo*	VIII	a	g-f'	d	c-b	a	g-f'	g	f-e'	VII	UNTRADITIONAL
All.	*Bene fundata est*	III	a	g-a'	d	c-d'	a	g-a'	e	d-e'	V	UNTRADITIONAL
Off.	*Domine deus simplicitate*	VI	c'	g-g'	f	c-c'	c'	g-g'	f	c-c'	IV	version of TRADITIONAL
Com.	*Comus mea*	V	g	g-e'	c	c-a	G	g-e'	f	f-d'	V	version of TRADITIONAL

Legend: TRAD = Traditional (PWD manuscript) melody (occasionally substituted for an UNTRADITIONAL one)

Example 13.2: *Benedicat te hodie* (first stave, 1485, fol. 35^r; second stave, Vatican, BAV, ms Ott. lat. 501, fol. 43^r)

Be - ne - di - cat te ho - di - e do - mi - nus de - us

Be - ne - di - cat te ho - di - e do - mi - nus de - us

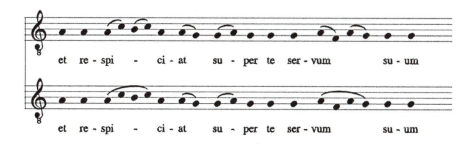

et re - spi - ci - at su - per te ser - vum su - um

et re - spi - ci - at su - per te ser - vum su - um

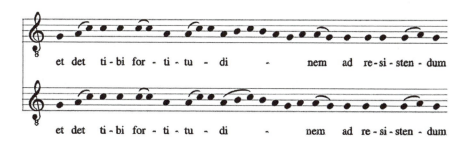

et det ti - bi for - ti - tu - di - nem ad re - si - sten - dum

et det ti - bi for - ti - tu - di - nem ad re - si - sten - dum

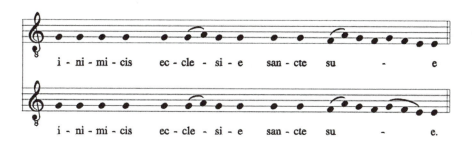

i - ni - mi - cis ec - cle - si - e san - cte su - e

i - ni - mi - cis ec - cle - si - e san - cte su - e.

untraditional settings – more than half – are in mode III; the eighth third-mode chant, the offertory *Sperent in te*, is a version of the traditional Gregorian melody.

None of the untraditional third-mode melodies, which might be described as meandering compared with their more incisive Gregorian counterparts, is obviously based on another, though most incorporate the *g–a–c'* motive and some use *c'* as a reciting pitch. This is not to say that traditional third-mode chants had no impact on the music editor of the 1485 print. The beginning of the untraditional verse *Bene fundata est* and its alleluia both seem to borrow music from the opening phrase of the familiar hymn *Pange lingua* (Example 13.3; cf. *GT*, p. 399 (mode V)). Still, assuming the user of the 1485 edition recognized the resemblance, he would have needed to sing the melody with *b flat*s throughout; the version copied by the scribe of US-CAh Typ. 217 would have also required *e' flat*. The 1543 edition was the first to use *e'* as the final. Note also that the verse of 1485, although brought to a more suitable conclusion in Plannck's edition of 1497, was still incomplete in the edition of 1543. All subsequent prints pick up this change; neither manuscript copy does, this being one indication among many of their having stemmed directly from the *editio princeps*.

One could also single out for further discussion the four remaining alleluias in Table 13.2. The first two, with the verses *Diffusa est* and *Lauda anima mea*, traditionally relate to one another and to other medieval alleluias of a type associated with the eighth-mode alleluia with the verse *Dominus in Sina* (*GT*, p. 236). As illustrated in Example 13.4, the music editor of 1485 abbreviated the first of these in a manner consistent with the late fifteenth century. But he also took it upon himself to adapt the third and fourth alleluias in the series, those with the verses *Redemptionem* and *Adorabo* to the same abbreviated version of the type-melody. The latter chant is given in Example 13.5.

A certain indecisiveness in the untraditional setting of the verse is again evident, but a more serious problem of transmission attracts attention. As indicated in Table 13.2 and illustrated in Example 13.5, three of the alleluias of 1485 are pitched a major second higher than one would expect, opening on *g* rather than *f*. The user of this and editions up to 1543 would either have repositioned the C clef to the fourth from the third highest line, where it was printed, or sharpened both *f* and *c'* to arrive at what is arguably the correct melody – 'correct' in the sense that Plannck printed the first of the four related alleluias at the proper pitch level, that he did the same in the 1497 edition, that the scribes of the manuscript copies adjusted the untraditional settings by changing at least some of the pitch levels, and, most decisively, that the 1543 music editor rendered all four melodies on *g*.

That the version of the alleluia *Adorabo* in US-CAh Typ. 217 (opening on *c*) would have required *f' sharp* suggests, perhaps surprisingly, that users of the prints would not have been overly challenged to sing the melody with 'diatonic ficta'.[19] If this possibility be granted, we would have rare evidence in chant of what Gaston

---

[19]This term and the concepts underlying it are discussed in Margaret Bent, 'Diatonic *Ficta*', *EMH* 4 (1984), pp. 1–48.

Example 13.3: *Alleluia* v. *Bene fundata* (first stave, 1485 fol. 207ʳ; second stave, 1497, fol. 156ʳ; third stave, 1543, fol. 161ᵛ)

Example 13.4: *Alleluia* v. *Diffusa est gratia* (first stave, GT, p. 413; second stave 1485, fol. 43^V)

Example 13.5: *Alleluia* V. *Adorabo* (first stave, 1485, fol. 207ʳ; second stave Cah Typ. 217, fol. 230ʳ; third stave, 1543, fol. 161ᵛ)

Allaire called 'singer's solmization', a transposing technique similar to the modern movable *do* system of *solfeggio* which he supposed to have been operative in the late fifteenth – early sixteenth centuries.[20] Why the higher pitch level was chosen for three of the four alleluias, and whether by the 1485 music editor or Plannck, remain open questions. But if either were a singer prone to questionable musical judgements we might have a basis for understanding the odd clef positions and perhaps also the nondescript character of many untraditional melodies.

Indeed only a few of these and some reworkings in the *editio princeps* could be described as artful. Arguably the best reworking among the chants under consideration is the gradual *Miserere mei deus miserere* (Example 13.6; cf. *GT*, p. 63). Here the traditional first-mode melody was reduced to a neumatic texture, and its phrases evenly balanced. The sense of symmetry was enhanced by the application of musical rhyme: note the similarity of cadences near the midpoints of both respond and verse ('*miserere mei*' and '*liberavit me*') and at the end of the respond ('*mea*') and in the verse ('*de celo*' and '*obprobrium*'). That a revised melody could exhibit this level of competence suggests the activity of a music editor who could rise to an occasion, even if most of his work is no better than competent, and sometimes lacks modal regularity.

Challenges to authenticity

The musical problems evident in many of the 1485 chants, be they revisions (even the best of which are not typically 'Gregorian') or untraditional chants, together with the lack of prior manuscript evidence for them, raise questions of authenticity. Might the print versions be simple mistakes, misprints, or mere filler between the revised rubrics and liturgical texts? A very few earlier manuscript pontificals do contain melodies of dubious reliability, presumably copied by text scribes with little understanding of music. Moreover, pontificals (like missals) are books for celebrants, not choruses. Couldn't a cantor have simply consulted a church's manuscript pontifical, antiphoner, and gradual for items his singers would need for the occasional special service?

The answer to both questions is no, and for three reasons. First, from a commercial standpoint printing nonsense, even musical nonsense, would have detracted from the value of the prints, the audiences for which would have included not just bishops and ecclesiastical institutions (and their cantors), but ambitious clerics hoping to ascend into the upper reaches of the church hierarchy, particularly in Rome.[21] One

---

[20] *The Theory of Hexachords, Solmization and the Modal System*, Musicological Studies and Documents 24 (American Institute of Musicology, 1972), pp. 34–43, 59–61. Plate III reproduces a table of hexachords build on *f, g, a, b flat, c', e',* and *e' flat* from the Giunta gradual of 1499–1500.

[21] On the market for printed chantbooks see Stanley Boorman, 'Early Music Printing: Working for a Specialized Market', in Gerald P. Tyson and Sylvia S. Wogonheim, eds, *Print and Culture in the Renaissance: Essays on the Advent of Printing in Europe* (Newark, 1986), pp.

Example 13.6: *Miserere mei Deus* (first stave, 1485, fol. 76ʳ; second stave, BVA, ms Ott. lat. 501, fol. 90ʳ)

imagines that errors of any kind would also have detracted from Plannck's reputation as a printer. And if not to sell books, why would he have included more melodies than the manuscripts provided, enough that the users need not bother cross-referencing other service books? As to Plannck's musical competence one cannot be certain, but at least he was experienced with notation, having been the founder of type for the first book with chant printed in Rome more than a decade earlier, a Roman missal of Ulrich Han (1476), indeed the second book in history printed with movable music type.[22]

Second, about a quarter of the chants in the PWD were not sung in the office or mass and thus could not have been found in antiphoners and graduals. Additionally, the PWD was less widely disseminated in fifteenth-century Italy than the prior recensions, the pontificals of the Roman Curia, which contained fewer chants and a different ordering, rendering them impractical for use in PWD services; in northern Europe, the PWD competed with a greater variety of regional pontificals than circulated in Italy. This means that, assuming a cantor were inclined to copy PWD chants for rehearsal, his source would have been either a relatively rare PWD manuscript or a more widely available print. (Single-leaf copies and gatherings of pontifical chants do survive from an earlier period – they are usually now bound with complete manuscript pontificals – but I have yet to find a handwritten copy of chants from the *editio princeps*.) It is reasonable to suppose further that the same cantor would have approached the untraditional melodies in ways similar to the scribes of the deluxe manuscripts: he could have substituted familiar traditional melodies for some untraditional ones and rendered others performable through his own musical expertise, if not first-hand experience with the melodies themselves.

Finally, why would later scribes and subsequent music editors, particularly those of the 1543 Giunta edition, have addressed the problems of the untraditional printed melodies if they were mistakes, misprints, filler, or nonsense? These individuals may have considered the *editio princeps* reflective of Curial Roman practice and printed the problematic melodies out of respect for that institution, but this begs the question of Plannck's own second edition, which preserves the same chants with only rare differences. (They were not printed from the same plates; the contents, print areas, and paginations are all different.) Certainly the music scribe of I-Rvat Ott. lat. 501, who worked somewhere in Italy and perhaps in Rome and may have heard some of the chants performed or even sung them himself, would not have been so easily gulled. Would he have sent to an important patron a work of many months that was so littered with nonsense, even if he made some of it more performable? All indications, in other

---

[22]Meyer-Baer, *Liturgical Music Incunabula* 21, no. 119. The missal's colophon is reproduced with English translation in Mary Kay Duggan, *Italian Music Incunabula: Printers and Type* (Berkeley, 1992), p. 80.

words, lead us to suspect that the untraditional, abbreviated, and revised melodies in the *editio princeps* were intended to replace earlier ones in manuscript circulation.[23]

If the *editio princeps* was an attempt to create an authoritative version of the pontifical, such was not yet attainable.[24] Plannck may have lacked the technical means to represent accurately the melodies he had been handed. Apart from inevitable mistakes and misreadings of his copy, his selection of type was limited, the printing process primitive and cumbersome, and (given his wide activity as a printer of many different kinds of books) his knowledge of plainchant likely inferior to that of most music scribes. There may also have been problems with the printer's copy itself, particularly in the case of melodies with finals that were not easily reconciled with basic chant theory. The scribes who copied the chant into the deluxe manuscripts corrected some of the 'singer's solmization' (if such it was), clarifying and reworking some of the untraditional and revised melodies according to their own musical experience, which evidently encompassed an approach to singing chant that allowed for diatonic *ficta*. Editors and typographers in Brescia, Venice, and Lyons were less inclined to do so and merely tidied up earlier print versions – that is, until 1543, when the pitch levels and other features of untraditional chants in the *editio princeps* were reconciled with the widely understood rules of modality. In sum, this Venice edition and earlier attempts to salvage the *editio princeps* chants establish their authenticity and provide useful guides to reconstructing them editorially.

That such is a worthwhile undertaking as a historiographical project is suggested by the fact that the men who edited the texts of the *editio princeps* were the same masters of ceremonies who, two years before its publication, supervised the inauguration of the Sistine Chapel in 1483. Although the Sistina was not consecrated in the manner outlined in the pontifical – it was the popes' private chapel, built on ground already blessed – we do know that a new altar was installed there and that this must have been duly consecrated.[25] If it is mere coincidence that many of the untraditional melodies, including some mass chants, are designated for the consecration of an altar or dedication of a church, it is a coincidence that demands further exploration.

---

[23] Although there is no discussion of chant in the preface to the *editio princeps*, the text editors refer disparagingly to the unfaithful transmission of liturgical texts owing to a superabundance of scribes. See Borders, 'The 1485 *Pontificale romanum*', p. 16.

[24] On the existence of variants in the printing into the eighteenth century, see Bernard Cerquiglini, *In Praise of the Variant: A Critical History of Philology*, trans. Betsy Wing (Baltimore, 1999).

[25] Borders, 'The 1485 *Pontificale romanum*', pp. 18–19.

Chapter 14

The double office at St Peter's Basilica on *Dominica de Gaudete*

Joseph Dyer

One of the most distinctive features of the early medieval Roman liturgy was an observance known as a 'double office'. Attested from the end of the eighth century, this consisted of vigils (generally of one nocturn) celebrated late at night, followed by a full matins of three nocturns that began at the usual time in the early hours of the morning.[1] Vigils lacked both the introductory versicles and the invitatory. There was no hymn either, but since Rome eschewed hymns in the office, this absence is not remarkable. The earliest reference (Roman or otherwise) to double offices occurs in Ordo romanus 12, which introduces its description of such offices with the title 'De festis sanctorum, qualiter apud romanos celebrentur'.[2] Double offices at Rome did remain most closely linked to the feasts of especially honoured saints, but they were also celebrated on a few other auspicious days of the liturgical year. (See Table 14.1

An earlier version of this chapter was presented as part of a paper read at the symposium 'Music in Sacred Space' at Wesleyan University (Middletown, CT) on November 22, 2003.

[1]The bibliography on nocturnal prayer is very large. Various viewpoints on the controversial questions about its origins and development are expressed in Anton Baumstark, *Nocturna laus. Typen frühchristlicher Vigilienfeier und ihre Fortleben vor allem im römischen und monastischen Ritus*, Liturgiewissenschaftliche Quellen und Forschungen 32 (Münster, 1957); Paul Bradshaw, *Daily Prayer in the Early Church*, 2nd edn, Alcuin Club Collection 63 (London, 1983); Camillus Callewaert, *Liturgicae institutiones tractatus secundus. De breviarii romani liturgia*, 2nd edn (Bruges, 1939); Herbert Goltzen, 'Nocturna Laus. Aus Arbeiten zur Geschichte der Vigil', *Jahrbuch für Liturgik und Hymnologie* 5 (1960), pp. 79–88; Jean-Michel Hanssens, *Nature et genèse de l'office des matines*, Analecta gregoriana 57 (Rome, 1952); Josef Jungmann, 'The Origin of Matins', in *Pastoral Liturgy* (New York, 1962), pp. 105–122; Robert Taft, *The Liturgy of the Hours in East and West: The Origins of the Divine Office and its Meaning for Today* (Collegeville MN, 1986), especially pp. 165–190 (with bibliography); Paul Tirot, 'Vigiles et matines: liturgie monastique et liturgie cathédrale', *EG* 22 (1988), pp. 24–30.

[2]OR 12.23, in Michel Andrieu, ed., *Les ordines romani du haut moyen-âge*, 5 vols, Spicilegium Sacrum Lovaniense 11, 23–24, 28 and 29 (Louvain, 1931–1961), vol. 2, p. 465 (hereafter Andrieu).

below.) Indeed, Ordo romanus 12 also describes in some detail a double office for Christmas, a feast that invited a heightened degree of solemnity.[3] It is not quite as easy, on the other hand, to understand why the third Sunday in Advent, known as 'Dominica de Gaudete' from the first words of the introit of the Mass (Philippians 4:4–6), merited such a distinction.[4] The station for the Sunday was the Vatican basilica,

Table 14.1: Roman double offices

Amalar, *De ordine antiphonarii*	Ordo romanus 12	*Liber politicus*
		Dom. de Gaudete 1 papal 2 papal/clerical
Christmas 1 papal 2 clerical St Stephen St John Evangelist Holy Innocents	Christmas 1 clerical [OR15] 2 papal De festis sanctorum	Christmas (SMM) 1 clerical 2 papal
		Epiphany 1 papal 2 papal/clerical
St John Baptist		St John Baptist [see OLat]
Sts Peter + Paul 1 papal 2 papal St Laurence Assumption		St Peter 1 papal 2 papal Assumption

---

[3] OR 12.4, in Andrieu, vol. 2, pp. 460–461.

[4] The passage from Philippians ('Rejoice in the Lord!') also provides the text for the first responsory of vigils in the Old Roman antiphoners. This responsory, *Gaudete in domino*, is extremely scarce, being represented in merely five per cent of the more than 800 manuscripts surveyed by Dom Hesbert for the *Corpus antiphonalium officii* project. Even more extraordinary is the fact that only in the two Old Roman antiphoners (mss Vatican, BAV, Archivio S. Pietro, B 79, and London, BL, add. 29988) does it occupy first place among the responsories of matins. See René-Jean Hesbert, 'L'antiphonaire d'Amalaire', *Ephemerides liturgicae* 94 (1980), p. 185.

Mallio, *Descriptio* ('nocturnales stationes')	BAV, ms S. Pietro, B 79 [BL, add. 29988]	Ordinals of Gregory X and Innocent III
Dom. de Gaudete	*Dom. de Gaudete* 1 clerical 2 clerical Christmas [BL]	*Dom. de Gaudete* papal vespers only Christmas (SMM) 1 ? [clerical] 2 papal
Epiphany Ascension Pentecost St Peter (+ oct.)	St Peter [BL] 1 clerical 2 clerical St Laurence Assumption	St Peter 1 papal 2 papal

and the ceremonial was far more elaborate than any of the other Roman double offices. It included a vigils office *ad corpus* in the crypt beneath the main altar and matins sung in the choir and altar precinct, the whole preceded by a nocturnal perambulation of the basilica with stations at several of the altars.

Details about both offices are available in two principal sources: (1) a description in an ordo compiled in Rome shortly before the middle of the twelfth century and (2) rubrics and music in a late twelfth-century antiphoner from St Peter's basilica.[5] The first of these sources, the *Liber politicus*, is a guide to papal services compiled *ca* 1140/43 by one Benedict, canon of St Peter's basilica, at the request of Cardinal Guido de Castello.[6] For this Sunday Benedict provided the cardinal with ample details about

---

[5] The double office on *Dominica de Gaudete* is listed among the 'nocturnales stationes' in a nearly contemporary description of the basilica by Pietro Mallio. See Mallio, '*Descriptio basilicae Vaticanae* 55', in Roberto Valentini and Giuseppe Zucchetti, eds, *Codice topographico della città di Roma*, 4 vols, Fonti per la Storia d'Italia 81, 88, 90 and 91 (Rome, 1940–1953), vol. 3, p. 434. A like expression appears in a rubric for this Sunday in the St Peter's Antiphoner (B 79, fol. 11). The other double offices mentioned by Mallio are Epiphany, Ascension, Pentecost, St Peter and the octave, and St Andrew.

[6] Guido was at the time cardinal priest of S. Marco; he later became Pope Celestine II. The *Liber politicus* is edited with notes by Paul Fabre and Louis Duchesne, *Le Liber Censuum de l'église romaine*, Bibliothèque des Écoles françaises d'Athènes et de Rome, 2nd series, 6/1–2 (Paris, 1910), vol. 2, pp. 141–171, especially 143–144 (hereafter *Lib. pol.*). For a description and interpretation of the procession and liturgy on 'Gaudete' Sunday see Sible de Blaauw,

the arrival of the papal court at the Vatican from the Lateran, housing accommodations, the procession through the basilica before vigils, and the arrangement of the papal and basilical clergy during vigils and matins.[7] The antiphoner (BAV, Archivio S. Pietro, B 79) contains the music of the office sung by the canons in Old Roman chant; it is also furnished with a few rubrics.[8] The canons' office in this twelfth-century antiphoner was not, as we shall see, identical to that of the papal court.

Origin of Roman double offices

Double offices were celebrated at Rome primarily on the feasts of the most prominent saints, and an explanation for their existence can be sought in the history of how sanctoral feasts began to be commemorated at Rome.[9] Initially, the annual commemoration of a martyr's *natalitia* into heavenly glory was observed exclusively at the place of his or her burial. This meant inevitably one of the suburban cemeteries, since in the Roman world burials within the city were forbidden.[10] (Certain suburban cemeteries also continued to expand because burial places in close proximity to a martyr's gravesite were much sought after by the Christian faithful.) Beginning in the seventh century, the ancient Roman taboo against disturbing the mortal remains of the de-

---

Cultus et decor. Liturgia e architettura nella Roma tardoantica e medievale, 2 vols, Studi e Testi 355–356 (Rome, 1994), pp. 688–690.

[7] The very same observance was repeated on Epiphany and Pentecost (*Lib. pol.*, 147 and 157), but no further details are provided in either context. Thus the vigils *ad corpus* were not occasioned by any special Petrine connection with the feasts. The other double offices treated by Benedict are *Dominica de Gaudete*, Christmas (at S. Maria Maggiore), St Peter, and Assumption (*Lib. pol.*, pp. 143, 145, 157, 158).

[8] The text of the antiphoner was published by Giuseppe Maria Tomasi in Antonius Franciscus Vezzosi, ed., *Responsoria et antiphonalia Romanae Ecclesiae*, Opera omnia (Rome, 1749), vol. 4.

[9] On the development of festal offices see Camillus Callewaert, 'Les offices festifs à Rome avant la règle de saint Benoît' and 'De distinctione duplicis, semiduplicis, simplicis', in *Sacris erudiri* (Steenbrugghe, 1940), pp. 149–168 and 179–183, and *Liturgicae institutiones tractatus secundus*, pp. 58–60; Pierre Jounel, 'Le sanctoral romain du 8e au 12e siècles', *La Maison-Dieu* 52 (1957), pp. 59–88.

[10] At Rome exceptions were made only for the imperial family. For recent surveys of Christian burial practices in late antiquity see Anna Maria Nieddu, 'L'utilizzazione funeraria del suburbio nei secoli V e VI', in Philippe Pergola, Riccardo Santangeli Valenzani, and Rita Volpe, eds, *Suburbium: il suburbio di Roma dalla crisi del sistema delle ville a Gregorio Magno*, Collection de l'École française de Rome 311 (Rome, 2003), pp. 545–606 (with bibliography); and Vincenzo Fiocchi Nicolai, 'L'organizzazione dello spazio funerario', in Letizia Pani Ermini, ed., *Christiana loca: lo spazio cristiano nella Roma del primo millennio* (Rome, 2000), pp. 43–58; and 'Strutture funerarie ed edifici di culto paleocristiani di Roma dal III al VI secolo', in Ivan Di Stefano Manzella, ed., *Le iscrizioni dei cristiani in Vaticano*, Inscriptiones Sanctae Sedis 2 (Vatican City, 1997), pp. 121–141.

ceased began to weaken, inevitably so, given the impossibility of protecting the venerable sites from plundering during the unsettled times that followed the dissolution of Roman authority in the West. The suburban cemeteries became prey to treasure hunters as well as pious relic collectors. Translation of a martyr's body to an urban church or monastery created a new focal point of veneration, and such translations increased over the eighth and early ninth centuries. Several of the popes sponsored wholesale removals of bodies, saintly and not so saintly, from the catacombs. Gradually at Rome the veneration of the martyrs on the anniversaries of their deaths formed itself into an urban liturgical calendar. The problem then arose of honouring the saints with a suitable office without interrupting the regular hebdomadal round of psalms, not to mention the scriptural pericopes, sermons, and homilies of the Fathers read at the night office.

A solution was devised by Pope Gregory III (731–741), who established an oratory within the walls of St Peter's basilica in honour of Christ, the Blessed Virgin, and the saints. Here he placed relics of apostles, martyrs, and confessors that had been transported from the remote cemeteries for safety. So that their memory would not be neglected, 'he decreed that in the oratory dedicated to their name ... vigils should be celebrated daily according to the existing order by the monks of the three monasteries serving the basilica and that masses on their feast days be celebrated in the same place'.[11] The early eighth-century homiliary from the Roman church of Sts Philip and James, known as the homiliary of Agimond after its scribe, has readings for two offices of St Peter and two of St Paul.[12] In each case the rubrics preceding the readings of the first office read 'in vigilias' and the second 'in secunda vigilia'. These vigil offices were not a replacement for the daily office, but a supernumerary obligation.

---

[11]'Hic fecit oratorium intro eandem basilicam, iuxta arcum principalem, parte virorum, in quo recondivit in honore Salvatoris sanctaeque eius genetricis reliquias sanctorum apostolorum vel omnium sanctorum martyrum ac confessorum, perfectorum iustorum, toto in orbe terrarum requiescentium. Quorum festa vigiliarum a monachis trium monasteriorum illic servientium cotidie per ordinem existentia atque nataliciorum missas in eodem loco celebrare.' Louis Duchesne, *Le liber pontificalis* (Paris, 1884–1892), vol. 1, p. 417. The oratory, chosen by Gregory III as his burial site, was located on the left side of the front of the central nave (no. 38 on the plan of Tiberio Alfarano, pp. 59 and 186, and Figure 14.1, no. 21 below; Tiberius Alfaranus, *De basilicae vaticanae antiquissima et nova structura*, 1571).

[12]Cited by Michel Huglo, 'Le chant "vieux-romain"'. Liste des manuscrits et témoins indirects', *Sacris erudiri* 6 (1954), p. 115. See also Réginald Grégoire, *Homéliaires liturgiques médiévaux: analyse de manuscrits*, Biblioteca degli Studi Medievali 12 (Spoleto, 1980), pp. 362–371 (St Peter, nos 77–85 and 86–97; St Paul, nos 95–104 and 105–114); Antoine Chavasse, 'Le sermonnaire d'Agimond. Ses sources immédiates', in Patrick Granfield and Josef Jungmann, eds, *Kyriakon: Festschrift Johannes Quasten*, 2 vols (Münster in Westfalen, 1970), vol. 2, pp. 800–810; Antoine Chavasse, 'Le sermonnaire des Saints Philippe-et-Jacques et le sermonnaire de Saint-Pierre', *Ephemerides liturgicae* 69 (1955), pp. 17–24.

Roman double offices for the Feast of Saints

Ordo romanus 12 must be dated after 795, for it closes with the remark that readings from vitae of the saints, heretofore confined to offices in churches dedicated in their honour, began to be read also at the Vatican during the time of Pope Hadrian (772–795).[13] Its description of a sanctoral double office is both representative and instructive. The first (vigil) office began in the evening ('sero ad vigilias peragendas') with the psalmody, the usual opening versicles and invitatory being omitted.[14] The antiphons of the vigils are drawn from the proper of the saint, or *commune*, if no *proper* texts exist. At this time the number of psalms was flexible (nine, six, or five), but is it not clear whether they were specially chosen for their appropriateness to the feast.[15] Such was probably the case, since the description of the second office in OR 12 specifies that 'ad nocturnas' (i.e. matins) the psalms were to be 'cotidianos de feria'.[16] The readings (three, five, seven, or nine), on the other hand, must be 'de ipso natalicio pertinentes'. Thus both of the double offices described by OR 12 (vigils and matins) were mixed. Some items were special to the saint or to his or her title to sainthood (apostle, martyr, etc.); others were accepted from the occurring day of the week.

The omission of opening versicles and invitatory at vigils has been regarded as a mark of antiquity, given their absence, e.g., on the last three days of Holy Week. Benedict of Nursia (*ca* 480–550) imposed the obligation of singing *Venite exultemus* (Ps. 94) near the beginning of the night office, but it cannot be concluded that he did not borrow this – as so much else – from the Roman basilical monasteries.[17] It is unlikely that the vigils portion of the double offices can be regarded as a remnant of a pre-Benedictine basilican office; hence the absence of an invitatory does not argue one

---

[13]'Passiones sanctorum vel gesta ipsorum usque Adriani tempora tantummodo ibi legebantur ubi ecclesia ipsius sancti vel titulus erat. Ipse vero tempore suo renovere iussit et in ecclesia sancti Petri legendas esse instituit'. OR 12.25, in Andrieu, vol. 2, p. 466.

[14]Cf. the rubric in the Antiphonary of St Peter's (fol. 173) for the double office on the feast of St Andrew: 'Sero ad vig[ilias] ca[n]tamus sic[ut] ca[n]tavimus ad matut[inas]'.

[15]Raymond LeRoux argued for a single nocturn in the earliest saints' offices, and he referred to the several instances in the St Peter's Antiphoner when this type of office preceded matins. Gradually a second and a third nocturn were added, thus eventually leading to a full festive sanctoral office; see Le Roux, 'Aux origins de l'office festif: les antiennes et les psaumes de matines et de laudes pour Noël et le 1er janvier selon les cursus romain et monastique', *EG* 4 (1961), p. 125.

[16]OR 12.24, in Andrieu, vol. 2, p. 24. OR 12.4 lists the eight (*proper*) responsories of Christmas vigils, but the twelve psalms of matins are also 'cotodianos'; Andrieu, vol. 2, pp. 460–461.

[17]*Regula monachorum* 9; Timothy Fry *et al.*, eds, *RB 1980: The Rule of St. Benedict in Latin and English with Notes* (Collegeville MN, 1981), p. 202. Callewaert, however, suggests a Benedictine invention in 'Les prières d'introduction aux différentes heures de l'office', in *Sacris erudiri* (Steenbrugghe, 1940), pp. 135–144, especially 139. See also Pio Alonzo, *L'antifonario dell'ufficio romano*, Monografie Liturgiche 3 (Subiaco, 1935), pp. 63–65; and Pierre Salmon, *L'office divin au Moyen Age*, Lex Orandi 43 (Paris, 1967), pp. 38–39.

way or another about the history of these offices. Indeed, Benedict gives no evidence of being aware of 'double offices' to celebrate feasts of saints. Chapter 14 of the Rule ('In nataliciis sanctorum qualiter agantur vigiliae') calls for saints' days to be celebrated like the Sunday office, not with a (modified) replication of the night office.[18] Benedict's further instruction that the psalms, antiphons, and readings should be 'ad ipsum diem pertinentes' has suggested to most interpreters that the psalms were not those of the daily *cursus* (which must thus have been omitted), but selected for their appropriateness to the saint being honoured. This is not the solution of the Roman double offices, which try to respect both the ferial *cursus* and the uniqueness of the saint's day.

The Roman double offices fascinated the Frankish liturgist and bishop Amalar of Metz (*ca* 775 – *ca* 859) on one of his visits to the city. He mentions these offices several times in the *Liber de ordine antiphonarii*, an extensive prologue prepared for the (now lost) revision of the antiphoner he was compiling for the diocese of Metz. Amalar described succinctly the principal features of the Roman usage:

> On the greatest festivals of the saints it is the custom of our holy mother, the Roman church, to perform two offices during the night, which offices are entitled 'de vigiliis'. The first of them, sung at the beginning of the night, is performed without alleluia. But the other, which begins about the middle of the night and ends at daybreak, does have alleluia both with the antiphons of the third nocturn and with the antiphons of matins [i.e., Lauds].[19]

Amalar confirms that the Romans solemnized with double offices the feasts of Christmas, St Stephen, St John the Evangelist, Holy Innocents, St John the Baptist, St Peter, St Lawrence, the Assumption of the Virgin, and St Andrew. In addition to the clear predominance given to saints' days, one notices the absence of any mention of Dominica de Gaudete, obviously because it was absent from the Roman antiphoner at Amalar's disposal.

The double office on the feast of St Stephen was the first sanctoral double office Amalar encountered in the Roman antiphoner; his comments about it can legitimately

---

[18] 'In sanctorum vero festivitatibus, vel omnibus sollemnitatibus, sicut diximus dominico die agendum, ita agatur, excepto quod psalmi aut antiphonae vel lectiones ad ipsum diem pertinentes dicantur.' *Regula monachorum* 14; Fry, *RB* (1980), pp. 208–209.

[19] 'In praeclarissimis festivitatibus sanctorum consuetudo est sanctae matris nostrae Romanae ecclesiae duo officia peragere in nocte, quorum officia praetitulantur de vigiliis. Primum eorum, quod canitur in initio noctis, sine alleluia peragitur; alterum vero, quod habet initium circa medium noctis et finitur in die, habet in tertia nocturna in suis antiphoniis alleluia, et in antiphonis de matutino'. Jean-Michel Hanssens, ed., *De ordine antiphonarii* 59.5, in *Amalarii episcopi opera liturgica omnia*, 3 vols, Studi e Testi 138–140 (Vatican City, 1948–1950), vol. 3, p. 96. Honorius of Autun (*ca* 1080 – *ca* 1137) cites a custom ('more antiquo') of a papal vigils without invitatory followed by a clerical matins (*Gemma animae* 3.6; *Patrologia latina* 172:644). His example of Christmas is borrowed from Amalar, but his confusion of these liturgical vigils with the sometimes disorderly fourth-century nocturnal gatherings at the tombs of the martyrs suggests that he had little familiarity with double offices.

be taken as representative of features common to sanctoral double offices. He says that the vigil office, celebrated 'circa vespertinam horam', was usually (*vulgo*) called 'proper', while the later office of matins was either ferial or drawn from the common of the saints ('sive de propria feria, seu de communibus sanctis').[20] This remark might imply a combination, not two alternatives, one exclusive of the other. This interpretation accords with the witness of OR 12 that the psalms of vigils were *proper* 'aut de apostolorum aut cuiuslibet sanctorum', while at the matins office the psalms were 'cotidianas de feria'. Other elements of the matins office were *proper*, including the readings and responsories.[21] Amalar respected this Roman custom in his Messine antiphoner by including a double office for the saints so honoured by the Romans,[22] but this urban custom was not widely accepted north of the Alps.

Table 14.1 compares double offices in Roman sources from the early ninth to the early thirteenth century. Given the diversity of the sources, they contain varying types and amounts of information. OR 12 (and probably OR 15, though the text may be garbled) is a series of notes on the office. The responsories of Christmas vigils are listed, and the ordo offers a rather extensive list of instructions on how the feasts of saints are celebrated 'apud romanos'. Amalar can be considered 'Roman' inasmuch as he describes urban-papal practice. *Dominica de Gaudete*, the principal focus of this chapter, does not appear until the 1140s with the *Liber politicus*, which delineates the liturgical activities of the papal court. The double offices in St Peter's Antiphoner, a book intended for the private use of the canons, are exclusively clerical. Mallio's list in the *Descriptio basilicae Vaticanae* is merely incidental to his main purpose: recording the important relics, tombs, and inscriptions of the basilica. By the time of the court ordinals of Innocent III (1198–1216) and Gregory X (1271–1276), attention to double offices has diminished markedly. On the eve of *Dominica de Gaudete* the court celebrated a solemn vespers that retained, in the incensations during the psalmody, only a reminiscence of the elaborate ritual of the *Liber politicus*.[23] As one can see from Table 14.1, the feasts of Christmas and St Peter were the most persistent presence of double offices over the centuries.

---

[20] *De ord. ant.* 17, in Hanssens, *Amalarii episcopi*, vol. 3, p. 53. For Amalar's references to the other double offices, see *De ord. ant.* 59–63, in *ibid.*, vol. 3, pp. 96–98.

[21] 'Lectiones aut tres, aut quinque, aut septem, aut si voluerit novem, de ipso natalicio pertinentes leguntur; responsoria vero de ipso die sanctorum.' OR 12.24, in Andrieu, vol. 2, p. 466).

[22] 'Ex romano antiphonario posui duas vigilias in nostro antiphonario. Primam solet apostolicus facere in initio noctis, quae fit sine invitatorio.' *De ord. ant.* 60, in Hanssens, *Amalarii episcopi*, vol. 3, p. 97.

[23] An indication that the 'Gaudete' Sunday observance had lapsed by the thirteenth century is the silence of Censius Savelli, who relished such detail; he makes no mention of it. See Fabre and Duchesne, *Le Liber censuum*.

Elsewhere I have discussed double offices observed at the Lateran basilica contemporary with the *Liber politicus* of Canon Benedict.[24] The Lateran canons celebrated double offices on a much larger number of occasions than Benedict cites, but they were not thereby honouring a venerable Roman tradition preserved only partially by the papal court and the canons of St Peter's. On the contrary, the reform canons of the Lateran had brought with them from Lucca an ordo with 'vesperae maiores' for feasts both of universal and of local significance.[25] These 'vespers' were a combination of a one-nocturn *vigilia* (anticipating the first nocturn of matins of the feast). They consisted of three psalms and antiphons, three readings 'de festivitate', two responsories, a *capitulum*, verse, Benedictus [*sic*], and closing prayer. Between the readings the altars, clergy, and people were incensed. The Lateran canons adapted the Lucchese practice to the new circumstances by honouring saints whose remains were enclosed in altars and chapels of the Lateran basilica. The Lucchese *vesperae maiores*, subsequently transported to the Lateran, may trace their ultimate origins to a Roman inspiration, but that is a question yet to be fully explored.

Dominica de Gaudete

Canon Benedict of St Peter's report on *Dominica de Gaudete* at the Vatican concerns itself not only with the liturgy but also with the practical details of housing the papal entourage and the distribution of various remunerations. Composing his *Descriptio* of St Peter's in the 1180s, Pietro Mallio was far less interested than Benedict in the liturgy and more concerned about how much each cleric in attendance received for performing his official duties. Benedict says that members of the court arrived at St Peter's on horseback towards evening and each received a cash distribution according to clerical rank. Most were given five *solidi* 'pro cenatica'. Housing had been prepared in a hostel known as the 'Domus Agulie' (*aiguillia*, pointed stick) because of its proximity to the great Egyptian obelisk, then still in its original site on the south side of the basilica.[26] The guestmaster had to provide lodging for the clergy and stabling for

---

[24]See my 'Double Offices at the Lateran in the Mid-twelfth Century', in John Daverio and John Ogasapian, eds, *The Varieties of Musicology: Essays in Honor of Murray Lefkowitz* (Warren, MI, 2000), pp. 27–46. The source of information on the Lateran customs has been edited by Ludwig Fischer, in *Bernhardi cardinalis et Lateranensis ecclesiae prioris Ordo officiorum ecclesiae lateranensis*, Historische Forschungen und Quellen 2–3 (Munich–Freising, 1916).

[25]Martino Giusti, 'L'*Ordo officiorum* della cattedrale di Lucca (Bibl. cap. 608)', in *Miscellanea Giovanni Mercati*, 6 vols, Studi e Testi 121–126 (Vatican City, 1946), vol. 2, pp. 523–566; Pierre-Marie Gy, 'L'influence des chanoines de Lucques sur la liturgie du Latran', *Revue des sciences religieuses* 58 (1984), pp. 31–41.

[26]The obelisk, weighing 340 tons, was transported from Egypt by Caligula in 37 BC and erected on the *spina* of his circus (later renamed in honour of Nero) at the Vatican. Since 1586 it has stood in the piazza before new St Peter's.

their horses, but he was paid separately for providing dinner, when that was requested.[27] This arrangement, Benedict informs his cardinal patron, applies to all *stationes nocturnales* throughout the year.

The course of the two Advent offices is outlined in Table 14.2. It should be read in conjunction with the ground plan of the basilica (Figure 14.1, adapted with permission from Sible de Blaauw, *Cultus et Decor*, Fig. 26).

Table 14.2: Vigils and matins of *Dominica de Gaudete* at St Peter's (*Liber politicus*)

Location	Ritual
ad sanctum Leonem	*Media nocte*, a mansionarius [sexton] prepares the thurible; the cubicularii, bearers of *faculae*, and the camerarii carrying candles take up positions in front of the pope, who incenses the altar dedicated to Pope St Leo I, located on the west wall of the south transept.
porticus pontificum	Procession moves along the north aisle.
ad sanctum Gregorium I	The pope incenses Gregory's altar at the eastern end of the north aisle and the separate altars of St Sebastian and St Tiburtius [and Gorgonius].
duo altaria in mediana ac crucifixos	A visit to altars in the nave dedicated to the apostles. Sts Simon and Jude and Sts Philip and James.
ad sudarium Christi quod vocatur Veronica	The pope incenses the adjacent altars of the Veronica and St Mary at the end of the outer north aisle.
ad sanctum Pastorem iuxta arcum triumphalem	This altar on the right side of the central nave before the transept is also incensed.
ad corpus	The ancient altar in the crypt beneath the raised presbyterium is incensed. All take their seats; the paraphonista and the schola begin **vigils**: an office of one nocturn without invitatory (3 psalms, 3 readings, 3 responsories, Te deum, closing prayer). (Table 14.3)
ad altare maius	The main altar of the basilica is incensed by the pope.

---

[27]The 'fast food' industry prospered in medieval Rome. It was more energy efficient – and far safer in the flammable housing stock of the period – to purchase food cooked in commercial ovens.

ad pectorale ante altare	For **matins** the [cardinal] deacons stand on one side of the enclosure inside the column screen of Gregory III, the bishops on the other [left] side.
in choro	The cardinals [priests] take their places in the choir with the canons of St Peter's. The cubicularii and camerarii place their *faculae* before the pope, who begins matins with the usual 'Domine labia mea aperies'. The office (with invitatory) consists of a full three nocturns, followed immediately by lauds.
[main altar]	**Mass** is celebrated by the pope with the singing of Gloria in excelsis. After receiving the *laudes* from the deacons, subdeacons and notaries, he returns crowned to the Lateran, 'sicut mos est'.[28]

The procession assembled in the vast interior of Constantine's basilica in front of the altar of the sainted Pope Leo I (Figure 14.1, no. 19), attached to the west wall of the south transept. Although Benedict does not mention it, the basilica was specially illuminated for nocturnal stations, so that the procession did not have to make its way in semi-darkness.[29] The altar of St Leo stood adjacent to a door that gave access to the basilica from the outside. Having gathered at this point, the procession started toward its ultimate goal: the presbyterium in the apse. A roundabout route was taken, accompanied (according to the antiphoner of the basilica) by the chanting of 'psalmos speciales et letaniam'.[30] The general notion of what a *letania* might have been like is clear enough, but what identified the psalms as 'special' is not. The term was sometimes applied to the seven penitential psalms, but the reason why these should be chosen on such an occasion is far from evident. Perhaps they were selected for their appropriateness to Advent.

---

[28] On the papal use of the crown see Sible de Blaauw, 'Contrasts in Processional Liturgy: A Typology of Outdoor Processions in Twelfth-century Rome', in Nicolas Bock, *et al.*, eds, *Art, cérémonial et liturgie au Moyen Âge: Actes du colloque du 3ᵉ Cycle Romand de Lettres, Lausanne-Fribourg, 24–25 mars, 14–15 avril, 12–13 mai 2000* (Rome, 2002), pp. 357–394.

[29] Mallio, *Descriptio* 43, in Valentini and Zucchetti, *Codice topographico*, vol. 3, pp. 425–426. I owe this reference to de Blaauw, *Cultus et decor*, vol. 2, p. 688.

[30] B 79, fol. 11. The entire rubric reads: 'antequam cantetur matutinum, facimus processionem, cantando psalmos speciales et letaniam per ecclesiam, et sub confessione beati Petri cantemus vigilias trium lectionum'. The antiphoner lists only the incipits of the items of this office, since they are all notated in the following matins. The antiphoner gives none of the rubrical detail of Benedict, save to mention that the vigil office takes place 'sub confessione beati Petri'.

Figure 14.1: St Peter's Basilica: 11–12c disposition (adapted from deBlaauw,
      Cultus et decor, **Fig. 26)**

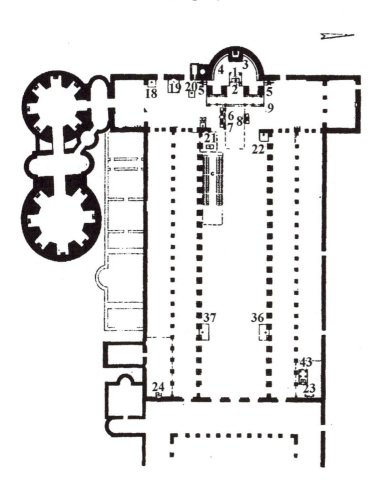

1 Main altar	19 Oratorio of St Leo
2 Confession	20 Altar of St Sixtus
3 Cathedra	21 Altar of S. Maria de Cancellis
4 Clergy benches (subsellia)	c Canons' choir
5 Entrance to the Crypt	22 Altar of St Pastor
6 Ambo (Gospel)	23 Altar of St Mary
7 Paschal candlestick	24 Oratory of St Gregory
8 Ambo (Epistle)	36 Altar of Sts Philip and James
9 Altar 'de ossibus apostolorum'	37 Altar of Sts Simon and Jude
18 Oratorio of St Hadrian	43 Altar of the Veronica

The next piece of topographical information offered by Benedict ('incedens per porticum pontificum') indicates the direction of the procession. The porticus pontificum, to which Pietro Mallio makes frequent reference in his *Descriptio basilicae Vaticanae*, appears to have been a general name for the area in the south aisle, 'nam in illo loco sunt sepulturae sanctorum pontificum'.[31] Mallio mentions it first in conjunction with the altar of Sts Processus and Martinianus, and a note on Alfarano's plan (at no. 19) states that many popes and cardinals were buried in this area. A further note on the plan (at no. 63) identifies the altar 'of Urban VI and many popes' about halfway down the aisle.

Though dedicated to the first pope who bore that name, the oratory of St Leo was also the burial site of three other Pope Leos (II, III, IV).[32] A few steps away stood the oratory where Pope Hadrian I (Figure 14.1, no. 18) was buried (epitaph by Alcuin) and on the west wall of the south transept the grave of Urban II (not shown on plan). The rubrics of the Antiphoner of St Peter's state only that the canons, in the absence of the papal court, went singing 'per ecclesiam' on their way to the first station of the procession.

The procession halted at the magnificent Oratory of Gregory I (Figure 14.1, no. 24) at the eastern end of the south aisle. This had been built by Gregory IV (827–844) to guarantee the safety of his eponymous predecessor's remains, which some Frankish monks had attempted to steal.[33] He also placed there the bodies of Sts Sebastian, Gorgonius, and Tiburtius, hence the reference to their altars in the *Liber politicus*. After the incensation of this altar, the procession turned into the central nave, pausing at the sixth intercolumniation at two altars, dedicated to Sts Simon and Jude and Sts Phillip and James, respectively, which faced each other across the nave (Figure 14.1, nos. 37 and 36). The 'ad crucifixos' identification refers to the presence of two large crucifixes (each weighing 200 lbs), one of gold, the other of silver, above these altars.[34]

The next station, 'ad sudarium Christi ... et altare sanctae Mariae', required the procession to retrace its steps towards the end of the outer north aisle. Against the inner wall of the basilica's façade John VII (705–707) built a splendid oratory, which he chose as his burial site (Figure 14.1, no. 23).[35] Nearby (Figure 14.1, no. 43) stood

---

[31]Mallio, *Descriptio* 15, in Valentini and Zucchetti, *Codice topographico*, vol. 3, p. 394. For other references see vol. 3, p. 473. This is also the opinion expressed in a footnote to excerpts from the *Liber politicus* published in *ibid.*, p. 210 n. 2.

[32]Alfarano, no. 38; the altar is no. 14 on Alfarano's plan. Mallio described the oratory of Leo IV and its furnishings in great detail (Mallio, *Descriptio* 12, in Valentini and Zucchetti, *Codice topographico*, vol. 2, pp. 391–393).

[33]*Liber pontificalis*, vol. 2, p. 74; Mallio, *Descriptio* 24, in Valentini and Zucchetti, *Codice topographico*, vol. 3, p. 413.

[34]Mallio, *Descriptio* 12, in Valentini and Zucchetti, *Codice topographico*, vol. 3, p. 392; see also de Blaauw, *Cultus et decor*, pp. 670–671, 674, 680.

[35]Alfarano, pp. 106–107 (no. 114 on plan); Mallio, *Descriptio* 21, in Valentini and Zucchetti, *Codice topographico*, vol. 3, pp. 410–411. A number of mosaics from the decorative

an oratory that contained one of the basilica's most precious relics: the cloth with which Veronica wiped the Saviour's face on the way to Calvary.[36] The procession must then have returned to the nave, since the next station was the altar of St Pastor, located on the north side of the triumphal arch (Figure 14.1, no. 22) opposite the canons' choir and altar of S. Maria de cancellis (Figure 14.1, no. 21). Here another incensation took place, in honour of the titular saint of the basilica, Peter under his title of shepherd of souls.[37] From this point it was only a short distance to the steps that led beneath the presbyterium (Figure 14.1, no. 5) to the annular crypt that gave access to the apostle's grave, site of the vigils office.

The creation of the crypt was a project of Gregory I (or one of his advisors). The floor of the apse was raised 1.45 metres, thereby creating an elevated presbyterium and yet permitting access to the apostle's tomb.[38] Access to Peter's grave was provided by a passageway under the presbyterium along the curve of the apse leading to a corridor that permitted access to the rear of the monument. An earlier altar was preserved there, evidence that masses at the tomb were not unusual. The exposed top portion of the Constantinian *memoria* to the apostle, 1.25 metres above the new floor level, served as an altar. In front of the altar, two sets of stairs at right angles to the presbyterium led up to the elevated podium. The set of six twisted vine-scroll columns that had originally supported the fastigium over the Constantinian *memoria* were moved into a single line at the edge of the raised presbyterium. This made the liturgy more visible from the nave, but it also emphasized the division between clergy and laity. When six more matching vine-scroll columns became available in the early eighth century, a gift to Pope Gregory III from Eutychius, the Byzantine exarch of Ravenna, these were immediately employed to create a trabeated screen (perhaps adorned with silver statues)

---

programme of this chapel have survived; see Guglielmo Matthiae, *Mosaici medievali delle chiese di Roma*, 2 vols, 2nd edn (Rome, 1967), vol. 1, pp. 215–224, and vol. 2, plates XXVII–XXVIII. One of the most frequently visited of these, part of a beautiful romano-byzantine Adoration of the Magi, has found a less than glorious refuge on the wall of the souvenir shop at S. Maria in Cosmedin.

[36]Alfarano, pp. 107–108 (no. 115 on plan); Mallio, *Descriptio* 27, in Valentini and Zucchetti, vol. 3, p. 420 ('De oratorio Veronicae'). The canons returned to this altar, adjacent to S. Maria ad praesepe, a few days later to celebrate the first mass of Christmas between their vigil office and matins (B 79, fol. 25).

[37]Alfarano, p. 60 no. 1. It was beside this altar in the nave that Callistus III (1455–1458) installed an organ 'metaliis lignisque deauratis exornata sex columnis porphireticis sustentata ad concentus cantus chori et Basilicae decorem suffecta' (*ibid.*, pp. 60–61).

[38]See the most recent survey by Sible de Blaauw, 'L'arredo liturgico e il culto di San Pietro', in Mario D'Onofrio, ed., *Romei e giubilei: il pellegrinaggio medievale a San Pietro (350–1250)* (Milan, 1999), pp. 271–277. In the same volume, see a beautifully illustrated catalogue of an exhibition held at the Palazzo Venezia (22 October 1999 – 26 February 2000), and Pierluigi Silvan, 'L'architettura della basilica medievale di San Pietro', pp. 249–261. There are countless studies of the architecture of old St Peter's that (with the notable exception of the work of Sible de Blaauw, especially *Cultus et decor*) take little account of the liturgy celebrated within its walls.

located in front of the raised presbyterium on the floor level of the basilica. This created a new enclosed space three metres deep, the *vestibulum altaris* reserved for the clergy; it played a part in the celebration of matins on *Dominica de Gaudete*, as the *pectorale*, which the pope, cardinal bishops, and deacons occupied during matins.

Figure 14.2: St Peter's Basilica. Reconstruction of the raised prebyterium and annular crypt with the outer screen of vine-scroll columns added by Gregory III

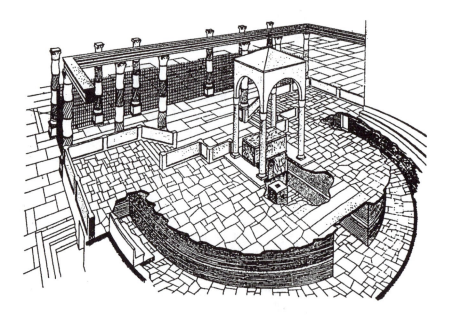

Vigils and matins

Descent into the semi-darkness to the crypt (Figure 14.2) for the vigils *ad corpus* must have been a delicate undertaking. Because of the narrowness of the space in the annular crypt and the corridor that led to Peter's grave, and the fact that the necessary candles and incense would not have helped 'air quality', only a few members of the assembled retinue could have assisted at vigils.[39] The paraphonista and schola cantorum began vigils, in which those assembled in the crypt participated. (Acolytes, cubicularii, basilicarii, a deacon, regional subdeacon, and a bishop are mentioned, in addition to the singers.) For those who could follow the office only at a distance the psalmody, responsories of the choir, and the hardly comprehended readings emanating from the underground recesses of the vast basilica must have produced a strange effect. Given the lateness of the hour and the fact that the third Sunday of Advent was not a major feast, the presence of laity other than those who lived in the vicinity of St Peter's is unlikely. Table 14.3 compares the rubrics for vigils in the *Liber politicus* with the musical contents of the St Peter's Antiphoner.

Table 14.3: *Dominica de Gaudete* at St Peter's: vigils

Liber politicus	Archivio San Pietro, B 79
Ant. Ex Egypto vocavi	Ant. Ex Egypto vocavi
[Ps. Beatus vir (1)]	Ps. Beatus vir (1)
Ant. Ecce apparebit dominus supra nubem candidam	Ant. Querite dominum dum inveniri potest
[Ps. Quare fremuerunt (2)]	Ps. Quare fremuerunt (2)
Ant. Ecce veniet dominus quem Johannes predicavit	Ant. Ecce veniet dominus quem Johannes predicavit
[Ps. Domine quid multiplicati sunt (3)]	Ps. Domine quid multiplicati sunt (3)
Reading: Gaudens gaudebo	
Primicerius cum scola cantat responsorium.	Resp. Gaudete in domino
	Vs. Estote parati
	Resp. Ecce apparebit
	Vs. Ecce dominator
Te deum	Te deum
Oratio	Oratio dominice

---

[39]Sible de Blaauw estimates that the space around the altar of the crypt was no larger than 3.50 x 6 metres (*Cultus et decor*, p. 689).

Vigils consists of a single nocturn of three psalms, the first three psalms of the Psalter; the papal office of the *Liber politicus* undoubtedly had the same arrangement. The *Liber politicus* and the St Peter's Antiphoner differ, however, in the choice of the second antiphon. The books used by the papal singers had as the second antiphon of vigils *Ecce apparebit dominus supra nubem*, an antiphon assigned by the St Peter's Antiphoner to the fourth Sunday of Advent (first nocturn, second antiphon; fol. 17). Neither corresponds to the Gregorian arrangement.[40] Basilicarii, papal officials of sub-diaconal rank, read three passages from the prophecy of Isaiah (*Gaudens gaudebo*; Isaiah 61:10–63:16). The responsory that follows the first reading, *Gaudete in domino*, with the verse *Estote* (common to B 79 and add. 29988), is extremely rare in the Gregorian tradition: Hesbert found this combination only in an antiphoner from Silos (London, BL, add. 30850). Its Roman authenticity is guaranteed by Amalar, who, not finding *Gaudete in domino* in the Messine antiphoner, says that he took care to insert it.[41] The Roman practice of singing the Te deum as the replacement of the ninth responsory only 'in natalitiis pontificum', valid in the ninth century, no longer applies.[42] Here it replaces the final responsory of the single nocturn of vigils. The closing prayer of the papal vigils, pronounced by the pope himself, was replaced by the Lord's Prayer in his absence.

Vigils having concluded, the participants emerged from the crypt to take their places for matins. Meanwhile the pope incensed the altar above the grave of the apostle. Not all of the clergy took up places in the canons' choir on the south side of the nave (Figure 14.1, no. 21). Benedict says that the pope, after having incensed the altar, 'descendit ad pectorale ante altare'. This must mean that the pope and deacons occupied one side (right) of the space between the two rows of twisted columns that screened the presbyterium, and the bishops the other (left).[43] If Benedict meant only the (seven) cardinal deacons and (seven) cardinal bishops, there would be more than enough space in this nine-foot wide enclosure to accommodate them comfortably.

---

[40]The other Old Roman antiphoner (ms London, BL, add. 29988) has no vigils and a different arrangement of antiphons for the first nocturn of matins: *A finibus terre*, *Ex Egypto vocavi*, *Qui post me venit*. Yet another indication of the idiosyncrasy that sets this document apart from the St Peter's antiphoner. Benedict offers no information about the chants or psalms of matins.

[41]*De ord. ant.* 10.1, in Hanssens, *Amalarii episcopi*, vol. 3, p. 41. Amalar implies that the responsory *Ecce apparebit* stood in second place in the Roman antiphoner: 'Responsorius *Gaudete in domino* plenus est consolationis verbis. *Ecce apparebit dominus* ipse configit in capite regem regum, qui venturus est liberare pauperes et afflictos de manu potentiae secularis. Utrumque demonstrant presentes responsorii.'

[42]See Amalar, *De ord. ant.*, Prol.7, in Hanssens, *Amalarii episcopi*, vol. 3, p. 14.

[43]This seems to be the obvious meaning of the rubric, as also interpreted by Duchesne (*Lib. pol.*, p. 160 n. 16); de Blaauw, however, places the two groups on the raised altar podium (*Cultus et decor*, pp. 690–691). Mallio mentions 'in virga ante pectoralia, .III. lampades' in his aforementioned description of the nocturnal illumination of St Peter's for stations (*Descriptio* 43, in Valentini and Zucchetti, *Codice topographico*, vol. 3, p. 425).

(Very rarely in the Middle Ages did the number reach the canonical seven.) Perhaps the entire party that had just completed vigils in the crypt occupied places in the *pectorale*. The cardinal priests and the canons of St Peter's took their places in the canons' choir in the nave ('cardinales in choro cum canonicis ecclesiae'). The position of the schola cantorum is not specified. (See Table 14.2: 'in choro'.) Most probably they occupied places in the canons' choir, as they did on the feast of St John the Baptist at the Lateran. Given the distances in a very resonant building separating all the participants, it is difficult to imagine that they would have a very easy time of singing (and staying) together.

    The pope himself intoned the introductory versicles of matins, and the schola (*cantores*) took up the invitatory. The canons enjoyed their special prerogative of chanting the three readings of the first nocturn (*Gaudens gaudebo* – read during vigils by basilicarii)[44] and the responsories that followed them. (The other responsories were sung by 'cantores et basilicarii'.) Bishops of the papal court read two passages (readings 4 and 5) from the letter of Pope Leo I to Bishop Flavianus of Constantinople (*De Incarnatione?*).[45] Readings 6 and 7 (from the same letter?) are assigned to cardinals. The eighth reading, by the *prior basilicarius*, is drawn 'de expositione epistole "Gaudete in domino semper"'. The pope takes the final reading from a homily, perhaps also by Leo I, on the text from Philippians that gave its name to the Sunday.[46] After the singing of the Te deum, lauds follows immediately.

    In both B 79 and the British Library antiphoner matins has the expected dominical structure.[47] The first nocturn consists of twelve psalms in groups of four under three antiphons (1, 2, 3, 6 / 7, 8, 9, 10 / 11, 12, 13, 14). They disagree about the order of antiphons. For the first nocturn of matins the St Peter's Antiphoner repeats the three antiphons of vigils with the twelve psalms just mentioned, but the British Library antiphoner has the antiphons *A finibus terre*, *Ex Egypto vocavi*, and *Qui post me venit*. While the two antiphoners also disagree about the antiphons for the next two nocturns, there is virtual unanimity about the responsories, even to having the same ordering of the five responsories included in the third nocturn. At Christmas there is almost complete unanimity between them for vigils and matins.[48]

---

[44]Early office books – the seventh-century 'Roman homiliary' reconstructed by Réginald Grégoire (VL 3836, third part of a homiliary compiled by the Roman priest Agimond) and the tenth-century St Peter's homiliary in BAV, ms S. Pietro, C 105 – assign this reading to Epiphany. Neither contains the season of Advent. See Grégoire, *Homéliaires liturgiques médiévaux*, pp. 150 and 235.

[45]Epistula 28; *PL* 54, cols 755–781.

[46] Leo, *Tractatus* 32: see PL 54, cols 237–240, and Corpus Christianorum Series Latina 138, pp. 165–169. The traditional rubric about omission of a response to the pope's 'Jube, domine, benedicere' – 'nullus benedicit eum nisi Spiritus Sanctus' – is duly noted (*Liber pontificalis*, p. 144).

[47]For a useful overview of the structure (and a comparison with the Benedictine Office) see Roger E. Reynolds, 'Divine Office', in *Dictionary of the Middle Ages*, vol. 4, pp. 221–231.

[48]Cf. B 79, fols 25ᵛ–29ᵛ and BL, add. 29988, fol. 21ᵛ–25ᵛ.

As far as one can determine from Benedict's account, the resident canons played only a minor role in what was a special devotional act of the papal court.[49] The canons' antiphoner does not, moreover, accord completely with the description of vigils that Benedict provides. Rather, it illustrates what the canons would have done in the absence of the papal court on *Dominica de Gaudete*.[50] If the curia did not make an appearance at St Peter's for a *statio nocturnalis*, the canons assumed their responsibilities (for appropriate remuneration, of course). Pietro Mallio set out a schedule of payments, 'si vero curiales non interfuerint'.[51] This must have been a not unusual circumstance during the many absences of the papal court from Rome in the turbulent era that witnessed the formation of the commune. The responsibility for these nocturnal stations thus fell frequently on the canons. *Dominica de Gaudete* was paradigmatic: 'sic facimus per omnes stationes nocturnales'.

By the end of the twelfth century the double office on *Dominica de Gaudete* had already fallen into desuetude in the papal rite, but a reminiscence of its incensations and visits to altars in the basilica had been incorporated into vespers celebrated there.[52] It represented the model for papal incensations for solemn vespers at St Peter's throughout the year. During the singing of the third vespers psalm, the pope incenses the main altar; then, passing 'per viam ex parte vaticani', i.e., to his right, and descending from the elevated presbyterium, he incensed the altar in the choir. Finally, crossing over to the edge of the north transept, he also honoured with incense the nearby altar 'ubi fuerunt ponderata ossa apostolorum' (Figure 14.1, no. 9). The peculiar name derives from the legend (reported by Alfarano) that this altar incorporated a square piece of porphyry on which Pope Sylvester divided and weighed the bones of the apostles (in order to divide them equally between the two basilicas erected in their honour), when he consecrated St Peter's.[53] The pope returns to his place in time for the

---

[49]Whenever the papal court showed up for a liturgical event at the Lateran, the canons were relatively marginalized. See my 'Double Offices at the Lateran', especially pp. 37–42.

[50]Obviously, the hierarchical arrangement of the participants would have had no meaning for a canonical office.

[51]Mallio, *Descriptio* 55, in Valentini and Zucchetti, *Codice topographico*, vol. 3, p. 434. Mallio says that the canons used to receive twelve *solidi*, but in his time only seven *solidi lucenses* for each stational visit.

[52]The ordinal of Innocent III cites only the readings and (eleven) responsories of matins; there is no mention of vigils. See S. J. P. van Dijk and Joan Hazelden Walker, *The Ordinal of the Papal Court from Innocent III to Boniface VIII and Related Documents*, Spicilegium Friburgense 22 (Freiburg, Switzerland, 1975), p. 108.

[53]According to Alfarano (p. 35), this was one of the seven privileged altars of the basilica, which, if all were visited, merited an indulgence equal to that gained by a visit to all seven principal churches of Rome. On special festivals, even greater spiritual benefits accrued to the devout. See Nine Robijntje Miedema, *Die römischen Kirchen im Spätmittelalter nach den 'Indulgentiae ecclesiarum urbis Romae'*, Bibliothek des deutschen historischen Instituts in Rom 97 (Tübingen, 2001), p. 337. The altar (no. 9 on Alfarano's plan and in Figure 14.1 above) was located to the north of the outer row of columns that stood before the presbyterium; see also de Blaauw, *Cultus et decor*, p. 672.

fifth antiphon of vespers, *Iuste et pie* (the only antiphon mentioned by name), to carry out a curious ceremony. The *primicerius urbis* pre-intoned this antiphon for the pope, who rewarded him by placing a gold coin on his tongue.[54] The Ordinal continues with a summary of the office of matins. Absent from first place is the traditional Roman responsory *Gaudete in domino*; now the series begins with *Ecce apparebit.*

Later in the century the papal court still sought out St Peter's on 'Gaudete' Sunday, as confirmed by the Ordinal of Gregory X (1271–1276). Though a rubric explains that a 'duplex officium' was merited 'propter festum stationis', this does not signify a double office but rather the liturgical rank of the day.[55] As it was in the time of Innocent III, the principal *Dominica de Gaudete* observance for the papal court was a solemn vespers on the Saturday before. Gregory's ordinal offers no details about the incensations, only a rubric about the unusual manner in which the primicerius received his 'payment'. Once vespers had been concluded the court departed: 'dictis vesperis, omnes recedunt'.

How long any of the double offices persisted anywhere in Rome after the twelfth century is a question beyond the scope of this chapter. Radulph de Rivo (d. 1403), something of a liturgical antiquarian, gives the impression that a double office was still observed on some feasts. The *vigilia* consisted of a single nocturn (no invitatory, three psalms, three antiphons, three readings, three responsories, the usual versicles, Pater noster, and Te deum). Radulph mentions the feasts of St Peter and Christmas, but these vigil offices had the full nine psalms and readings.[56] His historical description is well informed, but he may have been reporting on an admired, idealized past.

Finally, the presence of a solemn double office on 'Gaudete' Sunday still lacks an explanation. First attested before the middle of the twelfth century, its date of origin or the motivation for creating so distinctive an observance cannot be established, owing to the lack of sources, either from St Peter's or the papal court. The observance did not survive in the papal rite for more than a few decades. And the canons of St Peter's continued only for a while one of the most 'atmospheric' observances of the Roman liturgy.

---

[54]Oblique reference to this is made in an interpolation to the *Liber censuum* of Censius Savelli: 'in sabbato de *Gaudete* pergit ad vesperas ad sanctum Petrum, ubi dominus papa eidem primicerio adnuntiando antihonam *Iuste et pie vivamus*, dat unum marabutinum vice ipsius projiciens' (Fabre and Duchesne, p. 291, n. a).

[55]Van Dijk and Walker, 'The Ordinal of the Papal Court', pp. 550–551.

[56]Cunibert Mohlberg, ed., *De canonum observantia*, propositio 21, in *Radulph de Rivo: der letzte Vertreter der altrömischen Liturgie*, 2 vols (Münster in Westfalia, 1915), vol. 2, p. 123.

Chapter 15

Philip the Chancellor and the conductus prosula: 'motetish' works from the School of Notre-Dame

Thomas B. Payne

Philip the Chancellor (d. 1236), the noted theologian, homilist, and poet who lived and worked in Paris during the late twelfth and early thirteenth centuries, has enjoyed an increased celebrity over the past years as a contributor to the musical repertory associated with the cathedral of Notre-Dame of Paris.[1] Although his primary activity lay in fashioning texts to songs, his large number of attributed works, along with the potent information supplied by his relatively well documented life, shows that Philip is as integral to the history of this music as the more famous composers Leoninus and Perotinus. The knowledge gleaned from Philip's involvement in the creation of compositions can thus significantly aid our understanding of musical development during the Notre Dame era. In this study I want to pay particular attention to Philip's position as the co-creator of new and unusual types of musical works, and how these pieces may inform our assessment of the early growth of the motet, which was perhaps the most exceptional and prosperous musical creation of the Notre Dame school.

Among the large number of song texts ascribed to the Chancellor are a small but coherent group of unusual compositions that add a single syllabic text to the tenor part culled from the closing melisma of a polyphonic *conductus cum caudis*. Although these so-called 'conductus prosulas' quite clearly recall older techniques of prosulation (such as the addition of syllabic texts to melismas in monophonic plainchant), these particular works within the Notre Dame repertory are striking because they set poetry

---

[1]For some recent examples see Peter Dronke, 'The Lyrical Compositions of Philip the Chancellor', *Studi medievali* series 3, 28 (1987), pp. 563–592; my studies *'Associa tecum in patria*: A Newly Identified Organum Trope by Philip the Chancellor', *JAMS* 39 (1986), pp. 233–254; 'Poetry, Politics, and Polyphony: Philip the Chancellor's Contribution to the Music of the Notre Dame School' (Ph.D. diss., University of Chicago, 1991); *'Aurelianis civitas*: Student Unrest in Medieval France and a Conductus by Philip the Chancellor', *Speculum* 75 (2000), pp. 589–614; and David A. Traill, 'Philip the Chancellor and F10: Expanding the Canon', *Filologia mediolatina* 10 (2003), pp. 219–248. For a survey of some of the earlier literature see my *'Associa tecum'*, notes 1–7.

to the newly composed voices of a polyphonic model.[2] The knowledge of such melismatic concordances is telling in several ways, for it can secure a rhythmic realization for a syllabically written melody before the advent of a notational system that could express such details. Additionally, one of the most noteworthy aspects of these texted caudae is that the techniques that spawned them mirror the methods that produced the earliest motets. Just as the motet originated from the addition of words to discant clausulae, these conductus prosulas arose through the overlay of newly fashioned poetic texts onto previously composed polyphonic music. Although our knowledge of the origin of the Notre Dame motet is hampered somewhat by the fact that no examples can presently be dated with any certainty, I would contend that information gathered from a study of certain members of the conductus prosula repertory – ones that do suggest their probable time of composition – can aid in our assessment of the motet's creation and early cultivation.

Conductus prosulas – those works that share their music with the final cauda of a conductus – constitute a very small cache of pieces. (I have listed these in Table 15.1, along with their corresponding cauda sources.) In fact, modern scholars in cataloguing and discussing these pieces frequently include them under the mantle of the conductus.[3] Even medieval scribes, when they organized the carefully planned sources that today transmit the bulk of the Notre Dame repertory, are not always consistent in their placement of these works, though there is evidence that on several occasions they regarded these prosulas as a separate species of composition and grouped them together in the sources.[4] What remains especially striking though, is that for the seven discrete pieces that use material culled from a conductus melisma, three of these poems are specifically attributed to Philip in medieval sources.[5]

As Table 15.1 shows, the four apparent exceptions to the Chancellor's sole involvement in the production of conductus prosulas occur in the examples of *Anima iuge lacrima*, *Crucifigat omnes*, and the two contrafacts of *Crucifigat*, *Mundum renovavit*, and *Curritur ad vocem*. The two contrafacts, however, may be omitted from consideration as true conductus prosulas. They appear once each in two manuscripts copied outside of Paris[6] and in direct proximity to *Crucifigat*.[7] The circumstances of their

---

[2]A discussion of these works is contained in chapter 4 of my dissertation ('Poetry, Politics, and Polyphony').

[3]See, for example, the two standard catalogues of the conductus repertory: Gordon A. Anderson, 'Notre Dame and Related Conductus: A Catalogue Raisonné', *Miscellanea musicologica: Adelaide Studies in Musicology* 6 (1972), pp. 152–229, and 7 (1973), pp. 1–81; and Robert Falck, *The Notre Dame Conductus: A Study of the Repertory* (Henryville PA, 1981), pp. 138–256.

[4]Described in my 'Poetry, Politics, and Polyphony', pp. 234–242.

[5]For the attributions of these works to Philip, see Falck, *Notre Dame Conductus*, pp. 188 (*Bulla fulminante*), 219 (*Minor natu*), and 254 (*Veste nuptiali*).

[6]Manuscript sources cited in this paper are abbreviated as follows: *CB*: Munich, BS, latin 4660 (*Carmina burana*); *Cl*: Paris, BNF, n. a. fr.13521 (*La Clayette*); *F*: Florence, Biblioteca medicea-laurenziana, Pluteus 29.1; *LoB*: London, BL, ms Egerton 274; *StS1*: Stary Sącz,

survival thus suggest that they most likely came into existence only through the substitution of new lyrics to the immensely popular *Crucifigat*, rather than from a new and independent texting of a closing conductus cauda.[8] With this evidence of an apparent predilection on Philip's part for troping melismatic polyphony, it is appropriate to venture whether the two remaining conductus prosulas, *Crucifigat omnes* and *Anima iuge lacrima*, may also be his efforts, and whether he alone is responsible for the cultivation of these unusual pieces.

Table 15.1: Texts written to conductus caudae (conductus prosulas)

a Notre Dame compositions

Text Incipit	Melismatic model (final cauda)	Author of text
Anima iuge lacrima	Relegentur ab area (à3)	——
Bulla fulminante	Dic Christi veritas (à3)	Philip
Crucifigat omnes	Quod promisit ab eterno (à2)	——
Minor natu filius	Austro terris influente (à2)	Philip
Veste nuptiali	Dic Christi veritas (à3)	Philip

b Peripheral contrafacts of Crucifigat omnes (unattributed)

Mundum renovavit	Curritur ad vocem	

If the uncommon technique that produced *Crucifigat* were not enough, other details arise to support Philip's hand in the composition of its text. Here not only does the content of the poem suggest his authorship in terms of its rhetorical flourishes, but the incident for which the poem was fashioned also points to him as the probable author.

Biblioteka Klasztoru SS. Klarysek, D.2; *Stutt*: Stuttgart, Württembergische Landesbibliothek, 9; *W1*: Wolfenbüttel, HAB, Cod. Guelf. 628 Helmst.

[7]*Mundum renovavit* is unique to the Insular manuscript *W1*, and is written in the margin next to a transmission of *Crucifigat*. Its text is religious and concerns the sanctity of the Virgin Mary. *Curritur ad vocem* appears only in two German sources, *CB* and *Stutt*. In *CB* it occurs directly after a presentation of *Crucifigat*; in *Stutt* only the second strophe of *Curritur* is presented, and the work is intermingled with a transmission of strophe I of *Crucifigat* and the host conductus, *Quod promisit ab eterno*. The criticism of pecuniary greed in *Curritur* relates arguments that are similar to the ones that surface in Philip the Chancellor's conductus prosula *Bulla fulminante* (see below), but the lack of a central Notre Dame source for this piece raises serious objections to its inclusion in the main Notre Dame prosula corpus.

[8]A further pair of contrafacted prosulas surfaces with the examples of *Bulla fulminante* and *Veste nuptiali*, both of which share the music of the final cauda from the three-part Notre Dame conductus *Dic Christi veritas*. In this case, however, both of these texts as well as that of the model are attributed to Philip the Chancellor. Their connection to the main Notre Dame repertory is therefore much more obvious.

To take the points in order, the text of this Crusade song features several stylistic characteristics that are especially prominent in Philip's works.[9] I have provided the entire poem as Example 15.1. Its opening lines feature a call for the complete destruction of the Islamic forces that inhabit Jerusalem. It summons a personified 'second cross', that is, the crusading Christian forces, to crucify the occupiers. The anger and severity of this passage are echoed throughout Philip's attributed corpus; and, as is also common in his poetry, the dissatisfaction is not confined to the Saracen faction, for the delay of the Christian army to hasten to their mission is likewise rebuked in the failing of their Mosaic leader to heed the call to arms (lines 26–27). The third strophe of the lyric warns ominously that faith must be maintained with deeds, and failure to come to the aid of the Holy Land will spell certain damnation. This poem is not so much an entreaty as a threat.

Example 15.1: Text of *Crucifigat omnes*[10]

I	Crucifigat omnes,		May a second cross of the Lord,
	Domini crux altera,		the new wounds of Christ,
	nova Christi vulnera!		crucify them all!
	Arbor salutifera		The tree that brings salvation
	perditur; sepulcrum	5	is lost, a foreign
	gens evertit extera		people has forcibly overthrown
	violente. Plena gente,		the tomb. Though once filled with
	sola sedet civitas.		people, the city sits forsaken.
	Agni fedus rapit edus;		The goat plunders the lamb's covenant;
	plorat dotes perditas	10	the bride of Zion laments her lost
	sponsa Syon. Immolatur		dowries. Ananias is
	ananias; incurvatur		immolated; David's horn is
	cornu davit; flagellatur		cast down; the innocent man is
	mundus.		put to the lash.
	Ab iniustis abdicatur	15	He through whom the world is
	per quem iuste iudicatur		justly judged is renounced
	mundus.		by the unjust.
II	O quam dignos luctus!		O what worthy laments!
	Exulat rex omnium;		The king of all is banished;

[9]On Philip's poetic style see especially Dronke, 'The Lyrical Compositions', *passim*, as well as Traill, 'Philip the Chancellor and F10', *passim*, and my '*Aurelianis*', p. 599.

[10]Translations of Latin texts throughout this article are my own. Because of the frequent irregularities in poetic scheme caused by the overlay of these prosula texts to pre-existent music, as well as their rampant use of interlinear rhyme, I have frequently used the musical phrases to help determine line breaks in the poems. The text of *Crucifigat* given here presents the transmissions found in *F*, fol. 231^V (strophes I–II), and *CB*, fol. 13^r (strophe III, not found in *F*). The following readings from these sources have been emended: *F*: 32,3: promere; *CB*: 44,1: reputeris, 50,1–2: et ad vitam.

	baculus fidelium	20	the staff of the faithful
	sustinet opprobrium		endures the disgrace
	gentis infidelis.		of an infidel people.
	Cedit parti gentium		The total part yields to the
	pars totalis. Iam regalis		gentiles' faction. Now the royal
	in luto et latere	25	land labours in mud and brick.
	elaborat tellus. Plorat		It laments that its
	Moysen fatiscere.		Moses has grown weak.
	Homo, Dei miserere.		Man, have pity on God.
	Fili, patris ius tuere.		Son, defend your father's right.
	In incerto certum quere.	30	Seek the certain among the uncertain.
	Ducis		Earn the gifts of the
	ducum dona promerere		leader of the leaders,
	et lucrare lucem vere		and gain the light
	lucis		of the true light.
III	Quisquis es signatus	35	Whoever you are, inscribed
	fidei karactere,		with the sign of the faith,
	fidem factis assere.		maintain that faith with deeds.
	Rugientes contere		Annihilate the lions'
	catulos leonum.		roaring cubs.
	Miserans, intuere	40	Merciful one, look upon
	corde tristi dampnum		Christ's injury
	Christi.		with a saddened heart.
	Longus Cedar, incola,		Rise up, distant dweller in
	surge. Vide, ne de fide		Kedar. Take care, lest you are
	reproberis frivola.	45	chastened for your sorry faith.
	Suda, martir, in agone,		Sweat, martyr, in the contest,
	spe mercedis et corone.		with the hope of reward and crown.
	Derelicta babylone,		Now that Babylon has been abandoned,
	pugna!		fight!
	Pro celesti regione	50	Prepare yourself for the heavenly
	aqua vite te conpone.		realm, for the water of life.
	Pugna!		Fight!

Other parallels with Philip's acknowledged lyrics occur in the use of paradox and in the evocation of biblical motifs. The opening strophe of *Crucifigat* brings these two facets together in a list of indignities that demonstrate how the capture and occupation of Jerusalem has inverted the events of the Bible. Scriptural images now appear in the present, but horribly distorted: Jerusalem is filled with people, but now lies desolate; Ananias, one of the three youths who escaped the deadly furnace in the book of Daniel, is burned to a crisp; David's horn is lowered in defeat rather than raised in triumph; and Christ, who should be sitting on the judge's bench, is tried and punished by criminals.[11]

Along with the technical and stylistic features of *Crucifigat omnes*, some valuable details from Philip's life indicate that he may have had a personal stake in the events that occasioned the writing of this text. Though *Crucifigat omnes* is often considered as a response to the 1187 capture of Jerusalem which prompted the Third Crusade,[12] Ernest Sanders suggested in an article from 1985 that it was rather the Fifth Crusade of 1217–1221 – and specifically the delay of Holy Roman Emperor Frederick II to take up the cross – that occasioned this poem.[13] Not only did this new assignment to 1219–1220 help to clarify some rather arcane references in the poetry, but Sanders also remarked that such a chronology put *Crucifigat* temporally close to the only other dated conductus prosula: Philip's *Bulla fulminante*, generally considered to hail from 1222–1223.[14]

With a possible later date for *Crucifigat omnes*, the suggestions for Philip's authorship are further enhanced with the knowledge that the expedition to the Fifth Crusade counted two of his uncles among the campaign. These were Walter, who was then the chamberlain of the king of France, and the bishop of Paris, Peter of Nemours.[15] Peter and Walter probably arrived in the Holy Land sometime in the fall of 1218 as part of the outfit accompanying the infamous Cardinal Pelagius, at whose feet has been laid much of the blame for the failure of the enterprise. Shortly before the crusaders seized the strategically important city of Damietta at the mouth of the Nile (only to lose it shortly thereafter), Jerusalem and some of its surrounding lands had been offered in treaty to the Christians, a gift that they had refused at the insistence of Pelagius.[16]

Both of Philip's uncles died before they could return to France; and with the death of Bishop Peter, Philip lost one of his chief supporters.[17] Events in the chancellor's life

---

[11]For these biblical echoes, see Daniel 1:6–7, 3:8–25, 3:88–97; Luke 1:69; Matthew 27:26; and Romans 3:6.

[12]The 1187 date, as well as the attribution of *Crucifigat* to Philip, is defended most recently by Traill in 'Philip the Chancellor and the Third Crusade', a paper given at the tenth Annual ACMRS conference in Tempe, Arizona, February 2004. I regret that I have not been able to see this paper before completing this chapter, but I would like to thank Professor Traill for bringing his work to my attention.

[13]Ernest H. Sanders, 'Style and Technique in Datable Polyphonic Notre Dame Conductus', in *FS Anderson*, vol. 2, pp. 505–530. For the specific claims of the later date for *Crucifigat*, see pp. 513–518.

[14]For more on *Bulla fulminante* see below.

[15]On Philip's family see my 'Poetry, Politics, and Polyphony', pp. 36–41.

[16]On these points see James M. Powell, *Anatomy of a Crusade: 1213–1221* (Philadelphia, 1986), p. 117; and Steven Runciman, *A History of the Crusades*, 3 vols (Cambridge, 1955), vol. 3, pp. 154–155, and 161–162.

[17]Powell, *Anatomy of a Crusade*, p. 221, says that Walter returned home, but this is contradicted by Emile Louis Richemond, *Recherches généalogiques sur la famille des Seigneurs de Nemours*, 2 vols (Fontainebleau, 1907–1908), vol. 1, pp. 69–70. Walter's obit. is given as 26

following this loss show that he now began to suffer greater difficulties in the execution of his authority, particularly in his role as the overseer of the university of Paris. It is worth noting that as far as his datable poems show, it is only after his uncle's death that his bitter criticism of injustice and corruption begins to turn toward ecclesiastical circles.[18]

Even though there are apparently no specific references to Philip's relatives in the text of *Crucifigat omnes* the collective circumstances of the poem, its origin as a trope to a Notre-Dame conductus melisma, its language and rhetoric, and the fact that the chancellor's family members were involved in the Fifth Crusade make the likelihood of his authorship compelling. Even if Philip himself had never pledged to take up the cross, he had formerly proclaimed his desire for the liberation of the Holy Land, and specifically the city of Jerusalem, in his earliest datable poem, *Venit Jhesus in propria,* probably from 1187. One should have very few misgivings in crediting him with the text of *Crucifigat omnes*.

Similarly, *Anima iuge lacrima*, the second anonymous conductus prosula, also has features beyond its manner of composition that relate it to works familiar in Philip's corpus. (The text is given as Example 15.2.) Here the poet resorts to one of his most treasured forms, the Latin *altercatio* or poetic debate, a favourite medieval poetic genre related to the vernacular *jeu parti*. In Philip's works in this vein, instead of the typical confrontation between two named poets that appears so often in troubadour and trouvère poetry, he typically pits allegorical or symbolic figures in a disputation that concerns questions of salvation.[19] In Strophe I of *Anima iuge*, as in his similarly designed poems *Homo natus ad laborem tui status* and *Quo vadis quo progrederis*, the Flesh seeks to persuade the Soul to save itself by leaving behind the coarse, sinful nature of the body. Then in Strophe II, the Soul has its say in a voice dripping with sarcasm, as it chides the Flesh for hastening its own ruin instead of thinking of the rewards of heaven. The dispute is now at an impasse, and a final third strophe invokes a personified Reason to quell the charges of the Flesh through fear of eternal torment. As in *Crucifigat omnes* and a host of Philip's other conductus and motets, the threat of future retribution by a severe judge is the most potent force for changing one's character.

October 1219 in Benjamin Guérard, ed., *Cartulaire de l'église Notre Dame de Paris*, 4 vols (Paris, 1850), vol. 4, p. 174; but see also Richemond, vol. 1, p. 70. On Peter of Nemours see Powell, *Anatomy of a Crusade*, p. 237. Nemours's obit. is usually given as 14 December 1219, as in Guérard, *Cartulaire* , vol. 4, p. 199; but see Richemond, vol. 1, pp. 137–138, for an earlier possible death date of September 1218.

[18] See my 'Poetry, Politics, and Polyphony', p. 222.

[19] Other examples of this poetic species among Philip's works include *Homo natus ad laborem tui status* and *Quo vadis quo progrederis* (both between the Body and Soul), *Quisquis cordis et oculi* (between the Heart and Eye), *Inter membra singula* (between the Belly and the rest of the Body's members), and *Vitia virtutibus* (between the Virtues and Vices).

Example 15.2: Text of *Anima iuge lacrima*[20]

[The Flesh warns the Soul]

I	Anima, iuge		Soul, weep
	lacrima, difflue.		incessantly, let it flow.
	Dilue saucie		Wash away the filth of
	sordes conscientie.		your injured conscience.
	Fac tibi tutum.	5	Make yourself safe.
	Luteum vas, exue lutum,		Strip off this vessel of clay,
	subitus exitus		this filth, lest death soon
	pium ne propositum		forestall your devout
	perimat. Meritum		purpose. Let your worth
	redimat vite	10	compensate the injuries
	dampna perdite.		of a life lost.

[The Soul responds]

II	Caro, spiritui		What, Flesh, are you
	quid subderis?		subject to a spirit?
	Quid, tenui		Are you stymied
	flatu suspenderis?	15	by some feeble fart?
	Ad solita revertere.		Return to your accustomed haunts
	Via trita curritur libere.		Run freely on the beaten path.
	Stes legi divitum.		Persist in the law of the rich.
	Vetitum licitum.		Consider, as you will,
	putes ad libitum,	20	the forbidden as licit,
	Devia		caring for the deceits
	curans, non de patria,		owed to the nature of flattery,
	nature debita		and not of heaven.
	culture. Letos age dies,		Make your days joyful,
	leves requies.	25	your amusements light.
	Cure tedium		Beware of weariness,
	sit, quod iuvat pium.		for that would befit a pious man.

[The Appeal to Reason]

III	Lis hec, ratio,	Reason, let this quarrel
	tuo iuditio	come to an end

---

[20]The source for this version of the text is *F*, fol. 433ᵛ, which transmits the following emended readings: 1,2: iugi; 3,2: sautie; 11,1: dapmna. For the opening lines of this poem, I depart from the manuscript sources and certain other editions (including the one in my dissertation ('Poetry, Politics, and Polyphony', pp. 801–802)) by construing 'iuge' adverbially and 'lacrima' as an imperative. Such a reading allows the thoroughgoing internal rhymes of lines 1 and 2 to emerge.

finem subeat.	30	through your judgement.
Cohibeat		Let the dread of a
carnis impetus		fair judge halt the
iusti iudicis metus.		charges of the flesh.
Expietur anima,		Let the soul, the victim
carnis victima.	35	of the flesh, be appeased.
Libere servitutis		Let penitence flourish freely
opere, spe salutis,		through the work of servitude,
vigeat penitentia.		the hope of salvation.
Gratie pateat patrie via.		Let the road of heavenly grace lie open.

It is apparent that many factors argue for Philip the Chancellor as the sole poetic impetus behind the creation of the conductus prosulas. These five pieces, which relate closely to the motet in their manner of conception, are also significant because they can offer testimony that may help to fix more securely the time of the motet's creation and early cultivation. We have already heard claims that *Crucifigat omnes* may be dated from approximately 1220; and a second conductus prosula, Philip's celebrated *Bulla fulminante* (Example 15.3), also may be placed around this same time. Although the timing of this particular piece is also in dispute,[21] I would argue that the circumstances of this latter poem, in fact, are directly relevant to Philip's biography.

Example 15.3: Text of *Bulla fulminante*[22]

I	Bulla fulminante		With a bull of lightning
	sub iudice tonante,		wielded by a thundering judge,
	reo appellante		summoning the defendant
	sententia gravante,		in oppressing terms,
	veritas supprimitur,	5	truth is suppressed, torn limb
	distrahitur, et venditur,		from limb, and sold for profit,
	iustitia prostante.		while justice prostitutes herself.
	Itur et recurritur		You have to run back and forth
	ad curiam, nec ante		to the curia, before you
	quid consequitur	10	achieve anything more than
	quam exuitur quadrante.		being stripped of your purse.
II	Pape ianitores		The Pope's gatekeepers
	Cerbero surdiores.		are deafer than Cerberus.
	In spe vana plores,		You will only mourn an empty prospect,
	nam etiam si fores	15	even if you were Orpheus,

---

[21]It has been placed around 1200 by Benedikt Konrad Vollmann, ed., *Carmina burana: Texte und Übersetzungen* (Frankfurt, 1987).

[22]The source for the version presented here is *LoB*, fol. 38ᵛ, the only transmission of this piece that also furnishes the melody in a readable form.

	Orpheus, quem audiit	to whom Pluto, the god of the
	Pluto deus tartareus.	underworld, hearkened.
	Non ideo perores,	Don't even try to beg,
	malleus argenteus	unless the silver knocker
	ni feriat ad fores 20	raps upon those doors
	ubi Proteus	where Proteus changes his
	variat mille colores.	shape a thousand times.

III Si queris prebendas, — If it is prebends you are seeking,
frustra vitam pretendas. — the experience you offer is worthless.
Mores non commendas 25 — Do not recount your good conduct
ne iudicem offendas. — lest you vex the judge.
Frustra tuis litteris — In vain will you support yourself with
inniteris; moraberis — your learning; for you will be
per plurimas kalendas. — kept waiting for months on end.
Tandem expectaveris 30 — Eventually, you will end up waiting for
a ceteris ferendas, — rewards farmed out to others,
paris ponderis — unless you solicit them
precio nisi contendas. — with a bribe of equal value.

IV Iupiter dum orat — As long as Jupiter begs for
Danem, frustra laborat. 35 — Danae's favours, he labours in vain,
sed eam deflorat — but he deflowers her easily
auro dum se colorat. — once he turns himself to gold.
Auro nil potencius, — Nothing is more powerful than gold,
nil gratius; nec Tullius — nothing is more dear; even Cicero
facundius perorat. 40 — never argued more eloquently.
Sed hos urit acrius, — But gold consumes more ardently
quos amplius honorat. — those it honours most.
Nichil iustius — Nothing is more fitting than when
calidum Crassus dum vorat. — Crassus gulps his molten drink.

Bulla fulminante was the very first piece in the Notre Dame repertory ever to be furnished with a date.[23] The crux of its placement centres on the phrase in lines 8–9 'Itur et recurritur / ad curiam' ('you have to run back and forth to the curia'), which most likely refers to two specific journeys made by the chancellor to Rome.[24] The first voyage was initially provoked by Bishop Peter's excommunication of several Parisian masters who had attempted to set up statutes for independent government within the university. This condemnation would have occurred sometime before June of 1218,

---

[23]By Paul Meyer, 'Henri d'Andeli et le Chancelier Philippe', *Romania* 1 (1872), pp. 195–196, 198–199.

[24]For a fuller narrative of the following events, see my 'Poetry, Politics, and Polyphony', pp. 58–64.

when the prelate departed for the Fifth Crusade. On 24 February of the following year Philip in his uncle's absence extended this sentence to include those masters and students who had attempted to aid the ex-communicates, despite several appeals on their part to the pope. His actions resulted in a university-wide strike, and as a consequence he was commanded to journey to Rome to face judgement on the matter. The Chancellor's accusers failed, however, to appear during the specified term, and he was acquitted with a full pardon.

Philip's second trip was occasioned for the same reasons and suffered the same outcome. In 1221 certain masters and students repeated their assertion of independence from the cathedral chapter. They appealed anew to the pope, who set the matter before several ecclesiastical judges. Philip now had to travel to Rome again; but, as before, the absence of one of the contending parties resulted in a mistrial. On top of this, he was additionally dismayed by the provisional decision that went into effect pending the outcome of the trial. The resulting 'bulla fulminans' deprived him of much of the authority he had wielded as chancellor, including the demolition of his prison for university offenders and the repeal of his excommunications.

Thus, although the dates for both *Crucifigat* and *Bulla fulminante* remain in contention and the dates for the activity I am suggesting could change, the evidence delineated here argues for the production of Philip's conductus prosulas in the years around 1220. The small number of these works – a mere five pieces – and their convincing connection to a single poet also indicates that they probably represent only a slight detour from the path of texting polyphony that was eventually to concentrate on troping discant clausulae to make motets.

Philip's conductus prosulas are related to the conventions of the early motet by more than their use of preexistent music as a source for syllabic texts. Like the motet, which is built upon a rhythmicized melisma torn from a Gregorian chant, the conductus prosula also uses a smaller portion from a larger composition – in this case a detached closing cauda – for its melismatic source. It therefore draws on the very same procedure of the dismemberment of a larger piece that gave rise to the motet and, conceivably, may have come into being around the same time and coexisted with it. The characteristics of one particular conductus prosula, Philip's newly attributed *Anima iuge lacrima*, supply even further indications of a partnership with the early motet. The bonds are so close in this instance that it is worthwhile to consider the possibility of a mutual reliance of these genres upon each other.[25]

Anima iuge strays far beyond the standard features of the conductus prosula. It features the requisite syllabic text fitted to a conductus melisma, but it surpasses the other works of this type by setting two additional strophes of text to music not

---

[25]A related claim has been made by Mark Everist in his 'Reception and Recomposition in the Polyphonic *conductus cum caudis*: The Metz Fragments', *Journal of the Royal Musical Association* 125 (2000), pp. 135–163, where he targets the motet as the impetus behind the redaction of Notre Dame conductus into mensural notation in later manuscript sources.

otherwise derived from the melismatic source.[26] This trait is further complicated by the transmission of this singular work in two widely differing formats in the three sources that preserve it. In the manuscripts *F* and *StS1*[27] it appears, as do most of the other prosulas, in a format similar to that of a monophonic conductus, with its three strophes copied out successively. However, an alternate design is proposed by the third source, *La Clayette (Cl)*.[28] Here, in a codex whose musical portion is otherwise devoted exclusively to motets, *Anima iuge* appears in a disposition that suggests its strophes are to be combined polyphonically, rendering a composition consisting of three simultaneously sounding texts. As both Leo Schrade and Manfred Bukofzer have demonstrated independently, the various voices do concord extremely well, thanks to the assistance provided by the mensural notation of *La Clayette*.[29] This results in a work that is virtually indistinguishable from a number of otherwise unrelated motets that possess a freely composed, fully texted tenor.[30] (I have supplied a transcription of the opening of the piece in Example 15.4.)

Owing to the hybrid nature of this unique piece, which derives from a conductus cauda yet imitates the texture, style, and form of the motet, it is clear that an aesthetic quite different from that of the other prosulas is in effect. With the presence of these correspondences to the motet in mind, it is reasonable to suppose that some of its features might well have informed Philip's composition of *Anima iuge*. In this piece, the polyphonic complex of separately texted voices with varying phrase lengths quite successfully reproduces the same type of audible structure noticeable in the works that surround it in *Cl*. Only the melismatic configuration and rhythmic ostinato of the typical motet tenor are missing.[31] With these features, *Anima iuge* can be viewed as a singular experiment, a lone endeavour as it were, to merge the features of the conductus prosula with the techniques and sounds of the motet.

Other features relating to the motet may also suggest why Philip should have chosen this particular cauda for such a role. Unlike all the other conductus prosulas,

---

[26]Although the music for these additional strophes does not rely completely on the cauda, Leo Schrade notes some interesting correspondences among the melodies of these additional stanzas, the duplum voice of the appropriated cauda, and music from other parts of the source conductus *Relegentur ab area*. See his 'Unknown Motets in a Recovered Thirteenth-century Manuscript', *Speculum* 30 (1955), pp. 408–409.

[27]*Anima iuge* occurs in *F* on fol. 433[V] and in *StS1* on fol. 3[V].

[28]The music of this codex is edited in Gordon A. Anderson, *Motets of the MS La Clayette: Paris, Bibliothèque nationale, nouv. acq. f. fr. 13521* (Rome, 1975).

[29]Leo Schrade, 'Unknown Motets', pp. 404–412; Manfred Bukofzer, 'The Unidentified Tenors in the Manuscript La Clayette', *AnnM* 4 (1956), pp. 257–258. These two scholars made this discovery at approximately the same time.

[30]For these works see Friedrich Gennrich, *Bibliographie der ältesten französischen und lateinischen Motetten* (Darmstadt, 1958), nos 1183–1219b; see also Hendrik van der Werf, *Integrated Directory of Organa, Clausulae, and Motets of the Thirteenth Century* (Rochester NY, 1989).

[31]All the other pieces in *Cl* conform to the typical delineation of the motet genre, with a melismatic tenor segment disposed in some sort of rhythmic pattern.

the tenor voice of the appropriated cauda for *Anima iuge* consists primarily of ternary and duplex longs. Its imposing rhythmic stride is only occasionally broken by shorter

Example 15.4: *Anima iuge lacrima*, opening of polyphonic version (F, fol. 433ᵛ)

values.[32] Such a design, compounded with a penchant for phrases disposed in units of four or eight longs, evokes the manner of numerous fifth-mode tenors from Notre Dame and Ars Antiqua motets. As is evident in Example 15.5, the opening measures in particular recall one of the most favoured clausula and motet tenor patterns.

---

[32]The rhythms used by the tenor melody of *Anima iuge*, both as a cauda voice and as a prosula, appear variously represented in the sources. A trochaic division of the long is used for the transcriptions given here. This interpretation follows the indications of all the cauda sources

Example 15.5: a *Anima iuge lacrima*, opening of tenor melody, *F*, fol. 433^v;

b Opening of tenor from discant clausula *Nostrum*, *F*, fol. 157^v, 2nd setting

Above this underpinning the two added voices unfold with more varied rhythms. Their diversity is especially elegant: long–breve patterns in the duplum and triplum are judiciously mingled with phrases or motives composed of single or duplex longs, as though all the different parts were intentionally designed to complement the melodic shape and the sounding texts of the others (see Example 15.4).

The phrase structure of the whole piece is likewise sophisticated, and particularly akin to the motet in featuring sections where variously shaped phrases are interwoven, and sections where internal cadences are punctuated with simultaneous rests in all the parts. The disposition of the phrases in *Anima iuge lacrima* can be seen in graphic form in Figure 15.1.

But particularly interesting in light of the combination of the parts, the diversity of their rhythmic activity, and the contrasts in their phrase structure is the related programme of the three texts of *Anima iuge*. As we have seen, this piece is an altercation, a quarrel between the Soul and the Flesh. Each of these two personae occupies a specific vocal part that symbolically represents its character. The first strophe contains the complaint of the Flesh, which in medieval theology typically represented a lower, corrupt order, since it was initially composed of earth and embodied the sinful nature

---

except for *W1*, fol. 98^r, where the fifth-mode cauda is transmuted into a faster first rhythmic mode. The *Cl* version of *Anima iuge* features an iambic division of the long, except in occasional places in the triplum and duplum, where it is trochaic. This may indicate remodelling from an originally trochaic rendering. For the *Cl* reading of *Anima iuge* see Anderson, *Motets of the MS La Clayette*, p. 5.

of mankind. This particular entity is given the original tenor part from the source cauda, the lowest voice in a polyphonic setting when the voices were written in score. Analogously the Soul, which inhabits Strophe II, appears in the various sources as either a duplum[33] or a triplum voice,[34] a placement suggestive of its superiority over the Flesh's coarser nature, as well as its closer proximity to God.

Figure 15.1: Phrase structure of *Anima iuge* in numbers of longs (total = 80 longs)

Triplum:

```
8.......4...4...4...4...8.......8.......6.....
        4...12..........4...4...10........
```

Duplum:

```
3..7......8.......6.....8.......14............
        4...4...12..........4...10........
```

Tenor:

```
4...4...4...4...4...4...8.......6.....8.......
        4...4...8.......4...4...10........
```

The relationships between the texts of *Anima iuge* are therefore extremely suitable for the polyphonic performance of this composition. Its use of various simultaneously performed sets of lyrics along the lines of the double- and triple-texted motet is justified completely by the substance of the poetry. Just as the various characters in this work argue among themselves, so the music contributes to the sense of confrontation by presenting the texts concurrently. A more illustrative way of setting one of Philip's poetic debates in polyphony can scarcely be imagined.

The succession of strophes is particularly ingenious in the transmission of *Anima iuge* in *La Clayette*. While in *F* the three stanzas are presented in a linear sequence – the charge of the Flesh (I), the response of the Soul (II), and the judgement by Reason (III) – the disposition in *Cl* reverses the order of strophes II and III. With such an ordering only the simultaneous performance of all three texts obviates the irrational series of strophes in this source. Not only does this emphasize that the three parts of *Anima iuge* are indeed intended to be combined polyphonically (for otherwise the scheme of the text in *Cl* would make little sense), but the fact that in *La Clayette* the conciliatory strophe addressed to Reason actually falls between those of the clashing Body and Soul demonstrates that the role of reason in the conflict was not lost on the scribe. In this instance the placement of the third stanza between the other two in *Cl*

---

[33] As in *F* and *StS1*.
[34] As in *Cl*.

functions as an actual physical mediator that literally separates the two warring factions from each other.

Philip's newly attributed *Anima iuge lacrima* thus shares many stylistic features with the motet. Although we cannot be certain whether the path of influence is from prosula to motet or vice versa, what remains is the likely prospect that this unusual example of a conductus prosula closely parallels motet practice and quite conceivably arose as the result of an aesthetic quite similar to that of its more prevalent counterpart. By going beyond the techniques shared by the conductus prosula and motet in the texting of melismas, to incorporating the textures, phrase structures, and polytextuality typically associated only with the motet, *Anima iuge*, in effect, completely synthesizes the practices of the two genres.

With my contention that the evidence of the datable conductus prosulas indicates a period of cultivation in the early 1220s, and with the close connection of these pieces to the motet in their reliance on melismatic polyphony and their use of segments drawn from larger compositions, we may now be in a position to evaluate when the cultivation of motets was in full flower. In addition, further evidence derived from poems by Philip the Chancellor may help to secure a limit for the period in which the motet may first have appeared.

Just as Philip added texts to conductus caudae to fashion prosulas and to discant clausulae to make motets, he also troped melismatic sections culled from the music of three- and four-part organa.[35] (I have supplied a list of these in Table 15.2.) Like the conductus prosulas, the five different texts that make up this equally small repertory of texted organa can also be associated exclusively with him. Every one of these works is attributed to the Chancellor in medieval sources,[36] and it is also notable that each of the organa that he used for his models has been ascribed to the composer Perotinus by either medieval or modern authorities.[37] Like Philip's tropes to conductus, these five organum prosulas also provide a contact point with the motet, not only in the manner in which they were written, but in their reliance on polyphony initially composed in the environment of the Christian liturgy.

Philip's organum prosulas, though, differ from his motets and conductus prosulas in one key respect. Their concordant organal sources comprise the complete solo intonations of their supporting chants, an integral component of the genre as defined by Notre Dame practice. This feature contrasts starkly with the use of the detached segments of chant that make up the tenors of clausulae and motets, as well as the use of disembodied caudae taken from melismatic conductus that provide us with the examples of the conductus prosulas. The employment of these comprehensive portions in the organum prosulas thus represents a more conservative treatment, since it pre-

---

[35]See my '*Associa tecum*', for an investigation of these pieces and for support of the following discussion of *Associa tecum in patria*.

[36]For the attributions see Gordon A. Anderson, 'Thirteenth-century Conductus: Obiter dicta', *MQ* 58 (1972), p. 361.

[37]For the modern ascription of the three-part *Sancte Germane* organum to Perotinus see my '*Associa tecum*', pp. 245–247.

serves the integrity of the original organal source. A further example of such conservatism in Philip's tropes is evident in the fact that his texts to organa never fail to echo the sound and sense of the words of the supporting chant through the comprehensive application of rhyme, assonance, and quotation. (An instance of this practice appears in Example 15.6.) Such strict textual interdependence is not always present in motets, even in the examples that Philip himself authored, and it makes only rare appearances in his texts to conductus caudae. All these features substantiate the hypothesis that Philip's organum prosulas preceded chronologically the creation of both the motet and the conductus prosula, and probably motivated the conception of both these species.

Table 15.2: Texted sustained-tone organal compositions (organum prosulas)

Text incipit	Melismatic Model (organum)	Author of text
Vide prophecie	Viderunt [omnes] (respond, à4)	Philip
Homo cum mandato dato	[Viderunt] omnes (respond, à4)	Philip
De Stephani roseo	Sederunt principes (respond, à4)	Philip
Adesse festina	Sederunt principes (verse, à4)	Philip
Associa tecum in patria	Sancte Germane [Eligi] (respond, à3)	Philip

Example 15.6: Organum prosula *Vide prophecie / Viderunt:* relationships between prosula and tenor texts

Prosula text		Tenor (chant) text
Vide prophecie		VI=
finem adimplete!		
Fugit umbra die,		
quia lux prophete		
progenies est Marie.	5	
....		
Vide,		-DE-
sydus singulare,		
tuum salutare.		
Stelle signo fulgide		
quod radiat hoc mare,	25	
arride, confide.		
Stella preside,		
viam preside		
quam pro*vide*		
magi pro*viderunt.*	30	-RUNT

We are extremely fortunate to have one organum prosula whose composition has been dated: *Associa tecum in patria*, whose identity as an organum prosula was revealed in 1986.[38] This work is a poem in honour of Saint Eligius which despite its subject is set to music drawn from the organum triplum *Sancte Germane*. The likely impetus for the composition of this particular text has been traced to the gift of a relic of Eligius from Noyon to Paris in 1212. This event was accompanied by the addition of a new feast in Eligius's honour, and it also served to enhance his status and rank at the other celebrations that took place in his name at Notre Dame. Moreover, it is significant to note that at this time Philip was employed as an archdeacon in the service of the cathedral chapter of Noyon and therefore would have had additional incentives to honour this saint with a prosula to commemorate the event.[39]

Though *Associa tecum* is at present our only example of an organum trope whose time of composition has been postulated, some support for fixing it as the latest of all the organum prosulas surfaces in an observation of the musical style of its model. When compared to the other organa for which Philip fashioned texts, *Sancte Germane*, the organal model for *Associa*, reveals techniques that appear to be later practices, particularly its frequent use of the iambic patterns of the second and third rhythmic modes and the virtual absence of voice exchange.[40] Consequently, if we accept the dates given for the composition of the organum and conductus prosulas and allow for the likely potential of temporal overlap between the different genres, the entire spectrum of datable and stylistic information suggests that the date of around 1210 for the creation of the motet originally proposed by Ernest Sanders in 1967[41] seems very close to the mark, though a period of origin slightly subsequent to this would also fit the evidence.

If all of the proposed dates hold up under further scrutiny, such an ordering would propose the ensuing scenario for the creation and cultivation of organum and conductus prosulas and the early motet. Around the turn of the century Philip, impressed by the novel sounds of the monumental organa tripla and quadrupla of Perotinus, set the first known poems to melismatic Notre Dame polyphony in his organum prosulas. Such a process created songs that faithfully preserve the sound, structure, sense, and function of the music they embellish, while disclosing for the first time the potential of using the newly fashioned modal rhythms in a syllabic texture. The chancellor's final undertaking in this genre resulted in a tribute in the year 1212 to Eligius, the patron saint of his Noyon archdeaconry. In later years, at some point between this date and the beginning of the next decade, it appears that Philip shifted his attention to the troping of conductus caudae. In these more independently con-

---

[38]See *ibid.* for this and the following points.

[39]Dronke, 'Lyrical Compositions', p. 583, dismisses the attribution of *Associa* to Philip, which I attempt to refute in 'Poetry, Politics, and Polyphony', pp. 116–119.

[40]See my '*Associa tecum*', pp. 245–246, and 'Poetry, Politics, and Polyphony', pp. 313–321 for these claims.

[41]See his 'The Question of Perotin's Oeuvre and Dates', *Festschrift für Walter Wiora zum 30. Dezember 1966* (Kassel, 1967), pp. 243–245.

ceived pieces, created from melismatic counterpoint that first saw light as segments of a larger polyphonic work, a clear parallel is evident with the newly emergent genre of the discant clausula and its own form of prosula, the motet. Such relationships indicate that at the time of the cultivation of the conductus prosulas all the conditions necessary for the formation of the motet were present. It therefore seems tenable to assert that the motet probably arose around the same time as the conductus prosula, at some point soon after the year 1212, and that Philip, in troping organa and conductus caudae, probably also had a hand in the introduction of this newest Notre Dame genre.[42] However, by the time of the most advanced conductus prosula, *Anima iuge lacrima*, probably executed sometime after the datable *Bulla fulminante* of 1222–1223 and probably well before Philip's death in 1236, the motet had claimed pride of place and imposed its own style on its now moribund relative.

But even if my linear and perhaps overly logical sequence of events should be revised through new dates supplied for any of the pieces touched on in this chapter, Philip the Chancellor's efforts in constructing these prosulas still leave an indelible impression. The more one learns of his activities, the more his presence seems not only inescapable, but vital for our understanding of the musical activities of the late twelfth and early thirteenth centuries. His contributions to music not only serve to revise our estimation of his role in its evolution, but also to enhance our appreciation of its historical growth. If one of the duties of a musicologist is to chart the history of this music, then Philip the Chancellor appears as one of the best guides through the complex maze of works and workings that constitute the Notre Dame school.

---

[42]I have elsewhere argued for Philip as the primary creative force behind the motet. See 'Poetry, Politics, and Polyphony', pp. 555–564.

Chapter 16

Vox – littera – cantus: aspects of voice and vocality in medieval song

Philip Weller

Qualities of voice are difficult to capture, or even to intuit, in the Middle Ages. Medieval sources in the realm of both speech and song generally hide more than they reveal of the characteristic timbres, accents, and articulations that constitute the distinctive physical properties of language in all its varied manifestations. This perhaps should hardly surprise us. Relevant documentary material – either of an evocative kind or more concrete and informative – is less available than for later eras.[1] Yet this very elusiveness is in many ways part of the fascination. Something overheard or half-perceived exerts a potent charm that something fully stated and fully grasped can somehow never quite match. The sense of mystery is part of the search, both as enticement and (in part) as reward. The past is by definition always gone, and with it is gone the reality of the immediate apprehension of language, as of all other forms of living social and artistic expression. Yet in the face of this loss there is still the impulse, not simply to reconstruct but to re-enact, in and for the present, whatever among the surviving materials invites such re-enactment. Voices and habits of speech, in their very directness of impact, yet also in their transience and vulnerability to time, are perfect examples of the contrast between the almost effortless immediacy of a present and familiar culture and the difficulty of access of an absent or remote one. In any event, the search for 'old songs' to include in current performing repertories is, and always has been, intimately bound up with the whole cultural process of revival and (re)invention,[2] over and above the basic need for archival preservation. Archaeological and (re)creative types of activity in this sense complement one another and flow together within the same channel. What can be materially preserved is by definition only

---

[1] A great deal of the surviving evidence relating to the singing voice has now been brought together in one place in Timothy J. McGee, *The Sound of Medieval Song: Ornamentation and Vocal Style according to the Treatises* (Oxford, 1998).

[2] For a recent brilliant analysis of how the Middle Ages themselves created a repertory of 'old songs' for the present see Michel Zink, *Le Moyen Âge et ses chansons, ou un passé en trompe-l'oeil* (Paris, 1996), trans. Jane Marie Todd as *The Enchantment of the Middle Ages* (Baltimore, 1998).

ever partial and always needs completing in essential ways. And it is precisely the tension between what can be known and what cannot that gives the performative dimension of music, as of certain kinds of texts intended primarily for live delivery, its special challenge and excitement – and of course its sense of danger and uncertainty as well – within the broader scheme of history and historical thought.

But if there is one thing that can be said for certain about the arts of poetry and song in the medieval period, when the balance between oral and written modes was much more evenly weighted than in later times, it is precisely that performativity is one of their basic historical conditions. It is not simply that in the Middle Ages performance was 'applied to' text as a mode of presentation. Rather, living utterance was the primary ontological – as well as social and psychological – locus of language, which writing served to support and enrich, as *aide-mémoire* and as an added source of detail and complexity.[3] And this can be said as much of the skilled and artful uses of language as of common parlance or officialese (though it is clear that in certain special cases writing was indeed fundamental, as for example in the production of written charters and other documents for the regulation of legal or administrative matters, or in questions of biblical and theological authority).

Paul Zumthor famously coined the term *mouvance* to express the idea that textual differences between versions of many kinds of poems, and especially of songs, really represent far more than just local or incidental variation. They are, he argued, the characteristic result of a much more radical – and often powerfully interventionist – attitude to 'versions' and 'readings' on the part of performers.[4] This was true, he suggested, of both the poetic and the musical component of songs, but particularly of the latter. The speaking and singing voice was a necessary integrating force within all medieval poetry, one that helped to shape the form as well as the presentation of the poetic message. And it is the signature of vocality within the very substance of the poetic text that serves to give it its distinctive expressive edge and grain. This, I shall maintain, was an intrinsic and accepted part of the nature of both language and poetry as the Middle Ages understood and used them. Being part of an oral tradition always meant being part of a 'performance culture', and this was an ever-present factor in the creation and production of medieval song, in whatever language or context. It was a fundamental (hence to us often invisible) condition of its making – one which survived in brilliant fashion even when it also participated in a written tradition. Performance context, contigencies of sound, the impact of live delivery, and the fact of communication 'in the moment' are as fundamental to the historical reality of medieval song as is our knowledge of its textual sources and the conditions of their production. Text and

---

[3]Studies of the interdependence of orality and literacy are very numerous. For a stimulating range of essays on a variety of topics approached from different perspectives see A. N. Doane and Carol Braun Pasternack, eds, *Vox intexta: Orality and Textuality in the Middle Ages* (Madison, WI, 1991).

[4]Paul Zumthor, *Essai de poétique médiévale* (Paris, 1972), pp. 65–75, and 'Intertextualité et mouvance', *Littérature* 4 (1981), pp. 8–16; Frank R. Akehurst and Judith M. Davis, eds, *A Handbook of the Troubadours* (Berkeley, 1995), pp. 13–14, 320–322.

voice, script and sound, writing and memory – all work together, in a state of collaborative and finally productive tension, to shape and give expression to poetic ideas of many kinds, in different ways according to the needs and specific nature of the project in hand.

No reader or performer of medieval poetry and song can, in the end, afford to bypass this rhetorical and physical – and indeed social – dimension of text. This is perhaps true most of all with songs, where performers need to take account of the rich but complex aesthetic potential of the idea of the 'twofold' or 'double' melody (in John Stevens's apt and memorable phrase).[5] The interplay of verbal and musical patterns between the two poetic-melodic strands, and the counterpoint of different qualities of 'accent' and 'number', offer the resourceful performer a wide range of rhetorical and expressive possibilities for any and every live performance. Moreover these two strands, as distinct yet complementary parts of a greater and more articulate whole, are both embraced within the domain of vocality, in its broadest range of meaning. In this sense, knowledge of the literary and notational materials of a song will always need to extend far beyond the realm of philology and textual scholarship. Yet these are essential disciplines on which the whole project of interpretation and performance ultimately depends. There needs to be a concrete point of departure, a set of initial stimuli from which we first derive something valuable that speaks to us, elicits a response, and thus serves to trigger the whole process of (re)discovery and re-enactment. The primary historical and textual materials are in this sense crucial to the enterprise, and not at all arbitrary. Such basic givens need to be present and kept in mind throughout the evolving and dynamic process of interpretation, and should be reflected, however subtly and implicitly, in the final outcome, in what is actually 'produced'. Any performance of a song needs to respect the textual data, while still going beyond it to arrive at a fully internalized and articulate account of the human and expressive content, as well as of the poetic substance and versified form. Song attains its proper mode of being when the free play of interpretation – simultaneously linguistic *and* musical – is set to work on the surviving textual materials.

The fundamental condition of this interpretative work is that of vocality, of the expressive authority of voice in the moment of performance.[6] The mind is guided and to an extent constrained by what is textually given, yet is at the same time liberated to explore more freely the horizons of what is not. And so the initial poetic clues need to be sufficiently clear both to claim our attention in the first place, and then to fire the imagination – human as well as historical. Part of this process crucially involves the voicing and physical articulation of what otherwise would remain silent, uncontaminated by the contingencies and compromises of real-time performance, yet also

---

[5]John Stevens, *Words and Music in the Middle Ages* (Cambridge, 1986), pp. 496–499.

[6]Stephen G. Nichols, 'Voice and Writing in Augustine and in the Troubadour Lyric', in *Vox intexta*, pp. 137–161; Paul Zumthor, *La poésie et la voix dans la civilisation médiévale*, Collège de France: Essais et Conférences (Paris, 1984), *La lettre et la voix: de la "littérature" médiévale* (Paris, 1987), and 'Les marques du chant: le point de vue du philologue', *Revue de musicologie* 73 (1987), pp. 7–17.

remaining below the full realization of its expressive potential, as conveyed through the human agency of the body. Voices are of their nature transient. Hence with time they inevitably fall silent, and are succeeded by other voices. But those that are figured within texts, as rhetorical and literary constructions, and even those that survive simply as a latent presence, remain potentially available to later ages.

It is one of the glories as well as the frustrations of the Middle Ages that the human sounds of singing and speaking seem to be described or hinted at in the sources in so many ways in so many places, and yet remain finally beyond our grasp. There are countless medieval texts both poetic and prosaic which appear to contain, at a sub-liminal – and sometimes at a more explicit – level, the timbres and rhythms of the human voice. But these voices which we think we 'hear', in and beyond the text, are only ever on the verge of being vocalized in any clearly understandable or recoverable way. And yet it is a major achievement of medieval literacy that, to an alert reader, it so often manages to convey something very real of the richness and depth of its own orality: of its oral roots, and of the soil in which speech and writing have combined to produce the literary growth which has handed down to us whatever we now possess in the form of texts. And as part of this oral substrate we have been given – generally in potential rather than actual form, it is true – something of the 'vocal substance' of those texts we choose to study and seek to re-enact. Bringing out this dimension of text is the task of performers, as informed interpreters of the past who work in the present within the medium of a living communicative tradition. That is one reason why performers are as much guardians of the text as scholars are, in a complementary rather than antagonistic way – because they maintain the necessary active skills of reading and interpretation with a view to performance, and of linguistically grounded vocal production, which are components of medieval song as essential as the details of its textual profile.

This is the view from the modern side. But what, we may ask, of the Middle Ages themselves? How might medieval musicians and audiences have understood the contingency not just of performance *tout court*, as a radically recreative activity and the natural medium of poetry and song, but more specifically of the way 'voice' acts in an expressive – yet also defining, even assertive – capacity to affirm and substantiate text whenever it is uttered? More concretely still, would they have had a clear aes-thetic appreciation of the diversity of human voices and what they were capable of or best suited to? The evidence presented here suggests that they would. (By using the deliberately vague 'they' I mean to suggest the idea of a human and social category of theoretically limitless variety and extension.) The purpose of this essay, then, is to show that the medieval mind was at times capable of thinking very clearly and subtly about qualities of voice, both as a physical entity with distinctive characteristics, and as it might be applied to different kinds of music and musical idioms.

In Gerald of Wales's *Gemma ecclesiastica*, written during the last years of the twelfth century, we find a humorous – and very human – 'real life' anecdote illus-trating to perfection how the performance of secular song, in this case a dance song of the *carole* type, might impinge on the maintenance of good order in the conduct of church ceremonial.[7] The high-minded Gerald of course regards this is an outrageous infringement of ecclesiastical discipline (as too did the relevant bishop). And although the tone of his writing seems relatively even-handed for this emphatic and often vehemently moralistic writer, we are left in no doubt as to his clear disapproval. The anecdote occurs in connection with Gerald's citation of a 'canon' or ruling, apparently from one of the church councils held at Toledo during the earlier Middle Ages (*habemus ex concilio Toletano* ...), forbidding unseemly behaviour, and specifically the inappropriate use of singing and dancing (*saltatio* is the word used), in and around church buildings. This seems to have been a general proscription, but was taken to apply with particular force to all such 'secular' activity during the solemn moments of liturgical ceremonies – in particular at the consecration, one of the most sacred of all the ritual actions of the mass.

Gerald cites the Toledo pronouncement as stating that 'the people may not be permitted to dance, nor to indulge in songs, in the solemn celebration of holy things' (*saltationibus et cantilenis in sanctorum solemnitatibus populi vacare non debeant*). Those who ought to attend soberly and respectfully to the divine offices, it observes, are all too often 'intent on practising unseemly and scandalous gestures and dances, not only singing bad [i.e. infamous and inappropriate] songs, but also noisily disrupting the offices of the priests and other religious persons' (... *saltationibus turpibus invigilant, cantica non solum mala canentes, sed et religiosorum officiis obstrepunt*). The Toledo injunction thus appears to be a relatively early recorded case of official measures being taken against the kind of popular clamour and agitation that at times accompanied even the more solemn passages of the mass liturgy, instances of which are well attested in later times, when they seem to have occurred most often at the elevation. The dramatic raising of the host was a later accretion to the consecration, marking outwardly this moment of great inner mystery and solemnity, which by reason of the priest's gesture and its almost theatrical framing was thereby transformed into a crucial physical as well as theological motif within the grand spectacle of the mass. The elevation of the host became more or less general practice in the western church during the course of the thirteenth century.[8] In time it not unnaturally became a strong visual focus for personal devotion, and the occasion for paraliturgical musical items, as well as for spoken and sometimes physically demonstrative kinds of veneration on the part of the laity (who of course throughout the entire Middle Ages would have viewed such actions as spectators from afar, that is, from a position beyond the rood-screen dividing chancel from nave). The fact that such spontaneous demonstrations of popular affection for the mysteries of the faith were for the most part unsolicited and undesired by the clergy, as being disrespectful and out of keeping with the seriousness of the

---

[7]J. S. Brewer and James F. Dimock, eds, *Giraldi Cambrensis opera*, 8 vols, Rolls Series (London, 1861–1891), vol. 2, pp. 119–120.

[8]Peter Browe SJ, *Die Verehrung der Eucharistie im Mittelalter* (Munich, 1933; reprinted Rome, 1967), pp. 28–39.

occasion, rarely seems to have acted as a serious impediment to their recurrence. And so these joyful and celebratory expressions continued with a frequency and a vigour that are easily attested to by the proscriptions and denunciations that occur in a variety of written forms and contexts. But we must return to consider the second part of Gerald's discussion.

In best scholastic fashion, Gerald goes on to provide the *exemplum* (that is, the exemplary proof or 'instance') that is needed to demonstrate the force of the general point and so clinch the argument. The example is intended to show the application, and hence the viability, of the moral theory in the everyday world by bringing in a particular concrete example from that world. It is one of the innumerable situations where, contrary to the received view, medieval attitudes show a very direct and engaged approach to the immediate realities of events and experience. Gerald wishes to show with all the practical force at his command why secular song, especially when accompanied by dancing, is inadmissible in any sacred context. And so he narrates the anecdote referred to above, presenting it as if it had been drawn straight from life (notice the carefully recorded details of time and place), in order that it may appear in as empirical and convincing a guise as possible:[9]

> And an example [of this] is that of a priest, in England in the region of Worcester (*in Anglia Wigorniae finibus*) in recent times (*nostris diebus*), who, having listened all night long to a certain short phrase of a song being sung repeatedly – as they were in the habit of doing – many times over (a practice which they call 'the refrain')[10] in the *caroles* which were being danced [lit. 'led, conducted'] all around the church (*in choreis circiter ecclesiam ductis*), out of the remains of his thoughts (*ex reliquiis cogitationum*), and given that the mouth tends to speak out of the fullness of the heart (*quoniam ex abundantia cordis os loqui solet*), and even though it was in the morning when he was clothed in priestly vestments for mass, standing at the altar ready to give the blessing to the people, namely 'Dominus vobiscum', instead [of these words] pronounced that same [refrain], in English, in the presence of all and singing in a loud voice (*coram omnibus alta voce modulando*), as follows: *Swete lamman dhin are*, the sense of which may be rendered as 'Sweet love, your lover begs your favour' (*Dulcis amica, tuam poscit amator opem*).

The beauty and charm of the story are self-evident. So too is its humour, at least to a modern mind, if not to that of a stern twelfth-century disciplinarian. But of what are we actually being told here, apart from the illicit and forbidden nature of such practices in the eyes of the church? Of the sheer popularity of song and of dance, certainly, in these inappropriate circumstances, but also in those more suitable, though dozens of other medieval anecdotes would have told more or less the same tale, in straightforwardly censorious, no-nonsense terms. But Gerald's discussion, in its modest and still rather conservative way, opens up further perspectives. He describes in greater

---

[9]Brewer and Dimock, *Giraldi Cambrensis Opera*, vol. 2, p. 120.

[10]Gerald here offers an ingenious attempt at Latinizing the vernacular term *refrain*, cleverly glossing it as 'refectoriam seu refractoriam'.

detail than we might expect the actual mechanism by which the dance song has its effect. And in the very act of outlining the workings of this mechanism he also tells us, unwittingly and almost despite himself, a great deal more about his beliefs concerning the influence of music over human perception and behaviour. At times like this he almost seems to be a distant – and obviously quite unsystematic – follower of the kinds of proto-scientific explanation that were becoming more common and widespread as a result of the great intellectual expansion of the twelfth century. Gerald does not 'demonize' or even just moralize the phenomena in the anecdote, but gives them a plausible functional description, albeit one of a straightforward and commonsensical rather than a deeply technical kind. His commentary, though necessarily brief, does not remain at the level of moral polemic, but, by carefully suggesting a sequence of physical and psychological events, gives an account of how the thing came to happen as it did. In other words, he constructs a model – partial and modest in its pretensions, it is true, but interesting none the less and above all significative of a mentality that is no longer content merely to attribute such happenings to unseen spiritual agencies (to malefic incantations or demons, for example), but seeks instead a more graspable explanation in terms of the here-and-now of human functioning and experience.

It is the physical sonority, and above all the insistent patterns of sound, that seem to affect the poor cleric's brain and go on to disrupt his memory at the crucial moment, early the following morning, as he stands in front of the altar facing the people. And indeed, it is surely the role of memory that is being referred to in Gerald's phrase *ex reliquiis cogitationum*, 'out of the remains of his thoughts'. The priest's presence of mind is clouded by the confused but still very present and potent recollections of the sounds of the previous night. These recollections remain so near the surface of his mind, and disturb his perceptions so insistently, that he can only utter the lover's refrain in place of the words of the priestly blessing. Gerald's originality is to have placed this kind of simple, proto-scientific explanation in an otherwise common-parlance, moralizing context; and it shows much for his clarity of vision that he adopts this approach. There are many further observations that could be made in relation to this little incident and its description. But the point we need to hold on to here is that it is in the first place the sound of the song, its vocality and its body-rhythms, rather than just its structural properties and formal or stylistic features (important though these may have been), which made their impact on the cleric's mind all the more fateful.

Such an empirical and experiential approach to phenomena in the sphere of music and memory, in particular regarding the perceptual impact and 'catchiness' of songs, was not an isolated occurrence. This is shown by a short passage drawn from one of the early chronicles of the newly formed mendicant orders – in this case that of the Dominicans, as recorded in the *Vitae fratrum* (1259–1260) of Gerardus de Fracheto (Gérard de Frachet, d.1271).[11] This little story offers another instance of the problem, so vividly described by Gerald of Wales, when a tuneful song melody haunts the

---

[11]Benedictus Maria Reichert, ed., *Fratris Gerardi de Fracheto vitae fratrum Ordinis Praedicatorum, necnon cronica ordinis 1203–1254* (Rome, 1897).

memory and will not go away. It concerns a brother, who, prior to becoming a Dominican, had greatly indulged his 'secular' taste for songs and singing, yet without taking sufficient account of the frivolity and vanity involved in such pleasures. He had been made to suffer for this oversight later on, after entering the order:[12]

> There was a certain friar of the Roman province, who in the secular world (*in seculo*, i.e., before he became a friar) had taken great pleasure and delight in hearing and singing secular songs (*in audiendis et cantandis secularibus cantilenis fuerat delectatus*), yet had not given heed to the fact that he ought to avow a vanity of this sort, and so, being placed in [a condition of] grave weakness and infirmity, had these very songs [sounding] almost continuously in his ears and in his mind, in such a way that he experienced not pleasure as before, but only vexation and a not inconsiderable discomfort.

> Frater quidam in provincia Romana, qui in seculo multum in audiendis et cantandis secularibus cantilenis fuerat delectatus, nec adverterat quod confiteretur huiusmodi vanitatem, in infirmitate gravi positus, dictos cantus quasi continue in aure et cerebro habebat, et inde non delectationem ut prius, sed vexacionem et penam non modicam sustinebat.

The 'punishment' here stems directly from the misdemeanour. And it is not so much a theological as a psychological one: the friar is tormented by the very sounds from which he had previously (but also naively and incautiously) derived so much enjoyment. This example emphasizes the difference between the conduct appropriate to a 'free man' of secular status and that expected of a member of a religious order, even one of the mendicant orders, which were still in a very real sense 'out in the world' by comparison with the established monastic institutions. This relative freedom of the mendicants, a freedom which was nevertheless still disciplined by the kinds of behavioural codes and conventions alluded to in the passage above, acted during the thirteenth century as something of a counterbalance to the sometimes excessive freedom of action claimed by the much more independent and often vainglorious secular clergy. There can be no doubt that, along with the strong institutional reforms and political reorganizations of the early thirteenth century, there gradually emerged in the decades either side of 1200 – and then stretching right the way through the new century – a clear softening of attitude on the part of at least some priests, in particular of the urban clergy, towards the secular culture among which they lived and worked.[13] The presence and attitude of the church in urban communities all over Europe began to

---

[12]*Ibid.*, pp. 100–101. I owe the knowledge of this passage to Christopher Page, *The Owl and the Nightingale* (London, 1989), pp. 125 and 237 n.59.

[13]The situation in France, centering on Paris, is illuminatingly charted in Page, *The Owl and the Nightingale*. For the emergence of a distinctively urban way of thinking in central Italy see, e.g., George Holmes, 'The Emergence of an Urban Ideology at Florence, *ca* 1250–*ca* 1450', *Transactions of the Royal Historical Society* 5/23 (1973), pp. 111–134. For a collection of studies on the theme of religion in medieval urban communites see David Abulafia *et al.*, eds, *Church and City 1000–1500. Essays in Honour of Christopher Brooke* (Cambridge, 1992).

change along with, and in response to, the changing social and economic profiles of the communities themselves. Evidence of this change is discernible among the ecclesiastical hierarchy of the cathedrals and collegiate churches in the greater towns and cities, beginning with such eminent figures as John of Salisbury and Peter the Chanter in the twelfth century. But it can be seen to operate even more, and certainly in a very different way, among the friars, whose ministry was a distinctively urban one and practised very much among the people, during the early and middle decades of the new century.

The intellectual and artistic ferment of the twelfth century – written of with good reason and surely justifiable enthusiasm as a 'renaissance'[14] – was a movement towards cultural renewal of extraordinary sweep and intensity that was expressed most strongly in the major centres, and especially in Paris, but which extended with varying intensity and scope almost the length and breadth of western Europe. (This occurred not least as a result of the dissemination of new thought and ideas by the scholars and students who were drawn in such extraordinary numbers to the Parisian schools from elsewhere for periods of study of varying length.) Following on from this great opening up of ideas on many levels, and accompanied also by a new vigour of art and language, the cultural unfolding of the early thirteenth century took a variety of paths which differed from place to place and from region to region. On the one hand, there was a seemingly quite conscious and deliberate move towards consolidation and institutionalization across a broad sweep of Europe that can be seen to have operated during the pontificate of Innocent III (r. 1198–1216). This resulted in a number of internationally important, as well as many more localized, events: the capture of Constantinople and the establishment of a Latin empire in the East (1204); papal approval of the Franciscan movement (1210); the beginning of Frederick II's concurrent rule over the German empire and the kingdom of Sicily (1212); the convening of the great Fourth Lateran Council, and the granting of statutes to the University of Paris (both 1215). On the other hand we find the mendicant orders functioning as a great source of new social and religious energy, but scarcely (at least not in the very early years) of consolidation. On the contrary, the friars represented much that was new and radical, not only in the religious sphere; and their contribution was a major – perhaps the major – force for social and cultural rejuvenation in the new century:

> The founding of the Franciscan and Dominican orders demonstrates the continued vitality of medieval civilization in the early thirteenth century. The product of the institutionalization of asceticism in the twelfth century – the religious orders working in the world – was used to meet the consequences of the new piety and the new learning and to reassert the leadership of the church in European society, thereby completing the basis of the new consensus that Innocent [III] had set out to construct. [...] The

---

[14]Charles Homer Haskins, *The Renaissance of the Twelfth Century* (Cambridge MA, 1927); Richard W. Southern, *The Making of the Middle Ages* (London, 1953; reprinted 1993), and 'The Place of England in the Twelfth-century Renaissance', *History* 45 (1960), pp. 201–216; Christopher Brooke, *The Twelfth-Century Renaissance* (London, 1969); Robert L. Benson and Giles Constable, eds, *Renaissance and Renewal in the Twelfth Century* (Oxford, 1982).

development of thought, religion and culture in the thirteenth century was largely the working out of the implications of the Dominican and Franciscan ideals.[15]

The move towards a new consensus meant, among other things, that at least some clerical thinkers not only began to take a more tolerant and even appreciative attitude towards secular music, but were also prepared to defend its virtues theoretically and philosophically, in written treatises, if not necessarily in the more popular and public genre of sermons. As a result, song – both sacred and secular – came to enjoy a more prominent and above all a more widely accepted position than it had done before among the élites. Nowhere can this be more clearly seen than in the *Cronica* of the Franciscan writer Fra Salimbene de Adam (1221–87), perhaps the most comprehensive, and certainly the most enjoyable, of the general chronicles of the early years of the order.[16] What is particularly striking in this fascinating historical survey is just how widespread, and how absolutely normal, the use of music among the urban populations of north-central Italy seems to have been. It was certainly accepted as a fully integrated part of the social scene. Salimbene expresses admiration for good music as he does for evidence of piety or good morals or divine inspiration; and yet he is never surprised at the fact that music should take its place, quite naturally, within the habits and customs of his time. The range of musical topics covered in the *Cronica* is striking, as is the detailed and informed way in which they are treated (as we shall see, Salimbene was himself an educated and literate musician). Moreover, like the great French theorist Johannes de Grocheio (fl. *ca* 1300), though within a much narrower range, he finds a location and a context for his discussions of musical practice that are in the fullest sense of the word social and cultural, yet without sacrificing the fine-grained attention to detail they both so evidently valued. This openness to observation and to 'things as they are', and the willingness to work with the givens of social and cultural practice, while not relinquishing the insight that comes from a sensitive critical and classificatory approach to evidence and materials, represents a real step forward in the tradition of thinking and writing about music. It surely justifies seeing Grocheio's *De Musica* in particular as one of the great intellectual achievements of the high medieval era, and also justifies the more general view of the period from the late eleventh to the early fourteenth century as one of often radical and energetic development in the theoretical and critical, as well as the practical and compositional, domains of music.

The broad framework of the *Cronica* is, not surprisingly, constructed in a straightforwardly chronological way. But it contains along the way a large number of designated excursus-type passages dedicated not only to major events and to cultural and religious concerns of the time, but also to giving brief descriptions of a series of

---

[15]Norman F. Cantor, *The Civilization of the Middle Ages* (New York, 1993), p. 428.

[16]Oswald Holder-Egger, ed., *Cronica fratris Salimbene de Adam ordinis minorum* (Hanover/Leipzig, 1905–1913), Monumenta Germaniae Historica, 'Scriptores' 32. See also the new edition by Giuseppe Scalia: *Cronica*, 2 vols, Corpus Christianorum continuatio medievalis 125A/B (Tournai, 1998–1999). My detailed study of 'Music in the *Cronica* of Fra Salimbene de Adam' is forthcoming.

notable personalities and striking incidents. The result is supremely vivid as well as clear and informative. As an initial example of the rapid sketches of individuals, we shall briefly consider the case of a certain Fra Guidolino, described by Salimbene as 'a literate and educated man, and a good singer' (*litteratus homo et bonus cantor*) who also knew and expounded the Bible well, wrote beautifully, and was generally of honest and holy life, besides loving his brother friars as he was supposed to.[17] Such a listing of talents and skills and moral 'good points' forms an absolutely standard component of Salimbene's succinct eulogies of his fellow Franciscans and others whom he considers worthy of praise. But where the material warrants it he goes much further, both in his descriptions of events and in the portraits of individuals. And the great merit of the more extensive discussions he gives us in these cases is, as we shall see, that they usually are – or appear to be – based on first-hand knowledge and exper-ience. In the case of Fra Guidolino, the extra information we are given relates directly, and at an informed technical and aesthetic level, to the friar's skill in singing and to his vocal attributes. Salimbene makes the well-judged observation that

> He sang very finely indeed in melodious song (that is, broken song), and in plainchant his singing method was better than his voice, for he had a very slender and elegant voice.

> Optime cantabat in cantu melodiato (id est cantu fracto), et de cantu firmo melius cantabat, quam vocem haberet, quia valde gracilem vocem habebat. [*Cronica*, p. 552]

Here we catch a real hint – indeed, rather more than a hint – of expert musical comment. Guidolino's voice is described as *gracilis*, a term which implies a certain elegance and flexibility, as well as the more prosaic idea of thinness or slenderness. This kind of voice, Salimbene argues, precisely because of its flexibility, is more suited to the melodic elaborations of figured music than it is to the simpler grandeur and sonority of plainchant. What seems to me especially striking here is not just that these kinds of functional and aesthetic judgement about the appropriateness of particular voice types to different kinds of vocal idiom are made, but that they give rise to a subtler threefold distinction between physical voice, vocal technique, and melodic style. For although Guidolino's voice is, by virtue of its lightness and grace, not naturally suited to the performance of chant, Salimbene implies that he makes up for this with his acquired skill in singing, or what would in the era of *bel canto* have been termed his 'method' (*de cantu firmo melius cantabat, quam vocem haberet*). In other words, 'calibre' of voice is distinguished from vocal 'technique', and both are equally important when considering questions of style and idiom. What qualifications Salimbene himself may have had for making these kinds of observation, we shall soon discover.

But before embarking on this phase of the discussion it will be useful momentarily to recall that Salimbene's chronicle paints a vivid and at times highly suggestive (if inevitably rather sketchy) picture of the popular devotional activities, in part initiated

---

[17]Holder-Egger, *Cronica*, p. 552.

and certainly participated in by the friars, that give us a context for the prehistory of the *lauda* as a musical genre and of the *devotio moderna* as a new form of humane piety. The documented history of the institutionalized 'Compagnie dei laudesi' does not begin until the middle decades of the thirteenth century; and the genre itself, as an identifiable poetic and musical entity, also belongs to a slightly later period than we are considering here.[18] Salimbene's account instead offers us descriptions of some of the earliest social and cultural manifestations of this new secularizing impulse in religion, out of which the widely disseminated practice of *lauda* singing, connected in its origins to the Franciscans' encouragement of the 'laudes domini', emerged. Processions, informal assemblies, enthusiastic public speaking and moral exhortation, inspired preaching and singing in church or in the open air and apparently happening at all times of day – these were all part of the great religious ferment which, once its forces had been channelled and its challenge met, was to produce such striking developments on all levels of society through the ensuing decades:

> It was in the year 1233 [...] that the 'Alleluia' [time] began, [...] that is to say, a period of quietness and peace, during which warlike weapons were entirely absent – a period of serenity and happiness, of joy and exultation, of praise and jubilation. They sang songs in praise of God (*cantilenas cantabant et laudes divinas*), soldiers and infantrymen, city dwellers and country folk, young men and virgins, old men and children. And this Devotion was in all the towns of Italy. And I observed how, in my own city of Parma, every district wanted to have its own banner (*vexillum*) whenever there was a procession; which [banners] were duly made, and [they] placed on [each] banner the type of martyrdom of their [patron] saint. [...] And they came from the outlying rural districts into the city with their banners, in great throngs (*societatibus magnis*), men and women, boys and girls alike, in order to listen to the preachers and to praise God. They sang with voices of God, rather than of man (*et cantabant dei voces et non hominis*), and all men walked in [the way of] salvation, so that it was as if the prophecy had been fulfilled which said: 'let all the ends of the earth consider and turn again to the Lord; and let the families of all the peoples worship in his sight' [Ps. 21: 28].[19]

But Salimbene had almost as much to say about technical and aesthetic questions of singing as he did about the beginnings of the *devotio moderna*; and it is with this that we shall be primarily concerned here. We have already observed the distinctions he made, *à propos* of Fra Guidolino, between physical qualities of voice, skill in vocal method, and the kinds of music different voice types could be made to sing. These ideas were developed at much greater length in Salimbene's discussion of two outstanding singers and musicians, both of whom he knew personally and had studied

---

[18]Blake Wilson, *Music and Merchants: The Laudesi Companies of Republican Florence* (Oxford, 1992), pp. 28–33 and ch. 1–2 *passim*. See also the documentary evidence and dates reported in Gilles-Gerard Meersseman, 'Note sull'origine delle Compagnie dei Laudesi (Siena 1267)', *Rivista di storia della chiesa in Italia* 17 (1963), pp. 395–405, and *Ordo fraternitatis*, 3 vols (Rome, 1977).

[19]Holder-Egger, *Cronica*, p. 70.

with: Brother Henry of Pisa ('frater Henricus Pisanus') and Brother Vita of Lucca ('frater Vita de civitate Lucensi').

Brother Vita possessed an elegant and flexible voice, not unlike that of Fra Guidolino, but clearly far superior to it in both intrinsic quality and vocal method. Indeed, Salimbene went so far as to claim that

> [he was] in his time the finest singer in the world in both kinds of singing, that is, in plainchant and in broken [or figured] song. [And] he had a lovely, delicate voice, delightful to hear and full of subtlety.

> melior cantor de mundo [erat] tempore suo in utroque cantu, scilicet firmo et fracto. Vocem habebat gracilem sive subtilem et delectabilem ad audiendum. [*Cronica*, p. 183]

His gently persuasive and at times ravishingly beautiful singing was so marvellous to hear that

> there was no one so austere or severe that they would not willingly hear him. He sang in the presence of bishops, archbishops, cardinals, and the Pope, and they all gladly listened to him. And if anybody were to speak while Brother Vita was singing, he would cause the words to resound which are taken from *Ecclesiasticus* 32: 'you shall not impede the music'.[20]

> non erat aliquis adeo severus, qui non eum libenter audiret. Coram episcopis, archiepiscopis, cardinalibus et papa cantabat et libenter audiebatur ab eis. Si quis loqueretur, cum frater Vita cantaret, statim Ecclesiastici verbum resonabat [...]: *Non impedias musicam*. [*Cronica*, p. 183]

There was clearly much musical talent in the family: Salimbene tells us that 'Brother Vita's mother and sister were both excellent and delightful singers' (*optime et delectabiles fuerunt cantatrices*). Yet it seems likely that he must also have studied singing seriously at the technical level, as an *ars*. Certainly he felt he ought to pass on what he knew: Salimbene tells us that 'he was my singing master in his native city of Lucca in the year 1239, when there was that terrible eclipse of the sun'.[21] In any event, Brother Vita had a good enough technique (as well as a sense of duty to his adoring public) that, whenever he might have been tempted to refuse to sing because he was ill or indisposed, he did not do so:

> So generous (*ita curialis*) was he with his singing that he never made any excuses if he was asked to sing, on the grounds that his voice was in poor condition or impeded by a cold, or any other of those reasons that singers give when requested to perform (*nec occasione vocis laesae sive a frigore impeditae vel aliqua alia de causa...*), so that no

---

[20]I.e., *loquere maior natu decet enim te: primum verbum, diligenti scientia; et non impedias musicam*: 'it falls to you, as the greater by birth, to speak: as one who, putting the word first, delights in knowledge; and you shall not impede the music' (Eccl. 32: 4–5).

[21] *Chronica*, p. 183.

one could apply to him the verses written by Horace: 'All singers have this fault, that they never are prepared to sing when asked to do so among friends.'[22] [*Cronica*, p. 183]

Henry of Pisa, on the other hand, had a rather different kind of voice. In his character sketch Salimbene first attributes to him the usual list of excellent moral qualities, before going on specifically to discuss his vocal prowess:

> Brother Henry [...] was a handsome man, of only medium height, generous, courteous, jovial and lively (*largus, curialis, liberalis et alacer*). He knew well how to converse with all sorts and conditions of men, getting along well with them and adapting to everyone as an individual, respecting their habits and personalities. Moreover, he was on good terms (*gratiam habens*) both with his fellow friars and with lay people, a gift which is given to few.

> He was a celebrated preacher (*sollemnis predicator*), well loved by both clergy and people. Then, too, he was skilled in calligraphy and miniature painting – which some call illumination, because the book is so to speak 'illumined' by the illustration – as well as in musical notation (*notare*); and he knew how to compose (*invenire*) the most beautiful and delightful melodies (*cantus pulcherrimos et delectabiles*), whether these were elaborate and florid (*modulatos, id est fractos*) or in the straightforward unadorned style of plainsong (*firmos*).

> He himself was a fine and highly regarded singer (*sollemnis cantor*), and his voice was full and sonorous (*vocem grossam et sonoram*), so that it seemed to fill the whole choir. His bell-like upper register (*quillam*)[23] was indeed very fine-grained, light, high, and clear, but also lovely, gentle, and ravishing beyond measure (*subtilem, altissimam et acutam, dulcem, suavem et delectabilem supra modum*).

The last two sentences amount to a rapidly penned encomium of Brother Henry's vocal method and singing style. And we can only marvel at the sureness of touch displayed by Salimbene, both in choosing which qualities to praise and in finding the most eloquent mode of expression for praising them. Nonetheless he was not, or at least not quite, a disinterested observer. He enjoyed a close and very friendly relationship with Brother Henry throughout his life, and also studied singing with him in the early years ('during the period of Gregory IX [r. 1227–1241] he was my guardian and

---

[22]*Omnibus hoc vitium est cantoribus, inter amicos / Ut nunquam inducant animum cantare rogati* (Horace, *Satires*, 3, 1, 2).

[23]'Quillam' is probably a latinized form of the Italian word *quilio* (or, more rarely, *quilia*), referring to the high register of a voice which has a clear and penetrating, and sometimes vibrant, quality. (The term may also be related to *squillo/squillare*, as in, e.g., 'una voce squillante e in quilio'). Alternatively, there may be a case for emending *quillam* to *squillam*, taking the well attested meanings 'vox acuta' and 'bell / little bell' and relating them metaphorically to the clear, bell-like upper register of a well-schooled voice. There are many variant but probably cognate forms of this word: see Du Cange, *Glossarium mediae et infimae latinitatis*, rev. edn, 8 vols (Paris, 1840–1850), vol. 6, p. 269, s.v. 'skella'; Jan Frederick Niermeyer, *Mediae latinitatis lexicon minus*, (Leiden, 1976), p. 944, s.v. 'scella'.

mentor in the *custodium* at Siena, as well as being my singing master').[24] Salimbene hence profited in his youth from the advice and expertise of two gifted singers, and we can perhaps now begin to see where his confidence in exercising his taste and judgement came from, and also why he lavished such care on his musical descriptions. But even granted this background, the acuity and vividness of both these portraits still seem to me astonishing, especially at this great distance of time.

It is clear that, with a voice of broader and perhaps richer quality than that of Brother Vita, Brother Henry nevertheless had just as great a technical command, which enabled him to negotiate the high notes of his upper register with such apparent ease and elegance and beauty of tone. Nevertheless, Salimbene was clear in his own mind that Brother Vita's voice was 'more suited to the chamber than to the choir' (*vox eius magis pertinebat ad cameram quam ad chorum*), whereas in Brother Henry's case the reverse was probably true ('his voice ... seemed to fill the whole choir'). Expert vocality was not Brother Henry's sole musical gift, however, since he is also credited with great skill and considerable productivity in composition:

> [He] composed many songs (*cantilenas*) and many sequences (*sequentias*), including the text (*litteram*) and music of one entitled *Christe deus, Christe meus, Christe rex et domine!* which he modelled on the singing of a young woman as she was walking through the cathedral at Pisa (*ad vocem cuiusdam pedisequae, quae per maiorem ecclesiam Pisanam ibat cantando*), her song being in Italian: *E s' tu no cure de me / e no curaro de te* ('If you care not for me, I'll not care for thee').

This charming vignette of a girl murmuring her love song inside the great cathedral at Pisa, and being overheard by an entranced Brother Henry, will serve to remind us (if we need reminding) how open to the world the Franciscan mind-set really was, and also, more generally, just how enmeshed was the idiom of secular with that of sacred song, even if later historiography has tended to draw a much stronger line of demarcation between sacred and secular forms of expression. The beginning of the quotation moreover gives us a strong and vivid picture of the songmaker as a poet-singer fashioning his own texts and then performing them to his own music, that is entirely in accord with the holistic view of song in this period as a true amalgam of poetic and musical components. Not that Brother Henry always set his own texts, however. Salimbene informs us that he composed melodies to a considerable number of poems by his great contemporary Philip the Chancellor, and also to one of the Victorine sequences, when he apparently substituted for the original 'rough and awkward tune' 'a wonderful melody' of his own composition, which unlike the one it replaced was 'well

---

[24]The following anecdote shows just how close this relationship was, at both the human and the musical levels, and also demonstrates a clear sophistication on Salimbene's part in negotiating the relationship between sound and notation: 'Then once, when he was guardian (*custos*) of the *custodium* in the convent at Siena, and he lay ill in bed in the infirmary and was unable to write down his music, he called me to him and I became the first person to take down one of his songs directly from his singing (*et fui primus, qui eo cantante notavi illum cantum*)'.

adapted for singing'.[25] Here we get a strong impression of the free circulation of poems, and also of the freedom with which singers and musicians appropriated a wide variety of poetic texts to their musical purposes. And it reinforces the sense of sequences in particular as a fundamentally adaptable genre that of course had a strong role in the liturgy and in various paraliturgical contexts, but which also functioned independently as poetry and song in the broader sense. Moreover, Brother Henry's evident care for what might make a song idiomatic and attractive brings the whole domain of composition and the associated question of style back into the realm of vocality and the distinctive aesthetic and expressive qualities of the singing voice.

Nor was this all compositional activity exclusively monodic, for '[he] composed another song, setting the following text to three-part music (*litteram cum triplici cantu*): *Miser homo, cogita / facta creatoris*' (we may note that the incipit *Miser homo* has a strong resonance of the work of Philip the Chancellor). And sometimes subsidiary vocal parts would be added to an existing melody, not necessarily by the same composer, so that, for example, when Brother Vita

> wrote the following sequence [...] together with Thomas de Capua [...]: *Virgo parens gaudeat*, [...] he asked Henry of Pisa to set it to music, which he [then] did, making a delightful and beautiful melody, delightful to hear (*delectabilem et pulchrum ad audiendum suavem*), while Brother Vita [himself] wrote the secondary melody, that is, the countermelody (*secundarium cantum, id est contracantum*). And indeed, whenever Brother Henry had written a simple (*simplex*, i.e., monodic, single-line) melody, he [Brother Vita] would willingly compose a secondary melody to go with it.

For Brother Vita too was very active as a composer, and 'composed words and music of the sequence *Ave mundi spes, Maria*, as well as many other songs in florid or figured melody (*multas cantilenas de cantu melodiato sive fracto*), in which the secular clergy take such great delight (*in quibus clerici saeculares maxime delectantur*)'. Here we need to recognize the absolute congruity of the practical knowledge of the voice, with its instinctive sense of what is vocally idiomatic and expressive, and the poetic discernment coupled with musical inventiveness that together go to make the art of composition fully effective.

But in considering the technical and stylistic aspects of these songs and the kinds of vocal performance they might have received, we should not lose sight of the broader expressive and social purposes such singing was designed to serve. And here too, Salimbene offers some delightful anecdotes. Brother Vita was clearly something of a visionary, or at least a man with a profoundly artistic and at times almost mystical temperament, which caused his behaviour to verge on the eccentric. Yet he was loved and indulged by all, even by the most eminent and illustrious:

---

[25]Et in illa sequentia: *Iesse virgam humidavit* delectabilem cantum fecit, et qui libenter cantatur, cum prius haberet cantum rudem et dissonum ad cantandum. (Litteram vero illius sequentiae fecit Ricardus de Sancto Victore, sicut ut multas alias fecit sequentias.)

[And] if a nightingale was singing in a hedge or thicket, he would cease his singing and listen to it carefully, not moving but staying as if rooted to the spot, afterwards taking up his song again, so that one could hear in alternation these two wonderful voices coming from each in turn (*et ascultebat eum [lisignolum] diligenter nec movebatur de loco, et postmodum resumebat cantum suum, et sic alternatim cantando voces delectabiles et suaves resonabant ab eis*).

Several times [Brother Vita] left the order of St Francis, and several times rejoined, belonging in between times to the order of St Benedict; and, when he wanted to rejoin the Franciscans, Pope Gregory IX always dealt indulgently with him, on account both of his love for St Francis, and of the suavity of his singing.

And so it was precisely this suavity of singing that was in the end his greatest and most precious gift. Its sheer persuasive force was such that it once produced a truly astonishing effect that has, to my knowledge, no precedent in the anecdotal literature:

Once for example he sang so ravishingly (*ita delectabiliter cantavit*) that a nun who was listening to him threw herself down from a window in order to follow him – something which she was not then able to do, since she broke her leg in the act of falling (*ex casu illo sibi tibiam fregit*). Certainly this was not the kind of listening referred to in the last chapter of the *Song of Songs*, where it says: 'you who sit in the gardens, [while] your friends listen, let me also hear your voice' (*quae habitas in hortis amici auscultant fac me audire vocem tuam*).

Such, then, was the transporting beauty of Brother Vita's singing. And it is noteworthy that Salimbene reports this little tale delightedly, with scarcely a hint of reproach towards either the nun or Brother Vita himself. He simply accepts it, as no doubt we should too, as a beautiful demonstration of the miraculous expressive powers of truly inspired singing. And at least the poor nun enjoyed a few brief moments of airborne bliss.

We have seen instances of how the physical characteristics and expressive qualities of the singing human voice were understood and appreciated, at least on occasion, by medieval sensibilities. But the paradox of vocal expression – as something with the potential for supreme beauty and persuasiveness, yet morally ambiguous and even untrustworthy unless guided by reason and conscience – was an experiential problem that had been lived through by great Christian figures well before the era of the high Middle Ages. Pre-eminent among these was undoubtedly St Augustine. To Augustine, the voice was the self-inscribing of the body in language, in speech, in song, in all forms of human utterance. As such it was subject to the irrational and passionate impulses of all physical life. Yet it was also, in its origins, a God-given thing, animated by the breath of life (*pneuma, spiritus*) and capable of articulating thoughts from the human soul, thus able to show the light of reason and embody the creature's proper response to the creator. Song, in its largest sense, was implicated in – and intimately bound up with – this paradox of voice. Augustine famously recounted in the *Confessions* how, at the time of his conversion and baptism in Milan in 387,

I wept profusely in [hearing] your hymns and songs, deeply moved [as I was] by the voices of your church sounding so sweetly! Those voices flowed into my ears, and the truth was delightfully instilled into my heart; and so the emotion of my piety increased, and my tears ran over, and I was happy in my weeping.

Quantum flevi in hymnis et canticis tuis, suave sonantis ecclesiae tuae vocibus commotus acriter! Voces illae influebant auribus meis, et eliquabatur veritas in cor meum, et extaestuabat inde affectus pietatis, et currebant lacrimae, et bene mihi erat cum eis.[26]

The expressive force of this vocal music inspired in him emotion of an intensity which, though physically insistent and in a sense deeply seductive (*commotus acriter... et currebant lacrimae, et bene mihi erat cum eis*), was nevertheless in essence devotional – Augustine refers to it as *affectus pietatis* – because of the controlling presence of the sacred texts and the 'safeness' of the truth they embodied. The songs conveyed that truth, and their communicative power was harnessed to it, since the words guaranteed the reliability of the emotion. But the power of music and of the voice would both remain, in a more ambiguous form, when the texts were not there or could not be relied upon, or else when they were of a quite different kind from the 'hymns and songs' of the church. This potential ambiguity was a source of lifelong anxiety for Augustine. When in a later passage of the *Confessions* he thinks back and recalls his tears, he betrays something of the neurotic self-doubt that drove him to seek to reassure himself that it was indeed by 'the things that [were] sung' that he had been moved, and precisely not by his sheer delight in the music of the song. He even goes so far as to confess that 'the pleasures of the ears had most powerfully engaged and subdued me; but you [O God] did set me free and liberate me' (*voluptates aurium tenacius me implicaverant et subiugaverant, sed resolvisti me et liberasti me*; *Confessiones* 10. 33. 49). He knew very well and felt very keenly both the beauty and the intensity of the human voice. But he also distrusted them.

Augustine too had been scandalized by the habit of unseemly singing and dancing in sacred places, in particular when he had witnessed displays of inappropriate celebration in the church at Carthage where the shrine of St Cyprian was situated. In words that recall to a remarkable degree those of Gerald of Wales, he described in a sermon how 'profane songs and dances [had been] driven forth from the church where St Cyprian is buried' (*cantica profana et saltationes pulsae de ecclesia, ubi sepultus Cyprianus*). This had happened

not very many years ago, [when] a wanton and pestilential plague of dancers had infested this very place: here, the whole night long, infamous things were sung, and there was dancing [also] by those singing.

---

[26]*Confessiones*, 9. 6. 14. I have used James J. O'Donnell, ed., Augustine, *Confessiones*, 3 vols (Oxford, 1992).

Aliquando ante annos non valde multos etiam istum locum invaserat ... pestilentia et petulantia saltatorum. Per totam noctem cantabantur hic nefaria, et cantantibus saltabatur.[27]

From this we can see that the popular use of secular or secularizing song in sacred contexts, and the very close relationship of dance to song (this latter being the more dangerous of the two, in clerical eyes), was a constant factor to be reckoned with throughout the Middle Ages, from the fourth to the fourteenth century.[28] The basic situations repeated themselves, albeit with considerable – and for us highly diverting – variation of local detail, over wide tracts of geography and time. And the underlying tensions seem to have been remarkably similar, despite the vast cultural difference between the late antique world of Jerome, Ambrose, and Augustine, and the high medieval one of the centuries prior to the Black Death.

Augustine's homilies (*Sermones*) and commentaries on the psalms (*Enarrationes in Psalmos*) contain many incidental discussions of music, cast in a variety of discursive modes (moralizing, allegorical, exhortatory). They are particularly rich in their references to singing of different kinds, and also, from time to time, to the dance. And if they tend to offer less psychological detail and insight, they also show a broader social and cultural range than the intensely subjective and inward observations found in the *Confessions*. Augustine's attitude towards frankly profane and – as he would have seen it – frivolous songs never really changed. In the first place, he considered that they had no proper moral content, and that they were consequently vain and useless, if not actually corrupting:

Let no one let his heart turn towards theatrical songs

Nemo convertat cor ad organa theatrica [*PL* 36, col. 279]

For what reason should we go around delighting in vain songs which are productive of nothing, [and which,] while they may be sweet at the time, afterwards soon grow bitter? Human souls ensnared by such profanities of songs are made weaker

Quare ambularemus delectati vanis canticis nulli rei profuturis, ad tempus dulcibus, in posterum amaris? Talibus etenim turpitudinibus cantionum animi humani illecti enervantur [*PL* 38, col. 79]

In contrast, the words of the Psalter, and by extension the sound of psalms being sung wherever, from close at hand or in the distance, are

a sweet sound, a lovely melody, [which exists] both in the singing and in the intellectual meaning

---

[27]*Sermones*, 311. 5. 5; *PL*, p. 38, col. 1415.

[28]Peter Dronke, *The Medieval Lyric* (London, 1968), ch. 6, 'Dance Songs', especially pp. 186–189. Christopher Page, in *The Owl and the Nightingale*, ch. 1, 'Minstrels and the Clergy', and ch. 5, 'The *Caroles*, the Pulpit and the Schools', refers to similar proscriptions and discussions within his chosen period, 1100–1300.

Ista enim verba Psalterii, iste dulcis sonus, ista suavis melodia, tam in cantico quam in intellectu ... [*PL* 37, col. 1729]

To discern meaning while still appreciating the insinuating beauty of musical – specifically vocal – sonority was to take song in all its plenitude and richness, and to respond to it in its fully realized nature.

This, or something very close to it, was Augustine's theory of song. The twofold danger he foresaw and feared was that musical beauty would become a pleasurable end in itself, or that the sheer force and energy of musical rhythm (in the extended, late antique sense of the word) would spill over into physical dance:

We don't celebrate games for demons [i.e., false gods], as is often done for the delight of those being worshipped, the depravity of which tends rather to corrupt the worshippers; but here the holiness and the solemnity of the martyrs is celebrated – [and so] there is no dancing. [...] May that impudence and wantonness [of dancing] be absent, and may things return to what they should be. Listen, rather, to what requires to be [heard and] understood in wisdom. He who sings, teaches and instructs; he who dances, merely does. For what is dancing, but a being in harmony with the song by a motion of the limbs? What, then, should be our song? I will not perform or sound forth. That is not my function. For I am a [sacred] minister more than [I am] an actor ...

[Q]uia non celebramus daemoniis ludos, ubi solent ista fieri in eorum delectationem qui coluntur, et immunditia sua solent suos depravare cultores, sed celebratur hic sanctitas et solemnitas martyrum; [et] non hic saltatur [...] Absit ut redeat adhuc illa petulantia: audite potius quid velit intelligi sapientia. Cantat, qui praecipit; saltat qui facit. Quid est saltare, nisi motu membrorum cantico consonare? Quod est canticum nostrum? Non proferam ego, non sit meum. Melius minister sum, quam actor [*PL* 38, col. 1416]

Augustine therefore allows songs that teach, that impart knowledge and a certain kind of truth, that embody and convey the intelligible part of the message of scripture. Dancing was merely a mechanical activity, more or less; singing *per se* remained still too close to the life of the body to fully command his respect and trust; but song ennobled the voice through the dignified character of the thought contained within its verbal component. And it was in this dynamic equilibrium between the direct, persuasive beauty of the voice, and the rational content and devotional intensity of religious texts that he found an acceptable form of human vocality – one that did not suppress its physical and aesthetic characteristics, but rather caused it to enter into a higher union with words and ideas.

The attainment of such an equilibrium was hard won, however. In this as in other things, Augustine obsessively sought self-knowledge and self-mastery. He observed himself closely and intimately, as he hovered on the very limits of the equilibrium he aspired to, on the brink of giving in to musical pleasure:

And even now, in those sounds which your words and eloquence animate, and which are sung with a sweet and skilful voice, I confess I still take some solace and content-ment – though not so much as to be ensnared, since I remain free to go when I choose.

Nunc in sonis quos eloquia tua cum suavi et artificiosa voce cantantur, fateor, aliquantulum adquiesco, non quidem ut haeream, sed ut surgam cum volo. [*Confessiones*, 10.
33. 49]

At one point he indicates more clearly and more knowingly what he thinks the
'secret power' of song is: what it consists in, and why it is so irresistible. His discourse
here, as in so many other places, is saturated in the language of Roman rhetoric, of
Cicero and Quintilian and other lesser known names. His points also are registered
against a generalized conceptual background of neo-Platonic ideas. And so, quite apart
from what he tells us explicitly, we begin to learn just why the whole rich inheritance
of his pagan culture was so difficult to overcome or relinquish when he had once made
the transition to Christianity, and also how profoundly the struggle to be true to his
new beliefs, almost despite his natural inclinations and the depth of his long-meditated
education, came to mark the whole of his mature existence:

> Yet sometimes, too, it seems to me that I give them [i.e., songs and singing] more
> honour than is due to them. [...] For all the different affections and emotions of the
> spirit have their varied and appropriate modes [of expression], in both voice and song
> (*in voce atque cantu*), and are aroused by a mysterious inward affinity; [and in this
> way] my delight in the physical pleasure [of singing] has often overcome and deceived
> me, when the perceptions of the senses are not accompanied by reason, and are not
> content to be quietly subordinate, but try to run on ahead, and lead ...

> [A]liquando enim plus mihi videor honoris tribuere, quam decet, [...] et omnes affectus
> spiritus nostri pro sui diversitate habere proprios modos in voce atque cantu, quorum
> nescio qua occulta familiaritate excitentur; sed delectatio carnis meae [...] saepe me
> fallit, dum rationi sensus non ita comitatur ut patienter sit posterior, sed [...] etiam
> praecurrere ac ducere conatur.[29]

None the less, despite his unceasing doubts and anxieties, his final judgement of
human vocality was a fundamentally cheerful and positive, though also a somewhat
qualified, one:

> And so, now that [I know] I am moved not by the singing itself but by the things which
> are sung, and [moreover] sung with a pure and flowing voice and with very suitable
> melodic inflections, I recognize the great utility of this institution [i.e., of music and the
> singing of sacred poetry]. And so it is that I fluctuate between the danger of pleasure
> and the experience of [spiritual] health.

---

[29] *Confessiones*, 10. 33. 49. There are many passages in Cicero and Quintilian dealing with
the *pronuntiatio* of classical rhetoric which resonate here, of which this is but one example:
'Omnis motus animi suum quendam a natura habet vultum et sonum et gestum: totumque
corpus hominis et eius omnis vultus omnesque voces, ut nervi in fidibus, ita sonunt ut a motu
animi quoque sunt pulsae' (Cicero, *De oratore*, 3. 57. 216). The idea of the mysterious power of
the voice and of gesture, as exercised by the orator, is a frequent one in rhetorical theory; and
the doctrine of musical affect as a 'playing upon the soul' is commonly encountered in Platonic
and neo-Platonic philosophy.

[E]t nunc ipsum quod moveor non cantu, sed rebus quae cantantur, cum liquida voce et convenientissima modulatione cantantur, magnam instituti huius utilitatem rursus agnosco. Ita fluctuo inter periculum voluptatis et experimentum salubritatis [*Confessiones* 10. 33. 50]

Still his obsessive fear remains, that whenever he is moved by strong emotion without the security of words, he will veer off into uncharted and potentially dangerous regions of pleasure. The lure of the physiological affect aroused by the singing voice is intense, and powerful. And so it needs, for Augustine, the corrective pressure and the restraining influence of the justifying word, which remains the ultimate source of the sacred content of the song. In the passage just quoted he has set out specifically to praise, and in a sense to 'approve', the beauty and the lyric expressiveness of human vocality. Yet he cannot help including a high-minded and in the end mistrustful caveat, one that perhaps tells us more about his complex psycho-pathology than it does about the mere scrupulousness of his conscience. But, just as importantly, it also tells us a great deal – and very eloquently, I think – about the immediacy and intensity of his aesthetic response to singing in itself, in its own nature.

Augustine scarcely ever addresses the topic of song 'in its own nature' directly. But one startling exception to this occurs in the marvellous commentary to Psalm 32, where for once he approaches in a distinctly positive frame of mind the question of 'pure singing'. Here he views it as an ecstatic response to an emotion of joy that lies beyond words, hence beyond rational articulation. And in attempting to find turns of phrase that will somehow describe this state of the soul, as expressed through the agency of the body and the voice, he beautifully anticipates the classical medieval theory of the *jubilus* in the alleluia. In the first place, this commentary demonstrates that he was acutely aware of the value – simultaneously aesthetic and spiritual – of really good vocal performance. He recommends that, when 'any man asks how he should sing to God', the answer should be:

Sing to him, but [be sure you] do not sing badly. For he does not want his ears to be offended. Sing well, my brothers. And when someone says to you: 'Sing that you may please him', if [this refers to] an experienced musical listener, and if you are anxious at having to sing without having had much musical instruction, take care lest you displease the artist: because what the unskilled listener will not notice in you, the [true] artist will find fault with. Who would dare to offer to sing well to God, who is such an expert judge of a singer, such an acute examiner of everything, such a listener? When will you be able to present such a polished singing technique that you do not offend such perfect ears?

Canta illi, sed poli male. Non vult offendi aures suos. Bene cane, frater. Si alicui bono auditori musico, quando tibi dicitur, Canta ut placeas ei, sine aliqua instructione musicae artis cantare trepidas, ne displiceas artifici: quia quod in te imperitus non agnoscit, artifex reprehendit: quis offerat: Deo bene cantare, sic iudicanti de cantore, sic examinanti omnia, sic audienti? Quando potes afferre tam elegans artificium cantandi, ut tam perfectis auribus in nullo displiceas? [*PL* 36, col. 283]

Here God is portrayed as an expert, indeed perfect, listener. Hence the maximum exercise of vocal skill is seen as a *sine qua non* in the performance of sacred songs. And by invoking the authority of the divine presence, Augustine liberates himself to talk more freely about this aspect of singing. He makes room for himself to discourse a little on the perfection of voice and vocality that he desires, by momentarily casting God in the role of a connoisseur of fine singing. The great late antique orator in him must surely always have enjoyed the spectacle of a skilled and polished performer in full flight as an experience of the highest cultural and aesthetic value. But his conscience and his newly adopted Christian values would not have allowed him to indulge this taste very often. And in any case, his vision is not in the end an elitist or aristocratic one. He saw the surge of joy that exults wordlessly and gives a new melismatic and ecstatic expressivity to the human voice as something not just God-given, but given to all, from the leisured and the learned to the labourer in the fields:

> See then how he gives you a way of singing: do not seek for words, as though you can somehow 'explain' what God delights in. Sing in jubilation (*in jubilatione*). [...] But what is singing in jubilation? It is understanding, yet being unable to explain in words, what is sung in the heart. Just as, indeed, those who sing, whether at the harvest or in the vineyeard, or in any arduous and fatiguing work, when they have begun to exult with happiness in the song-texts, nevertheless turn away from the syllables of the words, as though filled with so much joy that they cannot express it verbally, and so move into a sound of jubilation.

> Ecce veluti modum cantandi det tibi: noli quaerere verba, quasi explicare possis unde Deus delectatur. In jubilatione cane: [...] Quid est in jubilatione canere? Intelligere, verbis explicare non posse, quod canitur corde. Etenim illi qui cantant, sive in messe, sive in vinea, sive in aliquo opere ferventi, cum coeperint in verbis canticorum exsultare laetitia, veluti impleti tanta laetitia, ut eam verbis explicare non possint, avertunt se a syllabis verborum, et eunt in sonum jubilationis [*ibid.*]

Such moments of cloudless enthusiasm are all the more precious for their relative rarity in Augustine. For he is usually much more circumspect, and also more rigorous, both with others and with himself – indeed sometimes too much so, as he occasionally admitted. For the most part we should surely assume that the singing and appreciation of songs, throughout the Middle Ages, was a much less problematic activity than it was for Augustine, even where religious scruples might be thought to be involved. The openness of Franciscan spirituality to the transporting beauty of vocal melody offers clear evidence of this. The flourishing tradition fostered by the Franciscans of singing *laude* (more generally *lode* or *lodi*, 'praises') is just one example among many of the new uses for sacred song in the secular sphere – often with texts in the vernacular – that are encountered over the course of the thirteenth century. The emergence of the *lauda* and other song genres of similar kind marks the point at which the sheer exaltation and intensity of, say, sung troubadour and trouvère lyric passes triumphantly over into the domain of the sacred, without losing contact with the world. And this is surely a crucially important part of the meaning behind St Francis's desire that he and his followers should become 'God's jongleurs'.

The traditions and typologies of medieval song are multifarious; so too are its contexts and the uses to which it was put. Yet our understanding of the very different responses of, say, Augustine and the early Franciscans, and of the much more diverse range of audiences and contexts for secular music described by an author such as Johannes de Grocheio *ca* 1300, all point towards a shared sophistication and intensity of appreciation of the utility, as well as the beauty, of song in all its richness and variety. All of which amply justifies Gerald of Wales's observation that, properly discerned and fully entered into, musical experiences of many kinds will have the power, *internas et ineffabiles comparant animi delicias*,[30] 'to provide inward and indescribable delights of the soul'.

---

[30]Brewer and Dimock, *Giraldi Cambrensis Opera*, vol. 4 (1867), p. 154.

Chapter 17

Ambrosian processions of the saints

Terence Bailey

The Milanese cult of the saints reached its impressive culmination in the high Middle Ages. By about 1100, the time of the earliest detailed service books, processions featuring an immense repertory of special chants[1] were customary from one or other of the city's two ancient cathedrals[2] to the site of the principal celebration (with intermediate stations at churches on the way and on the way back) for all the fifty-or-so saints' festivals with items entered in the antiphoners and the Manuale.[3] *Proper* chants are not given in every instance, but a special section of the *commune sanctorum* provided any not specified, and circumstances make clear that such processions were a normal feature of all these occasions.[4]

In Milan a saint's festival was always celebrated over two days, beginning on the day before the date assigned in the calendar. Lengthy processions took place on both. Detailed descriptions – disordered, unfortunately, and incomplete – are found in the 'Beroldus',[5] an ordinal named after the twelfth-century cathedral functionary who claimed authorship and did certainly write some parts.[6] Further information about the

---

[1]More than 500 of these 'psallendae' are entered in the antiphoners.

[2]Both destroyed to make room for the present, enormous, Duomo.

[3]*Manuale ambrosianum*, Part 1 (Milan, 1905), 'Psalterium et kalendarium', etc.; Part 2 (Milan, 1904), 'Manuale ambrosianum ex codice saec.xi olim in usum canonicae Vallis Travaliae'. The Manuale contains more or less what is found in the antiphoners, but only the texts of the chants.

[4]It seems out of the question, however, that such elaborate ceremonies were customary for every one of the saints' festivals entered in the Ambrosian calendar, many of them not even mentioned in the service books.

[5]Transcribed by the indefatigable scholar of the Ambrosian liturgy, Marco Magistretti, *Beroldus, sive ecclesiae ambrosianae mediolanensis kalendarium et ordines* (Milan, 1894). Magistretti published what he found in the three main manuscripts and did not attempt to correct the errors and contradictions. In this chapter I have (usually without comment) altered his punctuation, corrected obvious misprints, and chosen between the readings of the three manuscripts. I have also suggested a few emendations. Lacunae shown simply with six dots (......) were noted by Magistretti; those indicated in brackets ([......]) are my suggestions. Ellipses are shown in the usual way (...).

[6]He identifies himself at the beginning:

processions, usually with very little detail, has survived in the Manuale, in the antiphoners, and in a few later documents. In what follows I have brought together (and
translated, for those who will find it useful) the principal rubrics concerned with the
processions. In order to avoid the tiresome repetition of Latin terms I have employed
what I take to be English equivalents for the orders of the clergy and the accoutrements of the liturgy, some of these choices obvious, some not so obvious. If the latter,
I have added a note to clarify my usage.

Processions on the eve of saints' festivals[7]

The vigiliae date back to the time of St Ambrose himself, who instituted public, penitential, preparation for the festivals of the martyrs. This consisted chiefly of fasting and
wakefulness – this 'vigil' occupied by prayer and recitations that included a large
number of psalms.[8] The vigiliae of Milan preserved these essential features into the
fifteenth and even sixteenth centuries. The general rubric is as follows:

> In vigiliis sanctorum quando ordinarii canunt psalmos, semper canunt tertiam in ec-
> clesia hyemali, deinde proficiscuntur ad festum cum processione cantando cantus
> letaniarum secundum diem cui ipsa ecclesia festi ipsius data est. Si primo data est
> incipiunt *Domine deus virtutum*, si secundo, *Quem deprecamur*, si tertio, *Dei genitrix*.

> For the vigils of the saints when the clergy of the week[9] sing the psalms[10] they always
> sing tierce in the winter church, after which they set out in procession for the festival

---

Ego Beroldus, custos et cicendelarius ejusdem ecclesiae [ambrosianae mediolanensis] quidquid vidi
et audivi et scriptum reperi, huic nostro libello tradere disposui ...

I, Beroldus, *custos* and *cicendelarius* of the [Ambrosian Church of Milan], have collated and passed on
in this my little book what I have heard and observed and found in writing ...

and later, by means of an acrostic, as the author of one long section (*Beroldus*, pp. 35, 67). The
ordinal contains references to Bishop Olrich 'of blessed memory', who died in 1125. The oldest
copy, the 'Ambrosiano', is probably of the twelfth century. In the remainder of this chapter
page numbers alone, whether in the notes or in the text, refer to Magistretti's publication of
the Beroldus.
    [7]Vigils were also held for the Minor Dedication. This festival was celebrated by the cathe-
dral clergy in important Milanese churches on the anniversary of their foundation. By the
Middle Ages most churches were dedicated to saints, and this perhaps explains why the day was
treated in certain respects as though it were a saint's feast.
    [8]This is reported by Paulinus (a contemporary of the Saint) in chapter 13 of his *Vita sancti
Ambrosii*, Pellegrino, Michele, ed., *Paolino di Milano, Vita di S. Ambrogio* (Rome, 1961), p.
68.
    [9]When all the appearances in the Beroldus of *ordinarii*, *ordinarios* and *ordinariis* are
considered (the word is never used in the singular), it is seen to be the counterpart of *heb-
domadarii* and *septimanarii*. Compare the beginning of the general rubric presently under
discussion:

singing the chants of the [Great Litany] according to the day assigned to the festival-church. If the given day is the first they begin with *Domine deus virtutum*, if the second, *Quem deprecamur*, if the third, *Dei genitrix*.

The 'always' in this passage is significant. It makes clear that the vigils procession started in the winter cathedral even in the summer season. This is confirmed by the rubric for the Feast of the Nativity of St John the Baptist, which in Milan as elsewhere is celebrated in the summer:

> But returning on the vigil of [the Nativity of] St John the Baptist they sing this psalm, *Deus, deus meus, respice* with its psallenda, i.e., *Maior prophetis*, as far as the Eastern Gate, then *Benedictus dominus deus Israel quia visitavit* on the way to the winter church.[11]

The Three-Day Litany, an important penitential observance featuring lengthy processions, was held in Milan on the Monday, Tuesday, and Wednesday following Ascension.[12] The relationship to the the saints' festivals is clarified in a fifteenth-century

---

> In vigiliis sanctorum quando ordinarii canunt psalmos, semper canunt tertiam in ecclesia hyemali, deinde proficiscuntur ad festum cum processione (p. 57)

and the following obviously parallel passage (cited more fully later, where the reference is given):

> in vigiliis ejusdem s. confessoris Simpliciani ebdomadarii majoris ecclesiae [the Winter Church] illuc psallendo euntes psalterium finiant

The term *ordinarii* may not have include the lower orders:

> In vigilia festivitatum quas ordinarii faciunt et celebrant, sonito vespere, vadunt ad festum ordinarii et lectores et custodes (p. 63)

As for the interchangeability of the terms *septimanarius* and *ebdomadarius*, compare:

> et quando appropinquant ecclesiae hyemali septimanarius ostiarius cum observatoribus [ostiariis] sonant omnia tintinnabula (p. 59)

> ostiarius ebdomadarius cum observatoribus [ostiariis] omnia tintinnabula sonare debet (p. 113).

> porrigit subdiacono, cujus septimana est, candelabra accensa (p. 56)

[10]'Sing the psalms', certainly meant in a general sense, i.e., 'execute the offices'.

[11]The Latin is given below.

[12]The Gallican Church, and perhaps originally the Ambrosian, held these processions within Eastertide, in spite of their penitential character. The Beroldus (p. 122), but not the early antiphoners, also specifies items for the 'Gregorian' litany ('De letaniis s. Gregorii') on 25 April – evidently a late addition in imitation of the Roman practice. These penitential processions were held on many other occasions as well: on three days in the last (the sixth) week of the Ambrosian Advent, on the first day (Monday) of the Ambrosian Lent, and every Wednesday and Friday of that season.

source:[13] when the site of the principal liturgy of the saint was located in a part of the city visited on one of the days (over the three days, all six divisions of the city were included), the chants sung on the way to that church were those sung on the corresponding day of the Litany. In the antiphoners and in the Manuale the psallendae assigned in the Beroldus (*Domine deus virtutum*, etc.) are *not*, in fact, those that begin the processions, but the second, the second, and the seventeenth, respectively. This is one of many instances of disagreement between the sources for the Ambrosian liturgy.

The procession to the principal site of the saint's liturgy stopped at intervening stations, the same, presumably, as those on the corresponding day of the annual Great Litany. Information about the stations in the Beroldus, in the antiphoners, and in the Manuale is incidental, unsystematic, and incomplete. What took place and where during the Three-Day Litany seems to have been detailed in the *rotuli letaniarum*,[14] which do not survive. We do know that on Day One, before the procession set out from the cathedral, ashes were blessed and distributed (in the form of a cross on the forehead) to the clergy, and later, on the way to the first station at the church of St Simplicianus, to the laity, men and women. Whether ashes were also distributed in the processions on the eve of saints' festivals is not known. On Day One of the Great Litany at least three stational churches were visited, among them those of St Ambrose, St Nazarius, and St Lawrence; on Days Two and Three there were different, unrecorded, stations. Lessons were read and their responsories sung at these various locations. The length of the proceedings may be gauged from the number of chants assigned: the antiphoners provide twelve responsories for Day One, ten for Day Two, and twelve for Day Three; as for psallendae: twenty-two are given for the first day, twelve for the second, and thirty-nine for the third. These penitential chants of the Great Litany were used for the saints' vigils only on the way to the festival church; for vespers, the vigils office (see below), the procession of return to the winter church, and the stations on the way back the antiphoners provide many additional antiphons, responsories and psallendae that are not penitential in character.

In the procession to the festival church complete psalms were sung with the psallendae. This is disputed. The late Ambrosian missals say, 'the psallendae are repeated once, with the *Gloria patri* between'.[15] But this does not preclude psalms, and in any case the later practice is not necessarily the earlier: the history of chant provides many examples of substantial psalmody later curtailed. On the matter of psalms in the processions, the monks of Solesmes are categorical: the psallendae 'are not associated with any psalmody except that of the *Gloria patri*'.[16] But in the antiphoners, in dozens of cases, differentiae are assigned to the psallendae even if no recitation is specified. And recitation *is* specified in many instances: in the antiphoners it is usual that the first psallenda of the morning processions of the saints (on the day of their festival) is

---

[13]*Libro primicerii majoris* ('de omnibus annualibus faciendis per clerum'), a manuscript in the chapter library of the Duomo cited by Magistretti (*Beroldus*, p. 57, n. 103).

[14]They are mentioned in the Beroldus (p. 57).

[15]'Psallendae semel repetuntur interjectio versu: *Gloria patri*'.

[16]'Elles ne sont associées à aucune psalmodie que celle du Gloria Patri'. *PM* 6, p. 23.

assigned a psalm verse, as are the psallendae sung in the procession between the baptistries after matins on Christmas, Epiphany, Palm Sunday, the feast of the Major Dedication (and other occasions). These last are examples where specific verses were assigned. But an eleventh-century epigraph from the church of St Simplicianus[17] makes the case for complete psalms, indeed a complete Psalter, in the penitential processions on the way to the saints' vigils:

In vigiliis ejusdem s. confessoris, Simpliciani, ebdomadarii majoris ecclesiae, illuc psallendo, euntes psalterium finiant.

For the vigils of this same holy confessor, Simplicianus, the hebdomadaries of the principal church,[18] singing as they go, complete the Psalter.

and we will see later that complete psalms sung with psallendae were specified in the procession back to the cathedral.

The Beroldus also includes (19), among other things I have excised in the passage below, something of the constitution of the processions for the Three-Day Litany:

Et in his tribus diebus ebdomadarius et major ostiarius vicissim portant crucem auream ante presbyteros et diacones cardinales ... . Et illi duo qui sunt post illos qui portant cinerem debent portare unam crucem ante subdiaconos, alteram ante notarios ... . Et duo minores similiter ebdomadarii portant crucem vicissim ante primicerium presbyterorum ... . Similiter duo minores ostiarii vicissim portant crucem ante vicecomitem ... .

And on these three days the hebdomadary [ostiary] and the major ostiary[19] alternately carry the gold cross in front of the cardinal[20] priests and [cardinal] deacons ... . And the two [ostiaries] who follow those that carry the ashes are to carry one cross in front of the subdeacons and another in front of the notaries ... . And similarly two minor hebdomadary [ostiaries] alternately carry the cross in front of the chief priest [of the

---

[17]Cited by Magistretti (*Beroldus*, p. 57, n. 104), but he draws the wrong conclusion.

[18]I.e., the *ordinarii* of the winter cathedral.

[19]Concerning *custodes*, *cicendelarii* and *ostiarii* (pp. 35–36):

Sexdecim custodes adnotantur sub cimiliarcha suo praescripti quorum octo majores et octo minores sunt; ita tamen quod quatuor majorum vocantur cicendelarii et quatuor ostiarii. Et hi octo majores jacent in secretario ad custodiendum thesaurum ecclesiae, sed tantum bini per ebdomadam, unus cicendelarius et alter ostiarius.

Sixteen *custodes* are registered under the cimiliarch [the keeper of the treasury], eight of whom are major and eight minor; of the major, four are called *cicendelarii* and four *ostiarii*, and these eight sleep in the treasury guarding the treasure, but only two per week, one a *cicendelarius* and the other an *ostiarius*.

[20]'Cardinal', applied to priests and deacons (but never to subdeacons), seems to mean no more than that they were on the roster of the cathedral. The decuman priests (see below) were not, although twelve of them had certain privileges in the Winter Church (see Magistretti, *Beroldus*, p. 171, n. 63).

decumans[21]] ... . Similarly, two minor ostiaries alternately carry the cross in front of the viscount ... .

This description, to do mainly with the crosses, obviously omits other items.[22]

On arriving at the church where the saint's vigil was to be held, and after some preliminaries (the triple *Kyrie*, versicles and responses, the *Te deum*), the clergy, sang (another!) complete Psalter, divided into three equal parts by lessons (when these were assigned[23]) and responsories. For these 150 psalms antiphons are not specified. Perhaps none was employed; perhaps those of the ferial sequential recitation served. A penitential mass[24] followed, and then vespers of the saint.

Following vespers, was a procession back to the cathedral:

in his omnibus festis quando revertuntur veniunt cum processione in ecclesiam hyemalem cum psallenda quae fuit in vesperis intonata, cum singulis versibus sui

---

[21]Compare:

ostiario observatore portante crucem ante primicerium decumanorum, ex qua postea accenditur pharus (p. 61)

et ostiarius observator portat crucem argenteam ante primicerium presbyterorum cum qua postea accendit pharum (*Beroldus*, p. 117, Magistretti's note 245; cf. *Manuale*, p. 221)

The Milanese decumans were the seventy-two, later one hundred, 'priests of the pre-eminent basilicas of Milan'. Certain of them were allowed to celebrate the liturgy in the cathedral (see Magistretti, *Beroldus*, p. 171, n. 65). Concerning the name, cf. the ancient Roman officer, the *decumanus*, 'collector of tithes'.

[22]Lamps, for example, although they are not mentioned elsewhere:

In vigilia sanctorum Protasii et Gervasii, et s. Laurentii, et in ordinatione s. Ambrosii, et s. Stephani, et depositione s. Ambrosii clerici istarum ecclesiarum portant thesaurum de secretario sancta Mariae, et lampadam, excepto in s. Stephano, quando observator cicendelarius portat lampadam (p. 57).

In the vigils of SS Protasius and Gervasius (as in those of St Lawrence, the Ordination of St Ambrose, St Stephen, and the Deposition of St Ambrose) the clergy of these churches carry items from the treasury of [the Winter Cathedral], and a lamp, except on the feast of St Stephen, when an observer acolyte] carries the lamp.

From this it emerges also that some of the participants in the processions might be clergy not belonging to the cathedrals. For the meaning of 'observer' and the translation, 'acolyte' see below.

[23]'One [before] *Quid gloriaris*, the other [before] *Domine exaudi* (Unam in *Quid gloriaris*, alteram in *Domine exaudi*'). These are Psalms 51 and 101. See *Beroldus*, pp. 57–58. Bugati, in his memorial of St Celsius, describes the saint's vigils and says that the clergy divided into three groups each of which sang, *in turn*, its third of the Psalter. *Memorie storico-critico intorna le reliquie ed il culto di S. Celso* (Milan, 1782), p. 129, cited in *PM* vol. 6, p. 13.

[24]With a single sung item, a cantus (the Ambrosian counterpart of the Gregorian tract). On twenty-one occasions the usual chants were provided for a vespers mass *de sancto*. Whether this replaced the *missa in ieiunio* or was sung in addition is not known.

psalmi quem minor notarius et minor lector vicissim indicant, excepto in vigilia s. Dionysii quam finiunt ante altare ubi ejus corpus requiescit et in s. Protasii quam finiunt in ecclesia s. Vitalis et in s. Naboris quam finiunt ante altare s. Materni et in s. Satyri quam finiunt ante altare s. Ambrosii et quando canunt vesperum cum vigilia.

in all these feasts, when [the clergy] return, they come in procession to the winter church [singing] the psallenda that was begun [after[25]] vespers, with each verse of its psalm, which a minor notary and a minor lector announce[26] alternately, except for the vigil of St Denis, which they terminate in front of the altar where his body lies, and of St Protasius, which they terminate in front of the altar of St Maternus, and of St Satyrus, which they terminate in front of the altar of St Ambrose, and whenever they sing vespers with a vigil.

It must not be presumed that the alternation between the notary and lector was the same as that in antiphonal psalmody, that is, verse by verse. If that were so it would seem the lectors and notaries would not be separated in the procession, and as we will see later it appears they were. We will also see later that this list of vigils that concluded at an external site is not complete.

The last of the exceptions mentioned ('and whenever they sing vespers with a vigil') calls for comment, first, because of the ambiguity of the term *vigilia*. This word, in the singular and plural, was used in Ambrosian books to refer generally to the first day of the saints' *biduum* (the following examples are all taken from the Beroldus):

in vigilia et festo s. Laurentii sic fit pastus et omnis conditio sicut in vigilia sanctorum Protasii et Gervasii ...

in festo ss. apostolararum Philippi et Jacobi ad s. Protasium in campo, in vigilia ad vesperas ...

in vigiliis sanctorum quando ordinarii canunt psalmos ...

In vigiliis translationis s. Nazarii ...

---

[25]The rubric for this procession is always 'psallentium post vesperas'; only one psallenda is ever assigned.

[26]The exact meaning of *indicat* is unknown. The verb is used nine times in the Beroldus, always with reference to a lector starting a chant for others, most often for the deacon:

tunc major diaconus vadit ad cornu altaris et cantat. L ibi ad cornu altaris sicut in alia, primicerio lectorum indicante sibi et cantante (p. 89)

debet diaconus, qui legit evangelium in pulpito, adnunciare Pascha, primicerio lectorum apud eum stante, et sibi indicante, sic dicendo: *Noverit caritas vestras* ... (p. 80)

diaconus incipit psallentium, primicerio lectorum praedicente, vel indicante ei (p. 65)

I have translated *indicare* simply as 'intone'. Magistretti (*Beroldus*, p. 194, n. 135) suggested *praeintonare*, but that adds nothing to the argument.

However, in the phrase 'vesperum cum vigilia', the last word refers to an idiosyncratic Ambrosian office much like vespers,[27] with a hymn,[28] lessons (sometimes[29]), responsories, psalms, and antiphons, although without the *Magnificat*.

This vigils office, sung[30] after vespers before the return to the winter church, seems to be a feature of the vigiliae of all the saints included in the antiphoner,[31] and thus the general rule given just above, prescribing the immediate return after vespers, would seem never to apply. The awarding of distinctions over time to more and more occasions that did not originally have them is an easily demonstrable pattern in the Ambrosian (and other) liturgies; it is a kind of ecclesiastical 'inflation'. The obvious explanation for many of the evident contradictions in the Beroldus is that different parts of the ordinal belong to different periods – the rubric presently at issue from an earlier time when there were far fewer vigiliae than later.

The continuation of the passage just considered includes another regulation superseded by later developments in the Liturgy:

> (... canunt vesperum cum vigilia.) Sed in vigilia s. Joannis Baptista revertendo dicunt hunc psalmum, *Deus, Deus meus, respice* cum sua psallenda idest *Maior prophetis* usque ad portam orientalem, deinde *Benedictus dominus deus Israel quia visitavit* usque in ecclesiam hyemalem. Et quando appropinquant ecclesiae hyemali septimanarius ostiarius cum observatoribus [ostiariis] sonant omnia tintinnabula donec in ecclesiam pervenerint.

> But returning on the vigil of [the Nativity of] St John the Baptist they sing this psalm: *Deus, Deus meus, respice* with its psallenda, i.e., *Maior prophetis*, as far as the Eastern Gate, then *Benedictus dominus deus Israel quia visitavit* on the way to the winter church. And when they approach the winter church, an ostiary of the week and the observing[32] [ostiaries] together sound all the bells until [the returning clergy] have all entered.

Maior prophetis is assigned in the antiphoners and the Manuale for the procession after vespers. These books do not mention Psalm 21 or the Canticle of Zacharia (*Benedictus dominus deus Israel*), but they contain much more: a vigils office, consisting of the usual three responsories (no lessons are specified) and three antiphons with psalms (this, perhaps, was the content of the station at the Eastern Gate) four

---

[27]See, below, the excerpt concerning the Translation of St Victor, where the vigils office is actually referred to as vespers.

[28]Cf. 'Incoepta vero vigilia et hymno ... ' (p. 59). Which hymn is never specified.

[29]Et si lectiones leguntur in vigilia ... (p. 59).

[30]Presumably in the stational church.

[31]The office is not always specified, nor are all the items always included, but what would be needed was available in the *commune sanctorum*.

[32]Magistretti (*Beroldus*, p. 145, n. 2) writes: 'by this term, even today, is designated the one who is to succeed the hedomadary officer, when his week is completed' (quo vocabulo, etiam in praesens, designatur qui primus post ebdomadarium, cujus transacta ebdomada, eidem in officio succedere debet).

more psallendae, another responsory, obviously to be sung at a subsequent station, and a final psallenda.

A few additional details of the procession of return after vespers, applying perhaps to more than the single[33] occasion mentioned, are given in the following:

In vigiliis translationis s. Victoris et in passione Felicis et Fortunati martyrum ad vesperum, finita oratione post *Magnificat*, ordinarii procedunt ad ecclesiam s. Naboris: psallenda usque ad s. Naborem, *Elongavi*, etc., psalmus, *Exaudi deus orationem*, etc. Et statim postquam sunt extra ecclesiam cicendelarius ebdomadarius tollit candelabra de manibus subdiaconorum et extinguit; in altera vero ecclesia ad regias dat eadem accensa. Et eodem modo fit in translatione s. Nazarii in vigiliis.

Finito autem vespere, presbyter s. Naboris dat vinum et fruges omnibus ordinibus honorifice.

In the vigils of the Translation of St Victor [together with] the Passion of the Martyrs Felix and Fortunatus, the prayer after the *Magnificat* finished, the clergy of the week proceed to the church of St Nabor: the psallenda to St Nabor's, *Elongavi*, etc., the psalm, *Exaudi deus orationem*, etc. And as soon as they are outside the church, the hebdomadary acolyte[34] takes the candlesticks from the hands of the subdeacons and puts [the candles] out; at the entrance[35] to the next church, he lights them. And it should be done in the same way for the Translation of St Nazarius.

When vespers are finished, the priest of St Nabor's solemnly distributes wine and food to all the orders.[36]

---

[33]The feast of SS Felix and Fortunatus was celebrated together with the Translation of St Victor.

[34]*Cicendelarii* is more accurately translated as *lampmen*. But as their duties were the same as acolytes in the Roman and Gallican books (the care of the lights and service at the altar) it seems acceptable to employ the widely used term. *Cicendeli*, evidently oil lamps of lead employed within the church, are mentioned several times in the Beroldus:

Et cicendelarius accendit cicendelos, qui sunt in choro majori, in quibus archiepiscopus oleum impendit (p. 37)

Similiter etiam minor cicendelarius habet duodecim denarios de eadem camera [archiepiscopi] in opus plumbinorum, qui per totum annum sunt necessarii in supradictis cicendelis. Et iidem cicendelarii minores ponunt cicendelos per partes ecclesiae, sicut mos est (p. 75; see also pp. 40, 77)

Cicendeli were not specifically Milanese nor always of lead. See the interesting remarks in *Pilgrimage of Etheria*, edited and translated by M. L. McClure and C. L. Feltoe (London, 1919):

The word [*cicendela*] is used four times by S. Gregory of Tours. We also find the expression 'oleum cicindelis' in the Life of S. Nicetius, Bishop of Lyons, and that glass or pottery was probably the material is shown by the following: – 'Cicindela – de manibus super lapides lapsa est, quae nec versa est, nec fracta, nec extincta,' which occurs in Messianus Presbyter's Life of S. Caesarius of Arles.

[35]Cf. 'et intrant per regias occidentales' (p. 42).

[36]Thereby breaking the fast and ending the penitential observances of the vigil.

In the antiphoners, *Elongavi fugiens* is the single psallenda for the procession following vespers (there is no reference to Psalm 54, although this was probably understood, since it is the source of the chant's text), a procession leading to the site of the vigils office, which must have been the church of St Nabor. Following the items for this office three psallendae are entered, then another responsory, presumably for another station, and finally two more psallendae. It is interesting that in the excerpt cited just above, the vigils office at St Nabor's is referred to as 'vespers'.

The myriad details of the Milanese processions cannot all be recovered. For most occasions, only incidental particulars have survived. But from the Beroldus, the Manuale, and the antiphoners, and from a few later sources, we can piece together an unusually complete picture of the vigils procession for the Feast of St Lawrence. Much of the description given below must have applied generally, but in any case, it will give some idea of the complexity of the proceedings on a feast no more important than several others in the Milanese calendar.

The first station, the site of the penitential observances and the vespers of the great martyr's liturgy, was obviously the basilica of St Lawrence. In the Manuale *Manducabunt pauperes*, sung in the procession after vespers, is assigned Psalm 21 (from which the text is taken), to be sung 'eundo in ecclesiam hyemalem[37] (on the way [back] to the winter church)'. It would seem that this psallenda, especially since it was protracted with psalm verses, was meant to serve for the whole procession of return. But it appears that this rubric was superseded, for, in fact, much else intervened: the antiphoners show that a vigils office followed, at a location not mentioned, after which was a procession (for which there are nine psallendae) 'ad s. Eustorgium', where there was another station.

For this station, very exceptionally, we have some further information:[38]

> Ante altare sistunt omnes in gremio ecclesiae: L notarii, *Meruit esse*. v. *Spectaculum*, oratio, *Indulgentium tuam*.

> All stand in front of the altar in the middle of the church: the L of the notaries, *Meruit esse*, the verse, *Spectaculum*, the prayer, *Indulgentium tuam*.

At this same station, as is mentioned elsewhere, the archbishop was received ceremonially by the local clergy (41):

> In vigilia s. Laurentii, finitis lectionibus et antiphona cum psalmo, archiepiscopus cum toto clero vadit ad ecclesiam s. Eustorgii. Cantato L *Meruit esse*, intrat in canonicam ipsius ecclesiae et ibi honorifice accipit potum cum toto clero tribus vicibus datum a canonicis ipsius ecclesiae.

> During the vigils of St Lawrence, after the lessons and the antiphon with psalm, the archbishop goes with the whole clergy to the church of St Eustorgius. After the

---

[37] *Manuale*, p. 330 (Magistretti's ms M).

[38] Ex *Caeremon. ambros. Horatii Casati*, a manuscript of the sixteenth century cited by Magistretti (*Beroldus*, p. 188, n. 109).

responsory, *Meruit esse*, is sung he enters the hall of the canons[39] of this church, and there in the presence of the entire clergy of the three districts solemnly accepts the draught offered by them.

The lessons mentioned were presumably those of the vigils office immediately preceding; the last item of which, in the antiphoners, is the antiphon *Gratia dei sum* with Psalm 69.

After this station at the church of St Eustorgius was another procession for which eight psallendae are provided, then one responsory, then two final psallendae.

Magistretti, citing a sixteenth-century manuscript,[40] offers more information about the final two stations. After the ceremonies at St Eustorgius:

> revertuntur eodem ordine ad ecclesiam s. Laurentii, sive ad cappellam s. Genesii prope eandem ecclesiam: – L Lectoris *Stans ad ignem*. v *Exaudiat te*. – Oratio *Deus mundi creator*. – Deinde psallentium ad s. Laurentium ... . Ante altare majus s. Laurentii, omnibus genuflexis, magister scholarum cum quatuor pueris faciat litanias quae cani solent ad eandem ecclesiam s. Laurentii in statione tridui litaniarum. Quibus finitis oratio: *Beati martyris tui*, etc. Finita vigilia duo minores cicendelarii debent portare duo thuribula in ecclesiam majorem in secretario.

> they return in the same order to the church of St Lawrence, or rather to the chapel of St Genesius near that church: the responsory of the lector, *Stans ad ignem*, the verse, *Exaudiat te*, the prayer, *Deus mundi creator*; then the procession to St Lawrence's ... . In front of the main altar of St Lawrence, after all have genuflected, the master of the scholars and four boys perform the litanies[41] sung at the station in the same church of St Lawrence during the three days of the Great Litany. This finished, the prayer, *Beati martyris tui*, etc. After vigils is finished, two minor acolytes are to take the two thuribles [back] to the treasury.[42]

From this it appears – contradicting, of course, the earlier direction 'eundo in ecclesiam hyemalem' – that vigils on this occasion concluded at St Lawrence's.

There is perhaps an exception to the general arrangements for saints' feasts. The Beroldus and the Manuale describe (see below) the morning procession to the basilica of St Ambrose for the feast of his deposition; they say nothing about the previous day. But cues added in the margin of an antiphoner of the thirteenth century,[43] do specify

---

[39]'Canonica' sometimes means no more than 'a church' (cf. 'ecclesiam sive canonicam de Feghine vallis'), but circumstances suggest that a hall ('[aulam] canonicam'?) was meant. It is unlikely that the canons of St Eustorgius had a separate chapter-house for their meetings.

[40]Ex *Caeremon. ambros. Horatii Casati* (*Beroldus*, p. 188, n. 109).

[41]Presumably, a long series of invocations with responses.

[42]Two thuribles do not, of course, constitute all of the 'treasure' that would be returned to the Winter Church. One perhaps sees in such particular details the hand of Beroldus, himself a *cicendelarius*.

[43]Vimercate, Chiesa plebana di San Stefano, ms B, fol. 119[V].

the usual items for vespers *de sancto*[44] on the eve of that feast.[45] A psallenda is cued for the procession of return after vespers (no vigils office is mentioned). The feast is not obviously different from the others; the question is whether the usual penitential observances before vespers would have taken place on the first day of the *biduum*. The deposition of the eponymous bishop was celebrated on the Wednesday and Thursday of Easter Week, when such observances would seem inappropriate. It should be remembered, in this respect, that the usual Gallican dates for the Major Litany were changed in Milan so that they would occur only after Eastertide. A penitential vigil would, of course, have been held earlier in the year for St Ambrose's other feast, that of his ordination.

I have drawn attention to certain inconsistencies in the service books suggesting that vigils processions of the saints had not always been as frequent as they later became. There is a further indication, this time unmistakable. The long section containing the general rubric for saints' vigils (cited at the beginning of this chapter) is followed, with no intervening heading, by another, 'Concerning lesser festivities', or, in the two later redactions of the Beroldus, 'Here begins the ordo for minor festivals, how things are to be done at vespers':[46]

> In vigilia festivitatum quas ordinarii faciunt et celebrant, sonito vespere, vadunt ad festum ordinarii et lectores et custodes et schola s. Ambrosii et mares et foeminae. Tunc cicendelarius ebdomadarius portat duo candelabra et duos cereos, et unus duorum minorum custodum ebdomadarius debet portare albam et amictum et pluviale. Presbyter vero illius ecclesiae ubi festum celebratur debet dare thuribulum et incensum cicendelario et unam candelam, unde accendat thuribulum et cereos [etc.]

> On the vigil of festivals celebrated and executed by the clergy of the week, after vespers is signalled, the clergy of the week, the lectors, the custodians, and the Company of St Ambrose,[47] men and women, go [without procession[48]] to the feast. Then a hebdomadary acolyte brings two candlesticks and two candles,[49] and one of the two minor

---

[44]Another antiphoner, Vimercate ms D, fol. 14^r, contains the following: 'Note that today two vespers are sung, the first of the Resurrection, the second of St Ambrose' (Nota quod hodie dicuntur duo vesperi, primus de resurrectione, secundus de sancto Ambrosio).

[45]And for matins and mass on the day itself.

[46]'De minoribus festivitatibus'; 'Incipit ordo minorum festorum in vesperis, qualiter sit agendum' (p. 63).

[47]The *schola S. Ambrosii* were twenty *vetuli*, i.e., pensioners, ten men and ten women – also referred to as *veglones* (*veglonissae*). See Magistretti, *Beroldus*, p. 157, n. 11. They had a special dwelling: >in proprio hospitali veglonum ... ' (p. 16).

[48]See below. The word *vadunt* gives nothing away. Compare 'vadant cum processione in ecclesiam hyemalem ... '; 'archiepiscopus cum toto clero vadit ad s. Euphemiam sine processione' (pp. 128, 124). The clergy obviously went in some sort of order, but that is not to say 'in procession'.

[49]Any distinction in the Beroldus between *candela*, *cannella* and *cereus* cannot be recovered. *Cannella* and *candela* are certainly interchangeable: 'et benedictis candelis, archiepiscopus dat cannellas quamplures primicerio decumanorum, quas ille iterum dat sacerdotibus

hebdomadary custodians is to bring the alb, amice, and chasuble.[50] The priest of the church where the feast is celebrated is to give the thurible and incense to the acolyte and one candle, from which he is to light the thurible and [other] candles [etc.]

The first words of the general rubric ('For the vigils of the saints when the clergy of the week sing the psalms') and the first words of the *ordo* just above make clear that the directions apply in similar circumstances. But in the the festival described in the latter rubric there was no procession: we read that custodians carry the alb, amice, and chasuble to the festival church: in a procession, these vestments would have been worn by the celebrants. None of the other solemnities that the Manuale and antiphoners make clear had become a normal part of saints' festivals are mentioned – and what could these 'minor festivals' be, other than saints' feasts? The second ordo (belonging to an earlier stratum of the Beroldus than the first) must have been superseded by the 'inflation' referred to above: in later times there *were* no 'minor' saints' festivals, except perhaps those mentioned in the calendar but not in the antiphoners, and it's more than doubtful that the cathedral clergy were involved publicly on those occasions.

Processions on the morning of saints' festivals

'Concerning the festival days, the manner of the procession'[51] is the heading, but the rubric, like many others in the Beroldus, is not only incomplete, it is, for the unwary, misleading. What at first appears to be a list of the participants in the order of their apearance in the processions has been vitiated (as a comparison with other descriptions makes clear) by the insertion of various extraneous details.

---

suis' (p. 81). It is tempting to think that *cerei* were specifically wax candles, but *candelae*, *cannellae* and *cerei* were all three used on the altar and it seems unlikely that tallow would be acceptable. Since *cerei* were (in the Beroldus) always lit with a *candela*, there is a suggestion that the former were larger than the latter, an impression that is strengthened by two other references, to 'a *cereus* weighing three pounds and a half' and to one 'weighing one pound and a half' ('quatuor cereos, habentes per singulos tres libras cereae et dimidiam', p. 59; 'deferunt archiepiscopo cereum unum ponderis librae unius', p. 124).

[50]The *Catholic Encyclopedia* entry on the cope begins: 'Known in Latin as *pluviale* or *cappa*'. In twelfth-century Milan there was a distinction – indeed, much is made in the Beroldus of changing from one to the other. The *pluviale*, originally rainwear for use outdoors, was in Milan also worn indoors and was also referred to as the *casula*, i.e., chasuble: 'archiepiscopus indutus pluviali vel casula, debet incipere tertiam' (p. 47). The *cappa* may have been an article of everyday wear, since the *pluviale* seems to have been donned in preparation for liturgical solemnities. On one occasion at least, the *cappa* was worn outdoors: 'Et ipsemet custos portat eandem crucem ad s. Petrum in vinea cum subdiacono observatore. Et ibi subdiaconus expoliat se cappa' (p. 123). I have translated *pluviale* as *chasuble*, and *cappa* as *cope*. In the Beroldus the word *planeta* (=chasuble) is also used.

[51]De diebus festivitatum, qualiter processio fiat in eisdem (p. 65).

In altero die, sonito signo, congregato clero in ecclesia majori, unus duorum minorum custodum ebdomadariorum dat pluviale presbytero ebdomadario, clerico suo recipiente cappam, et portat ad festum albam et amictum subdiacono. Et diaconus ebdomadarius similiter induit se pluviale, clerico suo sibi porrigente, et cappam recipiente.

Tunc presbyter ebdomadarius dicit ante altare *Dominus vobiscum* et diaconus incipit psallentium, primicerio lectorum praedicente[52] vel indicante ei, et post illum subsequente cum suis eandem antiphonam. Et sic ebdomadarii omnium ordinum specialiter vadunt ad praedictum festum.

Antecedente schola s. Ambrosii tota cum cruce argentea, ostiario ebdomadario praecedente presbyterum cujus ebdomada est cum cruce argentea vel aurea, et si pharus est in festo observator ostiarius portat crucem argenteam ad accendendum pharum, et ebdomadarius subdiaconus palam portat calicem magnum coopertum, et cicendelarius observator portat patenam cum manutergio volutam sumptam de camera archiepiscopi et cazulam argenteam et fabiolum argenteum et duas alas textus evangeliorum et vas aquarium quod dicitur *aquamanile*. Et cicendelarius ebdomadarius portat candelabrum unum cum cereo et duo corporalia [......] similiter et reducit calicem magnum cum coopertura, quem subdiaconus palam portat ad festum.

The next day,[53] the signal sounded and the clergy having gathered in the principal church, one of the two minor custodians of the week gives the chasuble to the hebdomadary priest (his clerk having taken back the cope) and carries to the festival the alb and amice for the subdeacon.[54] And similarly the hebdomadary deacon puts on a chasuble, his clerk having handed it to him after taking back the cope.

Then the hebdomadary priest sings, *Dominus vobiscum* in front of the altar, and the deacon starts off the procession, the chief lector having announced [the antiphon], that is to say, intoned [it] for him; and behind him is [the chief lector], the rest of the lectors following, [singing] the same antiphon.[55] And all the orders of the hebdomadaries, in their own way as follows, go to the festival.

---

[52]The earliest manuscript of the Beroldus has *praecadente* in place of *praedicante*.

[53]I.e., the second day of the *biduum*, the actual date entered for the feast in the calendar.

[54]This passage is perhaps corrupt. Elsewhere, more than once, we read that the subdeacons wore albs in the procession. Consider the following:

Subdiaconus ebdomadarius omni die dominico dare debet quatuor denarios custodibus ebdomadariis. Et per hunc conventum custodes debent eos induere in missa vel in vesperis aut in matutinis, quoties opus fuerit. Et si tempus pluviae fuerit, iidem custodes portabunt vestes usque ad festum, sin autem subdiaconi portabunt camisium indutum tantum (p. 36).

Every Sunday a hebdomadary subdeacon is to give four *denarii* to the hebdomadary custodians. And for this consideration the custodians are to vest them for mass, vespers or matins, as often as required. And if it is raining, the same custodians will carry the vestments to the feast, but if not, the subdeacons will carry [them], each wearing only the *camisium* [there is little doubt that *camisium* = alb]

[55]Psallendae are sometimes called antiphons in the service books. This passage is very difficult, but compare the following:

postea dicit *Dominus vobiscum*, tunc diaconus ebdomadarius incipit psallentium, primicerio lectorum indicante, et eodem statim cum suis (p. 97)

Preceding with a silver cross is the whole Company of St Ambrose; the ostiary of the week, with a cross of silver or gold, precedes the hebdomadary priest; and if the feast has a *pharus*[56] the observing ostiary carries the silver cross for lighting it; and a hebdomadary subdeacon carries, in plain view, the great covered chalice; and the observing acolyte carries, wrapped in a costly handtowel, a paten from the chamber of the archbishop, a *cazula*[57] of silver, a *fabiolus*[58] of silver, the two wings[59] of the text of the Gospels, and the water vessel, which is called *aquamanile*.[60] And a hebdomadary acolyte carries one candlestick with a candle, and two corporals,[61] [...] and similarly brings back the great covered chalice that the subdeacon carried in plain view to the festival.

What follows immediately in the Beroldus is a description of the preparation for mass at the stational church (the first sentence seems to be an insertion that belongs later), but the passage is worth including here because it provides more information about the ritual objects carried in the procession:

Et duo observatores octo minorum custodum portant calicem offerendarum in quem colligitur vinum quod offertur, et porrigunt aquam cum aquamanile presbytero et diacono et subdiacono ebdomadariis ad abluendas manus. Et in introitu illius ecclesiae ubi festum celebratur presbyter ejusdem ecclesiae debet dare quinque candelas cruci

---

tunc primicerius lectorum cum suis incipit antiphonam ... (p. 41)

postremo primicerius lectorum sequitur cum suis canendo ... (p. 61)

[56]Magistretti (*Beroldus*, p. 192, n. 123), says 'globum ex gossypio', 'a globe of cotton'. Cf. *Ordo mysterii seu officii in ecclesia modoëtiensis*, ed. Anton-Francesco Frisi, in *Memorie storiche di Monza* (Milan, 1794), vol. 3, p. 196 (Monza is near Milan):

Cum intramus chorum custos, levata cruce aurea cum candelis accensis desuper ponit ignem in corona lampadarum tota circumdata et cooperta bombice, quod dicitur pharum.

When we enter the choir a custodian, raising up the gold cross with burning candles upon it, lights what is called the pharus, a crown of lamps entirely surrounded and covered with silk

[57]Magistretti suggested that this is the same as a *catiola*, 'a sieve through which the wine was poured into the chalice' (cf. Joseph Braun, *Das christliche Altargerät* (Munich, 1932), p. 286); cf. *Beroldus*, p. 52: 'vinum oblationis fusum est per catiolam argenteam in calicem aureum fundit'. However the only other appearance of *cazula* in the Beroldus does not seem to support Magistretti, but rather to suggest that the *cazula* was a vessel for mixing the wine: 'et cicendelarius ebdomadarius portat ... cazulam, unde colatur vinum in sacrificio' (47).

[58]The word appears only once in the Beroldus. Joseph Dyer has suggested privately that *fabiolus* (or *fabiolum*) might be derived from *favillae* (glowing ashes) and mean a censer.

[59]Perhaps ivory *garde-feuilles*, See Magistretti, *Beroldus*, p. 192, n. 124.

[60]The the *aquamanile* was often in the form of an animal. Six items seems rather a lot for one person to carry, and it may be that a few words identifying one or more other clergy have been accidentally omitted. It is certain that another lacuna follows a few words later.

[61]Fine cloths on which the consecrated hosts were placed or with which they were covered, perhaps carried in something to protect them. St Charles Borromeo, archbishop of Milan from 1563 to 1584, refers to a *sacculus corporalis. Acta Mediolanensia.* (Milan, 1683), vol. 1, p. 524.

vetulorum, alteri cruci videlicet aureae dat septem, si argentea fuerit quinque, et cruci vetulorum tres. Et si pharus habetur dat iterum septem ostiario observatori ex quibus accendat pharum; cicendelario ebdomadario dat [...][62] thuribulum et incensum et unam candelam unde cereum accendat. Hoc peracto, sacerdos paratus accedit ad altare, solus confessione ante [altare] acta, cum subdiacono et diacono ebdomadariis. Tunc magister scholarum incipit ingressam.

And the two observers of the eight minor custodians bring up the chalice of the offerings, in which is contained the wine for the sacrifice, and hand the hebdomadary priest, deacon and subdeacon the water and the *aquamanile* for washing their hands. And when [the procession] enters the church where the festival is celebrated, the priest of that church is to present five candles for the cross of the pensioners; for the other cross, viz the one of gold, he gives seven (if it is the silver, five), and for the [other] cross of the pensioners, three; and if there is a pharus he gives another seven to the observing ostiary to light it.[63] And to the hebdomadary acolyte he gives [a candle to light] the thurible, incense, and one candle to light the [large?] candle. This done, the priest, vested, the prayer before the [altar] having been said alone, approaches the altar with the [hebdomadary] subdeacon and the hebdomadary deacon. Then the master of the scholars begins the ingressa.[64]

The information in the general rubric is supplemented in the more detailed description, below, of the morning procession on certain of the more important festivals. Although this repeats some information already presented, it comes closest to establishing the order of the participants:

In ordinatione s. Ambrosii, et s. Petri, et sanctorum Nazarii et Celsi, et s. Laurenti, et s. Simpliciani, et depositione s. Ambrosii, et s. Stephani, sonato signo, pontifex induitur sacris vestibus quasi ad missam canendum, et omnes diaconi dalmaticis et omnes subdiaconi albis et presbyteri cardinales et primicerius decumanorum et primicerius lectorum et magister scholarum qui habet septimanam et ille qui fert textum evangeliorum et qui portat crucem auream et [...] scuticam s. Ambrosii, omnes induti pluvialibus.

Tunc quatuor cicendelarii debent thuribula accendere et candelabra praeparare tanta quot subdiaconi induti albis et dare in manibus eorum. Sed sciendum est quia minor lector semper tantum portat textum evangeliorum in s. Ambrosii ordinatione et depositione et s. Laurentii, et s. Stephani palam et alter qui sequitur portat librum. In ceteris vero festivitatibus in quibus palam portatur textus evangelii major custos octo minorum custodum semper portat textum et alter qui sequitur portat librum praeter si quando praedicti faciunt ebdomadam, et alii qui sequuntur faciunt istud. Item duo minores custodes semper in his festivitatibus praedictis portant missalem et epistolam excepto si

---

[62]Since thuribles were carried in the processions to the stational church ('Et notandum quia in omnibus istis festis ante psallentium incoeptum quatuor cicendelarii debent praeparare et dare thuribula et candelabra accensa subdiaconibus ad portandum in processione') it would seem that some words are missing here, and that the priest of stational church gave the acolyte not a thurible, but a candle to light the thurible. See Magistretti, *Beroldus*, p. 117, n 245. Cf. *Manuale*, p. 221.

[63]Presumably the seven candles were placed inside the pharus.

[64]The Ambrosian counterpart of the Gregorian introit.

faciunt ebdomadam, tunc reliqui qui sequuntur faciunt idem. Et duo custodes observatores octo minorum vadunt ante pontificem cum flagellis praeparando viam, sed si acciderit quod duo majores octo minorum fuerint observatores alii qui sequuntur faciunt hoc officium ante archiepiscopum quia illi majores portant textum evangelii et librum.

Schola vero s. Ambrosii praecedit cum cruce argentea deinde clerus minorum presbyterorum sequitur, ostiario observatore portante crucem ante primicerium decumanorum ex qua postea accenditur pharus. Post hunc sequitur primicerius notariorum cum suis et cum quatuor magistris scholarum, deinde subdiaconi cum thuribulis et cereis accensis, post quos sequuntur presbyteri cardinales ante quos ostiarius ebdomadarius portat crucem auream. Deinde sequuntur diaconi ante quos palam portatur textus evangelii. Item vero sequitur archiepiscopus, ante quem sua crux portatur a notario. Postremo primicerius lectorum sequitur cum suis canendo, eodem incipiente,[65] vicissim canendo cum notariis et reliquo clero ... vadunt ad monasterium s. Protasii in urbe.

For the Ordination of St Ambrose, and for the feasts of St Peter, SS Nazarius and Celsus, St Lawrence, St Simplicianus, the Deposition of St Ambrose, and St Stephen, the pontiff,[66] after the signal is sounded, puts on the sacred vestments as though for singing mass. All the deacons are in dalmatics, and all the subdeacons in albs; and the cardinal priests, the chief decuman, the chief lector, the master of the scholars for the week, he who carries the text of the Gospel, he who carries the golden cross and [he who carries] the shield of St Ambrose are all in chasubles.

Then the four acolytes should light the thuribles and prepare candlesticks, and hand [both] to all the subdeacons in albs. Note that for the Ordination and Deposition of St Ambrose, and for the feasts of St Lawrence and St Stephen, the [first] minor lector always carries, uncovered, the text of the Gospels, and the second [minor lector] follows, carrying the book[67] (for the other feasts when the text of the Gospel is carried uncovered the first of the eight minor custodians always carries the [Gospels], the second following with the book), unless the above-mentioned are the hebdomadaries, then the next in order have these duties. Also, in all the above-mentioned festivals, the [first] two of the minor [observing] custodians carry the missal and the Epistles, unless they are the hebdomadaries, then the next in order do so. And the two [next in rank] of the eight minor observing custodians walk in front of the pontiff with lashes to clear the way, but if it should happen that these two [carry the missal and Epistles] those next in order perform this service in front of the archbishop.[68]

The Company of St Ambrose precedes with a silver cross; the [decumans] follow, the observing ostiary carrying before their chief the cross with which the pharus is later lit; the chief notary is next, with the other notaries and the four masters of the scholars. Then the subdeacons with thuribles and lighted candles. After them follow the cardinal priests, before whom the hebdomadary ostiary carries a gold cross. The deacons follow, before whom is carried, in plain view, the text of the Gospel. Next is the archbishop,

---

[65] Here I have omitted the redundant words *sequentibus suis.*

[66] I.e., the archbishop.

[67] It is difficult to say which book is meant; it can't be the Missal or the Epistles, since they are mentioned just below. Subsequently, when the order of the procession is given, only the Gospels are mentioned. The text may be faulty.

[68] This passage in the Beroldus is contradictory and obviously corrupt.

preceded by his cross carried by a notary. Following after is the chief lector, who intones, and the other lectors singing alternately with the notaries and the rest of the clergy ... .[69] And they go to the monastery of St Protasius in the city.

We read here once again that the lectors and notaries sang alternately. The words that follow are hopelessly ambiguous: they may mean that the rest of the clergy merely followed or that they took part in the singing.

The general rubric ('Concerning the festival days, the manner of the procession') calls for the clergy to set out from the winter church. But (leaving aside for the moment exceptional occasions when it began in neither of the cathedrals[70]), it seems, rather, that the starting point was the winter church for half the year (beginning with the first Sunday of October) and the summer church for the other half (beginning on Holy Saturday). We read plainly (117) that on the Feast of the Deposition of St Ambrose the morning procession to his basilica began in the summer church: 'In depositione s. Ambrosii archiepiscopus vadit cum processione ab ecclesia aestiva usque ad ecclesiam s. Ambrosii.' And note also the following (123–124), where the reference to the alleluia (not, of course, sung in the penitential mass of the vigil) makes it clear that it is the morning procession *in die* that it meant:

> In natali s. Victoris processio fit de ecclesia aestiva ad s. Victorem 'coelum aureum', id-est ad s. Satyrum (ubi ejus corpus requiescit), et ibi presbyter observator debet cantare missam usque ad epistolam, *Assecutus es*. Statim cum processio venerit in chorum puer magistri scholarum incipit *Alleluja de Posuisti*, et observator diaconus dicit evangelium ... . Finito evangelio diaconus ebdomadarius incipit psallentium et vadunt ad s. Victorem, qui dicitur 'ad corpus'.

On the feast of St Victor the procession is held from the summer church to St Victor's of the Golden Ceiling, [also called] St Satyrus's (where his body lies) and there the

---

[69]I have omitted some details about the vestments, information already given in other citations.

[70]The case of Purification is given below in full; two others occasions are mentioned in the Beroldus, the Translation of St Nazarius:

> In altero die, sonito signo, archiepiscopus cum toto clero vadit ad s. Euphemiam sine processione, et ibi diaconus incipit psallentium ... ad s. Celsum (p. 124)

> On the day of the festival, the archbishop with all his clergy go to St Euphemia's without procession, and there the deacon starts off the procession ... to the church of St Celsus

and the Exaltation of the Cross:

> In altero die, sonito signo, omnes majoris ordinis vadunt ad s. Ambrosium sine processione ... et presbyter, induto pluviali, diaconus ebdomadarius incipit ibi psallentium usque in ecclesiam aesti-vam (p. 126).

> On the day of the festival, the signal sounded, all those of the major orders go to the basilica of St Ambrose without procession ... and there, the priest having put on the chasuble, the hebdomadary deacon starts the procession to the Summer Church

observing priest is to sing mass as far as the Epistle, *Assecutus es*. As soon as the procession enters the choir the [head] boy of the master of the scholars begins the *Alleluia de Posuisti*,[71] and the observing deacon reads the Gospel .... When the Gospel is finished the hebdomadary deacon starts the procession off [again], and they go to the church of St Victor called 'ad corpus'.

In the antiphoners and in the Manuale nothing is provided for stations in the morning processions of the saints; only psallendae are entered, never responsories or antiphons. But stations were certainly an important feature, even if they are mentioned only incidentally, as in the direction given just above for the Feast of St Victor. The interesting intersection of the cathedral liturgy and the liturgy of the stational church on that occasion was a feature of other festivals as well. Consider the following, unusually detailed, entries.[72]

For Assumption:

In assumptione s. Mariae presbyter observator canit missam in ecclesia hyemali .... Finito evangelium, archiepiscopus cum toto clero vadit ad ecclesiam s. Simpliciani indutus sicut legitur. Finito psallentio in atrio ejusdem ecclesia, presbyter observator debet cantasse missam usque ad epistolam super altare s. Johannis de dedicatione minori. Post haec statim cum intrant chorum s. Johannis puer magistri scholarum canit *Alleluja* cum versu, *Templum Domini*. Observator diaconus legit evangelium, *Egressus Dominus Jesus perambulabat Jerico*. Finito evangelio, procedunt ad altare s. Simpliciani. (125)

For the Assumption of Holy Mary the observing priest sings mass in the winter church[73] .... After the Gospel the archbishop with all his clergy go to the church of St Simplicianus vested as may be read [elsewhere]. By the time the procession ends in the atrium of that church the observing priest [of the church of St John the Baptist] should have sung the mass of the Minor Dedication[74] up to the Epistle at the [main] altar of St John's. Immediately after this, as they enter the choir of St John's,[75] the [head] boy of the master of the scholars sings the *Alleluia* with the verse *Templum domini*. The observing deacon reads the Gospel, *Egressus dominus Jesus perambulabat Jerico*. When the Gospel is finished, they proceed to the [main] altar at St Simplicianus's.

For the Deposition of St Ambrose:

---

[71]Boys were featured in the singing of the alleluia.

[72]See also *Beroldus*, pp. 61–62, 124–125.

[73]In the Middle Ages, the Winter Cathedral was dedicated to the Blessed Virgin.

[74]It seems that this was also the anniversary of the celebration of the dedication of this church. The day was crowded: the entry for 15 August in the calendar (included by Magistretti in his *Beroldus*) is 'Assumptio s. Mariae, et translatio s. Sisinii, Martyrii et Alexandri; et depositio s. Simpliciani in ecclesiae sua' (p. 9).

[75]Magistretti, *Beroldus*, p. 227, n. 262, suggested that this church of St John (the Baptist) was adjacent to the Basilica of St Simplicianus, so close that no processional chants were needed. This is not entirely convincing.

Mane ad psallentium ad s. Ambrosium archiepiscopus induitur sicut ad canendam missam et diaconi dalmatica subdiaconi alba presbyteri cardinales cum primicerio presbyterorum et primicerio lectorum et ...... cum illo qui portat textum evangeliorum et qui bajulat crucem auream cum magistro scholae s. Ambrosii cum flagello, omnes isti induuntur pluvialibus, et hoc eodem ordine procedunt in pentecosten et in festo s. Petri; sed tamen in festo s. Petri omnes diaconi portant manipulum ductum per capitium et sacerdotes induti planetis portant manipulum simili modo, et, in festo s. Nazarii, et s. Laurentii, et in Assumptione s. Mariae, et in ordinatione s. Ambrosii, et in festo s. Stephani, et s. Johannis evangelistae sic induuntur ut supra docuimus excepto festo s. Petri in quo aliquantulum differtur sicut supra legitur. ...

In the morning procession to the church of St Ambrose the archbishop is vested as though for singing mass, the deacons in dalmatics, the subdeacons in albs, the chief priest[76] with the [other] cardinal priests, the chief lector and ...... with him who carries the text of the Gospels, him who carries the gold cross, and the master of the Company of St Ambrose with his lash – all these vested in chasubles – and they go forth similarly attired[77] on Pentecost and on the Feast of St Peter; however on the Feast of St Peter all the deacons wear maniples tied round the neck,[78] and the priests dressed in chasubles wear the maniple in the same way. On the feast of St Nazarius, St Lawrence, Assumption, the Ordination of St Ambrose, St Stephen, and St John the Evangelist they dress as described above, except on the Feast of St Peter, when there is a slight difference, as is prescribed above. ...[79]

The Manuale then lists the processional chants sung on the way to the Ambrosian Basilica, but in a rubric entered between the fourth and fifth psallenda (there are thirteen to come), we learn, incidentally, of a station:

... iv *In conspectu agni.* Hic archiepiscopus statim cum exierit de ecclesia s Georgii, habens virgam pastoralem in manu, incipit hanc antiphonam excelsa voce versus in meridiem, et primicerius lectorum statim subsequitur, *Dicant nunc judaei.*

... iv *In conspectu agni.* The archbishop, directly after he comes out of the church of St George, his pastoral staff in his hand, facing south, begins this antiphon[80] in a loud voice, and the chief lector follows immediately[81] with *Dicunt nunc Judei.*

As might be expected, on the Feast of the Purification (Candlemas) the procession was exceptional:

---

[76]The *primicerius* of the cardinal priests seems to be the the archpriest. Cf. 'archipresbyter aut archidiaconus, vel alii presbyteri aut diaconi cardinales' (p. 36), but cf. Magistretti (*Beroldus*, p. 171, n. 63), where it is said the archpriest was the chief of the decumans.

[77]Literally, 'in the same order', but *ordine* is certainly used here in the sense of *modo*: it is the vestments that are being described.

[78]See Magistretti, *Beroldus*, p. 190, n. 112.

[79]*Beroldus*, Magistretti's note 245, p. 117; cf. *Manuale*, p. 221. I have omitted here a passage that repeats, using similar language, information found in rubrics from the Beroldus already presented in this chapter.

[80]Here again, a psallenda is referred to as an antiphon.

[81]It seems that no psalm was sung with this psallenda.

Mane facto et[82] sonito signo, pontifex cum clero sine processione vadit ad ecclesiam s. Mariae quae dicitur Bertrade, et duo minores presbyteri decumanorum qui fecerant baptismum in sabbato sancto portant ideam ad praedictam ecclesiam cum scala. Et legatus primicerii [decumanorum] quaerit duas a pontifice corrigias quas ponat in idea et liget super scalam. Et presbyteri illius ecclesia praeparant librum et aquam et incensum cum thuribulo cum quibus benedicit candelas.

Et benedictis candelis, archiepiscopus dat cannellas quamplures primicerio decumanorum quas ille iterum dat sacerdotibus suis. Et omnes clerus accendit cannellas ad psallentium. Archiepiscopus vero dicendo *Dominus vobiscum*, et diaconus ebdomadarius incipit psallentium.

Prima crux vetulorum praecedit omnes cum cannellis quinque sursum accensis et ostiarius observator similiter portat crucem ante primicerium decumanorum cum septem canellis accensis et septimanarius ostiarius portat crucem auream ante sacerdotes et levitas et duo presbyteri quos praediximus induti planetis portant ideam post lectores usque in ecclesiam hyemalem et tertius et quartus observator ostiarius sonant tintinabula. (81–82)

When day breaks and the signal has sounded the pontiff goes with the clergy, not in procession, to the church of Holy Mary that is called Bertrade, and the two minor priests of the decumans who performed the baptism on Holy Saturday carry the image [of the Virgin] to the above-named church on a cart.[83] And from the pontiff a deputy of the chief [of the decumans] gets two straps that he attaches to the image and ties to the cart. And the priest of this church [St Mary's, Bertrade] makes ready the book and water and incense in a thurible with which [the archbishop] blesses the candles.

After the candles are blessed, the archbishop gives a great many to the chief of the decumans, which he in turn gives to his priests. And the clergy all light the candles for the procession.[84] And the archbishop himself having sung the *Dominus vobiscum*, the hebdomadary deacon starts the procession on its way.[85]

The first cross of the pensioners,[86] surmounted by five lit candles, precedes all, and the observing ostiary carries similarly in front of the chief of the decumans a cross with seven lit candles, and a septimanary ostiary carries the cross of gold in front of the priests and levites,[87] and the two priests mentioned above, vested in chasubles, following the lectors, carry the image [of the Virgin] to the winter church, and [there] the third and the fourth observing ostiary ring the bells.

---

[82]The oldest manuscript of the Beroldus has 'altero die' (the next day) in place of 'mane facto et'.

[83]See Magistretti, *Beroldus*, p. 197, n. 147.

[84]The antiphoners contain the usual items for vespers, the procession after vespers, and the vigils office, but nothing for a procession to the baptistry, and from this we may infer that the usual solemnities of the vigil, although not mentioned in this rubric, took place at the stational church prior to the procession of return.

[85]All three manuscripts of Beroldus read 'Archiepiscopus vero incipit psallentium dicendo *Dominus vobiscum* et diaconus ebdomadarius incipit psallentium'. I have taken for granted that the first 'incipit psallentium' is an error in copying.

[86]I.e., the Company of St Ambrose.

[87]I.e., the deacons.

The order of the processions

Although some of the saints' processions are described in Byzantine detail, the information is not sufficient – even if there were no lacunae – to collate into general rules that would serve for every eventuality. Setting out clearly what modern readers would like to know was not the intention of Beroldus in compiling the ordinal. He and no doubt earlier contributors to the ordinal that bears his name seem to have inserted peripheral details just as they came to mind, details that distract from any logical exposition. This said, some very general remarks can be ventured.

The essential purpose of the processions, whether on the eve or the morning of the feast, was to convey the celebrants and liturgical accoutrements to the site of stational liturgy. This is as in the early Roman processions, and must date from a time when the site of the stations, originally *martyria*, had no permanent clergy. This observation allows us to conjecture that certain features mentioned only for the vigils processions or only for the processions on the day of the feast were part of both.

The detailed rubric given earlier for the feasts of the Ordination of St Ambrose, St Peter, SS Nazarius and Celsus, etc. seems to be the most reliable for the order of the participants it mentions, although others not mentioned may have been among them. I have included (in parentheses) additional information gleaned elsewhere from Beroldus and also (in brackets) some reasonable conjecture, but I have not tried to identify all the custodians, acolytes, or ostiaries who carried the crosses and other ritual objects. What follows is not certain, and as far as the order of the participants is concerned, lacks a convincing rationale:

First, preceded by a silver cross, the twenty members of the Company of St Ambrose (each carrying a ferule, the master of the order also carrying a lash)

Preceded by a silver cross, the chief priest of the decumans (with his ferule) and the other decumans

[Preceded by a cross?] the chief notary (carrying a ferule) and the other notaries

(Carrying ferules) all four masters of the scholars [accompanied by the boys?]

Preceded by a cross, [the chief subdeacon?] the hebdomadary subdeacons, with thuribles and lighted candles (one carrying the great covered chalice) [and the rest of the subdeacons?]

Preceded by a gold cross, the archpriest (with his ferule) and the cardinal priests

(Preceded by a gold cross and a text of the Gospel, the archdeacon, with his ferule) [the hebdomadary deacon?[88]] and the other cardinal deacons

[Preceded by a cross, the viscount, carrying a ferule and accompanied by his retinue?]

---

[88]The Beroldus never refers to more than one hebdomadary deacon, although frequently to 'hebdomadary subdeacons'.

Preceded by notary carrying a gold or silver cross, and two custodians with lashes to clear the way, the archbishop (with his pastoral staff and mitre) [or in his absence the hebdomadary priest?]

Preceded by a silver cross, the chief lector (carrying his ferule) and the other lectors

We read again and again that the hebdomadary deacon started the procession off, but it is not likely that he actually set out before everyone else, even if it were not said more than once that the Company of St Ambrose went first. Similarly unspecified is the position of the hebdomadary subdeacon carrying the covered chalice. The viscount is named only in the description of the Three-Day Litany, but a remark (apparently out of place) in the Beroldus[89] seems to say that he and his servants walked in procession in front of the archbishop on a number of occasions.

There were certainly other participants not mentioned, on at least five occasions clergy from other churches who carried objects from the cathedral treasury to the site of the festival. And, although we are only told that the officers appointed for the week (the *ordinarii*) went in procession, the observing clergy are sometimes assigned duties en route ('the observer deacon reads the Gospel'). And it is not inconceivable – considering that all the decumans and cardinal priests were included – that the off-duty (as it were) custodians, ostiaries, and acolytes came along in some ordered fashion, especially since we read of the presence of the lay clerks at the site of the festival.[90] Ferules, like an army officer's baton a sign of the dignity of office, may have been carried by others not specified.

The position in the processions of the numerous ceremonial objects mentioned in the Beroldus (there were perhaps others that were not named) cannot now be determined. In addition to candlesticks and thuribles we read of the pharus and a lamp; and for mass, in addition to the covered chalice mentioned above, of the paten, corporals, the *cazula*, and the *aquamanile*. We read also of various books – the Gospels, the

---

[89]Cf.:

... ad domum vicecomitis, qui in Natale Domini et s. Stephani et in s. Johannis evangelistae et in Resurrectione Domini et secunda feria et tertia feria post Resurrectionem praecedit archiepiscopum parando sibi viam servitoribus suis praecedentibus cum flagellis ligneis et scissis (p. 36).

... to the residence of the viscount, who on the feasts of Christmas, St Stephen, and St John the Evangelist (and on Easter, and the second and third days after Easter) precedes the archbishop, his [the viscount's] servants going first to clear the way with lashes made of wood and thongs.

[90]Page 29:

In eodem festo omnes presbyteri, et diaconi cardinales et omnes subdiaconi et omnes notarii et primicerius decumanorum, primicerius lectorum et quatuor magistri scholarum, *omnes isti cum singulis clericis,* et omnes lectores cum omnibus custodibus omnes isti comedunt cum abbate ipsius monasterii ubi festum celebratur.

On that day all the priests and cardinal deacons, all the subdeacons, all the notaries, the chief decuman, the chief lector, and the four masters of the boys, *all of these with their clerks,* and all lectors, all custodians [i.e., acolytes and ostiaries] – all of these dine with the abbot of the monastery where the feast is celebrated.

Epistles, the missal, perhaps the Old Testament – and also of the *fabiolus*, the ivory(?) *garde-feuilles* of the Gospels, the shield and lash of St Ambrose;[91] perhaps, in the vigils processions, ashes to be distributed along the way.

As for the vestments, the directions are nothing like complete and are sometimes ambiguous. It seems that the archbishop or hebdomadary priest were 'vested as for mass', the archbishop with a mitre; the other priests and the deacons wore dalmatics (on some occasions with maniples); the subdeacons, albs (*alba, camisia*). We read of many in the procession who wore chasubles (*pluvialia, casulae, planetae*) over their shoulders: the archbishop, the hebdomadary priest, the deacons and subdeacons, the cardinal priests, the decumans, the chief lector, the master of the scholars, 'he who carries the text of the Gospel', 'he who carries the gold cross', and even the twenty members of the Company of St Ambrose. In view of this last, it seems likely that chasubles were worn by all the lectors (not just the *primicerius*), by the notaries, and by any others belonging to the higher orders.

Whether in other great cities processions were as frequent and complex as they were in Milan is simply not known: we have no other document comparable in detail to the Beroldus. But that Milan would be unrivalled in these respects seems unlikely – except, notably, in the size of the repertory of special chants – and scholars may fairly look to the Ambrosian tradition when they seek to complete their fragmentary picture of the Christian Liturgy of Western Europe in the high Middle Ages.

---

[91]'Flagellum [magistri scholae] s. Ambrosii?' (p. 62). This may be nothing more than the lash carried in front of the Company of St Ambrose.

Chapter 18

Patterns and paleography: revisions, variants, errors, and methods

Andrew Hughes

> [Analysis of musical variants] is recognized as a critical research operation, yet there is no description of its methods. Nor is there a theory of the various strategies available to the researcher ...[1]

It gives me much pleasure to write this contribution honouring Bryan Gillingham, who has been such a good friend, inspiring scholar, adviser, and swift publisher of so many important and varied volumes. When asked to contribute, I was already preparing a similar article for another colleague. That is to be a comparison and analysis of the variants in a single plainchant in some 150 manuscripts of the main office for Thomas Becket of Canterbury, with some attention to the implications for performance of the different versions. Kay Slocum has published the most recent and comprehensive account and edition of the Becket offices.[2] Data and evidence for my analysis were accumulated and set aside several years ago and, in the frequent way of such things, I found it necessary to relearn, re-examine, and revise the methods devised for the project. This study, then, is an attempt to rationalize the procedures that I thought were needed to produce reasonably secure results. This process itself raised questions in sufficient quantity to suggest that the chapter that follows might be of general interest, as a foundation for more specific analysis. Although the procedures may seem like counsels of perfection, they can only be guidelines rather than mandates. The opportunity to prepare linked pieces in different publications, usually not practical, was also tempting.

The conclusions drawn from the process of comparison, although an end in themselves, could also lay the foundation for editing. For that task James Grier has provided a masterly and comprehensive manual and theory. Grier's book should be close at hand for all who deal with variants: firstly, for the emphasis on the meticulous codicological description for every source used, concisely laid out in his Appendix C; and for his useful insights into the methods and accuracy of scribes, more extensive

---

[1]Wayne C. Booth, Gregory G. Colomb, and Joseph M. Williams, *The Craft of Research* (Chicago, 1995), p. 244.
[2]Kay Slocum, *Liturgies in Honour of Thomas Becket* (Toronto, 2004).

than can be reviewed here.[3] An edition, involving choice, may use only a limited number of sources; a comparison, however, must record all versions. This fact presents the scholar with problems of documentation to be recalled later.

Perhaps I have spent too much of my professional life thinking about processes and devising methods, and agonizing over precise terminology, rather than addressing the scholarly issues themselves: 'theory pursued for its own sake ... divorced from the reality of the [repertory it analyses]'.[4] Partly these obsessions were necessitated by the repertories I undertook to study. Large and virtually unexplored, for analysis of detail to be possible at all they required the adoption of untried methods. The advent of the computer promised relief from the tedium of manual indexing and sorting, and a reasonable expectation of some success, but of course brought its own peculiar constraints on what was possible. The deficiencies or limitations of early programmes, of the kind available a quarter-century ago, and the inexorable requirements of computers for consistent 'spelling' and unmistakably unambiguous and distinct 'terms', in conjunction with reasonably transparent ways of referring to complex analytical issues forced the rethinking of approaches: these and some limitations and solutions are described in my article 'Large projects and small resources'.[5]

Here, I wish to examine the methods for analysing that most intractable of repertories, and indeed one of the most contentious issues within that repertory: the problem of plainchant and its variants. Since practically every scholar who deals with plainchant has to grapple with this issue, and probably everyone has attempted it, reviewing or even comprehensively listing earlier work in this field would be a massive task, better left for a bibliographical endeavour. The liturgical bibliographies periodically published in *The Journal of Plainsong and Medieval Music* run to some 13,000 entries, many of which are relevant in one way or another, but are not identifiable in the indexes.

Any discussion of this matter entails the comparison of tunes in more than a single source. Anyone who has made an edition from more than one source has of necessity had at least to record variants, without necessarily analysing them. Only briefly and as required will I rehearse the kinds of variants, the complexities of presenting them, the ambiguities hidden in any conclusions, and the significance that attaches to those conclusions. Most of these matters have been described and discussed many times as individual issues. Nowhere do I recollect an attempt to address them comprehensively, although James Cowdery sets out some very interesting thoughts about a quite different melodic tradition, some of which are relevant for our purposes.[6]

It seems astonishing that musicologists have not adopted a consistent method for recording this kind of analysis with respect to plainsong. One can perhaps attribute this

[3]James Grier, *The Critical Editing of Music: History, Method, and Practice* (Cambridge, 1996).

[4]John Caldwell, review of Grier, in *The Journal of the Plainsong and Medieval Music Society* 6 (1997), p. 175.

[5]See *FS Steiner*, pp. 521–45.

[6]James R. Cowdery, *The Melodic Tradition of Ireland* (Ohio, 1990).

reluctance to the high degree of subjective interpretation and judgement that such analysis often requires, as will be apparent from some of the later examples. Because no consensus has arisen, even on some major points, each scholar feels entitled to forge his or her own methods, *ad hoc*, often unstated, and to include or exclude various features.[7] Since the reliability of so much of this work has to be taken on trust, a point to be repeated later, it would seem sensible, in a process so fraught with ambiguities, to establish some consensus about what needs to be done. Laying out the variants one under the other and counting occurrences is only the beginning, even if some attempt is present to interpret the statistics.

My chief experience has been with late medieval plainsong, where the difficulty of interpreting early notation is much less of an issue. Much of what is set out will be applicable, with modifications, to other repertories, including polyphonic music. With examples drawn from my own work with the versified office of Thomas of Canterbury, what follows is for the most part theory. Citing other examples from the repertory in general would require the availability of comprehensive lists of the matters to be described. These lists do not yet exist, and no one has attempted to compile them. For most of the matters described, I have seen examples in manuscripts, without realizing the necessity (or having the time) systematically to collect them. I will attempt to lay out a minimal and general set of features that might be considered in any comparison of melodies, and to present methods of recording the evidence.

To reach reasonably secure conclusions, the recording of evidence should be comprehensive. An analysis that includes, for example, details of trivial variants may offer new insights. Otherwise they cannot even be taken into account. Some textual scholars in fact have emphasized the importance of analysing 'minor communicators' – that is, the insignificant words such as 'and' and 'for' – on the grounds that authors use them without thought and thus may unconsciously reveal stylistic preferences. Cowdery has some useful insights, suggesting that significance lies in the variable passages of a tune.[8] My own preliminary investigation of the word *et* in plainsong reveals some odd and interesting usages.[9] Even though its creative aesthetics are quite different from those of language, by analogy one might claim for plainsong that for analysis it is not the modally stable and structural notes that are important, but how one moves from one to another. Certainly minor details are important.[10]

Music can be learned, too, from material that superficially seems less interesting, such as tones. Meticulous work done by one of my research assistants, David Adam,

[7]Grier, *Critical Editing*, p. 10.

[8]Cowdery, *Melodic Tradition*, p. 74.

[9]See page 38 in 'Chantword Indexes: A Tool for Plainsong Research', in Paul Laird, ed., *Words and Music* (Binghamton, 1993), pp. 31–50.

[10]Grier, *Critical Editing*, p. 231.

reveals that even responsory verses (supposedly formulaic) are extremely variable, allowing much latitude for abbreviation and free extension.[11]

An inclusive approach, in any case, relieves the scholar of having to distinguish between trivial and substantive variants, ornament and structure, important and subordinate elements, or between formula and innovation, all of which, as David Hughes, Timothy McGee, and many other scholars have demonstrated, are non-trivial tasks laden with ambiguity.

Encoding and documentation

Perhaps the most serious problem impeding chant analysis in the past has been the inability of most scholars to know and retain in memory even a small part of the chant repertory. Even clerics saturated in the daily modern practice of chant can hardly know and recollect historical repertories closely enough to locate immediately the various details that are necessary for comprehensive analysis. Electronic storage of chant repertories in a searchable form brings infinite possibilities not available to earlier generations. Facsimile representations in electronic form do not yet allow the kind of ready searching that is necessary. The recording of chants must be in alphanumeric characters, accessible to all researchers so that the results can be checked, at least against the 'transcriptions' – encoding – and available facsimiles. Desirable though it may be, checking against the original manuscripts is normally impractical. For extensive comparisons, there is usually far more detail than any one person could reasonably be expected to check: I estimate the documentation alone for a forthcoming article would occupy some 200 pages.[12] The accuracy and judgement of the researcher must be taken largely on trust. Citation of multiple examples enables a reader to assess, up to a point, the reliability of the judgement, if not of the initial transcription. The use of conventional music or facsimiles may severely limit such citations, given the economics of publication. Here, a truly transparent alphanumeric encoding may help.

Here is not the place to describe such methods, of which there are several, but it will be necessary briefly to explain the system I use.[13] Adopting the essential principle that the encoding should be as transparent as possible, and must allow the reader to sing the chants at sight, I use numerals and a few symbols for the pitches, treating the final of the mode as 1. To allow the ready association of syllable with musical motive,

---

[11]David Adam will report on these features in the third volume of my edition of *Lambeth Palace, Sion College ms. L1; the Noted Breviary of York (olim Sion College ms Arc.L.40.2/L.1)*, Publications of Mediaeval Musical Manuscripts 25/1–3 (Ottawa, 2000–2001).

[12]'Echoes and Allusions: Sources of the Office for St Dominic', in Pierre-Marie Gy and Leonard E. Boyle, eds, *Aux origines de la liturgie dominicaine: le manuscrit Santa Sabina XIV L.1*. (Paris-Rome, 2002). Pp. 279–300.

[13]Full specifications of the system are in my *Late Medieval Liturgical Offices: Resources for Electronic Research (Sources and Chants)*, Subsidia Medievalia 24 (Toronto, 1996), chapters 7 and 8.

I attach the melodic representation to each word of the item, identifying syllables with dots. Thus, in mode 1 ending on *d*, the encoding *Dominus.123=2,.01.1* represents the pitches *deffe cd d*, where the *f* is a repercussive pitch, and the second *e* is a plica (see Example 18.1).

Example 18.1: (hypothetical) *Dominus*

Do-   mi- nus

Below, after a necessary exploration of features that might be present in an analysis, is a complete chant, Example 18.13, in conventional stemless noteheads. A presentation in any other kind of modern notation would clearly be misleading. In hypothetical examples and those that represent a base version, ligatures are indicated only by the spacing of the symbols. An alphanumeric encoding of the pitches, of course, does not represent the intervals, but these can easily be deduced by the reader and more easily examined by a computer programme. Although singers reading from this encoding can easily perform plainsong at sight, none that I have encountered like to use the system. Musical notation always conveys information that cannot be transmitted by letters and numbers. This visual factor is especially true of medieval notation, in which the spacing of symbols is especially crucial. The extremely concise nature of the notation, for instance, conveys a sense of phrasing quite different from that of most modern notation.[14]

Nevertheless, this system allows for the economical presentation of numerous examples in analytical studies, where the accumulation of evidence may be extremely large, and conventional examples of actual music much too prodigal of space (see note 12). It also allows for the electronic storage and easy searching of text, melody, syllable setting, and one or two rudimentary matters of notation.

Terminology

Textual analysis or textual criticism, the comparison and analysis of variants, often with the intention of reaching an archetype, has a long tradition and well established methods. The techniques include the analysis of the words in addition to the paleographical features of the letters.

The word 'text' sometimes refers to a book in general. Some scholars use it to refer to the liturgical book as a whole. Some use 'chant' to refer to the texts of plainsongs. Although acceptable in very general work where the precise meaning is unimportant,

---

[14]See my *Style and Symbol: Medieval Music, 800–1453*, IMS, Musicological Studies 51 (Ottawa, 1989), p. xxvii.

for specific and careful designation these practices seem unacceptably ambiguous. Adopting such a usage for 'text' would justify referring to the melodic analysis, our principal objective, as 'textual' analysis. Obviously, we must separate text from melody, just as we distinguish the words that are sung from the chant that sets them. My coinage of 'sungtext' avoids the ambiguity of an unqualified 'chant'. Two other coinages will be useful. Reflecting my belief, unexpressed at the end of a previous paragraph, that plainsong can most easily be analysed, initially, as a series of settings of individual words, I proceed from 'chantwords', individual words concatenated to their melodies. The term 'text', then, refers to the words themselves. The melodic motive attached to a word is a 'melodyword'. The melodyword is the principal object of the recording and analysis of variants. This method of working with plainsong is quite productive.[15] And experience has shown it to be by far the most transparent and practical method for the electronic comparison of plainsongs.

The comparison and analysis of small motives makes it possible to arrive at some useful conclusions even when tunes recognizable as 'the same' differ considerably. Cowdery, for example, cites tunes whose contours are generally the same but incorporate much variation, and tunes that are recognizable 'because of the melodic motives used, not because of their particular sequence'. Nevertheless, 'unless one is content with turning up interesting curiosities, one must eventually grapple with the problem of [comparing and identifying whole tunes]'.[16]

Complete comparisons of plainsongs will include textual analysis in its conventional sense, incorporating the paleographical details of the scripts, as well as the differences in letters and words and punctuation. The textual transmission may, of course, be entirely separate from that of the chant.[17] For the sake of simplicity this process may have to be carried out separately and later collated with the musical and notational analysis. That collation may prove intractable.

What then shall we use for a 'textual' analysis of the pitches and notation? For certainly, both those elements ought to be subjected to an equally rigorous investigation. Some small notational minutiae may no doubt be safely set aside, on the grounds that they would make as little difference to the melodic line or performance of plainsong as similar character differences would make to literary texts. Other notational features, such as plicas, repercussive pitches, and slight misalignments of stave and pitch symbol, for instance, are more crucial and should be observed where possible.

Pitch and notation analysis

Perhaps by analogy with texts, pitch analysis might implicitly include the paleographical aspects. But to emphasize the necessity of taking the paleographical ele-

---

[15]'Chantword Indexes', pp. 31–50.

[16]Cowdery, *Melodic Tradition*, pp. 73, 80, 89ff, 95, and Examples 35 and 36.

[17]Grier, *Critical Editing*, p. 75.

ments into account, and since they involve more features than those of letters and punctuation, it might be wise to describe them as notational analysis. The encoding described above does not incorporate specific information about the notation, as the chantword shown makes clear: additional coding attached to the chantword makes the result much harder to read. Some information can nevertheless be gathered. Plicas are always marked, with commas; a two-pitch rising interval, for example, must be a podatus ligature and descending a clivis; separate symbols within a syllable may be marked with an apostrophe. Such marking is especially important in melismas. Thus, in mode 3 ending on *e*, the form *contemptus.21,.2'3'21'14'32,.1* would signify on the syllable *con* a single symbol on *f* with a plicated *e*, on the syllable *tem* two single symbols and a clivis followed by a podatus on *ea*, and a single symbol on *g* with a plicated *f*. Example 18.2 is a rather crude imitation of what some original notation might look like:

Example 18.2: (hypothetical) *contemptus*

con-temp-　　　　tus

Attempts to indicate more notational details here were abandoned as too complex. In addition, for adequate information to be included about so many features would require access to the original manuscript.

A new research project, Nota quadrata, supervised by John Haines,[18] aims to describe and categorize the varieties of square notation of the later Middle Ages. The results of this project will perhaps eventually allow us to qualify the notation with terms similar to those of scripts, such as 'single-' or 'double-bowed letter a', so that a unified encoding might be simpler. For the moment, minute variations in the notation can be taken into account through observation of the originals. But generally, some small differences in notational symbols may be as little important (for certain topics at least) as variants in letter shapes. Others, such as a consistent use of plicas where other sources have no ornament or have raised the ornament to the status of a full pitch clearly indicate differences in performance that ought to be brought into the equation: they are not just differences in the melody, but differences in the ear with identical pitch sequences. Some orthographical differences, such as the difference between rectangular pitches with and without a stem, or between rectangular and rhomboid symbols, may carry meanings we as yet do not understand.

Let us move from minute differences of shape to other differences, such as those of position and layout. In these matters, several must be taken into account, as far as possible. Photographic reproductions are perfectly adequate for one of the most important matters to be noted: the position of line ends and page breaks. These are

---

[18]www.notaquadrata.ca.

places where mistakes are often made because of the extra care the notator has to exercise to remember custodes, clefs (anticipating the range beyond so that the clef is suitable), and accidentals. Trying to keep certain initials at the left margin and the right margin neat, usual features of medieval manuscripts,[19] a scribe (or designer) is some- times forced to employ turnovers or wraparounds at the ends of a texts that are incon- venient for the notator: might a notator adjust cadences at such places? Example 18.13 shows two such instances.

At the end of a gathering, in addition to these extra symbols that must be added, a scribe conventionally places a cue word pointing to the next gathering. Occasionally such a cue word is placed at the end of every page (or at least the verso of a leaf), suggesting the possibility that he is writing on separate leaves, which might need to be reordered, rather than on bifolia: this was still the practice of the early twentieth- century British civil service. These cue words can lead to erroneous dittography in copies. Although the words sometimes anticipate in detail and colour and abbreviation of the subsequent word (see note 19), I recollect no manuscript in which the music is anticipated. These features may or may not affect the melodic line.

More dependent on the quality of photographic reproduction are erasures, expunc- tuations, and marginal additions. John Haines has worked extensively on the first of these.[20] The last may have been trimmed off at some time, or may have been clipped by a photographer, and may be apparent only by means of carets in the writing area. All these paleographical features directly affect the melodic line. So, too, does the position of accidentals, which in many cases do not immediately precede a relevant pitch, and which could affect pitches other than the one on the same line or space.[21]

The system described here shows details of the melody, and adds evidence about texts, text-setting, and some notational and paleographical matters. Although intriguing in themselves, these kinds of evidence, especially if presented in tables or algebraic formulas, should of course be complemented by narrative conclusions to justify the purpose of the exercise.

So let us turn to the reasons for comparing plainsongs. A statement of purpose should surely precede the presentation of the evidence, since the purpose may well dictate what steps are necessary, what methods are used, and what features are includ- ed or excluded. Conclusions should revisit the purpose and, of course, may illuminate

---

[19]See my article 'The Scribe and the Late Medieval Liturgical Manuscript: Page Layout and Order of Work', in Robert A. Taylor *et al.*, eds, *The Centre and its Compass: Studies in Medieval Literature in Honor of Professor John Leyerle* (Kalamazoo, 1993), pp. 151–224; and *Medieval Manuscripts for Mass and Office: A Guide to their Organization and Terminology* (Toronto, 2nd edn, 1986).

[20]'Erasures in Thirteenth-century Music', in John Haines and Randall Rosenfeld, eds, *Music and Medieval Manuscripts* (Aldershot, 2004), pp. 60–88.

[21]See John Haines, *Manuscript Accidentals: Ficta in Focus*, Musicological Studies and Documents 27 (Rome, 1972), and Margaret Bent, 'Diatonic "ficta"', *EMH* 4 (1984), pp. 1–48, and *Essays on Musica Ficta* (New York, 2001).

reasons other than those initially stated. In the first of the purposes laid out below, for instance, material bearing on the second purpose may well appear.

I begin with comparisons that, it seems to me, are most likely to produce interesting and convincing conclusions.

1 *Assessment of variants and ornaments.* We may compare tunes in an attempt to obtain a general sense of which kinds of variants or ornaments are preferred in which manuscripts. Crucial in this endeavour is an examination of the notation. If the sources can mostly be dated reliably and securely placed within a Use or geographical area, much might be learned about local dialects and performance preferences. Unfortunately, these conditions are unlikely to be met very frequently.

The comparison of tunes in different Uses or repertories probably presents more difficulties and uncertainties than comparing tunes within the same corpus. It may be possible to use the variants as a means of establishing or confirming such codicological data.

2 *Grouping of sources.*[22] Given a sample of adequate size and a sufficient number of points of similarity, it may appear that certain sources are related, even if the direction of the relationship cannot be established or confirmed. An identical location of the sources may lend some weight. With respect to the sources of the Becket office, two books sharing most variants immediately come to mind. Both are in the National Library of Scotland in Edinburgh, mss Adv. 18.2.13A and B.

3 *Synecdoche*: unless we can establish that the part really does represent the whole, comparisons of only a single tune, or even a single office, or even a single section of a book can only hint at wider affinities, since individual elements may have been copied from different exemplars. In the case of early printed liturgical books whole sections – the complete Psalter, for instance – may be reprinted in an otherwise new edition.

4 *Influence.* Using comparison, we may wish to assert the direction of influence. Scholars of early chant have provided reams of evidence demonstrating reciprocal interchange between Rome and Gaul. Reliable demonstration of direction – ancestry or descent – requires a dating of the sources more accurate than is normally the case for most liturgical books.

5 *Stemma.* James Grier, whose book has already been mentioned, has provided the most thorough and comprehensive introduction to this topic for musical scholars.[23] To construct a reliable stemma – a filiation of the sources with the common intention of arriving at an archetype – will be the least feasible of the options for any medieval music, except possibly for a very limited number of sources that can be securely dated and related. Few such collections come to mind. We would need to work with a coherent

---

[22]Grier, *Critical Editing*, p. 5.

[23]*Ibid.*, p. 69, n. 9, lists other useful texts.

group of sources derived from the same place of use over several years. Generally, far too many sources are missing. Owain Tudor Edwards has estimated that only 0.17 per cent of Sarum Antiphonals that existed at the time of the sixteenth-century Reformation now survive.[24]

Of those manuscripts that do survive, even if they can be situated reliably within a liturgical Use – manuscripts of Orders such as the Dominicans, Franciscans, or Cistercians come to mind – locating them within specific institutions may be difficult.

Contamination

The problem of contamination arises with respect to directional relationships and any attempt to construct a filiation.[25] All scholars who have compared texts know that some criteria will lead to the conclusion that source A descends from B, others will suggest the reverse, indicating that some back and forth process of copying may have occurred. With respect to liturgical books, we simply do not know how notators (or scribes in general) copied: was it the same kind of process as is well established for a literary book or a manuscript with continuous text? We may suspect that many sections of liturgical books were copied from libelli, or even piecemeal by individual items, using several exemplars, and even from reference books such as Tonaries that were not for practical use in choir. In such circumstances, the dangers of contamination are very real.

At the moment, such complexities cannot be taken into account in general or on any rational basis, although in individual cases we may have enough facts to make tentative conclusions possible.

Date, place, and purpose

Numerous matters complicate all of these approaches. The difficulty of dating is perhaps one of the most pressing. Because liturgical books are very conservative, dating by script may be quite misleading. Illuminations are probably more reliable. John Haines has very sensibly chosen, as a starting point for his Nota quadrata investigation into late medieval square notation, to assemble a list of musical manuscripts whose dates can be established firmly from direct evidence, in a parallel to the various *manuscrits datés* publications of the past decades, only one of which even refers to music.[26]

---

[24] Owain Edwards, 'How Many Sarum Antiphonals Were There in England and Wales in the Middle of the Sixteenth Century?', *RB* 99 (1989), pp. 155–180.

[25] Grier, *Critical Editing*, pp. 74–5.

[26] Andrew G. Watson, ed., *Catalogue of Dated and Datable Manuscripts in Oxford Libraries* (Oxford, 1984), no subject index; Charles Samaran and Robert Marichal, eds,

Another factor is our almost complete lack of information as to when – or rather, how frequently – liturgical manuscripts were revised. Although we know when certain Uses were revised, such as Sarum in the early fourteenth century, we have no sense, for this Use and for most liturgical manuscripts generally, how long it took a scribe to copy a big and complex book such as a noted breviary. Are estimates from other kinds of book, often much simpler in content, to be trusted? The frequent presence of *ad hoc* additions on blank leaves or appended gatherings for offices such as Corpus Christi or newly established saints, and the great expense of copying, suggest that revisions must have been infrequent. Even if revisions were made once for each generation, and a single link is missing, we are faced with sources that may be separated by almost a century. Tastes, notations, modal preferences, the style and extent of melismas, and any number of other things may have changed: injunctions about uniformity and prohibitions of non-canonical items may have been issued. What we perceive as variants or errors may in fact be legitimate revisions.

Authorized revisions, to make books conform to a specific exemplar, as with the Dominican liturgy in the second half of the thirteenth century, or to Roman Use in particular, as at the end of that century, or to specific musical 'rules', as with Cistercian chant in the twelfth century, may have resulted in the destruction of non-conforming books. Those that survive may give us the false impression that uniformity was more common than was in fact the case. The apparent remarkable uniformity of early melodies in 'the earliest notated manuscripts ... despite the difference in neumatic script' is interesting.[27] It suggests either that the scribes were more careful with the musical notation than is probably true of any later repertory, or that there is something about the repertory that we still do not fully understand, or that only sources accurate and conforming to the canon were allowed to survive. We know that other non-canonical liturgical material was destroyed. Does what survives of chant exist because it conforms?

For too many sources, for example, we have no secure knowledge of whether they were used in choir, for the body of singers or a special *schola* or for a soloist, or for reference, or simply for transmission itself. Each of those circumstances may affect our knowledge of the places associated with the book and the reliability of its contents. Nevertheless, for every book used for comparison, we should try to distinguish the place of use from the liturgical Use and, if possible, from the place of writing. The provenance (a singularly ambiguous term, used here to mean only the general history

Catalogue des manuscrits en écriture latine portant des indications de date ... , 7 vols (Paris, 1959–1984), no subject index; Marie A. C. Mazzoli *et al.*, eds, *I manoscritti datati della provincia di Trento* (Florence, 1996), no subject index; François Masai *et al.*, eds, *Manuscrits datés conservés en Belgiques*, 6 vols (Brussels, 1968), subject index refers to music, with simply the abbreviation 'mus.' in the ms descriptions; Viviana Jemolo, ed., *Biblioteca nazionale centrale di Roma in catalogo dei manoscritti in scrittura latina datati e databili 1* (Turin, 1971), no subject index; Gerard I. Lieftinck, ed., *Manuscrits datés conservés dans les Pays-Bas*, 2 vols (Amsterdam, 1964), no relevant index.

[27] Alejandro E. Planchart, 'Old Wine in New Bottles', in *FS Hucke*, pp. 41–64.

of the book) will be useful only to establish whether there were later places of use, or revisions for Uses, other than the original.

Error, variant, revision

No scribe copies with one hundred per cent accuracy. Ways of ascertaining the accuracy of a scribe are well known. Some of them transfer easily to notators. Surely, before speaking about variants, we must try to establish some criteria for judging the accuracy of a notator. Other than using the material to investigate the types of errors and causes themselves, there seems little point in analysing differences in an obviously faulty witness as variants: they may be errors. Although provided with a grammar and a syntax, music, of course, lacks semantic meaning. The lack of this check available with texts is at its most severe with plainsong, lacking in harmony and regular metre.

What features can we use? To some of the following questions, which may have to be asked for each item compared, there are uncertain or even at present no answers.

a) What are the first places associated with, and what is the later provenance of, the sources? Naturally, in a preliminary stage any comparison should start with a battery of codicological questions about every source used: its date, its place of origin, its place of use, its liturgical Use. To include the comprehensive details listed by Grier will rarely be possible:[28] even if such things are securely known (rarely the case for liturgical books), the apparatus of documentation may be overwhelming, a point to be raised again below.

b) Is the manuscript neat? Neatness does not, of course, confer accuracy. Rather, we might ask: is the manuscript obviously careless?

c) Are textual scribe and notator equally neat? Is there any evidence they are the same person? Does the ink differ?

d) Are there helpful intersections between the ink or paint of text, chant, stave, and any illuminations? Could such paleographical matters help to establish whether the notator was placing his notes to avoid collisions with existing material?

e) Does the notator consistently place his notes high or low on the stave-line or -space?

f) Is there anything in the plainchant that looks odd? One phrase in the chant I plan to analyse for the companion article has always engaged my curiosity. Although not extreme, it is apparent to the eye and perhaps to the ear but will be much less so in any encoding:

---

[28]Grier, *Critical Editing*, Appendix C.

Example 18.3: Vespers 1, Magnificat antiphon, *Pastor cesus*, mode 1 (base)

... cru- o- ris   pre-   ci-   o   o   le- tus do- lor   in ...

Encoding: ... *cruoris.3.4.321 precio.23.21.1'5764'5345 letus.1.3 dolor.43.21 in.0* ...

Yet a sudden and seemingly inexplicable shift out of the surrounding range is not without reason in some cases.[29]

g)   Are there transpositions by a third? This most obvious of musical errors, and one of the easiest to make, results from writing the notes on stave-lines and -spaces adjacent to the correct ones. The out-of-range result produced by this error, though, is not necessarily immediately evident to the eye, although faulty intervals and articulations on wrong pitches may make it evident to the ear. Semitones and intervals such as tritones in unacceptable modal positions usually make it clear that this transposition is an error. When such signs are lacking – for a very short motive, say – it may not be easy to establish which version is correct and which made by error: possibly, indeed, both may be 'correct' if each is established by a large number of witnesses. Only a comparison with a base version known or taken to be correct may reveal the matter. I will have more to say about base versions, and the counting that may be necessary to establish valid readings.

h)   Other transpositions may present similar difficulties.[30] Does the plainsong end on a pitch not one of the normal Finals? Some transpositions seem to work modally: a tune in the F mode, for example, with a flat in the signature, may when transposed up a fifth retain the flat so that the contours of the melody and flavour of the pitch *b* are preserved, but not the position of the semitone. Transposition by a second is puzzling, suggesting that the tune may have been copied from a notation insecure as to pitch (there are plenty of such sources, even in the later Middle Ages), or from a faulty performance, or to resolve modal difficulties. But once again, which of the two versions is correct may have to be established by numerical or stylistic means.

i)   Was the book originally designed to accommodate music? To this question the answer is clearly no if the lines are too close together to accommodate

---

[29]See page 43 and plate 5 in my article 'Literary Transformation in Post-Carolingian Saints' Offices: Using All the Evidence', in Sandro Sticca, ed., *Saints: Studies in Hagiography*, Medieval and Renaissance Texts and Studies (Binghamton, 1995), pp. 23–50.

[30]Grier, *Critical Editing*, pp. 131–132 and Examples 4-9 and 4-10.

even unheighted neumes. If the answer seems to be yes, was the book prepared by a knowledgeable and careful designer? We have all seen early manuscripts in which the neumes extend well beyond the writing area into the margin, and often curve upwards to accommodate more than the margin can hold. What conclusions can such a practice offer? That the designer or scribe knew there was to be music, but not the extent of the music itself? That the notator knew a different, more elaborate version than the scribe? ... knew an old version in which melismas were preserved? ... or, especially in the case of very early repertories, knew a version that incorporated the new style of melismatic *melodiae*? ... that the notator indulged in creative initiative?

j)   Is the spacing of musical symbols regular and consistent? Quite difficult to observe are subtle squeezings and spacings of the notation to allow for a designer or a textual scribe who left too little or too much space for the music. Melismas and cadences and the ends of lines are places to observe.

k)   Is there evidence of scribal initiative? Because of the fewer semantic and linguistic constraints, the notator may have more flexibility, at least with new plainsongs for the Office. In Example 18.3, for example, the scribe may have heard something rather different from what he wrote, and exercised some discretion from an expert knowledge of music theory, a matter to be explored in the companion article.

l)   Does the book show signs of use? If it has thumbtags, a very practical addition, do these indicate use in choir or in a reference context? Are there corrections? In the same hand and ink? An obviously later hand or ink could indicate revisions rather than errors.

m) Are there erasures or expunctuations or other of the conventional signs of correction? Some books were certainly proofread, and that process may be specifically acknowledged.

n)   Does anything suggest oral rather than written transmission (e.g., was the book written from dictation)? It may not be possible to distinguish between this practice and one in which the notator wrote from memory. Textually, a literate and careful scribe is unlikely to write *missus aroma* when hearing *missus a Roma*.[31] Such a fault might suggest oral transmission to a casual scribe who did not recognize the error, and a book not proofread or well used. Can circumstances be found for plainsong to parallel such textual conditions?

o)   Working from dictation and even more so when working from memory, a notator, mishearing or misremembering, has choices, mostly quite limited. Between a *d* and a *g*, for instance, he may write an *e* or an *f*. The chances of one or the other appearing seem to me to be 50:50. The result may be a trivial variant, but the value and causes of such differences have to be

---

[31] Such a passage occurs in the versified office printed in AH 45, no. 13.

weighed. Similarly with a poorly performed leap from *e* to *g*: is there an intervening *f*? Does the reverberance of the chamber in which the singing takes place have any bearing? Any scribe working from dictation must be subject to the performance skills of the singer(s).

p) Is the nationality of the singers likely to affect the melody? Differences in pronunciation and accent, articulation and punctuation, and the position of clusters of consonants or diphthongs, conventionally associated with plicas, might well affect the character of ornamentation, if not the main pitches of a plainsong.[32]

Complicating all of these purposes, of course, is a single feature that, in fact, may confound every analysis. Plainchant is a living repertory.[33] Dead, traditional, or sacrosanct texts such as the Classics, Boethius, the Church Fathers, or the Bible are written and, for the most part, stable, not subject to the performers' preferences or mistakes. They are also texts for reading or speaking, not subject to the limitations and ranges of the singing voice. How many tunes were varied simply because a local choir was unable satisfactorily to sing them? Parish churches, required to have the full set of liturgical books, including antiphonals and graduals, could surely not have had singers competent to sing really complex plainsongs correctly. How many major institutions would have been able to set aside a special body of singers with time to rehearse chants? It may be true that resident clerics sang plainsong every day and for much of the day. But some chants are sung only once a year; others, especially when newly composed, are unfamiliar. How many tunes of the later non-canonical repertory are varied because unfamiliar tunes were brought into line with conservative taste? In the Becket office, for reasons that are unclear at the moment, manuscripts now in Trier provide, for some of the usual tunes, different and equally new melodies. If local cantors had such licence for complete items, why not for individual motives within melodies?

Counting

Many published comparisons are simply lists of the witnesses without ranking their value. But by judging the frequency of particular occurrences, the preferred version might be derived. That result, or in very optimistic cases an archetypal version, is occasionally a stated or implied aim. Several reservations may be entered to this process. The numerical preponderance of a particular variant, especially if associated with a short melodic motive, has to be weighed for significance against the context, in

---

[32]See Timothy J. McGee, A. George Rigg, and David N. Klausner, eds, *Singing Early Music: The Pronunciation of European Languages in the Late Middle Ages and Renaissance*, Music Scholarship and Performance (Bloomington, IN, 1996); see also Cowdery, *Melodic Tradition*, p. 34.

[33]Grier, *Critical Editing*, pp. 68–9.

which other motives may have different values. In other words, the parts have to be weighed against the whole, and individual parts may conflict. It is unclear how this problem can be resolved and described in narrative that is transparent to the reader, even if comprehensible to the researcher.

Given the rather limited melodic possibilities for plainsong – predominantly stepwise movement, with a tendency to counter movement in one direction by movement in another – what are the probabilities that variants occur simply by chance? In these circumstances, it may be rather easy for 'two scribes to make the same error independently'.[34] What are the chances that the *same* variant is found in the *same* place in a sample of chants, compared with the population from which the sample is taken? What are the criteria for choosing the sample? How does the loss of so many sources affect the issue? For reliable results, and to overwhelm the possibility of chance or coincidental resemblances or differences, a very substantial number of comparisons may be required from witnesses produced in corresponding circumstances.

But as we have seen, the more witnesses are used, the more troublesome is the presentation of the evidence. I sense that proper statistical methods might need to be employed: even after some investigation and several enquiries, I have no idea how they might be applied.

Despite these reservations, which may be the result of theorizing, in practice one can usually arrive at an acceptable version. That version will probably be a conflation, not generally now regarded as appropriate for an edition. It may, however, be useful for the base version.

The base version

A base does not have to be accurate. It is simply a universal measure against which differences can be recorded. The more closely the base resembles the version that emerges from a consensus of the sources, however, the fewer differences will have to be noted. A conflation using at each point the version provided by the majority of witnesses would be ideal. The result of that compilation would be a hypothetical text that depends on the 'editor's critical understanding of the work'.[35] But to determine what the majority of witnesses deliver – what the consensus is – the sources have to be compared against each other and the differences tabulated and counted, a process that is the object of the exercise. That process is obviously circular. The task of comparing versions should perhaps be delayed until the scholar has examined the material in sufficient detail and is already in a position to know, without statistical confirmation, which versions are at least reliable.

---

[34] *Ibid.*, p. 65.
[35] *Ibid.*

Methods

Here are some categories of variants that might be examined, with some practical suggestions as to how they might be represented for electronic searches. Few of the categories are entirely unambiguous. I record each of these categories in a database, so that flexible rearrangements, grouping, and counting can be carried out.

It is not necessary to lay out the full details, but to simplify the description of the categories some information may be useful. For each of the types described, it is useful to assign a single character. Mnemonic symbols are convenient, and upper- and lowercase letters allow two related variants to be brought together in electronic searches, which typically find both cases when lower case is specified. Uppercase letters typically refer to added, or longer, or more emphatic elements, and lowercase to the opposite. The characters I use are bolded. The symbols here, for reasons which will become obvious, are not those of the encoding, an unfortunate but unavoidable circumstance. No approach can possibly cover every situation.

General

1) Motives identical to the melodyword, the principal focus of the details to be recorded, need no symbol, but a positive indication that a comparison has been made is useful. The symbol = is appropriate.
2) When material is obscured, as in erasures or when in the gutter, a ? may be used, or appended to any of the symbols.
3) The usual symbols [ ] can note omissions in the manuscript, with a bold **i** for illegible **[i]** where necessary.
4) Often, too, pitch symbols sit a little high or low on the line (less often in the space). I mostly use a ? for this category, too, although **U** for 'move pitch up to produce what is recorded', and **u** for the opposite might be considered.

Category 1   This category deals with variants that, except for one or two strictly limited types, do not affect the sequence of pitches, the melody itself, although they may affect the performance result. For the most part, of course, they involve notation.

1a   *repeated pitches*

i)   When tunes are adapted to different texts, where there are fewer or more syllables, identical pitches may be omitted or repeated, often on the reciting pitch or Final of the mode. To signify such variants an **R** seems appropriate when more pitches are present, and **r** when fewer.

ii)   A very common variant is the omission or addition of repercussive pitches, that is, a repeated pitch not articulated with a separate syllable. As noted above, repercussive pitches in the encoding are marked with =. This symbol not being available in upper- and lowercase, a letter was chosen. Assuming that repercussive pitches are held without articulation, I use **H** (held) for the addition, and **h** for the omission of such pitches.

Example 18.4: Matins responsory 1, *Studens livor*, mode 1 (base, and Germany, Erfurt, Amploniana (Wissenschaftliche Allgemein-Bibliothek der Stadt) ms 44, fol. 29ᵛ)

... pri- vi-   le-   gi- o.

(See also Example 18.9.)

1b *plicas*

Another common variant is the hardening of plicas (**P**) into full pitches, or vice versa (**p**). Occasionally a plica is added where none is in the base, or is omitted altogether. For these features, a comma (**,**) (paralleling the symbol in the encoding) and a dot ꝫ (encircled for clarity in handwriting: the plica comma minus its hook) or 0, zero, seem appropriate.

Example 18.5: Lauds antiphon 1, *Granum cadit*, mode 1 (France, Metz, BM ms 461, fol. 132ᵛ)

Gra- num ca- dit ...

The base has no plica: should the plica pitch be *e*? This plica is particularly interesting since it decorates a nasal consonant cluster split between two words.

Example 18.6: Matins antiphon 8, *Strictis Thomas ensibus*, mode 8 (base, and Germany, Trier, Bistumsarchiv ms 480, p. 331)

... en-   si-   bus ...

Is the first *g* sung ornamentally in the Trier manuscript, by observing the nasal consonant cluster in the text?

1c *new lines, pages, or columns*

The slash / or double slashes // are a common symbol for such occurrences: within the melodyword the symbols will have to be added at the appropriate point, e.g. *123.1/2.32.1.*

Example 18.7: Matins invitatory, *Assunt Thome*, mode 2 (base, and Germany, Trier, Bistumsarchiv ms 480, p. 328)

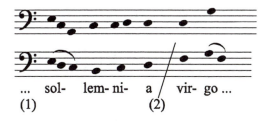

Is the new line responsible for this variant: the *f* perhaps an error by transposition of a third?

1d *ligatures and neumes*

The letter **l** or **n** signifies ligatures or neumes that are interestingly different from the base. In practice only that fact can be recorded: additional details must be gained from direct inspection of the notation.

1e *dialects*

The exchange of *e* and *f* or *b* and *c* in certain dialects of plainsong is well known, if not systematically documented. The letter **d** signifies differences from the base version.

1f *accidentals and clefs*

Accidentals often act as clefs. The precise position of these symbols, denoted by **a** and **^** respectively, needs to be shown in the melodyword. The accidental is almost never used except to mark a *b* as flat or natural, and other instances will need to be flagged, perhaps with a **!** for 'odd: investigate'. Clefs are specified further, using the pitch-letter and line or space, thus: ^c4 or ^f4 & c2 or ^b2. Summaries with the end-of-line symbols, accidentals and clefs concatenated give a quick indication that a notator is competent. The series ^f3//////// would signify a very long piece for which a single clef was suitable, whereas ^f3/^f4^f3a/^c4/a/^f3/ would signify several changes of clef and accidentals (clefs), many probably not necessary.

1g *text underlay*

   i) the letter **s** marks the distribution of syllables under the melodyword when distinctly different from that of the base, a circumstance ascertainable only when the underlay is really clear, something that is not always the case.[36]

   ii) when the distribution is different as a result of an adjustment of repercussive pitches, uppercase **S** is useful. See Example 18.4.

1h *word distribution*

The system described here works by chantwords. Occasionally, however, the distribution of words with respect to the melody differs. Thus, the base may have *Dominus.1.2.324321 Deus.0.1* and the variant *Dominus.1.2.32 Deus.4321.01*. This would attract a **w** for the first chantword an uppercase **W** (longer) for the second. See Example 18.13.

Category 2   In the second category, the melody is distinctly different from the base, but still recognizable as the same. Some judgement is required here, of course.

2a *exchanged pitches*

I limit the exchange to a maximum of two pitches (single pitches exchanged), using **x**. Thus *Dominus.1.32.1* and *1.23.1*. Larger exchanges, such as *1.3201* and *1.0132*, a more substantial variant, would require some other specification.

Example 18.8: Lauds antiphon 2, *Totus orbis martyris*, mode 2 (base, and Germany, Trier, Bistumsarchiv ms 480, p. 332)

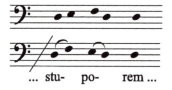

... stu-   po-   rem ...

2b *transposition (up or down)*

   i) *by a step*: the letter **t** specifies a maximum of two pitches transposed up or down by one step and **T** a longer segment.

---

[36]See Cowdery, *Melodic Tradition*, p. 34.

Example 18.9: Vespers 1 Magnificat antiphon, *Pastor cesus*, mode 1 (base, and
Germany, Trier, Bistumsarchiv ms 495, fol. 237^V)

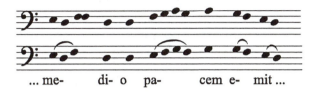

... me-   di- o   pa-   cem e-   mit ...

ii) *by a third*: this most common error attracts the letter **e**.

2c *additional or omitted pitches (including filled-in 3rds and 4ths)*

    i) for a maximum of two consecutive pitches the symbols > (greater than) and
< (less than) suffice. If both should be relevant for the same melodyword,
an alternative specification might be preferred, such as **v**.

    ii) for more than two consecutive pitches, as when a fifth is filled in or
reduced, the letter **f** works.

    iii) additional phrases: if the whole contour is present with an inserted,
appended, or prepended phrase, or if the variant lacks a complete phrase
present in the base, the symbols + and – serve. The phrase could be as short
as three pitches, the next step up from < and >.

2d *dittography*

Motives immediately repeated, or omitted where present, attract the symbol ".

2e *other variants*

    i) melodywords that use only the same pitches, but jumbled: **j**. The uppercase
J may serve when beginning and end pitches are identical, as with this
example from the Thomas office:

Example 18.10: Lauds antiphon 3, *Totus orbis martyris*, mode 3 (base, and
Scotland, Edinburgh, National Library ms Adv. 18.2.13.A, fol. 43)

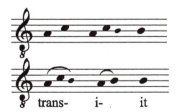

trans-   i- .   it

Is it possible here that the notator has anticipated one motive as a result of eyeskip, then replaced the *c* with a *b* because it made a recognizable cadential motive? Or is the base version wrong, because the plica ought to sit above the nasal cluster? Or does the plica decorate the double vowel? The weight of evidence here favours the base version.

ii) variants: miscellaneous indescribable variants within a clearly similar melodic contour: **v**.

Example 18.11: Vespers 1 Magnificat antiphon, *Pastor cesus*, mode 1 (base, and Germany, Trier, Bistumsarchiv ms 486, fol. 261 and ms 501a, fol. 212)

... in tri- sti gau- di-   o grex re- spi- rat ...

iii) other: this category, for which **o** may be used, is a catch-all for substantially different melodic contours within a context recognizable as close to the base.

Example 18.12: Vespers 2, Magnificat antiphon, *Felix locus*, mode 1 (base, and Germany, Trier, Bistumsarchiv ms 480, p. 333. Ms has *exulem* for base *presulem*)

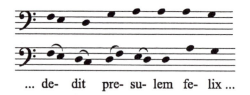

... de- dit   pre- su- lem fe- lix ...

Category 3   Here the melody as a whole, or a substantial segment within the same melody, differs from the base.

3a *partial*

Some complete phrases are identical, and others are similar, and others differ completely. Ex. 2:3 on page 43 of my *Style and Symbol* shows such a case. See note 14.

3b *modal*

The tune or segment is obviously different but in the same mode (**m**), and using some of the same formulas.

3c *different*

Not equal: #.

A complete example:

Example 18.13: Matins invitatory, *Assunt Thome* (base, and France, Bayeux, BM ms 73, fol. 18ᵛ. Slashes show new lines; asterisks points of variants)

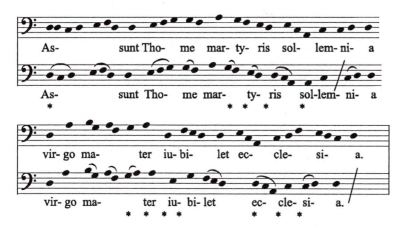

The encoding with the summary codes would be:

text	base	variant	code	comment
Assunt	1=01'231.1	101'231.1	'h	repercussive pitch omitted
Thome	234.43		=	
martyris	5.43.21	543.21.10*	sWt	syllable setting differs: material borrowed from next melodyword with one pitch transposed
sollemnia	20*.0.01.1	*.0./01.1	w/	w compensates for W in previous melodyword. Is the new line after the second syllable responsible?
virgo	1.5		=	
mater	64534.5	645345.5	>	one extra pitch (which should be highlighted in the handwritten copy)
iubilet	1.321.1	2.4.321	v	varied (some pitches recognizable)

ecclesia   20*.013.210.1   10*.0.01.1/   o/   much shortened, perhaps because of
the new line at the end. The cadence
on 'sollemnia' is imitated.

Conclusions

Fully to implement all the recommendations I suggest here, as with those advocated by Grier, requires an effort beyond the time, energy, and patience of many scholars, and some aspects will require learning a whole set of complex skills, paleographical or technological. Ideally, the purposes outlined above should be supported by every one of the recommendations. Some, however, must be set aside until we have far more secure information (e.g. about pronunciation, its effect on music, and the purpose of particular manuscripts). This information may be hidden in the dense prose of books that have no obvious or immediate bearing on plainsong – Chronicles, Customaries, Records of Visitations, and other such books that exist in large quantities. Very few musicologists can economically examine thousands of sentences for the one that is relevant. We have to rely on the scholars of such material who, in general, are notably unhelpful about such matters.

Some of the recommendations must be taken into account with any comparison. A stemma should require every one. To be entirely convincing, so should the grouping of sources and the elucidation of influence. Some useful information for these two purposes, however, can be obtained without the full panoply of textual, pitch, and notational analysis.

But these gloomy prospects should not deter exercises in the topic. We have so little information about many matters that the systematic collection of a few pieces of data alone would be useful. Significant results may ensue from just the counting of variants, even out of their larger melodic context. Here are some sample questions for which the investigation of individual categories of variants might lead to a fuller understanding:

- Are variants, or errors, or certain categories of them, related to the mode?

- ... to the genre?

- ... to the liturgical occasion?

- Are plicas limited to certain pitches of the mode?

- Does the splitting of words over lines or wrapped to the end of a subsequent line affect notation?

- Are certain aspects of performance, e.g. plicas and repercussives, implied and understood as a local tradition even when not visible in the notation?

- What is implied by changes in the notation that do not affect the melody?

- Are clef changes necessary, and what is the significance of unnecessary repetitions of the same clef?

- Do clefs or accidentals in irrational places within the line possibly suggest where new lines were in the exemplar from which the copy was made?

- How do singers interpret unheighted neumes, whose newly composed melody – e.g. those in some manuscripts of the Becket office – cannot be in their memories?

- Why are certain tunes, normal in the majority of sources, replaced entirely in a few?

- Are certain words more likely to attract variants or errors? Are they insignificant words?

- Are there regional preferences, other than the well-known dialect difference regarding semitones?

Preliminary investigation, counting, and analysis of the data already accumulated for the Becket chants are encouraging. Finding some answers to the apparently trivial questions about chant may make it easier to ask the right ones about the larger and more general issues.

Chapter 19

Notker in Aquitaine

Alejandro Enrique Planchart

When I was still young, and very long melodies – repeatedly entrusted to memory – escaped from my poor little head, I began to reason with myself how I could bind them fast. In the meantime it happened that a certain priest from Jumièges (recently laid waste by the Normans) came to us, bringing with him an antiphonary, in which some verses were set to the sequences; but they were in a very corrupt state. Upon closer inspection I was as bitterly disappointed in them as I had been delighted at first glance.

Nevertheless, in imitation of them I began to write *Laudes deo concinat orbis universus, qui gratis est redemptus*, and further on *coluber Adae deceptor*. When I took these lines to my teacher Iso, he, commending my industry while taking pity on my lack of experience, praised what was pleasing, and what was not he set out to improve, saying, 'The individual motions of the melody should receive separate syllables.'[1]

Thus Notker, monk of St Gall, writing around 880 to Liutward, bishop of Vercelli, in the dedicatory letter that precedes what he called a *Liber hymnorum*, a 'Book of Hymns'. The *Liber* is a collection of Notker's pieces that correspond to the 'verses to the sequences' brought by the monk of Jumièges to St Gall. These verses were called *prosae* by the mostly anonymous authors who added them. Notker's successors in Germany called them *sequentiae* or sequences, although in the Frankish west, where such compositions appear to have originated, a distinction was made between the melody, which was called *sequentia*, and the words which were called *prosa*.

Concerning the origins of this genre and its relationship to the Gregorian repertory imposed by the Carolingian rulers on their realm in the century after the meeting of King Pepin and Pope Stephen II in 754, as well as to the repertories of Gallican chant sung in Francia before the advent of Gregorian chant, it may be useful to recall that by 800 Gregorian chant was itself a very new repertory, less than half a century old, and that, according to the recent work of Kenneth Levy, a good deal of it, particularly the offertories of the mass, was laced with melodies derived from the Gallican tradition.[2]

---

[1]Notker, *Prooemium* to his *Liber hymnorum*. Latin text in Wolfram von den Steinen, *Notker der Dichter und seine geistige Welt*, 2 vols (Bern, 1948), vol. 2, pp. 8–10, 160. English translation in Richard Crocker, *The Early Medieval Sequence* (Berkeley, 1977), pp. 1–2.

[2]Kenneth Levy, *Gregorian Chant and the Carolingians* (Princeton, 1998); 'A New Look at Old Roman Chant', *EMH* 19 and 20 (2000), pp. 81–104, 173–197.

Scholars have long noted that what might be the earliest mention of the new 'post Gregorian' genres comes from Amalarius of Metz, writing in the 830s, who mentions 'haec iubilatio quam sequentiam vocant'.[3] By 848 the Council of Meaux sought to stamp out some of these innovations with the following decree:

> On account of the thoroughly damnable depravity of those who, delighted with novelty, fear not to interpolate their fancies into the purity of the old uses, we declare that no clerk and no monk should presume to add, interpose, recite, mumble, or sing those compositions called proses or other such fabrications in the Angelic Hymn, that is, 'Gloria in excelsis deo,' or in the sequences that are often sung in the solemn alleluia. Where this is done let [the practice] be abandoned.[4]

A notable aspect of this decree is that it tacitly places the *sequentiae* among the 'old uses', and condemns only the proses and newer items: the additions to the Gloria, that is, Gloria tropes. These are precisely the kinds of compositions that turn up, together with a few introit tropes, in the earliest collections that transmit the new genres.[5] The council of Meaux was as effective in this endeavour as King Canute was in turning the tide; tropes and proses proliferated for the next two hundred years, and if the tropes for the most part fell into disuse in the course of the thirteenth and fourteenth centuries, new proses continued to be composed, and numbered in the tens of thousands at the time of their official suppression by the Council of Trent. Indeed, the effects of the interdict of the Council of Trent have been overrated. The council fathers allowed four proses to remain in the liturgy: *Victimae paschali laudes* for Easter, *Veni sancte spiritus* for Pentecost, *Lauda Sion salvatorem* for Corpus Christi, and *Dies irae* for the mass of the dead. A fifth, *Stabat mater dolorosa* for the feast of the Sorrows of the BVM, was added in the seventeenth century. But a large number of churches and monasteries kept their own repertory in their liturgy until the nineteenth century and beyond. The seventeenth-century chant books of the Cathedral of Cambrai, used until the French Revolution, included twenty proses,[6] and the same conservatism can be documented in numerous churches in France, Germany, and northern Italy. The proses had their revenge in other ways as well: few liturgical texts are as well known or so

---

[3] Jean-Michel Hanssens, ed., *Amalarii Episcopi opera liturgica omnia*, 3 vols, Studi e Testi 138–140 (Vatican, 1948–1950), vol. 2, p. 304.

[4] 'Propter improbitatem quorundam omnino dampnabilem, qui novitatibus delectati puritatem antiquitatis suis adinventionibus interpolare non metuunt, statuimus ut nullius clericorum nulliusque monachorum in Ymno angelico, id est "Gloria in excelsis deo", et in sequentiis quae in Alleluia sollempniter decantari solent, quaslibet compositiones, quas prosas vocant, vel ulla fictiones addere, interponere, submurmurare aut decantare presumat. Quod si fecerit deponatur.' Cited with a discussion of the authenticity of the source in Gabriel Silagi, 'Vorwort des Herausgebers', in *Liturgische Tropen*, Münchener Beiträge zur Mediävistik und Renaissance Forschung 36 (Munich, 1985), pp. vii–viii.

[5] Munich, BS, clm. 14843, and Verona, BC, ms XC (85), both with tropes and *prosae*; Autun, BM, ms 28 S, and Paris, BNF lat., ms 17436, with *sequentiae* and *prosae*.

[6] Cambrai, BM, ms A 84.

ubiquitous in their musical settings as the *Dies irae*, *Stabat mater*, or *Lauda Sion*, and in the case of the *Dies irae* its opening strains can be heard time and again embedded in violin studies, symphonies, piano concertos, and even Bugs Bunny cartoons. As a poetic and musical genre, proses or sequences eventually had an immense influence in the central and late Middle Ages, giving rise or decisively influencing such genres as the conductus, the carol, the Latin *cantio*, and the German *leise* (and, through it, the chorales of the Reformation), the *lai*, and even the instrumental *estampie*. For example, the *Vida de Santo Domingo de Silos*, by Gonzalo de Berceo (fl. 1220–1240), the earliest Castilian poet known to us by name, begins as follows:

> En el nomne del Padre,   que fiço toda cosa,
> et de don Ihesu Christo,   fijo de la Gloriosa,
> et del Spíritu Sancto   que egal d'ellos posa,
> de un confessor sancto   quiero fer una prosa.
>
> Quiero fer una prosa   en romanz paladino
> en qual suele el pueblo   fablar con so vezino,
> ca non só tan letrado   por fer otro latino,
> bien valdrá, commo creo,   un vaso de bon vino.[7]

This vast repertory of proses and sequences was of enormous importance, influencing the history of music and of literature in the Middle Ages and the early Renaissance. In the nineteenth century, as interest in the Middle Ages reawakened, this repertory came to be recognized as a cultural treasure of a number of European nations. Most of the sequence repertories were uniformly anonymous, and thus it is not surprising that early in the twentieth century Notker's authorship of the sequences ascribed to him in the tradition of St Gall and even the veracity of his story in the letter to Liutward were questioned,[8] to the point that Jacques Handschin had to argue for both the reasonableness and indeed the modesty of Notker's story.[9] Notker's only claim was that he thought he could write better *versus ad sequentias* than what he saw in the antiphonary from Jumièges, not an unreasonable claim from a man whom modern literary scholars can proclaim 'one of the few great poets between the Gospel and Dante, who ... once and still after six hundred years has won a universal validity'.[10] It is also of

---

[7]'In the name of the Father, who made everything, and of Sir Jesus Christ, son of the Glorious Lady, and of the Holy Ghost, who is on a par with them, I want to make a prose about a holy confessor. I want to make a prose in common language [lit: public romance], the one folks use to speak with their neighbours, for I am not so lettered as to do another in Latin, it will be, I think, well worth a glass of good wine.' Brian Dutton, ed., Gonzalo de Berceo, *Obras completas, IV. La vida de Santo Domingo de Silos* (London, 1978), p. 35.

[8]See Clemens Blume's introduction to *Liturgischen Prosen erster Epoche*, AH 53 (Leipzig, 1911).

[9]Jacques Handschin, 'Über Estampie und Sequenz I', *Zeitschrift für Musikwissenschaft* 12 (1929), p. 11 n. 2, and 'Trope, Sequence, and Conductus', in Anselm Hughes, ed., *Early Medieval Music up to 1300*, New Oxford History of Music 3 (London, 1954), p. 148.

[10] Steinen, *Notker*, vol. 1, p. 7.

some interest to note, from Notker's account, that his teacher Iso was already acquaint-ed with the west Frankish tradition that was so new to his young student and able to correct some of the stylistic errors in Notker's first effort.[11]

In any case, Notker's texts show a very different literary sensibility from that of the early proses written west of the Rhine, even when imitating them. Crocker describes the general style of the ninth-century proses and Notker's position within it in the following terms:

> These texts unfolded in vigorous series of free rhetorical periods, cast, in Notker's case, in the sonorous cadences of classical diction, in the case of his West Frankish models, in a more exuberant diction rich in with assonance. In either case, the texts were in prose.

The difference in diction and approach can be experienced more easily by direct contact with the works than by explanation, although the bulk of Crocker's study is a detailed comparison of Notker's pieces with their West Frankish models, particularly in terms of structural changes that Notker made in order to adapt the models to his own rhetorical vision. My concern at this point is not with the changes Notker made but with the nature of the poetic imagery, the sense of structure, and rhetoric on both sides of the Rhine. For this we may turn to some examples.

My first example, *Celebranda*, is one of the grandest of the West Frankish proses, which I give preceded by its *sequentia* (see Examples 19.1 and 19.2). The melody may be as old as those used by Notker, although its oldest source dates from 923–936.[12] It is likely, however, that Notker never came across this melody, for his models were from the north of France, and none of the proses based on this melody was apparently known outside Aquitaine and Spain.[13] Further, the melody is one of a small number of *sequentiae* where the purely melismatic flow is interrupted a number of times by fragments of metric verse that were eventually incorporated into the text of every prose set to it, and Notker would not have countenanced such an intrusion.[14] But

---

[11]Iso's point stressed the syllabic setting of the texts. Notker's account continues as follows: 'Hearing that I immediately corrected those which fell under *ia*; those under *le* or *lu*, however, I left as too difficult; but later, with practice, I managed it easily'; Crocker, *Early Medieval Sequence*, p. 1. Still, the East Frankish settings of *sequentiae* and even more the Italian ones, often written under the spell of the German tradition, proved always more hospitable to oc-casional multi-note neumes and small melismas than the West Frankish settings.

[12]PaN 1240, fol. 47^r–47^v (text only), PaN 1084, fol. 243^r (text and music).

[13]See Guido Maria Dreves, *Prosarium lemovicence: Die Prosen der Abtei St Martial*, AH 7 (Leipzig, 1889; reprinted New York, 1961), nos 15, 20, 24, 27, and 29, and the notes to no. 21 in AH 53.

[14]There are less than a dozen such partially texted *sequentia* in the surviving sources. Their origins and *raison d'être* remain unclear; the only extended study of them is Bruno Stäblein, 'Zur Frühgeschichte der Sequenz', *AMw* 18 (1961), pp. 1–33, but see also my 'An Aquitanian Sequentia in Italian Sources', in Wulf Arlt and Gunilla Björkvall, eds, *Recherches nouvelles sur les tropes liturgiques* (Stockholm, 1993), pp. 371–393, where I show that some of these *sequen-tiae* go back to the middle of the ninth century.

Celebranda is in many ways the epitome of the West Frankish and even more the Aquitanian taste in such works.

Example 19.1: *Sequentia* for the prose *Celebranda*, (Paris, Bibliothèque Nationale de France, *fonds latin*, 1118, fols 132ᵛ–133ʳ)

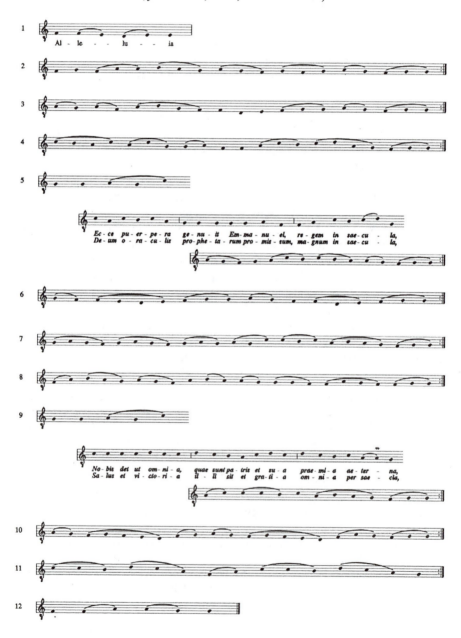

Example 19.2: Prose *Celebranda* (Paris, Bibliothèque Nationale, *fonds latin*, 1118, fols 151^r–152^v)

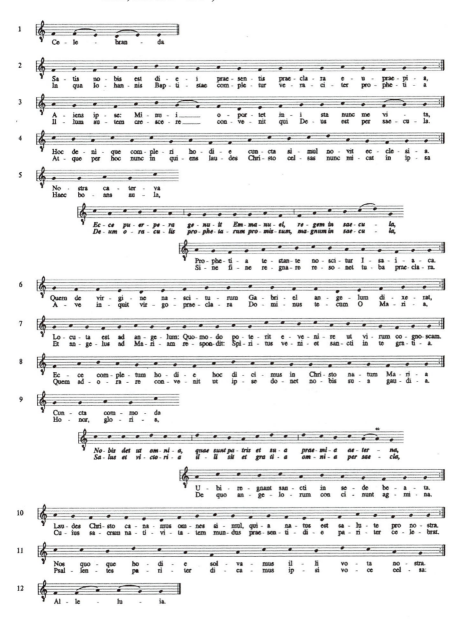

Translation of *Celebranda satis nobis*[15]

1	Celebrate
2a	We must the glorious excellence[16] of the present day,[17]
2b	On which the prophecy of John the Baptist is truly accomplished.
3a	Saying in person: 'It is meet that I should diminish now in this life,
3b	But it is right that he should grow who is God throughout all ages.'
4a	That this is being fulfilled[18] today the whole church together knows
4b	And it is for this that, uttering lofty praises to Christ, in it [the church] now
5a	our congregation shines forth:

> **Behold, she who laboured gave birth to Emmanuel, the King for ever,**
>> As known from the witness of Isaiah's prophecy.

5b	May this hall, shouting that

> **The God promised by the oracles of the prophets, great for ever,**
>> reigns for ever, resound to the clear trumpet

6a	Of whom the angel Gabriel had said that he was to be born of a virgin
6b	'Hail', he said, 'O illustrious Virgin, the Lord be with you, O Mary.'
7a	She spoke to the angel: 'How this may be, that I may know a man?'
7b	And the Angel answered Mary: 'The grace of the Holy Ghost shall come upon you.'
8a	Behold, we say, this is accomplished today in Christ born of Mary.
8b	Whom it is meet to worship that he may bestow his joys upon us.
9a	All good things

> **May he grant us, us all that is his father's and eternal rewards**
>> Where the saints reign in the blessed throne.

9b	Honour, glory,

> **Salvation and victory be to him, and grace for all time**
>> About which the angels sing their songs.

10a	Let us all sing praises to Christ, since he was born for our salvation.
10b	Whose holy birth the whole world celebrates together on this day.
11a	Let us too today fulfil to him our vows
11b	Singing psalms, let us together say to him with a loud voice:
12	Alleluia!

---

[15] I gratefully acknowledge the assistance of Leofranc Holford-Strevens with this translation.

[16] *Eujprevpeia*, splendour, excellence.

[17] The differences between Latin and English word order make it virtually impossible to convey the separation of line 1 and line 2a imposed by the music, when the meaning is 'We must celebrate ...'. Still, here I use as a linguistic precedent the famous slogan of New York's Consolidated Edison: 'Dig we must'.

[18] *Denique* has the force of 'that it is *this* that is being celebrated'. [LH-S]

The prose tells us, in a slightly rambling manner, the story of the Annunciation, the sayings of John the Baptist, the prophecies of Isaiah, and the birth of Christ, interspersed with short prayers and exclamations of joy and praise, all leading to the final alleluia (see the translation following Example 19.2). Rhetorically the prose resembles nothing so much as some of those wonderful Victorian mansions that still survive in New England, where several generations of owners added a room here, a porch there, and a couple of turrets elsewhere, with an eye more for splendour than for unity, and which yet remain in their overgrown variety magnificently arresting examples of architecture.

Upon this text the preexistent melody of the *sequentia* imposes a sense of unity, and even some symmetry through the constant reiteration of the cadence on G, not only at the end of every line but the first, but also at the end of the metric-verse section in lines 6 and 10. The cadential note, of course, brings out the assonance in all those places, but it goes further, for in lines 2, 3, 4, 5, 8, 9, 10, and 11 it creates a musical rhyme with the extended cadential pattern *a g f g g* – a favourite cadential pattern in many *sequentiae*, often used in them as an approach to both *g* and *d*, but seldom with the single-minded insistence found in *Celebranda*.

One trait found in many of the West Frankish *sequentiae* but not in *Celebranda* is a range shift, often of a fifth up, about halfway through the melody. Some melodies return to the range of the opening at the end, while others remain in the higher range. In *Celebranda* the effect of a range shift is achieved through the music of the two lines with the metric verses. Both of them open with a gesture similar to that of a psalm intonation,[19] aiming in this case at the *c'* above the final, not the *d'*. In the first of the two only the beginning and the end of the music for the metric verses remains in the higher range, while most of the verse is recited on *g*. Still, at the end of the line the music climbs to the highest note of the entire melody, *d'*, before leaping down to *g* at the end of the metric verse, the most dramatic gesture in the entire piece. The music for the second set of metric verses begins with the psalm tone intonation, but this time the recitation of the verse remains in the high range, hitting the high *d'* four times. Even in the midst of the prose text the metric verses stand out musically because of the prominent use of repeated notes, which has been prepared by the use of a psalm-tone intonation at the beginning of the verse. The poet of *Celebranda* underscored these shifts and articulations by using assonance at the end of the intonation in the lines that incorporate the metric verses (which have interior assonance), so that each of those lines has three points of articulation in both the music and the text.

Part of the excitement of the work lies in the manner in which the two strains of text reinterpret through their own accentuation the phrasing of the music. Perhaps the most noticeable examples of this are the end of line six, with the change from 'Prophetia testante noscitur Isaiaca' to 'Sine fine regnare, resonet tuba praeclara', and the end

---

[19]In effect it is a literal quotation of the initium of the eighth-tone intonation for the introit psalms and for the Magnificat.

of line nine, changing from 'hoc dicimus in Christo natum Maria' to 'ut ipse donet nobis sua gaudia'.

For all its rambling nature, the text creates a feeling of a headlong rush – urged on by the exclamations that dot the phrases – to the final alleluia, which despite its shortness is rendered all the more impressive in sound because in all likelihood the entire prose (after the first word) was delivered alternately by the two sides of the choir, both sides joining in the final alleluia.

As may be seen below in Example 19.3, however, this kind of rhetoric appears to be quite foreign to Notker's style; further, the Latinity of the West Frankish *prosatores*, not only in the ninth century but in the tenth and the eleventh as well, sometimes left a good deal to be desired, so one wonders what exactly Notker might have meant by the phrase 'they were in a very corrupt state' (*sed iam tunc nimium vitiati*) when speaking of the proses in the antiphonary that came from Jumièges.

Example 19.3: Notker, *Scalam ad caelos subrectam* (after Crocker, *The Medieval Sequence*)[20]

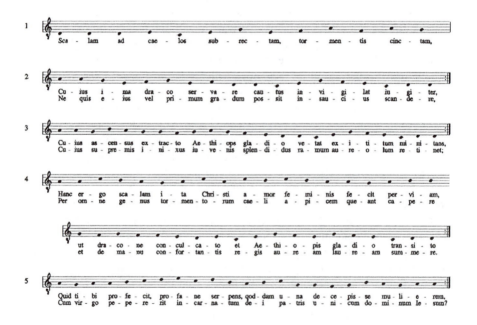

---

[20] There is no critical edition of the music for the Notker sequences. Crocker's transcriptions, based upon the text edition of Steinem, and the manuscript tabulations by Henry Marriott Bannister (Oxford, Bodleian Library, lat. Lit. MSS c 11–15), are at this time the most reliable by far.

Example 19.3, continued

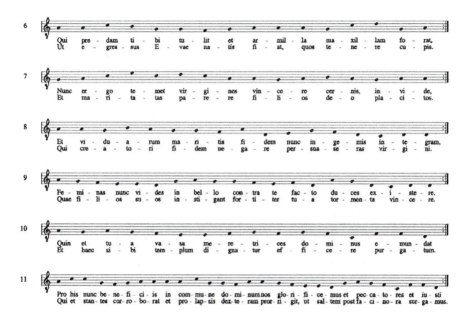

Translation of *Scalam ad caelos subrectam*[21]

1   A ladder stretching up to heaven, circled by torments

2a At whose foot an attentive dragon stands on guard, for ever awake

2b So that no one can climb to the first rung and not be torn

3a The ascent of the ladder barred by an Ethiop, brandishing a drawn sword, threatening death,

3b While over the topmost rung leans a young man, radiant, a golden bough in his hand

4a is the ladder the love of Christ made so free for women that, treading down the dragon and striding past the Ethiop's sword,

4b Way of torments of every kind they can reach heaven's summit and take the golden laurel from the hand of the strength-giving king.

5a What good did it you, impious serpent, once to have deceived a woman,

5b Since a virgin brought forth God incarnate, only-begotten of the Father:

6a He who took your spoils away and pierces your jaw with a hook

6b To make of it an open gate for Eve's race, whom you long to hold

---

[21] Cited from Peter Dronke, *The Medieval Lyric*, 3rd edn (Cambridge: D. S. Brewer, 1996), pp. 41–42.

7a   So now you can see girls defeating you, envious one,

7b   And married women now bearing sons who please God.

8a   Now you groan at the loyalty of widows to their dead husbands,

8b   You who once seduced a girl to disloyalty to her creator

9a   Now you can see women made captains in the war that is waged against you

9b   Women who spur on their sons bravely to conquer all your tortures.

10a   Even courtesans, your vessels, are purified by God,

10b   Transmuted into a burnished temple for him alone.

11a   For these graces let us now glorify him together, both the sinners and those who are just,

11b   Him who strengthens those who stand and gives his right hand to the fallen, that at least after crimes we may rise.

Example 19.3 gives us a particularly good idea of what is probably Notker's mature style. Of his surviving *versus ad sequentias* it is the last in liturgical order (being for the Common of Holy Women) in the *Liber hymnorum*. It is set to a tune known only east of the Rhine and not, like many of his earlier pieces, to a melody imported from the West. It was apparently sung only in Germany, although by the middle of the eleventh century it had been copied at the Old Minster in Winchester, which, to the best of my knowledge, is the only repository of this piece west of the Rhine.[22]

Both Crocker and Peter Dronke have commented extensively on this text, Crocker in terms of its relationship to the tune and Dronke with a particularly sensitive literary analysis. Dronke, following Steinen, shows that Notker has deliberately conflated with the image of Jacob's ladder two dreams recorded by St Perpetua (d. 203), one concerning combat with a dragon and the other with an Ethiop. Notker begins (see the translation following Example 19.3) with a dream-like sequence, carrying a single line of thought through lines 2a–4b.[23] Lines 5a–10b are a single defiant apostrophe to Satan, with references to Job and the Harrowing of Hell, and end with a remarkably inclusive description of the triumph of women over the devil's machinations, where not just virgin martyrs, who were the traditional image of holy women, but wives, widows, and even courtesans serve in the fight against evil. The final two lines are a doxology where, continuing the inclusive language of the previous lines, both the just and the sinner praise God.

The melody of *Scalam ad caelos* (see Example 19.3), unlike that of *Celebranda*, has a remarkable amount of internal variety, and the approaches to the cadence differ considerably from line to line. Nevertheless, the linear drive of Notker's text imposes upon it a sense of unity in much the same way as the melody of *Celebranda* unifies the otherwise scattered text of that prose. Notker's is surely not the original text for this *sequentia*. It survives with what Steinen regards as a tenth-century

---

[22]Oxford, Bodleian Library, ms Bodley 775, fol. 175[V].

[23]Dronke, *The Medieval Lyric*, 3rd edn (Cambridge, 1996), pp. 42–43.

Alemmanic text (see Example 19.4), but since this agrees better with the structure of the melody than Notker's, Steinen's date might well be off by a half century.[24] The inspiration is the *Canticum trium puerorum* in the apocrypha of the Book of Daniel (3:57–88, 56, sung at Lauds).

In this text (see the translation following Example 19.4) the different aspects of God's creation called to sing the alleluia underpin the difference in the approach to the cadence in each new verse, and the word 'alleluia' sung to the cadence pattern calls attention to the cadences, which are identical in lines 2–4, then 5 and 7, 8 and 9, and 10 and 11. Only lines 1 and 6 have an independent cadence, and that of 6 is a variant of the cadence in 5 and 7. Thus the music and text call our attention to the alleluia, culminating in the string of alleluias at the end of the sequence. In a sense this piece carries conceit of *Celebranda* to its ultimate form. As with *Celebranda*, the rhetoric of *Cantemus cuncti* is extremely different from that of Notker, and not a single one of the *versus ad sequentias* that can be ascribed to Notker ever uses the rhetorical approaches found either in *Celebranda* or in *Cantemus cuncti*.

Example 19.4: Anonymous, *Cantemus cuncti melodum nunc* (after Crocker, *The Medieval Sequence*)[25]

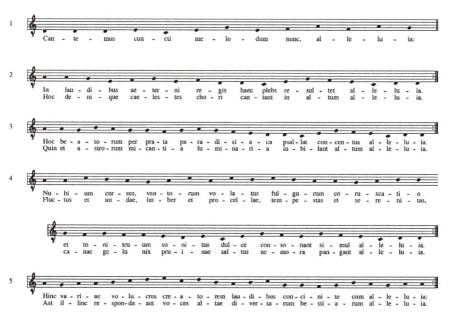

[24]Steinen, *Notker*, vol. 1, pp. 293–295. Steinen is surely right that the sequence comes from outside the St Gall orbit, but that in itself makes the dating even more problematic and opens the possibility of a contemporary of Notker as its creator.

[25] There is no critical edition of this music; the melody above, based on the notes of Henry Marriott Bannister, is that found most often in German sources. Italian manuscripts have a large number of small and large variants. The text contains emendations suggested by Leofranc Holford Strevens.

Example 19.4, continued.

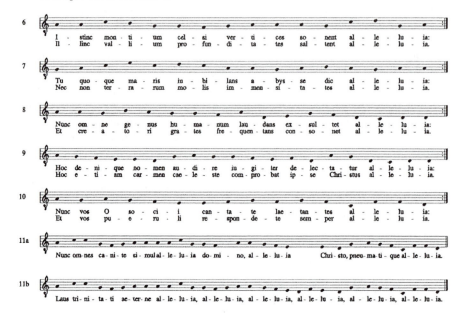

Translation of *Cantemus cuncti melodum*[26]

1   Let us all sing this melody, Alleluia.[27]

2a   Let this congregation echo the praises of the Eternal King, Alleluia.

2b   And this then let the heavenly choirs sing to the heights, Alleluia.

3a   This let the concordance of the blessed sing throughout the fields of paradise, Alleluia.

3b   Nay, let the gleaming lights of the stars cry aloud, Alleluia.

4a   Let the courses of the clouds, the flying of the winds, the flash of the lightnings, and the sound of the thunderbolts sweetly join in sonsonance, Alleluia.

4b   Let the waves and the billows, the rain and the gales, storm and calm, hoarfrosts, ice, snow, frosts, woods, and groves perform Alleluia.

5a   On this side, ye various birds, sing together your Creator's praises with Alleluia.

5b   On that side let the loud voices of divers beasts answer Alleluia.

6a   On this side let the lofty peaks of mountains sound Alleluia.

6b   On that side let the depths of valleys dance Alleluia.

7a   And thou too, vast deep of the sea, say Alleluia.

---

[26] Translation by Leofranc Holford Strevens.

[27] *Melodum* is a barbarism, it could stand for *melodiam* or the adverb *melodus*, i.e., Let us sing melodiously, Alleluia.

7b   And also the immensities of the mass of the earth, Alleluia.

8a   Now let the entire human race rejoice in praise, Alleluia,

8b   And flock together to join in sounding thanks to the Creator, Alleluia.

9a   This is the word He constantly delighteth to hear, Alleluia.

9b   And this heavenly song Christ Himself approveth, Alleluia.

10a   Now do ye, my companions, sing with rejoicing, Alleluia,

10b   And ye, little boys ever replying Alleluia.

11a   Now all sing together Alleluia to the Lord, Alleluia to Christ, and to the Spirit, Alleluia,

11b   Praise to the eternal Trinity, Alleluia, Alleluia, Alleluia, Alleluia, Alleluia, Alleluia.

Even a relatively cursory glance at the text edition of the surviving repertory of Aquitanian proses in volume 7 of the Analecta Hymnica[28] will reveal that the great majority share much of the rhetorical world of *Celebranda*; and Crocker's detailed comparison of Notker's *versus ad sequentias* with their putative West Frankish models also reveals a considerable gulf between the poetic world of the Western Franks and that of Notker, though not necessarily that of other East Frankish poets. It is thus no surprise that Notker, as his letter to Liutward states, did not think much of the literary merits of the texts he saw in the antiphoner from Jumièges.

The West Franks returned the compliment. Table 19.1 shows the concordance of Notker's *versus ad sequentias* outside German-speaking areas until the beginning of the twelfth century.

Table 19.1: Concordance of Notker's *versus ad sequentias* outside Germany

---

1   Natus ante saecula

Aquitaine: PaN 1118 (no music)

France: Apt 18, As 695, Cai 60, Cai 78

North Italy: Ber 40608, BoU 2824, Civ 56, Civ 58, Civ 79, Gor, Ivr 60, Mod 7, NY 797, Ox 340, Ox 341, Ox 222, Pad 16, Pad 20, Pad 57, RoC 1741, RoN 1343, To 17, Ud 2, Ud 78, Vol 39, Vro 107

South Italy: MC 318

2   Hanc concordi

France: Me 452

---

[28]Dreves, *Prosarium lemovicense.*

North Italy: Ber 40608, BoU 2824, Civ 56, Civ 58, Civ 79, Gor, Mod 7, Novara, NY 797, Ox 340, Ox 341, Ox 222, Pad 20, Pad 47, Pad 16, Pad 57, Pst 121, RoC 1741, RoN 1343, To 17, To 18, Ud 2, Ud 78, Vol. 39, Vro 107

South Italy: Ben 34, Bod 74 (OR), MC 318, MC 546, Vat 5319 (OR)

3   Iohannes Iesu Christo

England: Cam 710, Dur 5, Ox 148, PaA 135

France: Apt 18, Cai 60, Cai 78, Me 452, PaA 1169, PaN 10508

North Italy: Ber 40608, BoU 2824, Civ 56, Civ 58, Civ 79, Gor, Ivr 60, Mod 7, Mza 75, Mza 76, NY 797, Ox 340, Ox 341, Ox 222, Pad 20, Pad 47, Pad 16, Pad 57, Pia 65, Pst 121, RoA 123, RoC 1741, RoN 1343, To 17, To 18, To 20, Ud 2, Ud 79, Vce 146, Vce 161, Vce 162, Vol. 39, Vro 107

South Italy: Ben 34, Bod 74 (OR), MC 318, MC 546, Vat 5319 (OR)

Spain: Hue 4

Norman Sicily: Ma 19421, Ma 20, Ma 288, Ma 289

4   Laus tibi Christe

France, PaA 1169

North Italy: BoU 2824, Civ 56, Civ 58, Civ 79, Gor, Ox 340, RoA 123, RoC 1741, RoN 1343, Ud 2, Vro 107

5   Gaude Maria virgo

Nothing outside Germany

6   Festa Christi omnis

France: As 695, Cai 60, Cai 78, Me 452

North Italy: BoU 2824, Civ 56, Civ 58, Civ 79, Gor, Ivr 60, Ox 340, Ox 341, Pad 20, Pad 16, Pad 57, RoC 1741, RoN 1343, To 17, Ud 2, Ud 78, Vce 161, Vro 107

South Italy: Ben 35, MC 318, MC 546

7   Concentu parili hic te Maria

England: Bod 775, LoC 14

France: Apt 18, Me 452

North Italy: Ber 40608, BoU 2824, Civ 56, Civ 58, Civ 79, Gor, Mod 7, NY 797, Ox 340, Ox 341, Pad 20, Pad 16, RoA 123, RoC 1741, RoN 1343, To 17, Ud 2, Ud 78, Vce 146, Vce 161, Vce 162, Vro 107

South Italy: Ben 35, MC 318

8 Laudes salvatori voce

England: Bod 775, Cam 710, LoC 14

France: Lo 8C13, As 695, Cai 78, Me 452

North Italy: Aquileia, Ber 40608, Civ 56, Civ 58, Civ 79, Gor, Mod 7, Ox 340, Ox 341, Pad 16, Pia 65, To 17, Ud 2, Ud 78, Vol 39, Vro 107

South Italy: Ben 39, Ben 40, MC 318

Norman Sicily: Ma 19421

9 In qui prius

Nothing outside Germany

10 Christe domine laetifica

Nothing outside Germany

11 Agni paschalis esu

France: Cai 60, Me 452

North Italy: Aquileia, Ber 40608, Civ 56, Civ 58, Civ 79, Gor, Ox 340, Ox 341, Pad 16, To 17, Ud 2, Ud 78

12 Grates salvatori ac regi

France: Me 452

North Italy: Ox 340, Ox 341, Pad 16, Ud 2, Ud 78

13 Laudes deo concinat

North Italy: Ox340

14 Carmen suo dilecto

France: Me 452

North Italy: Ox 341, Pad 16

15 Haec est sancta sollemnitas

France: Lo R8C13, Me 452

North Italy: Ber 40608, Gor, Ox 341, Pad 16, Pad 20, Ud 2, Ud 78, Vro 107

16 Iudicem nos inspicientem

Nothing outside Germany

17 Laus tibi sit

Nothing outside Germany

18 En regnator caelestium

Nothing outside Germany

19 Laeta mente canamus

North Italy: BoU 2824, RoN 1343

20 Summi triumphum regis

France: Me 452, PaN 13252

North Italy: Ber 40608, BoU 2824, Civ 56, Civ 58, Civ 79, Gor, Ox 340, Ox 341, Pad 16, Pad 20, RoA 123, RoC 1741, RoN 1343, To 17, Ud 2, Ud 78

South Italy: Ben 38, Ben 39, Ben 40, MC 318

21 Christus hunc dies

Nothing outside Germany

22 O quam mira sunt deus

North Italy: BoU 2824, RoC 1741, RoN 1343

23 Sancti spiritus assit nobis

Aquitaine: Apt 17, PaN 778, PaN 887, PaN 1086, PaN 1132, PaN 1136, PaN 1177, PaN 1871

England: Bod 775, Ca 710, CC 473, LoC 14, Ox 148, PaA 135

France: Ang 96, Apt 18, As 695, Ber 155, Cai 60, Cai 61, Cai 78, Me 452, PaA 1169, PaN 10508, PaN 1087, PaN 1235, PaN 9449

North Italy: Ber 40608, Bol 7, BoU 2824, Civ 56, Civ 58, Civ 79, Gor, Ivr 60, Mod 7, Mza 76, NY 797, Ox 340, Ox 341, Pad 20, Pad 47, Pad 16, Pad 57, Pia 65, Pst 121, RoA 123, RoC 1741, RoN 1343, To 17, To 18, To 20, Ud 2, Ud 78, Vce 146, Vce 161, Vce 162, Vol 39, Vro 107

South Italy: Ben 34, Ben 35, Ben 38, Ben 39, Ben 40, Bod 74 (OR), MC 318, Vat 5319 (OR)

Norman Sicily: Ma 19421, Ma 20, Ma 288, Ma 289

Spain: Hue 4, PaN 495, Vic 105, Vic 106

24 Benedicto gratias deo

Nothing outside Germany

The table shows that Notker's *versus ad sequentias* had a very limited circulation west of the Rhine, in contrast to their ubiquitous presence in East Frankish manuscripts, and a relatively widespread distribution in Italy that included deep inroads into the Beneventan region (indicated as South Italy in the table) and a presence in two of the three surviving graduals with Old Roman music (indicated with OR in the table).

A summary of the West Frankish concordances in Table 19.1 is as follows: out of thirty-nine pieces by Notker we find two in Aquitaine, twenty-three in France, ten in England, and four in Spain, while nine pieces apparently did not circulate outside Germany. The mere statistics are deceiving, however, because ten of the French concordances are restricted to the Cambrai 60 and 78, Metz 452, and Apt 18, sources from the linguistic border between German and French in the Middle Ages. If these sources are placed within the German tradition, as early twentieth-century liturgists tended to do, the number of French concordances drops to thirteen, and the number of pieces restricted to the German area rises to nineteen. In most cases the French concordances consist of a handful of manuscripts, as opposed to what we find in the Italian peninsula. In the south of France we encounter only two pieces, *Natus ante saecula*, copied without music in PaN 1118 (a gigantic anthology most likely compiled around Tolouse between 996 and 1000 by an omnivorous scribe who apparently went out of his way to copy all the repertory he knew of[29]) and *Sancti spiritus adsit nobis gratia*, copied in sources ranging from the early eleventh to the twelfth century in Apt, Aurillac, Limoges, and perhaps in Moissac, Narbonne, and Toulouse, including manuscripts from the Abbey of Saint-Martial de Limoges.

Clearly *Sancti spiritus adsit nobis gratia*, Notker's piece for Pentecost set to the music of the magnificent West Frankish prose for Ascension, *Rex omnipotens die hodierna*, was the most widespread of his works outside Germany and the only one used to any extent in Aquitaine. One possible explanation for this is its presence in PaN 1087, a gradual from Cluny dating from the second half of the eleventh century.[30] Cluny, as is well known, was opposed to the singing of tropes and severely restricted the number of proses sung to the *sequentiae* during the year.[31] The manuscript transmits only nine proses in the main hand and three more as later additions at the end of

---

[29]See Alicia Doyle, 'The Repertory of Tropes in Paris, Bibliothèque Nationale *fonds latin* 1118: A Comparative Study of Tenth-Century Aquitanian Concordances and Transmission' (Ph.D. diss., University of California at Santa Barbara, 2000).

[30]*Le graduel romain, édition critique par les moines de Solesmes: II Les sources* (Solesmes, 1957), p. 97, dates it between 994 and 1048 because the office of St Odilo is copied by a later hand, but see Meyer Schapiro, *The Parma Ildefonsus: A Romanesque Illustrated Manuscript from Cluny and Related Works* (New York, 1964).

[31]See Pierre Marie Gy, 'Les tropes dans l'histoire de la théologie', in Gunilla Iversen, ed., *Research on Tropes* (Stockholm, 1983), pp. 10–11; David Hiley, 'Cluny Sequences and Tropes', in Claudio Leonardi and Enrico Menestó, eds, *La tradizione dei tropi liturgici* (Spoleto, 1990), pp. 125–138, and 'The Sequence Melodies Sung at Cluny and Elsewhere', in *FS Hucke*, pp. 131–135.

the manuscript.[32] Further, in the Cluny customary composed around 1079–1080 for Abbot William of Hirsau in order to provide William with information about Cluniac practice, one of the monks of Cluny, Ulrich von Zwettl (1029–1093), has this to say about how *Sancti spiritus adsit nobis gratia* came to be sung at Cluny:

> But although not all the French care very much for the proses of the Germans, the blessed father Odilo [abbot of Cluny from 996 to 1048], being pressed and then allying himself with our countrymen, nevertheless maintained that this one only, *Sancti spiritus adsit nobis gratia*, might be sung on this day in our community.[33]

Cluny took over and reformed a number of Aquitanian abbeys in the eleventh century, notably Saint-Pierre de Moissac in 1048 and Saint-Martial de Limoges in 1063. The Cluniac takeover might have led to the abandonment of tropes or at least the composition of new tropes in the Aquitanian houses, something that disturbed Adémar de Chabannes, who interpolated in his redaction of the *Liber Pontificalis* an appeal to the authority of Pope Hadrian I for the practice of singing tropes.[34] But as a rule, during the eleventh century the Cluniacs did not, by and large, interfere with the liturgy of the houses they took over. And one of the notable aspects of the transmission of *Sancti spiritus adsit nobis gratia* in Aquitaine is that it spread to a few establishments, such as the Basilica of St Anne in Apt, that did not come under Cluniac authority.

In other words, the Cluniac influence is only part of the story; the other part may be found in the traditions of Aquitaine itself. Twenty-four manuscripts that transmit proses, *sequentiae*, or both survive from the Aquitanian region, and many of these transmit tropes as well. In the case of the introit tropes, for example, I have been able to show that a comparison of the repertory for a given feast in the different manuscripts allows us to determine which pieces represented the basic Aquitanian repertory for that feast, and which were more local, that is, restricted to Saint-Martial, or Aurillac, or another of the centres in the region.[35] The case with the *sequentiae* and the proses is not much different. The proses for Easter and Eastertide may serve as an example. Table 19.2 gives the proses for Easter and Eastertide in the Aquitanian manuscripts.

At first glance the table presents what appears to be a confusing picture, but some patterns can be discerned. The earliest Aquitanian collection of proses, the liturgically disorganized *congregatio prosarum* of PaN 1240, transmits five proses for the Easter season (with unrelated pieces intervening among them) and a sixth one

---

[32]The repertory is given in Hiley, 'Cluny Sequences', p. 127 (omitting two of the three additions).

[33]'Quamvis autem omnes Galli non magnopere curent de prosis Teutonicarum, tamen beato Patre Odilone adnitente et de nostratibus aserente, haec sola, *Sancti spiritus adsit nobis gratia*, obtinuit ut in nostro loco in isto die cantaretur' (PL 149, 672); see also Hiley, 'The Sequence Melodies', p. 139.

[34]See Gy, 'Les tropes', p. 10.

[35]See my 'On the Nature of Transmission and Change in Trope Repertories', *JAMS* 41 (1988), pp. 215–249.

added later in the tenth century. Three of them are international, known in different western regions but not in Germany, and three are purely Aquitanian pieces. By the third quarter of the tenth century, when the old repertory of PaN 1084 was compiled, the establishment where the manuscript was first copied had what appears to be a well ordered series for the entire week of Easter which used three of the proses found in PaN 1240 with six others that are clearly Aquitanian in origin (even though several of them were known in Italy). The immense series in PaN 1118 is typical of that manuscript, in which the compiler attempted to gather repertories from several establishments and copied them in apparent disorder. Only the first two proses carry liturgical rubrics, and the manuscript has all the earmarks of an anthology of pieces from which the cantor could pick at will. PaN 887, again from an undetermined establishment but copied before 1050, provides rubrics for all but one of the proses, and what we have is a series similar to that found in PaN 1084. But PaN 887, like PaN 1240, shows considerable evidence of northern French influence in its repertory.[36] It has all the proses found in PaN 1240, but the beginning of the series is entirely made of international pieces, including one piece also found in German sources, *Stans a longe*, which was most often used as one of the proses for the Sundays *infra annum*. Similarly, for Feria 4 the manuscript has *Candida contio*, a prose normally associated with a number of different confessors throughout Europe.[37] Despite its late date PaN 887 shares a number of traits with PaN 1240, and my sense is that its repertory may well reflect the stages of both the trope and prose repertories around 950.

The same still unstable tradition is reflected in PaN 1120, the earliest full troper to survive from Saint-Martial de Limoges. The manuscript still has a number of imported works left without music by the scribes, and the proses around Easter include pieces rubricated for St Martin and St Germain. The prose for St Martin might be there because it is melodically associated with the Easter alleluia *Pascha nostrum* which also served as the melody for a number of other alleluia texts. A small majority of the proses in PaN 1120 are pieces already found in PaN 1240.

PaN 1138/1338 is the proser copied by a Saint-Martial monk who gave his name as Rogier.[38] Despite the lack of explicit rubrics, the proses seem to be a planned cycle for the entire Easter Week with two proses for Easter day (not an uncommon occurrence in the manuscripts). It appears that the entire cycle was newly composed, for most of the pieces are unica, although four of them found their way into later collections. In most respects, however, Rogier's Easter cycle is entirely exceptional and outside the normal tradition of the Aquitanian prosers, and it represents an extraordinary burst of creativity that remained relatively isolated.

---

[36]*Ibid.*, pp. 226–229.

[37]See AH 53, p. 392.

[38]This Rogier, as James Grier has shown, is not Rogier de Chabannes, cantor of Saint-Martial and uncle of Adémar. See Grier, 'Roger de Chabannes (d. 1025), Cantor of Saint-Martial de Limoges', *EMH* 14 (1995), pp. 56–57.

Table 19.2: Easter and Eastertide proses in Aquitaine, 925–1100[39]

Order	Source and incipit	Feast	Rubric	Notes	Origin[40]
	PaN 1240, St Martial, 923–936 (proses in an added appendix at the beginning of the troper)				
X	Prome casta contio	[Easter]	Prosa de alleluia Eduxit dominus		F/E
	(proses in the *congregatio prosarum*, all without music)[41]				
A	Fulgens praeclara rutilat	Easter	Prosa in resurrectione domini		IN
B	Laetabunda nunc imminet	Easter	In Pascha		A
C	Dic nobis quibus e terris nova	Easter	In Pascha		IN
D	O beata et venerabilis virgo	BVM in Easter	Prosa de sancta Maria		A
E	Creator poli rexque terrae	Feria 2	Feria II in Pascha		A

---

[39] A number of Aquitanian manuscripts do not have a prosarium but only a sequentiarium (PaN 909, 1133, 1134, 1135), others have both a prosarium and a sequentiarium (PaN 1084, 1118, 1121 (prosarium mostly lost), 1137, 1871). The sequentiaria apparently represent an earlier tradition and even in those manuscripts that have both there is often no direct correlation between the prosarium and the sequentiarium. Thus the sequentiaria are omitted from this table.

[40] A = Aquitanian (including Pyrenees); E = English; F = French; I = Italian; IN = International; A/F = Aquitanian but with some French concordances; A/I = Aquitanian but with Italian concordances; F/E = North French or English origin, most likely North French.

[41] This is not a true prosarium — that is, a liturgically ordered collection of proses — but a collection of proses and prosulae to the alleluia and the offertory that makes three or four 'passes' through the liturgical year, each 'pass' with a large number of gaps.

PaN 1084, unknown, later Aurillac, repertory of 10c/2 (proses in a *prosarium* with an extended appendix)

E	Creator poli rexque terrae	Feria 2	Feria II in Pascha	A

PaN 1084, unknown, later Aurillac, repertory of 10c/2 (proses in a *prosarium* with an extended appendix)

Main series

1-A	Fulgens praeclara rutilat	Easter	In Pascha	[Easter]	IN
2	Clara gaudia festa paschalia	-	Alia	[Vespers]	A/I
3	Nunc exsultet omnis mundus	-	Alia	[Feria 2]	A/I
4	Adest enim festa paschalia	-	Alia	[Feria 3]	A
5	Laudes deo omnis sexus consona[42]	-	Alia	[Feria 4]	A
6-X	Prome casta contio carmina	-	Alia	[Feria 5]	F/E
7	Gaudet tellus exsultetque mundus	-	Alia	[Feria 6]	A
8	Haec dies quam excelsus ipse	-	Alia	[Sabbato]	A
9-D	O beata et venerabilis virgo	-	Alia	[Octava]	A

Appendix, first series

B	Laetabunda nunc imminet	Easter	Psa de Resurrectione	A

Appendix, second series

3	Adest enim festa paschalia	Easter	De Pascha	A
	Gaudens mater pange laude	Easter	De Resurrectione	A/F

---

[42] Variant incipits: Laudes deo sexus omnis, and Laus deo nostro sit, cf. AH 53, 81.

Order	Source and incipit	Feast	Rubric	Notes	Origin
	Haec est vera redemptio et celsa	-	no rubric		A
	Hodie sollemnitas sollemnitatum	Easter	De Resurrectione		A
	Adest enim festa paschalia	Easter	no rubric		A
	PaN 1118, Toulouse or Auch, 996–1000 (proses in a *prosarium*)				
C	Iubilate deo omnes arva qui	Easter Vigil	In vigilia paschae		IN
B	Dic nobis quibus e terris nova	Easter	In die sancto paschae		IN
6-X	Laetabunda nunc imminet in terris	-	Alia		A
	Prome casta contio carmina organa	-	Alia		F/E
5	Laudes deo omnis sexus consona	-	Alia		A
	Vexilla regis prodeunt	-	Alia[43]		A
	Miserere facti hominis miserere	-	Alia		A
1-A	Fulgens praeclara rutilat	-	Alia	no music	IN
2	Clara gaudia festa paschalia	-	Alia		A/I
	Ecce visit radix david leo de	-	Alia		IN
	Cuncta simul instantia christo	-	Alia		A
4	Adest enim festa paschalia	-	Alia		A
	Sollemnem diem celebrat plebs	-	Alia	no music	A
7	Gaudeat tellus exsultetque mundus	-	Alia		A

[43] Normally this text is for the Finding of the Cross.

9-D	O beata et venerabilis virgo	-		Alia	A
	Festus adest nobis cunctis nimium	-		Alia	A
	Arvae polique conditori alacres	-		Alia	A
	Gaudens mater pange laude saecula	-	no music	Alia	A/F
	Haec est praeclarae sollemnitatis	-	no music	Alia	A
	Haec est vera redemptio et celsa	-		Alia	A
	Hodie sollemnitas sollemnitatum	-	no music	Alia	A
8	Haec dies quam excelsus ipse	-[44]		Alia	A

PaN 887, provenance undetermined, 11c/1
(proses in a *prosarium*)

1-A	Fulgens praeclara rutilat	Easter		De pascha	IN
6-X	Prome casta contio carmina	[Feria 2]		no rubric	F/E
C	Dic nobis quibus e terris nova	Feria 3		Feria III	IN
	Candida contio melos concrepa	Feria 4		Feria IIII	IN
	Stans a longe qui plurima	Feria 5		Feria V	IN
B	Laetabunda nunc imminet in terris	Feria 5		De eadem	A
E	Creator poli rexque terrae	Feria 6		Feria VI	A
	Sollemnem diem celebrat plebs	Feria 6		Feria VI	A
4	Adest enim festa paschalia	Sabbato		Sabbato	A
9-D	O beata et venerabilis virgo	Octave		Octabas paschae	A

[44] Despite the Christmas-like text, both PaN 1084 and PaN 1118 give this piece at the end of the Easter cycle.

Order	Source and incipit	Feast	Rubric	Notes	Origin
	PaN 1120, St Martial, 1010 and 1020 (proses in a *prosarium*)				
1-A	Fulgens praeclara rutilat	Easter	Prosa in pascha domini		IN
	Exsultet nunc omnis chorus		De alleluia pascha nrm[45]		A/F
B	Laetabunda nunc imminet in terris	Eastertide	Prosa de resurrectione		A
	Stans a longe qui plurima		De planctu publicani		IN
C	Dic nobis quibus e terris nova	Eastertide	De resurrectione		IN
	Candida contio melos concrepa	S Germain	Prosa de sco Germano[46]		IN
6-X	Prome casta contio carmina organa	Eastertide	De resurrectione		F/E
	PaN 1138/1338 [originally a single MS now dismembered], Limoges, *ca* 1040 (proses in a *prosarium*, the Easter series all in 1338)				
Rog 1	Alleluia hoc pium recitat plebs	Easter Vigil	In vigilia Paschae	[Vigil]	
Rog 2	Rutilat per orbem praeclara dies	Easter	In die sanctum Paschae	[Easter]	
Rog 3	Magne et pie hac die rex exsultat	-	Alia	[Easter]	
Rog 4	Caelica terrenaque simul turba	-	no rubric	[Vespers]	
Rog 5	Adest pia ac salutifera paschalis	-	Alia	[Feria 2]	
Rog 6	Clara resonent nunc organa	-	Item alia	[Feria 3]	
Rog 7	Laudum laeta psallat poemata	-	Alia	[Feria 4]	

[45]Extra rubric: 'De sancto Martino'.
[46]Partly without music.

Rog 8	Turba proclama laeta laude corona	-	Alia	[Feria 5]	
Rog 9	Alleluia quoniam vita resurrexit	-	Alia	[Feria 6]	
Rog 10	Omnigena contio redempta	-	Alia	[Sabbato]	
Rog 11	Canat omnis turba fonte renata	-	Alia	[Octave]	

PaN 903, St Yrieix, *ca* 1050
(proses in a *prosarium*, lacuna at the start of the Easter series)

1-A	[Fulgens praeclara rutilat]	Easter[47]		rubric lost	IN
2	Clara gaudia festa paschalia	Easter vespers		Item ad vesperos prosa	A/I
4	Adest enim festa paschalia	?[48]	Alia prosa		A
Rog 5	Adest pia ac salutifera paschalis	?	Item alia prosa		A
6-X	Prome casta contio carmina	?	Item alia		F/E

PaN 1871, Aurillac, *ca* 1050
(proses in a *prosarium*)

Rog 1	Rutilat per orbem praeclara dies	Easter	In die Paschae	[Easter]	A
1-A	Fulgens praeclara rutilat	-	Alia	[vespers?]	IN
	Gaudent ecce per omnem cuncta	-	Alia	[Feria 2]	A/I
Rog 5	Adest pia ac salutifera paschalis	-	Alia	[Feria 3]	A
4	Adest enim festa paschalia	-	Alia	[Feria 4]	A
Rog 4	Caelica terrenaque simul turba	-	Alia	[Feria 5]	A
2	Clara gaudia festa paschalia	-	Alia	[Feria 6]	A/I

---

[47]Starts on fol. 186ʳ with [*Victor*] *ubique morte superata.*

[48]These could be either for Feriae 2–4 or Sundays 1–3 after Easter, the next prose is for Ascension.

Order	Source and incipit	Feast	Rubric	Notes	Origin
Rog 6	Clara resonent nunc organa	-	Alia	[Sabbato]	A
3	Nunc exsultet omnis mundus quia	Octave of Easter	Octabas paschae	[Octave]	A/I
	Later additions				
	Iubilate deo omnis arva	Easter vigil	In Vigilia Paschae		A
	PaN 1119, St Martial de Limoges, between 1051 and 1062 (proses in a *prosarium*)				
1-A	Fulgens praeclara rutilat	Easter	Prosa in pascha		IN
	Praecelsa ad modum et clara nimis	Easter	De pascha		A
B	Laetabunda nunc imminet in terris	-	no rubric		A
	Stans a longe qui plurima	Eastertide	Prosa in resurrectione dni		IN
C	Dic nobis quibus e terris nova	-	Alia		IN
6-X	Prome casta contio carmina	-	Alia		F/E
	PaN 1132, St Martial, 11c/2 (after 1063) (proses in a *prosarium*, in two series)				

First series

Order	Source and incipit	Feast	Rubric	Notes	Origin
1-A	Fulgens praeclara rutilat	Easter	Prosa in sancto paschae		IN

Second series

Order	Source and incipit	Feast	Rubric	Notes	Origin
C	Dic nobis quibus e terris nova	Feria 2	Feria II in Pascha		IN
6-X	Prome casta contio carmina organa	Feria 3	Feria III in Pascha		F/E
B	Laetabunda nunc imminet in terris	Feria 4	Feria IIII		A

PaN 1136, St Martial, 11c/2 (after 1063)
(proses in a *prosarium*)

1-A	Fulgens praeclara rutilat	Easter	In resurrectione	IN
B	Laetabunda nunc imminet in terris	-	Alia prosa	A
C	Dic nobis quibus e terris nova	-	Alia	IN
6-X	Prome casta contio carmina	-	no rubric	F/E

PaN 1137, St Martial, 11c/2 (after 1063)
(proses in a *prosarium*)

1-A	Fulgens praeclara rutilat	Easter	De resurrectione	IN
	Praecelsa admodum et clara nimis	Easter vespers	Prosa de resurrectione ad vesperas	A
C	Dic nobis quibus e terris nova	-	Item alia	IN
6-X	Prome casta contio carmina	-	Item alia	F/E
B	Laetabunda nunc imminet	-	Item alia	A
	Stans a longe qui plurima	-	no rubric	IN

Apt 17, Apt, Ste Anne, 11c/2
(proses within the formularies)

1-A	Fulgens praeclara rutilat	Easter	Prosa	IN
	Laudent ecce per orbem cuncta	Feria 2	no rubric	A
	Ecce vicit radix david leo	Feria 3	Prosa	IN
	Dei ista fratres carissimi	Feria 4	Prosa	A/I
	Sancta cunctis laetitia festa	Feria 5	Prosa	A
2	Clara gaudia festa paschalia	Easter Vespers?	Prosa in Pascha	A/I

Order	Source and incipit	Feast	Rubric	Notes	Origin
	PaN 779, Arles, 11c/2 (proses within the formularies)				
1-A	Fulgens praeclara rutilat	Easter	Prosa		IN
2	Clara gaudia festa paschalia	Easter Vespers	Ad vesperas		A/I
3	Nunc exsultet onmis mundum	Feria 2	Prosa		A/I
	Agnus dei christus rex	Feria 3	Prosa		A
	Laudent [Gaudent] ecce per omnes cuncta	Feria 4	Prosa		A/I
4	Adest enim festa paschalia	Feria 5	Prosa		A
	Ecce vicit radix david leo	Feria 6	no rubric		IN
9-D	O beata et venerabilis virgo	Octave	Prosa		A
	Vera lux erat amunculo	–[49]	Alia[50]		A
6-X	Prome casta contio carmina organa	–	Alia		F/E
	Gaudeat tellus exsultetque mundus	–	no rubric		A
	Cuncta simul instantia christo	–	no rubric		A
	Rex aeterne dominator conserva	–	no rubric		A/I
	PaN 1086, Limoges, St Leonard, 12c/1				
1-A	Fulgens praeclara rutilat per	Easter	In Die Sco Pasche		IN

[49]These five proses copied in immediate succession may be for the five Sundays after Easter. They are followed immediately by the tropes for Ascension.

[50]This prose escaped the attention of the editors of Analecta Hymnica; it survives only in PaN 779.

	Chant	Occasion	Rubric	
	Victimae paschali laudes immolent	vespers	In Pascha ad Vp	IN
	Mane prima sabbati surgens dei	Feria 2	In Pascha Fr II	IN
	Sexta passus feria die christe	Feria 3	Fr III in Pascha	IN
	Salve dies dierum gloria dies	Feria 4	Fra IIII	IN
4	Adest enim festa paschalia	Octave	In Octab Pasche	A
	PaN 1177, Moissac?, 12c (proses in a *prosarium*)			
1-A	Fulgens praeclara rutilat	[Easter]	no rubric	IN
Rog 5	Adest pia ac salutifera paschalis	-	Alia	A
	PaN 778, Narbonne, 12c (proses in a *prosarium*)			
1-A	Fulgens praeclara rutilat	Easter	Prosa ad missam maiorem	IN
2	Clara gaudia festa paschalia	Easter vespers	Alia prosa ad vesperas	A/I
4	Adest enim festa paschalia	?	Alia ad vesperam[51]	A
	Laudent ecce [incipit]	Sunday 1	Dca I in Oct Pasche Psa	A
	Gaudeat tellum [incipit]	Sunday 2	Dca II in Oct Pasche	A
	O alma prima [incipit]	Sunday 3	Dca III in Oct Pasche	A
	Praecelsa admodum [incipit]	Sunday 4	Dca III	A
	Praecelsa admodum et clara	-	Prosa	A
	Splendent ecce novi rutilantia	Sunday 5	Dca V in Oct Pasche Psa	A
	Laudent ecce per omnem cuncta	Sunday 1	Dca I in Oct Pasche	A

[51]The final word of the rubric is almost illegible.

Order	Source and incipit	Feast	Rubric	Notes	Origin
Rog 5	Adest pia ac salutifera paschalia	-	Alia Psa		A
	Victimae paschali laudes immolent	-	Alia Prosa		IN
C	Dic nobis quibus e terris nova	-	Alia Prosa		IN
	Cuncta simul instantia christo	-	Alia Psa	no music	A
	Gaudeat ecclesia innovant gaudia	Octave	In Octabas Pasche Psa		A

PaN 903 is missing a folio with the beginning of the Easter prose, but the rubric that assigns *Clara gaudia* to Easter vespers allows us to determine that *Fulgens praeclara* began the series, which is, like all the series in PaN 903, relatively restricted. With the exception of *Adest pia ac salutifera*, which is taken from PaN 1338, all of the proses are part of the general Aquitanian repertory already present in PaN 1084.The mid-eleventh-century Aurillac proser in PaN 1871 presents a picture similar to that of PaN 1084. The first and last rubrics, together with the numbers of proses, indicate that we have here a complete series for the Easter week. Except for *Fulgens praeclara* the series of PaN 1871 shows no contact with the traditional Saint-Martial repertory that is represented not only in PaN 1240 and 1220 but in the later Saint-Martial manuscripts as well, but it does incorporate four of the proses in PaN 1338.

The later Saint-Martial prosers in PaN 1119, 1132, 1136, and 1137, essentially retain proses A, B, C, and X of the collection of PaN 1240, sometimes with the addition of *Stans a longe* (already in PaN 1120) and *Praecelsa admodum et clara*, a new prose whose earliest appearance is in the additions to PaN 1121, where, like *Stans a longe*, it is entered as a dominical prose, probably for one of the Sundays after Easter – the position it occupies in PaN 778.

As for the later prosers: Apt 17 shows an almost total independence from the central Aquitanian tradition, PaN 779 transmits a number of proses from the Aquitanian tradition together with later works, and the two larger prosers from the twelfth century give us, for all intents and purposes, a new repertory.

All the manuscripts, even those originating at Saint-Martial, show a good deal of variation in the proses for the days after Easter or the Sundays between Easter and Pentecost, a variability reflected in the case of those manuscripts that do not provide a clear or implied liturgical assignment by the order in which the proses are copied. The tradition for Easter Sunday itself, however, is nearly universally stable. From the *congregatio prosarum* of PaN 1240 to the late sources, the prose for Easter Sunday is *Fulgens praeclara*. Out of seventeen *prosaria* only PaN 1118, 1338, and 1871 do not have *Fulgens praeclara* and the main Easter prose, and in 1338 and 1871 the main Easter prose, *Rutilat per orbem*, is in fact a textual parody of *Fulgens praeclara* that uses the same melody and incorporates the partial text of its *sequentia*[52] (in PaN 1871 *Rutilat* is followed immediately by *Fulgens*).

In terms of Easter Sunday itself the evidence of the *sequentiaria* is equally conclusive: the first *sequentia* for Easter in PaN 887, 909, 1121, 1133, 1134, 1135, 1136, and 1137 is *Fulgens praeclara*. Only the very large and relatively disordered *sequentiaria* of PaN 1084 and 1118 do not place this *sequentia* at the start of the Easter series.

For the feast of Pentecost, the picture of repertorial stability presented by the main prose for Easter Sunday is reflected in the series of introit tropes for the day, as shown in Table 19.3.

---

[52]This was noted by Dreves in AH 7, p. 69.

Table 19.3: Introit tropes for Pentecost in Aquitaine

Order	Source and incipit	Cue	Rubric	Notes	Origin[53]
	PaN 1240, St Martial, 923–936				
A=3	Psallite cum laude cantate deo[54]	Spiritus domini	in Pentecost	no music	IN
A2	Discipulis flammas infundens	Spiritus domini	no rubric		IN[55]
	PaN 1084, uncertain, repertory 10c/2, later Aurillac and St Martial				
Original Series					
Intro 1	Inclita refulget dies	Spiritus domini	Tropos in Pentecosten		A/F
A1	Paraclitus sanctus postulans	Spiritus domini	A1		A
A2	Discipulis flammas infundens	Spiritus domini	Alios		IN
A3	Psallite candidati spiritus	Spiritus domini	A1		IN
A4	Sanctus en veniens sanctorum	Spiritus domini	A1		A
A5	Doxa patri ke yo ke agio	Spiritus domini	Alios	Greek doxology	A

[53] A = Aquitanian (including Pyrenees); E = English; F = French; I = Italian; IN = International; A/F = Aquitanian but with some French concordances; A/I = Aquitanian but with Italian concordances.

[54] Opening verse survives only in PaN 887 and 1240; it is an introductory verse for the verses that follow *Psallite candidati spiritus* in the other Aquitanian tropers.

[55] This is a uniquely Aquitanian reworking of an international trope, *Discipulis flammas infudit*.

Additions in the late tenth century in Aurillac

B1	Mystica paracliti virtutum	Spiritus domini	De Pentecosten		A
B2	Praeclarus nunc dies adest	Spiritus domini	Al		A
Intro 2	Hodie spiritus sanctus descendit	Spiritus domini	Al	no music	A
Intro 3	Hodie descendit spiritus sanctus	Spiritus domini	no rubric		A
PaN 1118, Toulouse or SW France, 996–1000					
Intro 2	Hodie descendit spiritus sanctus	Spiritus domini	In Die Pentecosten	Tropos Ad Missa Maiore	A
Intro 1	Inclita refulget dies	Spiritus domini	Alios		A/F
A1	Paraclitus sanctus postulans	Spiritus domini	Alios	Ps. Exsurgat deus	A
B1	Mystica paracliti virtutum	Spiritus domini	Al	Ps. Emitte / Gloria	A
A2	Discipulis flammas infundens	Spiritus domini	Alios	Ps. Confirma hoc	IN
B2	Praeclarus nunc dies adest	Spiritus domini	Al	Ps. Factus est	A
A4	Sanctus en veniens sanctorum	Spiritus domini	Al		A
A3	Psallite candidati spiritus	Spiritus domini	Alio		IN
A5	Doxa patri ke yo ke agio[56]	Spiritus domini	Ad Gla	cue added later	A
PaN 887, Uncertain, 11c/1					
A/3	Psallite cum laude cantate deo	Spiritus domini	In die Pent		IN
A2	Discipulis flammas infundens	Spiritus domini	Alios	Ps. Exsurgat deus	IN
B1	Mystica paracliti virtutum	Spiritus domini	Alios	Ps. Confirma hoc	A
A4	Sanctus en veniens sanctorum	Spiritus domini	Alio	Gloria patri	A
A1	Paraclitus sanctus postulans	no cue[57]	no rubric		A

---

[56] Not the gloria but the doxology.

Order	Source and incipit	Cue	Rubric	Notes	Origin
Intro 1	Inclita refulget dies	Spiritus domini	Ad R		A/F
	PaN 1834, St Martial, *ca* 1000				
Intro 1	Inclita refulget dies[58]	Spiritus domini	Dmc Sca Pentecosten		A/F
A1	Paraclitus sanctus postulans	Spiritus domini	Alium		A
A2	Discipulis flammas infundens	Spiritus domini	no rubric		IN
A4	Sanctus en veniens sanctorum	Spiritus domini	no rubric		A
A3	Psallite candidati spiritus	Spiritus domini	no rubric		IN
B1	Mystica paracliti virtutum flamma	Spiritus domini	no rubric		A
A5	Doxa patri yo ke agio	no cue	It Gloria in Greco		A
	PaN 1120, St Martial, 1010–1020				
Intro 1	Inclita refulget dies	Spiritus domini	Domc Sci Pent		A/F
A1	Paraclitus sanctus postulans	Spiritus domini	Alios		A
A2	Discipulis flammas infundens	Spiritus domini	Alios		IN
A4	Sanctus en veniens sanctorum	Spiritus domini	Alios		A
A3	Psallite candidati spiritus	Spiritus domini	Alios		IN
B1	Mystica paracliti virtutum flamma	Spiritus domini	Ite Alios		A

[57] In this source *Paraclitus sanctus postulans* and *Inclita refulget dies* are conflated as a single introduction, followed by the internal verses of *Paraclitus sanctus*.

[58] This introduction, which has no internal verses outside St Martial, was provided with a single internal verse at St Martial around 1000, *Cuncta regit cunctaque replet*.

A5	Doxa patri ke yo ke agio	no cue	Ite Gla in Greco		A
PaN 1121, St Martial, 1025–1028					
Intro 1	Inclita refulget dies	Spiritus domini	In Pentecosten Trophi		A/F
A1	Paraclitus sanctus postulans	Spiritus domini	Al		A
B1	Mystica paracliti virtutum flamma	Spiritus domini	Al		A
A2	Discipulis flammas infundens	Spiritus domini	Item Alios		IN
A4	Sanctus en veniens sanctorum	Spiritus domini	Item		A
A3	Psallite candidati spiritus	Spiritus domini	Alios		IN
A5	Doxa patri ke yo ke agio	no cue	Gla Greca		A
PaN 909, St Martial, 1028–1029					
Intro 1	Inclita refulget dies	Spiritus domini	In Sco Pent Tr		A/F
A1	Paraclitus sanctus postulans	Spiritus domini	Trop	Ps. Exsurgat deus	A
B1	Mystica paracliti virtutum	Spiritus domini	Trop		A
A2	Discipulis flammas infundens	Spiritus domini	Trop	Ps. Confirma hoc	IN
A4	Sanctus en veniens sanctorum	Spiritus domini	Ad Rep Tr		A
A3	Psallite candidati spiritus	Spiritus domini	Al Tr		IN
A5	Doxa patri ke yo ke agio	no cue	Grece Gla		A
PaN 1119, St Martial, 1050					
Intro 1	Inclita refulget dies	Spiritus domini	no rubric		A/F
A1	Paraclitus sanctus postulans	Spiritus domini	Aliu		A
B1	Mystica paracliti virtutum flamma	Spiritus domini	Alium		A
A2	Discipulis flammas infundens	Spiritus domini	Aliu	Ps. Confirma hoc	IN

Order	Source and incipit	Cue	Rubric	Notes	Origin
A4	Sanctus en veniens sanctorum	Spiritus domini	Aliu		A
A3	Psallite candidati spiritus	Spiritus domini	Aliu		IN
A5	Doxa patri ke yo ke agio	no cue	Item Gla in Greco		A
	PaN 903, St Yrieix, *ca* 1050				
Intro 3 =	Hora est – Hodie descendit	Spiritus domini	In Die Sco Pentecosten		A
Intro 1	Inclita refulget dies	Spiritus domini	Ad Pl [sic]	Ps. Exsurgat deus	A/F
A2	Discipulis flammas infundens	Spiritus domini	It Al	Gloria patri	IN
A4	Sanctus en veniens sanctorum	Spiritus domini	Al		A
	PaN 1871, Aurillac, ca 1050				
Intro 3	Hodie descendit spiritus sanctus	Spiritus domini	De Pentecosten Tropos		A
Intro 1	Inclita refulget dies	Spiritus domini	Alios		A/F
A 1	Paraclitus sanctus postulans	Spiritus domini	Alios	Ps. Exsurgat deus	A
B 1	Mystica paracliti virtutum	Spiritus domini	Ite Alios		A
A2	Discipulis flammas infundens	Spiritus domini	Alios Si Placet		IN
A4	Sanctus en veniens sanctorum	Spiritus domini	Alios		A
A3	Psallite candidati spiritus	Spiritus domini	Alios		IN
B2	Praeclarus nunc dies adest	Spiritus domini	Ite Alios		A
	-	Todo neumatu	Grecum Officium	Introit in Greek	-
	-	Ps. Apotes	-	Greek psalm	-
[A5]	-	Doxa patri ke yo	Gla	Greek doxology	-
	Apt 17, Apt, Ste Anne, 11c/2				

					A/F
Intro 1	Inclita refulget dies	Spiritus domini	Tr in Pentct		A
A1	Paraclitus sanctus postulans	Spiritus domini	Tro	Ps. Exsurgat deus	A
B 1	Mystica paracliti virtutum	Spiritus domini	no rubric		IN
A2	Discipulis flammas	Spiritus domini	It Tr	Gloria patri	A
B2	Praeclarus nunc dies adest	Spiritus domini	no rubric	Ps. Confirma hoc	A
A4	Spiritus adveniens sanctorum[59]	Spiritus domini	Item		A
A3	Psallite candidati spiritus	Spiritus domini	no rubric		IN
Intro 2	Hodie spiritus sanctus descendit	Spiritus domini	Item Tropi		A
New	Spiritus almus adest cunctorum	Spiritus domini	Item Trop	unicum	A
	PaN 779, Narbomne, 12c				
Intro 1	Inclita refulget dies	Spiritus domini	no rubric		A
A1	Paraclitus sanctus postulans	Spiritus domini	Alios	Ps. Exsurgat deus	A
B1	Mystica paracliti virtutum	Spiritus domini	Aliu	Ps. Confirma hoc	A
A2	Discipulis flammas infudit	Spiritus domini	Alios	Ps. Emitte Spiritum	IN
A4	Sanctus en veniens sanctorum	Spiritus domini	Alium		A
A5	Doxa patri ke yo ke agio	Spiritus domini	Ad Gla[60]	Gloria patri	A
A3	Psallite candidati spiritus	Spiritus domini	Ad Rp		IN

[59] Despite the first word variant (a common occurrence in Apt 17), this is the same trope as *Sanctus en veniens*.
[60] The cue however is the Introit *Spiritus domini*, the text of the trope is the Greek doxology.

A full performance of the introit, as would be required in a major feast such as Pentecost, theoretically involves four repetitions of the introit antiphon as follows:

Antiphon – Psalm – Antiphon – Doxology –

Antiphon – Verse ad repetendum – Antiphon

In practice, however, the Aquitanian manuscripts, for the most important feasts of the year, almost invariably suggest a fifth repetition: a single introductory trope, without interpolatory verses, leads to an introit cue without a psalm indication; then the second introit trope of the series, usually with interpolatory verses, leads to the corresponding introit cues, which are followed by a cue to the psalm verse. In this respect the practice is somewhat similar to that which in England was called a *versus ante officium*, where a trope-like composition serving as an introduction to the mass as a whole was followed by the normal number of tropes.[61] In this way a complete performance of the introit in Aquitaine could include five tropings of the antiphon.

The two tropes in PaN 1240 are versions of international tropes found on both sides of the Rhine) and probably go back to the ninth century, before the division of the empire. *Psallite cum laude* conflates with the interpolatory verses of *Psallite candidati* a first verse that survives only in PaN 1240 and 887; *Discipulis flammas* is the Aquitanian version of the international trope with a similar beginning.

By the middle of the tenth century an Aquitanian tradition has apparently emerged. The main series of PaN 1084 consists of an introduction to the mass as a whole and four antiphon tropes, which cover the most extended possible performance of an introit, this time with the older international opening verse for *Psallite candidati*. The fifth 'trope' is not quite that but rather the introit's doxology in transliterated Greek, possibly a misunderstood remnant of the *missa graeca* sometimes used by the Carolingians for Pentecost.[62] In the late tenth century, when PaN 1084 was taken to Aurillac, a supplement of two tropes and two introductions, one of them without music, were added in a later fascicle.

The series of PaN 1118 represents a conflation of the two series in PaN 1084, presenting the cantor with a choice of introductions and a choice of tropes. It is significant, however, that neither of the introductions has a psalm verse attached to its introit cue. It is the first trope with interpolatory verses, *Paraclitus sanctus*, that carries the first cue for a psalm verse.

---

[61]In northern France these are called *Tropi ad processionem*, and neither there nor in England are they cued to the introit. In Aquitania they always are, but invariably without a psalm cue. See Planchart, *The Repertory of Tropes at Winchester*, 2 vols (Princeton, 1977), vol. 1, pp. 234–240.

[62]Other such remnants, particularly the full introit, the Greek Gloria in excelsis, Sanctus, and Agnus dei appear also in the Pentecost mass in Aquitanian sources. See Charles Atkinson, 'Zur Enstehung und Überlieferung der Missa graeca', *AMw* 39 (1982), pp. 113–145, and 'Further Thoughts on the Origin of the *missa graeca*', in *FS Hucke*, pp. 75–94.

PaN 887, a troper that often aligns itself with PaN 1240 and shows traces of northern influence,[63] presents an expansion of the series in PaN 1240, keeping the first verse of *Psallite cum laude* and treating this piece as an introduction, since the psalm follows the troping with *Discipulis flammas*. The cues to the psalm and doxology after *Mystica paracliti* and *Sanctus en veniens* seem to require a reversal in the order of these two pieces in performance. What follows is a conflation of the trope *Paraclitus sanctus* and the introduction *Inclita refulget* marked 'Ad repetendum'.[64]

PaN 1834 presents another ordering of the first series of PaN 1084 (with tropes A3 and A4 reversed) plus a piece from the second series. This will be the Saint-Martial repertory for the next half century. The series of PaN 1834 is duplicated exactly in PaN 1120 and in neither source is the Greek doxology treated as a trope (that is, cued to the incipit of the introit); the rubrics properly identify it as a doxology. The series has one supernumerary trope, and it is tempting to see the change in the last rubric in PaN 1120 as a indication that this is an ad libitum piece that may be substituted for one of the others.

PaN 1121, 909, and 1119 subject the earlier Saint-Martial series found in PaN 1834 and 1120 to a single alteration, placing *Mystica paracliti* after *Paraclitus sanctus* and dropping all the intervening tropes by one place. The psalm cues and the rubrics in PaN 909 confirm my hypothesis that the final trope of the series is the supernumerary one; here the psalm verse appears after *Paraclitus sanctus*, the verse *ad repetendum* appears after *Discipulis flammas*, and therefore *Sanctus en veniens* is given the rubric 'Ad rep[etendum] tr[opi]'.

PaN 903 presents a simpler performance of the introit with four statements of the antiphon, but it conflates the introduction *Hodie descendit* with the famous Easter introduction *Hora est, psallite* and treats *Inclita refulget dies* as a trope, and not as an introduction. In this respect it places itself slightly apart from the central Aquitanian tradition.

The series in PaN 1871, from Aurillac,[65] is closer to the series in PaN 1084 than to that of the Saint-Martial tropers. It presents the cantor with a choice of two introductions (note that in this case it is the third trope that has the psalm incipit), one from the first series of PaN 1084 and the other from the second, followed by six tropes culled from both series. Two of them would be supernumerary pieces and indeed *Discipulis flammas* has the rubric 'Alios si placet'. The entire series is followed by the complete introit in Greek together with its psalm and doxology.

---

[63]See note 29 above.

[64]These kinds of conflations and the special relationship between PaN 887 and 1240 affect other feasts as well; see my 'On the Nature of Transmission', pp. 227–229, and David Hughes, 'Further Notes on the Grouping of the Aquitanian Tropers', *JAMS* 19 (1966), pp. 3–12.

[65]The usual assignation of PaN 1871 to St Pierre de Moissac, based upon Henry Marriott Bannister, 'Un tropaire-prosaire de Moissac', *Revue d'histoire et littérature religieuse* 8 (1903), pp. 554–581, is no longer tenable; see my 'Fragments, Palimpsests, and Marginalia', *JM* 6 (1988), pp. 293–339.

The two late tropers Apt 17 and PaN 779 present a different picture. Apt 17 is closer in its repertory to PaN 1118, while PaN 779 is closer to the Saint-Martial tradition, but in both cases the trope series is much looser and one has the impression that these sources offer the cantor an anthology from which to choose the tropes for a performance of the introit. This impression is conveyed in particular by the variety of psalm verses appended in PaN 779.

In spite of the differences I have noted, the repertory throughout Aquitaine, and for more than a century, is remarkably stable and consistent. This consistency applies even to matters of order: notice how the reordering of *Sanctus en veniens* and *Psallite candidati spiritus*, which took place between 975 and 996, was retained in all subsequent sources throughout the entire region until the end of the eleventh century. The repertorial stability evidenced by the prose for Easter Sunday and the introit tropes for Pentecost is, however, entirely absent in the case of the prose for Pentecost. The Aquitanian proses for Pentecost are given in Table 19.4.

In considering Table 19.4 we should note that Eastertide consists of the week of Easter (where each day has its own liturgy), followed by the five Sundays after Easter, that is, twelve occasions where a prose 'De resurrectione' is appropriate. Whitsuntide lasts only to the Saturday after Pentecost. By the tenth century the Sunday after Pentecost was Trinity Sunday, a festival with its own character, which marks the beginning of the long summer season. This might be one of the explanations for the smaller number of proses for Pentecost in the manuscripts.

One would suppose that the small number of proses would lead to a repertorial stability, but this is emphatically not the case for Pentecost. Out of twenty-five proses in Table 19.4 fifteen appear only once for Whitsuntide. Some of them are proses that survive today as unica; that is the case of *Spiritus sanctus procedens, Rex mundi dominator, Adest sancta dies, Pangamus carmina sancta*, and *Clara voce dans gaudia*. Others are borrowed from other feasts, usually those close to Pentecost: Trinity, in the case of *Benedicta sit, O alma trinitas deitas*, and *O alma trinitas deus* (this last often used also for All Saints and the Common of Saints); Ascension, in the case of *Praecipua aderit nobis*; the Sundays *infra annum* in the case of *Christe tua agmina*, one of the proses surviving in the earliest collections, although with a narrow concordance. Four – *Eia musa, Qui procedis, Lux iocunda*, and *Cantantibus hodie* – are Whitsuntide proses from outside Aquitaine that filtered into the region relatively late, and one, *Alma chorus domini*, most likely for Trinity or for the Sundays *infra annum*, is widespread and received a large number of different liturgical assignments in the more than fifty manuscripts that transmit it. Of these, *Christe tua agmina, Alma chorus*, and the three proses for the Trinity also appear in the Aquitanian manuscripts with liturgical assignments outside of Whitsuntide. The same is the case for the prose *Nunc exsultet* in PaN 1240, which appears for one or another of the feasts in Easter Week in PaN 779, 1084, 1118, and 1871 (see Table 19.3), and also in all Italian and

Spanish sources.[66] The text of *Nunc exsultet* has virtually nothing to do with Pentecost: the prose deals with the Harrowing of Hell and the resurrection of Christ; in other words, its imagery is entirely connected with Eastertide.[67]

The same sense of an unstable tradition is seen in the proses that open the Pentecost series. While in the case of Easter the principal prose for Easter Sunday is *Fulgens praeclara* in fourteen out of nineteen cases (and two of the five series that do not start with *Fulgens praeclara* are second or third series in manuscripts where the main series starts with it), in the case of Pentecost we have twelve proses, out of a total repertory of twenty-five, each of which might serve as the main prose for Pentecost in one or another of the series. The situation is given in Table 19.5.

A further demonstration of the instability of the tradition is presented by the prose *Ad te summe celsa laus*, a work that, like *Celebranda satis nobis* and *Fulgens praeclara*, makes use of a *sequentia* with a partial text. *Sequentia* and prose both come down to us with two different melodies: melody 1 appears in PaN 1084 (*sequentia*), 887 (prose and *sequentia*), 1118 (*sequentia*), 903 (prose), 1871 (*sequentia*), and 1177 (prose); and melody 2 appears in 1121 (sequentia),[68] 909 (*sequentia*), Rogier (prose), 1132 (prose), 1133 (*sequentia*), 1134 (*sequentia*), 1136 (prose and *sequentia*), 1137 (prose and *sequentia*), and the late appendix of PaN 1084 (prose). Melody 1, which cites the incipit of the alleluia *Spiritus domini*, goes back at least to 950, while the earliest source for melody 2 is PaN 1121, copied between 1025 and 1028 (the prose has music in PaN 1120), and it is restricted to manuscripts from Saint-Martial.

Of those in Table 19.5 the two that appear as the main prose for Pentecost in the largest number of sources are *Laudiflua cantica* (used in that manner wherever PaN 887 was copied, and as well as in Saint-Martial, St Yrieix, Aurillac, Arles, and Narbonne), and Notker's *Sancti spiritus* (used in that manner at Saint-Martial (after 1063), St Leonard, and Narbonne, and found also where PaN 887 was copied, namely, Apt, and Moissac). Oddly enough the most widespread of these pieces within Aquitaine was *Ad te summe celsa laus*, which, if we leave *Sancti spiritus* out, is probably also the oldest of the Aquitanian pieces specifically for Pentecost.

---

[66] The prose itself is not in PaN 1118, but the sequentiarium of PaN 1084 assigns it to Easter, and most likely it is one of the untitled melodies in the *sequentiarium* of PaN 1118. Within the troper of PaN 1118, however, the trope to the *sequentia* for Easter Monday, *Immortalis filius dei*, is cued to *Nunc exsultet*.

[67] This was already noted by Bannister in AH 53, p. 129.

[68] With the incipit *Salve regnans*, probably the incipit of a prose that no longer survives, it might have been in the proser of PaN 1121. The same incipit appears in the *sequentiarium* of PaN 1134 but connected to the melody of *Almiphona iam gaudia*.

Table 19.4: Proses for Pentecost and Pentecost week in Aquitaine

No.	Source and incipit	Cue	Rubric	Notes	Origin[69]
	PaN 1240, St Martial, 923–936 (proses in the *congregatio prosarum*)				
1	Nunc exsultet omnis mundus	Pentecost	In Pentec	no music	A/I
	PaN 1084, undetermined, main repertory of 10c ex. later Aurillac and St Martial (proses in a *prosarium* with an extended appendix)				
Main series					
2	Cantemus organa pulchra satis	Pentecost	In Pentecosten		A/F
3	Orbis conditor regressus est[70]	-	Al		A
Appendix, first series					
4	Spiritus sanctus procedens	Pentecost	De Pentecosten		A/u
Appendix, second series					
5	Praecipua aderit nobis (no music)[71]	Pentecost	Psa de Pentecosten		A/u

[69] A = Aquitanian (including Pyrenees); E = English; F = French; I = Italian; IN = International; A/F = Aquitanian but with some French concordances; A/I = Aquitanian but with Italian concordances; F/E = North French with English and Aquitanian concordances.

[70] Some verses erased.

[71] Found in PaN 1118, also without music, for Ascension.

No.	Title	Season	Rubric	Notes	Mode
6	Canat cuncta per orbem creata	-	De Sps Dni		A

Later additions, *ca* 1050

No.	Title	Season	Rubric	Notes	Mode
7	Ad te summe celsa laus alleluia	Pentecost	In Pentc P	melody 2	A
8	Laudiflua cantica det mens nostra	-	no rubric		A

PaN 1118, Tolouse or SW France, 996–1000 (proses in a *prosarium*)

No.	Title	Season	Rubric	Notes	Mode
3	Orbis conditor regressus est in	Pentecost	Psa in Die Sco Pentecosten		A
6	Canat cuncta per orbem creata	Pentecost	Alia prosa de Sps Dni	no music	A
2	Cantemus organa pulchra satis	-	Alia		A/F

PaN 887, undetermined, 11c/1 (proses in a *prosarium*)

No.	Title	Season	Rubric	Notes	Mode
8	Laudiflua cantica det mens nostra	Pentecost	De Pentecost		A
7	Ad te summe celsa laus alleluia	Pentecost	De Pent	melody 1	A
2	Cantemus organa pulchra satis	-	Alia		A/F
9	Sancti spiritus adsit nobis gratia[72]	Pentecost	In die Pentec		G
10	Resonet sacrata iam turma diva[73]	Pentecost	De Pentecosten		F/E
11	Rex mundi dominator die hodierna	-	Item alia		A/u

PaN 1120, St Martial, 1010–1020 (proses in a *prosarium*)

---

[72] After the proses for the Trinity.
[73] Between St Stephen and St John Baptist.

No.	Source and incipit	Cue	Rubric	Notes	Origin
1	Nunc exsultet omnis mundus quia	Pentecost	In Pentecosten	no music	A/I
12	[Christe] tua agmina iubilant	-	no rubric	no music	IN/u
13	Alma chorus domini nunc pangat	-	no rubric	no music	IN/u
7	Ad te summe celsa laus[74]	Pentecost	De Pentecosten Prosa	no music	A
	PaN 1121, St Martial, 1025–1028 (the *prosarium* of the manuscript is largely lost, only the last six folios survive)				
8	Laudiflua cantica det mens nostra[75]	[Pentecost]	no rubric	part no music	A
	PaN 909, St Martial, 1028–1029 (the manuscript did not have a *prosarium*)				
Both proses are later additions					
8	Laudiflua cantica det mens nostra	[Pentecost]	no rubric		A
14	Adest sancta dies hac praeclara	Pentecost	Prosa in Pentecosten de All Sps Dni		A/u
	PaN 1138–1338, Limoges, *ca* 1040 (two parts of a dismembered manuscript) (proses in a *prosarium*)				
10	Resonet sacrata iam turma diva	Pentecost	In Sco Pent	Fascicle 8	F/E
8	Laudiflua cantica det mens nostra	-	no rubric		A
7	Ad te summe celsa laus alleluia	Pentecost	In Pent	melody 2	A

[74] Later addition at the end of the codex.
[75] Later addition at the end of the codex.

2	Cantemus organa pulchra satis	Pentecost	De Pentecosten	fascicle 19	A/F
	PaN 903, St Yrieix, *ca* 1050 (proses in a *prosarium*)				
8	Laudiflua cantica des mens nostra	Pentecost	In Die Sco Pentecost Psa		A
7	Ad te summe celsa laus alleluia	-	It Al	melody 1	A
	PaN 1871, Aurillac, *ca* 1050 (proses in a *prosarium* with two series)				

First series

15	Pangamus carmina sancta resultant	Pentecost	In Pentes		A/u

Second series

8	Laudiflua cantica det mens nostra[76]	Pentecost	In Pentecoste		A
16	[Almiphona iam]...per climata[76]	-	no rubric		F/E
10	Resonet sacrata iam turma diva	-	Alia		F/E
2	Cantemus organa pulchra satis	-	Item Alia ubi supra		A/F
3	Orbis conditor regressus est	-	Alia		A
6	Canat cuncta per orbem creata	-	Alia ubi supra		A
	PaN 1119, St Martial, *ca* 1050 (proses in a *prosarium*)				
8	Laudiflua cantica det mens nostra	[Pentecost]	no rubric		A

---

[76]Beginning erased.

No.	Source and incipit	Cue	Rubric	Notes	Origin
	PaN 1132, St Martial, after 1063 (proses in a *prosarium* with two series)				
First series					
9	Sancti spiritus adsit nobis gratia	Pentecost	Psa de S Sps		G
7	Ad te summe celsa laus alleluia	-	Alia	melody 2	A
Second series					
15	Almiphona iam gaudia caeli	Feria 4	Fr IIII in Penthecosten[77]	F/E	
	PaN 1136, St Martial, after 1063 (proses in a *prosarium*)				
9	Sancti spiritus adsit nobis gratia	Pentecost	De Pentecosten		G
7	Ad te summe celsa laus alleluia	-	Alia	melody 2	A
16	Almiphona iam gaudia caeli	Pentecost	Alia Psa Pent		F/E
8	Laudiflua cantica det mens	-	Alia Psa Pulcriora		A
	PaN 1137, St Martial, after 1063 (proses in a *prosarium*)				
17	Benedicta sit beata trinitas	Pentecost	De Pentec		F/E/u
18	O alma trinitas deitas et	Pentecost	It Al de Pent		F/E/u

---

[77] Separated from the Pentecost proses by several Eastertide pieces.

No.	Incipit	Occasion	Rubric	Melody	Code
19	O alma trinitas deus es et unitas	-	It Alia		F/u
8	Laudiflua cantica det mens nostra	Pentecost	Ite Al de Pentecosten		A
7	Ad te summe celsa laus alleluia	-	Ite Alia	melody 2	A
	Apt 17, Apt, Ste Anne, 11c/2				
	(proses within the mass formularies)				
20	Eia musa dic quaeso praeclara	Pentecost	no rubric		IN/u
9	Sancti spiritus adsit nobis gratia[78]	-	Psa		G
	PaN 779, Arles, 12c				
	(proses within the mass formularies)				
8	Laudiflua cantica det mens nostra	Pentecost	Prosa ad Missa		A
21	Clara voce dans gaudia canat	Vespers	Sqr Prosa ad vesperas		A/u
3	Orbis conditor regressus est sui	In Octave	Alie per Octab		A
15	Almiphona iam gaudia caeli	Octave	In Octabas		F/E
	PaN 1086, Limoges, St Leonard, 12c				
9	Sancti spiritus adsit nobis gratia	Pentecost	In die Pentecoste		G
22	Qui procedis ab utroque genitore	Feria 2	Fra II Alia		A/F/u
23	Lux iocunda lux insignis qui	Feria 3	Fra III		F/E/u
	PaN 1086, Limoges, St Leonard, 12c				
9	Sancti spiritus adsit nobis gratia	Pentecost	In die Pentecoste		G

[78] Inserted in a fascicle among the tropes for the nativity of the BVM.

No.	Source and incipit	Cue	Rubric	Notes	Origin
22	Qui procedis ab utroque genitore	Feria 2	Fra II Alia		A/F/u
23	Lux iocunda lux insignis qui	Feria 3	Fra III		F/E/u
	PaN 1177, Moissac, 12c				
7	Ad te summe celsa laus alleluia[79]	[Pentecost]	no rubric	melody 1	A
9	Sancti spiritus adsit nobis gratia	Pentecost	In Pentecosten Psa		G
24	Veni sancte spiritus et emitte[80]				IN
	Pentecost	Psa			
	PaN 778, Narbonne, 12c (proses in a *prosarium*)				
9	Sancti spiritus adsit nobis gratia	Pentecost	Prosa ad Missa Maiore		G
25	Cantantibus hodie cunctis una	Vespers	Alia Psa ad Vprs		A/u
24	Veni sancte spiritus et emitte	-	Ala	upper writing	IN
3	[Orbis conditor regressus est]	-	rubric lost	lower writing	A
8	Laudiflua cantica det mens nostra	-	Alia Prosa		A

[79] Later addition.

[80] Separated from the previous prose by 20 folios. Copied between a prose for the BVM and one for Easter.

Table 19.5: Main prose for Pentecost in the Aquitanian manuscripts

Incipit		Sources as main prose	Also in Pentecost series
1	Nunc exsultet omnis mundus	PaN 1240, 1120	-
2	Cantemus organa pulchra	PaN 1084/1	PaN 1118, Rogier,[81] 1871
3	Spiritus sanctus procedens	PaN 1084/2	-
4	Praecipua aderit nostris	PaN 1084/3	-
5	Orbis conditor regressus est	PaN 1118	PaN 1084, 1871, 779, (778)
6	Laudiflua cantica det mens	PaN 887, 1121, 903, 1119, 1871/2, 779	PaN 1084, 909, Rogier, 1136, 1137, 778
7	Resonet sacrata iam turma	Rogier	PaN 887, 1871
8	Pangamus carmina sancta	PaN 1871/1	-
9	Sancti spiritus adsit nobis gratia	PaN 1132, 1136, 1086, 778	PaN 887, Apt 17, PaN 1177
10	Benedicta sit beata trinitas	PaN 1137	-
11	Eia musa dic quaeso	Apt 17	-
12	Ad te summe celsa laus	PaN 1177	PaN 1084, 887, 1120, Rogier, 903, 1132, 1136, 1137

[81]Rogier's proser, PaN 1138/1338.

Given the instability of the tradition, it is then not surprising that a 'foreign' work such as *Sancti spiritus* (one whose text was most likely not entirely appealing to Aquitanian sensibilities) made inroads into the repertory that no other specifically German piece penetrated. In a certain sense the Cluniacs did not have to push too hard in this case, since there was apparently no generally accepted prose for Pentecost as there was for a number of other feasts. It probably did not hurt that Notker chose as the tune for his text the melody of *Rex omnipotens die hodierna*, the Ascension prose that was almost without exception the main prose for Ascension, not only in Aquitaine, but in England, northern France, and the entire Italian peninsula (including the Roman basilicas where Old Roman chant was sung) in the tenth and eleventh centuries. The melody of *Rex omnipotens* could easily be described as the best-loved tune of any of the early *sequentiae*, and in the tenth and eleventh centuries the number of proses written in France, Aquitaine, England, and Italy that use that melody are legion.

The instability of the tradition for the prose in Pentecost that is apparent in the Aquitanian sources may have been a pan-European phenomenon before Notker wrote *Sancti spiritus*. Today we cannot see it quite so clearly, because *Sancti spiritus* attained early on an immense diffusion in the German-speaking lands and throughout Italy, and our evidence from west of the Rhine – particularly the crucial area of what is today northeastern France – is relatively late. Nevertheless, the earliest non-German sources with tropes and proses, Verona 90 and Munich 14843, have tropes for Christmas, Easter, and Pentecost, and proses for Christmas and possibly Easter but not for Pentecost.[82] The earliest collections of West Frankish *sequentiae* and proses outside Aquitaine[83] also appear, by and large, not to have pieces that are specific to Pentecost. Chartres 47 has a short aparallel *sequentia* found also in PaN 1084, where it is labelled 'Spiritus domini', but no western prose exists for it.[84] The two Winchester tropers, whose repertory might go back to the third quarter of the tenth Century, transmit the prose *Benedicta sit beata trinitas* (with its *sequentia*) for Pentecost. The *sequentiarium* in Angers 144 also shows *Benedicta sit* for Pentecost,[85] and so does the sequentiary of Cambrai 75.[86] PaN 1169 has *Benedicta sit* and *Sancti spiritus* as its proses within the

---

[82]Both manuscripts transmit the Christmas prose *Christi hodierna pangamini*, and Munich 14843 has the prose *Domine deus salvatio* immediately after the prosulas for the Easter Alleluia.

[83]The early *sequentiaria* have been the object of two important preliminary studies by David Hiley, 'The Sequentiary of Chartres, Bibliothéque municipale, MS 47', in Agostino Ziino, ed., *La sequenza medievale* (Lucca, 1992), pp. 105–118, and 'The Sequence Melodies', pp. 130–155. Anselm Hughes, *Anglo-French Sequelae* (London, 1934), based on the work of Henry Marriott Bannister, is useful but very limited.

[84]It is related to the alleluia *In te domine speravi* and its one prose, *Laus tibi sit*, an East Frankish work that is for Eastertide; see Hiley, 'The Sequentiary', p. 109.

[85]See Hiley, 'The Sequence Melodies', p. 143.

[86]Cambrai, BM, ms 75, does not give a liturgical assignment to any of its *sequentiae*, but the placement in the collection, separated only by a Marian *sequentia* from the *sequentia* for Ascension (*Rex omnipotens*), makes the association with Pentecost inescapable.

formulary for Pentecost, although it also has *Cantemus organa pulchra*, a true Pentecost prose from West Francia, copied together with *Ecce vicit radix David*, for Easter, between tropes for the Holy Innocents and a series of Agnus dei tropes. Not until we reach PaN 1149, copied around 1060 in Nevers, do we encounter proses specifically for Pentecost, *Almiphona iam gaudia* and *Resonat sacrata* indicated for the feast. Even later, in Cambrai 60 and Cambrai 78 we find *Fulgens praeclara* as the prose for Pentecost.[87]

Unlike other major feasts, where the West Frankish tradition yields proses of *sequentiae* with a specific connection to a given feast as early as the first half of the tenth century or the second half of the ninth, it appears that there was no tradition of proses specifically for Pentecost in the west until very late in the tenth century, and that this tradition was still not particularly strong in the eleventh. In this light Odilo of Cluny's decision to adopt Notker's *Sancti spiritus* as the single German prose to be used at Cluny appears to have been politically pragmatic and shrewd, giving comfort to the German brethren without opposing a strong tradition. The success of *Sancti spiritus* all through the west, even in Aquitaine, in the tenth and the eleventh centuries, is proof of his astuteness.

Appendix

Sigla	Place, library, ms number
Ang 96	Angers, BM 96
Apt 17	Apt, Basilique de Sainte Anne, 17
Apt 18	Apt, Basilique de Sainte Anne, 18
Aquileia	Missale Aquileiensis Ecclesiae (Venezia: Gregorio Gregorii, 1519)
As 695	Assisi, Biblioteca Comunale, 695
Ben 34	Benevento, BC 34
Ben 35	Benevento, BC 35
Ben 38	Benevento, BC 38
Ben 39	Benevento, BC 39
Ben 40	Benevento, BC 40
Ber 155	Berlin, Staatsbibliothek Preussischer Kulturbesitz, lat. theol. 8° 155
Ber 40608	Berlin, Deutsche Staatsbibliothek, 40608

---

[87]The use of *Fulgens praeclara* for Pentecost is attested in northern France (Cambrai 60 and 78, As 695, Pro 12, and RoA 435) and northern Italy (Pistoia, BC, 121). It is based on the references to Pentecost in verses 26–27 of the prose (see AH 53, p. 63). In the thirteenth century the tradition arose of ending the prose at Easter with verse 25 and adding verses 26–30 only at Pentecost. This is indicated in As 695, fol. 72ᵛ, by a rubric before verse 25: 'Istud residuum non dicitur nisi in die Pentecostes'. In a number of late sources this was accomplished by copying the prose up to verse 25 at Easter, and providing just the incipit as a cross reference, plus verses 26–30 at Pentecost. This misled Jeremy Yudkin in *Music in Medieval Europe* (Englewood Cliffs, 1989), p. 109, into giving as the prose in the mass for Pentecost the incipit, *Fulgens praeclara*, plus verses 26–30, although this leaves the verb 'fulgens' without a subject.

Sigla	Place, library, ms number
Bo 775	Oxford, Bodleian Library, Bodley 775
Bod 74	Cologny-Geneva, Bibliotheca Bodmeriana, 74
Bol 7	Bologna, Civico Museo Bibliografico Musicale, Q 7
BoU 2824	Bologna, Biblioteca Universitaria, 2824
Cai 60	Cambrai, BM 60
Cai 61	Cambrai, BM 61
Cai 75	Cambrai, BM 75
Cai 78	Cambrai, BM 78
Cam 710	Cambridge, UL 710
CC 473	Cambridge, Corpus Christi College, 473
Civ 56	Cividale dal Friuli, Museo Archeologico, 56
Civ 58	Cividale dal Friuli, Museo Archeologico, 58
Civ 79	Cividale dal Friuli, Museo Archeologico, 79
Dur 5	Durham, UL Cosin v.v.6
Gor	Gorizia, Seminario Teologico, I
Hue 4	Huesca, Archivo de la Catedral, 4
Ivr 60	Ivrea, BC 115 (olim Bollati LX)
Kil 29	Killiney, Dhun Muihre, B 29
Lo R 2B4	London, BL Royal 2 B IV
Lo R 8C13	London, BL Royal 8 C XIII
LoA 14	London, BL Cotton Caligula, A xiv
Ma 20	Madrid, BN Vitrina 20-4
Ma 288	Madrid, BN 288
Ma 289	Madrid, BN 289
Ma 19421	Madrid, BN 19421
MC 318	Montecassino, Archivio della Badia, 318
MC 546	Montecassino, Archivio della Badia, 546
Me 452	Metz, BM 452
Mod 7	Modena, BC, O. I. 7
Mza 75	Monza, BC, C 75
Mza 76	Monza, BC, C 76
Novara	Novara, Archivio Diocesano, ms s.s.
NY 797	New York, Pierpont Morgan Library, M797
Ox 148	Oxford, University College, 148
Ox 222	Oxford, Bodleian Library, Douce 222
Ox 340	Oxford, Bodleian Library, Canonici misc. 340
Ox 341	Oxford, Bodleian Library, Canonici misc. 341
PaA 1169	Paris, Bibliothèque de l=Arsenal, 1169
PaA 135	Paris, Bibliothèque de l=Arsenal, 135
Pad 16	Padua, BC, B 16
Pad 20	Padua, BC, A 20

Sigla	Place, library, ms number
Pad 47	Padua, BC, A 47
Pad 57	Padua, BC, E 57
PaN 778	Paris, BNF lat. 778
PaN 779	Paris, BNF lat. 779
PaN 887	Paris, BNF lat. 887
PaN 903	Paris, BNF lat. 903
PaN 909	Paris, BNF lat. 909
PaN 1084	Paris, BNF lat. 1084
PaN 1087	Paris, BNF lat. 1087
PaN 1118	Paris, BNF lat. 1118
PaN 1119	Paris, BNF lat. 1119
PaN 1120	Paris, BNF lat. 1120
PaN 1121	Paris, BNF lat. 1121
PaN 1132	Paris, BNF lat. 1132
PaN 1133	Paris, BNF lat. 1133
PaN 1134	Paris, BNF lat. 1134
PaN 1135	Paris, BNF lat. 1135
PaN 1136	Paris, BNF lat. 1136
PaN 1137	Paris, BNF lat. 1137
PaN 1138	Paris, BNF lat. 1138
PaN 1240	Paris, BNF lat. 1240
PaN 1338	Paris, BNF lat. 1338
PaN 1834	Paris, BNF lat. 1834
PaN 9449	Paris, BNF lat. 9449
PaN 10508	Paris, BNF lat. 10508
PaN 13252	Paris, BNF lat. 13252
PaN 495	Paris, BNF lat. n.a.l. 495
PaN 1177	Paris, BNF lat. n.a.l. 1177
PaN 1235	Paris, BNF lat. n.a.l. 1235
PaN 1871	Paris, BNF lat. n.a.l. 1871
Pia 65	Piacenza, BC 65
Pro 12	Provins, BM 12
Pst 121	Pistoia, BC, C 121
RoA 123	Rome, Biblioteca Angelica, A 123
RoA 435	Rome, Biblioteca Angelica, 435
RoC 1741	Rome, Biblioteca Casanatense, 1741
RoN 1343	Rome, Biblioteca Nazionale, 1343
RoV 52	Rome, Biblioteca Vallicelliana, C 52
To 17	Torino, Biblioteca Nazionale, F. III. 17
To 18	Torino, Biblioteca Nazionale, F. IV. 18
To 20	Torino, Biblioteca Nazionale, G. V. 20

Sigla	Place, library, ms number
Ud 2	Udine, Biblioteca Arcivescovile, 2
Ud 78	Udine, Biblioteca Arcivescovile, 78
Vat 5319	Vatican, BAV, Vat. lat. 5319
Vce 146	Vercelli, BC 146
Vce 161	Vercelli, BC 161
Vce 162	Vercelli, BC 162
Vce 186	Vercelli, BC 186
Vic 105	Vich, Biblioteca Episcopal, 105
Vic 106	Vich, Biblioteca Episcopal, 106
Vol 39	Volterra, Biblioteca Guarnacci, L. 3. 39
Vro 107	Verona, BC, CVII (100)
Wor 160	Worcester, Cathedral Chapter Library, F 160

Chapter 20

The *Historia Sancti Magni* by Hermannus Contractus (1013–1054)

David Hiley

A number of fortunate coincidences accompany this chapter. The year 2004 was an anniversary not only for the dedicatee of these lines but also for Hermannus Contractus, and it was more than appropriate that his *Historia Sancti Magni*, the cycle of chants in honour of St Magnus of Füssen, should have been noticed in time to be edited for the present volume. Among the many projects that Bryan Gillingham has taken under his benevolent wing, one of the more recent is the series 'Historiae', edited by László Dobszay, Barbara Haggh, and Ruth Steiner for the Study Group 'Cantus Planus' of the International Musicological Society. An essay on a *historia* therefore seems a suitable birthday contribution. The normal procedure in the series 'Historiae' is to edit not only chants but also prayers, lessons, and any other material necessary for the reconstruction of the liturgical celebration as fully as practicable. In the case of St Magnus this is not at present possible. The opportunity is taken here to present simply the chants, with a short introduction outlining their historical significance.

In a sentence that has already been quoted several times in the scholarly literature, Hermannus's disciple Berthold tells of the *historiae* that his beloved and much reverenced master composed:

> Cantus item historiales plenarios, utpote quo musicus peritior non erat, de sancto Georgio, sanctis Gordiano et Epimacho, sancta Afra martyre, sancto Magno confessore, et de sancto Wolfgango episcopo mira suavitate et elegantia euphonicos, praeter alia huiusmodi perplura, neumatizavit et composuit.[1]

> Being a *musicus* more expert than anyone else, he set to music and composed complete cycles of chants for *historiae*, for St George, SS Gordianus and Epimachus, St Afra the Martyr, St Magnus the Confessor and St Wolfgang the Bishop, harmonious in their wonderful sweetness and elegance, with very many others of this kind.

---

[1] Georg Heinrich Pertz, ed., *Monumenta Germaniae historica, scriptores, annales et chronica aevi salici* (1844; hereafter *MGH*), vol. 5, pp. 267–269 (here p. 268); PL 143, 25–30 (here col. 28).

Hermannus's productivity reminds one of those prolific Latin authors who composed biographies – *vitae* – not only of their own local patron saints but of others as well, the type of author recently called by Walter Berschin 'professional hagiographer'.[2] For example, Otloh of St Emmeram in Regensburg writes *vitae* not only of St Wolfgang of Regensburg but also of St Boniface of Fulda, St Magnus of Füssen, St Alto of Alto-münster (near Augsburg), and St Nicholas.[3]

Hermannus's offices for George and for Gordian and Epimachus have not yet been rediscovered, but the Afra and Wolfgang offices have been known for some time. In 1892 Wilhelm Brambach published a facsimile of the Afra office as found in a Karls-ruhe manuscript; a modern joint edition by Walter Berschin and myself has just ap-peared.[4] As long ago as 1894 Utto Kornmüller said he believed he had found the Wolfgang office; a transcription of the chants was published by Franz Stein in 1977, and a full critical, liturgical edition by myself in 2002.[5]

It seems just possible that Hermann composed all these offices with particular celebrations in mind. 1050 would have been the 300th anniversary of Magnus; that Hermannus composed the Wolfgang office for the saint's canonization in 1052 may be regarded as certain; 1054 was the 700th anniversary of Afra.

Two sources of Hermannus's *Historia de Sancto Magno* have survived, and in neither has the office previously been recognized. St Gallen, Stiftsbibliothek 388, is an antiphoner of the late eleventh century from St Gallen. (Its main text and neume hands are too early for a twelfth-century dating, but the presence of the *historia* for St Fides, whose relics were brought from Agen in Aquitaine by Abbot Ulrich III (1077–1121) near the start of his abbacy, gives a *terminus post quem*.) The Magnus office is entered on pp. 304–308, notated in St Gall neumes without significative letters or episemata. The other source is a two-volume manuscript antiphoner in Munich University Lib-rary, codex 2° 166–167, on fols. 171^V–177^V of the second volume. A hymn for the saint appears in the hymnary, on fol. 281^r. The description of the manuscript by Clytus

---

[2]Walter Berschin, *Biographie und Epochenstil im lateinischen Mittelalter* IV/1: *Ottonische Biographie, das hohe Mittelalter. 920–1220 n. Chr.*, Quellen und Untersuchungen zur latein-ischen Philologie des Mittelalters 12 (Stuttgart, 1999), p. 25, citing Petrus Subdiaconus (writing up to about 960), Adso of Montier-en-Der (died 992), Otloh of St Emmeram in Regensburg (died about 1070) and Sigebert of Gembloux (died 1112).

[3]Otloh's writings are edited in PL, vol. 146.

[4]David Hiley and Walter Berschin, *Hermannus Contractus (1013–1054): historia sanctae Afrae martyris Augustensis* (Ottawa, 2004).

[5]Utto Kornmüller, 'Der heilige Wolfgang als Beförderer des Kirchengesanges', in Johann Baptist Mehler, ed., *Der heilige Wolfgang, Bischof von Regensburg. Historische Festschrift zum neunhundertjährigen Gedächtnisse seines Todes (3.10.1894)* (Regensburg, 1894), pp. 140–162; Franz A. Stein, 'Das ältere Offizium des hl. Wolfgang in der Handschrift Clm 14872 aus St Emmeram zu Regensburg in der Bayerischen Staatsbibliothek München', in *Sacerdos et cantus gregoriani magister. Festschrift Ferdinand Haberl zum 70. Geburtstag* (Regensburg, 1977), pp. 279–302; see also my *Hermannus Contractus (1013–1054): historia Sancti Wolf-gangi Episcopi Ratisbonensis* (Ottawa, 2002).

Gottwald[6] lists the office among the items of the Sanctorale but does not identify it further (naturally enough, since only a summary catalogue is intended). The only other local saint in the book, Afra of Augsburg, indicates that it comes from South Germany, while the prominence given to Augustine and the secular or Roman cursus of the offices should mean a house of Augustinian canons. Gottwald suggests Diessen or Polling, but this cannot be right, since the numerous surviving breviaries from these monasteries do not contain this office, nor do they pay special attention to Magnus. The only South German house of Augustinian canons dedicated to Magnus was St Mang, Stadtamhof, Regensburg, but more proof will have to be sought before the manuscript can safely be assigned to St Mang. It is notated with square notation of the fifteenth century (see Figure 20.1).

The position of the office in the Sanctorale and the texts of the chants make it clear that Magnus of Füssen is being celebrated, his feast day falling on 6 September. That Hermannus is the author of the chants is naturally not indicated.[7] Berthold's statement that Hermannus composed such an office predisposes one to identify it with the chants in both manuscripts, but supporting arguments are clearly needed. The musical style of the chants strongly suggests Hermannus's authorship. While this is not such strong evidence as some sort of written attribution or identification (Berthold could, for example, have cited the opening items of each *historia*), it effectively places the onus of proof upon those who would argue against Hermannus's authorship. The two sources are complementary in this respect. If only the later manuscript had survived one might question the age of the chants, so progressive is their melodic style. From the neumes of St Gallen 388 alone the melodic style cannot be deduced, but the age of the source, made only about thirty years after Hermannus's death, makes it certain that we are dealing with Hermannus's compositions.

Structure

It is a fair assumption that Hermannus would have composed the *historia* for the Benedictine monastery of St Magnus at Füssen following the Benedictine cursus of the office, and would moreover have arranged the chants in numerical modal order. This is the case with Wolfgang of Regensburg, for whom Hermannus composed the following chants:

---

[6]Clytus Gottwald, *Die Musikhandschriften der Universitätsbibliothek München*, Die Handschriften der Universitätsbibliothek München 2 (Wiesbaden, 1968), pp. 22–24.

[7]The attribution of the Afra *historia* to him in Karlsruhe, Badische Landesbibliothek, Aug. LX, is exceptional, and may be understood in connection with the scribe's practice of indicating sources for all the texts in the manuscript.

David Hiley

Figure 20.1: Munich University Library, codex 2⁰ 167, fol. 171ᵛ

Hermannus Contractus: *Historia Sancti Wolfgangi*

Ad primas vesperas   mode
antiphona ad Magnificat 1 (the responsory is the twelfth in the night office)

Ad matutinas
   invitatorium   4

In primo nocturno
   antiphonae 1–6   1–6
   responsoria 1–4   1–4

In secundo nocturno
   antiphonae 7–12   7–8, 1–4
   responsoria 5–8   5–8

Ad cantica
   antiphona ad cantica   4
   responsoria 9–12   1, 3, 5, 7

Ad laudes
   antiphonae 1–5   5–8, 1
   antiphona ad Benedictus 2

Ad secundas vesperas
antiphona ad Magnificat 3

(The Magnificat antiphon of first vespers, the invitatory and the antiphona ad cantica of the night office stand outside the numerical series.)

Hermannus composed only nine responsories for the night office of the Afra *historia*. The provision of nine instead of twelve was quite common at this time: a majority of offices in the Sanctorale of the Hartker antiphoner (St Gallen, *ca* 1000), for example, have only nine *proper* responsories. Others could be taken from the Commune sanctorum if required. In extant monastic sources of the Afra office the number of twelve responsories is made up with the responsory from first vespers and two from the Commune virginum. Hermannus's original series for Afra was as follows:

Hermannus Contractus, *Historia Sanctae Afrae*

Ad primas vesperas   mode
   responsorium   3
   antiphona ad Magnificat   3

Ad matutinas
   invitatorium   4

In primo nocturno

antiphonae 1–6   1–6
responsoria 1–3   1–3 (responsory 4 is taken from the Commune
                                      virginum)

In secundo nocturno
  antiphonae 7–12   7–8, 1, 3, 5, 7
  responsoria 5–7   4–6 (responsory 8 is taken from first vespers)

Ad cantica
  antiphona ad cantica   7
  responsoria 10–12   7–8, 1 (responsory 9 is taken from the Commune
                                      virginum)

Ad laudes
  antiphonae 1–5   1–5
  antiphona ad benedictus   6

Ad secundas vesperas
  antiphona ad Magnificat   7

(The responsory and Magnificat antiphon of first vespers, the invitatory and the antiphona ad cantica of the night office stand outside the numerical series.)

The Magnus *historia* as transmitted in both manuscripts follows the secular or
Roman cursus. It seems certain that the original order would have been that of the
Benedictine cursus, but in St Gallen 388 the thirteen antiphons normal for the Benedictine night office (6+6+1) have been put in three groups of three each, the remaining
four being allocated to prime, terce, sext and none respectively. These four are omitted
from Munich 167. Since St Gallen 388 marks the *differentiae* of the psalm tones with
the characteristic St Gall psalm-tone letters (*a, e, i, o, u, H, y, w*), it may be seen that
the numerical modal order is continued. The final Magnificat antiphon in St Gallen
388 is in mode 7, outside the numerical series, but Munich 167 has a different antiphon at this point in the numerically 'correct' mode 4. (It also adds an antiphon for the
psalms at first vespers.) The original series would have been as follows:

Hermannus Contractus: *Historia Sancti Magni*

Ad primas vesperas   mode
  responsorium   8
  antiphona ad Magnificat   1

Ad matutinas
  invitatorium   7

In primo nocturno
  antiphonae 1–6   1–6
  responsoria 1–3   1–3

In secundo nocturno

| antiphonae 7–12 | 7–8, 1–4 |
| responsoria 4–6 | 4–6 |

Ad cantica
| antiphona ad cantica | 5 |
| responsoria 7–9 | 7–8, 7 |

Ad laudes
| antiphonae 1–5 | 6–8, 1–2 |
| antiphona ad benedictus | 3 |

Ad secundas vesperas
| antiphona ad Magnificat | 7 |

(The responsory and Magnificat antiphon of first vespers and the invitatory of the night office stand outside the numerical series.)

In the transcription from Munich 167 at the end of this chapter, and in Table 20.1 below, the manuscript order (Roman cursus) is followed.

The chant texts

The texts of most chants refer to incidents in the life of St Magnus, through to his death and burial commemorated at the end of lauds and in the Magnificat at second vespers. The chants of first vespers, the invitatory and the final responsory of the night office are not narrative, but many of the others can be matched with particular passages in the *vita*. Here we must distinguish between at least two biographies or versions of the *vita*, the 'standard' life and a new version by Otloh of St Emmeram. The standard text was presumably known to Hermannus, while Otloh, by his own account, was persuaded to write a new one by his pupil and fellow monk Adelhelm, who would later be abbot of St Magnus in Füssen, and after that abbot of SS. Ulrich and Afra in Augsburg. Otloh says this was in the year 1067.[8]

---

[8]The standard version is edited in *Acta sanctorum* 2 (September), pp. 735–759, the other by Maurice Coens, 'La vie de S. Magne de Füssen par Otloh de Saint-Emmeran', *Analecta bollandiana* 81 (1963), pp. 159–227 (edition on pp. 184–227). The first text is supposed to date back in part to Theodore, one of Magnus's companions, and to have been revised and enlarged by Ermenrich of Ellwangen about 848, soon after the solemn reinterment of Magnus's mortal remains in 845. Further revisions would have been undertaken in St Gallen after the monastery had received a precious relic of the saint in 890, when a cell and church dedicated to the saint were built. How much the preserved text really contains of previously distinct *vitae* is, however, disputed. Coens, editor of Otloh's *vita*, argues that the preserved text was put together for the first time in Füssen or Augsburg in the tenth century, including borrowings from previous writings (the Columbanus and Gallus *vitae*, for example).

It would perhaps be surprising if the chant texts contained direct echoes of Otloh's text, since it remained little known. But if such quotations occurred they would obviously be an argument against composition by Hermannus, who died in 1054. (Since Otloh was also a musician, it might even be argued that he was the composer of the Magnus *historia*.) In fact, there are no obvious citations from Otloh's *vita*. It is true that the first antiphon of the night office, reporting Magnus's origins, might seem to echo Otloh:

5. Ant.	*Sanctus vir Magnoaldus Scotigene stirpis ex Hybernia insula fuit oriundus.*
standard vita:	*Tempore illo ... quidam frater nomine Magnoaldus ex praefata patria Hibernia procreatus, pulsare coepit aures beati Galli ...* (AASS, p. 735)
Otloh:	*In tempore illo ..... frater quidam nomine Magnoaldus, ex eadem Hibernia oriundus, ad beatum Gallum accedens ...* (Coens, p. 187)

Yet the word 'oriundus' is by no means uncommon. One might even argue that Otloh took it from Hermannus's antiphon. And it is perhaps significant that the antiphon text calls Hibernia an island and says Magnus (Magnoaldus) is of Scottish ancestry, information not found in the *vitae*.

The final antiphon of the *historia* relates how Magnus's body is laid to rest in a stone sarcophagus by Bishop Tozzo and ends with the customary supplications for aid under the saint's protection. Here the antiphon text uses the word 'lapideus' like the standard *vita*:

29. Ant. ad Mag.	*Magnificus tuus Christe confessor Magnus in sarcophago lapideo sibi divinitus procurato condigno honore ab episcopo Tozzone tumulatus ...*
standard vita:	*Finito itaque commemorationis obsequio, invenerunt ambo sarcophagum optimum lapideum ...* (p. 755)
Otloh:	*Cum igitur talia agerentur, interea querebatur saxum quod aptium esset ad faciendum sarcophagum ...* (Coens, p. 220)

But this detail is also too slight to be an argument for the standard *vita* rather than Otloh's version as the source for the chant texts. In Table 20.1 the corresponding passages in the *vitae* are indicated for each chant.

The number of texts for which there is no obvious correspondence already suggests a degree of independence from the *vitae*. And even when obvious parallels are present, the chant text usually goes its own way in choice of words. For example, the antiphon *Cumque virtute prepollens* (no. 12) concerns something that happens when Magnus holds the office of cellarer of the monastery under St Columbanus. One day beer is accidentally left running from the barrel into a jug, but, instead of spilling over, the beer as it were piles up into a sort of crown over the jug. This miracle is attributed to Magnus's intervention. The standard *vita* and Otloh describe it in similar terms, but only the author of the chant text likens it to the miracle of the Red Sea (when the waters piled up into walls to allow the passage of the Israelites): *Cumque virtute prepollens obediencie curam amministraret cellarii antiquo Maris Rubri miraculo celitus meruit decorari.* (The narrative continues in the next antiphon.)

In the responsory *Veniens vir dei Brigancium* (no. 15) Magnus restores a man's sight by wetting his eyes with his saliva: both *vitae* have the word 'saliva', but the antiphon uses 'sputus'. Coming to Kempten, Magnus finds the town full of snakes. Attacked by one dreadful serpent called Boas, he strikes it dead with his staff (bequeathed to him by St Gallus, cf. responsory 3). In the responsory *Cum Campidonam sanctus venisset* (no. 16) the chant and Otloh use 'baculus' for the staff, while the standard *vita* has the colloquial 'cambuta'. But only the chant refers to 'angues' (serpents), while the *vitae* call them 'vermes'. The antiphon *Ad preces eius plurima convolans* (no. 18) tells how a large flock of birds is caught through Magnus's agency, to provide food for the hungry monks. In the *vitae* the birds are 'aves', in the chant text 'volucres'. The chant texts were, therefore, newly composed, not centonized from the *vita*.

The responsory of first vespers of the *Historia Sancti Magni*, like that in the *Historia Sanctae Afrae*, is in Leonine hexameters. Many other texts are in rhyming prose. It will have been noticed (cf. Table 20.1) that the antiphons and responsories of the night office follow two different narrative cycles; the antiphons of lauds continue where the responsories of the night office leaves off.

In all these respects, including the degree of independence from the *vita*, the *Historia Sancti Magni* resembles Hermannus's Wolfgang and Afra offices, and there seems no strong reason to doubt his authorship of them all.

Musical style

Turning to the musical style of the chants, we may observe very much the same features as are so obvious in the Wolfgang and Afra offices. The Magnificat and Benedictus antiphons and the responsories are almost extravagantly melismatic. Authentic chants touch the upper octave or pass beyond it, plagal chants include both the lower fourth and the upper fifth and notes beyond. Several chants encompass both authentic and plagal ranges together (antiphons nos 3, 13, and 23, responsories nos 3, 16, 20, and 22). Most important is the way in which nearly all chants use the fifth above the finalis, the fourth below (in plagal modes), and the octave above (in authentic modes) as melodic goals, or as pillars on which to hang the free-flowing melismatic lines. Furthermore, there are frequent leaps not only between finalis and upper fifth but also between upper fifth and upper octave. I have analyzed this style in detail elsewhere, and also related it to Hermannus's concept of the modes as scale segments whose principal points are those same consonant notes of the modal octave, to be understood ultimately, no doubt, as an aural embodiment of the harmony of the whole

Table 20.1: *Historia Sancti Magni*

Historia Sancti Magni		mode	Vita (prima)	Vita Otlochi
Ad primas vesperas				
1	antiphona super psalmos	*Ad te clamantes*	8	–	–
2	responsorium	*Miris magnorum*	7	–	–
3	antiphona ad Magnificat	*Precelsi confessoris Christi*	1	–	–
Ad matutinas				
4	invitatorium	*Maximum regem cunctorum*	7	–	–
In primo nocturno				
5	antiphona 1	*Sanctus vir Magnoaldus*	1	735B	187
6	antiphona 2	*Hic divino instinctus amore*	2	–	–
7	antiphona 3	*Ubi per vere lucis*	3	–	–
8	responsorium 1	*Felicissimum beati Magni*	1	–	–
9	responsorium 2	*Beatus Magnus cum sancto Gallo*	2	742D, C	200, 196
10	responsorium 3	*Post sancti patris obitum Columbani*	3	742–743	200–201
In secundo nocturno				
11	antiphona 4	*Sub sancto itaque patre degens*	4	–	–
12	antiphona 5	*Cumque virtute prepollens*	5	735EF–736A	189–190
13	antiphona 6	*Nam ipsius ad vocem*	6	"	"
14	responsorium 4	*Triennio post beati Galli*	4	745	202, 203–204
15	responsorium 5	*Veniens vir dei Brigancium*	5	745–746	204
16	responsorium 6	*Cum Campidonam sanctus venisset*	6	746	205–206

In tertio nocturno

17	antiphona 7	*Iussione viri dei ursus poma*	7	736A–B	190–191
18	antiphona 8	*Ad preces eius plurima convolans*	8	736C–D	191–192
19	antiphona 9	*O vere mundum et purum*	1	-	-
20	responsorium 7	*Expulsis e Campidona demonibus*	7	748–749 (747)	208–211 ((208)
21	responsorium 8	*Vir deo amabilis*	8	749	213
22	responsorium 9	*Confessor domini sanctissime*	7	-	-

Ad laudes

23	antiphona 1	*Comperta virtutum beati Magni*	6	751–752	213–215
24	antiphona 2	*Cum ad pontificem Wicterpum*	7	752F	216
25	antiphona 3	*Accito ad Campidonam*	8	752D	215–216
26	antiphona 4	*Deo dignus diaconus Wicterpi*	1	cf. 752–753	cf. 217
27	antiphona 5	*Divina donante clemencia*	2	753	218
28	antiphona ad Benedictus	*Post transacta trium et septuaginta*	3	755	219–220

Ad horas

-	ad Primam	*In visione raptus divina*	4	738D	194
-	ad Tertiam	*Beatus Magnus in hac terra*	5	739A	-
-	ad Sextam	*Cum Italiam periturus*	6	739A–B	195
-	ad Nonam	*O felicem et salutiferam*	7	-	-

Ad secundas vesperas

-	antiphona ad Magnificat (SGs)	*Inter varias mundi temptationes*	7	-	-
29	antiphona ad Magnificat (Mu)	*Magnificus tuus Christe confessor*	4	cf. 755	cf. 220

created world.[9] One example will suffice here, the seventh responsory of the night office *Expulsis e Campidona demonibus* (no. 20). The upper fifth of the modal scale is clearly accented. While the finalis is naturally the most important note, other possible cadence notes, such as one would find in a traditional office chant, are neglected. An easy way of testing this is to observe the notes on which each word ends, omitting monosyllables, since they cannot be expected to attract much melodic weight. Many word endings are strongly marked by means of the subtonal ending *f–g–g* or *c'–d'–d'* (sometimes called the 'Gallican' cadence). The end notes may be listed as follows (subtonal endings in bold italic):

Expulsis e Campidona demonibus,	*d' **d' g***
relictoque inibi ad Christi famulatum Theodoro,	*d' **d'** d' **d'** g*
vir beatus ad Wicterpum Auguste presulum venit,	*d d'**c' c'** g*
eiusque permisso et auxilio	*g g **d'***
Fauces Alpium peciit.	*g **g** g*
V. Cum prius horribilem Christi virtute draconem peremisset.	*g **d'** c' **d' d' d'***

In all there are nine endings on *g*, twelve on *d'*, one on *d* and three on *c'*. That makes twenty-two endings on 'consonant' notes, only three on others. Nearly half the endings on *g* (five) and *d'* (five) are subtonal.

There is no space here for a more comprehensive statistical analysis, but readers are invited to test chants in various modes for themselves. The Magnificat antiphon at first vespers, the fourth and fifth antiphons of lauds, and almost any of the responsories are particularly 'consonant' in this sense. The style is not uncommon in chants of the twelfth century and later, but Hermannus is the earliest composer to achieve such a high degree of 'consonance', if we may so call it, in his melodies.

Finally, there is space to draw attention to only one of the melodic 'fingerprints' sometimes encountered in Hermannus's melodies. In the responsory at first vespers *Magis magnorum* (2), after bouncing back and forth between finalis, upper fifth, and upper octave at 'radiis fulgens', the melody leaps up a fifth to *d'* and another third to *f'* before sweeping down beyond the finalis and cadencing subtonally (marked 'x'). Similar phrases follow from the Wolfgang and Afra offices: for example, in the Wolfgang

---

[9]'Das Wolfgang-Offizium des Hermannus Contractus – Zum Wechselspiel von Modustheorie und Gesangspraxis in der Mitte des XI. Jahrhunderts', in Walter Berschin and David Hiley, eds, *Die Offizien des Mittelalters. Dichtung und Musik*, Regensburger Studien zur Musikgeschichte 1 (Tutzing, 1999), pp. 129–142; 'Die Afra-Gesänge des Hermannus Contractus. Liturgische Melodien und die Harmonie des Universums', in Manfred Weitlauff and Melanie Thierbach, eds, *Hl. Afra. Eine frühchristliche Märtyrerin in Geschichte, Kunst und Kult*, Jahrbuch des Verein für Augsburger Bistumsgeschichte 38, Ausstellungskatalog des Diözesanmuseum St Afra (Augsburg, 2004), pp. 112–119.

responsory *Eximie presul* or the Afra responsory *Postquam novellam*.[10] Singing such melodies, it is easy to appreciate Berthold's admiration of his master's achievements, and to marvel at Hermannus's imagination and audacity in leaving the traditional style of office chants so very far behind.

---

[10] Hiley, *Historia Sancti Wolfgangi Episcopi Ratisbonensis*, p. 2; Hiley and Berschin, *Historia sanctae Afrae martyris Augustensis*, p. 53.

Hermannus Contractus (1013-1054) - Historia sancti Magni

AD PRIMAS VESPERAS

1. Antiphona super psalmos *Ad te clamantes*

Ad te claman-tes tu-i-que in om-ni-bus ad-iu-to-ri-um im - plo-rantes nostri sin-gu-la-ris sancte Mag-ne pa-tro-ne iu-gi-ter nos digne-ris pro-pi-ci-us ex - au-di-re. Ps. De die.

2. Responsorium *Miris magnorum*

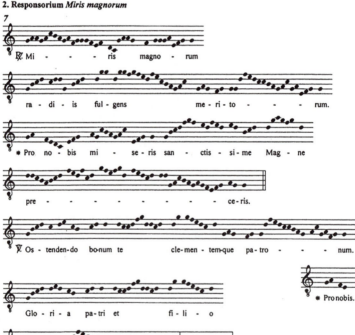

℟. Mi - ris magno - rum ra - di - is ful - gens me - ri - to - - rum. * Pro no - bis mi - se-ris san - ctis - si - me Mag - ne pre - - - - - - - ce-ris. ℣. Os - tenden-do bo-num te cle-men-tem-que pa-tro - - - num. Glo - ri - a pa-tri et fi - li - o et spi-ri-tu - i san - cto. * Pro nobis.

* Pro nobis.

3. Antiphona ad Magnificat *Precelsi confessoris Christi*

Pre-cel-si confes-so - ris Christi, tam me-ri - tis quam nomine Mag - ni,

na - ta - lis assunt nobis fe-sta di - e- i, qua de - po- si - ta

gra-vi car-nis hu-ius sar-ci - na e-ter-na la - bo-ris su-i

gau - dens ad-ep - tus est pre-mi- a:

un - de nunc e-ius un - a- ni-mes lau - di-bus in-sis - ta-mus,

ut et nos tan- ti a-pud de - um pa-tro-ni per - pe-tim suffra-gi - a

sen - - ci - a- mus. Ps. Magnificat.

AD MATUTINAS

4. Invitatorium *Maximum regem cunctorum*

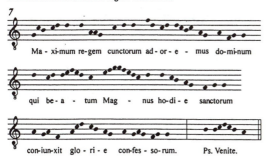

Ma - xi-mum re-gem cunctorum ad - or - e - mus do-mi-num

qui be- a - tum Mag - nus ho-di - e sanctorum

con-iun-xit glo - ri - e con-fes - so- rum. Ps. Venite.

In Primo Nocturno

5. Antiphona 1 *Sanctus vir Magnoaldus*

San-ctus vir Mag-no-al-dus Sco-ti - ge - ne stir-pis

ex Hy-ber-ni - a in-su-la fu - it   o - ri-un-dus.   Ps. Beatus vir.

6. Antiphona 2 *Hic divino instinctus amore*

Hic di - vi - no in-stin-ctus a-mo-re mun-di ce-pit nugas ce-de-re   et Christi gym-na-si-a

ty - ro-num men-te de-vo-ta cre-bri-us vi - si - ta-re. Ps. Quare fremuerunt.

7. Antiphona 3 *Ubi per vere lucis*

U - bi per ve-re lu - cis   pre-conem be-a-tum Gallum ex-ci - ta-tus,

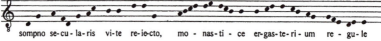

sompno se-cu - la-ris vi-te re-ie-cto, mo - nas-ti - ce er-gas-te-ri - um re - gu-le

strenu-us est o - pe-ra-tor in - gressus.   Ps. Domine quid.

8. Responsorium 1 *Felicissimum beati Magni*

℞. Fe-li-cis-si-mum be-a - ti Mag - ni spe-ci - a - lis pa - tro-ni

re-co-len - tes transi-tum. ＊ Un-a-ni - mi - ter om - nes

glo - - - ri - fi - ce - mus do - mi - num.

℣. Qui ab oc - ci - du - is fi - ni - bus mundi

ta - lem no - bis fe - cit so - lem o - ri - ri. ✳ Unanimiter.

9. Responsorium 2 *Beatus Magnus cum sancto Gallo*

℞. Be - a - tus Mag - nus cum san - cto Gal - lo plu - ri - mis

in hac re - gi - o - ne vir - tu - ti - bus de - cla - ra - tus,

a Io - han - ne e - pis - co - po Con - stan - ci - en - si.

✳ In di - a - co - na - tus est gradum pro - mo - tus.

℣. Sic - ut ip - si dis - cedens sanctus predi - xe - rat Co - lumbanus. ✳ In diaconatus.

10. Responsorium 3 *Post sancti patris obitum Columbani*

℞. Post san - cti pa - tris ob - i - tum Co - lum - ba - ni

be - a - tus Magnus ad e - ius ce - no - bi - um mis - sus.

re - co - len - tes transi - tum. ✳ Un - a - ni - mi - ter om - nes

＊E-pis-tolam ab-so-lu - ci - o-nis et ba - cu-lum e - ius

fe-li-ci re - - - - tu-lit Gal - lo.

℣. Ut in-ter-dic-tum per hec si - bi cognosce-ret

of-fi - ci-um es-se per - missum. ＊Epistolam.

Glo-ri - a pa-tri et fi-li-o et spi-ri-tu - i san - cto. ＊Epistolam.

In Secundo Nocturno

11. Antiphona 4 *Sub sancto itaque patre degens*

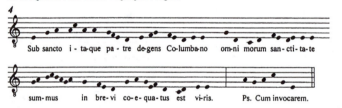

Sub sancto i - ta-que pa-tre de-gens Co-lumba-no om-ni morum san-cti-ta-te

sum-mus in bre-vi co-e-qua-tus est vi-ris. Ps. Cum invocarem.

12. Antiphona 5 *Cumque virtute prepollens*

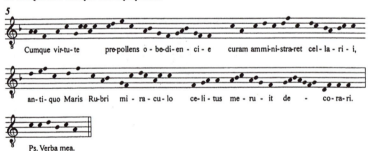

Cumque vir-tu-te pre-pollens o - be-di - en - ci - e curam ammi-ni-stra-ret cel - la - ri - i,

an-ti-quo Maris Ru-bri mi - ra - cu-lo ce-li-tus me-ru-it de - co-ra-ri.

Ps. Verba mea.

13. Antiphona 6 *Nam ipsius ad vocem*

Nam ip- si-us· ad vocem cum minister currens prope-ra - ret,   liquor quem e-du-li- o proflu-entem

ob-li - tus re-li-quit   su-pra vas quod in-flu-e-bat,   mirum in mo-dum so-li-da-tus

cu-mu- lum   ef- fe-cit.   Ps. Domine dominus noster.

14. Responsorium 4 *Triennio post beati Galli*

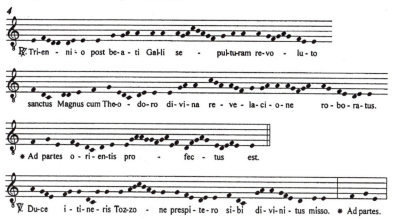

℟. Tri-en - ni - o post be-a - ti Gal-li se -   pul-tu-ram re-vo - lu - to

sanctus Magnus cum The-o - do-ro di-vi-na re - ve- la-ci- o- ne   ro - bo - ra-tus.

✱ Ad partes o - ri - en-tis pro -   fec - tus   est.

℣. Du-ce   i - ti-ne - ris Toz-zo - ne prespi- te- ro si-bi   di - vi-ni- tus misso. ✱ Ad partes.

15. Responsorium 5 *Veniens vir dei Brigancium*

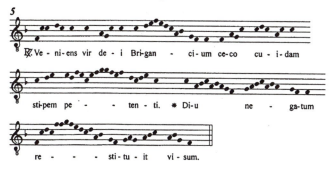

℟. Ve - ni- ens vir de - i Bri-gan -   ci- um ce-co   cu - i- dam

sti-pem pe - - ten - ti. ✱ Di-u   ne - ga-tum

re - - - sti - tu - it   vi - sum.

℣. O - ra - ci - o - nem do-mi-no fun-dens et o - cu-los e - ius spu-to su - o li - ni - ens.

✻ Diu.

16. Responsorium 6 *Cum Campidonam sanctus venisset*

℟. Cum Campi-do-nam sanctus ve - nis - set

et plenum ser-pen - ti - bus op - pi - dum in-ve - nis - set,

pridem ho-mi-ni-bus in-ha - bi - ta-bi - lem.

✻ Di - vi - no ser-vi - ci - o lo-cum red - - - di - dit ha - bi-lem.

℣. In-gen - tem i - bi Bo - am in no-mi-ne do - mi - ni

ba-cu-lo ne - ci sternens, re-li - quosque angues in fu-gam ver - tens. ✻ Divino.

Glo - ri-a pa - tri et fi - li - o et spi - ri - tu - i san - cto. ✻ Divino.

In Tertio Nocturno

17. Antiphona 7 *Iussione viri dei ursus poma*

Ius- si - o - ne   vi- ri   de- i   ursus poma dis-crevit

et op- ti- ma que-que in usum ser-vo - rum Christi in - tac- ta servavit.   Ps. Domine quis.

18. Antiphona 8 *Ad preces eius plurima convolans*

Ad   pre- ces   e- ius plu- ri- ma convolans co - pi - a   vo - lu-crum

san-ctis   se   vi-ris ul-tro-ne-um   pre- bu- it   e-sum.   Ps. Domine in virtute.

19. Antiphona 9 *O vere mundum et purum*

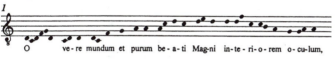

O   ve- re mundum et purum be- a- ti Mag-ni in-te- ri- o- rem o- cu-lum,

quo corpo-ra-li-ter ab-sen-ci - a   in spi-ri-tu me - ru- it con-spi-ce- re   presen-ci - a.

Ps. Domini est terra.

20. Responsorium 7 *Expulsis e Campidona demonibus*

℟. Ex-pul-sis e   Cam - pi- do-na de - mo - ni- bus,

re- lic - to - que in- i- bi ad Chri - sti fa - mu-la-tum The - o - do- ro,

vir be-a-tus ad Wic-ter-pum Augus-te pre-su-lem ve-nit,

e-iusque per-mis-so et au - xi-li-o.

✱ Fau-ces Al-pi - um pe - - - ci - it.

℣. Cum pri-us hor - ri-bi-lem Chri-sti vir-tu-te dra-conem per-e-mis-set.

✱ Fauces.

21. Responsorium 8 *Vir deo amabilis*

℟. Vir de - o a - ma-bi-lis, a-ma-tor so-li-tu-di-nis,

e-lec-tum si-bi ex-co-lens lo-cum, o-ra-to-ri-a et cel-las con-struxit.

✱ At-que thetras de-monum in-de pha-lan - ges pro - - - pul - sa-vit.

℣. Ie - iu-ni-is vacans o-ra-ci-o-ni-bus in-vi-gi - lans.   ✱ Atque thetras.

22. Responsorium 9 *Confessor domini sanctissime*

℟. Con - fes-sor do-mi-ni sanctis-si-me me-ri-tis et no - mi-ne Mag - ne

sup-pli-cum vo-ta tu-o-rum pi - e que-su-mus su-sci - pe.

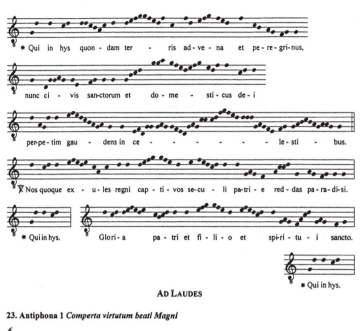

* Qui in hys quon - dam ter - ris ad - ve - na et pe - re - gri-nus,

nunc ci - vis san-ctorum et do - me - sti - cus de - i

per-pe - tim gau - dens in ce - - - - - - le - sti - bus.

℣. Nos quoque ex - u - les regni cap - ti - vos secu - li pa-tri - e red - das pa - ra-di-si.

* Qui in hys.   Glori - a   pa - tri et fi - li - o et   spi-ri - tu - i   sancto.

* Qui in hys.

AD LAUDES

23. Antiphona 1 *Comperta virtutum beati Magni*

6

Com - per - ta vir-tu-tum be-a-ti Magni   fa - ma,

Pi- pi - nus prin - ceps lo-cum quem san - ctus in - co - lu - it

re- gi - a lar-gi - ci-o - ne do - na-vit.   E u o u a e.

24. Antiphona 2 *Cum ad pontificem Wicterpum*

7

Cum ad pon - ti - fi - cem Wic - ter- pum ve-nis - set vir   de - i

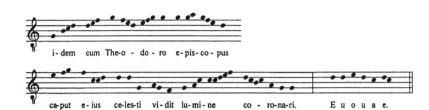

i- dem cum The-o - do - ro e-pis-co- pus

ca-put e- ius ce-les-ti vi-dit lu-mi- ne co - ro-na-ri. E u o u a e.

25. Antiphona 3 *Accito ad Campidonam*

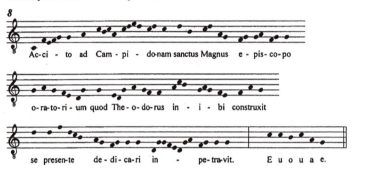

Ac-ci - to ad Cam-pi - do-nam sanctus Magnus e - pis-co-po

o- ra-to-ri - um quod The-o- do-rus in - i - bi construxit

se presen-te de - di-ca-ri in - pe-tra-vit. E u o u a e.

26. Antiphona 4 *Deo dignus diaconus Wicterpi*

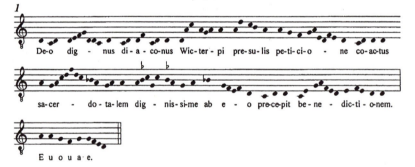

De-o dig - nus di-a - co-nus Wic-ter - pi pre-su- lis pe-ti-ci-o - ne co-ac-tus

sa-cer - do- ta-lem dig - nis-si-me ab e - o pre-ce-pit be-ne - dic-ti - o-nem.

E u o u a e.

27. Antiphona 5 *Divina donante clemencia*

Di-vi - na do-nan-te clemen-ci - a vir do-mi-ni ur - so monstran - te

et ob-se-que-lam ad nu-tum e - ius pre - ben-te ve - nas fer- ri

ad u-sum pos-te- ri - ta- tis me-ru- it   in-ve- ni-re.   E u o u a e.

28. Antiphona ad Benedictus *Post transacta trium et septuaginta*

Post trans-ac - ta tri - um et sep-tu-a-gin - ta an-norum cur - ri - cu- la

be-a - tus Mag - nus me-ri- tis e - ta- te et sancti-ta- te ple-nus

ex hu-ius in-co-la- tu vi - te morta-lis Christo vo - can-te

ad e - ter- na trans- i-vit gau - di- a pa-tri- e ce- les-tis,

al - le - lu-ia al - le - lu- ia.   Ps. Benedictus.

AD SECUNDAS VESPERAS

29. Antiphona ad Magnificat *Magnificus tuus Christe confessor*

Mag-ni - fi - cus tu- us Christe con - fes - sor Magnus

in sar-co-pha-go la-pi - de- o si- bi di - vi-ni-tus pro - cu- ra-to

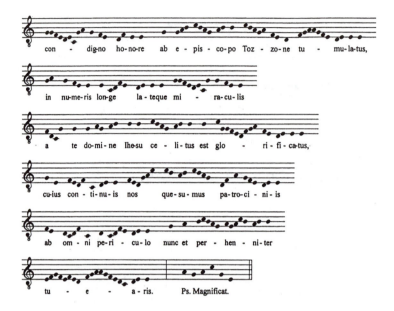

con - dig-no ho-no-re ab e - pis - co-po Toz - zo-ne tu - mu-la-tus,

in nu-me-ris lon-ge la - teque mi - ra-cu- lis

a te do-mi - ne Ihe-su ce - li-tus est glo - ri - fi-ca-tus,

cu-ius con - ti-nu-is nos que-su - mus pa-tro-ci - ni - is

ab om - ni pe-ri - cu-lo nunc et per - hen - ni - ter

tu - e - a - ris.   Ps. Magnificat.

30. Hymnus *Deus piissime*

1. De - us   pi - is - si - me   pa - ter dig - na - re   al - tis te vo - ci - bus
2. Qui ti - bi me - ri - tis   pla-cu - it   san-ctis   hu- iusnunc pre-ci - bus
3. Sit pa - tri glo - ri - a   na-to   co - ro-na   san-cto spi - ri - tu - i

ut   col-lau - de-mus   in   pa-tro-ni al - mi   no - mi - ne Mag-ni.
ad - es - to   pi - us   et   tu de-us nos - tris   ig - nos - ce no-xis.
iu - bi-lent   cun-cti   par   po-tes-tas tri - ni   u - ni e - ter-no.

Publications of Bryan Gillingham

Abbreviations used:

CAUSM   *Journal of the Canadian Association of University Schools of Music*
CUMR   *Canadian University Music Review*
ML   *Music and Letters*
MR   *The Music Review*
SMUWO   *Studies in Music from the University of Western Ontario*

BOOKS

The Polyphonic Sequences in Codex Wolfenbüttel 677. Binningen, 1982.
Saint-Martial Mehrstimmigkeit. Binningen, 1984.
Medieval Polyphonic Sequences. Ottawa, 1985.
Modal Rhythm. Ottawa, 1986.
Paris, Bibliothèque nationale, fonds latin 1139. Ottawa, 1987.
Paris, Bibliothèque nationale, fonds latin 3719. Ottawa, 1987.
B.N., fonds latin 3549 & B.L., Add.36881. Ottawa, 1987.
Cambridge, University Library Ff.i.17(1). Ottawa, 1989.
Beyond the Moon: Festschrift Luther Dittmer (with Paul Merkley). Ottawa, 1990.
Secular Medieval Latin Song: An Anthology. Ottawa, 1993.
Indices to the Notre-Dame Facsimiles. Ottawa, 1994.
A Critical Study of Secular Medieval Latin Song. Ottawa, 1995.
The Social Background to Secular Medieval Latin Song. Ottawa, 1998.
Chant and Its Peripheries: Essays in Honour of Terence Bailey (with Paul Merkley). Ottawa, 1998.

ARTICLES

'Modal Rhythm and the Medieval Sequence', *SMUWO* 1 (1977), pp. 105–123.
'The Proemium to Notker's Liber ymnorum', *CAUSM* 8 (1978), pp. 73–81.
'Four Pre-Transitional Polyphonic Sequences', *CAUSM* 9 (1979), pp. 25–52.
'British Library Ms Egerton 945: Further Evidence for a Mensural Interpretation of Sequences', *ML* 61 (1980), pp. 50–59.
'Social and Musical Matters Pertaining to J. C. Bach's Third Set of Keyboard Concertos', *MR* 42 (1981), pp. 225–237.
'St. Martial Polyphony', in Luther Dittmer, ed., *Gedenkschrift Gordon Athol Anderson*. Binningen 1984.
'Atavism and Innovation in a Late Medieval Proser', *SMUWO* 10 (1985), pp. 79–103.
'Medieval Polyphony in a Cividale Manuscript', *CUMR* 6 (1985), pp. 239–253.

'Lambeth Palace Ms 457: A Reassessment', *ML* 68 (1987), pp. 213–221.

'A New Etiology and Etymology for the Conductus', in Bryan Gillingham and Paul Merkley, eds, *Beyond the Moon: Festschrift Luther Dittmer*. Ottawa, 1990. Pp. 100–117. Repr. *MQ* 75 (1991), pp. 59–73.

'The Sequences in Paris, B. N. fonds latin 5247 and Relationships with Others in Mensural Sources', in Agostino Ziino, ed., *La sequenza medievale. Atti della Convegno Internazionale, Milano 7–8 Aprile 1984*. Lucca, 1992. Pp. 87–104.

'The Conductus as Analgesic', *CUMR* 14 (1994), pp. 49–59.

'An Archetype for the Chorale St Antoni', *Currents in Musical Thought* 4 (1995), pp. 109–124.

'Turtles, Helmets, Parasites and Goliards', *MR* 55 (1998), pp. 249–275.

'The Centrality of the Lost Cluniac Musical Tradition', in Bryan Gillingham and Paul Merkley, eds, *Chant and Its Peripheries*. Ottawa, 1998. Pp. 241–256.

'The Social Context of "Goliardic" Song: Highway, Court and Monastery', *Dalhousie Review* 82 (2002), pp. 75–90.

'Ceremonies and the Unceremonious at Twelfth-Century Cluny', in László Dobszay, ed., *The Past in the Present: Papers Read at the IMS Intercongressional Symposium 23–28 August 2000*. Budapest , 2003. Vol. 2, pp. 253–270.

'The Transmission of Two Secular Songs', *StM* 45 (2004), pp. 105–117.

BOOK REVIEWS

Terence Bailey, *The Processions of Sarum and the Western Church* (Toronto, 1971), *CUMR* 2 (1981), pp. 236–237.

Iain Fenlon, ed., *Early Music History I* (Cambridge, 1981), *CUMR* 3 (1982), pp. 222–225.

Jan W. Herlinger, *The Lucidarium of Marchetto of Padua* (Chicago, 1985) *CUMR* 6 (1985), pp. 341–342.

James V. McMahon, *The Music of Early Minnesang* (Columbia, SC, 1990), *Notes* (September 1992), pp. 80–81.

Nicky Losseff, *The Best Concords: Polyphonic Music in Thirteenth-Century Britain* (New York, 1994) *Notes* (September 1995), pp. 82–84.

Christoph März, *Die weltlichen Lieder des Mönchs von Salzburg* (Tubingen, 1999), *ML* 81 (2000), pp. 437–438.

Die Klöster als Pflegestätten von Musik und Kunst (Halberstadt, 1999), *ML* 81 (2000), pp. 438–441.

PERFORMANCE EDITIONS

All of the following were edited with Donald Beecher, Dovehouse Editions, Ottawa.

Viola da Gamba Series

1	Christopher Simpson, *Divisions for Treble and Bass Viols* (1979)
2	William Gorton, *Twelve Airs for Two Bass Viols* (1979)
3	John Jenkins, *Divisions in A Minor* (1979)
4	Le Sieur de Machy, *Pièces de viole* (1979)
5	John Ward, *Six Airs* (1979)
6	Giovanni Coperario, *Twelve Fantasias* (1979)
7	John Jenkins, *Six Airs and Divisions* (1979)
11	Christopher Simpson, *Divisions for Two Bass Viols* (1980)
13	John Withy, *Twenty-Two Airs* (1980)
14	John Jenkins, Robert Whyte, and Charles Coleman, *Four Duos* (1980)
15	John Jenkins, *Divisions in G Minor* (1981)
44	Anon., *Two Suites* (1984)

Baroque Series

10	William Young, *Two Sonatas* (1983)
13	John Blow, *Sonatas* (1983)

Italian Renaissance Consort Series

2	Girolamo Frescobaldi, *Ten Ricercars* (1980)
3	Girolamo Frescobaldi, *Five Canzonas* (1980)
5a	Jacques Buus, *Ricercari a quattro* (1983)
5b	Jacques Buus, *Ricercari a quattro* (1984)

Also with Donald Beecher:

Andrea Falconiero, *Il Primo Libro di Canzone, Sinfonie, Fantasie...* Part I. Hannacroix, NY, 2002.

BOOKS PRODUCED AS GENERAL EDITOR OF THE PUBLICATIONS OF THE INSTITUTE OF MEDIAEVAL MUSIC

Publications of Mediaeval Musical Manuscripts: Facsimiles

14	Paris, Bibliothèque nationale, Ms fonds latin 1139, ed. Bryan Gillingham. 1987. ISBN 0-931902-54-1

15 Paris, Bibliothèque nationale, Ms fonds latin 3719, ed. Bryan Gillingham. 1987. ISBN 0-931902-55-x

16 Paris, Bibliothèque nationale, Ms fonds latin 3549, and London, British Library, Ms Add. 36,881, ed. Bryan Gillingham. 1987. ISBN 0-931902-56-8

17 Cambridge, University Library, Ms Ff.i.17 (1), ed. Bryan Gillingham. 1989. ISBN 0-931902-62-2

18 Paris, Bibliothèque nationale, Ms fonds latin 7211, ed. Alma Santosuosso. 1991. ISBN 0-931902-68-1

19 Florence, Biblioteca nazionale centrale, Ms Conventi soppressi, *F.III.565*, ed. Alma Santosuosso. 1994. ISBN 0-931902-90-8

20 Oxford, Bodleian Library, Ms. Lat. Liturg. b. 5, ed. David Hiley. 1995. ISBN 0-931902-93-2

21 Utrecht, Bibliotheek der Rijksuniversiteit, Ms 406 (3.J.7), ed. Ruth Steiner. 1997. ISBN 1-896926-03-7

22 Aberystwyth, National Library of Wales, Ms. 20541 E (The Penpont Antiphonal), ed. Owain Edwards. 1997. ISBN 1-896926-06-1

23 Oxford, Bodleian Library, Ms e Mus. 126 (The York Processional), ed. David Hiley. 1998. ISBN 1-896926-06-17-7

24/1 Avranches, Bibliothèque municipale, Mss 236, 237, ed. Alma Santosuosso. 1999. ISBN 1-896926-29-7

24/2 Paris, Bibliothèque nationale, Ms fonds latin, 10509, ed. Alma Santosuosso. 2003. ISBN 1-896926-54-1

25/1 London, Lambeth Palace, Sion College Ms L1 (The York Breviary, vol. 1), ed. Andrew Hughes. 2000. ISBN 1-891926-26-6

25/2 London, Lambeth Palace, Sion College Ms L1 (The York Breviary, vol. 2), ed. Andrew Hughes. 2000. ISBN 1-896926-27-4

26 Paris, Bibliothèque nationale, Ms fonds latin 1143, ed. Vincent Corrigan. 2001. ISBN 1-896926-30-4

27/1 Salamanca, Archivo de la Catedral, Ms 5, ed. James Boyce. 2001. ISBN 1-896926-38-x

27/2 Salamanca, Archivo de la Catedral, Ms 6, ed. James Boyce. 2001. ISBN 1-896926-39-8

27/3 Salamanca, Archivo de la Catedral, Ms 7, ed. James Boyce. 2001. ISBN 1-896926-40-1

27/4 Salamanca, Archivo de la Catedral, Ms 8, ed. James Boyce. 2001. ISBN 1-896926-41-x

28 Šibenik, Monastery of the Conventual Francisicans, *Liber sequentiarum et sacramentarium*, ed. Dujke Smoje. 2003. ISBN 1-896926-49-5

29 Vilnius, Academy of Sciences, Department of Manuscripts, Ms F22-95, ed. Ike de Loos and Victoria Goncharova. 2003. ISBN 1-896926-50-9

30 St Omer, Bibliothèque municipale, *L'antiphonaire de la Paix des Princes chrétiens*, ed. Jean-François Goudesenne. 2003. ISBN 1-896926-55-x

31 Utrecht, University Library, Ms 16 H 34, ed. Ulrike Hascher-Burger. 2004. ISBN 1-896926-60-6

Musicological Studies Series

45   Bryan Gillingham, *Medieval Polyphonic Sequences: An Anthology*. 1985. ISBN 0-931902-51-7

46   Bryan Gillingham, *Modal Rhythm*. 1985. ISBN 0-931902-52-5

47   Terence Bailey, *The Ambrosian Cantus*. 1987. ISBN 0-931902-53-3

48   Paul Merkley, *Italian Tonaries*. 1988. ISBN 0-931902-57-6

49   Paul Helmer, *The Mass of St James*. 1988. ISBN 0-931902-58-4

50/1   Terence Bailey and Paul Merkley, *The Antiphons of the Ambrosian Office*. 1989. ISBN 0-931902-60-6

50/2   Terence Bailey and Paul Merkley, *The Melodic Tradition of the Ambrosian Office-Antiphons*. 1990. ISBN 0-931902-64-9

50/3   Terence Bailey, *Antiphon and Psalm in the Ambrosian Office*. 1994. ISBN 0-931902-83-5

51   Andrew Hughes, *Style and Symbol*. 1989. ISBN 0-931902-61-4

52   Alma Colk Santosuosso, *Letter Notations in the Middle Ages*. 1989. ISBN 0-931902-63-8

53   Bryan Gillingham and Paul Merkley, *Beyond the Moon: Festschrift Luther Dittmer*. 1990. ISBN 0-931902-65-7

54   Joseph A. Diamond, *A Tradition of Three Tropes*. 1991. ISBN 0-931902-67-3

55/1   CANTUS Index. *An Aquitanian Antiphoner: Toledo, Biblioteca capitular, 44.2*. 1992. ISBN 0-931902-71-1

55/2   CANTUS Index. *Piacenza, Biblioteca Capitolare 65*. 1993. ISBN 0-931902-79-7

55/3   CANTUS Index. *Linz, Bundesstaatliche Studienbibliothek 290 (183)*. 1996. ISBN 0-931902-96-7

55/4   CANTUS Index. *Cambrai, Médiathèque Municipale, 38, and Impr. XVI C4*. 1995. ISBN 0-931902-98-3

55/5   CANTUS Index. *The Zwiefalten Antiphoner: Karlsruhe, Bad. Landesbibl., Aug. perg. LX*. 1996. ISBN 0-931902-43-6

55/6   CANTUS Index. *An Utrecht Antiphoner: Utrecht, Bibl. der Rijksuniversiteit 406 (3.J.7)*. 1997. ISBN 0-896926-05-3

55/7   CANTUS Index. *Four Klosterneuburg Antiphoners*. 1998. ISBN 1-896926-14-2

55/8   CANTUS Index. *Salamanca, Archivo de la Catedral, 5, 6, 7, 8*. 2001. ISBN 1-896926-33-9

56   Paul Merkley, *Modal Assignment in Northern Tonaries*. 1992. ISBN 0-931902-72-x

57   Máire Egan-Buffet, *Les Chansons de Claude Goudimel*. 1992. ISBN 0-931902-73-8

58   Lulu Huang Chang, *From Confucius to Kublai Khan: Music and Poetics Through the Centuries*. 1993. ISBN 0-931902-75-4

59   Harry B. Lincoln, *The Latin Motet: Indexes to Printed Collections, 1500–1600*. 1993. ISBN 0-931902-80-0

60/1 Bryan Gillingham, *Secular Medieval Latin Song: An Anthology.* 1993. ISBN 0-931902-81-9

60/2 Bryan Gillingham, *A Critical Study of Secular Medieval Latin Song.* 1995. ISBN 0-931902-91-6

60/3 Bryan Gillingham, *The Social Background to Secular Medieval Latin Song.* 1998. ISBN 1-896926-11-8

61 Susan Fast, *Johannes de Muris:* Musica speculativa. 1994. ISBN 0-931902-85-1.

62/1 Nancy van Deusen, *The Cultural Milieu of the Troubadours and Trouvères.* 1994. ISBN 0-931902-87-7

62/2 Nancy van Deusen, *The Medieval West Meets the Rest of the World.* 1994. ISBN 0-931902-94-0

62/3 Nancy van Deusen, *Tradition and Ecstasy: The Agony of the Fourteenth Century.* 1997. ISBN 1-896926-01-0

62/4 Nancy van Deusen, *Design and Production in Medieval and Early Modern Europe.* 1998. ISBN 1-896926-13-4

62/5 Nancy van Deusen, *Medieval Germany: Associations and Delineations.* 1998. ISBN 1-896926-22-3

62/6 Nancy van Deusen, *Issues in Medieval Philosophy.* 2001. ISBN 1-896926-36-3

62/7 Nancy van Deusen, *Performing Ecstasies: Music, Dance and Ritual.* 2004. ISBN 1-896926-68-1

63 Bryan Gillingham, *Indices to the Notre-Dame Facsimiles.* 1994. ISBN 0-931902-88-6

64 Joan Halmo, *Antiphons for Paschal Triduum-Easter in the Medieval Office.* 1995. ISBN 0-931902-92-4

65/1 Barbara Haggh, *Two Offices for St Elizabeth of Hungary.* 1995. ISBN 0-931902-97-5

65/2 David Hiley, *Historia Sancti emmerammi.* 1996. ISBN 0-931902-42-8

65/3 Roman Hankeln, *Historia Sancti Dionysii Areopagitae.* ISBN 1-896926-12-6

65/4 Roman Hankeln, *Historia Sancti Erhardi.* 2000. ISBN 1-896926-23-1

65/5 James Boyce, and William Coleman, *Officium Presentationis Beate Virginis Marie in templo.* 2001. ISBN 1-896926-32-0

65/6 Jean-François Goudesenne, *L'office romano-franc des saints martyrs Denis, Rustique et Eleuthère.* 2002. ISBN 1-896926-43-6

65/7 David Hiley, *Historiae Sancti Wolfgangi Episcopi Ratisbonensis.* 2002. ISBN 1-896926-45-2

65/8 Juri Snoj, *Two Aquileian Poetic Offices.* 2003. ISBN 1-896926-53-3

65/9 Zsuzsa Czagány, *Historia de Sancta Martha hospita Christi.* 2004. ISBN 1-896926-61-4

65/10 Hermanus Contractus. *Historia Sanctae Afrae martyris.* Ed. David Hiley and Walter Bershin. 2004. ISBN 896926-62-2

66 Máire Egan-Buffet, *Adrian Le Roy,* Traicté de musique. 1996. ISBN 0-931902-99-1

67   Kathleen E. Nelson, *Medieval Liturgical Music of Zamora*. 1996. ISBN 0-931902-40-1

68   Robyn Smith, *French Double and Triple Motets in the Montpellier Manuscript*. 1997. ISBN 1-896926-02-9

69   Karl Kügle, *The Manuscript Ivrea, Biblioteca capitolare 115*. 1997. ISBN 1-896926-04-5

70/1   Paul Helmer, *Le premier et le secont livre de Fauvel*. 1997. ISBN 1-896926-08-8

71/1   Jean Mallet and André Thibaut, *Les manuscrits en écriture bénéventaine de la Bibliothèque capitulaire de Bénévent*, vol. 2. 1984. ISBN 1-896926-09-6

71/2   Jean Mallet, and André Thibaut, *Les manuscrits en écriture bénéventaine de la Bibliothèque capitulaire de Bénévent*, vol. 3. 1997. ISBN 1-896926-10-x

72   Bryan Gillingham and Paul Merkley, *Chant and Its Peripheries*. 1998. ISBN 1-896926-16-9

73   Dolores Pesce, *Guido d'Arezzo's* Regule Rithmice, Prologus in Antiphonarium, *and* Epistola ad Michahelem. A critical text and translation. 1999. ISBN 1-896926-18-5

74   Joseph Szövérffy, *Lateinische Conductus-Texte*. 2000. ISBN 1-896926-24-x

75   Hans Tischler, *Conductus and contrafacta*. 2001. ISBN 1-896926-29-0

76   David Wulstan, *The Emperor's Old Clothes: The Rhythm of Medieval Song*. 2001. ISBN 1-896926-31-2

77   John Emerson/Lila Collamore, *Albi, Bibliothèque municipale Rochegude, Manuscript 44*. 2002. ISBN 1-896926-44-4

78   Mark Stewart and David Wulstan, eds. *The Poetic and Musical Legacy of Heloise and Abelard*. 2003. ISBN 1-896926-51-7

79   Terence Bailey, *The Transitoria of the Ambrosian Mass*. 2003. ISBN 1-896926-52-5

80   George Sawa, *Music Performance Practice in the Early* ^C*Abbāsid Era*. 2004. ISBN 926-64-9

81   Heinz Ristory, *Denkmodelle zur französischen Mensuraltheorie des 14. Jahrhunderts*. 2004. ISBN 1-896926-67-3

Collected Works

VIII/4   Johannes Galliculus, *Isagoge de composicione cantus*, ed. Arthur Moorefield. 1992. ISBN 0-931902-74-6

XI/2   Antoine de Févin, *Masses (II)*, ed. E. Clinkscale. 1993. ISBN 0-931902-82-7

XI/3   Antoine de Févin, *Lamentations, Magnificats, Motets and Chansons*, ed. E. Clinkscale. 1994. ISBN 0-931902-89-4

XI/4   Antoine de Févin, *Opera Dubia, Fragments and Intabulations*, ed. E. Clinkscale. 1996. ISBN 0-931902-41-x

XII/2   Cristóbal Galán, *Obras litúrgicas*, ed. John Baron and Daniel Heiple. 1991. ISBN 0-931902-69-x

XII/3   Cristóbal Galán, *Obras litúrgicas*, ed. John Baron and Daniel Heiple. 1992. ISBN 0-931902-70-3

XII/4   Cristóbal Galán, *Solos, dúos y tríos*, ed. John Baron and Daniel Heiple. 1993. ISBN 0-931902-78-9

XII/5   Cristóbal Galán, *Cuartetos/Quartets*, ed, John Baron and Daniel Heiple. 1995. ISBN 0-931902-95-9

XII/6   Cristóbal Galán, *Cuartetos, Quintetos y Sextetos*, ed. John Baron and Daniel Heiple. 1998. ISBN 1-896926-15-0

XII/7   Cristóbal Galán, *Sextetos y Septetos*, ed. John Baron and Eric Vogt. 2002. ISBN 1-896926-46-0

XII/8   Cristóbal Galán, *Octetos*, ed. John Baron and Eric Vogt. 2003. ISBN 1-896926-56-8

XIII   Robert de Févin, *Masses and Motet*, ed. E. Clinkscale. 1993. ISBN 0-931902-77-0

XIV/1   Francisco Peñalosa, *Twenty-Four Motets*, ed. Jane Morlet Hardie. 1994. ISBN 0-931902-84-3

XIV/2   Francisco Peñolosa, *Lamentations of Jeremiah*, ed. Jane Morlet Hardie. 1999. ISBN 1-896926-19-3

XV   Melchior Neusidler, *Intabolatura di Liuto* (1566). 1994. ISBN 0-931902-86-x

XVI/1   Jean Maillard, *The Masses*, ed. R. Rosenstock. 1997. ISBN 1-896926-07-x

XVII/1   Capella Sistina 51, Bioblioteca apostolica vaticana: Liber Missarum, ed. Rex Eakins. 1999. ISBN 1-896926-21-5

XVII/2   Capella Sistina 51, Biblioteca apostolica vaticana: Liber missarum (2), ed. Rex Eakins. 2000. ISBN 1-896926-25-8

XVII/3   Capella Sistina 51, Bioblioteca apostolica vaticana: Liber missarum (3), ed. Rex Eakins. 2001. ISBN 1-896926-25-8

XVII/4   Capella Sistina 51. Biblioteca apostolica vaticana: Liber missarum (4), ed. Rex Eakins. 2004. ISBN 1-896926-59-2

XVII/5   Capella Sistina 51. Biblioteca apostolica vaticana: Liber missarum (5), ed. Rex Eakins. 2004. ISBN 1-89692-66-57

XVIII   Hans Tischler, *The Songs of the Master Trouvère: Gace Brulé*. 2001. ISBN 1-896926-34-7

XIX   Hans Tischler, *The Circle Around Gace Brulé: Four Famous Early Trouvères*. 2002. ISBN 1-896926-42-8

XX   Hans Tischler, *The Earliest Laude: The Cortona Hymnal*. 2002. ISBN 1-896926-47-9

XXI   Terence Bailey, *The Transitoria of the Ambrosian Mass*. 2002. ISBN 1-896926-48-7

XXII   Jane Hardie, *The Lamentations of Jeremiah. Ten Sixteenth-Century Prints*. 2003. ISBN 1-896926-57-6

XXIII   Donald Beecher, *Orazio Vechhi, Le Veglie di Siena.* 2004. ISBN 1-896926-58-4

Theorists in Translation

13   Johannes Galliculus, *The Introduction to Song Composition*, trans. Arthur Moorefield. 1992. ISBN 0-931902-76-2

14   Allen Scott, *Nikolaus Gengenbach's Musica Nova: Newe Singekunst.* Commentary, critical edition, translation, facsimiles. 1996. ISBN 0-931902-44-4

15   Alexander Rausch, *Opusculum de musica ex traditione Iohannis Hollandrini.* 1997. ISBN 1-896926-00-2

16   Peter Slemon, Introductorium musicae *of Johannes Keck.* Commentary, critical edition, translation, facsimiles. 2001. ISBN 1-896926-35-5

Bibliography

For the sigla see Bibliographical abbreviations, pp. vii–viii; short references refer to complete entries in the Bibliography.

Abulafia, David, Michael J. Franklin, and Miri Rubin, eds. *Church and City 1000–1500. Essays in Honour of Christopher Brookest.* Cambridge, 1992.

Adam, Adolf. *The Liturgical Year, Its History and Its Meaning after the Reform of the Liturgy.* New York, 1981.

———. *Foundations of Liturgy: An Introduction to Its History and Practice.* Collegeville, MN, 1992.

Agustoni, Luigi. 'Die Frage der Tonstufen SI und MI', *Beiträge zur Gregorianik* 4 (1987), pp. 47–101.

Alfarano, Tiberio. *See* Cerruti.

Allaire, Gaston. *The Theory of Hexachords, Solmization and the Modal System.* American Institute of Musicology. Musicological Studies and Documents 24. Rome, 1972.

Alonzio, Pio. *L'antifonario dell'ufficio romano.* Monografie liturgiche 3. Subiaco, 1935.

Anderson, Gordon A. 'Thirteenth-Century Conductus: *Obiter dicta*', *MQ* 58 (1972), pp. 349–364.

———. 'Notre Dame and Related Conductus: A Catalogue Raisonné', *Miscellanea musicologica: Adelaide Studies in Musicology* 6 (1972), pp. 152–229, and 7 (1973), pp. 1–81.

———. *The Latin Compositions in Fascicules VII and VIII of the Notre Dame Manuscript Wolfenbüttel Helmstadt 1099 (1206).* 2 vols. IMS. Brooklyn, 1972, 1976.

———. *Motets of the MS La Clayette: Paris, Bibliothèque nationale, nouv. acq. f. fr. 13521.* American Institute of Musicology. Rome, 1975.

———. *Notre-Dame and Related Conductus: Opera Omnia.* IMS. Collected Works 6. 9 vols. Henryville, 1979–1988.

Andrieu, Michel. *Les ordines romani du haut moyen-âge.* 5 vols. Spicilegium sacrum lovaniense 11, 23–24, 28, 29. Louvain, 1931–1961.

———. *Le pontifical romain au moyen-âge.* 4 vols. Studi e Testi 86–88, 99. Vatican City, 1938–1941.

Antolín, Guillermo. 'La encuadernación del libro en España', *Revista de archivos, bibliotecas y museos* 26 (special issue, 1922).

———. 'Notas acerca de la encuadernación artistica del libro en España', *Boletin de la Real academia de la historia* 89 (1926), pp. 294–308.

Apel, Willi. 'The Central Problem of Gregorian Chant', *JAMS* 9 (1956), pp. 118–127.

———. *Gregorian Chant.* Bloomington, IN, 1958.

Arens, Fritz. 'Ein Blatt aus den mainzer Karmeliterchorbüchern', *Jahrbuch für das Bistum Mainz* 8 (1958–1960), pp. 341–346.

Aribo. *See* Waesberghe.

Atkinson, Charles. 'Zur Enstehung und Überlieferung der Missa graeca', *AMw* 39 (1982), pp. 113–145.

———. 'Further Thoughts on the Origin of the *Missa graeca*', in *FS Hucke*, pp. 75–94.

Aurelian of Réome. *See* Ponte.

Bailey, Terence. *The Intonation Formulas of Western Chant*. Toronto, 1974.

———. ed. *Commemoratio brevis de tonis et psalmis modulandis*. Ottawa, 1979.

———. *The Ambrosian Cantus*. IMS. Musicological Studies 47. Ottawa, 1987.

———, and Paul Merkley. *The Antiphons of the Ambrosian Office*. IMS. Musicological Studies 50/1. Ottawa, 1989.

———, and Paul Merkley. *The Melodic Tradition of the Ambrosian Office-Antiphons*. IMS. Musicological Studies 50/2. Ottawa, 1990.

Baldwin, John W. *Masters, Princes and Merchants: The Social Views of Peter the Chanter and his Circle*. 2 vols. Princeton, 1970.

Baltzer, Rebecca A. 'Aspects of Trope in the Earliest Motets for the Assumption of the Virgin', *Current Musicology* 45–47 (1991), pp. 5–42.

———. 'The Polyphonic Progeny of an *Et gaudebit:* Assessing Family Relations in the Thirteenth-Century Motet', in Dolores Pesce, ed., *Hearing the Motet: A Conference on the Motet in the Middle Ages and Renaissance*. Oxford, 1996. Pp. 17–27.

———. 'The Little Office of the Virgin and Mary's Role at Paris', in *FS Steiner*, pp. 463–484.

Bannister, Henry Marriott. 'Un tropaire-prosaire de Moissac', *Revue d'histoire et littérature religieuse* 8 (1903), pp. 554–581.

Baroffio, Giacomo. 'I libri con musica: sono libri di musica?', in Cattin *et al*, eds, *Il canto piano nell'era della stampa*, pp. 9–12.

Baumstark, Anton. *Nocturna laus. Typen frühchristlicher Vigilienfeier und ihre Fortleben vor allem im römischen und monastischen Ritus*. Liturgiewissenschaftliche Quellen und Forschungen 32. Münster, 1957.

Baxter, J. H. *An Old Saint Andrews Music Book*. London, 1931; repr. New York, 1973.

Beare, William. *Latin Verse and European Song: A Study in Accent and Rhythm*. London, 1957.

Becker, Gustav. *Catalogi bibliothecarum antiqui*. Bonn, 1885; repr. Hildesheim, 2003.

Benson, Robert L., and Giles Constable, eds. *Renaissance and Renewal in the Twelfth Century*. Oxford, 1982.

Bent, Margaret. 'Diatonic "Ficta"', *EMH* 4 (1984), pp. 1–48.

———. *Essays on musica ficta*. New York, 2001.

Bentas, Christos J. 'The Treatise on Music by John Laskaris', *Studies in Eastern Chant* 2 (1971), pp. 21–27.

Berceo, Gonzalo de. *Obras completas IV. La vida de Santo Domingo de Silos*, ed. Brian Dutton. London, 1978.

Bernhard, Michael. *Studien zur* Epistola de armonica institutione *des Regino von Prüm.* VMK 5. Munich, 1979.

———. *Clavis Gerberti. Eine Revision von Martin Gerberts Scriptores ecclesiastici de musica sacra potissimum (St. Blasien 1784).* Part 1. VMK 7. Munich, 1989.

———, ed. *Lexicon musicum Latinum medii aevi. Wörterbuch der lateinischen Musikterminologie des Mittelalters bis zum Ausgang des 15. Jahrhunderts.* Munich, 1992–.

———. 'Die Überlieferung der Neumennamen im lateinischen Mittelalter', in *Quellen und Studien zur Musiktheorie des Mittelalters* 2. VMK 13. Munich, 1997.

———, and Calvin M. Bower, eds. *Glossa maior in institutionem musicam Boethii.* 3 vols. Munich, 1993–1996.

Berno of Reichenau. *See* Waesberghe.

Berschin, Walter. *Ottonische Biographie. Das hohe Mittelalter, 920–1220 n. Chr.* Part 1. *Biographie und Epochenstil im lateinischen Mittelalter* 4/I. Quellen und Untersuchungen zur lateinischen Philologie des Mittelalters 12, 1. Stuttgart, 1999.

Blaauw, Sible de. *Cultus et decor. Liturgia e architettura nella Roma tardoantica e medievale.* 2 vols. Studi e Testi 355–356. Rome, 1994.

———. 'L'arredo liturgico e il culto di San Pietro', in Mario D'Onofrio, ed., *Romei e Giubilei: il pellegrinaggio medievale a San Pietro (350–1250).* Milan, 1999. Pp. 271–277.

———. 'Contrasts in Processional Liturgy: A Typology of Outdoor Processions in Twelfth-Century Rome' in Nicolas Bock *et al.*, eds, *Art, cérémonial et liturgie au moyen âge: Actes du colloque du Troisième cycle romand de lettres, Lausanne–Fribourg, 24–25 mars, 14–15 avril, 12–13 mai 2000.* Rome, 2002. Pp. 357–394.

Blume, Clemens. *Liturgischen Prosen erster Epoche.* AH 53. Leipzig, 1911.

Bogaert, Pierre-Maurice, ed. *Judith.* Vetus Latina: Die Reste der altlateinischen Bibel 7/2. Freiburg, 2001.

Bonniwell, William R. O. P. *A History of the Dominican Liturgy, 1215–1945.* New York, 1945.

Boorman, Stanley. 'Early Music Printing: Working for a Specialized Market', in Gerald P. Tyson and Sylvia S. Wogonheim, eds, *Print and Culture in the Renaissance: Essays on the Advent of Printing in Europe.* Newark, 1986.

Booth, Wayne C., Gregory G. Colomb, and Joseph M. Williams. *The Craft of Research.* Chicago, 1995.

Borders, James. 'The 1485 *Pontificale romanum* and its Chants', in Cattin *et al.*, eds, *Il canto piano nell'era della stampa*, pp. 13–28.

Bower, Calvin. 'The Grammatical Model of Musical Understanding in the Middle Ages', in Patrick J. Gallacher and Helen Damico, eds, *Hermeneutics and Medieval Culture.* Albany, 1989. Pp. 133–145.

Boyce, James John, O. Carm. 'Die Mainzer Karmeliterchorbücher und die liturgische Tradition des Karmeliterordens', *Archiv für mittelrheinische Kirchengeschichte* 39 (1987), pp. 267–303. Translated as 'The Carmelite Choirbooks of Mainz and the Liturgical Tradition of the Carmelite Order', in *Praising God in Carmel.* Washington, DC, 1999.

——. 'Two Antiphonals of Pisa: Their Place in the Carmelite Liturgy', *Manuscripta* 31 (1987), pp. 147–165.

——. 'The Carmelite Choirbooks of Florence and the Liturgical Tradition of the Carmelite Order', *Carmelus* 35 (1988), pp. 67–93.

——. *Catálogo, Archivo de música gregoriana. Cantorales: 52 Manuscritos, Siglos XIV–XIX*. Salamanca, 1993.

——. 'Newly-discovered Manuscripts for an Old Tradition: The Salamanca Choirbooks', *International Musicological Society Study Group Cantus Planus. Papers read at Estergom and Visegrád*. Budapest, 1998. Pp. 9–28.

——. *Salamanca, Archivo de la Catedral, 5, 6, 7, 8: Printouts from an Index in Machine-Readable Form*. IMS. Publications of Mediaeval Musical Manuscripts 27. Ottawa, 2001.

——. 'The Carmelite Choir Books of Krakow: Carmelite Liturgy before and after the Council of Trent', *StM* 45 (2004), pp. 17–34.

Bradshaw, Paul. *Daily Prayer in the Early Church*. 2nd edn. Alcuin Club Collection 63. London, 1983.

Branner, Robert. *Manuscript Painting in Paris during the Reign of Saint Louis: A Study of Styles*. Berkeley, 1977.

Braun, Joseph. *Das christliche Altargerät*. Munich, 1932.

Breviary. The Hours of the Divine Office in English and Latin. 3 vols. Collegeville, MN, 1963.

Brewer, J. S., and James F. Dimock, eds. *Giraldi Cambrensis opera*. 8 vols. Rolls Series. London, 1861–1891.

Brockett, Clyde W., ed. *Anonymi* De modorum formulis *et tonarius*. CSM 37. 1997.

Brooke, Christopher. *The Twelfth-Century Renaissance*. London, 1969.

Browe, Peter, SJ. *Die Verehrung der Eucharistie im Mittelalter*. Munich, 1933; repr. Rome, 1967.

Bryden, John, and David Hughes, *Index of Gregorian Chant*. 2 vols. Cambridge, MA, 1969.

Bukofzer, Manfred. 'Caput: A Liturgico-Musical Study', in *Studies in Medieval and Renaissance Music*. New York, 1950. Pp. 217–310.

——. 'The Unidentified Tenors in the Manuscript La Clayette', *AnnM* 4 (1956), pp. 255–258.

Bulst, Neithard. *Untersuchungen zu den Klosterreformen Wilhelms von Dijon (962–1031)*. Pariser historische Studien 11. Bonn, 1973.

Callewaert, Camillus. *Liturgicae institutiones tractatus secundus. De breviarii romani liturgia*. 2nd edn. Bruges, 1939.

——. 'Les offices festifs à Rome avant la règle de saint Benoît', *Sacris erudiri* (1940), pp. 149–168.

——. 'Les prières d'introduction aux différentes heures de l'office', *Sacris erudiri* (1940), pp. 135–144.

Cantor, Norman F. *The Civilization of the Middle Ages*. New York, 1993.

Cardoso, Manuel. *Passionarium iuxta Capellae Regiae Lusitaniae consuetudinem. Accentùs rationem integre observans*. Leiria: Antonio de Mariz, 1575.

Casado, Juan Delgado. *Diccionario de impresores españoles (siglos XV–XVI)*. Madrid, 1996.

Castañeda, Vicente. 'Exposición de encuadernaciones de la colección Lázaro Galdiano', *Boletin de la Academia de laHhistoria* 106 (1935), pp. 377–388.

———. *Ensayo de un diccionario biografico de encuadernadores españoles*. Madrid, 1958.

Cattin, Guilio, Danilo Curti, and Marco Gozzi, eds. *Il canto piano nell'era della stampa: Atti del convegno internazionale di studi sul canto liturgico nei secoli XV–XVIII, Trento – Castello del Buonconsiglio, Venezia – Fondazione Ugo e Olga Levi, 9–11 ottobre 1998*. Trent, 1999.

Cerquiglini, Bernard. *In Praise of the Variant: A Critical History of Philology*. Translated by Betsy Wing. Baltimore, 1999.

Cerruti, Michele, ed. *Tiberii Alpharani de basilicae vaticanae antiquissima et nova structura*. Studi e Testi 26. Rome, 1914.

Chadd, David, ed. *The Ordinal of the Abbey of the Holy Trinity, Fécamp (Fécamp, Musée de la Bénédiction, Ms 186)*. Publications of the Henry Bradshaw Society 111, 112. London, 1999, 2002.

Chavasse, Antoine. 'Le sermonnaire d'Agimond. Ses sources immediates', in Patrick Granfield and Josef Jungmann, eds, *Kyriakon: Festschrift Johannes Quasten*. 2 vols. Münster in Westfalen, 1970. Vol. 2, pp. 800–810.

———. 'Le sermonnaire des Saints Philippe-et Jacques et le sermonnaire de Saint-Pierre', *Ephemerides liturgicae* 69 (1955), pp. 17–24.

Chomton, Abbé. *Histoire de l'église Saint-Bénigne de Dijon*. Dijon, 1900.

Cicconetti, Carlo, O. Carm. *La regola del Carmelo*. Rome, 1973.

Claire, Jean. 'Les répertoires liturgiques latins avant l'octoéchos: I. L'office férial romano-franc', *EG* 15 (1975), pp. 5–192.

Clarke, Hugh, O. Carm., and Bede Edwards, O.D.C., eds. *The Rule of Saint Albert*. Aylesford and Kensington, 1973.

Coens, Maurice. 'La vie de S. Magne de Füssen par Otloh de Saint-Emmeran', in *Analecta Bollandiana* 81 (1963), pp. 159–227.

Collamore, Lila. 'Charting the Divine Office', in *FS Steiner*, pp. 3–11.

Connolly, Thomas. 'Introits and Archetypes: Some Archaisms of the Old Roman Chant', *JAMS* 25 (1972), pp. 165–174.

Coussemaker, Edmond de, ed. *Scriptorum de musica medii aevi novam seriem a Gerbertina alteram*. 4 vols. Paris, 1894–1879; repr. Hildesheim, 1963.

Cowdery, James R. *The Melodic Tradition of Ireland*. Kent, Ohio, 1990.

Crocker, Richard. 'Hermann's Major Sixth', *JAMS* 25 (1972), pp. 19–37.

———. *The Early Medieval Sequence*. Berkeley, 1977.

Cutter, Paul, and Brad Maiani. 'Responsory, 3', *NG2*, vol. 21, pp. 222–224.

Deckert, P. Adalbert, O. Carm. *Die Oberdeutsche Provinz der Karmeliten nach den Akten ihrer Kapitel von 1421 bis 1529*. Rome, 1961.

Delisle, Léopold. *Le cabinet des manuscrits de la Bibliothèque impériale*. Paris 1874; repr. Hildesheim, 1978.

Desmond, Karen. '*Sicut in grammatica*: Analogical Discourse in Chapter 15 of Guido's *Micrologus*', *JM* 16 (1998), pp. 467–494.

Dician, Amelia, and Janina Loret–Heintsch, eds. *Inwentarz rękopisów Biblioteki Zakładu Narodowego im. Ossolińskich we Wrocławiu.* Wroclaw, Warsaw, Krakow, 1966. Vol. 3, *Rękopisy 11981–13000*.

Dittmer, Luther A. *Wolfenbüttel 1099 (1206)*. IMS. Publications of Mediaeval Musical Manuscripts 2. Brooklyn, 1960.

——. *Firenze, Biblioteca Mediceo-Laurenziana, Pluteo 29,1*. IMS. Publications of Mediaeval Musical Manuscripts10 and 11. Brooklyn, 1966–1967.

Doane, A. N., and Carol Braun Pasternack, eds. *Vox intexta: Orality and Textuality in the Middle Ages*. Madison, WI, 1991.

Dobszay, László. 'Offizium', *MGG*, vol. 2, p. 7, cols 593–609.

——. 'Experiences in the Musical Classification of Antiphons', *International Musicological Society Study Group Cantus Planus, Papers read at the Third Meeting, Tihany, Hungary, 19–24 September 1988*. Budapest, 1988. Pp. 143–156.

——. 'The Debate about the Oral and Written Transmission of Chant', *Revista de musicología* 16 (1993), pp. 706–729.

——. 'The Types of Antiphons in Ambrosian and Gregorian Chant', in Bryan Gillingham and Paul Merkley, eds, *Chant and its Peripheries: Essays in Honour of Terence Bailey*. IMS. Musicological Studies 72. Ottawa, 1998. Pp. 50–61.

——. *Corpus antiphonarum: Europai örökség és hazai alakítzás* [Corpus Antiphonarum: European Heritage and Hungarian Creation]. Budapest, 2003.

——. 'Concerning a Chronology for Chant', in Gallagher *et al*., eds, *Western Plainchant in the First Millennium*, pp. 217–229.

——. 'Antiphon Variants and Chant Transmission', *StM* 45 (2004), pp. 67–93.

——. *Ólatin liturgiák énekei* [Chant in the Old Latin Liturgies], Egyházzenei Füzetek [Church Music Guide Books] 1/13. Budapest, 2004.

——, and Janka Szendrei. *Antiphonen*. 3 vols. MMMA 5. Kassel, 1999.

Doyle, Alicia. 'The Repertory of Tropes in Paris, Bibliothèque Nationale *fonds latin* 1118: A Comparative Study of Tenth–Century Aquitanian Concordances and Transmission'. Ph.D. dissertation. University of California at Santa Barbara, 2000.

Dreves, Guido Maria, ed. *Prosarium Lemovicence: Die Prosen der Abtei St. Martial*, AH 7. Leipzig, 1889; repr. New York, 1961.

Dronke, Peter. *The Medieval Lyric*. London, 1968. 3rd edn Cambridge, 1996.

——. 'The Lyrical Compositions of Philip the Chancellor', *Studi medievali*, 3rd series, 28 (1987), pp. 563–592.

Duchesne, Louis. *Le Liber pontificalis. Texte, introduction et commentaire*. 2 vols. Paris, 1884–1892. Complemented by Cyrille Vogel, *Additions et corrections*. Paris, 1957.

Duggan, Mary Kay. *Italian Music Incunabula: Printers and Type*. Berkeley, 1992.

Dyer, Joseph. 'Double Offices at the Lateran in the Mid-Twelfth Century', in John Daverio and John Ogasapian, eds, *The Varieties of Musicology: Essays in Honor of Murray Lefkowitz*. Warren, MI, 2000. Pp. 27–46.

——. 'Old Roman Chant', *NG2*, vol. 18, pp. 381–385.

Dykmans, Marc. *Le pontifical romain révisé au XVe siècle*. Studi e Testi 311. Vatican City, 1985.

Edwards, Owain Tudor. 'How Many Sarum Antiphonals Were There in England and Wales in the Middle of the Sixteenth Century?', *RB* 99 (1989), pp. 155–180.

Erlande-Brandenburg, Alain. *Notre-Dame de Paris*. Paris, 1991.

Everist, Mark. *French Thirteenth-Century Polyphony in the British Library: A Facsimile Edition of the Manuscripts Additional 30091 and Egerton 2615 (folios 79–94v)*. London, 1988.

———. 'Reception and Recomposition in the Polyphonic *Conductus cum caudis*: The Metz Fragments', *Journal of the Royal Musical Association* 125 (2000), pp. 135–163.

Fabre, Paul, and Louis Duchesne, eds. *Le Liber censuum de l'Église romaine*. Bibliothèque des écoles françaises d'Athènes et de Rome. 2 sér., VI/1–2. Paris, 1910.

Falck, Robert. *The Notre Dame Conductus: A Study of the Repertory*. IMS. Musicological Studies 33. Henryville, PA, 1981.

Fassler, Margot. 'Representations of Time in *Ordo representacionis Ade*', in Daniel Poiran and Nancy F. Regalado, eds, *Contexts: Style and Values in Medieval Art and Literature. Yale French Studies*, special Issue. New Haven, 1991. Pp. 97–113.

———. *Gothic Song: Victorine Sequences and Augustinian Reform in Twelfth-Century Paris*. Cambridge, 1993.

Ferreira, Manuel Pedro. 'Music at Cluny: The Tradition of Gregorian Chant for the Proper of the Mass. Melodic Variants and Microtonal Nuances'. Ph.D dissertation. Princeton University, 1997.

Ferretti, Paolo M. 'I manoscritti musicali gregoriani dell'archivio di Montecassino', *Casinensia* 1 (1929), pp. 187–203.

Fiocchi-Nicolai, Vincenzo. 'Strutture funerarie ed edifice di culto paleocristiani di Roma dal III al VI secolo', in Ivan di Stefano Manzella, ed., *Le iscrizione dei cristiani in Vaticano*. Inscriptiones Sanctae sedis 2. Vatican City, 1997. Pp. 121–141.

———. 'L'organizzazione dello spazio funerario', in Letizia Pani Ermini, ed., *Christiana Loca: Lo spazio cristiano nella Roma del primo millennio*. Rome, 2000. Pp. 43–58.

Fischer, Ludwig. *Bernhardi cardinalis et Lateranensis ecclesiae prioris Ordo officiorum ecclesiae Lateranensis*. Historische Forschungen und Quellen 2–3. Munich–Freising, 1916.

Fischer, Pieter ed. *The Theory of Music from the Carolingian Era up to 1400*. 6 vols. Répertoire international des sources musicales B3. Munich–Duisburg, 1961–2003. Vol. 2: *Italy*. Munich, 1968.

Frere, Walter H. *Antiphonale sarisburiense*. London, 1901–1924.

Frisi, Anton-Francesco, ed. *Ordo mysterii seu officii in ecclesia Modoëtiensis. Memorie storiche di Monza* 3. Milan, 1794.

Froger, Dom Jacques. 'Les prétendus quarts de ton dans le chant grégorien et les symboles du MS H. 159 de Montpellier', *EG* 17 (1978), pp. 145–179.

Fry, Timothy, Imogene Baker, Timothy Horner, Augusta Raabe, and Mark Sheridan, eds. *RB 1980: The Rule of St. Benedict in Latin and English with Notes.* Collegeville, MN, 1981.

Gajard, Dom Joseph. 'Les récitations modales des 3ᵉ et 4ᵉ modes dans les manuscrits bénéventains et aquitains', *EG* 1 (1954), pp. 9–45.

Gallagher, Sean, John Nadas, James Haar, and Timothy Striplin, eds. *Western Plainchant in the First Millennium: Studies in the Medieval Liturgy and its Music.* Aldershot, 2004.

Gennrich, Friedrich. *Bibliographie der ältesten französischen und lateinischen Motetten.* Darmstadt, 1958.

Gerbert, Martin. *Scriptores ecclesiastici de musica sacra potissimum.* St Blasien, 1784.

Gevaert, François-Auguste. *La mélopé antique dans le chant de l'église latine.* Ghent, 1895.

Gillingham, Bryan. *Secular Medieval Latin Song: An Anthology.* IMS. Musicological Studies 60/1. Ottawa, 1993.

———. *A Critical Study of Secular Medieval Latin Song.* IMS. Musicological Studies 60/2. Ottawa, 1995.

Giusti, Martino. 'L'*ordo officiorum* della cattedrale di Lucca (Bibl. cap. 608)', in *Miscellanea Giovanni Mercati.* 6 vols. Studi e Testi 121–126. Vatican City, 1946.

Gmelch, Joseph. *Die Vierteltonstufen im Messtonale von Montpellier.* Veröffentlichungen der Gregorianischen Akademie zu Freiburg 6. Eichstatt, 1911.

Goltzen, Herbert. 'Nocturna Laus. Aus Arbeiten zur Geschichte der Vigil', *Jahrbuch für Liturgik und Hymnologie* 5 (1960), pp. 79–88.

Gottwald, Clytus. *Die Musikhandschriften der Universitätsbibliothek München.* Die Handschriften der Universitätsbibliothek München 2. Munich, 1968.

Gozzi, Marco. 'Il Graduale di Angelo Gardano (1591)', in Laura Dal Prá, ed., *Un museo nel Castello del Buonconsiglio: acquisizioni, contributi, restauri.* Trent, 1995. Pp. 399–414.

Graduale de sanctis iuxta ritum sacrosanctae romanae ecclesiae: Editio princeps (1614). Facsimile edition and appendix, ed. Giacomo Baroffio, Eun Ju Kim, and Manlio Sodi. Monumenta Studia Instrumenta Liturgica 10–11. Vatican City, 2001.

Graduale sarisburiense: A Reproduction in Facsimile of a MS. of the Thirteenth Century, ed. Walter Howard Frere. London, 1894; repr. Farnborough, 1966.

Graduale triplex. Solesmes, 1979.

Graduale Wirczeburgense. Wurzburg: Georg Reyer, 1496.

Grégoire, Réginald. *Homéliaires liturgiques médiévaux: analyse de manuscrits.* Biblioteca degli Studi Medievali 12. Spoleto, 1980.

Grier, James. 'Roger de Chabannes (d. 1025), Cantor of St. Martial de Limoges', *EMH* 14 (1995), pp. 53–119.

———. *The Critical Editing of Music: History, Method, and Practice.* Cambridge, 1996.

Grierson, Philippe. 'La bibliothèque de St. Vaast d'Arras au XIIe siècle', *RB* 52 (1939), pp. 117–140.

Guérard, Benjamin, ed. *Cartulaire de l'église Notre Dame de Paris*. 4 vols. Paris, 1850.

Guido of Arezzo. *See* Waesberghe.

Guilmard, Dom Jacques-Marie. *Tonaire des pièces de la messe selon le Graduale triplex et l'Offertoriale triplex*. Subsidia gregoriana 2. Solesmes, 1991.

Gümpel, Karl-Werner. 'Spicilegium rivipullense', *AMw* 35 (1978), pp. 58–59.

Gushee, Lawrence. 'The *Musica Disciplina* of Aurelian of Réôme: A Critical Text and Commentary'. Ph.D. dissertation. Yale University, 1963.

———, ed. *Aurelianus Reomensis*. Musica disciplina. CSM 21. Rome, 1975.

Gy, Pierre-Marie. 'Les tropes dans l'histoire de la théologie', in *Research on Tropes*, ed. Gunilla Iversen. Stockholm, 1983.

———. 'L'influence des chanoines de Lucques sur la liturgie du Latran', *Revue des sciences religieuses* 58 (1984), pp. 31–41.

Haggh, Barbara. 'Traktat *Musica disciplina* Aureliana Reomensis: proweniencja I datowanie [Musica disciplina Aureliani Reomensis and the Problem of the Date and Origin of the Treatise]', translated from English into Polish by Katarzyna Naliwajek, *Muzyka* (Journal of the Institute of Musicology, Polish Academy of Sciences, Warsaw) 45 (2000), pp. 25–78 .

———. 'Aurelian's Library', *International Musicological Society Study Group Cantus Planus: Papers Read at the Ninth Meeting, Esztergom & Visegrád, 1998*. Budapest, 2001. Pp. 271–300.

Haines, John. 'Erasures in Thirteenth-Century Music', in John Haines and Randall Rosenfeld, eds, *Music and Medieval Manuscripts*. Aldershot, 2004. Pp. 60–88.

Handschin, Jacques. 'Trope, Sequence, and Conductus', in Anselm Hughes, *Early Medieval Music up to 1300*. New Oxford History of Music 3. London, 1954.

Hansen, Finn Egeland. *H. 159, Montpellier: Tonary of St. Bénigne of Dijon*. Copenhagen, 1974.

———. 'Editorial problems connected with the transcription of H 159, Montpellier: Tonary of St. Bénigne of Dijon', *EG* 16 (1977), pp. 161–172.

———. *The Grammar of Gregorian Tonality: An Investigation Based on the Repertory in Codex H 159, Montpellier*. 2 vols. Copenhagen, 1979.

Hanssens, Jean-Michel, ed. *Amalarii episcopi opera liturgica omnia*. 3 vols. Studi e Testi 138–140. Vatican City, 1948–1950.

———. *Nature et genèse de l'office des matines*. Analecta gregoriana 57. Rome, 1952.

Hardie, Jane Morlet. 'Liturgical Books for Use in Spain 1468–1568: Puzzles in Parchment and Print', *Musica antiqua* 9/1 (1991), pp. 279–319.

———. 'Lamentations in Spanish Sources before 1568: Notes Towards a Geography', *Revista de musicología* 16 (1993), pp. 912–942.

———. 'Proto-Mensural Notation in Pre-Pius V Spanish Liturgical Sources', *StM* 39/2–4 (1998) , pp. 195–200.

———. *The Lamentations of Jeremiah: Ten Sixteenth-Century Spanish Prints*. IMS. Collected Works 22. Ottawa, 2003.

———. 'The Past in the Present: Some Liturgico-Musical Relationships between Toledo, Rome and Andalucía', in László Dobszay, ed., *The Past in the Present*. 2 vols. Budapest, 2003. Vol. 2, pp. 207–222.

Harris, Simon. 'The "Kanon" and the Heirmologion', *Music and Letters* 85 (2004), pp. 175–197.

Harrison, Frank, Ernest Sanders, and Peter Lefferts, eds. *Polyphonic Music of the Fourteenth Century*. Monaco, 1980, 1983, 1986.

Harrison, Frank, and Roger Wibberley, eds. *Manuscripts of Fourteenth-Century English Polyphony: A Selection of Facsimiles*. London, 1981.

Haskins, Charles H. *The Renaissance of the Twelfth Century*. Cambridge, MA, 1927.

Haug, Andreas. *Troparia tardiva. Repertorium später Tropenquellen aus dem deutschsprachigen Raum*. MMMA Subsidia I. Kassel, 1995.

Hesbert, René-Jean. *Corpus antiphonalium officii*. 4 vols. Rerum ecclesiasticarum documenta, Series maior, Fontes 7–10. Rome, 1963–1979.

———. 'L'antiphonaire d'Amalaire', *Ephemerides liturgicae* 94 (1980), pp. 176–194.

Hiley, David. 'The Norman Chant Traditions – Normandy, Britain, Sicily', *Proceedings of the Royal Musical Association* 107 (1980–1981), pp. 1–33.

———. 'Cluny Sequences and Tropes', in Claudio Leonardi and Enrico Menestó, eds, *La tradizione dei tropi liturgici*. Spoleto, 1990. Pp. 125–138.

———. 'The Sequentiary of Chartres, Bibliothèque municipale, MS 47', in Agostino Ziino, ed., *La sequenza medievale*. Lucca, 1992. Pp. 105–118.

———. 'The Sequence Melodies Sung at Cluny and Elsewhere', in *FS Hucke*. Pp. 130–155.

———. *Western Plainchant: A Handbook*. Oxford, 1993.

———. 'Das Wolfgang-Offizium des Hermannus Contractus – zum Wechselspiel von Modustheorie und Gesangspraxis in der Mitte des XI. Jahrhunderts' in Walter Berschin and David Hiley, eds, *Die Offizien des Mittelalters. Dichtung und Musik*. Regensburger Studien zur Musikgeschichte 1. Tutzing, 1999. Pp. 129–142.

———. *Hermannus Contractus (1013–1054): historia sancti Wolfgangi episcopi Ratisbonensis*. IMS. Musicological Studies 65/7. Ottawa, 2002.

———. 'Die Afra-Gesänge des Hermannus Contractus. Liturgische Melodien und die Harmonie des Universums', in Manfred Weitlauff and Melanie Thierbach, eds, *Hl. Afra. Eine frühchristliche Märtyrerin in Geschichte, Kunst und Kult. Jahrbuch des Verein für Augsburger Bistumsgeschichte 38. Ausstellungskatalog des Diözesanmuseum St. Afra*. Augsburg, 2004. Pp. 112–119.

———, ed. *Missale Carnotense (Chartres codex 520)*. MMMA 4. Kassel, 1992.

———, and Walter Berschin, eds. *Hermannus Contractus (1013–1054): historia sanctae Afrae martyris augustensis*. IMS. Musicological Studies 65/10. Ottawa, 2004.

Holder-Egger, Oswald, ed. *Cronica fratris Salimbene de Adam ordinis fratrum minorum*. Monumenta germaniae historiae. Scriptores 32. Leipzig, 1905–1913.

Holman, Hans-Jørgen. 'The Responsoria Prolixa of the Codex Worcester F. 160'. Ph.D. dissertation. Indiana University, 1961.

Holmes, George. 'The Emergence of an Urban Ideology at Florence, *c*.1250–*c*.1450', *Transactions of the Royal Historical Society*, Series 5/23 (1973), pp. 111–134.

Hornby, Emma. *Gregorian and Old Roman Eighth-Mode Tracts.* Aldershot, 2002.

Horste, Kathryn. '"A Child is Born": The Iconography of the Portail Ste.-Anne at Paris', *Art Bulletin* 69 (1987), pp. 187–210.

Hourlier, Jacques. 'Remarques sur la notation clunisienne', *Revue grégorienne* 30 (1951), pp. 231–240.

Hucke, Helmut. 'Musikalische Formen der Offiziumsantiphonen', *Kirchenmusikalisches Jahrbuch* 37 (1953), pp. 7–33.

———. 'Gregorianischer Gesang in altrömischer und fränkischer Überlieferung', *AMw* 12 (1955), pp. 74–87.

———. 'Die Gregorianische Gradualeweise des 2. Tons und ihre ambrosianischen Parallelen', *AMw* 13 (1956), pp. 285–314.

———. 'Zu einigen Problemen der Choralforschung', *Die Musikforschung* 11 (1958), pp. 385–414.

———. 'Karolingische Renaissance und gregorianischer Gesang', *Die Musikforschung* 28 (1975), pp. 4–18.

———. 'Das Responsorium', in Wulf Arlt and Max Haas, eds, *Gattungen der Musik in Einzeldarstellungen.* Berne, 1975. Pp. 144–191.

———. 'Towards a New Historical View of Gregorian Chant', *JAMS* 33 (1980), pp. 437–467.

———. 'Gregorianische Fragen', *Die Musikforschung* 41 (1988), pp. 304–330.

Hughes, Andrew. *Manuscript Accidentals: Ficta in Focus 1350–1450.* American Institute of Musicology. Musicological Studies and Documents 27. Rome, 1972.

———. *Medieval Manuscripts for Mass and Office: A Guide to their Organization and Terminology.* 2nd edn, Toronto, 1986.

———. *Style and Symbol: Medieval Music, 800–1453.* IMS. Musicological Studies 51. Ottawa, 1989.

———. 'Chantword Indexes: A Tool for Plainsong Research', in Paul Laird, ed., *Words and Music.* Binghamton, 1993. Pp. 31–50.

———. 'The Scribe and the Late Medieval Liturgical Manuscript: Page Layout and Order of Work', in Robert A. Taylor, James R. Burke, Patricia J. Eberle, Ian Lancashire, and Brian S. Merilees, eds, *The Centre and its Compass: Studies in Medieval Literature in Honor of Professor John Leyerle.* Kalamazoo, 1993. Pp.151–224.

———. *Late Medieval Liturgical Offices: Resources for Electronic Research (Sources and Chants).* Subsidia Medievalia 24. Toronto, 1996.

———. 'Large Projects and Small Resources', in *FS Steiner*, pp. 521–545.

———. *Lambeth Palace, Sion College MS. L1: The Noted Breviary of York (olim Sion College ms Arc.L.40.2/L.1).* IMS. Publications of Mediaeval Musical Manuscripts 25/1–3. Ottawa, 2000–2001.

———. 'Echoes and Allusions: Sources of the Office for St Dominic', in Pierre-Marie Gy and Leonard E. Boyle, eds, *Aux origines de la liturgie dominicaine: le manuscrit Santa Sabina XIV L.1.* Paris–Rome, 2002. Pp. 279–300.

Hughes, Anselm. *Anglo French Sequelae.* London, 1934.

Hughes, David G. 'Further Notes on the Grouping of the Aquitanian Tropers', *JAMS* 19 (1966), pp. 3–12.

——. 'Evidence for the Traditional View of the Transmission of Gregorian Chant', *JAMS* 40 (1987), pp. 377–404.

——. 'Communications', *JAMS* 41 (1988), pp. 566–575.

——. 'The Implications of Variants for Chant Transmission', in *FS Hucke*, pp. 65–73.

——. 'An Enigmatic Neume', in Bell Yung and Joseph S. C. Lam, eds, *Themes and Variations: Writings on Music in Honor of Rulan Chao Pian.* Cambridge, MA, and Hong Kong, 1994. Pp. 8–30.

——. 'The Alleluias *Dies Sanctificatus* and *Vidimus Stellam* as Examples of Late Chant Transmission', *Journal of the Plainsong and Mediaeval Music Society* 7 (1998), pp. 1–28.

——. 'Guido's *Tritus*: An Aspect of Chant Style', in *FS Levy*, pp. 207–221.

——. 'From the Advent Project to the Late Middle Ages: Some Issues of Transmission', in Gallagher *et al*, eds, *Western Plainchant in the First Millennium*, pp. 181–198.

Huglo, Michel. 'Le chant "vieux-romain". Liste des manuscrits et témoins indirects', *Sacris erudiri* 6 (1954), pp. 96–124.

——. 'Le tonaire de Saint-Bénigne de Dijon (Montpellier H. 159)', *AnnM* 4 (1956), pp. 7–18.

——. *Le graduel romain: Les sources.* Solesmes, 1957.

——. *Les tonaires: inventaire, analyse, comparaison.* Paris, 1971.

——. 'Les remaniements de l'antiphonaire grégorien au IXe siècle: Helisachar, Agobard, Amalaire', in *Atti del XVIII convegno di studi sul tema 'Culto cristiano e politica imperiale carolingia', Todi, 9–12 ottobre 1977.* Todi, 1979.

——. 'Grundlage und Ansätze der mittelalterlichen Musiktheorie', in Thomas Ertelt and Frieder Zaminer, eds, *Geschichte der Musiktheorie.* Darmstadt. Vol. 4, 2000, pp. 17–102.

——. *Les manuscrits du processionnal. RISM B* XIV 2, Index II.1. Munich, 2004.

——, and Manuel Pedro Ferreira. 'Cluniac Monks', *NG2*, vol. 6, pp. 63–65.

Huglo, and Joan Halmo. 'Antiphon', *NG2*, vol. 1, pp. 735–748.

Huot, Sylvia. *From Song to Book.* Ithaca, 1987.

Indino, Annarita. 'Il graduale stampato di Angelo Gardano (1591)', in Cattin *et al.*, *Il canto piano nell'era della stampa*, pp. 207–221.

Inguanez, Mauro. *Codicum casinensium manuscriptorum catalogus cura et studio monachorum S. Benedicti archicoenobii Montis Casini.* Rome, 1915–1951.

——. 'O Roma nobilis', *L'illustrazione vaticana* 4 (1933).

Jaeger, C. Stephen. *The Envy of Angels: Cathedral Schools and Social Ideals in Medieval Europe, 950–1200.* Philadelphia, 1994.

Jeffery, Peter. *Re-Envisioning Past Musical Cultures – Ethnomusicology in the Study of Gregorian Chant.* Chicago, 1992.

——. 'Communications', *JAMS* 49 (1996), pp. 175–179.

Jonsson, Ritva, ed. *Corpus troporum*. Studia latina stockholmiensia 21. Stockholm, 1975–. Vol. 1 (1975).

Jounel, Pierre. 'Le sanctoral romain du 8ᵉ au 12ᵉ siócles', *La Maison-Dieu* 52 (1957), pp. 59–88.

———. *Le culte des saints dans les basiliques du Latran et du Vatican au douzième siècle*. Collection de l'École française de Rome 26. Rome, 1977.

Jungmann, Josef. 'The Origin of Matins', in *Pastoral Liturgy*. New York, 1962. Pp. 105–122.

Jullien, Marie-Hélóne, and Françoise Perelman, eds. *Clavis scriptorum latinorum medii aevi: auctores Galliae, 735–987*. 2 vols. Turnhout, 1994, 1999.

Kallenberg, Paschalis, O. Carm. *Fontes liturgiae carmelitanae, Investigatio in decreta, codices et Proprium sanctorum*. Rome, 1962.

Karp, Theodore. *Aspects of Orality and Formularity in Gregorian Chant*. Evanston, IL, 1998.

———. 'A Serendipitous Encounter with St. Kilian', *Early Music* 28 (2000), pp. 226–237.

———. 'Some Notkerian Sequences in Germanic Print Culture of the Fifteenth and Sixteenth Centuries', in Gallagher *et al.*, eds, *Western Plainchant in the First Millennium*, pp. 399–428.

Kelly, Thomas F. *The Beneventan Chant*. Cambridge, 1989.

Kornmüller, Utto. 'Der heilige Wolfgang als Beförderer des Kirchengesanges', in J. B. Mehler, ed., *Der heilige Wolfgang, Bischof von Regensburg. Historische Festschrift zum neun-hundertjährigen Gedächtnisse seines Todes (3.10.1894)*. Regensburg, 1894. Pp. 140–162.

Krummel, Donald William, and Stanley Sadie. *Music Printing and Publishing*. New York, 1990.

La Fage, Adrien de. *Essai de diphthérographie musicale*. Paris, 1864; repr. Amsterdam, 1964.

Leach, Mark A. '*His ita perspectis*. A Practical Supplement to Guido of Arezzo's Pedagogical Method', *JM* 8 (1990), pp. 82–101.

Le Berrurier, Diane O. *The Pictorial Sources of Mythological and Scientific Illustrations in Hrabanus Maurus' De rerum naturis*. New York, 1978.

Lecca, Carlos Romero de, ed. *Ochos siglos de encuadernacion española*. Brussels, 1985.

Lefferts, Peter M. *The Motet in England in the Fourteenth Century*. Ann Arbor, 1986.

———. 'Motet' and 'Old Hall Manuscript', in *Medieval England: An Encyclopedia*. New York, 1998. Pp. 527–529, 560.

———, and Brian Seirup. *Studies in Medieval Music: Festschrift for Ernest H. Sanders*, ed. members of the Department of Music, Columbia University. New York, 1990.

Leroquais, Victor. *Les sacramentaires et les missels manuscrits des bibliothèques publiques de France*. Paris, 1924.

LeRoux, Sister Mary Protase. 'The *De harmonica institutione* and *Tonarius* of Regino of Prüm'. Ph.D. dissertation. The Catholic University of America, 1965.

LeRoux, Raymond. 'Aux origines de l'office festif: les antiennes et les psaumes de matines et de laudes pour Noël et le Ier janvier selon le cursus romain et monastique', *EG* 4 (1961), pp. 66–170.

Levy, Kenneth. 'Charlemagne's Archtetype of Gregorian Chant', *JAMS* 40 (1987), pp. 1–30.

———. 'On Gregorian Orality', *JAMS* 44 (1990), pp. 185–227.

———. *Gregorian Chant and the Carolingians*. Princeton, 1998.

———. 'A New Look at Old Roman Chant', *EMH* 19 and 20 (2000, 2001), pp. 81–114, 173–197.

Liber primo and *Liber secundus de tenebrae* and *Officium hebdomadae sanctae*. Salamanca: Mathias Gastius, 1582.

Lieftinck, Gerard I., ed. *Manuscrits datés conservés dans les Pays-Bas*. 2 vols. Amsterdam, 1964.

Little, Charles T. 'From Cluny to Moutiers-St-Jean: The Origin of a Limestone Fragment of an Angel at the Cloisters', *Gesta* 27 (1988), pp. 23–29.

Ludwig, Paul. 'Lamentations notées dans quelques manuscrits bibliques', *EG 12* (1971), pp. 127–130.

Magistretti, Marco. *Beroldus, sive ecclesiae ambrosianae mediolanensis kalendarium et ordines*. Milan, 1894.

———. *Manuale ambrosianum ex codice saec. xi olim in usum canonicae Vallis Travaliae*. Part 1. Milan, 1905.

Maiani, Brad. 'Readings and Responsories: The Eighth-century Night Office Lectionary and the *Responsoria prolixa*', *JM* 16 (1998), pp. 254–282.

Mallio, Pietro. 'Descriptio baslicae vaticanae', in Roberto Valentini and Giuseppe Zucchetti, eds, *Codice topographico della città di Roma*. 4 vols. Fonti per la storia d'Italia 81, 88, 90 and 91. Rome, 1940–1953. Vol. 3 (1946), pp. 375–442.

Martini, Pater Clemens. *Der deutsche Carmel, Ein Gesamtüberblick über die Provinzen von Niederdeutschland, Oberdeutschland und Sachsen des Stammordens u. l. Frau vom Berge Karmel in Deutschland, über die Tätigkeit u. das Wirken dieses Ordens auf deutschem Boden*. 2 vols. Bamberg, 1922. Vol. 1.

Masai, François, and Martin Witteck, eds. *Manuscrits datés conservés en Belgiques*. 6 vols. Brussels, 1968–1991.

Matthiae, Guglielmo. *Mosaici medievali delle chiese di Roma*. 2 vols. 2nd edn. Rome, 1967.

Mazzoli, Marie A. C., Donatella Frioli, Silvano Groff, Mauro Hausbergher, Marco Palma, Cesare Scalon, and Stefano Zamponi, eds. *I manoscritti datati della provincia di Trento*. Florence, 1996.

McClure, M.L., and C. L. Felto, eds and translators. *Pilgrimage of Etheria*. London, 1919.

McGee, Timothy J. *The Sound of Medieval Song: Ornamentation and Vocal Style According to the Treatises*. Oxford, 1998.

———, George Rigg, and David N. N. Klausner, eds. *Singing Early Music: The Pronunciation of European Languages in the Late Middle Ages and Renaissance*. Bloomington, IN, 1996.

McKinnon, James. 'Lector Chant Versus Schola Chant: A Question of Historical Plausibility', in Janka Szendrei and David Hiley, eds, *Laborare fratres in unum*. Spolia Berolinensia 7. Berlin, 1995.

———. *The Advent Project: The Later-Seventh-Century Creation of the Roman Mass Proper*. Berkeley, 2000.

———. 'Jerome', *NG2*, vol. 13, pp. 10–11.

———, ed. *Antiquity and the Middle Ages from Ancient Greece to the Fifteenth Century*. Englewood Cliffs, NJ, 1990.

Meersseman, Gilles-Gerard. 'Note sull'origine delle Compagnie dei Laudesi (Siena 1267)', *Rivista di storia della chiesa in Italia* 17 (1963), pp. 395–405.

———. *Ordo fraternitatis*. 3 vols. Rome, 1977.

Merkley, Paul. *Italian Tonaries*. IMS. Musicological Studies 48. Ottawa, 1988.

Meyer, Christian. *Mensura monochordi. La division du monocorde (IXe–XVe siècles)*. Paris, 1996.

Meyer-Baer, Kathi. *Liturgical Music Incunabula*. The Bibliographical Society Publication for the Year 1954. London, 1962.

Miedma, Nine Robijntje. *Die Mirabilia Romae. Untersuchungen zu ihrer Überlieferung mit Edition der deutschen und niederländischen Texte*. Tubingen, 1996.

Missale romanum: editio princeps (1570). Facsimile edition, Introduction and Appendix, ed. Manlio Sodi and Achille Maria Triacca. Monumenta liturgica concilii tridentini 2. Vatican City, 1998.

Mohlberg, Cunibert. *Radulph de Rivo, der letzte Vertreter der altrömischen Liturgie*. 2 vols. Louvain, 1911.

Molinier, Auguste. *Catalogue général des manuscrits des bibliothèques publiques de France*, vol. 6. Paris, 1887.

Moll, Jaime. 'Plantino, los Junta y el "privilegio" del Nuevo rezado', in Hans Tromp and Pedro Peira, eds, *Simposio internacional sobre Cristóbal Plantino*. Madrid, 1990. Pp. 9–23.

Monsignano, Frate Eliseo. *Bullarium carmelitanum plures complectens summorum pontificum constitutiones ad Ordinem Fratrum beatissimae, semperque virginis dei genitricis Mariae de Monte Carmelo spectantes*. Part 1. Rome, 1715.

Moore, Carey A. *Judith: A New Translation with Introduction and Commentary*. The Anchor Bible. Garden City, vol. 40. Garden City, NY, 1985. Pp. 31–37.

Moosburger graduale, München, Universitätsbibliothek, 2° Cod. ms. 156. Facsimile with an Introduction and Index by David Hiley. Veröffentlichungen der Gesellschaft für Bayerische Musikgeschichte. Tutzing, 1996.

Newton, Francis. *The Scriptorium and Library at Monte Cassino 1058–1105*. Cambridge, 1999.

Nichols, Stephen G. 'Voice and Writing in Augustine and in the Troubadour Lyric', in Doane and Pasternack, eds, *Vox intexta*, pp. 137–161.

Nieddu, Anna Maria. 'L'utilizzazione funeraria del suburbio nei secoli V e VI', in Philippe Pergola, Riccardo Santangeli Valenzani, and Rita Volpe, eds, *Suburbium: Il suburbio di Roma dalla crisi del sistema delle ville a Gregorio Magno.* Collection de l'École française de Rome 311. Rome, 2003. Pp. 545–606.

Niermeyer, Jan Frederick. *Mediae latinitatis lexicon minus.* Leiden, 1976.

Nowacki, Edward. 'Antiphon', *MGG*, vol. 1, pp. 636–660.

———. 'Studies on the Office Antiphons of the Old Roman Manuscripts'. Ph.D. dissertation. Brandeis University, 1980.

———. 'The Gregorian Office Antiphons and the Comparative Method', *JM* 4 (1985), pp. 243–275.

———. 'The Performance of Office Antiphons in Twelfth-Century Rome', *International Musicological Society Study Group Cantus Planus, Papers read at the Third Meeting, Tihany, Hungary, 19–24 September 1988.* Budapest, 1988. Pp. 79–91.

———. 'Contantinople – Aachen – Rome: The Transmission of *Veterem hominem*', in *FS Hucke*, pp. 95–115.

O'Donnell, James J., ed. *Augustine:* Confessiones. 3 vols. Oxford, 1992.

Officium hebdomadae sanctae. Salamanca: Mathias Gastius, 1582.

Page, Christopher. *Voices and Instruments of the Middle Ages.* London, 1987.

———. *The Owl and the Nightingale.* London, 1989.

Palazzo, Eric. *A History of Liturgical Books from the Beginning to the Thirteenth Century.* Collegeville, MN, 1998.

Passionarium oxomense noviter excussum: cui accessit cerei paschalis, fontisque benedictionis officium cum alijs. Burgo de Osma (Didacus Fernández) Corduba, 1562.

Passionarium romanum con canto toledano. Toledo: Juan de la Plaça, 1576.

Passionarium toletanum. Alcalá de Henares: Arnao Guillem de Brocar, 1516.

Patier, Dominique. 'L'office rythmique de Sainte Ludmila', *EG* 21 (1986), pp. 49–96.

Payne, Thomas B. '*Associa tecum in patria:* A Newly Identified Organum Trope by Philip the Chancellor', *JAMS* 39 (1986), pp. 233–254.

———. 'Poetry, Politics, and Polyphony: Philip the Chancellor's Contribution to the Music of the Notre Dame School'. Ph.D. dissertation. University of Chicago, 1991.

———. '*Aurelianis civitas:* Student Unrest in Medieval France and a Conductus by Philip the Chancellor', *Speculum* 75 (2000), pp. 589–614.

———. 'Philip the Chancellor', *NG2*, vol. 19, pp. 594–597.

Peebles, Bernard N. '*O Roma nobilis*', *American Benedictine Review* 1 (1950), pp. 67–92.

Pellegrino, Michele, ed., *Paolino di Milano*, Vita di S. Ambrogio. Rome, 1961.

Penney, Clara Louisa. *An Album of Selected Bookbindings.* New York, 1967.

Pertz, Georg Heinrich, ed., *Monumenta Germaniae historica, scriptores, annales et chronica aevi salici* 5. Berlin, 1844; repr. 1985.

Pesce, Dolores. *The Affinities and Medieval Transposition.* Bloomington, IN, 1987.

———. *Hearing the Motet: A Conference on the Motet in the Middle Ages and Renaissance.* Oxford, 1996.

———. *Guido of Arezzo's* Regule rithmice, Prologus in antiphonarium, *and* Epistola ad Michahelem. IMS. Musicological Studies 73. Ottawa, 1999.

Pfisterer, Andreas. *Cantilena Romana. Untersuchung zur Überlieferung des gregorianischen Chorals.* Paderborn, 2002.

Philippart, Guy. *Les légendiers et autres manuscrits hagiographiques.* Turnhout, 1977.

Phillips, Nancy. '*Musica* and *Scolica enchiriadis*: The Literary, Theoretical, and Musical Sources'. Ph.D. dissertation. New York University, 1984.

Planchart, Alejandro Enrique. *The Repertory of Tropes at Winchester.* 2 vols. Princeton, 1977.

———. 'Fragments, Palimpsests, and Marginalia', *JM* 6 (1988), pp. 293–339.

———. 'On the Nature of Transmission and Change in Trope Repertories', *JAMS* 41 (1988), pp. 216–249.

———. 'An Aquitanian Sequentia in Italian Sources', in Wulf Arlt and Gunilla Björkvall, eds, *Recherches nouvelles sur les tropes liturgiques.* Stockholm, 1993. Pp. 371–393.

———. 'Old Wine in New Bottles', in *FS Hucke*, pp. 41–64.

Poeck, Dietrich W. *Cluniacensis Ecclesia: Der cluniacensische Klosterverband (10.–12. Jahrhundert).* Munich, 1998.

Ponte, Joseph Perry. 'Aureliani Reomensis, *Musica disciplina*: A Revised Text, Translation, and Commentary'. Ph.D. dissertation. Brandeis University, 1961.

———. *Aurelian of Réome,* The Discipline of Music. Colorado College Music Press Translations 3. Colorado Springs, 1968.

Pontificale romanum: Editio princeps (1595–1596), Facsimile edition, Introduction and Appendix, ed. Manilo Sodi and Achille Maria Triacca. Monumenta concilii tridentini 1. Vatican City, 1997.

Powell, James M. *Anatomy of a Crusade: 1213–1221.* Philadelphia, 1986.

Raasted, J., ed. *The Hagiopolites: A Byzantine Treatise on Musical Theory.* Copenhagen, 1983.

Rajeczky, Benjamin. 'Népdal-történet és gregorián-kutatás' [Ethnomusicology and Chant Research], in Béla Gunda, ed., *Festschrift für Zoltán Kodály.* Budapest, 1943. Pp. 308–312.

———. 'Gregorián, népének, népdal' [Gregorian Chant, Folk Hymn, Folk Song], *Magyar Zenetörténeti Tanulmányok* [Studies in Hungarian Music History] 2 (1969), pp. 45–64.

———. 'Choralforschung und Volksmusik des Mittelalters?', *Acta musicologica* 46 (1974), pp. 181–192.

Reichert, Benedictus M., ed. *Fratris Gerardi Fracheto Vitae fratrum Ordinis praedicatorum,. necnon cronica Ordinis ab anno MCCIII usque ad MCCLIV.* Rome, 1897.

Reynolds, Roger E. 'Divine Office', in Joseph R. Strayer, ed., *Dictionary of the Middle Ages.* 13 vols. New York, 1984. Vol. 4, pp. 221–231.

Richemond, Emile Louis. *Recherches généalogiques sur la famille des Seigneurs de Nemours.* 2 vols. Fontainebleau, 1907–1908.

Righetti, Mario. *L'anno liturgico: il breviario*. Storia liturgica 2. 3rd edn. Milan, 1969.

Roberts, C. H. *Catalogue of the Greek and Latin Papyri in the John Rylands Library, Manchester*. 4 vols. Manchester, 1911–1952.

Roesner, Edward H. *Antiphonarium, seu, Magnus liber organi de gradali et antiphonario*. Codices illuminati medii aevi 45. Munich, 1996.

Rolland, Francisco Hueso. *Exposicion de encuadernaciones españolas siglos XII al XIX. Catálogo general ilustrado*. Madrid, 1934.

Roverius, Petrus. *Reomaus, seu historia monasterii sci Johannis reomaensis* [...]. Paris, 1637.

Runciman, Steven. *A History of the Crusades*. 3 vols. Cambridge, 1955.

Rusconi, Angelo. 'Teoria musicale e teorici italiani nel Medioevo. Studi, ricerche, edizioni 1988–2000', *Fonti musicali italiane* 5 (2000), pp. 7–42.

———. 'Il cod. 318 di Montecassino: Note sulla struttura e sul contenuto', in Michael Bernhard, ed., *Quellen und Studien zur Musiktheorie des Mittelalters*, vol. 3. VMK 15. Munich, 2001. Pp. 121–144.

Sabatier, Pierre. *Bibliorum sacrorum latinae versiones antiquae; seu vetus italica*. 2nd edn. Paris–Reims, 1751.

Saggi, P. Ludovicus, O. Carm. 'Constitutiones capituli Londinensis anni 1281', *Analecta Ordinis Carmelitarum* 15 (1950), pp. 203–245.

Salmon, Pierre. 'Le martyrologe-calendrier conservé dans le MS. L. 14086 de Paris et ses origines', *RB* 56 (1945–1946), pp. 42–57.

———. *L'office divin au moyen âge*. Lex orandi 43. Paris, 1967.

Samaran, Charles, and Robert Marichal, eds. *Catalogue des manuscrits en écriture latine portant des indications de date, de lieu, ou de copiste*. 7 vols. Paris, 1959–1984.

Sanders, Ernest H. 'The Question of Perotin's Oeuvre and Dates', in Ludwig Finscher und Christoph-Hellmut Mahling, eds, *Festschrift für Walter Wiora zum 30. Dezember 1966*. Kassel, 1967. Pp. 241–249.

———. 'Style and Technique in Datable Polyphonic Notre Dame Conductus', in *FS Anderson*. IMS. Musicological Studies 39. Henryville, PA, 1985.

Santosuosso, Alma Colk. *Letter Notations in the Middle Ages*. IMS. Musicological Studies 52. Ottawa, 1989.

———. *Firenze, Biblioteca nazionale centrale, Conventi soppressi, F.III.565*. IMS. Publications of Mediaeval Music Manuscripts 19. Ottawa, 1994.

Sauerländer, Willibald. *Gothic Sculpture in France, 1140–1270*. Translated from the German by Janet Sondheimer. New York, 1972.

Scalia, Giuseppe. *Cronica fratris Salimbene de Adam Ordinis fratrum minorum*. Corpus christianorum, continuatio medievalis 125/125a. 2 vols. Tournai, 1998–1999.

Schapiro, Meyer. *The Parma Ildefonsus: A Romanesque Illustrated Manuscript from Cluny and Related Works*. New York, 1964.

Schier, Volker. 'Propriumstropen in der Würzburger Domliturgie', *Kirchenmusikalisches Jahrbuch* 76 (1991), pp. 3–43.

Schlager, Karlheinz. *Alleluia-Melodien II ab 1100*. MMMA 8. Kassel, 1987.

Schmelowszky, Ágoston. *Rövid bevezetés a zsidó liturgiába* [A Short Introduction to the Jewish Liturgy]. Egyházzenei Füzetek [Church Music Guide Books] 1/13. Budapest, 2002. Pp. 53–62.

Schmid, Bernhold. *Der Gloria-Tropus Spiritus et alme bis zur Mitte des 15 Jahrhunderts*. Tutzing, 1988.

Schmid, Hans, ed. *Musica et Scolica enchiriadis, una cum aliquibus tractatulis adiunctis recensio nova post Gerbertinam altera ad fidem omnium codicum manuscriptorum*. VMK 3. Munich, 1981.

Schrade, Leo. 'Unknown Motets in a Recovered Thirteenth-Century Manuscript', *Speculum* 30 (1955), pp. 393–412.

Serrano, Mathilde López. *La encuadernación española*. Madrid, 1972.

Sevestre, Nicole. 'Tropes du propre de la messe: cycle de Noel', in Johnsson, ed., *Corpus Troporum*, vol. 1, pp. 275–304.

Silagi, Gabriel. 'Vorwort des Herausgegebers' in *Liturgische Tropen*. Münchener Beiträge zur Mediävistik und Renaissance Forschung 36. Munich, 1985.

Sinobas, Manuel Rico y. *El arte del libro en España* . Madrid, 1941.

Slocum, Kay. *Liturgies in Honour of Thomas Becket*. Toronto, 2004.

Smet, Joachim. O. Carm. *The Carmelites, A History of the Brothers of Our Lady of Mount Carmel*. 4 vols. Vol. I: *Ca. 1200 until the Council of Trent*. Rev. edn. Darien, IL, 1988.

Snow, Robert J. 'The Old-Roman Chant', in Willi Apel, *Gregorian Chant*. Bloomington, IN, 1958. Pp. 487–492.

Southern, Richard W. *The Making of the Middle Ages*. London, 1953; repr. Pimlico, 1993.

——. 'The Place of England in the Twelfth-Century Renaissance', *History* 45 (1960), pp. 201–216.

Stäblein, Bruno. 'Zur Frühgeschichte der Sequenz', *AMw* 18 (1961), pp. 1–33.

Staehelin, Martin, ed. *Die mittelalterliche Musik-Handschrift W1: Vollständige Reproduktion des 'Notre Dame'-Manuskripts der Herzog August Bibliothek Wolfenbüttel Cod. Guelf. 628 Helmst*. Wolfenbütteler Mittelalter-Studien, Band 9. Wiesbaden, 1995.

Steglich, Rudolf, ed. *Die Quaestiones in Musica; ein Choraltraktat des zentralen Mittelalters und ihr mutmasslicher Verfasser, Rudolf von St. Trond (1070–1138)*. Leipzig, 1911.

Stein, Franz A., 'Das ältere Offizium des hl. Wolfgang in der Handschrift Clm 14872 aus St. Emmeram zu Regensburg in der Bayerischen Staatsbibliothek München', in *Sacerdos et cantus gregoriani magister. Festschrift Ferdinand Haberl zum 70. Geburtstag*, ed. Franz A. Stein. Regensburg, 1977. Pp. 279–302.

Steinen, Wolfram von den, ed. *Notker der Dichter und seine geistige Welt*. 2 vols. Bern, 1948.

Steiner, Ruth, and Keith Falconer. 'Matins', *NG2*, vol. 16, pp. 128–129.

Stephano, Fratre. *Liber passionum et eorum quae a Dominica in palmis, usque ad vesperas Sabbathi Sancti inclusive, cantari solent*. Lisboa: Simon Lopez, 1595.

Stevens, Denis. 'Polyphonic Tropes in Fourteenth-Century England', in *Aspects of Medieval and Renaissance Music*, ed. Jan La Rue *et al*. New York, 1966. Pp. 768–784.

Stevens, John. *Words and Music in the Middle Ages*. Cambridge, 1986.

Stratford, Neil. 'La sculpture médiévale de Moutiers-St-Jean (Saint-Jean-de-Réôme)', in *Congrès archéologique de France, 144e Session: Auxois–Chatillonais*. Paris, 1989. Pp. 57–201.

Summers, William John. 'A New Source of Medieval English Polyphonic Music', *Music and Letters* 58 (1977), pp. 404–413.

———. 'The Repertory of Three-Voice Music Notated in Score from Fourteenth-Century England: English Discant and Free Settings'. Ph.D. dissertation. University of California, Santa Barbara, 1978.

———. *English Fourteenth-Century Polyphony: Facsimile Edition of Sources Notated in Score*. Tutzing, 1983.

———. 'The Effect of Monasticism on Fourteenth-Century English Music', in Marc Honneger and Paul Prevost, eds, *Actes du XIIIe Congrès de la Société Internationale de Musicologie, Strasbourg, 1982*. 2 vols. Strasbourg, 1986. Vol. 1, pp. 119–142.

———. 'English Fourteenth-Century Polyphonic Music: An Inventory of the Extant Manuscript sources', *JM* 8 (1990), pp. 173–227.

———. 'The Establishment and Transmission of Polyphonic Repertoires in England, 1320–1399', in Angelo Pompilio *et al*., eds, *Atti de XIV congresso della Societé internazionale di musicologia, Bologna*. 3 vols. Bologna, 1990. Vol. 3, pp. 659–672.

———. 'Fourteenth-Century English Music, A Review of Three Recent Publications', *JM* 8 (1990), pp. 118–141.

———. 'Cantilena', 'Manuscripts of Polyphonic Music', and 'Worcester Fragments', in Paul E. Szarmach, M. Teresa Tavormina, and Joel T. Rosenthal, eds, *Medieval England, An Encyclopedia*. New York, 1998. Pp. 160–161, 448–489, 818–819.

Suso, Carmen Rodriguez. *La monodia litúrgica en el Pais Vasco (fragmentos con notación musical de los siglos XII al XVIII)*. Bilbao, 1993.

Tacconi, Marica. 'Antifonario, con tonario di Oddone d'Arezzo', in Lorenzo Fabbri and Marica Tacconi, eds, *I Libri del duomo di Firenze. Codici liturgici e biblioteca di Santa Maria del fiore (secoli XI–XVI)*. Florence, 1997.

———. 'Liturgy and Chant at the Cathedral of Florence: A Survey of the Pre-Tridentine Sources (Tenth–Sixteenth Centuries)'. Ph.D. dissertation. Yale University, 1999.

Taft, Robert. *The Liturgy of the Hours in East and West: The Origins of the Divine Office and Its Meaning for Today*. Collegeville, MN, 1986.

Tardo, Lorenzo. *L'antica melurgia bizantina*. Grottaferrata, 1938.

Thurston, Herbert, S. J., and Donald Attwater, eds. *Butler's Lives of the Saints*. New York, 1963.

Tirot, Paul. 'Vigiles et matines: liturgie monastique et liturgie cathédrale', *EG* 22 (1988), pp. 24–30.

Tischler, Hans. *The Earliest Motets (to circa 1270): A Complete Comparative Edition.* 3 vols. New Haven, 1982.

Tomasi, Giuseppe Maria. *Responsorialia et antiphonaria romanae ecclesiae.* Opera omnia 4, ed. Antonio Francesco Vezzosi. Rome, 1749.

Tomaszewski, Bronisław Alfons, O. Carm. 'Dzieje Klasztoru OO. Karmelitów na Piasku w Krakowie, Wydanie II'. Doctoral dissertation. University of Krakow, 1970.

Traill, David A. 'Philip the Chancellor and F10: Expanding the Canon', *Filologia mediolatina* 10 (2003) pp. 219–248.

Treitler, Leo. 'Homer and Gregory: The Transmission of Epic Poetry and Plainchant', *MQ* 60 (1974), pp. 333–372.

———. 'Centonate Chant: Übles Flickwerk or *E pluribus unus?*', *JAMS* 28 (1975), pp. 1–23.

———. 'Oral, Written, and Literate Process in the Transmission of Medieval Music', *Speculum* 56 (1981), pp. 471–491.

———. 'The Early History of Music Writing in the West', *JAMS* 35 (1982), pp. 237–239.

———. 'Orality and Literacy in the Music of the Middle Ages', *Paragon: Bulletin of the Australian and New Zealand Association for Medieval and Renaissance Studies* 2 (1984), pp. 143–175.

———. 'Sinners and Singers: A Morality Tale', *JAMS* 47 (1994), pp. 137–171.

———, ed. *Strunk's Source Readings in Music History.* Revised edition. New York, 1998.

Trowell, Brian. 'Sight, Sighting', *NG2*, vol. 23, pp. 371–372.

Valentini, Roberto, and Giuseppe Zucchetti. *Codice topographico della città di Roma.* 4 vols. Fonti per la storia d'Italia 81, 88, 90, 91. Rome, 1940–1953.

Van der Werf, Hendrik. *The Emergence of Gregorian Chant: A Comparative Study of Ambrosian, Roman and Gregorian Chant.* 2 vols. Rochester, NY, 1983.

———. *Integrated Directory of Organa, Clausulae, and Motets of the Thirteenth Century.* Rochester, 1989.

Van Dijk, S. J. P., and Joan Hazelden Walker. *The Ordinal of the Papal Court from Innocent III to Bonface VIII and Related Documents.* Spicilegium Friburgense 22. Freiburg, Switzerland, 1975.

Vittenet, Alfred. *L'abbaye de Moutier-St-Jean.* Mâcon, 1938.

Vivell, P. Cölestin. ed. *Commentarius anonymus in Micrologum Guidonis Aretini.* Vienna, 1917.

Vogel, Cyrille. *Medieval Liturgy: An Introduction to the Sources.* Translated and revised by William Storey and Niels Rasmussen. Washington, DC, 1986.

———, and Reinhard Elze, eds. *Le pontifical romano-germanique du dixième siècle.* 3 vols. Studi e Testi 226–27, 269. Vatican City, 1963, 1972.

Vollmann, B.K., ed. *Carmina Burana: Texte und Übersetzungen.* Frankfurt, 1987.

Waesberghe, Joseph Smits van. *De musico-pedagogico et theoretico Guidone Aretino.* Florence, 1953.

———, ed. *De musica Aribonis.* CSM 2 (Rome, 1951).

———, ed. *Guido Aretinus, Micrologus.* CSM 4. 1955.

———, ed. *Expositiones in Micrologum Guidonis Aretini, Liber argumentorum, Liber specierum, Metrologus. Commentarius in Micrologum Guidonis Aretini.* Musicologica Medii Aevi 1. Amsterdam, 1957.

———, ed. *Bernonis augiensis abbatis de arte musica disputationes tradita. Pars A. Bernonis Augiensis de mensurando monochordo.* Divitiae musicae artis. Series A, liber 6. Buren, 1978.

Wagner, Peter. *Einführung in die gregorianischen Melodien III: Gregorianische Formenlehre.* Leipzig, 1921.

Wathey, Andrew, ed. *International Inventory of Musical Scores,* vol. B4, 1–2, Supplement. Munich–Duisburg, 1993.

Watson, Andrew G., ed. *Catalogue of Dated and Datable Manuscripts in Oxford Libraries.* Oxford, 1984.

Weber, Robert, ed. *Biblia sacra iuxta vulgatam versionem.* 2nd edn. Stuttgart, 1975.

Wellesz, Egon. *Eastern Elements in Western Chant.* Copenhagen, 1947.

Wilson, Blake. *Music and Merchants: The Laudesi Companies of Republican Florence.* Oxford, 1992.

Wollasch, Joachim. 'Das Patrimonium Beati Germani in Auxerre', in Gerd Tellenbach, ed., *Studien und Vorarbeiten zur Geschichte des grossfränkischen und frühdeutschen Adels.* Forschungen zur oberrheinischen Landesgeschichte 4. Freiburgim-Breisgau, 1957. Pp. 185–224.

Zimmerman, R. P. Benedict. O. C. D. *Ordinaire de l'ordre de Notre-Dame du Mont-Carmel par Sibert de Beka (vers 1312), publié d'après le manuscrit original et collationné sur divers manuscrits et imprimés.* Paris, 1910.

Zink, Michel. *Les voix de la conscience: parole du poète et parole de Dieu au Moyen Age.* Caen, 1992.

———. *Le Moyen Age et ses chansons, ou un passé en trompe-l'oeil.* Paris, 1996. Translated by Jane Marie Todd as *The Enchantment of the Middle Ages.* Baltimore and London, 1998.

Zumthor, Paul. *Essai de poétique médiévale.* Paris, 1972.

———. 'Intertextualité et mouvance', *Littérature* 4 (1981), pp. 8–16.

———. *La poésie et la voix dans la civilisation médiévale.* Collège de France. Essais et conférences. Paris, 1984.

———. *La lettre et la voix: de la "littérature" médiévale.* Paris, 1987.

———. 'Les marques du chant: le point de vue du philologue', *Revue de musicologie* 73 (1987), pp. 7–17.

———. 'An Overview: Why the Troubadours?', in F. R. P. Akehurst and Judith M Davis, eds, *A Handbook of the Troubadours.* Berkeley, 1995. Pp. 11–18.

General index

Index of incipits

Index of manuscripts cited

See also the extensive listings of manuscripts in the appendices of David Hughes, pp. 177–180, and Alejandro Planchart, pp. 363–366.

Abbreviations:

AC Archivo de la catedral
BA Bistumsarchiv
BAV Biblioteca apostolica vaticana
BC Biblioteca capitolare, Biblioteca capitular
BL British Library
BM Bibliothèque municipale
BML Biblioteca mediceo-laurenziana
BNF Bibliothèque nationale de France
Bod. Bodleian Library
BS Bayerische Staatsbibliothek
CL Cathedral Library

CR Cathedral reservado
DD Dom- und Diözesanmuseum
FR Fisher Rare Book Room
GC Gonville and Caius College
HAB Herzog August Bibliothek
LB Landesbibliothek
NLS National Library of Scotland
SA Basilique de Sainte-Anne
SB Staatsbibliothek
SS Chiesa plebana di San Stefano
Stf. Stiftsbibliothek
WLB Württembergische Landesbibliothek

Index of saints